The Reconstruction of the
Christian Revelation Claim

The Reconstruction of the Christian Revelation Claim

A Philosophical and Critical Apologetic

Stuart C. Hackett

BAKER BOOK HOUSE
Grand Rapids, Michigan 49506

ISBN: 0-8010-4283-6

Library of Congress
Catalog Card Number: 84-071850

The author used his own translation of Hebrew and Greek
texts for scripture references.

Printed in the United States of America

Contents

Preface

Thirty years have passed, and a proportionate volume of water has flowed under all the bridges of world history, since I first promised that world in the original edition of *The Resurrection of Theism* that I intended to follow that strident epistemological and metaphysical defense of a theistic world-view with a complete system of philosophical apologetics. This project would attempt to reconstruct the entire case for a Christian understanding of existence in the context of the principal perspectives of both Western and Eastern religious-philosophical thought. In my youthful vigor and enthusiasm, I thought, perhaps naively, that it would all come to fruition in the scope of something like a decade of my subsequent life. However, this was not to be, both because the circumstances of my personal and professional life did not afford me the necessary time, and because the problems involved in the execution of the task seemed to expand in geometric ratio and proportion as I began seriously to explore them. Yet the embryo of it all was there, both in thought and on paper, from those early days in the fifties which many of my generation would describe in retrospect as the best years of our lives. So it has taken the birth pangs of three decades of thought and research to bring that long-conceived intellectual child into the light of day for all to see. Still, the actual form of it has itself been in transition along the way. My dialogue with Oriental thought became a book in its own right under the title, *Oriental Philosophy: A Westerner's Guide to Eastern Thought* (1979). The present work, while in a sense a sequel to the book that contained my original promise, has become a wholly self-contained work that requires no familiarity with my previous work for its fullest comprehension, even if those earlier books help to illuminate the path to its door. In any case, after thirty years of reflection and three years of actual writing (during fifteen months of which I gave my whole professional energy to the task), here at last is the fulfillment of my youthful promise.

In the execution of all this, I have tried to cover, though never adequately, a vast reflective terrain. In retrospect and with untainted sincerity, I can almost say, with only modest reservation, that in these pages I have said virtually everything I always wanted to say about philosophy and the Christian understanding of existence, with all the complexities involved in their intricate relationship. In so doing, I have addressed myself to the principal problems of philosophy in the areas of epistemology, metaphysics, and even, though to a lesser extent, ethics or moral philosophy. Hence my analysis is a sort of critical investigation and introduction into the nature of philosophy itself. I have also grappled with the central concerns of the Christian world-view, so that I have provided a kind of focal analysis of Christian theology in an analogously critical context. Yet, in both of these dimensions, my main concern is not intellectual self-defense, either for myself or for other committed Christians with whom I am proud to take my stand. Instead, my far greater concern is to reach out in love to both the uncommitted and the otherwise committed in an attempt to build bridges that may possibly connect much that is in their thought world with much that is in the Christian thought world. It is my hope that such individuals will be neither cornered nor much less coerced, but rather brought to at least some insight into the notion that no one who commits himself to the Lordship of Christ is called upon to abandon anything of genuine truth or worth in the thought world in which he was previously growing, or surrender any genuinely self-fulfilling concern or involvement of his integral human status. In this way, perhaps such individuals will come to see that they are being invited to find their true human selfhood in Jesus Christ in whom all truth and goodness—from whatever mediate human source their elements may have been derived—are brought to fruition and fulfillment. If, as a result, any sincerely reflective person catches even a glimpse of a single ray of genuine light, I will view this labor of years as totally worthwhile. Of course, if any such person, following the lead of that single ray, finally walks, with illumination from many other sources as well, into the full light of the noonday sun, I will be over-whelmingly ecstatic.

Anyone who attempts the sort of task I have set for myself here must, of course, stand solidly on his own feet and assume full responsibility for all of his own commitments and even his shortcomings. However, no one—I least of all—can so stand without resting on the supportive shoulders of countless others who have guided him on his way. Much of that indebtedness will be obvious from the discussion itself: my own teachers, my teaching colleagues, whole generations of my students, the great company of all those who have become my friends only in their books. All have played an indispensable and significant role, and it would be provincial of me to single out any such persons by name to represent the debt I owe to all. But I do want to single out three sources of my obligation at the purely human level for special mention. First, I want to express my deep gratitude to the administration, trustees, and faculty senate of Trinity Evangelical Divinity School for granting me two sabbatical quarters in which to devote my full attention to writing. Second, I want to thank the entire editorial staff of Baker Book House, from the chief editors on down, for all the assistance and encouragement they have offered me in bringing this work to the public light of day. Above all, I want to dedicate this product of long years to my darling wife, Joan, who has never failed to stand by me through every difficulty, personal and professional. Without her sustaining motivation and relentless encouragement, I would long since have laid my pen to premature rest.

Stuart Cornelius Hackett
Deerfield, Illinois
January 1984

Introduction:
Philosophical Prolegomena

What follows is the intermingling of a personal pilgrimage with a systematic philosophical account, the record and expression of one individual's attempt to reconstruct the religious truth-claim of historic Christianity in the context of the problems and perspectives of metaphysical philosophy—all forged in the crucible of my own existential struggle to understand the meaning of human existence in the broadest possible framework of insight. Therefore, I am not concerned here merely with an abstract, logical analysis which aims to ground itself in universal foundational truths and then proceeds to attempt to incorporate the vast sweep of human experience into a rationally plausible conceptual world-view which might leave the most rigorous demands of the finest human mind (certainly not my own) at peace with existence—yet I *am* deeply concerned with that possibly ethereal goal. And again I am not here concerned merely with the production of a private diary of an intimately personal but inevitably idealized account of my own religious experience in which I might suppose myself to provide a kind of typical examplar for reflective individuals who are open to contact with the bottom (or top) of reality in such a way as to achieve that integral personal wholeness which might fulfill the deepest human longing for peace with existence—yet I am *also* deeply concerned with that possibly elusive goal. In my most intellectually alert and most religiously sincere moments, I stand firmly on the conviction that neither of these goals can be fulfilled at their human best unless both of them are relentlessly and agonizingly sought throughout an individual's entire lifetime. Systematic philosophy, I venture to suppose, cannot achieve its most mature stature without that pervasive sensitivity to Ultimate Reality which the pro-

I. Aim: An individual attempt to reconstruct the Christian truth-claim in philosophical context.

A. Not merely
1. a logical analysis which aims at rational objectivity,

2. or a personal account of religious experience which aims at personal wholeness;

B. but rather a comprehensive stance which combines sensitivity to Ultimate Reality with persistent concern for the goals of systematic philosophy.

11

pensity to religious experience provides; and religious experience, I further contend, cannot reach the ground and content of a full-orbed insight without the perspectival framework that rigorous, systematic philosophy aims to achieve—however incompletely and inadequately these goals may be realized even when fully joined together.

Of course, my own qualifications for such an investigation are as limited as anyone else's. In a sense, I approach the task as a professional, since I think and speak from a background provided by three decades in the philosophy and theology classroom, in both undergraduate colleges and graduate schools of theology. However, I also approach that task from over half a century of lived experience as a human being. During that time, I have certainly been chastened by those rebuffs and frustrations which inevitably manage to whittle to manageable proportions any illusion of absolute objectivity that might lead me to regard my convictions as incorrigible finalities. After all, I see clearly that I am not only a child of the West (although I have spent much of my professional life trying to understand and assess Oriental religious philosophy[1]), but that I have been nurtured and educated, and have lived, prospered, and worked in the most affluent part of it. And I further realize that my most carefully constructed systematic thought is influenced in its form and content by a multiplicity of historical, cultural, and even idiosyncratic personal factors which virtually defy adequate analysis.

On the other hand, in all these respects, I am not essentially unlike any other serious investigator who might attempt to approach such a task as I envision for myself here. No human thinker embodies truth in the abstract, and all face the restrictions that come from foibles generally similar to my own, even though the specific form of such limitations may vary from person to person, culture to culture, age to age. The fact that serious thinkers recognize their conceptual limits already puts each such investigator in a position from whch he may hope to approximate the rational objectivity in which truth consists by struggling to compensate for his recognized limits. To acknowledge a limit of this sort is already to take the first steps toward transcending it, even though the final steps are never taken.

The term *philosophical prolegomena* may certainly be misleading if it suggests that the style of my comments is to be that of specialized philosophical scholarship. Actually, the term simply means introductory comments about the approach and level, not to mention the style, in which I plan to carry through my objective. I certainly plan to discuss a considerable number of philosophical questions and to do some serious philosophy about these questions. But just as I intended in my work on Oriental philosophy, I really want to spread a feast of insight for that common man who is deeply and profoundly con-

II. My qualifications, though limited, combine a background in professional philosophy

with a chastened recognition of the restrictions placed on the aim at objectivity by my historical, cultural, and personal circumstances.

A. Yet such limits are inevitable for any human investigator,

B. and the clear acceptance of such obstacles constitutes a basis for the partial compensation for their influence, as well as a significant step toward objectivity.
III. This approach to be seriously philosophical in nature,

but as free as possible of the earmarks of technical scholarship, since it aspires to reach the common man who has a deep interest in such questions.

---

1. *Oriental Philosophy: A Westerner's Guide to Eastern Thought.* (Madison, Wisconsin: University of Wisconsin Press, 1979).

cerned about the meaning of existence and about the truth-claims of those developed perspectives which aim to enshrine that meaning. Hence, I have no intention of bogging down in the technical paraphernalia of academic scholarship—complex footnotes, extensive quotations, intricate bibliographical references, and the like. I certainly plan to discuss alternative positions, supporting arguments, and counter-arguments; but I hope to do so in the clearest and most straightforward manner that the nature of the subject matter and my own limited expressive capacity permit. If the discussion is to bristle with anything, let it be with clarifying insight, rather than with those weighty academic encumbrances which might well turn aside that very common man to whom I most want to speak.

> A. Hence a concern with positions, arguments, and counter-arguments,
>
> B. but set forth as clearly as possible without distracting encumbrances.

A quarter of a century ago, in the frenzied fervor and optimism of my youth, I wrote a book[2] in which I discussed rather technically questions about religious knowledge and theistic metaphysics. Like Hume's *Treatise*, the book fell stillborn from the press because of its heavy style and technical context. In retrospect, I do not want to reach that same audience again, although some of what I discussed there is set out in a different and, hopefully, more approachable style in this introduction. In all honesty, I have little to take back from what I said so long ago as far as substance and content are concerned. However, I certainly would not use the same style again, and I particularly regret the histrionic invective and sarcasm which pervaded that earlier analysis and which, as I see it now, may have turned away many whom I wanted to address.

> C. In these stylistic respects, I intend my project to stand in sharp contrast to an earlier book,
>
> although I have little to retract from the substance of that treatise.

Foundations of Religious Knowledge

Epistemology and the Problem of Starting Point

The Nature of Philosophical Investigation

There is, of course, no such thing as philosophy in the abstract, devoid of any essential reference to human persons or of any significant dependence upon them. A table of trigonometric functions, though concocted and arranged by human agents, is appropriate only if it involves no significant dependence upon them as persons. But a philosophy as such is the projection and possession of the human person, to whatever extent it may be replete with propositions whose truth-claims are logically independent of the distinctive individual

> I. No such thing as a philosophy in the abstract,
>
> A. for a philosophy is a distinctly human and personal project, even though its truth-claims have an independent logical status;

2. *The Resurrection of Theism.* (Chicago: Moody Press, 1957).

attributes of its proponent. For a man's philosophy is the sum or collection of basic beliefs by which, consciously or not, he makes substantive decisions, guides his conduct, and directs his activities toward the fulfillment of significant ends. Understood in this way, an individual's philosophy is an indispensable tool for managing his human life. To see this clearly, one need only ask himself why he made a certain moderately important decision as he did, rather than in some alternative way that would have been possible for him. If the "why" question is then understood in terms of purpose rather than natural causality, the answer to that question will, through very few intervening additional questions of the same sort, quickly come up against certain general beliefs about intrinsic values, moral duties, the nature of the individual's social and physical environment, and the like. With these beliefs, he will find himself at the very core of a perspective about the meaning of human existence—and that core will be the center of his philosophy.

Now if that is what is meant by a person's philosophy, then it seems evident that the individual has no option as to whether or not to have a philosophy, unless he can sincerely regard the paralysis of practical activity as such an option. The real option, therefore, is between absorbing one's perspective about existence in a haphazard, environmentally determined fashion (accidentally, as it were), on the one hand—and on the other hand, constructing his point of view in a reflective, self-determined manner that aims explicitly at a true and adequate insight which gives some promise of achieving genuine significance in life. For this reason, even though in a broad sense every thinking individual has a philosophy (because he has a core of basic beliefs), yet in a narrow sense only those persons are correctly regarded as students of philosophy who approach this core of beliefs in a distinctive way.

As I see it, the first phase of this process consists in the *conscious formulation* of one's basic beliefs. As I previously hinted, you can gain some success in this by tracing your immediate activities back to their purposive grounds. But, with rare exceptions, not even the great intellectual pioneers of civilization have proceeded solely in this way. They have instead been guided by the models provided by other persons who were either previously or contemporaneously involved in the same search for insight. Thus a cumulative tradition of philosophical investigation emerges so that individuals start, not from scratch, but from a general framework of procedure which provides clues as to what to look for and how to find it effectively.

But mere explicitness is scarcely the whole task, since it might easily result in a merely random list of beliefs which would suggest little about their relative significance. There must also be *coherent organization* of such a sort as to bring out the topical and logical connections of one's fundamental convictions so that they constitute an ordered perspective which can function as a framework for significant thought and activity. To the extent that one models his attempt on the achievements of other persons historically, he will find that the

Margin notes

B. and a person's philosophy is a core of basic beliefs indispensable to the intelligent direction of life.

C. Nor are these beliefs remote from decision making, since the logical steps from any decision to such basic beliefs are relatively few in a typical case.

II. Operating with a philosophy is hence virtually unavoidable.

A. But one can choose whether to absorb such a core of beliefs haphazardly, or to aim at achieving them in a self-reflective fashion.

B. Hence, a student of philosophy in the explicit sense involves himself in a concern with basic beliefs which aims at:
1. their conscious formulation through the guidance provided by the cumulative tradition of serious thought; and

2. their coherent organization in such a way as to bring out their logical relations to each other:

main alternatives for such an organization have already been worked out in the philosophical tradition.

One persistently illuminating (but not the only significantly useful) pattern of organization has consisted of the topical arrangement of basic beliefs according to their principal subject matter. However surprising it may seem, virtually all such beliefs can be arranged under three main subdivisions: knowledge, reality, and value. These in turn correspond with what have historically been the main areas of philosophical concern: (1) *epistemology* (the origin, nature, and limits of knowledge; the nature and tests of truth; and the relation of thought to its objects); (2) *metaphysics* (levels of reality and their reciprocal relations—especially nature, man, and ultimate reality); and (3) *axiology* (values: aesthetic, moral, and logical). Hence, epistemology raises such questions as: How does knowledge originate? What does a knowledge-claim consist of? What is meant by "truth," and how is it appropriately tested? How are our ideas related to their objects? Metaphysics deals with such issues as: What sorts of things are real, and how are these realities related to each other in the framework of being? What is the essential nature of man, and how is he related to his total environment? Is there an ultimate reality, either in the sense of a primordial substance of which all real things are composed, or in the sense of a real being whose existence is self-explanatory and whose activity is the ground of all other realities? And so the questions mount. Axiology, finally, probes questions of value: What is the basis of and what are the forms of beauty, and are there any universal standards for assessing the propriety of aesthetic judgments? What is the ultimate nature of moral obligation or duty, and how are the morally right and the morally good to be understood and related to each other (ethics)? What is the meaning of the contrast between truth and falsity as basic logical values? And so it goes, seemingly without end.

If a person becomes really serious about all this, or perhaps even if he merely dabbles in it, he will inevitably come up against a baffling and frustrating disclosure which must have been at least obscurely evident to him at the outset. He will discover both that some of his fundamental convictions either contradict or do not comport well with his other beliefs, and that various of his beliefs stand in contrast to those of other persons whose sincerity in holding those commitments is as genuine as his own. And if he is to go on with the investigation rather than give it up, he must engage in a *critical evaluation* which subjects his own beliefs to a comparative scrutiny equally as rigorous as that which he directs against the beliefs of those with whom he disagrees—for there is no plausible reason for him to give any special preference to his own convictions. In any case, he must find a way to reconstruct his beliefs so as to avoid internal contradictions among them and to give, at least to himself, a sincerely satisfactory account of why his own position on a given point is more plausible than alternative positions which he rejects. Not that the process of critical evaluation will be easy, simple, or straightforward.

a) a topical arrangement has proved traditionally useful,

b) and virtually all basic beliefs fall under three main subdivisions—
(1) epistemology,

(2) metaphysics,

(3) and axiology.
c) Sample issues in these areas of thought.

3. Critical evaluation must be made in such a way as to eliminate inconsistency from his own beliefs, while at the same time taking full account of the contrasting beliefs of other persons, without giving to his own beliefs any privileged status that he would not also assign to those of others.

a) This is a difficult enterprise, since it requires epistemological principles which are themselves disputable.

Carrying through this program will require him to have a theory of knowledge and truth, as well as a methodology for testing them, and such a theory and methodology are among the very issues about which serious students of philosophy disagree in the first place.

b) The philosophical task is hence not a short-range activity but a lifetime commitment which

(1) is essentially open-ended,
(2) and can never be more than an approximation of final truth,

And now it will be further clear that the distinctives involved in becoming a student of philosophy involve a lifetime commitment to a task which by its very nature can never be completed. It will not be like running a race or playing a game of chess; instead it will be analogous to becoming a good husband, or a good father, or, more basically, a good man. And such tasks are always open-ended. Of course, enormous consequences follow from this view of philosophical investigation. One should be pointed out immediately, namely, that the best efforts directed toward the formulation of a full-orbed philosophical position will at most be an approximation of a fully adequate position, so that such formulations are always subject to reconsideration and reconstruction. The recognition of this situation should, however, be no cause for discouragement or alarm; for it merely discerns the task as it really is and thus perhaps also saves one from the frustration of aiming at a finality which must always be sought but

(3) although some points may closely approach such finality.

can never be actually achieved. Some points, even in such a generally approximative system, may possibly be nailed down with a firmness that is tantamount to finality. However, if one were to suppose that he had achieved comprehensive, total finality in a philosophical system, he would by that supposition become the victim of the very sort of intellectual illusion which it is the point of philosophy to evade at all costs.

III. My present goal involves a philosophical approach to one version of the Christian understanding of existence, and hence a specific concern with religion.
A. definition of religion as involving

In the present context I am, as previously indicated, interested in the application of philosophical methodology to the clarification and critical investigation of a comprehensive religious perspective which I view as one possible version of what may be broadly characterized as the Christian understanding of existence. This specific orientation raises a number of preliminary questions about the relation between philosophy and religion. I would characterize religion as the total life response of man to what he comes to regard as ultimately and decisively significant for human destiny, and to whatever he views as depending on this sense of significance or as symbolizing it in some important way. A person responds to any situation not only in biological ways that human beings share to some extent with other living things, but also in distinctively human ways that uniquely characterize man among living things. One responds to a situation *intellectually*

intellectual, volitional, and emotional response to the ultimately significant as decisive for human destiny.

with a set of beliefs, *volitionally* with a set of decisions and their implementation in action, and *emotionally* with a variable complex of impulses, feelings, inclinations, and attitudes. Such a response is religious if it is directed toward that object which is regarded as ultimately decisive for the individual's (and therefore humanity's) destiny and is so regarded with an unconditional concern which transcends in its importance all the limited and conditional concerns of human reality.

How is philosophy to be related to religion thus understood? Since philosophy is concerned with basic beliefs and since religion is concerned with beliefs related to the religious object, it seems plausible to regard a person's philosophy as containing a broad cross section of beliefs which are identical with the intellectual aspect of his religious response, though here we would have to understand philosophy in the broad sense in which every thinking person has such a philosophy. It would be futile to attempt to resolve the question whether every individual has a religious response to reality in a sense analogous to that in which I suggested that any thinking person also has a philosophy; but it is perhaps reasonable to suppose that any mature individual has some sort of ultimate, unconditional concern, however implicit and unformulated it might be, which provides a basic groundwork for arranging his conditional concerns into a kind of hierarchy of ascending and descending levels of value or precedence. And if that is the case, then in that very broad sense it seems plausible to suppose that every thinking person has a partly realized propensity for religious response.

B. A person's philosophy, broadly construed, is identical with the intellectual aspect of his religious response.
1. It is pointless to debate whether every person has an explicit religious response,

2. but plausible to suppose that each individual has a structured hierarchy of concerns which constitutes a religious propensity.

The Methodological Priority of Epistemology

Since our concern here is with beliefs as a characteristic and unique human response to existence—although actions, decisions, attitudes, and emotions are important for the full expression of man's religious response—it will be appropriate to limit our attention to the philosophical and intellectual aspects of that response. Moreover, this limitation will direct our concern toward a complex of issues commonly regarded as belonging to the philosophy of religion. That discipline can therefore be defined as the comparative and critical study of alternative sets of religious beliefs, together with an analysis of the grounds urged in support of these alternatives and the critical counter-arguments directed against them.

I. Our interest here is in the intellectual aspect of the religious response and

therefore with the philosophy of religion as the critical study of religious alternatives.

Now since beliefs have to be directed toward a subject matter or toward objects to which such beliefs refer, and since it seems clear on little reflection that this subject matter will ultimately involve reality or existence, there is a sense in which metaphysics (which concerns itself with reality) takes priority over epistemology (which concerns itself with knowledge and truth). After all, there has to *be* something before there can be beliefs about it. Of course, there are beliefs about beliefs (that is what epistemology is really about), and in that sense beliefs are themselves a segment of reality. On the other hand, as students of reality, so to speak, we should desire above all else that our beliefs about reality (or about values, or about whatever else) should themselves be true and therefore embody adequate knowledge. When it is a question of procedure, then, in formulating and testing beliefs, one has to operate with a methodology or a theory of knowledge and truth; and in that sense, epistemology would seem to take priority over metaphysics. After all, unless one can trace his truth-claims back to ultimate standards or criteria of evaluation, he will have no plausible basis for regarding those claims as true. So, as a preliminary for assessing truth-claims of any sort, including religious truth-claims, it

A. In a sense, metaphysics takes priority over epistemology, since beliefs will have reality as their intended object,

B. but since we desire our beliefs to be true, we must operate with a methodology of knowledge and truth, so that procedurally epistemology takes priority over metaphysics.

seems essential to work out a methodology of assessment, or in other words, a theory of knowledge and truth.

C. Yet epistemological method is itself a matter of dispute.

1. Such argument always presupposes the sort of criteria being debated, so that the investigation is enormously difficult,

Yet this is no simple matter, since philosophers appear to argue endlessly about epistemology itself, and in so doing they inevitably employ a set of evaluative standards of the very logical sort which they purport to be critically investigating. Reflecting on this puzzle, a person might well decide that the whole investigation is impossible, or pointless, or both. And yet if that decision itself is not to be arbitrary and idiosyncratic, it will be itself grounded on the very sort of ultimate criteria which such a decision regards as impossible and pointless. So perhaps it is important to strive to achieve an epistemological method which one can sincerely regard as appropriate, even if the task seems enormously difficult. At the outset, an individual may have to set out with a sort of raw confidence in the operational principles which are implicit in his attempt to discover the foundations of genuinely objective knowledge-claims. But there is no special reason to suppose initially that he must end with an epistemological commitment which is as logically arbitrary as it must inevitably have seemed when he began the investigation.

2. and a person may have to begin with a raw confidence in his own cognitive capacity.

II. General prevalence of foundationalism as appealing to basic starting points for thought.

A. Much of what we claim to know can be argued from logically prior premises.

It has been the all-but-universal assumption of both Eastern and Western thought that all truth-claims must run back to certain foundational principles or starting points which function as indispensable (perhaps also necessary) presuppositions of all possible thought and knowledge. Nor is it difficult to understand the pervasive appeal of such a *foundationalism* as it has often been called. Much of what we claim to know is correctly regarded as known by arguments which provide premises from which the truth of the knowledge-claim may be logically derived by methods of valid inference. If these premises are themselves challenged, we may proceed to construct still further arguments from the premises of which our original premises may be derived by equally valid inference. In turn, if these premises are themselves challenged, we may proceed to reconstruct still further arguments from the premises of which our original premises may be derived by equally valid inference, and so on. But, of course, not all the premises of reasonable knowledge-claims can be known by inference from logically prior premises without logical limit. If that were the case, the proper vindication of any knowledge-claim would depend on an actually infinite series of logically prior premises, each of which could itself be vindicated only by an equally infinite series of analogous premises. Not only does such a view seem intrinsically absurd; but it would also follow that no finite thinker could properly claim to know anything at all, since he could never traverse, in any finite time span, an infinite series of premises. Hence, it seems plausible to claim either that knowledge is impossible, or else that proper knowledge-claims must be susceptible of vindication by a finite series of premises. It would follow in turn that the ultimate premises of any such series would have to be non-inferentially knowable, that is, knowable in some direct way rather than through the indirect way of being inferred from logically prior premises. Those ultimate starting points

1. But not all can be known in this way, since that would imply an actually infinite number of logically prior premises for every genuine knowledge-claim;

2. and hence there must be ultimate premises that are non-inferentially knowable in some direct way.

for knowledge would, therefore, be the foundational truths not only for knowledge-claims but also for foundationalism as a theory about the proper vindication of knowledge-claims.

But, of course, the overall plausibility of foundationalism in general does not settle a number of further issues about these foundational truths and their relation to particular knowledge-claims about the ordinary objects of common experience, such as tables, chairs, trees, and stones. For example, are these foundational propositions knowable with certainty? If so, with what sort and degree of certainty? Or might some of the foundational propositions have the status of being merely working assumptions to be adopted tentatively as making possible the coherent organization of a certain context of thought? There might, of course, be foundational propositions of both kinds— some of them having a certainty that characterizes their status as indispensable presuppositions of all possible, intelligible thought, and others being tentative preconditions of some limited context of thought. In any case, how would one arrive at a plausible set of foundational propositions, and what would be their relation to particular knowledge-claims?

Proposed answers to these and other similar questions proliferate into a variety of epistemological theories whose claims and counter-claims baffle even the most competent investigators. I have no intention of tackling an adequate analysis of all the complex issues involved. However, I do think it incumbent on me to steer what seems to me a generally plausible course through these murky waters, even if I cannot stop to attempt to dislodge all the hidden boulders beneath their surface.

One epistemological tradition (which I will call *pure rationalism*) holds in general that if knowledge is to be characterized by certainty, then two situations must prevail. First, the foundational propositions must themselves be logically necessary starting points for all possible thought and inference; and second, the whole body of derivative knowledge must be inferrable from these basic truths by logical methods alone without any essential dependence on contingent, factual statements whose content is grounded in particular experience (*deductivism*). The whole system, if actualized, would constitute, therefore, a logically ordered scheme or hierarchy of deductions such that one could reason logically backward in the system from any point to the ultimate axioms or starting points, and also logically forward to the whole set of logical derivatives. Since all the elements of the system are logically prior to and independent of particular facts of experience, it is convenient to refer to this feature of the elements by calling these propositions *a priori* propositions and to refer to the whole scheme as *rationalistic apriorism.* Some such general scheme as this seems to have been held by philosophers as otherwise diverse as Plato, Descartes, Spinoza, and (possibly) Hegel.

Now it is common for rationalistic apriorists to hold that no genuine knowledge can be derived from particular facts of experience, such as sensory perceptions. Whether correctly or not, these thinkers hold *a*) for genuine knowledge must be objectively, universally, and necessarily certain,

that no proposition constitutes genuine knowledge unless it is characterized by a certainty that is objective (its truth status is logically independent of factors relative to any given individual), universal (its truth status admits of no exceptions in particular cases), and necessary (the negation or denial of its truth status would generate a contradiction in the scheme of propositions in which it occurs). The rigor of these logical requirements is such that no proposition grounded in the particular facts of experience can possibly measure up to them. There are, for example, some experiential certainties—I can be introspec-

while experiential certainties are always subjective, particular, and contingent.

tively certain, perhaps, that I am hot or angry or depressed. But this is a certainty which is subjective in the sense that its certainty is accessible only to the individual who apprehends it about himself, while any judgment about these matters made by other persons will have to be inferred from behavioral observations and will, therefore, be objectively no more than probable. Again, an experience-based judgment will be particular rather than universal, both because it will be limited to a particular person and because it will not necessarily be unexceptionably true even of that person. Finally, experiential propositions are not necessary in the requisite sense but contingent. They may be true as a matter of fact, but their falsehood would generate no contradiction in the scheme of propositions in which they occurred. I may, for instance, be feeling depressed at a given time, but if I were not so depressed, that would generate no contradiction. Since, therefore, propositions based on particular facts of experience have at best a certainty that is subjective, particular, and contingent, rather than objective, universal, and necessary, it follows that such propositions cannot constitute genuine knowledge, according to pure rationalistic apriorism. Instead, such apprehensions may best be characterized as

b) Experiential judgments have the status of opinion or probable belief, though they may provoke the awareness of universal truth.

having the status of opinion or probable belief, although even in that limited status they may function to remind a given thinker of some universal truth that those opinions approximate or imperfectly exemplify. A round ball, for instance, may remind one of the concept of roundness which the ball imperfectly actualizes.

B. Pure Empiricism.
1. All genuinely informative knowledge is grounded in experience,
2. while non-experiential certainties are ultimately based on conventionally adopted axioms.
3. Hence, knowledge is basically *a posteriori.*

The main alternative epistemological tradition (which I will call *pure empiricism*) holds that if knowledge is to contain genuine information about actually existing entities, it must ultimately be grounded in those very particular facts of experience which pure rationalism rejects as a foundation. It also holds that there either are no certainties of the sort the rationalist appeals to, or, if there are any such certainties, none of them contains any genuine information about reality, but instead they are conventionally adopted axioms or corollaries deducible from these axioms by logical methods alone. Since, according to this perspective, all informative assertions are grounded in experience, it is convenient to refer to such propositions as *a posteriori*, that is, as logically dependent upon the particular facts of experience.

IV. Clarification through the analytic/synthetic distinction.

A. Thus,

We can make all this much clearer and more precise if we add to the already clarified distinction between *a priori* and *a posteriori* propositions, a further classification of such propositions as either *analytic* or *synthetic*. Simply put, an analytic judgment or proposition is one that is true (or false, as the case may be) by virtue of the definition of the subject term. The definition of a Euclidean triangle implies, in the context of that geometrical system, that the sum of its interior angles is equal to two right angles, because this property is logically deducible from the definition. The proposition, that such a triangle has interior angles the sum of which is equal to two right angles, is an analytic judgment. On the other hand, a synthetic judgment is one in which, if it is true, the predicate term (that which is judged about the subject) cannot be logically deduced from the definition of the subject term. I am, for example, wearing blue denim jeans, but that property is not deducible from anything essential to my being myself. The proposition is, therefore, synthetic, since it is not true (or false) merely by definition of the subject term.

Now what the pure empiricist holds is that (1) all synthetic judgments are *a posteriori*, that is, all nondefinitional judgments are based on empirical experience; and that (2) all *a priori* judgments (if there are any) are analytic. That is, all judgments whose truth-values are logically independent of empirical experience are true by definition in such a way that the ultimate grounds of the definitions run back logically to conventionally adopted axioms like those of a system of pure logic or mathematics. In contrast, the pure rationalist holds (1) that there are indeed synthetic *a posteriori* judgments, but they constitute merely some degree of opinion rather than genuine knowledge; (2) that the ultimate starting points, principles, and interpretive categories of knowledge are both *a priori* (if they were *a posteriori*, they would not possess the requisite type of certainty) and synthetic (they could not be analytic or true by definition, since they are the necessary presuppositions of all definition); (3) that the rest of genuine knowledge is a logically ordered series of analytic derivatives from the synthetic *a priori* starting points; and finally (4) that although there are conventionally grounded analytic truths like the linguistic and synonymous equivalences of an actual language (the word *bachelor* is thus equivalent in the English language to the phrase *unmarried adult male*), yet not all analytic truths are linguistically trivial in this way, since there are, as indicated in (3), analytic *a priori* derivatives of the synthetic *a priori* categories that are the ultimate foundation of all genuine knowledge.

It is clear on reflection that pure rationalism and pure empiricism are so related that they are logically contrary and cannot both be true as theories of knowledge. Yet it must not be overlooked that, from a formal, logical point of view, both of these positions might be false; for they are not genuine contradictories (if they were so related, at least one position would have to be true and at least one would have to be false). They are merely contraries, so that they cannot both be true. One way of spelling out this possibility explicitly runs as follows: Pure rationalism would be false if there were any synthetic *a posteriori* judgments that constituted genuine knowledge; and pure empiricism would be false if there were any synthetic *a priori* truths, i.e., any truths that were logically independent of empirical experience and yet

1. an analytic judgment is true or false by virtue of the definitions of its terms and their connectives,

2. while synthetic judgments are true or false on some other basis than definition alone.

B. Accordingly,
1. pure empiricism can be precisely defined

as can pure rationalism;

2. and it is clear that they are logically contrary, so that
a) they cannot both be true, but
b) they may both be false, since they are not formally contradictory.

C. Thus, a "third way" of epistemology embraces first principles of knowledge, but extends knowledge to include some experiential truths.

1. Such a rational empiricism or moderate rationalism is the view I find plausible myself.

2. Both pure rationalism and pure empiricism seem incoherent by appealing to the very sort of knowledge claims that they purport to reject by their arguments against the other view.

3. Rational empiricism combines the best of both views; *a*) for it accepts ultimate presuppositions and interpretive categories

which are synthetic *a priori*, while their formulation is open to revision;

also non-definitional in nature. This "third way" of epistemology has seemed eminently plausible to many traditional philosophers. Perhaps the most important historically was Immanuel Kant; but in my opinion, although they did not use our type of terminology, both Aristotle and Thomas Aquinas held substantially this moderate position in epistemology, although each stated the view in his own way and both have sometimes been claimed as empiricists by that tradition.

Bypassing such merely historical squabbles, we can refer to this moderate or in-between position as either *rational empiricism* (Kant's label) or *empirical (moderate) rationalism*. It is the substance of the position rather than the terminology that is important. I will immediately eliminate all suspense by acknowledging that I find such a rational empiricism or moderate rationalism to constitute, when appropriately expressed and qualified, the proper theory of knowledge. At the outset, it seems clear to me that both pure rationalism and pure empiricism are logically incoherent. When, for example, the pure rationalist argues against genuine empirical knowledge by claiming that such truth-claims vary with the changing efficiency of our sense organs and have no genuinely objective certainty, he seems to be founding his argument on the very sort of empirically grounded claims that he purports to dismiss as mere opinion by using these arguments. How else could such a rationalist claim to know about the limitations and characteristics of states of awareness that are grounded in sense perception? Furthermore, when the pure empiricist argues that all genuinely informative knowledge (all knowledge that is not trivially analytic or linguistically definitional) must be empirically derived and therefore *a posteriori*, so that there can be no synthetic *a priori* knowledge, it appears that he is making a claim which is not itself grounded in empirical data. Therefore, either, by his own logical classifications, he is merely giving a conventional definition which appears totally arbitrary, or else his thesis about knowledge is itself a non-empirical (synthetic *a priori*) dogma of the very sort that he purports to dismiss as ungrounded.

But why not opt for the best of both epistemological worlds? It seems plausible to maintain that there are indeed necessary presuppositions of all possible thought and being, for instance, basic logical laws (such as the principle of coherence or contradiction) and ultimate interpretive categories (such as the general principle of causal connection, or the relation of ground and consequence). Unless we are to regard these principles and categories as arbitrarily adopted definitions embodying conventional choice (since such concepts lie at the foundation of all reasoning, that would make all our deliberations and conclusions based on them capricious), we may as well regard them as synthetic *a priori* starting points which characterize both thought and being as a necessary structural framework, while at the same time being fully open to revision in the way in which we formulate and identify these foundational elements. All this would be a concession to the rationalistic tradition, yet we need not go overboard here and adopt the deductivist thesis of many rationalists that all genuine knowledge must be logically derivable from the ultimate principles and categories. Instead, we can again leave open the project of sketching out (always tentatively) the logical derivatives of the structural framework. And we can concede to the empiricist tradition that, while the structure or form of thought and being is *a priori*, yet much of the content must be extraneously supplied from empirical sources at all levels of experiential apprehension. Yet once more we need not attempt to argue that the truth-claim of synthetic *a posteriori* judgments (which could not be formulated without the use, whether consciously or not, of *a priori* interpretive categories) has the same sort or degree of certainty as properly formulated *a priori* judgments. Instead, we can accept as plausible knowledge-claims empirically grounded assertions whose certainty never objectively transcends some degree (however high) of probability, so that such judgments also are always revisable. I myself am inclined to regard empirical judgments of all sorts, not as literal descriptions of the objective properties of anything, but rather as practically useful formulations which make environmental adaptation more effective just in the degree that their claim on our thinking is warranted. I do not even object to calling this way of taking empirical truth-claims *symbolical pragmatism*, which would then mean precisely that empirical judgments regarded literally are to be viewed as symbols of practicality. Why, after all, should we suppose that the effects of our environment on our conscious awareness through our sensory capacities should result in a literal and pictorial description of objects themselves? But if such a symbolical pragmatism proves disturbing to any thoughtful person, he may of course simply set it aside for future reflection at his leisure.

All this is a sketch rather than a fully developed theory of knowledge, but it seems to me the only sort of sketch in which I can indulge myself in the present context. Nor do I claim any finality for the formulation of this position; I claim only that it is the clearest and most expressive formulation that I can offer at present and that it aims at a core of epistemological insight which I sincerely regard as essentially sound. Basically the whole of my epistemological approach can be summarized without concern for its involvement in the epistemological traditions of Western philosophy.[3] If there are basic principles and categories that make knowledge possible, then this acknowledgment means that ideally these starting points should be necessary presuppositions of all possible thought and being. Since they make intelligible thought possible, we can start by asking ourselves what it is to think intelligibly. And does not thinking intelligibly mean thinking in terms that stand for concepts which have a determinate (though possibly not consciously defined) meaning which sets the reference of the concept apart from whatever does not belong to it, and especially from whatever is so opposed to that concept that it

b) and it maintains that much of the content of knowledge is experiential in origin,

even though the degree of certainty of such judgments does not transcend probability.
(1) A possible symbolical pragmatism regarding empirical judgments,

(2) though this is not a crucial point at this juncture.

4. A concise formulation of my epistemological viewpoint is possible without involvement in Western philosophical tradition.
a) If basic categories make intelligible thought possible,

it seems clear that thinking intelligibly involves the principle of contradiction or coherence as such a basic category,

3. cf. my *Oriental Philosophy*, pp. 6—11.

would be unintelligible to affirm both that concept and its opposite of the same subject at the same time and in the same sense? The assumption here appealed to may be called the principle of *rational coherence* or the principle of *contradiction*, and may be stated propositionally as follows: All the concepts that intelligibly apply to the same subject of thought must be logically consistent in meaning, both with each other and with that subject. It follows that all the propositions that can meaningfully be thought to be true at the same time must likewise be consistent and therefore free from either explicit or implicit contradiction. Of course, the truth of this principle cannot be proven, since it is itself a part of the basis of every reasonable proof without exception. But it can be justified as reasonable, since nothing whatever can be intelligibly thought except by approximating conformity to that principle itself. As an evaluative standard for philosophical systems, the principle of rational coherence means that just to the extent that such systems contain contradictory elements, the truth-claim of the system will be unjustified in a formal logical sense.

A further basic principle emerges if we remember that the whole point of a philosophical view is to give a satisfactory explanation, in systematic form, of the general characteristics of the whole range of human experience. Providing such an explanation means giving an account of the nature of reality which, if it were true, would account for the general character of things being as they are, rather than otherwise. In this sense, a philosophical view aims at discovering and analyzing the cause or ground of things, and this aim is not realized fully in any identification of causes which themselves require further explanation of the same kind. No, it can reasonably be held that a philosophical system aims at tracing the character of things up to causes or explanatory principles which, though in a general way they explain all else, are themselves self-explanatory in the sense that they require no further causal grounding or argumentative basis. If anyone should ask why it should be necessary to provide such ultimate causal explanations, his very question could in turn be interpreted as illustrating this very necessity, since he is asking for precisely such a causal explanation himself. What this fact shows is that causal explanation is itself an ultimate interpretive principle or category, and that no one can reasonably dispense with it, unless he claims to do so in a purely arbitrary fashion. Whenever anyone asks for the justification of a factual truth-claim, he is asking for a causal explanation; but no further justification of that principle itself can be reasonably required, since it would itself be a part of the basis of any such justification. We may call this ultimate principle, thus clarified, the principle of *experiential relevance* or *explanatory capacity*. As a test for the adequacy and reasonableness of a philosophical system, this principle would require that such a system provide a satisfactory ultimate explanation of all the main features of the experienced world. And the truth-claim of such a system, from a factual point of view, would in that sense be proportionate to the comprehensive adequacy of its causal explanation of things.

[margin note, left:] though this principle cannot itself be proven precisely because it is such a basic category.

[margin note, left:] b) if a philosophy aims to provide a satisfactory explanation of the reason why things are as they are rather than otherwise, then this aim presupposes a causal explanation which runs back to self-explanatory grounds.

[margin note, left:] (1) Since such a causal principle can be challenged only on grounds that imply its use, it appears that causal explanation is itself an ultimate category of thought;

[margin note, left:] (2) and we can call this category experiential relevance or explanatory capacity.

In passing through these murky epistemological waters, I have of necessity left many a submerged and threatening rock of alternative theory not merely unsung but even unmentioned. This is not because these alternatives are historically insignificant, but rather because I feel constrained to chart a course which refuses to cross over from that degree of explanatory adequacy which I deem essential for clarity and persuasiveness to that ocean of technical and historical complexity which I fear might do more to disseminate confusion than to generate illumination. I would have no one suppose that I view myself as moving with smoothness and ease through these difficult waters. The element of struggle and even of anxious perplexity is never fully eliminated, not even when I actively man my intellectual oars with all the conceptual vigor that I can muster at my most lucid moments— and those moments are rare. I think I feel, with as much concern as any serious investigator of these issues, the enormous difficulties involved in aiming to lay bare and formulate the ultimate principles of thought and being without becoming self-deluded to the point of intellectual shipwreck in the process. But the relentless drive to understand the truth about reality and the hope of finally arriving in safer waters and docking at the port of my intellectual home are all so strong that I am willing to take the risks involved. I am particularly chilled and windswept by the thought that since ultimate starting points are foundations for all possible thought and cannot be vindicated by logically prior premises, there must be a sense in which any epistemological theory is characterized by a personal arbitrariness which threatens to engulf it in the dark night of idiosyncratic subjectivity. Some contemporary thinkers are so appalled by such thoughts that they have concocted the notion that there is something intrinsically wrong with the foundationalism that underlies virtually the whole of traditional discussions in epistemology. Armed with that notion and with trenchant criticism of certain easily discredited versions of foundationalism (such as deductionism), they attempt to work out an alternative to the epistemological enterprise itself. But whatever they call that alternative (coherentism or what else), in the end they inevitably run their own arguments back to foundational presuppositions of the very sort they attempt to discredit. So there is, as I see it, no alternative but to try to disclose those foundations. Trying to dispose of them seems alarmingly like trying to throw away an old boomerang, and when I see, as I clearly do, that my own reasoning here involves the use of those very principles and categories that make my own thinking possible, I inevitably come back to the raw confidence that the foundations of truth and knowledge for all of us are immediately accessible in the structure of our own conceptualizing, and, therefore, are at least as close to us as the air we breathe. In the end we have no recourse but to operate with this fundamental confidence; but we can certainly choose to do so in that atmosphere of self-conscious preoccupation which seems most likely to carry us toward the difficult goal of objective reasonableness.

c) The acknowledged historical selectivity of my position.

(1) While I never transcend a certain hesitancy about declaring myself on these issues,

still the possible value to be achieved makes the risks seem worthwhile.
(2) Since foundational principles are primitive starting points, I never fully escape the lurking sense of personal arbitrariness;
a) yet any proposed alternative to foundationalism seems inevitably to run its own claims back to analogous starting points,

b) and there is thus no real alternative but to try to formulate those ultimate principles that each person has at the basis of his own conceptualizing.

I. The question arises whether variation in objects of

knowledge requires a parallel variation in epistemological methods.

A. Possible objects of knowledge are commonly broken down into distinct types with clearly different logical properties.

B. And there is the *internal criterion* view to the effect that there are no general criteria of knowledge applicable to all types of objects.

II. This question is often viewed as particularly applicable to the religious sphere.

A. This is

1. partly because the religious object is sharply set off from other levels and types of reality,

so that the degree of conceptual clarity about the object is limited;

2. partly because the concepts used were originally applied to ordinary objects, so that their application to the religious object must be qualified, and therefore rendered partly mysterious;

3. and partly because extreme views regard the religious object as

The Application of Basic Epistemology to the Religious Sphere.

What has been so far elaborated applies to knowledge in general without any specific reference to the variable types of possible objects with which knowledge-claims may be concerned. But it seems at least initially plausible to suppose that, in view of the wide variety of such possible objects of knowledge, it might be necessary to have a corresponding variety of epistemological methods, each appropriate to some unique and distinguishable type of object. It would, of course, be self-stultifying to suppose that there should be a distinct method for every particular possible object. But there certainly are responsible philosophers who maintain that the spectrum of possible objects of knowledge can be broken down into a number of distinct spheres of awareness (e.g., the logico-mathematical object sphere, the physical object sphere, the psychological object sphere, the religious object sphere, and so on) whose characteristics are so distinct (if not unique) that these spheres call for extensive alterations in the methodology of knowledge that is appropriate for each. And there is even the *internal criterion* view (as I shall call it) that the methodologies appropriate to the spheres are wholly relative to the contexts in which they operate, so that there are no general criteria of knowledge which merely require specific adaptation from one sphere to another.

This sort of problem is frequently regarded as particularly pertinent to the religious sphere. In all the developed religious-philosophical perspectives, whether Eastern-Oriental or Western-Occidental, the ultimate object of religious concern has characteristically (though not unexceptionably) been so construed that it is regarded as, in itself, so set apart from other aspects of reality as to stand in sharp contrast to other levels and types of reality. This metaphysical aloofness has nearly always carried with it a parallel epistemological distance of such a nature that, at the very least, all attempts to achieve conceptual clarity about the essence and properties of the religious object are shrouded by an elusive fog of mystery which leaves the keenest intellect among us at least partly baffled if not fundamentally befuddled. Moderate versions of this perplexity argue, for example, that, since the concepts by which we attempt to understand the religious ultimate have their primary and original application to the objects and qualities of ordinary experience, any attempt to apply the determinate meanings of these concepts to that ultimate must be so qualified that their meaning is clouded by a vagueness and analogical significance which cannot be eliminated completely for even a single concept (like *power*, for instance). And could a sober-minded person recognize as an object of ultimate religious concern any reality whose properties were transparently clear to the careful and attentive mind? Mystery of the insoluble sort seems to pertain to the very essence of the religious object. More extreme versions of this perplexity extend its proportions to the limit of infinity, as it were, so that the religious ultimate is wholly beyond the discursive intellect and its conceptual determinations—in such a way that even qualified properties are viewed as perversions if applied to that object, and the object itself is said to be totally devoid of all qualities and to have no determinate characteristics whatsoever. It seems strange indeed that proponents of such a view about the ultimate should write so extensively concerning it in their profound treatises; but they develop various tactics for referring to what they regard as intellectually incomprehensible. Certain kinds of ascriptions, though not actually characteristic of the ultimate, are nevertheless such that they provoke and express in us an appropriate recognition of that object and a fitting response to its claim on us in some way or other. But here I must bypass the details and historical forms of such proposals in order to concentrate on the main issue concerning the application of general epistemology to the religious sphere of reality, thought, and discourse.

Now then it seems unquestionable that if there are basic general criteria of knowledge (ultimate starting points, necessary presuppositions of all thought, or however else such foundational principles and categories may be referred to), they will not be specifically applicable to every sort of possible object of awareness in the same way. The very distinction between the principles of rational coherence and experiential relevance suggests that, although basic interpretive categories provide the structure of all thought, there may be some truth-claims whose status can be determined on *a priori*, logical grounds alone (as in pure logic and pure mathematics, for instance). Yet there may be others which have an experiential content that makes their truth-claim such that their pertinence as an explanation of that content is an essential basis for settling the claim (as in judgments about empirical objects like tables, chairs, trees, and stones). There are no straightforwardly empirical observations which will settle the question whether 34 x 28 = 952, although one could look up this product in a sufficiently extended multiplication table. On the other hand, logical analysis and deduction alone will never settle the question whether I generally wear a blue denim cap when walking my dog on sunny days. One could not make judgments about the latter claim without using rational principles and logical categories (whether consciously or not); but it seems obviously impossible to settle the claim on these grounds alone. This suggestion, that ultimate criteria are applicable to different spheres of awareness in distinguishable ways, may be illustrated extensively, though I will spare myself the trouble of providing more than a single further illustration. It makes, for instance, perfectly good sense to say that two of my sweaters are exactly alike except that one is gray and the other is gold (though we suspect that there are some minute further differences in the number of stitches per inch, and so on, but such insignificant variations are taken for granted). But it makes no sense at all to say that two morally significant acts are exactly alike in every respect, except that one is morally right and the other morally wrong, for two acts cannot logically differ in moral quality without differing in some further respects, even though two sweaters can logically differ significantly in color alone. So it may

wholly beyond discursive intellect so that even qualified properties become perversions.

a) While proponents regard some properties as more fittingly applied to the religious object than others, *b*) yet even those are not actually characteristic of it.

B. Even if there are general criteria of knowledge, it seems clear that they are not applicable to all types of objects in the same way.
1. This claim is illustrated by the distinction between *a priori* judgments whose truth-status can be settled on logical grounds alone, and *a posteriori* judgments whose truth-status, though involving the use of logical principles and categories, can only be settled on empirical grounds.

2. The point is further illustrated by the fact that the grounds of intelligibility for sensory judgments are clearly, though only partly, distinct from the corresponding grounds for moral judgments.

3. Hence, the application of ultimate principles may vary from sphere to sphere.

plausibly be concluded that, in general, the application of ultimate principles of knowledge may differ logically in distinguishable spheres of awareness.

C. Yet this need not mean that the criteria are wholly internal to each sphere.

1. The internal criterion view is itself a general claim not confined to any limited sphere, so that it claims itself to be universally applicable,

a) and this in turn shows that it is incoherent and inconsistent with the content of its own assertion.

b) While this criticism rests on the principle of contradiction as universally applicable, the critic of it must rest on the same ground to render his own view intelligible.

2. General interpretive principles are in practice appealed to in all spheres, even if in theory this is denied.

D. But is the religious sphere an exception to the universal-criterion view?

But does all this mean that the criteria of truth or propriety for a given sphere are wholly relative or internal to that sphere? Self-reflection on the process involved here will, in my opinion, at least chasten, if it does not finally correct, the tendency to suppose such a radical methodological disjunction among the various spheres in which truth-claims are made. For the internal criterion thesis itself is a general perspective about the characteristics of knowledge and is therefore a truth-claim that is not confined to any limited sphere of subject matter. That means that the thesis is a universal proposal of the very sort that, as a thesis, it purports to deny. In making this critical claim, I am, of course, appealing to the principle of contradiction or rational coherence as itself a universal criterion, and I have no wish to disguise this fact. But what I am suggesting is that the thesis that criteria of truth are wholly internal to distinct spheres of awareness is incoherent and involves a sort of existential contradiction between *what* is being asserted and the *fact that* it is being asserted. On the other hand, my criticism to this effect involves no such incoherence since I openly acknowledge the very sort of universal criterion to which I here appeal. And if, in response, someone were to suggest that I am appealing to the very sort of criterion which the internal-criterion theorist rejects, then the answer is: First, that this observation, though true, does not remove the contradiction; second, that if my critic does not at least implicitly appeal to the principle of contradiction as a universal criterion, he will not be able to render his own view fully intelligible; and third, that I have no hesitation in supposing that if any sober-minded person becomes convinced that he is involved in such an existential incoherence in a position he holds, he will discard the position rather than continue consciously in the incoherence, unless he has some idiosyncratic, wholly personal reason for clinging to his thesis.

A further difficulty with the internal-criterion view is therefore that with very few exceptions general principles like rational coherence and experiential relevance are in practice appealed to by responsible investigators in all spheres of awareness, even if in theory the ultimate and universal status of such principles is denied. This is the case, admittedly, in the empirical sciences; but it is also the case in ethics, religion, and other analogous spheres. And if we find thinkers in every sphere implicitly appealing to such universal criteria in the confidence that such appeals will be decisive in regard to positions they investigate, it will be difficult to escape the plausibility of the view that there are indeed universal and ultimate principles and categories of knowledge, even though their application to various spheres will differ in relation to the logical status of particular judgments in that sphere.

However, there still remains the supposition that, while the universal-criterion view (as I will term it) may indeed be correct in relation to other spheres of awareness, nevertheless the religious sphere, concerned as it is with the ultimate object of religious concern, may constitute an exceptional case in which the otherwise universal criteria are simply not applicable either straightforwardly or with special qualifications. On reflection, it seems to me that there are no plausible reasons for making such an exception of the religious object. If an exception is made, then it will either be wholly arbitrary or else it will be based on certain formulable reasons which will in the end rest logically on the very sort of principles and categories which the exception would regard as inapplicable to the religious object. Such reasons might, for instance, argue that the religious object had characteristics or attributes which would render conceptual categories inapplicable; but arriving at a clear knowledge of these attributes and thus at a knowledge of the religious object itself would require that the individual had some way of consciously identifying that object and apprehending its properties in order to distinguish it from other objects of awareness. Yet this process would itself be conceptual in nature and finally be grounded in those very sorts of principles and categories which were supposed to be excluded from the knowledge of the religious object. It has been commonly held that the ascribing of determinate characteristics of a conceptual (is there any other?) sort would compromise the absoluteness or the infinity or whatever of the religious object. But it is clear that such an argument is itself an example of a high level of sophisticated conceptualizing. And while I certainly have not discussed all the arguments of this sort that have appeared historically, I have without exception found that such arguments involve and, in my opinion, succumb to the very sort of difficulty that I am discussing here.[4]

1. Such an exception would either be arbitrary or else based on the very sort of universal principles regarded as inapplicable; 2. and any attempt to view the religious object as having qualities which made conceptual categories inapplicable, would involve the use of just such categories in clarifying those qualities.

3. The claim that conceptual qualities would compromise the absoluteness of the religious object involves the same sort of difficulty.

Why, then, has the notion of the inapplicability of conceptual principles and categories to the religious object had such an enormous and pervasive fascination for a certain type of religious tradition and consciousness? So far as this is a question about psychological motivation, it is very difficult to provide anything even approaching a complete and adequate answer, since characteristically none of us is able to give a satisfactory account of the psychological motives underlying his own attraction to various positions and arguments. But I think I can offer some tentative suggestions toward a plausible answer. When a person is intensely involved in the awareness of some object of any sort, he is generally not self-reflective about the structure of awareness through which he apprehends the object, but is instead all but wholly absorbed in the object itself. In fact, such self-reflective analysis (typical for the critical-philosophical mood) may be detrimental to the fullness and integrity of the experience itself. In this way, it becomes easy to identify non-awareness of conceptual structure with the supposed absence of that structure. And if authentic religious experience is regarded as perhaps the most intense and absorbing of

E. Why has the notion of the inapplicability of concepts to the ultimate been so prevalent?

1. This is partly because absorption in an object typically obstructs any awareness of the structure through which it is apprehended, and such awareness may even be detrimental to the experience;

4. cf. my *Oriental Philosophy*, pp. 162–167.

all distinctively human experiences, then the sort of confusion involved in arguing afterward, from the lack of the awareness of conceptual categories to their assumed absence, is just what one might expect.

But there are also other reasons for the fascination we are reflecting about. To most individuals who analyze the ultimate object of their own religious experience, it seems clear that there are certain class concepts which are obviously inapplicable to the religious object. It cannot have the sort of material status that a rock has, for example; or, more generally, it cannot be confined to a limited space; or it cannot be essentially evil in the ethical sense. Since for most such persons the class of such unpredicable properties is very extended, it is an understandable transition of thought to suppose that *no* conceptually determinate properties can be identified which will not contain some basis for their inapplicability to the religious object. And thus the reasonable thesis—that the nature of the religious object excludes certain attributes—passes into the highly questionable (and to me wholly implausible) thesis that the nature of the religious object excludes any conceptually determinate attributes and is therefore immune to being known through ultimate rational principles and categories. A final suggestion would be that since the religious consciousness exalts its ultimate object above all finite realities, there is something demeaning or devaluating about knowing that object through the sort of categories and principles by which one apprehends these ordinary realities. Hence the suspicion arises that if one can know the religious object conceptually, he somehow stands above it so that it cannot be the true religious object after all. I must confess that I find this last line of supposition wholly baffling. As I see it, the intelligibility or rational knowability of any object of awareness enhances rather than diminishes its value; and in any case there is no reason why the religious object cannot be known precisely as *superior*, in being and attributes, to the finite mind.

From all this I conclude that there is no reason to regard the ultimate object of religious awareness as an exception to the general thesis that all knowledge ultimately is grounded in certain universal criteria which pervade the whole sphere of cognitive awareness, even though these criteria may be differently applicable to distinct segments of that sphere. In general, I further conclude, these universal criteria of knowledge have the character of being necessary foundations or presuppositions of all intelligible thought and being, so that they are the ultimate starting points or basis, in the logical sense, of all knowledge- or truth-claims. Yet it must not be supposed that every responsible thinker is consciously aware of the whole (or even of any part) of the structure of these foundational principles when he makes a particular truth-claim. The degree of this awareness will vary widely for different individuals, depending on their intellectual background and attitudes, and it will even vary for the same individual at different times and under altered immediate circumstances. And it may, I think, be said that even the most theoretically astute among us never achieve

Marginal notes:

2. but it is partly also because it is possible to move easily from one plausible thesis, that some categories are not applicable to the religious object, to a wholly implausible thesis, that no conceptual categories are applicable to that object;

3. and finally because it is supposed that it demeans the religious object for it to be known conceptually as other objects are known, so that this relation places the knower above the object, although in fact *a*) knowability enhances an object's value, *b*) and the religious object can be known precisely as superior to all finite objects.
F. Hence, I conclude
1. that the religious object is not an exception to the universality of the criteria of knowledge,
2. and that these criteria are necessary presuppositions of all thought and being;
3. although it does not follow that responsible thinkers are explicitly conscious of these principles,

a fully clear apprehension of these principles in their total structure and relationships, much less a fully adequate propositional and conceptual expression of them. The point is that such principles *actually are* the foundations of thought and being, however little and imperfectly conscious of them we may be in the actual operations of reasoning and making truth-claims. Analogously, we do not consciously consider the structure of our eyes when engaged in the activity of vision. We simply see with them, and we generally become self-reflective about our eyes only when some eyelash or speck of dust irritates them and interferes with their normal functioning. It follows from this that it is no criticism of the doctrine of such ultimate principles that most persons are not consciously aware of the foundation which these principles provide for their own process of thought and understanding.

or that any thinker's formulation of them is either adequate or complete, since such principles are the structure *through* which we think, rather than, as a rule, objects *about* which we think.

It is not my intention to develop here a logically inclusive analysis of the particular principles and categories which function as such logical starting points for thought. I would, in fact, maintain that any such analysis would, as I have suggested, be at best an approximation of the total structure and therefore a tentative formulation of it, in need of continuous reconsideration and possible revision. But I do maintain that the principles of rational coherence and experiential relevance, as I previously elaborated them, provide specific examples of these ultimate presuppositions. And even more explicitly, I find some version of Immanuel Kant's transcendental method an intuitively plausible way of getting at a fairly extended list of these categories. It was his contention that since such categories function to make intelligible thought possible, and since thinking is structurally cast in the form of judgments or propositions, then there must be as many basic categories as there are irreducibly basic types of logical judgment. Since, for example, judgments are either affirmative or negative, there would be corresponding categories of reality and negation to make these types possible. Using this general parallelism between judgments and categories, Kant, following traditional logic, came up with a list of categories which included such concepts as substance, causation, reciprocity, existence, possibility, and necessity. I am not maintaining that this method is the only possible one for getting at a plausible list of such ultimate principles; but I certainly do regard it as a fruitful approach to the problem. However, the further pursuit of this complex issue would lead to intricacies that would distract us from our main core of analysis. Instead, let each investigator plumb the depths and seek the foundational principles which lie at the root of his own thinking, to see if there does not emerge a set of principles whose similarity to Kant's list is so analogous that it would support the rational plausibility of such a general epistemological thesis.

III. It is beyond my purpose to develop a detailed analysis of basic principles and categories.
A. Any such analysis would be tentative in any case;
B. but
1. the principles of rational coherence and experiential relevance are examples,
2. and the general method of Kant, in deriving a list of such categories, seems plausible.
a) General procedure and results of this method.

b) While no exclusive claim is made for this method, it seems a fruitful approach;

C. and each person can attempt to think back to the foundations of his own thought to discover an analogous structure of basic principles.

Epistemological Approaches to the Evaluation of Religious Truth-Claims

In general, there are two significantly different attitudes toward ultimate criteria of knowledge or evaluative critical principles, both in general epistemology and in the more limited sphere of religious epistemology. While there is no established terminology for referring to these broad approaches, I find it useful to call them by the names *voluntaristic* and *rationalistic*, although this nomenclature might easily generate confusion if it is not clearly and carefully understood. The voluntaristic outlook holds that an ultimate commitment of will is the decisive basis for the status of such principles as standards, and it maintains that these fundamental criteria are logically dependent upon the overall metaphysical or world-view system that a man accepts, whether knowingly or not. From this point of view, evaluative principles are likely to vary from one system of thought to another, and there is no neutral ground of independent logic or reason by which one can decide between contrasting and opposing sets of criteria, since any given set is wholly internal to the perspective in which it operates. In the end, of course, the voluntaristic approach means that a given thinker can criticize another thinker's system only on grounds that imply his own commitment. Therefore, all decisions between systems are ultimately arbitrary—not merely in the sense that they often or even characteristically *are* arbitrary, but also in the sense that it is logically inevitable that they *must* be.

In contrast, the rationalistic stance holds that there are ultimate criteria of knowledge or evaluative principles which do not depend for their status as foundational principles on voluntary commitment to a particular overall world-view perspective, but rather reflect the nature of objective reason itself. Such an attitude maintains that the final grounds of all truth-claims, so far as those claims are reasonable, cut across alternative systematic perspectives and therefore need not reflect the special distinctives of any one such perspective. In a way, these categories would be metaphysical in their significance, both in the sense that they would pertain to the understanding of reality in such a way that nothing could exist or be clearly thought without conforming to them, and also in the sense that the consistent and proper use of these principles in relation to the real world would presumably point in one metaphysical direction rather than another. But such criteria would not be logical derivatives of that or any other metaphysical direction. Instead, these principles would be evaluative standards for arguing the reasonableness of any given metaphysical direction in relation to others, so that the rational propriety of *any* system of philosophy would then depend on the degree to which it reflected, and conformed to, those very principles. And it goes almost without saying that a proponent of the rationalistic attitude *need not* (and, in my opinion, *should not*) claim finality for any particular formulations of these principles, but may rather, with appropriate acknowledgment of his personal, historical, and cultural limits, regard such formulations as tentative and revisable in the light of further reflection. To put it more succinctly, rationalism in this sense is not necessarily dogmatism in any objectionable sense.

It will be immediately evident that my previously elaborated epistemological perspective is a particular version of the rationalistic attitude. However, it should be equally clear that I am far from stoutly maintaining either that it is the only plausible version or that the only possible alternative to the rationalistic stance itself is sheer intellectual insanity. Yet I feel it incumbent on me to analyze a selected variety of voluntaristic arguments and perspectives in religious epistemology in order to bring out their intrinsic claim and make the alternative approaches as clear as I possibly can.

II. My perspective is clearly a variety of rationalism as thus understood, but I hold its details with appropriate tentativity.

Voluntaristic Approaches

The main thesis of the voluntaristic outlook, then, is that evaluative criteria for assessing knowledge-claims are logically and therefore inevitably relative to some particular world-view perspective to which prior volitional commitment, whether fully conscious or not, has already been made. In religious epistemology, this type of approach, involving as it does a foundational faith-principle or belief-commitment, is commonly referred to as fideism (from the Latin *fides* = faith), although not all thinkers who take this stance are comfortable with this terminology. But while it is essential to voluntarism here that there are no logically independent or neutral criteria for objectively deciding among alternative world-view perspectives, most defenders of voluntarism do not hesitate to provide a rationale for the voluntaristic stance itself.

I. Although voluntarism regards evaluative principles as system-dependent and therefore as grounded in a faith-or belief-commitment,

nevertheless they provide a sort of rationale for voluntarism itself.

In general, supporting arguments for voluntarism are of three types: (1) from the *logical* status of evaluative criteria; (2) from the *psychological* motives that form the causal basis of belief-commitments; and (3) from the *religious* context to which ultimate criteria are applied. The *logical status* arguments urge, first, that no matter how neutral or logically independent ultimate epistemological principles purport to be, an analysis of their logical context invariably shows that they do in fact reflect some prior world-view commitment—indeed, if any such criteria were genuinely independent of any and all particular perspectival commitments, their very neutrality would make them practically useless for a decision among alternative world-views, so that the criteria would thus lack the chief virtue ascribed to them by rationalists. The second argument is that even defenders of rational objectivity acknowledge that ultimate truth-standards are inevitably arbitrary in the logical sense, since they are themselves the necessary presuppositions of all intelligible thought and cannot therefore be supported by any arguments which do not already rest on their ultimacy itself. The third claim is that the case for any particular metaphysical perspective through the use of these so-called neutral criteria is admitted by rationalists themselves to be, at best, no more than highly probable, so that the question inevitably arises whether this sort of probability comports well in practice with the sort of unconditional commitment which is essential to religious belief. (Can a religious believer seriously address in prayer, for example, a God whose existence he regards as merely probable?)

II. Such arguments are of three main types:

A. Logical status arguments which claim
1. that in fact all evaluative criteria do reflect world-view commitments when analyzed, since otherwise they would be useless;

2. that even rationalists admit that basic criteria are by nature logically arbitrary;

3. that logical cases for particular world views are no more than probable, while religious belief requires a commitment that is unconditional.

In terms of *psychological motives*, it is contended that belief-commitments are characteristically, if not universally, the determined ef-

B. Psychological motive arguments which claim:

1. that belief-commitments are the product of non-rational causal factors of which the individual is largely unconscious, so that rational objectivity is not practically possible;

fect of idiosyncratic—personal, cultural, and historical—influences that decisively shape the outlook of an individual in such a way that in practice he cannot achieve that independence of such causal factors which is required to occupy an intellectual position that corresponds to rational objectivity. Furthermore, these determining influences have two additional qualities which make the desired objectivity even more difficult. First, even the most introspective and culturally alert individual is conscious of no more than a very limited number of these factors, so that they produce their virtually inevitable effect without our conscious supervision. Second, such influences are nearly always non-rational—that is, although they *cause* our beliefs, they are not typically such that these causes provide any logically relevant reasons for the truth-claim of those beliefs. A simple (but all too common) example would be a case in which a person's deep respect and affection for some other individual leads him causally to accept some significant belief which that person also accepts, although, of course, it seems clear on reflection that the ground of the truth of a belief could logically never be the fact that any given individual believes it. But, of course, there are innumerable additional factors far more obscure than those involved in this example: such things as subconscious and suppressed fears and hostilities, odd mental tendencies and quirks, deeply ingrained tendencies grounded in historical and cultural patterns, and so on. How, then, can we plausibly suppose that the adequate grounding of the most important truth-claims (among which religious beliefs would rank at or near the top of the list) should be decisively dependent on rational criteria whose use is practically inaccessible to the individual?

2. that the motives which in fact underlie religious beliefs rarely have the logical character of rational arguments, but rather are emotional and authoritarian in nature,

Closely related to the previous psychological argument is the further contention that descriptive studies of the psychological motives underlying religious beliefs rarely disclose those motives as having the logical character of rational arguments grounded in supposedly objective criteria of evaluation. Instead, the typically religious person, when asked for an account of his motives for a religious belief-commitment, will respond by referring to emotional experiences and crises involving personality transformations, or to some traditionally grounded respect for religious authority (whether in an ecclesiastical teaching body or in an accepted oral or written standard of belief), or to similar influencing factors. And what is not accessible by such testimony is often discernible in the individual's behavior patterns. It seems clear that, just to the extent that one's belief-commitments importantly affect his destiny, decisions about those commitments are influenced by the individual's underlying hopes, desires, and emotive inclinations. In

and in particular reflect the state of a person's moral character, the causal influence of which one is largely impotent decisively to alter.

particular, it is often pointed out that the state of a person's moral character (however that may be assessed) plays a causal role in his attempt to decide belief-commitments. Since it is apparently not within the normal operation of the will to alter decisively the state of one's moral character, it becomes at least enormously difficult, if not practically impossible, to cope effectively with this moral state in such a way as to achieve a characteristically objective stance. In the language of Christian theology, this moral factor is commonly referred to as the noetic effect of sin. It is often contended that in the natural state of humanity, apart from efficacious divine grace, a man's eyes are so thoroughly blinded by the sinful condition of his character that he cannot discern and respond to the ultimate religious truth—everything in an individual's sphere of possible religious insight takes on the blurred cast of his distorted vision.

There are, finally, some deep *religious* concerns that, for many, appear safeguarded by the voluntaristic approach. If, as the rationalist outlook supposes, we make ultimate rational criteria, as exemplified in the structure of our own minds, the ground for assessing truth-claims about the religious object (God, for most Westerners); and if, therefore, we require any such claim to conform to the rational demand of these criteria, it appears to follow that we are exalting objective reason (and perhaps our own minds as its chief, undisputed exemplars) above the religious object itself. But this reversal is perhaps the essence of religious idolatry, since by this move we are in effect making a god out of objective reason. In any case, such an exaltation of reason is inconsistent, it is claimed, with the absoluteness required by the unconditionality of religious commitment. As one critic of rationalism put it: Making rational criteria the ultimate ground of religious truth-claims immediately discloses *what*, not *who*, the rationalist's god really is.

A similar religious argument concerns the concept of revelational authority: If we suppose that a revelation claim (that is, the claim that a certain body of insight is genuine religious truth) must be defended by rational arguments that are logically independent of the revelation-claim itself, are we not compromising the very nature of that authority by making objective reason, not revelation, the ultimate consideration? An assumption underlying this line of reasoning is that a genuine revelation must be self-authenticating or self-vindicating if it is to have the status of revelation at all. A more extreme form of this whole type of argument would go on to maintain that if objective reason is the ultimate criterion for the genuineness of divine revelation, then it ought to be intrinsically capable of acquiring the entire content of that revelation through its own operations on generally accessible data. If that is the case, then the very notion of divine revelation would be rendered vacuous. To avoid such conclusions, we should, it is claimed, revert to the thesis that revelation can only be volitionally appropriated, not rationally argued.

It is scarcely necessary to mention that not all thinkers in the voluntarist tradition employ all these arguments in support of this general approach, and the arguments that a given proponent does use are given varied emphasis from thinker to thinker, while some of the arguments are simply dismissed as ineffective by one voluntarist or another. Furthermore, representatives of this outlook vary as well in their emphasis on the sort of volitionally espoused factor which they take to be decisive for religious truth-claims. I would characterize the main division here as a distinction between *experiential* voluntarism

C. *Religious context* arguments which claim:
1. that decisive dependence on rational arguments places objective reason above the religious object in an idolatrous manner;

2. that if a revelation claim must be defended by logically independent arguments, then that would compromise the ultimacy of revelational authority,

and perhaps even mean that reason could achieve all genuine religious truth without revelation.

III. Voluntarism divides into two main perspectives, depending on the volitional factors viewed as decisive.

A. Hence, *experientialism* (emphasizing definitive religious experience as basic) and *revelationalism* (emphasizing authoritative revealed truth as basic), though the difference is not sharp.

and *revelational* voluntarism, the former emphasizing some sort of distinctively religious experience or awareness as a self-validating, non-rational (though not unintelligible in every case) foundation for religious truth-claims, the latter emphasizing a context of revealed truth (however that notion is construed) as an ultimate starting point for the vindication of such claims. The difference between these two emphases is, however, not particularly sharp, since a decisively religious experience is normally regarded as itself involving a revelatory disclosure, and every revealed truth runs back, as it were, to such a religious experience as the context of its manifestation. But a common divergence between these viewpoints emerges in the Christian tradition (though it appears also in other religions), in which revealed truth has often been regarded as originally limited to disclosures imparted to a closely limited and special group of recipients (such as prophets and apostles) in their religious experiences, while the genuine religious experience of other persons in the tradition is normally grounded in, and provoked by, the oral or written expression of these special recipients.

B. Experiential voluntarism subdivides according to the type of experience emphasized:
1. Pascal.

2. Kierkegaard.

3. Plotinus.

4. Schleiermacher.

5. Otto.

6. James.

Experiential voluntarism is of course further capable of subdivision into a wide variety of perspectives distinguished from each other by the sort of experience that is emphasized and the context of thought in which the experience itself is understood. A Blaise Pascal will emphasize the poverty of rational arguments to generate religious faith, and will put in the place of these arguments a knowledge of the heart, an intuitive and synoptic core of insight which grasps the meaning of existence as a whole and which is analogous to the intuited axioms of mathematical and other formal logical systems, although this intuited capacity transcends conceptual reason and rational principles. A Søren Kierkegaard will dismiss rational systems as fraudulent devices destructive of the very essence of genuine religious truth, and will argue that authentic religious faith involves a sort of anguishing personal commitment to a core of truth which, from the standpoint of rational objectivity, takes essential paradox as its ultimate form. A Plotinus will speak, with acknowledged ineptness, of an intuitive experience of insight in which the individual experiences undifferentiable oneness and indiscerptible unity with the ineffable One that is devoid of all determinate and rationally apprehended qualities. A Friedrich Schleiermacher will identify the essence of religious awareness as the feeling of absolute dependence on the Infinite All, and will proceed to interpret all religious doctrines as constructions upon this basic core of understanding in such a way that the propriety of these doctrines is precisely a function of the degree to which they both express and evoke this essential religious awareness. A Rudolf Otto will point to a unique, *a priori* schematism of non-rational awareness which characterizes all genuine religious experience and makes it irreducible to the dimensions of any sort of natural experience, while he continues to regard conceptual religious systems as analogous schematisms which (always imperfectly) attempt to understand the non-rational core of essential religion in rational terms. A William

James, finally, will regard what he vaguely refers to as the religious hypothesis as neither defensible nor refutable on rational grounds. But he will then go on to maintain that individuals have every right to exercise their will to believe in whatever version of that hypothesis will, above all others, enrich and fulfill the meaningfulness of life for that individual and for humanity at large, provided only that the particular form of the hypothesis does not, as it were, fly in the face of generally acknowledged scientific evidence. Yet the basic thrust of all these widely varying perspectives is analogous—a distinctive type of uniquely religious experience which becomes the foundation and clearinghouse for religious truth-claims.

And revelational voluntarism is similarly proliferated into an extensive variety of distinguishable forms. But here there is a significant further subdivision which turns on contrasting emphases about the concept of revelation itself, particularly in the Christian tradition. For one of these revelationist views, which I will call *illuminationism*, the stress rests upon a decisive experiential element which involves a personal encounter with God in the witness of the Holy Spirit, in such a way that the individual is specially enlightened to discern the essential religious truth. At the same time it is held that the prophetic and apostolic writings (the Christian Scriptures) function as a norm and instrument through which the quickening experience is communicated. In this vein, a Saint Augustine, though profoundly respecting and drawing on neo-Platonism, maintains that in the essential spiritual sense the individual does not first understand the rationale of the Christian faith and then believe. Rather, that individual is first moved to believe by the illumination brought to him through the witness of the Holy Spirit, and only then does he understand the spiritual truth with sufficient clarity. Or a John Calvin holds that although God is clearly revealed in the natural order and in the inspired Scriptures, yet the blindness of sin so distorts the vision of man that neither of these revelations results in genuine spiritual insight except in conjunction with, and as a result of, the regenerating act of the Holy Spirit through which alone the individual achieves clear understanding. Or, finally, an Emil Brunner, though acknowledging a revelation in nature and accepting the Scriptures as the norm through which the Spirit of God provokes spiritual awareness (but at the same time rejecting any static notion of the Scriptures as divine revelation), nevertheless argues that it is through personal divine encounter, indeed through spiritual truth as encounter, that an individual truly confronts and understands the word of God with the requisite clarity.

For the other revelationist view, which I will call *scripturalism*, although there is certainly a stress on the efficacious witness of the Holy Spirit, yet the main emphasis is on the Christian Scriptures as the basic presuppositional ground of the reasonableness of the Christian truth-claim. It follows that instead of arguing *to* scriptural authority from logically independent rational and experiential grounds, one argues instead *from* scriptural authority as foundational to the reasonableness or otherwise of any religious truth-claim whatever. The vol-

C. Revelational voluntarism likewise subdivides into:
1. *illuminationism* (which stresses an existential encounter with God, resulting in enlightenment to discern religious truth).

a) Augustine.

b) Calvin.

c) Brunner.

2. *Scripturalism* (which stresses the sacred Scriptures as the basic presuppositional ground).

a) Kuyper.

b) Van Til.

IV. Critical evaluation
of voluntarism:

A. This requires com-
mitment to a particu-
lar perspective about
evaluative criteria.
1. My procedure takes
the form of a personal
response and does not
presuppose absolute
objectivity.

2. Yet in giving such
criticism I am aiming
sincerely at a rational
objectivity which even
the voluntarist at-
tempts to achieve in
his own arguments,

while at the same time
I am struggling
against non-rational
influences.

untarist element consists primarily, from a philosophical point of view,
in the individual's commitment of will and intellect to that scriptural
authority as the ultimate starting point. In this vein, then, a thinker
such as Abraham Kuyper regards the principle of special revelation
(which achieves its fixed verbal form in the Christian Scriptures) as
the ultimate faith-principle of the Christian system, so that this principle has precisely the status of a basic axiom or foundational presupposition, with the result that no logically independent ground for this
principle is possible. A Cornelius Van Til argues that, although God is
clearly revealed in the natural order, human reason is so distorted by
sin that this clear manifestation is properly evident only to the man
who places himself on scriptural authority as a necessary epistemological starting point, with the characteristic corollary that the man himself can authentically operate from this starting point only if he has,
in conjunction with this epistemological commitment, also made that
faith-commitment which makes it evident that he has been regenerated by the Holy Spirit. Yet the basic thrust of both illuminationism
and scripturalism consists of taking revelational authority, however it
is spelled out in detail in either experiential or scriptural terms, as the
ultimate presupposition and ground for discerning the reasonableness
or otherwise of religious truth-claims.

If now we address ourselves to the critical evaluation both of
specific voluntaristic views and of the outlook in general, it is clear
that we can do so only by appealing to some perspective about the
basic criteria of knowledge and truth, criteria whose logical status is
itself at stake in the very issues which divide voluntaristic from rationalistic approaches. Since I have no wish to hide or even disguise this
situation, I readily acknowledge that here, as in all my critical work,
there is a sense in which my assessment takes the form of a personal
response, precisely because I cannot avoid making presuppositions
with which other thinkers might suppose themselves to be in disagreement. Nor do I imagine for a moment that I have succeeded in
transcending the influence of every possible idiosyncratic slant which
might in varying degrees distort my vision. However, if I seriously
thought that the basis of my criticism was, in the end, wholly personal
in that idiosyncratic sense, I should not expend the energy to elaborate
such criticisms as if they constituted significant difficulties. In appealing to criteria such as rational coherence and experiential relevance, I
am placing myself on a foundation which I sincerely take to be rationally objective in a sense that I have already elaborated. And in the
application of these standards to the assessment of voluntarism, I am
with equal sincerity aiming at the same rational objectivity which,
admittedly or not, the voluntarist himself aims at, both in defending
his position and in critically evaluating his own philosophical opponents. Yet I am at the same time struggling, with all the intellectual
energy I can muster, to compensate for the influence of those non-
rational factors likely to unbalance one who is intent on walking the
narrow track of truth, although, like any other finite thinker, I am
confident that I often lose my footing temporarily—sometimes with-

out even being explicitly aware of it. That is, in part, why philosophy is not, in the end, an isolated individual task but an inclusive community enterprise. We *need* each other to detect on our own eyes the very sort of obscuring film that we are earnestly trying to treat in the eyes of others.

For the sake of clarity, I find it best to begin my evaluation with a consideration of particular versions of voluntarism. Experiential voluntarism, then, takes as its starting point and foundational criterion some kind of self-authenticating religious awareness which then becomes the standard for assessing more limited and less fundamental religious truth-claims. However, it seems questionable whether religious experience can properly occupy this epistemological status. For one thing, the recognition and description of a particular type of experience as religious seems to presuppose a structure of interpretive principles, logically prior to the experience, in order to carry through this essential task of recognition and description, so that this structure would take epistemological (but not, of course, valuational) precedence over the religious experience itself. The presence of this interpretive factor becomes all the more obvious when we take account of the drastically different views of religious experience and its world-view significance, as these positions are expounded even by the limited number of thinkers touched upon in our own analysis. On reflection, it becomes apparent that the nature of religious experience itself, as well as the description of its implications, is in part (if not wholly) a function of the interpretive context which the individual, with whatever degree of explicit awareness, *brings to* the experience by way of anticipation. This thesis about religious experience—a thesis which I will call *interpretive contextualism*—may be put more simply and succinctly: *How* an individual *takes* a religious experience, and even his discernment that it *is* a religious experience, is in large measure a function of *what* the individual expects in such an experience, so much so that, in part at least, this expectation gives the experience its cognitive content. But this, of course, means that any truth-claims propounded on the basis of religious experience must be assessed, not through the experience itself as a criterion, but through the propriety and reasonableness of the interpretive framework which provided the experience with its structure and, to some extent, even its content. So there seem to be two factors that are logically prior to religious experience: First, the basic categories of intelligible thought (common, I have previously suggested, to all rational minds) which make it possible to identify and analyze religious experience as such; and second, the world-view context (however vaguely apprehended by the individual) which gives meaning and content to that religious experience.

All this becomes further evident when an individual appeals to his own (or anyone else's) religious experience as a basic criterion and then tries to square this claim with the very different account of the nature and significance of religious experience given by another individual as a personal account. If he dismisses the other's experience as

B. Critique of *experiential voluntarism:*

1. Recognition of an experience as religious presupposes a logically prior set of interpretive principles which are therefore more basic.

a) The wide variety of views based on religious experience also suggests that this variety is a function of different interpretive contexts.

b) Hence, it is plausible that the context provides much of the cognitive content of the experience.

c) Thus truth-claims based on experience should be assessed through evaluating the framework itself, since the experience is inseparable from it.

2. When a person gives criterial priority to his account of religious experience over the account of some other person, his procedure is either arbitrary or else it appeals to grounds logically independent of the experience.

a) If both experiences are regarded as authentic independent of their content, that is virtually the view here argued.
b) Otto argues for common structural components in all genuine religious experience, regardless of content, but sees the components themselves as pointing to a particular world-view.

C. Critique of *revelational voluntarism:*
1. This view has many of the problems of experiential voluntarism, except that, in Christian tradition, the interpretive context seems more obvious.

2. Appeal to the witness of the Holy Spirit raises the question of identifying that witness.

3. Scripturalism involves an appeal to the religious experiences of the biblical writers.

inauthentic or misinterpreted, then either that claim will be arbitrary, or else it will rest on grounds that are logically independent of religious experience itself, which is not therefore in practice the ultimate criterion of truth-claims ostensibly made on the basis of religious experience. The other alternative would be to regard the varying contents ascribed to religious experience as not essential to the experience itself, so that both individuals have, it may be admitted, a genuine religious experience, but proceed to understand it differently on grounds extraneous to the experience itself. But that is precisely interpretive contextualism as I understand it. A thinker like Rudolf Otto tries to cope with such difficulties by arguing that man as man has a unique *a priori* capacity for religious experience, such that the structural components of that experience are common to all genuine religious experiences, regardless of the historical context in which these experiences are understood by the individual. He then proceeds to argue that the structural components themselves point in the direction of a particular religious world-view as more plausible than its alternatives. Of course, Otto recognizes that truth-claims grounded in such an analysis are scarcely distilled from religious experience itself in any ultimate sense, but are rather based on a highly developed exercise of rational reflection. Whether Otto is right about all this, I am content, for the moment at least, to regard as an open question.

Revelational voluntarism is, as I see it, beset with similar problems. To the extent that revelational illuminationism is a reiteration of the experientialist emphasis on religious experience as a logical starting-point, it involves whatever problems that are conjoined to that view as previously analyzed—except that here the understanding of religious experience through an extraneous world-view context is, if anything, even more obvious through the interpretation of that experience in close correlation with, and dependently upon, the normative standard provided by the Christian Scriptures as refracted through the tradition of Christian theology. It seems also to be the case that the emphasis on the witness of the Holy Spirit raises difficult questions about identifying the felt inner witness as in fact the work of the Holy Spirit. The New Testament itself instructs believers not to regard every spiritual witness as that of the Holy Spirit. In fact, it urges those believers to test the "spirits" to see whether they are from God (1 John 4:1f.); and the tests proposed are doctrinal and ethical in nature, rather than being directly grounded in the inner witness.

But it is revelational scripturalism which focuses our attention on the principal problems in this particular epistemological approach. In the first place, the Christian Scriptures as such, even from the most traditional standpoint of orthodoxy, emerged from the religious experiences of the biblical writers themselves—not always out of what those writers took to be direct encounters with God (and I have no desire to challenge this way of taking the matter), but, at the very least, out of their awareness of the pervasive guidance of the Holy Spirit even in their activities of collecting data and reflecting on their meaning. This means that appealing to biblical authority as a starting point is also clearly an appeal to the epistemological ultimacy of religious experience.

A further difficulty here concerns the scripturalist thesis that the Christian Bible itself might (or should) be taken as the axiom-set of the Christian system in a way that is analogous to the foundational presuppositions of other systems and that therefore is veiled with at least parallel logical respectability. But such a thesis seems to me highly implausible for a wide variety of reasons. To begin with, the biblical writings contain materials at a large number of different logical levels and of such a nature that many of its propositions are argued as conclusions from other biblical statements or even from explicitly acknowledged extra-biblical grounds. To suppose that the conjunction of all these varied materials could constitute an axiom-set, composed either of logical primitives from which deductions are to be made or of interpretive structural principles by means of which all non-biblical data are to be understood and assessed—such a supposition is, at the least, very difficult to construe in any proper fashion, if indeed the proposal does not approach being positively baffling. And this perplexity is further compounded by the fact that, as in the parallel case of religious experience, the biblical statements are, neither singly nor in conjunction, either self-evident or self-interpreting, so that a structure of logically prior interpretive principles or categories is implied as a foundation for understanding the biblical propositions themselves.

Perhaps, however, it is not too much to say that the problems already suggested diminish to modest proportions indeed when compared with the puzzle that arises from the fact that the Christian Scriptures do not constitute the only claimant to the status of revelational authority. There are, after all, the Vedas and the Upanishads of Hinduism, the Zend-Avesta of Zoroastrianism, the Koran of Islam, not to mention such documents as the Book of Mormon and other similar treatises—all of which claim to be, in one way or another, authoritative religious revelations. In view of this proliferation of claimants, either the choice of one revelational authority (if any) is wholly arbitrary in a prejudicial and objectionable sense; or, alternatively, there are reasons for regarding one of the claimants as having a more plausible title to this claim; or, still alternatively, all the claimants should, regardless of their contrasting contents, be regarded as having equal claim to the title. On the assumption that the first and third alternatives cannot be taken seriously by the philosophically sincere, it follows that a revelation claim must be assessed in terms of reasoned argument. But if the argument is not to be viciously circular (in the logical sense), the reasons cannot be based on the religious authority itself, but must rather be extraneous to that authority. All this makes it quite clear that no claimant to the status of revelational authority can be correctly regarded as epistemologically ultimate or foundational. If, in response, it is argued that the same predicament of prejudicial arbitrariness confronts *any* proposed set of ultimate presuppositions, whether biblical or not, then I can only respond that this assertion, resting as it

4. Taking the Bible itself as an axiom set

a) overlooks the logical complexity and relations of the biblical statements themselves,

b) and fails to account for the fact that these statements are neither self-evident nor self-interpreting.

5. Since there are other claimants to revelational status,

the preference for one claimant would either be wholly arbitrary

or else would appeal to logically independent reasons,

nor is this difficulty wholly offset by the apparent arbitrariness of ultimate presuppositions in general.

must on some such foundation, renders itself equally arbitrary for the same reason, and, more generally, that my whole previous discussion of epistemology is an extended attempt to cope with this perplexity.

Reflecting in retrospect on my critical evaluation of both experiential and revelational voluntarism, I want to forestall a pervasive misunderstanding that might easily take form in the mind of the thoughtful reader. It would be a serious mistake to suppose that the intent of these criticisms was to dismiss either the genuineness or the value of either religious experience or revelation, however their relation to each other may be elaborated in detail. In fact, at a later stage of my argument, each of these concepts has a significant place in what I have termed the reconstruction of the Christian truth-claim. But in the present context we are considering the question, not of genuineness or value, but of epistemological ultimacy or priority. And it is my opinion that, objectively speaking, for reasons such as I have developed, neither religious experience nor revelation can logically occupy that role of ultimacy. On the other hand, subjectively speaking and in the context of psychological motivation, there is no reason why either religious experience or revelation or some combination of the two could not, in full consistency with my position about epistemology, occupy a status of basic adequacy or fundamental satisfactoriness for any given individual in terms of his own religious awareness. It is in this way that I understand the notion of resting in one's experience of God as a wholly satisfying ground-motive, or taking one's stand on revelational authority as a fully sufficient foundation beyond which the individual need seek no further basis for religious purposes. In effect, I am claiming here what should be obvious to anyone who has a profoundly fulfilling religious awareness—namely, that the richness, value, and satisfyingness of one's personal religious commitment and all its experiential consequences and overtones are in no sense impoverished by the lack of conscious systematic philosophizing for the individual to whom religious experience or revelational authority are subjectively adequate final appeals. Nor is there any reason to immerse such a person in the deep waters of abstract philosophy, provided that on his subjectively sufficient basis he does in fact find himself committed to those insights which form an activating context for moral and spiritual fulfillment. It is, after all, far more important that a man believes the right things in practice than that he does so for philosophically adequate reasons.

Suppose, finally, that we consider the general arguments for the voluntaristic stance in critical terms. There is, of course, a clear sense in which, so far as a person has a specific and at least partly explicit epistemological perspective, his act of accepting that point of view constitutes a volitional commitment to it. And it is even the case that, so far as one's self-analysis in making this commitment is transparent to himself, any reasons which he advances to render his commitment plausible will reflect the logical structure that these reasons are intended to justify. But it seems equally obvious that the truth-claim of the principles to which one volitionally commits himself is logically

---

D. The intent of the above criticisms is not at all to question the genuineness of religious experience or revelation.
1. The issue here at stake is rather one of epistemological priority.

2. It is fully compatible with my position for a given individual to rest on religious experience or revelational authority as a wholly satisfying ground-motive.

3. Nor is it essential for every person to be involved in abstract philosophy.

E. Critique of *voluntarism in general:*
1. While the acceptance of any epistemological perspective involves a volitional commitment,

independent of this piece of descriptive psychology about voluntaristic acceptance. Whether an interpretive principle or category is logically ultimate does not in any sense rest objectively on any individual's act of will in accepting that principle or category. To put it more succinctly: Truths and tenets (i.e., beliefs as held by persons) are logically distinct, so that whether a proposition is true is wholly independent of whether anyone believes it. And if, therefore, there are ultimate starting points for grounding truth-claims, their status as ultimate will not depend on anyone's volitional act of accepting them.

the truth or otherwise of ultimate interpretive principles is logically independent of this psychological fact, since truth and belief are distinct categories.

It is the point of the general arguments for voluntarism to assail the aim at that rational objectivity which is the rationalist's goal for thought. But suppose we ask about the logical status of the voluntarist's own arguments. When a voluntarist argues that presuppositions about foundational criteria of knowledge inevitably reflect the world-view standpoint of the person propounding them, and that therefore there are no rationally objective epistemological principles, he seems himself to be making a truth-claim that cuts across all such world-view standpoints and that therefore purports to transcend dependence on any particular standpoint, with the evident result that his argument reflects the very sort of rationally objective stance which, as an argument, it claims to reject as at least practically, if not theoretically, impossible. In this case, any such argument appears to commit an existential contradiction in making a claim that is inconsistent with the fact that it is being asserted. And this general logical difficulty seems applicable to every sort of supporting argument urged by the voluntarist for his own position. To illustrate selectively from the arguments previously analyzed: If indeed an individual's beliefs are characteristically (or even inevitably) determined by non-rational factors which compromise and effectively undermine the aim at rational objectivity, then the truth-claim made by this thesis, so far as it is a belief of the voluntarist, will by its own assertion be rendered equally ineffective as a claim about how beliefs originate. Or if, as a matter of fact, the moral state of an individual's character unavoidably distorts his judgment about questions decisively bearing on his well-being and destiny, then since this thesis is a claim of precisely this sort, it too will be unavoidably distorted and lack the descriptive objectivity necessary to render it a serious criticism. And so the original difficulty expands into an inclusive spiderlike web which appears to ensnare every such argument against the aim at rational objectivity. If, however, the proponent of these arguments forthrightly admits the subjectivity and pervasive relativity of his own critical claims, then these claims cease to constitute genuinely relevant objections and become instead merely interesting pieces of descriptive personal self-analysis.

2. The basic voluntarist thesis itself purports to describe the status of all epistemological presuppositions irrespective of their world-view context, so that it is contradictory in claiming for itself the very sort of objectivity that it intends to deny.

a) This difficulty applies to all the supporting arguments for voluntarism.

b) If such arguments are not intended to be rationally objective, they cease to be serious criticisms.

c) The full acknowledgement of obstacles to objectivity is in fact an important step toward counteracting their influence, so far as this is realistically possible.

Yet we must not make too much out of the general logical difficulty that has been elaborated. If we acknowledge, as I certainly do, the overall legitimacy of the aim at rational objectivity, that does not have to imply that the aim has been fully actualized by any individual in his struggle to achieve the goal. On the contrary, we can readily acknowledge that our belief-commitments are pervasively influenced by an extensive network of non-rational causal factors which incline us in one direction rather than another. We can recognize that the effort to achieve rational objectivity is at best only approximated by those among us who struggle the hardest and the most relentlessly to achieve it; and we certainly can admit outright that our moral state exerts a powerful influence on our most decisively existential belief-commitments. But to face up to all this is precisely the core of the struggle to achieve the very rational objectivity which has been challenged in its legitimacy by such admissions. For if, with full sincerity, a man becomes explicitly self-conscious about the factors which might unbalance the plausibility and objectivity of his judgments, he can then, in varying degrees, deliberately act to compensate for these influences by intellectually swimming upstream against those currents that threaten to sweep him away from his destination on the opposite shore. But, as we noted in an earlier context, success may be no more than modest, and results may be no more than partial. Yet that is no reason to surrender the struggle; it is rather a reason to engage in it with all possible care and exertion. We can therefore admit the premises of many voluntarist arguments without accepting their conclusions, and we can maintain that, however difficult the goal of rational objectivity may be in practice, it is not (indeed, it logically cannot be) impossible in principle.

3. The logical ultimacy of basic interpretive principles does not make them arbitrary in an objectionable sense, since such principles are foundational for all thought and being.

Nevertheless, all this does not respond to the whole of the voluntarist's case. We can also acknowledge that, in the logical sense, ultimate criteria are arbitrary in that, as ultimate, they cannot be argued from premises logically more basic than themselves. Yet we can claim that properly identified criteria of this sort are not arbitrary in the subjectively relative and objectionable sense, precisely because these principles function in practice as an interpretive structure which is foundational to all intelligible thought and being—that, in fact, is the very essence of their objectivity. Nor does the objectivity of these principles render them useless for metaphysical argument; for it is quite possible that the application of these categories to the broad context of experience may point in the direction of one sort of world-view rather than another, since such a world-view would not be *deducible from* the principles, but would rather *emerge from* their application in understanding reality as it confronts us from a common-sense point of view.

4. The probability status of conceptual systems is not inconsistent with the unconditional character of religious commitment,

And does the probability status of a world-view thus discerned necessarily run counter to the unconditional character of a genuinely religious commitment? To some extent this is a psychological issue about how certain responses fit together in the crucible of an individual's outlook; and in this sense, the comfort or cramping likely to be experienced by a given person here would be relative to his attitudinal framework and personality traits. As the good Bishop Joseph Butler repeatedly urged, most of us find no seriously disruptive obstacle in accepting this kind of probability as a framework for deciding our most agonizing human choices, even when they are of the greatest importance for determining our this-worldly destiny. Why then should we feel cramped at having to understand and decide our spiritual destiny in an analogous framework of probability? But more importantly, we may ask ourselves what it is to which religion calls us unconditionally. Perhaps it is not too much to suggest that it is not to the sort of conceptual system, with which philosophy is concerned, that we are thus unconditionally called, but rather to the ultimate reality toward which these conceptual systems point. Thus one can, if I may put it in Christian terms, be unconditionally committed to the reality of God, while at the same time regarding his philosophical system as, at best, a highly probable approximation to the truth about God and his relation to the world. In any case, the degree of plausibility and probability intrinsic to any such philosophical position can be reasonably judged about only through the sort of difficult intellectual struggle for objectivity which I have all along been attempting to defend as humanly legitimate.

since that latter is not directed toward conceptual systems, but toward the ultimate reality to which such systems point.

Nor, finally, does the admitted epistemological ultimacy of conceptual reason necessarily lead to any sort of religious idolatry. Such a claim might be immediately dismissed if one takes the view (not without proponents in the history of thought) that the objective structures of rationality, though exemplified in the finite entities that constitute the natural world order and in the minds of finite thinkers like ourselves, have their final and transcendent locus as constitutive structures of the Divine Mind. For, in that case, nothing is made prior to the reality of God by taking reason as epistemologically ultimate, since this would be to take as foundational those categories of thought and being which are essential aspects of God himself. But whether that view is adopted or not, it is clear that no worthy representative of the rationalistic stance would regard either finite entities or finite minds as the constitutive ground of rational principles, since such finite realities can only exist by exemplifying those principles in the structure of their being; and hence nothing finite is here exalted to the status of an object of worship. An effective way of seeing this point clearly consists in recognizing that, although I could not think intelligibly if my mind were not rationally structured, nevertheless, when the constitutive principles of this structure are explicitly understood, it is quite obvious that those principles in no way depend on my finite being for their truth-status as epistemologically ultimate. Far from it being the case that those principles depend on me (or any other finite minds, separately or in conjunction), it is rather the case that we are all of us dependent on the objective and independent status of those principles.

5. The ultimacy of conceptual reason is not idolatrous,
a) especially if the Divine Mind is itself the ultimate locus of rational principles;

b) but in any case rational principles, though illustrated by finite entities, are not to be viewed as grounded in them.

Musing reminiscently on the exposition and elaboration of voluntaristic approaches to religious truth-claims, however, I certainly cannot dismiss the voluntaristic premises without sensing the restraint that they reasonably place on the exercise of thought by such limited and harassingly encompassed beings as ourselves. Such considerations should provoke us to humility, tentativity, and revisability in our attitude toward the consequences of our own intellectual efforts; but they need not (and in my personal opinion, clearly do not) require us to surrender the aim at the only sort of rational objectivity which, as I

F. The voluntaristic arguments provide a basis for humility, but not for the surrender of the ideal of rational objectivity.

see it, can save the genuine and legitimate insights of thought from a sheer arbitrariness that would reduce those insights to complete existential irrelevance. However imperfectly, therefore, the sword of reason may be wielded in our trembling hands, the threat of irrelevance should make us rather bear the one effective weapon we have to use than surrender it to a foe whose own weapon is, by his admission, as dull as the one he would rend from our grasp.

Rationalistic Approaches

I. The main thrust of rationalism is that the basic criteria of truth are logically independent of any particular world-view.

In discernible contrast to the voluntaristic outlook, the main thrust of rationalism is the claim that the basic criteria for evaluating truth-claims, whether explicitly religious or not, possess a status of rational objectivity such that their truth-status is independent of any particular metaphysical perspective in contrast to its alternatives, even though the use of these criteria may, through their practical application in the task of explaining existence, point to the greater reasonableness of

A. The main argument for this contention is that otherwise all truth-claims would be arbitrary in a self-stultifying sense which would eliminate all objective knowledge claims.

some specific metaphysical option in the end. The principal defense of this rationalistic attitude consists generally in urging that unless there is some such set of objective standards or categories, not only would any choice among philosophical systems be purely arbitrary in some objectionable preferential sense, but any truth-claim for any proposition would be just as arbitrary, since all such claims presuppose the ultimacy of certain evaluative criteria of this sort. The end result of rejecting the aim at rational objectivity would then be a kind of self-eliminating scepticism which would implicitly (if not explicitly) deny the possibility of any objective knowledge whatsoever, including that

B. Hence the critique of voluntarism is already a defence of rationalism and vice versa.

of the knowledge-claim contained in this thesis itself. It should therefore be clear to the thoughtful reader that the supporting arguments for the rationalistic approach in general have already been elaborated in the general critique of voluntarism, so that there is no reason to reconstruct those arguments here. Analogously, it is equally evident that the general supporting arguments for voluntarism constitute the main negative criticisms of the rationalistic stance, so that, correspondingly again, these critical difficulties also require no further elaboration in the present context. Nor is there, finally, any need to expose again my own commitment in this controversy, since that also has been made abundantly clear in the whole previous development of my argument.

It is, however, one thing to find the rationalistic approach in general to be plausible, and quite another to elaborate an epistemological position in detail within the compass of the general rationalistic framework. And here again, as was the case with voluntarism, I see two sufficiently distinguishable rationalistic perspectives which are different enough to make the distinction between them worth elaborating. One of these positions approaches the task of religious apologetics with a general epistemology that clearly exemplifies *empiricism*, though not in the extreme form that would lead to the religious scepticism that emerges from the sort of radical empiricism characteristic of a David Hume or an A. J. Ayer. A Thomas Aquinas, for

II. Rationalism again divides into two main perspectives:
A. *Empiricism*

1. Aquinas.

example, argues that, although there are first principles of reason whose status is recognizable by the fact that their denial would be unintelligible, nevertheless all genuine knowledge finds its source in sensible effects, so that there is nothing in the intellect which was not first in sensation. A Joseph Butler, engulfed by the sweep of John Locke's empirical theory of knowledge, simply takes up the perspective thus bequeathed to him and purports to build his whole case for religious truth-claims on an analogical probability grounded basically in sense experience. An F. R. Tennant, finally, develops a critically alert epistemology which holds that ultimate interpretive principles themselves emerge from the mind's attempt to grapple with the broad thrust of empirical foundations. Yet all three, though accepting a qualified empiricism, are rationalistic in the sense that, however basic principles may originate, they nevertheless possess an objectivity that makes the development of a theistic world-view possible as a live option, or, in the case of Aquinas, as a demonstrable perspective.

2. Butler.

3. Tennant.

The alternative rationalistic stance, which I shall call *apriorism*, holds that there is a set of foundational principles which, though they function as an interpretive structure for apprehending the contents of empirical experience, are nevertheless logically independent of sense experience and therefore neither derived nor derivable from sense experience. A pure epistemological rationalist like Plato or Descartes would, as we suggested earlier, claim that while empirical experience might occasion or exemplify such *a priori* principles, nevertheless no genuine knowledge could be derived from such experience, since empirically derived propositions are never more than highly probable and therefore never transcend the status of mere opinion. A more moderate Leibniz, though still a pure rationalist of sorts, includes in the sphere of knowledge the contingent propositions exemplified in empirical experience, although it is perhaps not too much to say that his way of working out the distinction between necessary truths (which are absolutely *a priori* and independent of any possible empirical data) and contingent truths (which are *a priori* only in a qualified sense by being entailed in some possible universes but not in all) does not seem fully clear. And, in a sense, even Aristotle and Aquinas, though sincerely supposing themselves to be empiricists, can probably be claimed as moderate rationalists or rational empiricists, since they recognize the ultimate character of first truths of reason (like the laws of logic) which are not empirically grounded. Again all of these thinkers are conjoined in arguing that plausible, if not demonstrable, arguments for a theistic world-view can be launched with the proper use of such ultimate rational principles, whether or not they are regarded as requiring supplementation with empirical content.

B. *Apriorism.*
1. Such views regard foundational principles as, at least in part, logically independent of sense experience.
2. Thus
a) the pure rationalism of Plato or Descartes,

b) the moderate rationalism of Leibniz,

c) and even the views of Aristotle and Aquinas, who recognize non-empirical first truths of reason.

III. Previous analysis makes clear my commitment to *rationalistic apriorism.*
A. But the commitment to the ideal of rational objectivity is more important than the issues that divide apriorism and empiricism. In fact, a case can be made for the claim that empiricists invariably make use of *a priori* arguments of the sort they purport to deny.

It must be abundantly clear from my previous analysis that I myself side, in the main, not only with the rationalistic approach, but also with apriorism in epistemology; and I have already attempted to argue the plausibility of these two commitments in several earlier contexts. Here it only remains to comment, first, that what empiricism and apriorism have in common, in the acknowledgment of rational objectivity as an ideal goal for knowledge, is far more important, as I see it, than the technical, theoretical issue about interpretive principles which divides the two outlooks, so that, to put it in emotive terms, I claim both Plato and Leibniz, on the one hand, and Aquinas and Butler, on the other, as both friends and champions. As a second comment, I should like to observe that one can make a very respectable case for the thesis that even those who *claim* to be empiricists invariably make use of interpretive principles which are clearly non-empirical, so that even the intelligibility of their own supporting arguments rests on *a priori* grounds of the very sort that they purport to dismiss in rejecting apriorism. There are therefore, I venture to believe, no fully consistent empiricists; and I regard this claim to be as true of an admitted extremist like David Hume as it clearly is of more moderate empiricists such as John Locke or Joseph Butler.

B. My commitment, though sincere, is quite compatible with the recognition of valid elements in both voluntarism and empiricism.

In retrospect, then, though I am not without certain qualms about my own commitments, I find the approach of what I sometimes call rationalistic apriorism to be a plausible approach to the investigation of religious truth-claims. At the same time, I recognize sincerely and forthrightly the pervasive influence of non-rational factors in molding and influencing my personal belief-commitments (so much in concession to voluntarism). And I enthusiastically scan the vast sea of empirical experience as providing that extended ocean of content which keeps the vessel of reason afloat and provides the essential resistance to its conceptual oars (so much in concession to empiricism).

The Mind-Object Relation and the Religious Object

Epistemological Monism and Epistemological Dualism

I. The problem of the mind-object relation concerns the connection between objects and the ideas in which they are apprehended.

Knowledge invariably takes the form of ideas or conscious contents in the awareness of the subject or person who knows. And, irrespective of the type of object apprehended (God, other finite minds, physical objects, logical relations, mathematical formulas, and so on), the question unavoidably comes up, for a reflective individual, about the real (ontological) relation between objects and the ideas by which they are apprehended. The ordinary stance of unsophisticated common sense (which of course is culturally variable) assumes without question that the mind directly apprehends, without any obstructively intermediating factors, the ordinary objects of empirical awareness (sights, sounds, and so on) when these are not themselves reflected by some physical medium through such things as mirror images or echoes or the like. Now while this ordinary perspective has indeed been championed by sophisticated philosophers, it is not at all obvious, on reflection, that this way of thinking of the relation of ideas and objects is indisputably true as a sort of axiomatic starting point. After all, in ordinary conversation we also speak of hearing the voices of our friends in telephone earpieces, of seeing the president of the United States on the face of television picture tubes, and of noticing the color

A. Common sense supposes that ordinary objects are directly confronted in experience.

1. But this supposition is not an indisputable axiom;

2. nor do the patterns of ordinary conversation provide an unassailable standard here.

of a relative's shirt in a photograph. But while these things (and countless others of a similar sort) easily pass muster as fashions of speech, it takes no more than a moment's reflection to decide that none of these ways of talking is a literal expression of what is actually the case in such situations.

However that may be, it will be helpful, for the sake of achieving clear thinking here, to distinguish between two basic perspectives about what I shall call the mind-object or idea-object relation. Epistemological *monism* takes the position that ideas are, at least in some sense and to some extent, numerically identical with the objects of which they are ideas, so that it is the red pencil itself of which I am immediately aware in vision, for instance. Epistemological *dualism*, in contrast, maintains that the subject never apprehends objects directly, even in part, and that the ideas, through which that subject apprehends an object, are always numerically distinct from the object itself as a set of effects which, however indirectly and perhaps inadequately, rather represents or reconstitutes the object for the mind—so that it is precisely *not* the red pencil itself of which I am immediately aware in vision but instead a sort of reconstruction of it for thought. Monism itself admits of a further very important distinction between a position which holds that, while objects when apprehended are numerically identical with the ideas in which they are disclosed to us, nevertheless some of these objects, either in their entirety (*naive* monism) or in part (*critical* monism), are independently real apart from our ideas of them—I call this view *monistic realism;* and another position which holds that the being of these objects is wholly constituted by the idea or ideas in which those objects are perceived, so that there is no independent referent or object apart from the consciousness of it—I call this view *monistic idealism.* While further proliferations of viewpoint are possible, these distinctions are a sufficient account of the main positions for general epistemology.

The distinctions of viewpoint represented by these positions, though applicable to any object of thought, are perhaps easiest to understand if we think of the standard object as a referent of perceptual experience, such as our red pencil. And even here, with such a limitation, all sorts of absolutely ingenious arguments have been put forth to support one position or another. Since my main concern is with the application of these distinctions to religious epistemology and therefore to the religious object, I will rehearse only a limited number of what I regard as the more significant arguments in the area of perceptual objects.

I have no reason to obscure the clear implication that my previously developed epistemology involves some version of epistemological dualism as a corollary. For if, in fact, knowledge arises only through the application of a structure of interpretive principles to a content in some sense (different for different sorts of objects) distinct from, and normally extraneous to, the principles themselves, then it is clear that an object as thus known is numerically distinct from the object as possessing whatever independent status does in fact characterize it.

B. Two viewpoints can be clearly distinguished here:
1. epistomological *monism* (the idea and the object are in some sense numerically identical),
2. and epistemological *dualism* (the idea and the object are always numerically distinct).

C. Monism in turn divides into
1. monistic *realism* (the object, at least in part, is independently real apart from the idea of it);
2. and monistic *idealism* (the object consists entirely of the idea in which it is perceived).

D. The views are most clearly illustrated by reference to perceptual objects, though these will be considered in only a limited way.

II. My own previous position implies epistemological dualism through the claim that knowledge involves the synthesis of interpretive principles with a content distinct from them.

And since dualism is thus a corollary of my general theory of knowledge, it would seem to follow that it is supported by whatever argumentative plausibility attaches to the overall theory itself.

A. The phenomenology of perception supports dualism:
1. by recognizing a chain of causes between object and perception;

But there are numerous other considerations which point toward dualism as a correct analysis of the idea-object relation. In the case of a perceptual object (like our proverbial red pencil), the general phenomenology of perception supports dualism in at least three ways. First, the descriptive analysis of perception holds that the object itself impinges in some way on the sensory organ (eye, ear, and so on), produces a series of neural and other physico-chemical changes which, through complex intermediary causes, eventually affect the central nervous system and finally, in the case of a conscious impression, the brain itself, and only then does an object appear in consciousness as perceived. So, of course, the resultant content of awareness is clearly *not* the original object that presumably impinged on the sense organs.

2. by claiming that an idea must be *of* something other than itself;

Second, the analysis of an idea seems to involve the notion that, to be an idea, it must be an idea *of* something other than itself, since it essentially involves both an *act* of awareness and a *content* of awareness, so that the idea thus understood cannot be its own object so far as the latter has an independent status. Third and finally, in the case

3. by distinguishing between the properties of ideas and those of perceptual objects.

of perceptual objects, ideas and objects have mutually exclusive characteristics which would preclude their being identical. An idea, for instance, is clear or confused, adequate or inadequate, vague or explicit, and so on; but none of these properties can be intelligibly predicated of a perceptual object, which in turn has properties such as size, shape, weight, motion and direction—qualities which would be equally nonsensical if attributed to ideas.

B. Dualism is implied by the fact that the experienced content of a perceptual idea can vary independently of any change in the object.

A host of other puzzles, which would pose serious difficulties for epistemological monism, cease to be significant problems for dualism. When, for instance, I see my red pencil as double by pressing my eyeball, am I to suppose that, contrary to the testimony of my sense of touch, the pencil actually *is* double? But, of course, it would be double if idea and object were numerically identical; or worse still, it would itself be both double (to sight) and not double (to touch) at the same time. Nor will it help to suggest that the pencil has some properties, *as perceived*, which it does *not* have as existing independently of perception, so that the apparent doubleness is one such property, while certain other perceived properties (like the quality of *not* being double

C. Variations in perceptual perspective involve variations in perceptual ideas in relation to an unchanged object. But this is conceivable only if ideas and objects are distinct, since the notion of perspective does not apply to ideas as such.

as perceived by touch) characterize the object itself. For while, as a dualist, I fully accept this analysis, it implies that idea and object *as a whole* are not identical, since it is not a *part* of the pencil but the *whole* of it that I see as double when I press my eyeball.

There is also the general fact that, even as perceived, the objects of the senses are characterized by variations in perceptual perspective which change with altered circumstances of observation, while presumably the object itself remains relatively the same through all this variation. As I approach an object, my vision perceives it as increasingly larger; or if I sit closer to the band, its sound will be perceived much louder than as if I sat on the opposite side of the listening hall.

This fact itself implies the numerical distinctness of idea and object. But it is also the case that, if I contemplate an idea introspectively as a content of awareness, the notion of literal perspectival variation makes no sense at all—for there is no way to alter the literal perspective in which I contemplate an idea *as* an idea, since every idea is, so to speak, infinitely close to the mind that contemplates it. It is only when I interpret my ideas as representing objects, distinct from them *as* ideas, that the notion of literal perspective makes any sense. But of course this clearly involves epistemological dualism.

A final consideration is that unless conscious contents and independently existing objects are always numerically distinct, it would either be impossible for two distinct perceivers to perceive the same object simultaneously, since then their presumably separate ideas would be numerically identical—or else it would be necessary, if the same object were thus perceived by two perceivers, for those two perceivers to be numerically identical in that respect and therefore not to be distinct perceivers at all. Since it seems virtually indisputable (though not absolutely so, of course) that two distinct perceivers frequently do perceive the same object at the same time without destroying either the sameness of the object or the distinctness of the perceivers, it would appear that each does so through a conscious content of his own which is numerically distinct from the independent object itself.

D. Dualism is implied by the fact that the same object can be perceived by two perceivers at once through distinct contents of consciousness.

But if epistemological dualism is thus disclosed as so eminently plausible, it may be asked, why then has epistemological monism been such a fascinating obsession of so many philosophers otherwise so distinct from each other? While this question poses a highly controversial issue among philosophical experts, I think I can suggest, even without detailed historical elaboration, a plausible answer. For one thing, it has seemed to many thinkers that epistemological dualism is intrinsically sceptical in such a way as to question whether we can ever have any veridical perception of objects at all. If we never get at independent objects without intermediating causal factors, how can we be confident (much less sure) that there are any independent objects or that they have literally any of the properties that they appear to have when we experience them through our ideas? After all, we cannot, as it were, get outside the circle of our ideas to discern either whether the supposed independent objects exist or what qualities they have in themselves if they thus exist. But if some version of monism is true and we confront the objects themselves directly as numerically identical with our ideas of them, this sceptical issue appears to dissolve: How can there be any question about the being or character of objects which, as ideas, are immediately accessible to the activity of consciousness? Small wonder, then, that Bishop Berkeley, as a monistic idealist about perceived objects, decided to dispense with all qualms about any independent object by maintaining that the very being of sense objects consists in their being perceived by the mind— subjectively by finite minds, whose involuntary ideas are directly excited by the Divine Mind, and objectively by the act for itself of the

III. Monism has seemed plausible to many because they held that dualism entails scepticism, since it implies that we never get at objects directly.

A. Monism seems to eliminate this scepticism by placing the object directly before the mind,

hence, Berkeley's view that the whole being of the object consists in its being perceived by the mind (finite and/or Divine).

Divine Mind, without there being any objects whatever apart from minds and their ideas. In this way both religious and empirical sceptics seem to be silenced with one fell swoop of the philosophical bird of prey.

I have no intention of coping adequately here with all the aspects of this ingenious proposal, nor do I see any way that it can be ruled out of the philosophical court without further ado. But I must admit that I am deeply puzzled by Berkeley's position if it is intended as a means of eliminating the scepticism supposedly intrinsic in dualism. First of all, the proposal does not, I think, really avoid but merely relocates the sceptical question. For if the being of a sense object consists objectively in its being perceived by God, then that object is certainly numerically distinct from the object subjectively excited in my mind by God. And the question will follow—how do I know that these two distinct entities have any common properties at all, since, again, I cannot get at God's ideas directly? Furthermore, it seems unthinkable, as I understand it, to suppose that the whole being of an object could consist merely in its being perceived, for in that case there would be absolutely no content that was being perceived, if the act of perceiving thus constitutes *as act* its own content. Beside that, since being perceived is common to all perceptual objects, it would then be impossible, if the act of perceiving constitutes the whole being of the object, to explain how perceptual objects differ from one another in their existence and properties. If, to avoid these difficulties, it is held that at least the Divine Mind actively produces a content distinct from the Divine Act of perceiving and therefore having different properties in the case of different perceptions, that might be plausible. But it follows at once that the whole being of the object does not consist in its being perceived—which would be to surrender Berkeley's original theory.

But of course it may be urged that Berkeley's proposal is not really the best model for epistemological monism, however fascinating his position may be in other respects. The view that I have called *naive* realism need not detain us here for long. Such a monistic position maintains that all the properties of an object as perceived are, at the time of perception, numerically identical with the properties of the object as existing independently of its being perceived. But few reflective persons would dispute that in any context of perception at least some of the properties regarded as experienced are not properties of the object as existing independently, but are rooted in the context and conditions of perception. Much of our previous analysis has illustrated this point by referring to such things as variations of perspective. It seems plausible to suppose, then, that if we are to accept monism at all, it must be a *critical* monism which holds to only a partial identity of properties between the perceived object and the independent object. Thereby, some properties exhibit the requisite numerical identity and others are rooted in contextual and circumstantial factors. The cold honey, for example, actually is a viscous liquid as experienced, but (perhaps) the sweetness of its taste is dependent on the state of

1. But Berkeley's view does not eliminate possible scepticism, since there is a dualism between the object as perceived by God and the object as perceived by a finite mind.

2. If the *act* of perception wholly constituted its own object, then
a) there would be nothing that was being perceived,
b) and no way of explaining how perceptual contents differ from each other.

B. Naive realism is implausible here, since it seems clear that at least some properties of experienced content are not properties of the object itself.

C. So it must be a critical monism (if any):
1. Hence, a partial numerical identity between idea and object.

our taste buds in relation to certain unperceived properties of the honey itself which do not as such involve the property of sweetness.

Now if we are to accept such a critical monistic realism, we immediately have the problem of finding a criterion (simple or complex) for determining which of the properties as perceived are numerically identical with the properties of the independent object, and which are not. But no matter what criterion is proposed, the process surely involves critically considering the percept in order to determine its relation to the object; and this implies that percept and object are numerically distinct, rather than numerically identical. Perhaps it is not too much to say that, since my only knowledge of the independent object springs from my perceptions, if it were really the case that percept and object were numerically one, the thought of their identity could never occur to me and I would never have any reason for saying so.

2. But this view requires a criterion for identifying the numerically identical properties:
a) The application of the criterion involves considering the relationship of the perceptual idea to the object;
b) and that in turn implies dualism.

From all this, it begins to appear that monism is no less intrinsically sceptical then dualism is alleged to be. If either view is in difficulty here, then perhaps both views share this defect. That being the case, we are confronted here with a serious philosophical malady which, as a drastic illness, requires an equally drastic cure. As to the question whether there is any reason for believing that perceptions are effects of objects or realities that exist independently of their being perceived by finite minds, I think that many philosophers—including thinkers as diverse as Descartes and Kant, Locke and Berkeley—have suggested a plausible general answer: While it is, of course, impossible for us to know these causes apart from our awareness of them (we surely are "locked up" to the circle of our ideas), yet the fact that in normal perception (not to mention other modes of conscious awareness) we are involuntarily affected in what we discern, so that we cannot radically alter that content while considering it, implies that, precisely to the extent of that involuntary affectation, we are being acted on by an extraneous cause, a reality other than ourselves as knowers. As I see it, although this fact is not logically demonstrative, it is a virtually irresistible ground for believing in an independent causal basis for our perceptions.

D. So monism is no less sceptical than dualism.

1. Yet it is plausible to believe that our perceptual ideas are the effects of independent objects just to the extent that we are involuntarily affected in the awareness of those ideas, though this conclusion is not logically certain.

Now the element of scepticism creeps in when it is assumed that, in the case of sense perception, the qualities of objects as perceived, allowing for perspectival variations, should, for some supposedly standard perceptual viewpoint (for example, you are looking straight at the face of the clock in normal daylight without visual defects), exhibit a sort of pictorial correspondence to the properties of the object as existing independently. Since by hypothesis there is no way of perceiving this correlation, we tend on reflection to be sceptical about it and to search diligently for some way to achieve certainty about it—and hence the various puzzling solutions of both monism and certain kinds of dualism. But perhaps it is the underlying assumption of pictorial correspondence itself that is mistaken here. Since our perceptions are mediated by an intricate bodily apparatus that has properties of its own and is likely to intrude the properties of that

2. The element of scepticism enters through the assumption that ideas pictorially correspond to objects, while that relation is by nature imperceptible.

a) But that assumption is itself questionable, since the bodily apparatus of perception is likely to intrude its own properties into the process of perception, as certain physical theories imply.

apparatus into the process of perception (actually there is every reason to believe in just such an intrusion), why should we suppose at all that the perceived qualities of an object are its literal properties? A surface looks solid to us, but atomic and molecular physics tell us that it is mostly empty space. The same surface appears colored to us, but again we are rebuffed by physics into supposing that our experience of color is a subjective effect of certain properties of the surface which are not objectively colored at all. These disruptions of our pictorial assumption easily slip by us because of their familiarity, without, as a general rule, seriously disturbing our overall confidence in the assumption itself.

But on reflection it seems quite plausible to challenge the pictorial assumption as a whole and replace it in its entirety with a view about the content of our empirical awareness which comports more adequately with the generally acknowledged way in which that content reaches our conscious awareness. Why, after all, do the theories of physics run counter to the pictorial assumption? It is not, certainly, because the physicist, with all his technical apparatus, is able to perceive objects through sensory contents which disclose, to his vision for example, that objects, under more precise conditions of perception, no longer look visually colored or that their surfaces no longer appear solid either to sight or touch—although of course the color may take on a different hue and the surface a different experienced texture. No, the theories of the physicist are rendered plausible just to the extent that they become useful means for enabling us to adjust more adequately to our environment through prediction and control of its effects on us. And a part of what becomes predictable in this way would be our future perceptions themselves, just in proportion to the effectiveness of the theory in establishing a practically useful correlation between our perceptions and the elements of the theory, rather than involving any pictorial correspondence between *either* our perceptions *or* our theories, on the one hand, and the objects themselves on the other. Suppose, then, we stop thinking of *either* our perceptions *or* our theories as if they were pictorial representations of the literal properties of the objects themselves existing independently, and start thinking of *both* our perceptions *and* our theories as functionally adequate guides to successful activity and appropriate adaptation to environmental conditions. If we take perception and theory in this way, we will not be denying the propriety of either in fulfilling its appropriate function, but we will be divesting ourselves of the insoluble sceptical riddles that encumber any theory of pictorial correspondence—for we will be able to test the accuracy of both perception and theory by the only method that is actually available to us, namely, the test of functional effectiveness. I find it helpful to refer to this general position about perception and theory as *symbolical pragmatism—symbolical* because the elements of perception and theory are taken as signs rather than pictures of objects, and *pragmatism* because the propriety of these signs is found in their practical usefulness. As an illustrative means of clarifying my position here, I suggest that we

b) Physical theories run counter to the pictorial assumption, not because of a more precise technique of perception,

but because the theories are more adequate means of environmental adjustment through prediction and control.

c) If perceptions and theories are regarded as functionally adequate guides to successful activity, rather than as pictorial representations, the sceptical riddles of the pictorial view will dissolve.

3. This theory about perception may be termed *symbolical pragmatism,* since it regards perceptions as practically useful signs.

think of the relation between perceptions and objects as analogous to the relation between the perception of dots on a radar screen and the perception of the objects (airplanes, missiles, meteors, or what have you) that those dots symbolically represent. While the dots as perceived are in no sense pictures of the objects as perceived, they are useful guides to reacting to those objects in a way that comports with our goals of activity. And for all that reinterpretation, beautiful music will still sound as sweet, roses will still look as red (or whatever color), and velvet fabric will still feel as soft. Perhaps these experiences will acquire even richer significance for us, since we no longer need to entertain the slightest suspicion that in such experiences we are in any sense being deceived.

a) The radar screen analogy.

b) The richness of perceptual experience is in no way disturbed but rather enhanced by this way of interpreting it.

It is clear that if one accepts symbolical pragmatism as an account of the relation between either ideas or theories and the independent objects which they characteristically symbolize in thought, he is by that very fact also accepting epistemological dualism. Yet it is often argued that, however attractive such an account may be theoretically, the epistemological dualism it entails is counter intuitive by flying straight in the face of common sense. For does anyone, apart from the befuddlement he may have contracted from an exposure to philosophical conundrums, really believe, for example, that what he directly sees in visual perception are not tables and chairs themselves, but rather conscious images of them strained through the complex apparatus of the body which intrudes upon and pervasively influences the content of that image? The obvious answer to this challenge is the counterclaim that we often speak of our perceptual experiences in ordinary conversation as if those experiences constituted the identical presence of the objects themselves to consciousness—even though, on reflection, we know that this is only a concession to the uncomplicated style of conversation and not any sort of literal description. In an analogous way, as I long ago illustrated, we speak of the sun's rising and setting, of seeing a baseball game on the face of a television picture tube, or of hearing a friend's voice in the earpiece of a telephone. But to borrow a phrase from Bishop Berkeley out of context, in these things we must think with the educated and speak with the vulgar, so that theoretical complexity need not intrude on simple conversational efficiency.

4. Symbolical pragmatism clearly implies epistemological dualism.

a) Nor is the fact, that we often do not attend to this distinction any serious criticism of it, since that fact is a concession to conversational efficiency which comports with many obvious simplifications of ordinary speech.

b) What is called for here is not a different way of speaking, but a different way of thinking.

It is not my intention in this context to develop a thorough response to a final challenge which asks how, if perceptions do not provide us with an awareness of the literal properties of independent objects even with some critical sifting, we are ever to develop any satisfactory account of those literal properties at all. One way (but not the only possible way) of responding to this challenge, from the standpoint of symbolical pragmatism, is to reject the question as spurious on the ground that it rests on a misunderstanding. For if the decisive function of our ideas of objects, whether those ideas are perceptions or theories, is to make successful adaptation possible, the question of the literal properties of objects can be turned aside as impertinent and inconsequential. We can even maintain an agnositicism about such

5. As to the question how we are to get at the literal properties of objects if not through perception, *a)* the question may be turned aside as based on a misunderstanding, and replaced by an innocuous agnosticism at this point.

b) Or we can attempt to get at those properties through critical reflection on what they must be if they are to be free from contradiction and are to explain the functional effectiveness of theory and perception.

properties, but it will be a wholly innocuous agnosticism which makes no genuine practical difference. Still it is not necessary to leave the matter there, even if venturing beyond this innocuous agnosticism is an epistemologically risky business. For if sense perception provides no satisfactory account, we can at least give it a try with conceptual thought itself by asking ourselves what the literal properties of objects must be if they are to be essentially free from contradictions and if they are to provide an extensive correlation with the functional effectiveness of our perceptions and theories themselves. It is far beyond the scope of my present purpose to work this out in detail, but I have found much illumination here from thinkers otherwise as diverse as G. W. Leibniz, George Santayana, and Alfred North Whitehead. In any case, this difficult terrain requires no further exploration for our immediate task.

The Application of the Monist/Dualist Distinction to Theories of Religious Knowledge

I. Problems about the mind-object relation extend to every domain of thought, including the religious object.
A. Hence the monism/dualism distinction applies also.

1. But some variation in application is to be expected for different spheres.

2. For example, the relation between a universal concept and its object, as an essence, has such a variation.

It is obvious, of course, that problems about the mind-object or idea-object relation are not limited to the spheres of perception and the complex scientific analyses which purport to provide a theoretical explanation of those perceptions. In fact, these problems extend to every domain of thought right up to the level of the religious object itself. If, therefore, we accept the unity of epistemological theory in general for all contexts of thought, it seems plausible to transfer the monism/dualism distinction to each of those domains and therefore also to problems and perspectives concerning the relation of thought and conscious experience generally to the religious object as well. In making this contextual move from perception (and theories about its objects) to other spheres, we would expect some modification in the application of the distinction, as the type of thought content and the conditions for apprehending the objects of that type vary. As an illustrative example (although I have no intention of working through this level with systematic adequacy in this part of my analysis), consider the relation of a universal concept to its object. Without running through the proliferation of possible theories of a monistic or dualistic sort, I will assume, for the sake of my illustration, the dualistic thesis that the concept, as a content of my thought, is numerically distinct from the objective referent of which it is a concept, and that the object itself is an essence, nature, or quality which has a logical status quite independent of my concept of it. It turns out, in fact, that I actually believe these assumptions and therefore believe in real essences which may or may not be exemplified in particular instances— an admission at which some readers may fairly bristle at this juncture and perhaps may also forget that I am only developing an exemplary illustration. Suppose, further, that the object of my concept is the essence of triangularity as defined in Euclidean geometry—now the object of my concept here is not some particular triangular object (such as a drawing on a blackboard) but just triangularity itself. Quite unlike the case of perception, in which a mediating biological mechanism intrudes on the access of my thought to the object, here there is no such intrusion that can be identified or, as far as I can discern, even be conceived or construed. Either my concept is the concept of the objective essence of triangularity or not. If not, then I am conceiving some other essence whether I affix the term *triangularity* to it or not. And if so—that is, if my concept is that of triangularity itself— then there is no question of my concept being mistaken or intruded upon by some distorting intervening factor, since there is no such factor to consider. It follows that, quite differently from perception, we need no symbolical pragmatism to relieve us of sceptical twinges—for, although it is clear that my concept, as a construct and content of my conscious awareness, is numerically distinct from triangularity itself (since that essence is what it is whether I form a concept of it or not), it is equally clear that my access *to* any given essence by the medium of my concept is totally unencumbered and unobstructed. I may, of course, call some essence thus conceived by a conventionally inappropriate name, so that my language may be wrong in the sense of being ineffective for communication. But there can be no question for me that whatever essence I conceive is precisely that essence itself with all of its properties so far as I am conscious of them. I ask the reader not to boggle at the veritable plethora of assumptions which this extended illustration embodies, but merely to see the point of the illustration itself—namely, that there will be significant variations of detail when the monism/dualism scheme is transferred from one context (perception) to another (universal conception).

No doubt there will be analogous variations when the scheme is applied to the religious domain itself. It is clear, certainly, that much of the general epistemological position I have previously elaborated points in the direction of a viewpoint which would deny any numerical identity between religious ideas, as contents of conscious awareness, and any independently real referent or correlate of these ideas. If all thought involves the interpretive structure of rational principles and categories, which characterize the mind logically prior to and independently of experience, and which reconstitute for consciousness the objects of thought by means of ideas, then it is clear that the functioning of this structure, in the case of religious ideas, means that those ideas are in no sense numerically identical with any independently real referent. And if, as I also argued, religious experience itself is invariably pervaded by an interpretive context composed of various strata of thought to the extent that this context provides much of the content of the experience itself, so that religious experience cannot as such function as a foundational basis for assessing religious truth-claims—which therefore can be settled in principle only through a critical assessment of those interpretive contexts themselves—then it is equally the case that the religious ideas which compose religious experience cannot plausibly be regarded as numerically identical with any objective correlate. Yet this conclusion, if accepted, would leave open two radically contrasting perspectives about the relation of religious ideas to the religious object. One option would be the extreme

a) Since, unlike the case of perception, there is no mediating mechanism that obstructs the access of thought to its object as an essence, there is no question of the concept being mistaken in its apprehension of the object.
b) Thus there is both a distinction between concept and object, and yet an unobstructed access to the object, though there may be an impropriety of language.

B. A similar variation may be expected for the religious object.
II. My whole previous position implies a dualism between religious ideas and the religious object, primarily because all thought invokes an interpretive structure which reconstitutes objects of thought through ideas.

A. Hence religious ideas cannot be numerically identical with any objective correlate.
B. But two very different options would still be possible:
1. a subjectivism which denies an independent object;
2. and an objectivism which accepts an independent religious object.

subjectivist thesis that the religious object has no independent reality status but is constituted entirely by the religious ideas of the individual conscious subject. The other would be the moderate objectivist thesis that although the religious object has an independent reality status, nevertheless the religious ideas of the individual conscious subject are always numerically distinct from that religious object, so that the question of the adequacy of religious ideas, as characterizing the nature of that independent religious object, is left open for critical investigation and decision.

III. The monism/dualism scheme yields:
A. *Monistic religious idealism*—which holds that the religious object is numerically identical with religious ideas which constitute the sole status of that object.
1. Various alternatives are possible here:

If now we adopt the monism/dualism scheme for analyzing these two clearly opposed positions, I propose that we call the first (subjectivist) view *monistic religious idealism*—*monistic* because it holds that the religious object and the religious ideas are numerically identical for each conscious subject, since the sole status of that object is constituted entirely by those ideas; and *idealistic* because this view thus regards the religious object as mental in nature through its identity with the religious ideas of the conscious subject. Such a perspective further breaks down into a variety of alternatives which differ primarily in their explanation of the causal origin of religious ideas and in their viewpoint as to which context of religious ideas comports most effectively with the position's concept of the function of religion in human life. In this vein a *projectionistic* idealist, such as

a) Projectionistic idealism (Feuerbach, Sartre),

Ludwig Feuerbach or Jean Paul Sartre, would hold that religious ideas are a creative imposition on reality of a scale of values that represent an ideal of human selfhood that is itself relative to culturally and individually variable opinions about just such an ideal. A *psychiatric*

b) Psychoanalytic idealism (Freud),

or *psychoanalytic* idealist such as Sigmund Freud would regard religious ideas as a sublimated ideal of the father-image, acting on the conscious mind from the complex structure of the subconscious personal life of the individual. And a *humanistic* idealist such as John

c) Humanistic idealism (Dewey).

Dewey would regard a critically reconstructed concept of the religious object (he retains the word *God* here) as the clarified unification of ideal and integrative individual and social ends which long-range experience discloses as implementing human well-being. From this selective characterization and exemplification of monistic idealism it becomes immediately obvious that the main impact of any such perspective on religious ideas, as construed by persons who take them with ultimate seriousness, would be clearly negative and therefore

2. The main thrust of all these views is negative in its impact on religious truth-claims.

would represent an analysis of religious ideas from the standpoint of interpreters who regard those ideas as a disguised and largely misunderstood way of expressing some basically non-religious facet of human experience.

B. *Dualistic religious realism*—which holds that the religious object is distinct from religious ideas, but exists independently of such ideas.

At or near the opposite end of the spectrum of viewpoints would be the moderate objectivism which, in our parlance, I will describe as *dualistic religious realism*—*dualistic* because it holds that the religious object is in no sense numerically identical with the religious ideas of the conscious subject, but rather always numerically distinct from those ideas as contents of individual awareness; and *realistic* because such a position maintains that the religious object has a reality status that is quite independent on the ideas and experiences through which that object is apprehended by the conscious subject, while the relative adequacy of any context of religious ideas, construed as a representative characterization or description of the religious object, is left for critical analysis to decide. Again this general perspective subdivides into distinct varieties which differ primarily in the methodologies proposed for settling religious truth-claims, in the degrees of confidence to be vested in critical decisions of adequacy or inadequacy, and in the religious-philosophical milieu in which the whole project is carried out. There are, of course, various ways of breaking this down into types of position, but I have found it helpfully illuminating, for a cluster of typical Western perspectives, to distinguish two main subtypes on a dividing principle that relates to the degree of confidence in the independent reality status and characterization of the religious object as thus independent. I will accordingly refer to those dualistic views characterized by a high degree of objective confidence as *theistic* dualisms (since all the views I would classify here have a broadly theistic view of the religious object). And I will in turn designate as *agnostic* dualisms those positions characterized by a relatively low, or at least far more modest, degree of objective confidence. While I am not totally comfortable with this admittedly imprecise classification which will inevitably spawn a number of borderline positions, I find it, on the whole, more clarifying than any alternative classification with which I am presently familiar.

Theistic dualism, in turn, will involve various views which subdivide on lines not very dissimilar from those which divide rationalism and voluntarism (of the revelational type) in general religious methodology. Positions which find their core emphasis in defending theism through the use of what are regarded as rationally objective arguments for the existence of God on more or less universally accessible rational and experiential grounds, I will call *argumentative* theisms, although this stance has commonly been referred to as natural theology: Thomas Aquinas, with his fivefold proof for the existence of God, and F. R. Tennant, with his expansion of one of these proofs (the teleological) to cosmic proportions, will serve as appropriate examples, although there are many others. On the other hand, positions which throw all such arguments into question and find their own central thrust in uniquely revelatory events which they regard as providing a framework of plausibility for commitment, I will designate as *revelational* theisms: Calvin and his reformed heirs, along with so-called neo-orthodox thinkers such as Karl Barth and Emil Brunner (who perhaps also would align themselves with Calvin), may well serve as models for this approach. Numerous thinkers, including some whom I have indicated as examples of either argumentative or revelational theism, I will refer to as *combinational* theists, because they synthesize both argumentative and revelational elements in their framework of defense: Augustine, Thomas Aquinas, G. W. F. Leibniz, and Joseph Butler would all fall together here as exemplary paragons of this category, although of course they are not alone.

1. Various alternatives possible here on the basis of the degree of confidence regarding the reality and nature of the religious object:

a) *theistic* dualism (high confidence),

b) and *agnostic* dualism (modest confidence).

2. Theistic dualism further subdivides into:

a) *argumentative* theism (Aquinas and Tennant),

b) *revelational* theism (Calvin, Barth, Brunner),

c) *combinational* theism (Augustine, Aquinas, Leibniz, Butler).

3. Agnostic dualism also subdivides along lines determined by attempts to remedy the objective inadequacy of the case for any religious worldview:

a) The religious ethicism of Kant, which bases plausible religious belief (not knowledge) on the unconditional status of moral law and duty;

b) The religious empiricism of Schleiermacher and Otto, who ground religious truth-claims in the universal character of religious experience;

c) The religious pragmatism of Pascal and James, who defend religious belief on the ground that it enriches the meaning of life and may even be ultimately true;

Agnostic dualism, with at least a discernible contrast to the previous alternatives, encompasses all those who hold that the rationally objective or revelationally grounded case for a theistic perspective is at best indecisive and at worst possibly even religiously or critically perverse. And again these views will vary in terms of the interpretive context which they bring to bear in an attempt to shore up what they regard as the sagging and flimsy status of the bolder and more objective claims of various theistic dualisms. In this general atmosphere, for example, the *religious ethicism* of an Immanuel Kant courageously rejects all transcendental metaphysical truth-claims (including those of theism) as inappropriate candidates for genuine theoretical knowledge—on the ground that such claims violate Kant's limitation of genuine knowledge to the phenomenal (things as they appear to us, rather than as they are in themselves) and the empirical (objects of awareness that involve elements of sense experience, even though these elements are structured in the mind by a framework of *a priori* principles). Then the position goes on to reconstitute religious truth-claims by regarding them as plausible beliefs rather than pieces of genuine knowledge—beliefs, furthermore, whose title to rational plausibility is grounded in the claim that they make the unconditional claim of the objective moral law (which *is* a piece of possible knowledge, even though it is totally devoid of empirical elements) more fully intelligible to us so far as we are ideally rational beings.

Still in the agnostic arena as we have defined it, the *religious empiricism* or *religious experientialism* of a Friedrich Schleiermacher maintains that all religious truth-claims are constructs of religious experience as centered in the feeling or inner consciousness of absolute dependence, and the plausibility of such claims rests in their effectiveness as clarifying the nature of that experience. An alternative religious experientialism like that of Rudolf Otto, on the other hand, claims that a fundamental sense of the numinous, or the non-rational awareness of the religious object, pervades all religious experience and involves an *a priori* structure which apprehends that object as *mysterium tremendum et fascinans* (the overpoweringly fascinating sense of ultimate and impenetrable mystery). This viewpoint then goes on to interpret conceptual religious perspectives and rational schemes which purport (with no final success) to make the ultimate mystery intelligible.

In another dimension of the agnostic climate would be what I will term the *religious pragmatism* of Blaise Pascal and William James—a standpoint which again dismisses rationally objective arguments here as either indecisive (James) or religiously perverse (Pascal). But it then goes on to defend belief in the religious object as eminently reasonable on the practical ground that such a belief enriches and fulfills the meaning of life, even if it should turn out to be false—while the alternative of disbelief impoverishes our present life by depriving it of the sense of meaning and would lead to irreparable loss if the religious hypothesis turned out to be true. To put the matter more succinctly, man's religious situation is such that, although rationally objective grounds are missing or defective, the individual has every conceivable value to gain and no conceivable value to lose by opting for positive religious belief.

And in the final agnostic corner (for our merely illustrative purposes) would be the *religious existentialism* of a Søren Kierkegaard, for instance. Discarding all rational apologetics for theism as tainted with an approximative probablism (the infinite approximation process) which is totally inconsistent with the unconditionality of religious commitment, Kierkegaard opts for truth as subjectivity in emphasizing the urgency of concern with which one believes (rather than focusing on the objective content of belief), takes the form of paradox as the logical structure that alone correlates with subjectivity as urgent concern, and by a leap of faith lands squarely on Christian theism by regarding the central Christian doctrine of the Incarnation of God in Christ as the ultimate paradox. Or there is the alternative religious existentialism of a Karl Jaspers. He regards all the modes in which the individual apprehends the religious object as metaphorical and symbolic in nature, so that no translation of these symbols into conceptual terms which are literally characteristic of the religious object is possible even in principle. Jaspers therefore maintains that religious truth is possible only through a polar tension between subjectivity and objectivity in which the individual achieves authentic selfhood by confronting the transcendent reality of Being itself (the Encompassing, as he calls it) through symbolic dimensions of insight which are occupied merely to be transcended in succession.

But the scheme of perspectives, on the relation of religious ideas to the religious object, will not be systematically complete unless we add to monistic religious idealism and dualistic religious realism a third general type of viewpoint which I shall term *monistic religious realism*—*monistic* because it maintains that there is, for ideal religious experience, an overlapping numerical identity between the individual conscious subject's awareness of the religious object and that religious object itself, so that what is disclosed in such authentic religious experience is no representative surrogate or substitute for the religious object, but just the numerically identical present and therefore the immediately apprehended religious object itself. It is also *realistic* because the position agrees with dualistic religious realism in contending that the religious object has a reality status that is independent of the experience in which the individual apprehends that object, so that—quite in contrast to dualisms of any sort here, although there is a numerical identity with the object in the experience—the object is not wholly constituted by the elements of the experience as such. As with other general perspectives, monistic religious realism subdivides into various distinguishable types. We need not linger long over the prereflective *naive religious monism* of those religious persons who think of God as being characterized by every determinate quality in which they are aware of God in their religious experience. But there are two clearly distinct and well-developed positions here which call for considerably more attention. One of these, which I will call *critical*

d) The religious existentialism (1) of Kierkegaard, who emphasizes truth as a subjectivity which leads to the ultimate paradox of the Incarnation,

(2) or of Jaspers, who emphasizes the apprehension of Being itself through successive but always inadequate modes of symbolic insight.

C. *Monistic religious realism*—which holds to at least a partial numerical identity between authentic religious experience and the independently real religious object.

1. *Naive religious monism* may be passed over for two more fully developed forms.
2. *Critical monistic religious realism.*
a) This view holds to a partial identity which must be discerned from an admitted dualistic periphery through a process of critical testing;

monistic religious realism, argues that although much of the genuine religious experience of a given individual may be composed of elements that are not numerically identical with the properties of the independent religious object but are contributed by other individual and environmental factors, there is nevertheless—in religious experience at its best for such an individual—a partial identity or overlapping core in which the religious object is immediately present to the individual who can therefore, in a state of appropriate religious adjustment, recognize that core of identity through what is to him an indisputable criterion of its presence and reality. For such a view this identical presence of the religious object is surrounded, then, by a dualistic periphery of elements or factors which must be critically discerned as distinct from the authentic core of immediate divine presence through a process of verifying or testing. And a further duality is recognized here in the accompanying thesis that it is wholly reasonable to believe that the independent religious object has other properties or attributes which, though genuinely characteristic, are not immediately present in the religious experience either of a given individual or of all such individuals taken collectively. It is evident that for any such critical monistic realism the crucial distinguishing factor will be the criterion that is employed to carry through the critical analysis which divides the dualistic periphery from the core of identical divine presence. As an exemplar par excellence of this type of position, we may single out Douglas Clyde Macintosh, who develops the view with an elaborate historical backdrop and takes as the criterion of immediate divine presence a framework of eternal and absolute ideals of value (such as rationality, beauty, and goodness) which are construed as authentic ends for all times, places, and persons. The divine factor thus discerned will consist of all those aspects and forces (including human elements) in reality which are value-producing or contribute to the realization of

but regards the concept of a transcendent personal diety to be a plausible religious belief which goes beyond the core of identical valuational knowledge.

absolutely valid ideas. And if the term *God* is limited to this functionally operative causality in the production of valuable ends, then our religious knowledge of God so construed is being progressively verified in our experience and the discernment of these values as in process of realization is the identical and immediate presence of God. If the term *God* is extended to refer to the notion of these operative factors as the activity of a transcendent personal deity—conscious, intelligent, and purposively active—this is a religious intuition or faith which it is reasonable to believe, but which is not directly verified as religious knowledge in the sense in which the divinely functioning factors, making for the realization of enduring and permanent values, *are* definitely verified as knowledge.

3. *Extreme monistic religious realism.*
a) For other views, discursive concepts at least refer to the religious object as itself having determinate attributes,

The second well-developed monistic realism, which I will call *extreme monistic religious realism,* stands in considerable contrast to the previously elaborated perspective and indeed to all the determinate conceptual viewpoints which we have considered. However these alternatives may differ from each other, they share in common the general thesis that—whether as metaphorical symbols or as literal characterizations—discursive intellectual concepts at least point in the direction of a religious object that has determinate attributes, however obscure our identification and understanding of these attributes may be. But I use the term *extreme* of the perspective now being analyzed because it takes the position (if it can be called a position—adherents often refer to it as the no-view viewpoint or the post-gained no-knowledge) that the religious object wholly transcends all determinate properties, qualities, or attributes, so that intellectual concepts are wholly inept means of apprehending this absolute divine reality. Yet the position is indeed *monistic* in the most ultimate sense—for the religious object is in fact the only genuine reality there is—and it therefore embraces an all-inclusive monistic self-identity such that no identifiable entity whatever is numerically distinct or even finally distinguishable from it. In its most developed forms, this perspective embraces a view that I have called *phenomenal illusionism,* since it holds that while the realm of ordinary experience has a provisional reality as composed of conceptually distinguishable aspects, yet at the highest level of insight all these distinctions collapse, as it were, into the indiscerptible oneness of the religious object itself, so that the ordinary world is finally an illusion. Even the individual conscious subject is an aspect of this illusion; and fully authentic religious knowledge consists in the realization of the undifferentiable identity of the individual (who is thus not really an individual) with the absolute reality—a state in which all difference, distinction, and duality are unmasked as illusory and therefore absolutely excluded. As for models of this conceptually baffling perspective, the clearest examples are found in Oriental thought—in the Changtzu concept of the Tao in classical Taoism, in the blessed Dharmakaya of Mahayana Buddhism, and in the absolutely unqualified Brahma of Sankara's Non-dualistic Vedanta Hinduism. In all of these traditions the basic insight is itself, so to speak, non-dualistically identical, although the admittedly inadequate and misleading conceptually oriented language is different in each context. In Western thought, this type of perspective represents more of a tendency in various mystical philosophies, rather than a developed stance taken clearly to its ultimate limit and conclusion. Perhaps the most impressive example would be found in the Neo-Platonic philosophy of a thinker like Plotinus for whom the ineffable One or absolute Good at the summit of the hierarchy of being is above all differences and distinctions, although Plotinus explained the various levels of difference disclosed to ordinary experience and conceptual thought as somehow an overflow or emanation from the One in a way that is in principle incapable of clear conceptual explanation.

Reflecting in retrospect on the schematism of viewpoints thus elaborated concerning the relation between religious ideas and the religious object through the monism/dualism distinction, I must acknowledge at once that, in terms of critical response, it is my limited intention here merely to thread my way through this complex fabric of perspectives, rather than to attempt to unravel the fabric completely. To use a different metaphor, I spare myself the strength that would be required to remove from the bay of knowledge all the

Margin notes:

but the extreme view regards all such concepts as wholly inapplicable to the religious object, which has no determinate properties.

b) With rigorous monism,
(1) The view regards the religious object as the sole reality with nothing distinct from it.
(2) Phenomenal illusionism, a usual corollary, regards the realm of ordinary experience as ultimately unreal.

(3) Genuine religious knowledge thus is realized identity with the absolute religious reality.

c) Proponents of this outlook are prominent in Oriental thought,

but the Neo-Platonism of Plotinus is a close Western parallel.

IV. *Critical reflections* on this schematism.
A. My main intent will be merely to draw out the implications of my epistemology for these views, though other criticism will not be excluded.

hidden and exposed rocks that might obstruct the voyage of an inquirer—instead I shall merely attempt to steer a safe course through these obstacles to a port where I can dock with reasonable confidence at best. As a method of accomplishing this objective, I shall attempt to draw out the implications, for the monism/dualism controversy, of my previously elaborated epistemological position. That, at least, will be my main intent, although I shall not hesitate to engage in a peripheral skirmish beyond the scope of this intention, if it seems clarifyingly important to do so.

B. Given that previous epistemology, several corollaries follow:

If, then, we accept a theory of religious knowledge which embraces a general unity of epistemological method in general for all the fields of awareness, however diverse their subject matter, but allowing for variations in application for different types of objects—and if this method runs all truth-claims through a testing grid which involves *a priori* principles and categories as providing structure for experiential content for various levels of experience, so that the propriety of a truth-claim is a function of its conformity to what I have called rational coherence and experiential relevance (or explanatory capacity)—then several corollaries follow at once.

1. That the independent religious object will be numerically distinct from truth-claims that involve the formal synthesis of rational and experiential elements.

First it is clear that if there is an independently real religious object apart from our religious ideas, then that religious object will be numerically distinct from those religious ideas and thus some form of dualistic religious realism will be more plausible than any monistic perspective here—for the simple reason that a religious truth-claim will, so far as it is initially plausible in general, always involve a synthesis of rational and experiential elements that are thus distinct numerically from the object that such a synthesis representatively reconstitutes for thought.

2. That extreme monistic realism will be eliminated by purporting to identify the religious object as beyond conceptual categories which, for my view, are all-inclusive in their scope of applicability.

a) Extreme monists would reject this corollary,

Again, it will be an equally significant corollary that, since, for our epistemological theory, no object which purports to transcend all determinate attributes and therefore all conceptual categories, will be coherently identifiable as a reality for thought, any position that involves extreme monistic realism will for that very reason be highly implausible. It should be acknowledged, of course, that since advocates of that position claim that discursive conceptual principles and categories simply do not apply to the religious object, any criticism at any level to the effect that the viewpoint of extreme monistic realism is contradictory, inconsistent, or unintelligible in conceptual terms, will fall, as it were, on deaf ears, since such criticism presupposes the applicability to the religious object of the very conceptual principles that are judged inapplicable by exponents of the position. On this subject I have written at some length in my book entitled *Oriental Philosophy*, and I will not repeat myself here beyond the following general observation (which such monists would rule out as spurious) that there is no way to rule out the application, to any possible object of thought, of conceptual categories of thought—except by employing those same categories to distinguish between that alleged object and any other possible object to which those categories might apply. Here, perhaps, the Zen Buddhist silence is perhaps the only recourse. And if no

b) but there is no way to distinguish the religious object from other objects without using conceptual categories of this sort, so that silence is the only recourse and hence nothing is maintained.

determinate position is maintained, there would appear to be nothing to which any conceivable critical response might be addressed.

A final corollary of our epistemological position will be that the universal applicability of the general structure of knowledge to all possible objects of awareness will call into question any elements in various agnostic dualisms which involve the restriction of discursive conceptual principles to certain limited spheres of thought, and which at the same time postulate an object for plausible belief that is beyond those limits. All such restrictions will involve, as in the case of extreme monistic realism, a sort of pervasive existential contradiction between the inevitable *use* of conceptual categories to define or at least identify the spheres into which intellectual principles cannot enter, on the one hand—and the thesis propounded conceptually that conceptual categories are beyond their depth and limit in those spheres, on the other. This phenomenon can be variously illustrated in the tradition of agnostic dualism—for example, in Kant's evenhanded dismissal of all metaphysical knowledge-claims on the ground that the categories of the understanding are applicable for the attainment of genuine knowledge only within the limits of actual or possible sense experience; or in Kierkegaard's identification of truth with a subjective responsiveness whose only adequate objective form is that of logical paradox; or in Rudolf Otto's contention that the *a priori* and unique forms of religious awareness involve a dimension of insight whose elements are wholly non-rational and therefore insusceptible of being expressed in clear conceptual form. It is clear that, for the sort of dualistic religious realism that I regard as plausible, the issue here is not one that hangs on distinguishing between a level of reasonable belief and a higher (or at least distinct) level of genuine knowledge. For we have already acknowledged that religious world-views and their subordinate aspects exhibit at their human best no more than an approximation to the ideal of absolute metaphysical certainty from a logical point of view. And hence we can invite into our arena of reasonableness whatever support can be found in Kant's defense of religious belief on moral grounds, or in the eminently plausible wager to which we are urged by Pascal and James, or in the objective correlate of unique modes of religious awareness insisted upon by Otto, or even in Kierkegaard's thesis of personal confrontation with the unconditional claim of God. To refuse to call the sort of high-level probability that emerges, from these and many other lines of analysis, by the name of knowledge, would be to confine that term to a sphere of sterility and transform it into an elusive phantom. So let both agnostic and theistic religious dualists join hands here in facing up to the real issue.

Perhaps an invitation of the same sort may be extended to certain forms of critical monistic realism, especially in versions of the type that is propounded by D. C. Macintosh. Critically speaking, I find his repeated insistence that there is a partial identity or overlap between the immediate content of an individual's authentic religious experience and the objective dimension of the religious object both unsupported by plausible grounds and inconsistent with the method or criterion he

3. That any attempt to restrict conceptual categories to a limited sphere will be suspect in a similar fashion by necessarily using conceptual categories to define these spheres.

a) Examples of this difficulty in agnostic dualism.

b) Since religious world-views, on my position, are approximative at best in the logical sense, that reasonable probability can receive support from all the positive arguments of agnostic dualism, without argument about the terms *belief* and *knowledge*.

C. The position of critical monistic realism
1. is difficult to render intelligible, since the criterion for recognizing the purported identity implies merely a correlation, not an identity,

proposes for recognizing this identity and distinguishing it from non-identical aspects of the experience. This identity-claim, as I shall call it, is suspended on the single ground that certain aspects of genuine religious experience embody the recognition of an objective order of moral and spiritual value that subsists independently of individuals either singly or collectively, and that therefore this correlation between experienced content and objective reality means that on those points of correlation the two are identical. But, of course, this evidence or basis (which I fully accept as sound and thus have no reason to contest) does not actually imply any such identity. Instead, it implies the representative adequacy of the experienced content as reconsti-

so that the realism en-tailed is actually dual-istic.

tuting for thought the objective values in question—a conclusion that entails realism indeed, but a realism that is dualistic rather than monistic, since the correlation presupposes the numerical distinctness of the two entities (subjective content and objective value) that are the

2. Also, the applica-tion of a criterion to religious experience, in order to determine its relation *to* the ob-jective order, implies dualism directly.

terms of the correlation. On the matter of the criterion for recognizing the identity, it would appear that if the individual is required to apply a critical standard *to* his religious experience in order to determine the relation of the experience to an otherwise discerned objective order of value, then this whole procedure presupposes the non-identity of the experienced content with the objective order. If the two were really identical, the question of their relation could not even be raised (as it *is* not in the highest forms of extreme monistic realism). Here again it appears to be a sort of dualistic realism that emerges, rather than any type of monistic realism.

D. On the question whether the special status of the religious object would alter the monism/dualism scheme:

There is, however, the question whether the special character of the religious object might lead to some modification of the monism/dualism scheme for that particular object as over against other pos-sible types of object. We found, for example, that there was such a variation as between sense-objects and the objects of universal con-cepts. Is it perhaps the case that the distinctive status of the religious object is such that, while there could be no numerically identical presence to the individual conscious subject in the case of either sense-objects or the objects of universal concepts, nevertheless there could be such a numerically identical presence in the case of the religious object? Even if we assume the realistic thesis that the divine reality has a status in being that is in some sense independent of the individual conscious subject, it will not be possible to give a clear answer to this question until the precise character of that independent

this would depend on the precise character of the religious object. 1. Pantheism would imply a complete iden-tity of all ideas and ob-jects with the religious object.

status is itself determined. If, for instance, we accepted a version of metaphysical pantheism which held that the divine reality includes within itself all the things and processes of the experienced world-order as aspects of itself—but that these aspects were genuinely real as determinate and distinct from each other, so that, quite differently from the case of extreme monistic realism, all actual differences were maintained in the unity of the divine reality as a whole—then it would clearly be the case that *all* ideas in the minds of conscious subjects, and indeed those minds themselves and all objects that they could conceivably contemplate, would sustain a numerical identity with the divine reality just by literally being aspects of that reality, although it would be difficult to regard any particular aspects, whether ideas or not, as any more pertinent to the nature of that divine reality than any other such aspects, since the identity would be the same for all.

But if, in contrast to such a pantheism, we accepted a version of metaphysical theism which holds that the divine reality, though it is the creative, sustaining, and purposive ground of the contingent world order, is nevertheless wholly distinct from that order in its being—so that things and processes are in no sense aspects of that divine reality—a very different result emerges. One might suppose that, since for a typical theism of this type, God—while existing independently of the space-time universe—nevertheless is fully present and causally operative at every point in space and time, therefore God, as so construed, fully occupies all the space-time positions that ordinary things and processes occupy, and that God would thus be characterized by the requisite numerically identical presence that would make monistic realism in religious epistemology a live option. In my opinion, however, this line of reasoning would be a serious misconstruction of the type of theism we are considering here—for God does not, in this view, occupy space-time positions in the same sense in which contingent objects (and therefore also ideas as contents of individual finite consciousness) occupy space-time positions. Hence God's direct accessibility at all points in space-time is quite distinct from any numerical identity with the contingent and ordinary objects of space-time. Quite to the contrary, God should be so construed here that, though immanent within space-time, he is nevertheless wholly distinct from it. In an analogous but not wholly identical fashion, arithmetical truths (for example, $2 \times 2 = 4$), precisely because they hold independently of both space and time, are true at every point in space-time and in that quite distinctive sense wholly immanent within it. Contingent things and processes, on the other hand, do not in typical cases sustain such a transcendent relation to space-time and can therefore be immanent in space-time only by occupying a limited context of it. From all this it follows that, for such a version of theism, there can be no numerical identity between God and any content of the contingent order of things. And it will therefore also follow that the knowledge of God as the religious object can never be numerically identical with God himself in any aspect of the divine reality whatever, no matter how limited an aspect we might consider. It does not, however, follow that, for such a position, there can be no adequate knowledge of the religious object—such knowledge will be adequate just to the extent that the ideas which compose it are reconstructions for thought in the form of universal concepts which have as their objects essences which actually characterize the nature of the religious object. But that way of putting it again entails epistemological dualism, with all the implications about religious knowledge which such a dualism involves.

But in all this concern with the monistic aspect of what I have called critical monistic realism, it is important not to lose sight of the critical and realistic aspects of a position like that of D. C. Macintosh.

2. Theism yields a different result by emphasizing the distinction between God and all contingent entities.

a) Nor does God's presence and operation at all points of space-time imply any numerical identity with its contents.

b) On the contrary, God's immanence within space-time involves his being wholly distinct from its contingent contents.

c) Hence, the knowledge of God in finite minds could not be identical with God himself, although that does not imply that there can be no knowledge of God on dualistic grounds.

3. In any case, it is clear that not every aspect of religious experience provides a positive clue to the nature of the religious object.

On the critical aspect, it seems clearly correct that not every quality of religious experience can be taken as an appropriate clue to, much less an adequate reconstruction of, the religious object itself—for the core of adequacy, however that may be determined, is characteristically encircled by a periphery of aspects that are so obviously idiosyncratic, traditional, and cultural in their foundation that a critical line must be recognized as separating the core from that periphery, even though we can never draw that line explicitly with final confidence. And, as I see it, we have no recourse but to apply here, as in the whole of knowledge, those criteria of adequacy which disclose themselves to reflective thought as interpretive principles and categories which are presupposed in the possibility of all intelligible thought. As for the realistic aspect here, I see no reason not to agree with the general thesis that such reflective thought discloses an objective order of value, essentially moral and spiritual in nature, the ultimately adequate explanation and ground of which would be found in the object of a reasonable belief in a transcendent, personal divine reality. But the fuller elaboration of this point I shall reserve for a later context.

If then we again join hands with critical monistic realism (though with the qualifications previously elaborated), as we did previously with agnostic dualism subject to analogous reservations, what is the remaining crucial issue which all these allied perspectives inevitably face? In my opinion, this issue is clearly confronted in the position which I earlier referred to as monistic religious idealism—a perspective which identifies the religious object with the religious ideas of individuals singly and collectively, and then denies that the religious object has any straightforwardly independent reality status apart from the conjunction and accumulation of such ideas. Yet this issue is not as simple as it may appear, for the explanations of projectionist, psychiatric, and humanistic religious idealism are not wholly devoid of significance and plausibility. If we approach religious ideas in a critically constructive frame of mind, it may well appear that these ideas contain elements that are indeed projections of ideal human values, or extensions to cosmic proportions of elements grounded in family relationships and centering around father- and mother-images. It will be the task of critical assessment to recognize these elements and to decide whether they are, in particular instances, either a sort of disposable husk or, alternatively and much more importantly, significant analogical or metaphorical clues to the nature of the religious object itself. The issue, then, will not be whether religious experience involves such peripheral elements, but whether, when those elements are acknowledged and put in proper perspective, there is anything left in a critically assimilated sphere of religious thought which points toward the reality of the religious object as independent of the conjunction of such ideas and elements. Is the issue, then, perhaps after all statable in its simplest terms in that ancient and well-worn question, does God exist? This, in any case, is the decisive problem that any critical realism in religion must confront. And on this issue it will be of secondary importance whether that realism is monistic or dualistic, and whether

a) Whatever core of adequacy there may be will be recognized by the application of those principles which make knowledge in general possible.

b) It is plausible here to recognize objective value as ultimately grounded in a personal God.

E. The crucial issue for all these allied views (critical monistic realism, agnostic dualism, and theistic dualism) is clearly faced in monistic religious idealism, which denies any objective status to the religious object.

1. Religious ideas may well contain elements derived from the sources suggested by this orientation.

2. The issue will then be whether these elements may nevertheless point analogically to a religious object independent of these sources.

3. The question will then be whether God exists in this independent way—the real issue will therefore be between realism (of any sort) and monistic idealism.

such a dualism takes the stronger theistic form or the less ambitious but still realistic agnostic form. But I myself find the view that I have called combinational theistic dualism more plausible than any of its realistic alternatives. I shall try to argue in this framework of understanding, in order to show why I regard the united perspectives of realism as a more adequate stance than any version of monistic religious idealism, with its thesis that religious truth-claims of whatever sort have as their sole basis and referent the subjective ideas of finite conscious individuals.

Retrospective Summary on Religious Epistemology

As I pause on the threshold of this larger investigation in order to reflect in retrospect on the foundations of religious knowledge, I think it well to survey my results in brief compass. However, as I do so, I would have it clearly understood that these results are at best approximative and therefore always subject to reconsideration and restatement through a developing clarity in discerning those basic principles and categories which provide structure and grounding for both being and thought. With that reservation firmly in hand, I find myself committed to the ideal of rational objectivity that lies at the heart of perspectives I regard as rationalistic. But I aim at this ideal with an increasing awareness of all those factors which voluntarism identifies as pervasively distracting even the most diligent inquirer from the track of objective reasonableness, while at the same time I regard the developing awareness of these factors as making it possible for the individual to compensate in large measure for their influence.

Once inside the rationalist framework, of course, I confront the division between apriorism—with its emphasis on necessary starting points for thought which characterize the mind as interpretive structures prior to and independently of the particular data of experience— and empiricism—with its opposing thesis that both the structural form and the determinate content of knowledge find their sole source in precisely those data of experience. On this issue, I see a moderate apriorism as the more plausible stance, since I cannot regard the mind as deriving anything from experience unless *as* a mind it is antecedently characterized by interpretive principles which make the function of derivation possible. At the same time, my apriorism here involves only the general formal structures of knowledge—rational coherence and explanatory adequacy in terms of causal grounding, with whatever subordinate principles that involves. The determinate content of knowledge, in relation to existing particulars, I regard as arising through the application of *a priori* principles to experiential data at various logical levels (sense-objects, objects of universal concepts, and so on). And because of this experientially derived content in all existential knowledge-claims, I regard all such claims as both contingent and probable or approximative in nature, so that they are always subject to possible revision in relation to the expanding front of experience.

Turning to perspectives involving the idea-object or mind-object

I. While my conclusions are approximative and subject to review, they involve the following elements:

A. An aim at rational objectivity, tempered by the recognition of the influence of non-rational factors;

B. A moderate apriorism which involves interpretive structures that characterize the mind prior to experience, and a determinate content of experience to which those data are applied to gain knowledge;

C. A view of existential knowledge as contingent and probable.

II. Concerning the idea-object relation, my position involves these elements:
A. Epistemological dualism and the thesis that truth-claims are causal inferences from ideas to objects,

relationship, I find the framework of my general epistemology everywhere inclining me to the dualistic thesis that the idea of any object is always numerically distinct from the object itself as the referent of that idea. And since this thesis entails the conclusion that ideas at best are representative reconstructions which reconstitute the object for thought, it likewise follows that existential truth-claims are always causal inferences from ideas to their objective correlates (whether correctly or not—mistakes are possible here, perhaps even rampantly prevalent), except in the strikingly unique case of each individual's undeniable certainty of his own existence as a thinking subject—a certainty that is discerned in the direct activity of functioning as such a subject. *Cogito ergo sum* (not just Descartes's *cogito*, but every individual's *cogito* for himself) is not really a causal inference at all, but an expression of each individual's self-knowledge disclosed in the *act* of being a subject.

Nor do I see any reason for supposing that a general epistemological dualism is inapplicable to certain special types of objects. Instead, I discern a variation, for distinct types of objects, in the application of the dualism. Hence, I accept a symbolical pragmatism with respect to our knowledge of sense-objects and of scientific theories based on empirical analyses of these objects, while on the other hand I regard the essences which are the referents of universal concepts as unobstructedly accessible to thought, so that no symbolical thesis is pertinent in such cases. As to the religious object, finally, I found no reason to regard it as an exception to the dualism that pervades general epistemology, provided one accepts a realism as to the independent reality status of that religious object. But the real issues here remain to be investigated—either a realistic pantheism or a monistic idealism about the religious object would involve (but in strikingly different ways) the discarding of epistemological dualism in relation to the knowledge of the religious object. The crucial question at this stage— a question which involves a clear transition of emphasis from epistemology to metaphysics—is whether either of these alternatives is ultimately plausible, or whether, in contrast, some version of theism is more plausible in the place of both.

(margin notes)

except in the unique case of each individual's self-certainty in the *cogito*.

B. As applied to different types of objects, this involves:

1. symbolical pragmatism *re* sense-objects and scientific theories about them;

2. unobstructed access to universal essences;
3. and theistic dualism *re* the religious object.
III. But the truth-claim of theism, in contrast to pantheism or monistic idealism, remains to be settled.

The Development of the Concept of Revelation

The General Idea of Revelation

Whatever exists, in whatever realm of being or reality, under whatever limitations or restrictions, is in some sense self-disclosed. And in whatever sense it is self-disclosed, it is in that same sense and to that same extent self-revealed. For nothing can subsist in any mode or level of being unless it is determinate in nature and therefore either *is* a property (or conjunction of properties) or *has* a property (or conjunction of properties). And a property (quality, attribute, essence) is at least potentially, if not actually (in a relatively small number of cases), the object of a universal concept in some finite conscious subject or mind. But to be the object of such a universal concept even potentially is to be self-disclosed with that same potentiality; and to be thus self-disclosed involves at least a potential revelation of the nature of the reality in question to a knowing mind. I will take it as existentially indisputable, by any critically discerning investigator, that some knowing minds exist—since investigating a truth-claim is itself a function of reflective thought on the part of such a knowing mind. And if there were no knowing minds, then no actual truth-claim could either exist or be disputed. I will therefore also conclude from these considerations that being is essentially self-revealing as the potential object of universal concepts, and essentially self-revealed to the extent that being is the actual object of universal concepts. Reality, therefore, as a whole and in all its aspects, is an all-inclusive self-revelation.

But, in claiming this, I am not blithely ignorant of the fact that my argument presupposes a virtually incalculable number of assumptions, some of which at least are ardently disputed and most of which are potentially disputable. Yet that is the case with every non-trivially significant argument whatsoever. I can therefore hardly be expected to collect and analyze all the chips that fall to the ground otherwise unnoticed as I chisel my way toward a perspective on being. I have of course assumed that existence is universally intelligible to thought, that this intelligibility is understandable only in terms of the supposition that all being is determinate in character, and that thought is itself one of the modes of being that is thus intelligible, in this case to itself—although all this is but a comparatively negligible sample of my assumptions. But frankly I cannot make any sense at all out of the attempt to deny such assumptions, since that denial would involve the reintroduction of precisely analogous assumptions to make it intelligible as a denial. I will therefore make no further apology for incorporating such a network of assumptions, and I will merely suggest that their plausibility will finally consist in the extent to which they make possible a world-view which is characterized by rational coherence and explanatory capacity more fully than any alternative world-view with which I am presently familiar.

While therefore all existence is, in the sense elaborated, a revelation, the precise character of this self-disclosure will vary for different realms or levels of being, and within each level for different specific instances. If, for example, we consider the general realm of particular existing entities at the sub-levels of matter, life, and mind, it will appear, from a certain point of view, that a thing will be more explicitly self-disclosed to the extent that its relations to other things are externally determined and its capacity to respond to these other things is relatively limited—while a thing will be less explicitly self-disclosed to the extent that its relations to other things are guided in part by a principle of inner self-direction and its capacity to respond to these other things

I. All determinate being is at least potentially self-revealed by being the possible object of a universal concept in some knowing mind.

A. Since the reality of knowing minds is existentially indisputable,

it follows that reality is an all inclusive self-revelation.

B. Yet this claim involves a large number of disputed assumptions, only a few of which are here noted:
1. For example, that being, as determinate, is universally intelligible to thought as itself a mode of being;

2. but such assumptions can be denied only by other analogously intelligible assumptions.

II. The precise nature of self-disclosure will vary for different realms of being.
A. In general, a thing will be less explicitly self-disclosed to the extent that its relations to other things are guided by a principle of inner self-direction.

1. An inanimate object, for example, is subject to a rather full investigation by a qualified observer;

2. but living things are less explicitly self-disclosed just in proportion to their degree of complexity and inner direction;

3. and at certain points a capacity for self-concealment emerges.

B. The case of persons is more intricate still:
1. partly as an extension of the principle already explained;

2. and partly because of a qualitative contrast with other living beings.

a) Aspects of this difference.

b) The core of personal uniqueness.
3. Hence the degree of self-disclosure and self-concealment is optional for persons, though a person may also be pervasively concealed from himself,

is relatively complex, extended to a broad spectrum of variations, and susceptible of a multiple redirection and alteration in any response initiated. A stone, for example, is to a large extent externally determined in its relations to other things and its capacity to respond is largely limited to environmentally determined disintegrations in its substance (it can, for instance, be ground into smaller particles or split in two) or to externally caused changes in spatial position. And just for these reasons the practically significant properties of a stone are to a relatively high degree open to rather full investigation by an inquiring observer, even though its theoretically construed properties may be fairly complex. A living thing, on the other hand, whether plant or animal, is a far more difficult assignment, precisely because its relations to other things are in part directed by a principle of inner self-direction which is capable of responding to environmental changes in an extended variety of ways. And the more complex and intricate a thing is in its life-response, the less explicit it seems to be in its self-disclosure, so that an actual revelation of its nature may require a far more involved effort on the part of a would-be knower. At certain variable points in the sphere of living things, a capacity for self-concealment emerges which leaves the self-disclosure for any observer partly up to the option of the living thing in its self-directed response to the environment. Even a very highly trained observer may be frustrated in his attempt to photograph a highly elusive lioness in the wild.

If now we turn our attention to the case of living human persons, all this becomes infinitely more involved and complex. For a person appears to have the most far-reaching inner self-directedness and the most extended and variable response capacity known to us in the range of living things. And it seems plausible to suppose that this pervasive difference between persons and even the most developed sub-personal living things is to be partly accounted for, not merely by the further unfolding of capacities already present at those sub-personal levels, but also and perhaps decisively by a qualitative contrast exhibited in a self-conscious, intelligently directed, purposively oriented capacity for activity which persons possess and which is virtually absent at those other levels of life. This striking contrast expresses itself in a variety of forms—the ability to use language, the capacity to form universal concepts, the power to sublimate the influence of both environmental and biological pressures in order to aim consciously at the realization of an envisioned goal which those pressures might otherwise obstruct, to mention only a few of these forms. And since the core of a person's unique sort of being is largely resident in this overall, self-conscious, inner awareness and directedness, the degree to which a person is actually self-disclosed to other persons is very largely up to the option of that person, so that both the capacity for self-revelation and the capacity for self-concealment (though of course within limits) are enormously enhanced. So complex is the inner structure of personhood that it is not merely possible but actually characteristic for a person to be decisively concealed from his own watchful mental eye and therefore fundamentally confused about his own self-identity. As a result, the self-concealment of a person from other persons may and commonly does come about, even if that person is prompted by the strongest urge to self-communication. Therefore, the capacity for self-revelation to others in an authentic fashion is significantly possible only to the extent that an individual has at least gained an upper hand in the struggle to know his own inner self.

From all this it seems to follow that, if we arrange existing things in a sort of hierarchy, ranging from such things as stones to persons, then as we ascend this hierarchy reflectively, the capacity for self-disclosure becomes less explicit and more subject to the control of the reality being considered, so that while fuller self-revelation becomes possible, so does fuller self-concealment. Still it is clear that even at the highest level of this projected hierarchy of finite realities, no subject that is even externally accessible to a discerning observer can succeed in totally veiling himself. We unwittingly give ourselves away in certain of our acts, attitudes, habits, and responses, even when we do not intend such a disclosure. And an especially important way in which any existing thing thus reveals itself is found in the effects of its being and activity on other things in an extended variety of ways. Everything that exists leaves a sort of continuous trail that composes its path through being and discloses something—perhaps even a great deal—about its nature and significance. If, at the personal level, an individual has both a firm grip on the knowledge of himself and a settled resolve to self-revelation, then the total impact of his existence and activity on other persons may reach a remarkably high level of authentic self-disclosure through the conjunction of these two elements of self-knowledge and revelatory intent.

For finite knowers like ourselves, in any case, this entire revelatory exchange of being portrays itself to each individual conscious subject through the expression in each such subject of all the other facets of reality upon it. Nothing is actually disclosed to me except through effects of its being and activity which finally reach my consciousness, however indirectly through however extended and varied a complex of intervening or intermediary factors. To an extent that is crucially but not entirely dependent on my own will to recognize these effects or not, or even on my being blithely negligent and inattentive, I may achieve a relatively high degree of openness to the revelation of being. Alternatively, I may achieve a relatively complete solitary confinement, shut off from the light of being by a sort of self-absorption which filters this revelation through a self-composed grid that turns much of the light back to its source and, whether deliberately or not, allows only a dim and all-but-invisible ray to pass through to my explicit consciousness. At sub-personal levels of existence, the operation of such an obstruction is far less effective—for it is precisely at the level where controls over self-revelation and self-concealment reach their finite highest in persons that the capacity to deflect the light of revelation makes possible the most complete blindness.

so that genuine self-revelation requires a difficult struggle for self-knowledge.

C. Yet no subject succeeds in total self-concealment, since it reveals something of itself in its discernible qualities, and especially in its effects on other things.

1. This fact may reach a high degree of impact for persons.

2. For finite knowers, other realities are revealed through their effects in consciousness, although the degree of effectiveness depends on the degree of openness or its opposite.

a) In fact, resistance to the revelation of being is most fully possible for just such knowers;

b) but a receptive person traces effects to causes adequate to explain them.

(1) Other persons are known, and related to, in this way;

(2) and so are sub-personal levels of being.

(3) Eventually an inclusive overpattern of the whole of being reflects itself in such an open individual's mind through the sustained and active exercise of his whole capacity for thought.

III. To trace that causal network to its ultimate ground is to approach the ultimate object of religious concern as the cause of all contingent being.

A. This ultimate ground is not plausibly identifiable with the contingent world-order as a whole, since this whole would require causal explanation itself, although this point requires further reflection.

But when an individual's will is turned toward the light and his consciousness is openly receptive, his knowledge moves toward a goal of adequacy and completeness, precisely by tracing effects upon him to causes that he interprets as having the specific powers of being to explain their activity in producing those effects, whether in a relatively direct or indirect fashion. He comes to know other persons through the impingement of their being and activity upon him; he discerns patterns of that activity which he traces to relatively settled dispositions of character; and he responds to those persons with a reciprocal self-disclosure on his own part, confident that the network of causal connectedness that he thus discerns will effectively guide his activity in achieving an appropriate relationship to other individuals. Such a person must already have extended his vision of this causal network to include the rich and varied sub-personal levels of being as well; and he does so in a way that is not essentially different from the operation of his knowledge with respect to persons—although it does alter his stance peripherally in accordance with variations in the patterns of response that are disclosed to him at these levels. Then perhaps he begins to grasp with fuller awareness what has been guiding him unwittingly all along—namely, the sense of an elaborate framework of relationships among the parts of being, a framework which discloses a complex of analogies of various sorts and with varying degrees of similarity, so that the whole of being reflects itself, in the mirror of his consciousness, as a sort of all-inclusive, comprehensive overpattern which unites all its subordinate themes into a whole. In all of this, the open individual, as I shall call him, has of course brought to bear his whole capacity for intelligible thought—and he has used that capacity to follow, as it were, a single thread which leads from effects to causes and eventuates in the unveiling for him of a general pattern of being. It is also clear that the fewer stones he leaves unturned, the fewer causal trails he leaves untraced, and the fewer lines of connection he abandons without completing his analysis of them, the fuller by far will be the revelation of being to that individual. Will it be surprising, therefore, if such an individual presupposes, in his attempt to understand existence, that if being has an ultimate secret to disclose or an ultimate capstone to discover, it will bare itself to the eye of the person who sets his whole energy on tracing the analogical causal structure of being to its deepest foundation or ground?

To approach that depth of being in an individual's knowledge and awareness would be at the same time to approach the ultimate object of religious concern, as well as the ultimate and primary ground of the existence and qualities of all contingent and therefore finite entities whose functioning and relationships constitute the world order as a whole. Nor would it seem plausible to regard that ground of being as either a reciprocally dependent part of that world order or that order itself as an inclusive interdependent totality—for in either of these cases the reality confronted by the individual, though genuinely real, would simply not be the ultimate ground at all, since it would itself require the very sort of causal explanation that any lesser dependent part or totality of such dependent parts would likewise require. Not that the transcendent status of the depth of being—that is, its independence of all contingent, dependent entities of which it would be the final ground—is decisively settled by this transitional analysis. Far from it, since this question will continue to dominate much of my subsequent reflection. At this juncture, I am merely pointing out a direction for further thought.

Yet some insights about the ultimate reality seem clear even at the present stage of understanding. However that reality is conceptually understood in its relation to the contingent aspects of the world order, if it is to be the final foundation and ground of that order, it seems reasonable that it must possess that conjunction of attributes and characteristics, properties and qualities, which would make it capable of causally acting to produce and account for all the varied and complex levels of finite being—right up to and including the level of personal consciousness as exemplified, at the very least, in ourselves as precisely such persons. Furthermore, this ultimate causality would likewise need to be construed as providing the basis for all those objective realms of reality which finite persons reasonably recognize as independent of themselves, even though these realms are not empirically observable—such realms, for example, as those of moral value and logical structure. It is not initially impossible, of course, to think of the ultimate reality as some sort of homogeneous, primordial stuff from which all the presently recognizable levels of being emerged through a kind of inexplicably creative process in which there developed the whole range of complex qualities of which the original stuff was, at the outset, totally devoid. But just as it is not initially impossible to suppose such a development, however great a strain it may put on credulity, neither is it necessary to begin with such an assumption. It might at least be equally plausible, if not far more credible, to suppose that the ultimate reality itself possessed that total complex of properties which would both explain the complexities of the world order and at the same time be compatible with the nature of ultimate reality as itself requiring no foundation of being beyond itself.

And what would that view of this relationship add to our understanding of revelation in its broadest sweep? In the first place, such an outlook would suggest that the ultimate reality was itself intricately complex precisely by possessing all those properties, essentially and in the highest degree, which were recognizable and conceivable as properties of various levels of contingent things, especially those which are themselves characterized by a relatively high degree of complexity. Only those properties would be excluded whose essential nature would imply the sort of imperfection and contingency which would be inconsistent with the nature of ultimate reality itself as non-contingent and therefore self-existent. At the same time, the ultimate reality would have to be conceived as capable of producing things with essentially imperfect and contingent properties, but it could not itself be characterized by such properties without ceasing to be ultimate in

B. Provisionally:
1. The ultimate reality would have to have properties which could causally explain all contingent being, including persons;

2. and it would have to provide the basis for all objective realms of being such as moral value and logical structure.
C. Though explanation in terms of primordial stuff is not initially excluded, neither must it be initially assumed: it is at least equally plausible to view the ultimate reality as possessing all those qualities consistent with its ultimacy.

IV. Revelation would thus be extended.
A. While properties implying imperfection and contingency would be excluded from the ultimate,

it would have to be capable of producing things with imperfect and contingent qualities.
1. Personal mind might be the best analog here, though the logically incidental qualities of finite mind would be excluded;
2. nor could any sort of composition of parts be ascribed to the ultimate reality.
B. If the ultimate were construed as personal,
1. then it would have the fullest capacity for self-disclosure and self-concealment, so that the extent of its revelation to finite minds would be wholly subject to its personal will;

2. it would further express itself in ways characteristic of personal activity through conscious purpose, moral will, and aesthetic diversity;

3. and it would be plausible to expect finite persons and their linguistic self-expression to be significant vehicles of the revelation of the ultimate.

the highest sense. Perhaps the most plausible analog for construing the nature of the ultimate, as thus clarified, would be to conceive it as supreme personal mind, characterized by self-consciousness and self-determination in the fullest sense, but without supposing that the ultimate had any of those logically incidental qualities of mind as existing at the finite level—such qualities, for example, as subjection to temporal process or restriction to limited conscious content. On the other hand, no property whose definition implied a composition of parts (spatial extension, for instance) could be ascribed to the ultimate at all, since anything composed of parts would clearly be, for that reason, contingent in its nature.

If the suggestion that the ultimate reality is essentially personal is followed out (a point that is here merely put forth as possible, rather than being confidently decided), then considerable further insight emerges as well. A person has, as previously indicated, both the fullest capacity for self-disclosure and at the same time the most extensive ability for self-concealment, so that the degree of self-disclosure is potentially pervasive indeed but is guided by conscious purpose and deliberate intent. The power of will over self-disclosure is of course limited for finite persons—we inevitably leave a trail of revelatory clues about ourselves, even if we try very hard not to do so. But in the case of the ultimate personal mind, it is not antecedently unthinkable that the absolute reality could be incognito in the very world order of which it is the causal ground—and to those very finite minds (like our own) which in their highest exercise aspire to the knowledge of that ultimate personal mind. What this means is that the revelation of the ultimate is entirely grounded in the decision of its personal will to an extent that is only weakly mirrored by finite persons like ourselves.

We might further expect that the ultimate, as personal, would, in its deliberate conscious intent, manifest itself across the whole sweep of the contingent world order of which it would be the ground, in all those types of quality and activity which essentially characterize finite persons. Thus we would expect to find cosmic purpose operating in the production of valuable ends, moral will expressing itself in a framework of ethical obligation and value, and even, perhaps, aesthetic self-expression clothing itself in unimaginably vast and intricate forms of beauty at all levels of reality. Yet possibly the firmest expectation would be to find that ultimate personal reality distinctively self-disclosed in the history and personal expression of finite minds which would, on our hypothesis, be its most appropriate contingent models. And that self-disclosure might well take the humanly sophisticated form of ideas and even language as the vehicle of those ideas. In that case, we might expect human personal life and conceptual, linguistic expression to be among the most significant vehicles of the self-disclosure of the ultimate. That the historically developed Christian understanding of existence actually embodies much of this insight, is not, I think, an indispensable ground of the plausibility of that insight, epistemologically speaking. But, conversely, the plausibility of that insight itself, so far as it can be exhibited on rational and experiential grounds, may indeed well be one of the most significant foundations for holding to the reasonableness of the Christian understanding of existence.

Throughout my analysis of the general idea of revelation, I have been referring abstractly to the ultimate or absolute reality as the causal ground of all contingent being, to supreme personal mind as a plausible characterization of the ultimate through analogy with finite personal minds, and even occasionally to the ultimate as the object of religious concern or, more straightforwardly, the religious object. But now that I have proposed at some length the personal analog for understanding the ultimate in a preliminary and philosophically tentative sense, I intend now, not to discard that abstract mode of expression, but rather to extend and supplement that mode by referring to the ultimate in distinctly religious and personal terms. Hence, since I regard the term *God* (and its equivalent in other languages) as the most effective linguistic means of such religious and personal reference, I will not hesitate henceforth either to speak of the ultimate as God or to capitalize the term *Ultimate* and other similar expressions when they have this significance. Partly, this is a matter of linguistic convenience; but it is also partly an expression of the fact that my intention here is to reconstruct the Christian revelation claim in which such a personal view of the Ultimate is indisputably central. Yet I wish to make it abundantly clear that I intend to settle no point of philosophical substance by my preference for linguistic usage. Instead, I am merely adopting that usage as appropriate for pointing out the basic direction of my reflection. So let no one be either perturbed or beguiled by the mere form of speech, since the important issues of substance, which such forms suggest, have yet to be broached.

C. At this juncture I intend to extend the use of the personal analog by the free use of terms such as God, the Ultimate, and other similar expressions in capitalized form.
1. This is partly for convenience and partly an expression of my apologetic purpose.

2. But no question of substance is settled by this merely linguistic decision.

In general, then, we may provisionally think of revelation as referring to the self-disclosure of being at every level, from the frailest example of contingent reality to the Ultimate Itself as transcending all contingent reality, of which in some sense it is the causal foundation. And we may also construe the causal strand which, in varied and intricate ways, constitutes reality as an integral whole, to be the clue to both the nature and the direction of that pervasive self-disclosure. Since, finally, the Ultimate is the causal ground of all finite reality, we may conversely view the whole finite world order, and each of its constituent parts, as an inclusive and comprehensive revelation of the nature of that Ultimate, although the interpretation of that revelation is, of course, a still further work of reflective thought.

V. Summary on the general idea of revelation.

The Species of the Idea of Revelation

If, as I have maintained, reality, both as a whole and in all its aspects, is an all-inclusive self-revelation—and if the Ultimate Reality is Itself, in a multiplicity of ways, self-revealed in all the aspects of contingent reality—then it will clearly follow that the comprehensive unity of this pervasive revelatory character of being must take philosophical priority over any recognition of a distinction within that revelation into

I. Although the all-inclusive character of the revelation of being implies that its unity takes priority over any subdivision into types, still there is an almost universal tendency to distinguish between a *general* form of revelation that is universally accessible and a *special* form which is historically restricted.

A. While this distinction is virtually extended to all the principal world religious traditions,

it is effectively possible and even crucial to develop it in the single historical form of Christianity, since that comports with my apologetic aim.

B. The distinction between general and special revelation has often been cast into a rigid form which contrasts:
1. natural and supernatural,

2. universal and particular,

species or types. Yet, in virtually all religious-philosophical traditions in which the notion of revelation has been clearly recognized and analyzed, a marked distinction has been made, at least in relation to the Religious Object or God, between a sort of general revelation of God which is at least potentially accessible to every human person capable of reflective thought, regardless of his cultural, historical, and personal circumstances, on the one hand—and, on the other hand, a sort of special revelation precisely in the context of such particular circumstances, with the result that this disclosure is therefore limited in its accessibility for humanity as a whole, except so far as the content and implications of this revelation are themselves historically disseminated to broader segments of humanity—either by those to whom the revelation was first vouchsafed or by their successors in the receipt of this communication. This distinction is obvious in the Hebrew-Christian tradition. But it is likewise clearly present in Islam (the prophet Muhammed and the Qu'ran), in orthodox Hinduism (the seers and the sruti or sacred scriptures of the Vedas and the Upanishads), and even in Buddhism (in the Tripitaka of the Hinayana and the various Mahayana Sutras), although here the distinction is qualified and limited by certain peculiar features of early Buddhist tradition which I cannot here discuss since I have already dealt with them in my book *Oriental Philosophy: A Westerner's Guide to Eastern Thought.* It seems effectively possible to develop this distinction between general and special revelation, however, only by analyzing it in one of its broad historical forms. And since I am here ultimately concerned with the Christian revelation claim and its critical assessment, I regard it as crucial to analyze the distinction in that context primarily, although I will sometimes allude to its application in other contexts of religious tradition.

It should be acknowledged that in much traditional discussion the distinction between general and special revelation has been cast in the form of a fairly rigid, if not radical, dichotomy such that the comprehensive unity of revelation is, at the very least, compromised. General revelation has been identified with the revelation of God in the *natural,* empirically discernible realm of existence, so that the manifestation of God to persons takes the form of reasoning from more or less ordinary states of contingent existence, considered as effects requiring explanation, to God as their Ultimate Cause and Explanation. Special revelation has been identified with the revelation of God in a series of *supernatural,* historical interventions into the natural order, in such a way that the inherent possibilities of the natural order, however construed, would by themselves be inadequate to explain these events, which are thus unique, divine disclosures of a special sort. Or again, general revelation, precisely because its data consist of certain common features of the natural order which may become evident to any investigator who reflectively turns his attention to them, is said to be *universal* in its potential extent; while special revelation, precisely because it is transmitted in specific events in unique historical circumstances to selected individuals or groups, is said to be *particular* in its actual extent. Finally, general revelation has been regarded as primarily *epistemological* and *cognitive* in its impact on the human person, since its main result, where it is effective, is to make possible a knowledge of the existence and nature of God and of his relations to the contingent world-order—while special revelation has been referred to as primarily *soteriological* and *moral* in its impact, since, while it supplements the knowledge of God through general revelation, its principal thrust has been to confront and, in general, to solve the predicament of man's moral and spiritual alienation from God through the abuse of free choice.

3. epistemological/ cognitive and soteriological/moral.

It is not difficult to see, on careful reflection, that the two sides of the chasm dividing general revelation from special revelation are spanned by connecting conceptual bridges without which the distinction would be seriously questionable, if not unintelligible. If, as I have provisionally suggested, God is the Ultimate Causal Ground of the sum of those contingent entities that constitute the natural world order—and if this relationship of the world order to God entails, just for that reason, the comprehensive dependence of the so-called natural order on the supernatural (that is, on God as transcending the natural order)—then it follows that no natural agent can either exist or function except in dependence on the divine supernatural causality. Hence the natural order has no inherent possibilities apart from this inclusive relation of dependence. It would seem to follow as well, therefore, that the notion of an independent natural order, capable of operating on its own in the way implicitly assumed by the original distinction between the natural and the supernatural, is an implausible notion. This is not to say, of course, that finite things and processes have no intrinsic causal efficacy, nor is it to maintain that what we call the natural order has no generally operative patterns of regularity. But it is to point out that both that causal efficacy and those patterns of regularity are throughout actual and possible only through the supervening operation of divine causality, so that the whole of the world order and all that occurs within it would constitute a unitary spectrum of divine self-disclosure, even though some elements along that spectrum would make a far more striking impression of the divine causality than others to what I will hesitatingly call a typical observer. There is, nevertheless, a genuine distinction, but it clearly falls within this comprehensive unity.

C. But this rigidity is considerably moderated

1. by the pervasive dependence of the natural order on God as its supernatural Ground, so that the distinction falls within a comprehensive unity of divine self-disclosure;

A similar analysis applies to the distinction between the universality of general revelation and the particularity of special revelation. On the one hand, it seems plausible to suppose both that the recognition of particular events as revelatory of God is a universally open possibility for any human person who contemplates those events in the appropriate frame of mind, with the result that in that sense particular revelation is potentially universal—and that every human person capable of even a modicum of reflective understanding could recognize, in the particular circumstances of his own existence and of the existence of other persons with whose circumstances he either is or could become familiar, a distinctive revelation of God in such a unique context—at

2. by the universal openness of any set of particular events to interpretation as divine self-disclosure,

least there is no specific reason to assume otherwise at the outset. On the other hand, even if, as I surely believe and will try to maintain at length, there is a connected train of revelatory events which, properly understood, can be seen to have a clearly central and crucial role in God's historical self-revelation, it seems nevertheless to be the case that the recognition of these events as revelatory of God can achieve maximum impact only for a person who, whether consciously and explicitly or not, is prepared for this recognition by the influence of the comprehensive revelation of the Divine Reality in the whole world order. That, for example, Jesus Christ is God Incarnate, is perhaps the central thrust of the Christian truth-claim; but this thrust is fully intelligible only within a general theistic perspective in which God is antecedently recognized as the central reality. Here again, therefore, we confront indeed a distinction between universal and particular revelation, but it is nonetheless a distinction that falls within an un-fractured and comprehensive unity.

This unity appears a third time in the relation between the episte-mological-cognitive impact of general revelation and the soteriologi-cal-moral focus of special revelation. Certainly, in the Christian tradition and especially in the Johannine and Pauline literature of the New Testament, it is clear that an important and essential role of the Christian gospel is to provoke men to the knowledge of God both in the cognitive and in the moral and spiritual sense. There must, after all, be a recognition *that* God *is* real if there is to be a personal relationship *to* God *as* real. Conversely, God's revelation, in the exis-tence and character of the world order as whole, is certainly miscon-strued if it is thought of as providing no more than a basis for satisfying disinterested informational curiosity. It is rather a univer-sally accessible witness, provoking all those persons who discern its testimony to moral and spiritual commitment. If the Christian preoc-cupation with so-called natural theology has even a core of plausibility, then perhaps its most central conclusion, beyond that of the reality of God as Ultimate Cause, is the recognition that the objectivity of moral duty and obligation finds its final basis in God as essential or absolute Goodness. And to recognize that moral order in such terms is at the same time to be both morally judged by its standard and spiritually called to its fulfillment through a moral energy that God himself provides. For a final time, therefore, the inclusive unity of revelation embraces and synthesizes the distinction of its types.

The Philosophical and Systematic Implications of the Idea of Revelation

In developing the concept of revelation in this provisional and exploratory fashion, I have certainly made a generous context of assumptions for which I have provided little or no specific rationale or justification. To some extent, the reason for this procedure consists in the fact that no analysis of any concept is practically feasible unless some such set of assumptions is put forth as a context in which the

---

[margin notes:]

and by the recognition of general revelation as a necessary context for the understanding of particular revela-tion. The Incarnation of God in Christ, for instance, is fully intelli-gible only within a general theistic per-spective;

3. and finally by the essential element of knowledge in soterio-logical and moral rev-elation, as well as the motivation to moral and spiritual commit-ment in the epistemo-logical thrust of general revelation.

II. The unity of reve-lation thus synthesizes its distinct types.

I. The previous analy-sis of the concept of revelation involves nu-merous unjustified as-sumptions yet to be discussed.

analysis is to operate. Even if a deliberate attempt is made to trace all truth-claims in a given context to their epistemological foundations, it is probably the case that numerous theoretically justifiable assumptions would remain actually unjustified in that context, and it is certainly the case, provided my previous analysis of epistemological foundations is sound, that the foundational truths themselves would be unjustified—since it is the very nature of such first principles to be logically ultimate and therefore to function as necessary starting points for all arguments. Nevertheless, I openly admit that many of my assumptions, in clarifying the notion of revelation, clearly do not fall into this logically ultimate category and therefore call for explicit justification. At the same time, I frankly acknowledge that my best efforts at argument will doubtless leave many unjustified assumptions which, under altered circumstances or even with closer attention and scrutiny, it might otherwise be possible and important to argue from prior premises. Like every other historical investigator, I am, after all, a finite thinker, struggling toward the ideals of objectivity and completeness under the influence of a largely uncatalogued framework of propensities and circumstances which constitute the entire context of my existence as a person; and I have neither reason nor desire to mollify this point. More specifically, it is as clear to myself, as it should be to any other reflective person, that a considerable set of what will remain my unjustified assumptions has that status because my present purpose is itself restricted in a deliberate sense by the fact that I intend to clarify and assess the distinctively Christian revelation claim. Hence, a considerable mass of provocative and important issues will simply be bypassed just because they are largely peripheral to my central intent. On the other hand, I do not wish this candid acknowledgment to convey the impression that I have nothing important to say except to those who already largely agree with my course of thought and are therefore simply trying to derive solace from shoring up their shared convictions. On the contrary, I intend to address the substance of what I claim to every sincere and reflective person with the patience required to understand it.

If we understand revelation in the comprehensive way that I have proposed, then perhaps I can sketch in general the central substance that I actually do intend to argue. If causality is, as it were, the thread that runs throughout the warp and woof of being as a unitary revelation, then the initial question to be considered, so far as religious philosophy is concerned, is the question of the existence and nature of what I have already called the Ultimate Cause which constitutes the depth and final ground of this causal network—if indeed, as I suppose, the notion of such an Ultimate Cause (in religious terms, God) is a logically coherent one. This will involve what has been traditionally called natural theology in the framework of what I have already referred to as general revelation. And the argument will reach its terminus in a theistic conception of God as an absolutely necessary and transcendent Being, characterized by personal, intelligent will, and constituting essential or absolute Goodness. The relation of God, so

A. But no context of discussion can provide explicit justification of all its assumptions.

B. My best efforts will leave some justifiable assumptions undefended,
1. partly because of my finite limitations,

2. and partly because of my restricted goal;

3. but I nevertheless intend to address every sincere and reflective person with my argument.

II. In summary, I intend to argue:
A. that the causal network of being is grounded in God, theistically construed as its ultimate basis:

1. This will entail a version of natural theology as a reflection on general revelation,

2. and will embrace the notions of creation, preservation, and providence.

understood, to the finite world order will be construed as embracing creation, preservation, and providence—God as the creative Cause of the world order, as the sustaining Ground of its existence and functioning, and as its providential Director toward morally and spiritually significant ends, which are themselves grounded in God's nature as essential or absolute Goodness and the ultimate foundation of objective moral order.

B. that the core of the distinctively Christian revelation-claim, *viz.* the Incarnation of God in Jesus Christ, is both intelligible as a concept and plausible as a thesis:

Now, if there are plausible reasons for believing in theism as thus understood and argued, that plausibility will provide a general metaphysical context within which the central revelation claim of the distinctively Christian version of theism can be rendered provisionally intelligible and therefore also critically assessed. I take that central revelation claim to be the contention that the historically human individual known as Jesus Christ was and therefore is the theistic God Incarnate, both as the final historical self-manifestation of God and as the fully adequate solution to the problem of man's universal moral predicament of alienation from God and the consequent state of moral guilt and corruption that ensues. This will involve special revelation and what has been called revealed theology, but with the tempered recognition already clarified that both general and special revelation (and therefore also both natural and revealed theology) belong to the same inclusive continuum of revelatory self-disclosure. The notion of Jesus Christ as God Incarnate will of course call for an expanded and modified understanding of the concepts of both deity and humanity, as compared to what that understanding might plausibly have been apart from the notion of incarnation. This reinterpretation is, of course, striking indeed when objectively considered, but its long-standing familiarity in the tradition of Christian theology has dulled the contrast for those who are thoroughly conversant with that tradition.

1. This will involve the context of special revelation in union with general revelation,

2. and it will involve a modification in the notions of both deity and humanity;

C. and finally that God has carried his self-revelation to determinate and accessible expression in the written word:

If the expression of human thought in written language constitutes, as I have suggested, one of the most highly developed and even artistic forms of personal self-expression, it will not be surprising that the Christian revelation claim extends itself to the notion that God has carried his self-revelation not only to the extent of himself appearing as a historical human person, but also to the level of self-expression in the written word. This verbal manifestation includes not merely (though importantly) a general disclosure of religious insight in all the great written learning and literature of all human cultures and epochs, whether religious or not—but also, according to the Christian revelation claim, a particular and unique verbal self-unfolding in a series of writings vouchsafed through specifically selected and influenced individuals in a wide variety of personal circumstances across an extensive but determinate segment of human history resulting, of course, in the Hebrew-Christian Bible. The notion of a written revelation of the Ultimate is not, certainly, limited to the Hebrew-Christian tradition. But the claim that this particular literary collection, the Bible, is a uniquely authoritative particular manifestation of God in a sense that goes beyond that in which religious literature generally reveals God, is

1. partly through the verbal manifestation of all human cultures,

2. but specifically and uniquely through selected individuals in the production of the Hebrew-Christian Bible.

a significant element of the Christian claim. We are not disoriented to find, then, that Christians call this collection the Bible, or the Scripture (which simply means "the Book" or "the Writing"), with the implication that in a special sense nothing else is either a book or a writing in the same way. That claim too, however, must be elucidated and assessed.

PART I

Christianity and the Revelational Cosmos
A Philosophical Case for a Theistic Metaphysic

The Development of the Theistic Position

In the general projection of my thought through previous analysis, I have already put forth a brief, perhaps even bold, characterization of the position that I call *theism* and which I regard as an essential metaphysical context for rendering the Christian revelation claim initially and provisionally intelligible. But that preliminary sketch should now be filled in and adequately clarified before a supporting case can be reasonably developed. Certainly the meaning of a truth-claim must be elucidated before it can be argued. Taking the term *God* as the most appropriate term in our language for the Ultimate Reality in a theistic perspective, I propose to define God as an absolutely necessary Being, characterized by personal intelligent will, and constituting essential or absolute Goodness—a Being, furthermore, whose relation to the contingent world order (the space-time universe as an inclusive totality) is that of creative Causality, sustaining Ground, and providential Direction, while at the same time this Being transcends in existence and nature that world order of which it is thus the ultimate foundation. That God is absolutely necessary means that he is self-existent (contains the whole ground of his existence within himself in such a way as to have no dependence on any extraneous cause, however construed), and *self-explanatory* (is completely explicable by principles wholly intrinsic to himself in such a way as to require, or admit of, no explanation in terms of extraneous principles, however construed). Since God thus understood stands in contrast to every contingent entity and to the contingent world order as a whole—and since whatever is contingent does require explanation in terms of causes and principles that are extraneous to it, so that whatever is contingent can, without contradiction, be logically conceived not to exist (its non-

existence, even if it does in fact exist, is logically and consistently
thinkable)—then it follows that God, as absolutely necessary in existence and nature, cannot, without contradiction, be logically conceived not to exist. His non-existence, whether or not he actually exists,
is not logically and consistently thinkable, since otherwise his existence
and nature would, *per contra*, be contingent rather than necessary.)

b) it follows that God, as thus conceived, cannot consistently be conceived as non-exis-tent.

When I further define God as *personal intelligent will*, I mean that
God should be understood as having the capacity to act through
decision and implementation (*will*); that this capacity should be construed as characteristically directed toward the fulfillment of recognizable and significant ends (*intelligence*); and that this capacity so
directed is the activity of an agent whose essence involves self-
consciousness, that is, awareness of one's self as the subject or agent
of one's acts—as well as self-determination, that is, grounding of these
acts in the agent's intrinsic nature as principal cause, rather than in
any extraneous causes acting on the agent in a decisive rather than
merely influential fashion (*personality*). Furthermore, God, as thus
conceived, possesses these properties in a fully actualized manner, free
from the limitations and obstructions that are attached to personal
intelligent will in finite individuals or agents. This would mean that
while finite agents like ourselves are essentially possessed of these
same properties, they are not fully and perfectly so, with the result
that God alone is fully actualized personal Being, and thus constitutes
the ultimate model or paradigm of personhood in which we ourselves
fragmentarily and in varying degrees participate. Hence, far from it
being the case that God is a psychological projection on the human
model, it is rather the case—if theism is true—that man, in his personal
selfhood, is a realization, however limited, on the divine model. The
definition does not, of course, as I have so often explained, settle this
point; but it does clarify the point for a theistic metaphysical perspective.

2. God, as personal in-telligent will, has the self-conscious and self-determining ca-pacity to act toward the fulfillment of sig-nificant ends.

a) God possesses these properties in a fully actualized man-ner, and thus is the model of true person-hood in which finite persons participate only partially.

b) Hence, if theism is true, God would not be a projection on the human model, but quite the contrary.

What, then, does it mean to maintain that God should be conceived
as constituting *essential* or *absolute Goodness?* Negatively, it implies
that God is not to be thought of as embodying some standard of
goodness that is independent of or extraneous to his own being, but
that rather God constitutes or is the ultimate standard of goodness
itself—he is good just by *being* Goodness as such. If, on the contrary,
God were thought of as merely the highest personal instantiation of
an independent standard of goodness (say, an abstract and merely
logical essence), then God would not be the Ultimate Reality, since
that independent standard would then be metaphysically prior to God
and would be the ground of God's having this property. Whatever is
good by participating in essences or properties independent of it is
therefore contingent and dependent in its being—and that would
apply to every finite entity and to the totality of such entities as make
up the world order. Goodness, therefore, is intrinsic to God as an
essence or property; and whatever else is good has that quality
through a limited participation in, and embodiment of, the divine
goodness. This makes it clear that goodness, in its most inclusive sense,

2. God, as essential or absolute Goodness, *a)* constitutes that goodness just by being goodness itself;

b) does not partici-pate in a logically in-dependent standard of goodness which would then be metaphysi-cally prior to God; *c)* is therefore the es-sence of goodness through which all con-tingent goods possess worth by limited par-ticipation;

refers to the perfection or worth of being itself in God as the Ultimate Ground of being. But theism also involves the notion that God is the essence of ultimate moral or ethical goodness as an aspect of that inclusive ontological or metaphysical Goodness. And that means, in turn, that God is the ultimate standard of moral goodness or worth in an objective sense, so that whether acts, principles, states of character, and, generally, finite persons are morally good to whatever extent is dependent, not subjectively on culturally and individually variable states of opinion, preference, feeling, or response, but rather objectively on God's essential moral goodness as itself the independent standard of all finite moral worth.

d) constitutes the objective standard of moral goodness as an aspect of his metaphysical Goodness.

That God, for an adequately clarified theism, should be construed as the creative cause of the whole finite world order, and the contingent events and processes that compose it, not only means that God is the originating cause of the form and matter of the world and of the particular entities that combine these aspects, but it also means that God is the sustaining or preserving cause of all finite things, so that at every moment of their dependent existence they could neither exist nor function without operative divine causality—a sort of continuous divine creation of everything finite, so to speak. And since God is himself the ultimate Moral Agent, it is plausible to maintain that in the exercise of that agency he providentially directs the course of events toward the production and progressive development, in moral righteousness, of finite moral selves, and generally as well toward the fulfillment of morally and spiritually significant ends, although always in such a way as not to infringe, in any determining causal way, on the moral freedom of those finite moral selves. What this supreme moral purpose of God involves in detail is vast and comprehensive indeed; and some of it I shall attempt to spell out as I proceed.

4. God, as creative cause of the contingent world order, is the originating, continuously sustaining, and providentially directing ground of the order,

in such a way as to effect its culmination in the moral self-realization of finite selves without infringement on the genuineness of their moral freedom.

But I have also claimed, finally, that the theistic God should be thought of as transcending the contingent world order in his existence and nature. Basically, this implies that while God is fully present and operative at every point in the space-time universe (the divine immanence), nevertheless space and time are not forms of the being of God, who is therefore independent of both space and time, so that there is no literal change, transition, or process in God's existence and nature. In fact, it is precisely because God transcends space and time in this way that he can be fully present and operative *in* space and time at every point—for if God were subject to space and time, then his inclusive presence in them could only be conceived through God's being pervasively spread out or extended through them on the model of some diaphanous ether or gas, with the result that God could not be fully operative or present at *any* point in space and time. Although this view of God's nature does imply that God is not composite in the sense of having literal and distinguishable parts, it need not imply (and for me it *does* not imply) that God's Being is so totally simple that he cannot have a complexity of aspects that are conceptually distinguishable and related to each other in the intricate Divine Essence. If anything, God is, by contrast, the most complex of all beings, since the

5. God, as transcending the contingent world order,
a) is so related to that order that space and time are not forms of his being, so that he is beyond all change or process;

b) is therefore fully present and operative at every point in space-time;

c) is not any sort of literal composite, although this should not entail the notion that God is logically simple in nature,

(1) since that would imply that God was not knowable by conceptual reason,

(2) and it might even entail the non-existence of God.

d) is not to be construed pantheistically as including the entities and processes of the world in himself.

II. Theism has not always been understood this way:
A. nor do I claim finality for this version;
B. but I do claim:
1. that this version has fewer difficulties than its viable alternatives,
2. and that, given my epistemology, this version has a high degree of plausibility which supports the reasonableness of commitment to it.

C. Probability is thus our guide, but that should not deter us from the highest attainable degree of objective reasonableness.

notion of the divine simplicity would imply that no conceptually determinate properties were genuinely attributable to the Divine Essence, with the result that God would be totally unknowable through conceptual reason or discursive intellect. It might even be argued that the divine-simplicity view would logically entail the non-existence of God, since it seems plausible to maintain that whatever is real or exists must have certain determinate properties which distinguish it from other entities. And if God is transcendent in the way suggested, then that would logically eliminate, from theism so understood, any pantheistic view which included all the entities and processes of the world in God, and it would also eliminate any view which ascribed spatial or temporal qualities to the divine nature.

I certainly do not claim that every responsible theist would interpret what he called theism in precisely the same way that I have interpreted what I call theism; nor do I claim that my view of theism is totally free from apparent difficulties in understanding its meaning. But I do hold that other views of theism are, on the whole, encumbered with a considerably larger number of conceptual obstructions than the position that I have defined and intend now to argue. In keeping with my previously elaborated epistemology, however, what I have to offer are arguments whose premises I regard as highly plausible and whose conclusions I regard as following from them either with a high degree of probability or (sometimes, but rarely) with formal logical validity. At times, therefore, certain stretches of argument, given the ultimacy of my epistemological first principles, will approach the level of demonstration. But more often the thread of analysis will involve varying degrees of plausibility which at least render my conclusions rational as the subject matter of justifiable belief-commitment. In all this I join with the good Bishop Joseph Butler in maintaining that, for the most part, probability is the guide of life, and, I might add, the guide as well of the only sort of reasonable philosophy that is systematically possible for us. But let not this concession be a discouragement—we are not gods, but we are men, and we can aim, even if always incompletely, at the highest level of objective reasonableness we can attain, so that in our belief-commitments we can sincerely respect our choices without the slightest twinge of even a secret hypocrisy.

The Possibility of the Cosmos: A Conceptual Argument

I. Because my argument here is to be a conceptual one, I wish to summarize the ontological argument in order to distinguish it from my own.

A very ancient and provocatively fascinating argument for the existence of God is the so-called ontological argument which runs back historically at least to Saint Anselm of Canterbury (A.D. 1033–1109). Since I have previously written extensively about this argument in my earlier work, *The Resurrection of Theism,* I mention it here only because it is a purely conceptual argument which has no specific existential premise, but rather argues straightforwardly that the concept of God implies logically the objective, actual existence of God. Now, since I have called my argument in the present context a conceptual argument, I wish to consider the ontological argument briefly, with the explicit intent of distinguishing it from the argument I myself intend to propose. And let me bypass historical formulations here (from Anselm through Descartes, Spinoza, and Hegel, right up to contemporaries such as Norman Malcolm and Alvin Plantinga) and use my own linguistic formulation, although I claim no particular originality for this mode of expression. I have, then, already defined God as an absolutely necessary Being who, as such, stands in logical contrast to contingent beings which, precisely as contingent, can be logically conceived not to exist (that is, their non-existence is consistently thinkable even if in fact they actually exist). And I have even said that if God is an absolutely necessary being by definition, then that means that his non-existence is not logically conceivable or consistently thinkable; and hence his existence must, if we are to be consistent in our thought, be conceived as logically necessary. Now if God by definition is, in this way and in this sense, a logically necessary being, can we not immediately and soundly conclude that God must exist objectively and actually, since if he did not, his non-existence would be for that reason logically conceivable (on the ground that nothing could be the case in fact unless it was logically possible), and then God would not be an absolutely necessary but rather a contingent being— which would contradict the original definition of God as absolutely necessary.

> A. The ontological argument reasons, from the concept of God as an absolutely (and therefore logically) necessary being, to the objective and actual existence of God, on the ground that the denial of God's existence would contradict his definition.

Now whatever else is objectionable about this argument, I feel fully entitled to reject as impertinent one of the main historical objections to it alluded to by David Hume and formulated in detail by Immanuel Kant. Kant's objection was that the non-existence of a thing would be contradictory only if its existence were a property of the thing in the sense of following analytically from its conceptual definition. But, Kant continued, existence in this sense is simply not a property, so that, for example, a hundred possible (but non-existing) dollars and a hundred actually existing dollars are conceptually identical in their definition. And it therefore follows that to say of anything that it exists is not to ascribe to it any additional property that belongs to its conceptual definition, but rather merely to claim that the concept, as involving all its properties, corresponds to something actual. Of course, what Kant is actually claiming is that we cannot consistently conceive a contingent thing (a dollar, a chair, or a tree) which has existence as a property in the sense that its existence follows from its definition— and that is not overwhelmingly surprising, since, as I have myself maintained, it is the mark of a contingent thing that its non-existence is logically conceivable, whether it exists in fact or not, so that of course its existence could not be an essential property of it. In all this, I do not disagree with Kant. But then he proceeds to conclude that, because existence could not be consistently construed as a property of anything contingent, it follows that necessary existence cannot consistently be construed as an essential property of God, and that

> B. Kant's well-known objection to this argument is, in my opinion, incorrect:
>
> 1. Kant argues (correctly) that existence cannot be a conceptual property of any contingent thing,
>
> and then concludes (incorrectly) that necessary existence cannot be construed as an essential property of God.

2. But all that really follows is that God is not a contingent being.

therefore God's necessary existence is not logically deducible from the concept of God. But of course that does not really follow at all from Kant's premises; what actually follows is that God, if he is necessarily existent in our sense, is not a contingent being—but then no one who has ever seriously proposed the ontological argument ever supposed that God was a contingent being.

C. However, the onto-logical argument is in-conclusive in any case,

Unfortunately, however, I do not conclude from the invalidity of Kant's objection that the ontological argument is therefore sound, either in the version I have proposed or in any other version with which I am presently familiar. The argument starts from a conceptual definition of God; and, in my opinion, then, the most that can be logically deduced from such a concept, considered *as* a concept, is some other concept that is an aspect, facet, or part of the original, more complex concept. More pointedly, from the concept of God I can, I think, deduce the concept of his necessary existence, so that if

since it confuses the concept of God's nec-essary existence with his objective, actual existence—which are distinct from each other.

God is conceived at all in terms of my original defintiion, he must be conceived as absolutely necessary and therefore, in the sense ex-plained, as a logically necessary being. But the concept of necessary existence is not, in my opinion, the same thing as objective, actual existence, nor do I regard the latter as logically deducible from the former. We do not therefore, I think, correctly or consistently conceive God unless we conceive him as a logically necessary being; but we cannot reasonably deduce the objective, actual existence of God from this conceptual requirement. If God does in fact exist therefore, then his existence is logically necessary, since the concept of a God whose existence is merely contingent is, as I see it, logically incoherent and impossible.

II. My conceptual ar-gument is quite differ-ent:
A. Historical back-ground.

But it was not my original intention to discuss the ontological argument in this context. Instead, I wish to concentrate on a strikingly different sort of conceptual argument, the materials for which, in human thought, have been accessible at least since the time of Plato (427–347 B.C.) and have been utilized in various ways by explicitly Chris-tian philosophers beginning at least with Augustine (A.D. 354–430). I will, however, formulate the argument in my own way, without con-cerning myself in detail with this historical background beyond the passing acknowledgment of its existence.

B. Basic question: How is a contingent world order logically possible?

I begin with a question: How is a cosmos, a world order of contin-gent entities, logically possible or conceivable? Not that I question its existence at all—I simply assume *carte blanche* that such a world order does in fact exist and that I am an aspect of it. It is not that these points are unnegotiable, in my opinion, but simply that I assume them here as not likely to be seriously questioned by the majority of individuals to whom I am addressing (and even dedicating) my whole discussion. In my earlier elaboration of epistemology, I developed the

1. Foundational prin-ciples of knowledge are *a priori* conditions of all possible thought and being.

notion that all knowledge-claims or truth-claims run back to neces-sary starting points of thought which I characterized as *a priori*. Such principles are *a priori*, I argued, both in the sense that they are the ultimate presuppositions of all possible thought, so that they are in-terpretive structures, inherent in finite minds which employ them in all thinking about reality, whether those minds are explicitly conscious of those principles or not; and also (*a priori*) in the sense that these ultimate categories are necessary conditions of all possible existence, so that, for instance, nothing can conceivably exist unless all its properties are mutually compatible or consistent in the logical sense. Yet on reflection it becomes clear that although contingent objects of thought could not logically exist except in conformity with these *a priori* principles, nevertheless the principles themselves do not reciprocally depend on finite minds and objects. If I understand, for example, what the law of contradiction or the principle of causal connectedness means, it will be clear that these principles retain their objective status and validity independently of particular minds and objects, in the sense that the adequate propositional or judgmental expression of them would remain true whether or not any finite minds and/or objects even existed. I need these principles to exist, but they do not need me in order to be objectively true. From this analysis, it follows that a cosmos or world order is logically possible and conceivable only through the validity of those *a priori* principles of reason whose objective status is quite independent of the existence of that world order itself—composed, as it is, of a complexity and succession of finite entities and states of existence. In this way, the ultimate interpretive principles are metaphysically transcendent and therefore also metaphysically (as well as epistemologically) *a priori.*

a) But these principles, rightly understood, have an objective status that is independent of finite minds and objects.

b) Thus these principles transcend the realm of contingent being as necessary conditions of the possibility of that realm.

But while the transcendent objectivity of the formal principles of thought and being is a *necessary* condition for the existence of a world order, it scarcely even begins to be a sufficient condition of the existence of such a world order. It is further the case that no particular type of thing can exist unless its existence as that determinate type of thing is actually possible and logically conceivable. But that condition is in turn capable of fulfillment only if the specific properties or qualities that constitute any determinate type of thing, and hence its definition, are themselves actually possible and logically conceivable as attributes. Now the defining properties and qualities of any determinate type of thing constitute the essence or nature of that type of thing; and the defining characteristics of those properties and qualities constitute in turn the essence of the properties and qualities themselves. Now if, in fact, the properties or qualities in question happen to be simple and unanalyzable into further constituent elements, then those properties or qualities are themselves simple essences, while essences definable in terms of simpler properties may be called complex essences. Now clearly the objectivity and hence independent reality status of these essences is a further necessary condition of the existence of finite entities that make up any conceivable world order. If, for example, there were no such essence as triangularity, there could be no triangularly shaped objects (as clearly there are); and if there were no human essence or nature, then there could likewise be no particular human beings which exemplified that essence (as clearly there are). Now what follows from this, in general, is that there could be no world order, unless logically and ontologically (but not tempo-

2. The existence of any particular type of contingent thing is possible only if its conjoined properties are conceivable as essences of those properties.

a) If such essences were not objective and independent of such particulars, the latter could not logically exist.

b) Hence, there could be no actual world order if the essences of all the types and properties it contained were not ontologically prior to that order.

rally, of course) prior to that order there were also all those essences or natures which make the existence of the determinate types of entities which compose that order actually possible and logically conceivable—no metaphysically transcendent realm of essences, no world order (as clearly there is one)!

3. Since the realm of logically possible qualities and classes is indefinitely extended, it will follow that the present world order is only one of an indefinitely extended set of logically possible world orders.

But there is more: Since essences are thus ontologically prior to particulars and thus have a reality status independent of them, there is no reason to limit the transcendent realm of essences to those which make possible those entities which are or have been actualized in existence. But, on the contrary, there is every reason to suppose that the realm of essences is unimaginably extended to include all logically possible and consistently conceivable characteristics or qualities. This would in turn mean that the present world order (the contingent cosmos in its entirety both spatially and temporally) would be the actualization of a kind of complex cross section of that far more inclusive (indeed, indefinitely extended) realm of essences. And that would further mean that the world order itself was only one of an indefinitely extended set of logically possible and consistently conceivable world orders—so that an actual world order is only conceivable if there is some reason or explanation as to why, among all logically possible world orders, this particular one in fact exists. The question would then be, not why there is something rather than nothing, but rather why there is this particular thing (the cosmos) instead of all the logically conceivable alternative things (world orders) that might have existed.

a) But then there could only be an actual world order if there were some reason why it, rather than some other such order, is actual.

b) Summary of necessary conditions for the possibility of a contingent world order.

In general retrospect, then, among the necessary conditions for the existence of a cosmos would be: (1) the ontologically prior and transcendent realm consisting of the ultimate rational principles and categories which make thought and existence in general possible; (2) the equally transcendent and indefinitely extended realm of all logically possible characteristics or properties; and (3) a principle or operative ground of that concretion or selection, so to speak, which explains the being of the actual cosmos or world order as over against all the other possible world orders. And the question will now be: What is the most comprehensively adequate explanation of the fulfillment of these three conditions? That they *are* fulfilled I shall, in the present context, assume as beyond serious question—here I am, after all, enmeshed in that very cosmos or world order which is itself conceivable only through the fulfillment of these very conditions.

c) Crucial question: What is the most adequate account of the fulfillment of these conditions?

C. Since the ultimate principles which make thinking possible constitute the essential nature (in a structural sense) of what it is to be a mind at all,

If we reflect on those ultimate presuppositions, principles, or categories which make thought and existence possible in general, it becomes reasonably clear that these principles are such that, while particular objects like trees and stones could only exist in conformity with them, nevertheless the principles provide no distinctive clue as to the positive nature of these objects and other analogous ones. But the situation is strikingly different in the case of thought as a function of mind, for those ultimate principles of reason constitute the very essence of the structure of mind in its capacity for thinking and consciousness. To be a mind is precisely to be structurally constituted through those interpretive principles and categories which essentially characterize mind *a priori*, that is, logically prior to and independently of particular facts of experience. Of course, this structure is not necessarily the whole essence of mind (which may in fact have a substantial as well as a structural facet), but it is clearly an indispensable and positive aspect of that essence. The particular experiential contents of the mind are, in the case of finite minds, incidental or accidental to its essence as a mind—it would still be a mind and the same mind if its experiential contents were markedly different. But it would not be a mind at all if it were not structurally and formally constituted in an essential sense by those ultimate rational categories.

Now finite minds can only exist through instantiating or exemplifying these essential structures, while yet the structures themselves are ontologically independent of particular finite minds. And since nevertheless these principles, as independent, constitute the very essence of mind in its structural aspect, it is plausible to suppose that the most adequate explanation of the ontologically prior and transcendent status of these principles is to regard them as the essential structure of an Eternal Reason or Absolute Mind which, as thus constituted, is itself ontologically prior and transcendent, so that it is the ultimate locus, or mode of the transcendent objectivity, of the rational principles themselves. How, otherwise, would the transcendent objectivity of those principles be reasonably understood and interpreted?

And what, furthermore, of that indefinitely extended realm of essences involving all logically conceivable characteristics or properties? How can we most adequately construe its transcendent objectivity? To begin with, I note that, as essences, these properties and characteristics clearly belong to that same realm of essence that is the locus of the formal principles of reason. And if it is plausible to regard the Absolute Mind as precisely the locus of those principles, then it appears equally reasonable to regard the essences of all logically possible entities and their constituent properties as finding their ultimate locus in that Absolute Mind as well, since the formal structures of reason provide the skeletal framework, as it were, for the essences that make up that unitary realm. One might think of these essences of the classes of possible entities as models or archetypes in that Eternal Reason or Absolute Mind. Furthermore, if essences are logically prior to the particular entities that exemplify them in the contingent realm of existence, what other conceivable mode of objectivity could they possess other than as exemplars or forms which are themselves the objects and contents of Absolute Thought? Does it make any sense to claim that the various essences subsist merely as such and entirely without finding their locus in the way I have suggested? On reflection, the essences can be clearly regarded as constituting a unified and ordered hierarchy through the complex relations that any given essence has to others in an organized scheme. The facets of this organization are intricate indeed, and I have no intention here of providing a detailed analysis, but one unifying organizational thread would be found in the fact that essences define possible classes some of which

and since these principles transcend particular finite minds,

it is thus reasonable to regard them as constituting the essential structure of an Absolute Mind which is thus the transcendent locus of these principles.

D. Since the essences of these ultimate principles are continuous with, and comprise the framework of, the whole realm of essences, that realm itself would find its ultimate locus in the same Absolute Mind.

1. What other conceivable mode is there for the transcendent objectivity of the realm of essences?

2. If essences constitute an ordered hierarchy,

that fact is best understood through the operation of mind which is essentially ordering in its activity.

are subsets of others through the relation of genus and species (man, for example, is a subset or species of the more inclusive genus animal, and hence the essence of humanity is therefore a species of the essence of animality). Now it is my opinion that the intricate organizational complexity of the realm of essences is best understood as finding its ordered structure in the operation of mind, since mind is essentially ordering in its activity. And, hence, it seems plausible on these various lines of argument and analysis to maintain that Absolute Mind is also the locus of the realm of essences.

E. Since the actual world exists through an operation that is extensively analogous to directive selection in human experience,

and since such a selection is the functional essence of mind, this selection is plausibly attributable to the Absolute Mind.

Finally, there is the question of how to explain the existence of the actual world order rather than any other world order that is logically conceivable. Since the number of such logically conceivable possible worlds seems, like the realm of essences itself, to be indefinitely extended in number, it follows that the actual existence of one of these possible worlds (namely, the one in which we find ourselves) is the result of an operation that is quite analogous to directive selection among possibilities as exemplified in human choices among far more limited possibilities in the actual world. But is not this type of directive selection precisely the functional essence of mind in an operative sense, just as the rational categories are also its structural essence? And if that is the case, then does it not seem reasonable to conclude that the actual world exists, in contrast to other possible but non-existent worlds, precisely through the operation of directive selection on the part of the Absolute Mind?

III. The Absolute Mind thus construed is the God of theism in one of his previously defined aspects.
A. Thus God is the ground of the possibility of any contingently possible world order.

Again reflecting in retrospect, I conclude here that the actual cosmos is possible only through a realm of formal rational principles and property essences, together with the operation of a principle of directive selection, all of which are fully intelligible only through their convergence in Eternal Reason or Absolute Mind. But of course such an Ultimate Mind is precisely the God of theism in one of his aspects as previously defined; and hence, a cosmos or world order finds its possibility in the fulfillment of conditions which are themselves completely plausible only if God is real. More pointedly, if this cosmos or any cosmos is possible, then God exists as its ultimate ground and explanation. I am not, of course, naive about all of this; and I fully realize that at every step of argumentative tilling I have plowed up conceptual rattlesnakes which are poised to strike at the heart of the argument with their deadly venom. In the sequel, I will respond to some of these objections, but I cannot possibly respond to all. What I claim now, therefore, is modest: I claim merely that God is actually a reasonable explanation of the possibility of the world order on the assumptions I have attempted to make plausible.

B. But what is actually claimed in a provisional sense is that the theistic explanation is actually reasonable.

The Actuality of the Cosmos: A Causal Argument

The space-time universe—the interconnected totality of things, events, and processes in space and time—is not, of course, merely a possible cosmos; it is an actual one. Scientists and philosophers may, indeed, disagree between and among themselves about the nature and relationships of the ultimate constituents of the world order. They may wrangle endlessly about the patterns and relative regularities that characterize it, and especially about the nature of man and his place in that universe. But only the most sceptical amongst us would question the genuine reality of the cosmos on at least some (of course debatable) interpretation of it. And even on such a solipsistic outlook (the view that the world exists only as the mental content of a solitary individual mind), still this lonely locus of the apparently vast cosmos cannot, without befuddlement, question his own existence. If all else is sceptically swept away into the pit of nothingness, the *cogito* (the self as thinker) nevertheless stands unassailed by its own attempts at scepticism. But I shall cavil no further about this matter. I shall simply assume as beyond reasonable question that something—at least some individual thinker—does in fact indisputably exist.

And I will make another assumption as well, although it is one for which my previous discussion of epistemology has already provided rather ample preparation. In that earlier context I argued that the principle of causality (or of ground and consequence) is among the ultimate *a priori* principles of rational intelligibility, so that such a principle of causality is therefore a necessary presupposition of all possible and therefore also of all actual existence. It follows from this complex premise that nothing can exist unless it possesses an adequate explanatory ground, that is, a cause whose nature and relation to the existent entity are such that they provide a rationally satisfactory explanation of the fact that the entity exists and that it has the properties that it possesses and sustains the relations in which it stands to other things. Now if the entity in question is contingent (that is, dependent in its existence), then the adequate cause (however complex) of its existence, nature, and relations, will be extraneous or external to the entity itself. On the other hand, if the entity is self-existent and therefore self-explanatory, then that would mean that it contains the ground of its existence in its own nature, so that both the fact that it exists and the properties that it possesses are intrinsic to that nature. Such an entity would be precisely what I have previously defined as an absolutely necessary being—or, in religious language, God, in one of his basic aspects, as God is construed in my understanding of theism. Hence, any possible and therefore any actual being is either contingent or necessary in its existence; and I have assumed, in this context, that something exists, so that that something is either contingent or necessary in its existence. In actual practice, I am in fact assuming that something contingent (that is, dependent in its existence) is real beyond any serious question. But I am *not* at this point assuming that anything necessary exists—I am merely assuming that the concept of an absolutely necessary being is a logically consistent concept and therefore the concept of a possible being—an assumption which I clarified previously.

With this preliminary spadework completed, I can now state what

I. Assumptions underlying the argument:
A. that the space-time universe, in some sense, exists, even if only in the mind of an individual thinker;

B. that the principle of causality is an *a priori* presupposition of all possible and actual existence, so that:
1. whatever exists must have an adequate explanatory ground which accounts for its existence and properties;

2. any existing entity must either be contingent (and have an external cause) or necessary (and be self-existent);

3. and something, either contingent or necessary, exists,

though the actual existence of anything necessary is not here presupposed.

II. Statement and
clarification of the ar-
gument:
appears to be a straightforwardly simple (in the logical sense) argument for the existence of God as an absolutely necessary being; and I
will state it as a hypothetical syllogism in the form *modus ponens*.

A. Brief statement of
premises and conclu-
sion:

Premise 1: If anything exists, an absolutely necessary and transcendent being exists.
Premise 2: Something (I, at least, as a thinker) exists.
Conclusion: Therefore, an absolutely necessary and transcendent
being (i.e., God, as partly defined by theism) exists.

I shall waste no further time in discussing what I now merely point
out—that this is a logically valid argument, that is, an argument whose
the argument both
1. formally valid,
formal structure guarantees that if its premises are both logically
intelligible and also true, then the conclusion is also true, in the sense
that it could not possibly be false on condition of the truth of the
premises. I shall also not argue further that the premises and conclu-
2. and its premises
logically intelligible.
sion are intelligible. I submit that the only ingredient of these premises
that would even be questionable in its intelligibility would be the
concept of an absolutely necessary being—a notion which I have
already explained at length and which I will defend against certain
historically prominent objections in the sequel.

B. Truth-value of the
premises:

1. The second prem-
ise is indisputably
true, since its denial
would be existentially
self-contradictory.
In order therefore to decide whether an absolutely necessary being
exists, we have at present merely to decide whether the premises of
the argument are true. It should be clear on a moment's reflection that
the second premise, even though it is only contingently true, is actually
undeniable in the sense that no one can consistently deny it if he
understands its meaning—for he himself would have to exist in order
to deny the premise, and hence the act of denial would implicitly deny
its own content, so that it would be existentially self-contradictory. The
second premise of our argument therefore is indisputably true, so that
2. *Re* the first prem-
ise:
a) that which exists
may be necessary—
which establishes the
truth of the premise;
b) but if that which
exists is contingent,
(1) then by definition
such an entity has an
extraneous cause.
the only remaining question concerns the truth of the first and major
premise. If then anything exists, its existence is either necessary or
contingent. But if its existence is necessary, then we already have the
main thrust of the premise as true and have only to argue that a
necessary being must be transcendent (that is, must exist independently of the space-time universe).

Let us assume therefore the more difficult case—that our something which exists is contingent. Now it is an intrinsic and essential
mark of a contingent thing that it cannot exist alone, since by definition whatever is contingent depends for its existence and nature on
something external to itself. But, of course, one could suggest, it might,
in any case proposed, depend for its existence on other contingent
things, and these in turn on still others interminably. However, it can
(2) But the series of
such causes cannot
proceed interminably,
since in that case no
adequate causal expla-
nation of any part of
the series (or of the
whole series) will have
been given.
be plausibly argued that, in terms of our previously elaborated principle of causality, we have not really given any adequate causal explanation of an entity or a state of things if we merely explain the ground
of its existence by referring it to other entities and states which require
the same explanation themselves without logical limit. In fact, it may
reasonably be questioned whether we have actually provided any

genuine causal explanation of any of these entities in this way. It would be analogous to writing a bank check to cover a debt and then writing another check to cover the first and so on indefinitely without ever involving any actual monetary deposit to cover any of the checks—just as, in such a case, it could be reasonably argued that no debt had actually been paid at all, so in the case of contingent causes which must themselves in turn be construed as effects, it may, by parallel reasoning, be argued that no causal explanation of anything has actually been provided at all. Checks, after all, are only intermediate and not ultimate units of payment and exchange; and analogously contingent entities are only intermediate and not ultimate units of explanation in the context of causality.

Now this difficulty about contingent causes holds whether we think of these contingent entities and states as temporally succeeding one another (so that, for example, the writing I am engaged in now is in part viewed as the effect of events that occurred yesterday or in any case previously in time), or alternatively we regard these causes as all contemporaneous with the effect they are introduced to explain (so that, by parallel example, the effect which consists in my writing now could not be taking place unless all its necessary conditions—which together are sufficient to produce the writing—were presently existent and operative). In some ways this latter way of conceptualizing the causal order of the cosmos is clearly preferable. If we regard what happened yesterday (or at any previous time) as no longer existing or occurring, how could it provide even a part of the explanation of what is presently existing and occurring? But I will not at present dispute this point or attempt a choice between these two ways of viewing the causal order of the cosmos. For either way of construing the matter, if we refer only to contingent causes (and therefore also effects), it will still be the case that we have not provided any adequate causal explanation of any of the links in the causal chain. And something else will also follow in either of these methods of causal explanation, namely, that there would have to be, either successively or contemporaneously, an actually infinite series of contingent causes for even a single contingent effect to exist—since each contingent cause could only exist and operate through dependence on another and so on interminably. And the question then arises as to whether the notion of an actually infinite series, made up of particular and determinate parts which are themselves distinguishable, is a logically intelligible notion. What would be involved here is the notion of a contingent effect as possible only through a logically and/or temporally prior series of contingent causes which are actually infinite in number, and each of which causes is itself an effect and hence can exist only on the same supposition, and so on without logical limit. So what we are called upon to conceive here is not merely one actually infinite series of this sort, but rather an actually infinite series of actually infinite series of the same logical type.

To make the issue as clear as possible, we can identify the general properties which an actually infinite series would have to possess if it

c) It will be irrelevant whether these contingent entities are viewed as temporally successive or as contemporaneous with each other:

(1) Though the latter formulation may be preferable,

(2) in neither case will an adequate causal explanation have been given,
(a) since for either case an actually infinite series of contingent causes would be required to explain a single contingent effect;
(b) but it is questionable whether the notion of such a series is logically intelligible, since each element in the series would require the same sort of explanation for itself.

d) The concept of a supposed actually infinite series.
(1) Its properties;

(a) no first logical member,

(b) no principle for constructing particular members,

(c) composed of particular and determinate parts.

(2) Such a series:

(a) would be quite distinct from any mathematical notion of the infinite, since all such series are merely indefinitely extended, rather than actually infinite in the sense indicated above;

(b) turns out to be logically unintelligible to any person who adequately understands the elements of the notion involved.

could exist. At the outset, it could have no first logical member, since, if it did, then, no matter how many succeeding members it possessed, the number of identifiable members it possessed would at any point be a certain particular number of members from the first logical member, so that the series would be indefinitely extended without logical limit and would therefore not at any point be actually infinite in the number of logically prior members—which would contradict the notion of an actually infinite series. A further property of such a series, if it could exist, would be that it could have no principle for constructing particular members of it, since such a principle of construction is possible only if the operation involved has an identifiable starting point—and it is already clear that a series without a first member could not therefore have an identifiable starting point. Finally, if an actually infinite series of causes and effects could exist, it would have to be composed of particular and determinate parts which could be identified by some clearly intelligible rule of procedure, since otherwise we could not identify any particular cause in relation to any particular effect, and hence we could not reasonably speak of a series (which by definition has identifiable and related parts) at all, much less of an actually infinite series of causes and effects.

Now from this analysis of the properties of an actually infinite series (if it could exist), it will certainly be clear that we are not talking about any mathematical notion of the infinite here. For every such series, while it is indeed made up of particular and determinate parts, always has a first member and a principle or rule of construction for the logical generation of subsequent members. And, hence, any so-called infinite series in mathematics is in fact not actually infinite in number but rather indefinitely extended, since the number of members from the first member to any particular member is always finite. The series of whole numbers (or of odd numbers, or of even numbers, or of fractions generated between integers by any specific rule of construction, or of fractional series between integers generated by successive rules of construction, and so on) is, of course, indefinitely extended in precisely the sense clarified, since the number of members in the series between the first member and any subsequent member is always finite. In fact, it is the essence of the notion of a mathematically infinite series that there is no logically final member in the series, no particular number, for example, in the series of whole numbers, that is the largest possible number, or than which a still larger number cannot be generated. I am not, of course, a professional mathematician; but from all these considerations I see clearly that the actually infinite series, about which I am raising the intelligibility question, is certainly not the sort of indefinitely extended series which mathematicians refer to as infinite. And I am not therefore raising any question whatever about the mathematical concept of the infinite (which I would prefer to refer to as the indefinitely extended, for the sake of avoiding confusion).

We are now in a position to ask whether the notion of an actually infinite series, in the sense thus clarified, is a logically intelligible notion. And while I do not claim any universal consensus here or even the practical feasibility of ever achieving one, what I do claim is that the notion of such an actually infinite series is simply not logically intelligible to any person who fully and clearly understands what such a notion involves. To see this point, I find it helpful to cast the exposition in a particular context (although there is no special reason for choosing one possible context over another); and I will choose the series of temporal states or (broadly construed) events constituting successively the past history of the space-time universe. I shall further assume that any given state of the universe is properly understood as at least partly and in some sense an effect of temporally prior states of the universe, so that, for example, the present state of the universe is the effect of past states of the universe in this admittedly limited sense. Now select, at random, any state of the universe for consideration: How many previous states have there been if we adopt the thesis that the series of temporal states constituting the previous history of the universe has no first member and therefore no beginning? The answer will have to be: an actually infinite number of previous states in precisely the sense of our notion of the actually infinite. Yet each state of the universe, since, as I am assuming, it is particular and determinate, increases the number of previous states by one. And any number of states than which a still larger number can be conceived (and, in this case, can be actual, since we are discussing the states of a universe assumed to be actual) is certainly not an actually infinite number—which contradicts the original notion of an actually infinite number of previous states. If, now, we also assume that a contradictory state of things is both logically and metaphysically impossible— an assumption involved in the very fabric of our epistemology—then it will follow that the notion of an actually infinite number of temporally prior states of the universe, since it is contradictory in the way indicated, is logically and ontologically impossible, and hence is rationally unintelligible. And more generally it will follow that an actually infinite number of contingent causes and effects, whether construed as temporally successive or as contemporaneous, is also rationally unintelligible. Still more generally it will further follow that the series of contingent causes and effects must itself have, as its ground, an absolutely necessary cause, so that either an absolutely necessary being exists or the series of contingent causes and effects which constitutes the space-time universe does not exist. Since this last issue (that is, the existence of the space-time universe) is not at stake here— inasmuch as it is actually undeniable that something contingent exists—then it follows that an absolutely necessary being exists.

The one remaining point to be clarified would be the claim of the first premise and conclusion of our argument that the absolutely necessary being is transcendent in the sense of being ontologically independent of the space-time universe itself. It might be maintained quite otherwise, of course, as indeed it has been maintained by metaphysical naturalists from Democritus to Bertrand Russell, that if there is an absolutely necessary being, it may well be the space-time uni-

i) An actually infinite temporal series would be contradictory,

since prior to any given member of that series, there would already have been an actually infinite number of previous members, while at the same time each member of the series would increase by one the actual number of members.

ii) Since a contradictory state of things is logically and factually impossible, the concept of such an actually infinite series is unintelligible.

e) From all this it follows that:
(1) The temporal series has an extraneous ground,
(2) and thus an absolutely necessary being exists, if anything exists.

f) That the absolutely necessary being is transcendent is clear from the fact that the space-time universe cannot itself be this being since

(1) that universe is
made up of contingent
parts and is therefore
contingent as a whole;

(2) it is also contin-
gent in the sense that
its non-existence is
logically conceivable.

(3) As a temporally
successive series, the
universe must have
had a beginning and
therefore an extra-
neous ground.

C. Conclusion:
1. The first premise of
the argument is there-
fore true.

2. It follows that the
whole argument is
sound, so that God ex-
ists as the ground of
the actuality of the
cosmos.

3. Yet the argument
claims, not absolute fi-
nality, but rational
plausibility.

verse itself. But it is already clear from our previous argument that
this is not the case, for if the space-time universe is a complex of
contingent entities, states, events, and processes, then it appears that
the complex itself, as the conceptualized totality of that process, is
likewise contingent; not that a whole cannot have some qualities that
its constituent elements do not have, but rather that a whole cannot
have properties that are logically excluded by the properties of those
constituent elements—in this case, necessary existence in the whole is
logically excluded by the acknowledge contingency of the parts. But
this same conclusion can be arrived at from a consideration of the
fact that, as I have indicated in earlier contexts, the actual space-time
universe is only one among an indefinite number of logically possible
universes—and that means that its existence, as thus merely possible
in relation to the concept of that universe, is clearly contingent, since
it is the very definition of a contingent entity that both its existence
and its non-existence are consistently conceivable. Finally, if the space-
time universe is a temporally successive order (a thesis that I will
assume as beyond serious question by anyone who believes that the
space-time universe exists)—and if, as I have just now argued, the
notion of an actually infinite number of temporally successive states
is a contradictory notion—then it follows that the space-time universe
must have had a beginning in the sense that it must have had a first
temporal state. It will then follow that, since logically prior to that first
temporal state the universe can be construed as non-existent without
contradiction, that universe, or any other temporally and spatially
ordered universe, cannot be the absolutely necessary being, precisely
because, as I have previously argued, an absolutely necessary being is
a being whose non-existence is logically inconceivable by definition.
More simply: If the space-time universe has had a beginning, then it
must have an extraneous or independent causal ground; and whatever
has a causal ground outside itself is, again by definition, contingent
and not necessary in its existence.

From all this, it appears that, if there is an absolutely necessary
being, it must have an existence that is logically independent of the
space-time universe, and hence it also must be transcendent in the
sense thus defined. And that concludes my argument for the truth of
the first premise of the original argument, namely (*Premise 1*), if
anything exists, an absolutely necessary and transcendent being exists.
Since the religious equivalent of such a being is, by definition, God as
construed by my view of theism, I therefore conclude what I started
by claiming: If the cosmos or world order is actual (as it undeniably
is), then God exists as its necessary ground. As in the case of my earlier
argument from the possibility of the cosmos, I am not naively unaware
that the present argument, from the actuality of the cosmos, both
involves numerous assumptions which I have not explicitly defended
in the context, and at the same time calls forth a still larger number of
caveats from persons whose epistemological and metaphysical conceptions are strikingly different from my own. I do not therefore
suppose at all that the only alternative to accepting my conclusion

would be to embrace intellectual imbecility; on the contrary, I deeply respect those who strongly disagree with me. I merely claim that the argument displays that aspect of theism which it supports as a rationally plausible intellectual and personal commitment. I am not offering an absolute clincher but rather what I hope will be an appealing case, at least for some.

The Structure of the Cosmos: A Purposive Argument

Again, the space-time universe is, of course, not merely possible and actual, but determinate in character as displayed in the vast network of its specific and interrelated properties. And if we approach these intricately varied qualities with the previously argued persuasion that the universe is a complex effect of God as its ultimate causal ground, it is reasonable to expect that the determinate structure of that universe, so far as it is knowable to finite thinkers like ourselves, will reveal something more definite as to the essential nature of God beyond those attributes that previous arguments have disclosed. No doubt the various strands that make up, as it were, the texture of the unimaginably vast universe, strike different interpreters with an altering force that varies for each such individual. Yet varied as these strands and responses may be, there seems to be a kind of central core of integrative unity which binds them all around itself as a focal point—namely, the pervasive presence and all-but-overwhelming impression of a significant order which irresistibly draws reflective thought to the supposition of a sort of cosmic weaver or directive intelligence which stands behind it all as an essential aspect of its causal ground. Whether a person considers the ordered patterns of the starry heavens or the intricate structure of his own eyeball, he can avoid the supposition of intelligent causality only with a massive reinterpretation which puts the strongest imaginable strain on his natural credulity. But all this is, of course, not really an argument, although it certainly suggests one and provides the basic materials for it.

At the outset, we may ask what there is about varied natural patterns in the universe which draws us toward the supposition of directive intelligence. Basically, I think it is a certain general character that these various illustrations share in common—namely, that they all involve the relation of complex means, as structural elements, so as to make possible and produce a resultant state whose operation and arrangement have the appearance, on the cosmic scale of natural occurrence, of the sort of adaptive order that we would ourselves aim at when guided by conscious purposive intent. The production of artifacts such as houses, automobiles, or watches is an obvious and well-worn type of example; but the clear purpose involved in the activity of writing a book, delivering (or even composing) a lecture, or performing a musical piece on the classical guitar is just as fully

I. Various properties of the space-time universe presumably disclose some indication of the properties of its presumed causal ground.

A. Although the basis of such inferences is extremely intricate, there is a central core of insight which points clearly to directive intelligence as an aspect of the causal ground.

B. This suggestion is based on an analogy between various types of natural order and the sort of adaptive order that human agents aim at when guided by conscious purposive intent.

1. This analogy is often criticized as sheer anthropomorphism;

2. but the force of this criticism is turned away:
a) by the fact that virtually all reasoning is based on analogy, as disclosed in the universal concepts through which reasoning proceeds,

b) and by the fact that we find a basis, for believing in our own status as intelligent causes, in the significantly ordered results of our own operational activity.

C. It is also claimed that chance is a plausible basis of such significantly ordered results, so that there need be no recourse to conscious intelligent causality.

exemplary. This means, of course, that I am drawing an analogy between the directive intelligence involved in these human activities and the causal principle underlying the significant order in natural entities, events and processes. For this reason, an argument of this sort is frequently dismissed as sheer and objectionable anthropomorphism, as if we were congratulating ourselves by ascribing to the causal ground of all contingent being a quality that we regard as a constituent element of our own relatively insignificant existence and being. But what is involved here is not really that simple. Granted that the reasoning involves analogy, nevertheless it should be pointed out that virtually all reasoning about matters of fact involves analogy, with the possible (but not very plausible) exception of the direct description of a presently observed content of empirical awareness, so that the rejection of the analogical principle would be virtually tantamount to rendering all factual reasoning spurious. And if we add the point that all thought involves universal concepts expressed and symbolized in general words—and that this generality itself assumes a pervasive analogical structure in both thought and its objects—then the observation that the reasoning in my argument is analogical will be, if anything, a commendation rather than a criticism.

But there is a still deeper point to be made about the specific analogy (directive intelligence) involved in our particular argument. I have already explained in an earlier argument that directive selection or choice is the very essence of conscious intelligent activity from an operative or functional standpoint. We discern this essence in our own continuous involvement in activities that exhibit the adaptation of complex means to the achievement of consciously purposive and therefore previsioned ends; and we find the experiential basis for believing in our own status, as possessing intelligent will, in this very functional or operational activity. If therefore this same sort of significantly ordered result is observed in countless cases of natural arrangement, then the denial that this operational activity in nature is the work of purposive intelligent will would be very much like (if not precisely identical to) the contradictory act of ascribing and withholding the same essence to the same operative causal principle.

Another expedient for boggling at the force of this argument would be to appeal to chance in this context. After all, very significant results are sometimes achieved in human experience without any causal operation of the capacity of purposively intelligent activity on our part. For example, we just happen to buy the winning ticket in the lottery, or we just happen to roll a lucky seven with the dice, or we just happen to get four aces in a game of poker, and so on. Or another type of example: a friend just happens to be driving through an intersection with a green light while a careless driver runs the red light on the cross street and causes a serious accident; or a man just happens to attend a church service after which he meets the woman whom he eventually marries; and so on, more or less indefinitely. And is it not conceivable, then, by analogy with human experience, that all the types of significant order in the observable universe are more analogous to such happenings than they are to purposively directed activities?

In response to this oft-repeated suggestion, I will acknowledge at once that the chance explanation is logically possible in a particular case. It is even logically possible in what appear to be consciously purposive activities in ordinary human operations. Indeed, certain philosophers have argued that in fact causality is never purposive at all even in the clearest human examples—we act as we do because the material ingredients of our physical organisms are mechanically disposed as they are—and the supposition that even human purposes ever account for things being as they are, rather than otherwise, is a pure illusion which is itself the fleeting shadow of the same sort of physically determining causes. Perhaps all this is logically possible; but the question is whether it is rationally plausible as a satisfactory explanation—and I submit that it is not. In an earlier argument concerning the possibility of the universe, I suggested that the very principles involved in the notion of logical possibility are both objective and transcendent, and that such principles find their own most adequate explanation if they are regarded as having their ultimate locus in Eternal Reason or Absolute Mind. I further suggested that the fact that the present universe is only one of an indefinitely large number of logically possible universes itself is best explained through an operation of directive selection or purpose on the part of that Absolute Mind. Now if the very notions of logical possibility and directive selection are themselves rooted, as it were, in the Ultimate Mind—so that a universe is only possible as such through what I will call the creative activity of a purposive agent—is it not far more plausible that the instances of significant order in the universe are to be explained by the extended operation of that same principle of purposive intelligent activity, than to suppose, on the contrary, that all the marks of order in the universe are the result of the eternal churning of mindless matter through purely mechanical causality? The question virtually answers itself! Add to all this the fact that an indefinitely large number of those logically possible universes would be universes in which the sort of order we find in the present universe (for example, the cosmic progression from matter through life to mind) could not conceivably occur at all even in drastically altered form, and the case of teleology or purposive activity becomes strong indeed. As an example, consider a simple, logically conceivable universe composed of four concentric solid, frictionless spheres endowed with gravitational attraction. The future of such a universe is perfectly predictable (the spheres will impact at the common center and return to their original position and so on forever), wholly monotonous, and totally without any possibility of the origin of further order.

But to return to the original notion of chance explanation: All the limited human examples of chance that I enumerated (and any others that might be suggested) make sense only in a larger context of purposive order that makes the limited notion of chance intelligible. The game of dice, for example, is itself a purposive human activity,

1. Such a chance explanation is *prima facie* logically possible, even with respect to purported purposive causality in human experience.

2. But it is not rationally plausible:
a) Previous argument has grounded the notions of logical possibility and directive selection or choice in the Absolute Mind as the ground of the possibility of any universe at all,

so that the ascription of observed natural order to that same ground is far more plausible than the chance explanation, especially since many logically conceivable universes would involve no such analogously significant order at all.

b) Chance explanation is itself intelligible only within a more inclusive context of significant purposive order.

however trivial that purpose might be; and the man and woman, who met at a church service and later married, were both in pursuit of various intended goals, even if they did not intend marriage as an ultimate issue of that particular occasion. So chance makes sense (and therefore a merely restricted sense) only in a more inclusive context of purposive order; and when the notion is universalized—as it would be in the idea that all significant order in the universe is the product of chance or occurs wholly without purposive direction—then the notion ceases to be intelligible as a purportedly rational explanation. This fact can be most clearly seen in the previously mentioned thesis that all supposed cases of even humanly purposive activity are in fact devoid of any purposive causality and are therefore the product of purely mechanical and biological causes. For this thesis would then itself be, not the purposively directed explanation that it purports to be, but rather, by its own claim, the random product of purely mechanical and biological forces determining the activity of the theorist who makes this claim. And, in that case, there would be no reason why he or anyone else should believe it, since false statements (if indeed either true or false statements are conceivable on these terms) would by hypothesis be indistinguishably the product of the same sort of mechanical forces. From all this, I conclude that the notion of chance simply does not provide any rationally plausible explanation of the significant order in the universe, and that therefore the principle of purposively directed activity provides an overwhelmingly more reasonable explanation.

So far, I have been informally discussing the premises of this purposive argument without explicitly stating them. But now, perhaps, it is appropriate to be formally explicit:

Premise 1: All composites which involve the relation of complex means so as to produce a significant result, are composites of whose cause purposive intelligence is an indispensable aspect.

Premise 2: The space-time universe is a composite in which complex means are so related as to produce significant results.

Conclusion: Therefore, the space-time universe is a composite of whose cause purposive intelligence is an indispensable aspect.

Some explanatory comments regarding this explicit argument are in order. First, it is cast in a logically valid argument form,[1] so that if its premises are true, then its conclusion must also be true. A question may be raised as to what is meant by the phrase *significant result:* I regard a result or effect as significant if it involves a distinctive function or end which the means involved make possible and which has a comparatively greater assignable value than those means would be reasonably judged to possess prior to and apart from the produced

---

Margin notes:

(1) Hence, if the notion of chance is universalized, it ceases to be intelligible as an explanation.
(2) This fact is illustrated by the thesis which denies causal efficacy to human purposive activity, since the thesis would then contradict its own claim.

c) It is therefore reasonable to claim that purposively directed activity is a more plausible explanation than chance.
II. Formal statement and clarification of the argument.

A. Premises and Conclusion.

B. Explanatory comments.
1. The argument is logically valid in form.
2. Meaning of a significant result.

---

1. The technical designation given this form by formal logic is AAA.

result; often the effect is significant in this way precisely because it is itself a partial means in the emergence of a still further and more inclusive significant result. For example, an antibiotic medicine is a significant result precisely because it is itself a means for restricting disease and promoting health in a living organism.

Much of the previous analysis has been in support of Premise 1, the major premise of the argument, and I will consider that premise therefore as adequately supported for my purposes in the present context. The second or minor premise has been implied by numerous of the illustrations I have alluded to—it is simply not reasonably disputable that the universe, so far as it comes under observational scrutiny, is virtually bulging with instances of the defined type of significant order. In any case, so much has been written elsewhere, by so many different authors, about the extensive examples of adaptive order in the universe, that I have no intention of laboring the case here. While my bibliography contains a number of such works, I cannot resist the temptation to mention explicitly in my text itself the one work which has made the most profound impression of all this proliferated teleology on my own mind, namely, F. R. Tennant's monumental work, *Philosophical Theology.* Tennant maps out in detail four areas of adaptive order which I have already discussed at length in my own earlier work, *The Resurrection of Theism:* (1) the fitness of the inorganic material environment in the production and maintenance of life; (2) the internal adaptedness of organic beings; (3) the intelligibility of the world and its instrumentality in the realization of humanly previsioned ends; and (4) the temporal progressiveness of the cosmic process through the levels of matter, life, and mind, in an order of increasing assignable value. I shall, then, regard the second premise as also adequately supported.

Now if both premises of the argument may reasonably be construed as true and if the argument is formally valid, it is equally reasonable to regard the conclusion as true, so that the significant order in the universe may with full plausibility be believed to be the effect of the purposively directed activity of the Ultimate Mind or, in religious terms, God. And God, in turn, may be rationally viewed as essentially characterized by personal, intelligent will, precisely as theism construes the Divine Reality. But, as in the case of my earlier arguments, the strength of this argument is not that of absolute mathematical demonstration; it rather has the force of all but overwhelming reasonableness and probability. To ask more would be to demand too much; and to expect more would be to misinterpret the nature of the foundations on which the rational direction of the fullest human life rests.

C. The truth-value of the premises.
1. The first premise is previously supported.
2. The second premise:
a) is supported by an abundance of empirical illustrations,

b) is well expressed by F. R. Tennant,

c) is here assumed to be a true descriptive generalization.

D. The argument is therefore sound, so that:
1. the significant order of the universe may be attributed to divine purposive activity;
2. and God may be characterized as personal intelligent will.
E. Yet it is not demonstration but reasonable probability that is claimed.

The Climax of the Cosmos: An Anthropological Argument

It would perhaps be too ambitious to claim that man is himself, through the properties of his distinctively human nature, the climax of the cosmos at large. But it may not be too much to claim instead, on a more modest scale, that the unique properties of that human nature—properties that set man off from the rest of the natural order and put him, as it were, in a class by himself—are of such a sort that they put man at the top of the scale of finite beings known to us in ordinary human experience, and therefore in the genus, at least, of the sort of beings that would be the climax of the cosmos. Indeed, someone has somewhere wisely said that the essential difference between man and the highest ape is infinitely greater than that between the highest ape and a blade of grass. This difference, however, is not in the area of man's organic, bodily nature, however striking that may be—for in that respect man is really quite similar to apes and other mammals which together with him constitute the highest class of the vertebrates among living things. Nor is the difference found even in the capacity of man for goal-directed activity in circumstances where stimulus and response appear not to supply a fully adequate explanation of that activity—for certain other mammals have at least a minimal capacity for responding effectively to such circumstances, although man's capacity for such goal-oriented activity is far more widely extended and much more intricately developed. No, the uniqueness of man lies in his selfhood, his personhood, his essentially self-conscious and self-directing spiritual nature, and in all the capacities which that nature entails. We can, perhaps, distinguish between the signs or symptoms of selfhood, on the one hand, and the essential qualities of it, on the other. The former would include language, writing, artistic creativity along with aesthetic appreciation, scientific ingenuity and productivity, and in general all that comes together in cooperative human life to constitute what we broadly call culture. But all these are made possible by the essential qualities that enter into selfhood. It is quite true that other forms of life do not produce the ingredients of culture—they do not create music, or construct complex architecture on the imaginative scale that characterizes human society, or produce enduring artifacts which contribute to the efficiency and convenience of their activity; they do not develop language or any of its by-products; and especially they neither laugh nor even smile. But the underlying question is: Why not? In the end, it all comes back to a selfhood that human persons possess and that other animals simply do not exhibit in even a remotely analogous way.

What, then, are the essential qualities and facets of that selfhood? Certain higher animals other than man have consciousness or awareness. But they do not, so far as we can tell, have that reflective awareness in which they realize that they are conscious or aware, nor do they recognize themselves therefore as either subjects of their awareness or agents of their activity—they do not, to put it pointedly, have the notion of an ego or an "I". But human beings, on the contrary, do have precisely this reflective capacity which other animals lack. Closely conjoined to this subjectivity and inseparable from it is the capacity to conceptualize—to form class-concepts and therefore to apprehend the essences or universal natures which are the objects of these concepts. Hence, human beings have the capacity to recognize particular entities which exemplify or instantiate these essences—to apprehend triangularity and to recognize triangular objects, for example; or to apprehend the concept of a musical theme, to recognize a particular theme of this sort (say, the choral theme in Beethoven's Ninth Symphony) and the various ways in which it can be expressed vocally or instrumentally. This capacity for conceptualization is at the core of what we call thinking in the highest sense, and it is both a condition and an ingredient of reflective self-awareness.

b) involves the capacity to conceptualize and therefore to apprehend essences or universal natures, as well as particular things which exemplify them;

Self-awareness and conceptualization, in turn, make self-direction possible. They enable us to apprehend in present awareness the sought future goals of present activity, so that we can both consciously act in the pursuit of those goals and envision ourselves in the circumstances which those goals may actualize. And this self-directive capacity has a profoundly significant aspect which I shall call, following thinkers such as George Santayana and Max Scheler, *sublimation*. Even though self-awareness, conceptualization, and self-direction take place in the intimate context of organic, bodily existence, nevertheless this complex of mental and spiritual activity involves the capacity to redirect or even set aside, within limits, what otherwise would be the effect of animal drive or biological life-impulse. Of course, we are often blindly driven and even determined by such drives or impulses—and when we are, we are responding in ways that are inevitable for other living things. But they are not inevitable for us—we can mediate and govern our bodily impulses. And we can even deny ourselves the objectives toward which they impell us, although we cannot, of course, effectively reject their demands across the board, as it were. Or to use our original word here: Because I am an essential spiritual self, I can, as spirit, sublimate my animal drives and biological life-impulses. That I am able to do so may reasonably be held to imply that the capacity for sublimation means that man has, as the essence of his selfhood, a spiritual dimension which—precisely because it is capable of redirecting and even rejecting the otherwise determining influences of physiological forces—cannot be regarded as the product of those forces, but must rather be seen as the product of an immaterial ground or cause which neither inert nor living matter would be sufficient to explain.

c) makes self-direction possible,

as well as its characteristic expression in sublimation as the capacity to redirect the energy of animal drives to the pursuit of the goals of selfhood.

(1) As spiritual self, man can exercise directive control over biological life-impulses.

(2) Man has thus a spiritual dimension which cannot be reductively explained merely as the product of material and biological forces.

Of course, the emergence of this conclusion is by no means all clear sailing; entire edifices of metaphysical theory have been constructed which would militate against such a result. If, for example, we could accept a naturalistic theory of reality, with its view that the ultimate structural constituent of all substantially real entities is some sort of material particle, or unit of physical energy; and if we could accept the past temporal eternity of a universe thus construed—and if we could therefore reasonably suppose that the whole of what we might call mind or selfhood was either itself a purely physical complex, or could be regarded as a qualitatively distinct by-product of merely physical processes with no reciprocal causal efficacy on the part of the mind or selfhood thus explained (since on such a view all effica-

II. Critical problems with the argument.

A. A naturalistic view of mind, as either itself physical or as the by-product of wholly physical processes, would reverse the conclusion of the argument.

B. But such a view is
initially implausible:
1. because previous
arguments have made
it plausible to believe
that the natural uni-
verse and its proper-
ties require
explanation in terms
of a transcendent
spiritual ground;

cious causality would be purely material)—then the fulfillment of all
these conditions would involve a drastically different result. The thorough discussion of these possibilities I shall postpone for the next main
section of my analysis. However, we can already glimpse from the
previous development of these issues several plausible grounds for
regarding the conditions for this alternative explanation as subject to
very serious question. If the very possibility of a contingent cosmos or
world order is fully conceivable only through its dependence on a
transcendent realm of essence and directive selection; and if the very
notion of an actually infinite series of past temporal states of the
temporal universe involves a self-contradiction, whether that universe
is construed in mentalistic or materialist terms; and if the pervasion of
the universe by significant order or purposive adaptation is itself best
explained through an operation of transcendent self-directive mind
through its own operative causality—and these are the very claims
that our previous arguments have defended as plausible—then the
supposition that selfhood (self-awareness, conceptualization, and self-
direction) could now be explained in terms of material constituents,
which themselves require explanation on transcendent and essentially
immaterial or spiritual grounds, seems questionable indeed.

2. because selfhood,
with its distinctive as-
pects and properties,
is not the sort of result
that material particles
would or could con-
ceivably produce;
a) since the discerni-
ble properties of men-
tal states and physical
properties exhibit no
intelligible continuity,

But with more direct pertinence to the present argument, we may
ask whether selfhood, as we have analyzed it, is the sort of reality that,
through whatever intervening causal steps, ultimate material particles
in random interaction with one another would be sufficient to explain.
If, as an activity of the self, I introspectively analyze the constituent
aspects of my own awareness as directly disclosed to me in consciousness, it is clear that I do not find any of the ingredients I would expect
to find if this sort of reflective activity were a physical process—no
material particles impacting each other and moving off in various
directions, and certainly no spatial pattern of organization in any literal

so that mental states
could neither be, nor
be the product of
purely physical proc-
esses;

sense. But instead I might find ideas of which such things as material
particles would perhaps be the referent objects, and I also find various
percepts, concepts, memories, emotional states, and so on. Reciprocally, if I analyze material particles, again I do not find any of the
ingredients that normally accompany consciousness and its elements.
If it is suggested as a result that, although mental states are not
themselves physical, they are nonetheless the product of physiological
processes, then the question will be how to make that supposition
intelligible. What conceivable physiological processes, as normally described in physical terms, could result in mental states whose qualities
have no discernible continuity whatsoever with the qualities of physical states? Or more succinctly, how could moving particles produce
thoughts? It is not, as we shall see, that there have been no attempts
to propose answers to these questions; it is rather that the proposed
answers generate more problems than they solve. And if we can now
add, in the present context of analysis, the capacity for sublimation,
for setting aside the influence of animal drives and physical impulses,
it would appear that such an operation of the self implies that it has a
unique causal efficacy of its own—since if its energy for sublimation

b) since there would
then be no way to ex-
plain the mind's ca-
pacity to sublimate
physical drives and
impulses;

were borrowed, as it were, from physical sources, there would be no sublimation at all (which seems contrary to fact) but merely the struggle of various physical energies with one another.

Finally, selfhood involves a kind of pure subjectivity (sometimes called transcendental egoity) which no explanation, in terms of physical forces, is competent to account for. The self, as the subject of all its experiences, occupies a status that transcends any or all of the contents of its own awareness, and it is therefore not itself, as pure subject, an element of that which it witnesses. That does not mean that I am not aware of my subjectivity through ideas; it rather means that I, as subject, am always something ontologically distinct from those ideas, however they are construed. Now, that being the case, it seems to follow that physical forces or causes could never account for the self as such a pure subject, since physical forces could only produce physical states as effects. And while, as a self, I might be conscious of such states and forces, I could never correctly construe my subjectivity as identical with them or constituted through them.

3. because the self, as pure subject distinct from the objects of its awareness, could not be the effect of physical forces which could produce only physical states as effects.

Yet my selfhood, I contend, is admittedly contingent and finite, and therefore requires explanation in terms of an independent causal ground which is not contingent and which, as I now clearly discern, is not explicable in material or physical terms either. I suggest that this is another way of saying that the essential spiritual selfhood of man has its only adequate ground in the transcendent spiritual Selfhood of God as Absolute Mind. As always, this is not a rigorous demonstration, but rather a plausible, perhaps even a highly plausible, explanation. I might even characterize it as an activity of self-analysis in which I see that I could not be the self I am if God were not the Self he is. With modest apology to Descartes: *Cogito, ergo Deus est!* I think, therefore God is!

C. But finite selfhood, as contingent, does require an independent causal ground which cannot therefore be material: hence, God as Absolute Personal Mind.

The Value Dimension of the Cosmos: A Moral Argument

But selfhood, even on the human level, is not, of course, an isolated matter. It involves membership in what I will call the community of selves or persons, and this in turn engulfs all the relations in which persons appropriately stand in association with each other. In order to see what those relations themselves encompass, I propose to make what to some will seem an astounding assumption which I will expend little energy to defend as reasonable, since I firmly believe that it is an assumption which, for most of us, has but to be clearly understood in order to be accepted as virtually beyond serious question. That assumption is that persons, merely as such and just on account of their personhood, possess intrinsic value or worth. What that means is that persons are not to be construed as merely means or instruments of further ends, but rather as ends in themselves. Material objects,

I. Selfhood involves a complex of relationships to other persons, such that an adequate understanding of this complex involves the assumption that persons possess intrinsic value or worth.
A. This implies that persons are to be recognized and treated as ends and never merely as means to further ends.

human experiences, and even particularized human activities (solving a problem, playing a game of tennis, eating lunch, or listening to a musical performance) may all appropriately be regarded as possessing primarily, if not exclusively, extrinsic worth—that is, they are all means or instruments to further ends. But this, I shall assume, is not the case with persons. Because of their incidental social relations to us, they may inevitably find a place among the means to the achievement of our own personal goals; but if that exhausts their significance for us, then our regard for them lacks the propriety which it can only possess if we construe them as ends in themselves, along with our own personhood as similarly possessing the same sort of intrinsic worth.

B. The assumption, however, is a reasonable one:
1. because the significant and responsible choice of goals involves the implicit recognition of intrinsic personal worth as its ultimate rational basis, so that action toward any end implies the worth of persons as intrinsic ends;

While I have referred to this thesis of intrinsic personal worth as an assumption, it is certainly not a groundless assumption, in my opinion. Persons, as we know them on the human level, characteristically pursue goals which are, at least to some extent and in cases where something of recognized importance is at stake, the objects of their implicit or even explicit choice. Furthermore, they make value judgments about the worth of these goals—indeed, it is difficult to see how responsible choice can proceed at all here unless some alternative goals are judged as more deserving of our acceptance than others, since not to judge in this way would be to judge irresponsibly by allowing our goals to be determined by accidental causes (such as emotional whims, public sentiment, or political pressure) which contribute nothing to their worth in a rationally grounded sense. Now if a person introspectively analyzes the grounds which in his most lucid moments he would regard as appropriate for making such choices and such judgments of worth with respect to his own goals, he will, I think, clearly see that those goals are alone deserving of rational choice which implement or seem likely to implement his own personal well-being as a self and/or the analogous personal well-being of other selves whose circumstances are likely to be affected by his choices. In other words, in aiming at significant goals, a person implicitly accepts his own intrinsic worth and that of other persons as the rational basis of the worth of his choice, so that those goals themselves are judged appropriate, in the final analysis, because they are extrinsic means for actualizing the intrinsic worth of persons. Action toward any end, then, if it is rational, presupposes one's own worth as an intrinsic end. Otherwise, the whole process of making choices becomes trivial and absurd in the most objectionable existential sense.

2. because any other pursued goals are clearly instrumental means to the well-being of persons, so that such goals are to be evaluated in terms of their effect on personhood.

The same conclusion (namely, that persons possess intrinsic worth in a unique sense) can be illustratively discerned if we consider two further points: First, that any other proposed candidates for the status of intrinsic worth in this sense turn out to be patently ridiculous on analysis—the pursuit, for example, of power, wealth, knowledge, pleasure, or even health—all these ends are so obviously instrumental means to the well-being of persons as selves that any supposition that they are themselves intrinsically valuable becomes virtually ludicrous, except to a person who is self-deceived or confused. It may be good to pursue any or all of these goals, but not unconditionally; yet the recognition and acceptance of the intrinsic worth of persons is, on the contrary, the unconditional goal which makes all these conditional goals plausible within limits. And it then follows from this insight that personal well-being does not consist in every individual's getting what he wants as a matter of idiosyncratic preference or hedonistic pleasure—for preferences and pleasures are themselves to be evaluated by their role in fulfilling, or deteriorating, the meaning of personhood.

Now if persons are in this way possessed of intrinsic worth, it is further reasonable to believe that the community of persons is a moral or ethical community in which the members have duties and obligations toward themselves and each other as intrinsic ends, so that, at least in regard to persons, the universe is pervaded by an objective moral order which ideally defines the network and principles of these duties, obligations, and responsibilities. I call this moral order objective because the morally binding character of these principles is not a function of individually and culturally variable states of feeling, preference, opinion, or response. The authority of such principles is not constituted by our opting for them in any sense; it is instead an authority that we recognize and discover as binding on us precisely because conformity to these principles implements and expresses the intrinsic worth of persons whether any individual person accepts this authority or not—so that, far from it being the case that we legislate these principles by opting for them, it is rather the case that our legislative options are themselves to be evaluated by these principles considered as objective. How could I sincerely respect the moral authority of a principle whose binding force lay solely in my idiosyncratic preference? Of course, the doctrine of moral objectivism I am contending for here has been subject to a long tradition of negative criticism; and in due season I shall have to grapple with the main core of this criticism. Suffice it to say for now that, if there were no intrinsic moral worth in the objective sense, then there would be no reasonable standard for evaluating preferences themselves. And, in fact, without any objective intrinsic worth, there could, by definition, be no extrinsic or instrumental ends, since there would be no terminating goals of which such intermediate ends would be the means. Or shall we judge as reasonable the supposition that each end is an extrinsic means to other ends which are extrinsic to still others and so on without logical limit? That would reduce the pursuit of any of these ends to absurdity. Just as a contingent entity depends ontologically on an ultimately necessary ground, so an extrinsic goal depends morally on an intrinsically valuable end. If everything is, valuationally considered, for the sake of something else and nothing is for its own sake, then, in the last analysis, nothing can reasonably be judged to be for the sake of something else either.

We are now in a position to analyze the implications of the concept of intrinsic personal worth and of the objective moral order of being which that concept involves. It is not difficult to see that if moral authority, as I have urged, is objective to any particular finite self, then the ultimate basis of that authority cannot reasonably be identified

C. The community of persons, with reciprocal moral duties, constitutes an objective moral order which ideally defines these duties through moral principles.
1. Such an order and such principles are objective, since their authority is not constituted by our choices or preferences which are themselves to be evaluated by these principles.

2. This sort of moral objectivism is plausible since, if there were no objective intrinsic moral worth, there would be no reasonable standard for morally evaluating anything, and the pursuit of extrinsic goals would itself be reduced to moral triviality.

II. Implications of intrinsic personal worth and objective moral order:
A. If moral order is objective to finite selves, then it must have a basis other than the community of such selves, so that those selves have a derived, rather than an ultimate intrinsic worth.

B. This implied ultimate and intrinsic moral worth:

1. cannot be the impersonal order of nature or any part of it, since these have only extrinsic worth;

2. is therefore most plausibly identified as an aspect of transcendent personal selfhood in God as Absolute Personal Being.

III. But why must the absolute and transcendent good be personal in the theistic sense?
A. because intrinsic personal worth is the basic content of the moral good;

B. because moral obligation among human selves always involves responsibility to personal being;

C. because the transcendent good cannot be merely an abstract essence, since essences are themselves fully intelligible only as constitutive principles of Ultimate Personal Mind;

with that particular self or even with the whole community of finite moral selves, for that moral authority would retain its binding force even if any particular finite self had never existed. Granted that finite moral selves possess, as I have argued, intrinsic moral worth, this must in some sense be a derived, though genuinely intrinsic, moral worth. What that disclosure suggests is that there is an ultimate and unconditionally intrinsic moral worth that is independent of finite moral selves but yet participated in, or instantiated, by these finite selves. Clearly, this ultimate intrinsic worth could not attach to anything in the impersonal order of nature or to that order as a whole, since such impersonal entities, singly or collectively considered, have no more than an extrinsic or instrumental significance, not an intrinsic one in the sense we are here considering. It then follows that if there is an ultimate and absolute intrinsic good or worth, it must transcend both the impersonal natural order and also the realm of finite personal selves. But this Ultimate Good cannot, in that case, be less than personal in nature, so that the most plausible explanation of intrinsic moral worth is the supposition that it is ultimately an aspect of transcendent personal selfhood or the Absolute Mind which we have already confronted at the conclusion of earlier arguments. If that is the case, I could not possess derived intrinsic worth as a finite person unless God as Absolute Person possessed ultimate and unconditional intrinsic worth.

It will, however, be helpful to develop a frontal and summary answer to the following direct question. Granted that the Absolute Good, in the moral sense, must transcend the realm of contingent, finite entities and persons, why must that transcendent good itself be personal in the explicitly theistic sense? The argument just concluded provides a considerable part of the answer to this question, since it attempts to take intrinsic personal worth as the basic content of the good in the moral sense, and then attempts as well to argue that the derived intrinsic worth of finite persons must be grounded in the absolute and ultimate intrinsic worth of God as transcendent personal reality. There is also the further analogical argument that since every case of recognized moral obligation within actual human moral experience may plausibly be interpreted as involving the responsibility on the part of a person or persons to some person or persons as object of that responsibility—and since the transcendent good is the ultimate ground and object of all moral responsibility, even to finite persons—then it is reasonable to conclude that the transcendent good itself is, by this analogy with human moral experience, itself personal.

Again, if the transcendent objectivity of the good is accepted but its identity with Ultimate Personal Mind (God) is not acknowledged, then the good would have to be interpreted as some sort of abstract essence (Plato) or principle (Kant). But I have already urged in an earlier argument that the transcendent status of essences in general is fully intelligible only if these essences are regarded as constitutive principles of Ultimate Personal Mind. Hence, since the good is, by hypothesis in this case, at least a transcendent essence, its status also is fully intelligible only if the good is therefore such a constitutive principle of Ultimate Personal Mind or God, in the theistic sense.

It is important to be reminded, furthermore, that the ultimate intrinsic good must be wholly self-contained in its worth; and that would mean that the entire basis of its worth would be inherent in itself—for if it depended on anything else for its worth, its value would be extrinsic or instrumental in relation to that other entity and not really intrinsic at all in the posited sense. Now it clearly follows from this analysis that the transcendent good must be ontologically identical with self-existent being. But God is, by theistic definition, the only self-existent being. Indeed, a plurality of self-existent beings is rationally objectionable, since, if there were more than one such being, each would stand limited in its being by the others, and none would be truly self-existent and independent at all. Of course, my earlier arguments have concluded precisely the existence of God as a self-existent Being whose nature is that of personal intelligent mind and will. So, if the transcendent good is self-contained in its worth and therefore identical with God as self-existent Being, then the good must also be identical with God as Ultimate Personal Mind.

Perhaps the most notorious answer to the original question—why the ultimate good must be personal—is found in Immanuel Kant's principal argument for the reasonableness of belief in a personal God, although it should be made clear that Kant did not himself believe that the conclusion of this argument represented any genuine extension of speculative, theoretical knowledge in contrast to reasonable belief on moral grounds; and I myself, in expounding this argument, will not be bound by the details involved in Kant's way of posing it. If, as has been argued, the universe is an objective moral order, then within such an order moral obligation would imply, in part, both a responsibility, on the part of any moral agent, to make amends for immorality, and also an order of reality in which existence is both adapted to moral ends and at the same time involves effects proportionate to the state of one's moral conduct and character. More pointedly, reality would not be an objective moral order if there were not finally an ideal proportion between moral virtue and personal well-being, as well as between moral vice and personal ill-being. Moral agents, óther circumstances being equal, should enjoy precisely that state of overall well-being which matches the developing or deteriorating state of their moral character. Nor is this to be taken hedonistically, as if well-being were to be wholly defined in terms of the accumulated experience of pleasures and pains. It is rather to be understood in terms of the circumstances and means essential to provide an individual with the possibility of both being and becoming a better person through the implementation of respect for the moral law and acceptance of whatever truth about reality the authority of that law, correctly understood, would imply. However, the possibility of achieving such a state of moral well-being involves such an arrangement of the circumstances of persons as to constitute in effect a purposively adapted order of the entire universe. But such an adaptive order is

D. because the transcendent good can be self-contained in its worth only if it is identical with self-existent being—which previous arguments have identified with God as Ultimate Personal Mind;

E. because an objective moral order implies a proportion between the state of a person's moral character and the degree of his personal well-being, while the conditions for effecting such a proportion imply an adaptive order of the entire universe, of which God, as personal intelligent will, is the only adequate cause.

fully intelligible only as the complex effect of such a directive control over the universe as would require the operation of personal intelligent will—so that God, thus construed, is the only conceivable ground for the ideal proportion between moral virtue and well-being which an objective moral order of reality would require.

F. Hence, it is God, as Ultimate Personal Mind, who makes moral objectivity fully conceivable.

If, now, we put together in a single framework all of these considerations, in answer to the question why the transcendent good must be personal, they appear both singly and unitedly to provide a fully plausible basis for believing reasonably that God as Ultimate Personal Mind is the transcendent locus and even the reality of that essential or absolute goodness which alone makes moral objectivity fully conceivable. But I do not wish to leave this argument without responding to a very common rejoinder to the effect that if, as I have argued, morality is contingent in this way on the reality of God theistically construed, then it would follow that, if God did not exist, there would be no such thing as objective morality. And it might even follow as well that, if a person did not believe in the reality of God so understood, he would not for that reason be bound by moral law, since he would by hypothesis be deprived of any subjective basis for its authority. The last of these two suggestions is, I think, clearly mistaken, since a person is objectively bound by the truth and its implications for his existence, whether or not he accedes to that truth—so that believing even in the moral law (much less in God) is in no sense a necessary condition of its authority over the individual. Hence, the moral institution of life can clearly survive, even if without a fully adequate foundation in thought, whatever the idiosyncratic metaphysical beliefs of various individuals may turn out to be. And what of the suggestion that there would be no such thing as objective morality if God did not exist? That, I submit, is essentially correct—for if our previous arguments for the existence of God are essentially correct in their structure and conclusion, then it clearly follows that nothing at all would either exist or be conceivable; and, hence, objective morality, like all the rest of being and possibility, would, as it were, be swept away. It is, however, reasonably clear that this is not the case, else there would be nothing to discuss and certainly no one to discuss it. In fact, I think this last question (whether objective morality would cease if there were no God) boggles the mind of the average reflective individual only because (1) he does not fully understand the implications of the question, and (2) he confuses it with the earlier question as to whether *belief* in God is a necessary subjective condition of objective moral authority.

IV. The thesis that morality depends on God is often criticized as a questionable basis, since the reality of God is itself disputable.
A. But persons are bound by objective moral law, whether they believe in that law (and in its theistic basis) or not.

B. While it is correct that, on this view, there would be no objective morality if God did not exist, it is also the case, if our previous arguments are correct, that nothing at all would exist or be possible if God did not exist.

III. The overall case for theism consists in the conjoined conclusions of all the previous arguments as summarized here.

In summary retrospect, what then is the overall case for a theistic metaphysic? If the arguments I have just now concluded are indeed rationally plausible, then they constitute unitedly the radii or spokes of a sort of wheel of existence—with the reality of God, construed as transcendent personal mind constituting essential and absolute goodness, as the center or hub conjoining all these spokes in a common conclusion. If the world is possible only through a transcendent realm of logical principles and essences which explain that world only through the operation of an equally transcendent activity of directive selection; and if the actual world order does indeed require an adequate causal ground which does not itself require further causal explanation because its existence is necessary rather than contingent; and if the structure of the cosmos is thoroughly permeated with an adaptively purposive network of reciprocal arrangement and order which attest that the causal explanation of this structure involves the activity of intelligently directed choice with a view to significant ends; and if man himself, as the exemplary capstone of the cosmos, possesses a unique spiritual personhood which sub-personal and purely physical forces are insufficient reasonably to explain; and if, finally, the contingent world order involves and constitutes an objective moral order in which personal being stands as the core of intrinsic worth, while yet the intrinsic worth of finite persons is itself clearly derived in its basis or ground—then, since God, as theistically understood, provides a logical terminus for the direction in which all these facets of the cosmos point, it follows that a metaphysic with such a God at its heart is an eminently reasonable world-view indeed, so that the basis of this world-view is at the same time a wholly reasonable object of belief for any reflective person who fully (or even fragmentarily) grasps the force of its impact.

> A. Hence theism is a wholly reasonable object of belief on such reflective grounds.

But, of course, as I long ago conceded (and now, at least, without reluctance), the persuasive thrust of even the most plausible speculative arguments of this sort is person-relative. An objectively rational basis does not always, or perhaps even characteristically, provide a subjectively effective motive for commitment, since such motives are as variable in their result as the complex of altered factors which constitute the unparalleled uniqueness of individual persons. So, over virtually every line, if not every word, of such arguments as I have developed, there is a continually erupting storm of controversy. Not only would I be naive and uncritical if I failed to recognize this point in general, but I would as well be derelict in my philosophical duty if I did not discuss some of this controversy in detail. Even conceptual coins have always an opposite side to explore.

> B. But since the persuasive efficacy of argument is person-relative, all these arguments have generated negative controversy which calls for explicit discussion.

Viable Alternatives and Critical Objections

Logical Conventionalism and the Analytic-Empirical Objection to Theism

I. Since the arguments for metaphysical perspectives are based on epistemological foundations, some of the most serious objections against theism are challenges to its epistemological basis.

It will scarcely be surprising, to any who have followed the thread of my analysis as far as this, that the most serious objections to any metaphysical perspective, and therefore also to the theistic metaphysic as I have defined it, almost inevitably run back to the epistemological foundations which any metaphysical truth-claim, whether explicitly or not, involves and, in the last analysis, is called upon to provide. What I have argued, with respect to the reality of God, is clearly suspended on the epistemological basis which I spelled out at the beginning of this intellectual journey. But what if everything epistemological were reversed or even turned, as it were, on its head? Without concerning ourselves again with the alternatives in religious epistemology which, however contrasting among themselves, are nevertheless united in the defense of some sort of positive religious truth-claims, why not simply consider an alternative in general epistemology which, if plausible, would turn aside much of what my arguments have claimed?

I have leaned heavily and indispensably on a moderate rationalistic apriorism which posits synthetic *a priori* principles and categories as the starting-points for all knowledge-claims, and which regards such principles as necessary presuppositions of all possible thought and being. But what if all that is mistaken and some sort of pure empiricism is true, so that, even though all thought and knowledge-claims are based on logical foundations of some sort, these foundations are, in the end, a matter of conventional choice? Any reflective thinking will then rest on starting points of a sort, but they will not possess any ultimate necessity in an objective sense, since the particular starting points presupposed will be either implicitly or explicitly assumed by choice and will in that sense be arbitrary inasmuch as the thinker might have selected different assumptions. On the supposition that one wears clothes when he appears in public, it will then be necessary to be dressed for such appearances; but it is only some clothing or other that is required, not any particular set of clothes. Analogously, epistemological presuppositions of some sort are necessary for any thought or argument, but the particular presuppositions employed are a matter of arbitrary choice. However, just as custom has developed standards of propriety for clothing in a given culture, so logicians and other theorists have developed standards, even rules, of propriety for effective thinking. Hence, our actual choices in practice are largely limited by the tradition of logical structure, although in theory, at least, it might all have been quite otherwise, not merely for the symbols we use in expressing logical presuppositions, but also for the substance that such symbols express. We make our principles necessary simply by defining them as we do. As Lord Russell has suggested, the whole fabric of epistemology is of a piece with the great and equally necessary truth that there are three feet in a yard—an obvious convention adapted to our practical needs.

This sort of *logical conventionalism*, as it has been called, lands us squarely in the center of contemporary empiricism in epistemology, as I noted near the beginning of my whole discussion of epistemology in general. For such a view, there are indeed *a priori* truths and principles—*a priori* in the sense that these truths are insusceptible of empirical justification; but that is because they are made true by our decision. A similar fate awaits the doctrine of real essences as I have defended it in various previous contexts and especially in my first argument for theism. For a supposedly consistent empiricism, there are no real essences or natures; there are merely general terms which we conventionally adopt in order to facilitate linguistic reference to groups of similar things, and we are led into the confusion (or perhaps illusion) of believing in real essences merely because we mistakenly suppose that such general terms must have analogously general objects. From this sort of *nominalism* (universal terms are merely names and have no general objects) and from logical conventionalism, taken together, it will follow as well that the notion of logically possible universes, which would actualize different cross sections of an indefinitely extended realm of real essences, would also collapse into an experiment of pure imagination based on a notion of logical order and possibility which is entirely a product of our own implicit or explicit convention.

Now if all this is posited—if we accept a conventional theory of logical foundations, a denial of real essences, and a trivializing of the

A. If synthetic *a priorism* were replaced by a pure empiricism, then the logical foundations of knowledge-claims would be conventional and thus arbitrary by being the product of choice.

1. While there are accepted rules of propriety for such choices, yet in theory both the symbols and substance of logical presuppositions could be wholly otherwise.

2. *A priori* truths are thus non-empirical because they depend on the logician's decision.

B. For such a view, real essences are also denied in favor of a nominalism which regards general words as simply terms for referring to groups of similar particulars.

C. It would therefore result that the notion of logically possible universes would be based on a merely conventional concept of logical possibility;

and hence any argument for theism based on synthetic apriorism and realistic essentialism would be called into question.

II. Such an analytic empiricism also rejects the intelligibility of the concept of God as a necessary being.

A. For necessary existence could not be regarded as a property of God, since (*a la* Kant) existence is not a property at all.

B. Nor could the proposition that God exists be a necessary truth,
1. since existential truths are empirical and therefore contingent,

2. and necessary truths are all conventional and therefore existentially arbitrary.

III. It is even claimed that the proposition that God exists is not a genuinely meaningful and informative assertion.

A. Such a genuine assertion must be such that its truth would exclude certain conceivable states of affairs.

notion of logical possibility—then it is clear that my argument to God, based on non-conventional *a priori* principles, real essences, and a non-trivial concept of logical possibility, will be cast into serious jeopardy, if indeed it does not collapse altogether. And yet there is more: For the analytic empiricism which leads to such conclusions also proceeds to question the very concept of God as a necessary being and the informative status of any proposition which attempts to affirm that such a God (or any other transcendent metaphysical reality) exists. Theism, as I have defined it, entails the thesis that God exists necessarily rather than contingently. Now, according to the sort of analytic empiricism I am considering here, the thesis that God exists necessarily may be interpreted in two ways. First, it may mean that necessary existence is a property or conceptually predicated attribute of God (similar to holiness, justice, mercy, and so on); or, alternatively, it may be equivalent to the claim that the proposition "God exists" is a necessary truth. But neither of these meanings is plausible for such an analytic empiricism. The first is eliminated simply by accepting Kant's criticism of the ontological argument to the effect that existence is not a property or conceptually predicable attribute at all—since to say of anything that it exists is not to add to the concept of that thing, but merely to affirm that the concept, as fully explicated, applies to something actual—and if existence is thus not a property, so the objection runs, then necessary existence cannot logically be a property of God. The alternative interpretation, that the proposition "God exists" is a necessary truth, is, if anything, even more objectionable: First, because no genuinely existential truths are necessary, since all such truths are based on an empirical and therefore contingent awareness of reality—that is, if existential truths are all empirical, and if all empirical truths are contingent (even though they are true, their falsity would not generate any logical contradiction), then it follows that no existential truths can be necessary truths. Second, the proposition "God exists" cannot be a necessary truth, because, for logical conventionalism, the only truths that are necessary are those that are made true by definition, that is, by the conventional and synonymous equivalences of language, and which are therefore existentially arbitrary in the sense that they are purely formal and thus provide no information whatever about the reality or existence of anything. It follows, therefore, that the proposition "God exists" cannot be a necessary proposition since it purports to give the very sort of information about existence which necessary propositions, as purely conventional, cannot provide. More pointedly, the claim that "God exists" is a necessary truth is, for logical conventionalism, a clear contradiction in terms.

In this same context of logical theory, there emerges a serious question as to whether the proposition "God exists" is a genuinely meaningful and informative assertion. Of course, it *purports* to be meaningful and informative; but it is a necessary characteristic of every genuinely informative and determinate assertion that its particularity and definiteness of meaning exclude some conceivable states of empirical affairs in the sense that, if these states were the case, they would count against the original assertion. So if there is nothing that an assertion denies (nothing which, if it were the case, would count against the truth of the assertion), then there is equally nothing that the assertion affirms. For anything to be the case, other things, which might conceivably be the case, must be excluded—to affirm anything is to negate whatever would be inconsistent with that affirmation. But the proposition that God exists is commonly interpreted, by those who seriously believe it true, either in such a way that there are no conceivable states of affairs which, if they were actual, would render that proposition false by being logically inconsistent with it—or, alternatively, in such a way that, although there are conceivable states of affairs which would indeed militate against the proposition, there are none which would count decisively against it. It is a notoriously well-known device of religious believers to argue that, no matter what happens, no matter how bad the appearances are, God exists anyway. With the prophet Habakkuk the poetically inclined believer is ready to declare:

> For though the fig tree hold no fruit, nor vines their product yield:
> And though the olive bear no shoot, nor harvest fill the field:
> Though fleeting time my flock destroy, and herds no more endure:
> Yet God the Lord shall be my joy—Rejoice!
> I am secure!

(February 1972)

But if in this way the proposition that God exists is understood to be logically compatible with any conceivable state of empirical affairs, then that proposition is not a genuinely meaningful and informative assertion, since it is not sufficiently determinate to affirm or deny anything. On the other hand, the previous arguments in this section have shown that "God exists" is not a formal logical assertion either. And if all cognitively meaningful assertions must be either empirically or logically determinate, then, since "God exists" is neither of these, it is not a cognitively meaningful assertion, but falls in the class of pseudo-assertions which neither affirm nor deny anything.

In response to these various criticisms of theism from the standpoint of the type of analytic empiricism we have been considering, it seems clear that the fundamental basis of all these criticisms is found in the conventionalist theory of the nature of logical truth and its relation to language. But is such a conventionalism itself a plausible position? On the one hand, necessary truths are propositions whose denial would be logically self-contradictory; but on the other hand, it is claimed that these same truths are merely linguistic conventions or arbitrary linguistic equivalences which are adopted for theoretical and practical utility. However, conventions are precisely arbitrary (they could always be other than they actually are), contingent (if they were different, no contradiction would be entailed), and empirical (propositions expressing conventions are always based on descriptive, factual observation). Hence, if necessary truths are conventional in this way,

---

1. But religious believers commonly interpret "God exists" as consistent with any state of affairs, or at least as not falsifiable by any state of affairs.

2. It then follows that there is nothing that the theistic claim denies and therefore nothing that it affirms either.

B. Thus the claim that God exists is:
1. not a factually informative empirical assertion,
2. and not a formal logical assertion,
3. so that it is a cognitively meaningless pseudo-assertion.

IV. Now the logical conventionalism underlying these criticisms is itself implausible:
A. because conventions are by nature contingent, arbitrary, and empirically arrived at, so that there would then *be* no necessary truths at all, and the distinction between logical and empirical truth would dissolve;

they have all the marks of synthetic *a posteriori* or empirical propositions with which they are supposed to stand in logical contrast—and
it will then follow both that the distinction between logical and empirical truth collapses, and also that the thesis that necessary truths are
conventional is self-contradictory.

There is, of course, no question about the claim that the linguistic
and stipulative symbols which *express* logical truths are conventional—that is not being contested here. But the fact that necessary
truths can always be translated into other linguistic frameworks or
even other systems of symbolic logic without loss of meaning and
significance presupposes that these necessary truths themselves are
logically prior to, and independent of, the various linguistic and symbolic conventions through which they may be asserted. Basic logical
principles or interpretive categories (for example, the law of contradiction, or the principle of ground and consequence) stand true irrespective of the language in which they are expressed, so that it is the
language that is conventional, not the principles and categories themselves. That such principles and categories are *objectively* rather than
merely *linguistically* necessary is further evident from the fact that
their truth status is independent of our wills or preferences, as is not
the case with linguistic conventions in the same sense. It would be
difficult and inconvenient to change the standard usage of the word
table, although it would be possible; but it would be impossible coherently to reject the law of contradiction, so that it would be odd (though
true) even to speak of such a rejection as difficult or inconvenient—
which obviously illustrates the fact that we are in an entirely different
logical realm here. And it is further the case that such basic logical
principles and interpretive categories are embedded in any and all of
the various sets of logical axioms adopted by different systems of
symbolic logic—so that there is always a non-conventional necessity
of logical relationships that function as principles for deriving consequences from the logical primitives of any such system. That objective
logical truth stands behind and pervades the various alternative conventional logical symbolisms is evidenced, finally, by the fact that
logicians themselves recognize various criteria as tests of the adequacy of any given system of symbolic logic. The axioms of a well-
formed system, for example, must be logically consistent with each
other and therefore incapable of generating contradictory logical consequences—and it is clear that such a requirement is not itself merely
conventional but rather objective in its necessity. Whatever the ultimate principles of meaning and intelligibility are, they cannot themselves be constituted through conventional definition, since such
definitions could be adopted only through the use of principles of
intelligibility which are logically prior to all such conventional definitions. One would have to be thinking in accordance with the principle
of contradiction, for example, in order to recognize any meaning as
having a determinateness that excludes its opposite, so that the principle itself logically precedes all convention.

Consider, furthermore, the consequences of logical conventional-

B. because, although
the symbols that ex-
press logical truths are
conventional, those
truths themselves are
not:
1. since these truths
can be translated into
other linguistic sym-
bols without loss of
meaning, so that they
are clearly independ-
ent of the language in
which they are ex-
pressed;

2. since these truths
are independent of
our will and prefer-
ence, while that is not
the case in principle
with linguistic conven-
tions;

3. since the same
basic principles are
embedded in all the
different systems of
symbolic logic;

4. since logicians rec-
ognize logical tests of
adequacy for logical
systems in general, so
that those tests cannot
themselves be arbi-
trarily conventional;

5. and since the ulti-
mate principles of
meaning logically pre-
cede all conventional
definition;

ism for its own theory, for its criticism of theism (or any other metaphysical position), and for the validity of thinking in general. If the conventionalist's own logic is conventional and therefore objectively arbitrary, and if he can argue only in accordance with such a logic, then that will render the thesis of conventionalism itself arbitrary and implausible, since by hypothesis it will be grounded in contingent choice. Again, if the logic which charges theism with inconsistency is itself conventional (or if the principle of contradiction is itself per impossible regarded as conventional), then, since conventions are precisely historically contingent and arbitrary, it will follow that no argument based on such a logic will provide any objective basis for a criticism of theism or any other metaphysical perspective, and there will therefore be no objective way of deciding among such world-view alternatives. Finally, if all thinking depends on logical structure and all logical structure is conventional, then the validity of thinking in general will, by hypothesis, be totally undermined in the objective sense. It will then appear that the conventionalist will be able to take his own conclusions seriously only if he makes them an exception to his own rule and regards his claim as grounded in a logic of that very objective sort which his conventionalism purports to deny. All this brings us back clearly to the sort of synthetic apriorism or moderate rationalism which I have defended earlier and on which, in part, I grounded my first argument for theism. It follows that the notions of logical necessity and logical possibility cannot be plausibly trivialized in the way that the conventionalist insists, and that any criticism of theism based on such conventionalism will be put in serious question.

And what, in the next place, of the nominalism which denies real essences? It is clear at the outset that nominalism and logical conventionalism go hand in hand—for nominalism is precisely the view that general terms are merely conventional tags for similar groups of particular objects, so that such terms have no general or universal objects at all. Yet this thesis itself is intelligible only if its general terms stand for such universal objects as the thesis denies. If it is suggested that the actual objects of these terms are particular entities, then it may be asked in return how these particulars are to be identified apart from the various universal properties they exemplify, or even, more radically, how particulars of any given sort can even exist if there are no objective properties which define the objective essence of that class. Here again one must, unwittingly perhaps, be presupposing real essences in order to render his denial of such essences intelligible to himself—and that seems clearly to be a pervasive inconsistency of the greatest magnitude.

Again, is the concept of necessary existence—a concept which I regard as essential to theism—really self-contradictory? I have already responded to the view that, since existence is not a property, necessary existence cannot be a property of God, by contending that, while existence is not a property (part of the definition) of contingent things, it does not follow that necessary existence cannot be a property of God who, by definition, is not a contingent entity. And I will not here

---

C. because if the basis of all logic were conventional, it would follow:
1. that this claim itself would be arbitrary by its own thesis;

2. that such an arbitrary logic could furnish no objective criticism of any metaphysical thesis;
3. that the validity of thinking in general would be undermined because all thinking involves logical structure.

V. The nominalism conjoined with conventionalism is also implausible:
A. because its own claim is intelligible only if general terms have universal objects;
B. because particular entities could neither exist nor be identified if there were no objective universal properties.

VI. Nor is the concept of necessary existence self-contradictory as claimed:

A. because, so far as this claim has not been previously answered, it depends on the logical conventionalism just criticized;

repeat my argument on this issue as it appears in my earlier discussion of the ontological argument. As for the contention that the proposition "God exists" cannot be a necessary truth, since all existential truths are contingent and empirical: This claim is again itself dependent on the sort of logical conventionalism which I have already criticized above, so that the claim begs the question for its own thesis. Besides, here also it is the case only that existential truths about contingent and empirical matters of fact cannot be necessary truths, but, since the existence of God is, by hypothesis, not a contingent matter of fact, it does not follow that the proposition "God exists" is not a necessary truth. Such a conclusion will follow only from the admittedly arbitrary definitions of logical conventionalism.

B. because, if the claim that God necessarily exists were self-contradictory, so that the claim was necessarily false, the non-existence of God would still not follow, because the critic's own logic stipulates that no existential conclusion (affirmative or negative) can follow from a necessary proposition.

But let us suppose that the critic is right here and that the proposition "God necessarily exists" is self-contradictory. By the hypothesis of logical conventionalism itself, all propositions, to the effect that a given proposition is either consistent or contradictory, are themselves necessary propositions (that is, they are either necessarily true or necessarily false). But the conventionalist maintains also that no necessary proposition, since it is conventional in nature, can entail any existential assertion whatsoever, whether affirmative or negative. Now the proposition that the concept of necessary existence is self-contradictory is, on these terms, a necessary proposition. But if so, as a necessary proposition, it can entail no existential assertion. Hence, if we expand the proposition to the form "The proposition that God exists is a necessary truth, is a self-contradictory proposition," then, by the conventionalist's own logic, we can conclude nothing about the existence or non-existence of God. But, of course, the conventionalist critic here wants us to conclude precisely at least that God does not exist as defined, and perhaps that God cannot exist as defined. Yet neither of these conclusions can legitimately follow if no necessary truth can entail an existential conclusion. Hence, the claim that the concept of God's necessary existence is contradictory will no longer constitute any criticism of theism. The desired criticism will only follow for us if we allow ourselves to drift, imperceptibly to ourselves, between logical conventionalism and logical objectivism; but for logical objectivism, there need be no contradiction whatever in the concept of necessary existence, and hence no criticism of theism as so construed.

VII. It is claimed that the proposition that God exists cannot be a genuinely informative proposition, since there are no conceivable empirical circumstances that could logically count against it, while all informative propositions are empirical and therefore in principle falsifiable.
A. Elaboration of this claim.

A final piece of unfinished business, with the analytic empirical criticism of theism, remains—and that is the claim that the proposition "God exists," as generally interpreted by theistic believers themselves, is not a genuinely informative proposition, because it is commonly construed in such a way that no conceivable states of empirical affairs would count decisively against it, in the sense of constituting a sufficient ground for reasonably declaring the proposition false. It is part of the epistemological context of this criticism to suppose that there are only two classes of cognitively significant assertions: trivially analytic *a priori* statements whose truth value is decidable through the definitions of the terms contained in the statements, so that such propositions are either true or false by their meaning alone and are said to be logically determinate (this is part of the logical convention-alism analyzed above); and synthetic *a posteriori* statements whose truth-value is decidable, at least in principle and either directly or indirectly, through empirical observation, so that such propositions are either true or false on factual grounds external to their meaning and are said therefore to be empirically or factually determinate. Definitionally true (or false) statements of the first class, it is main-tained, will give us no information about reality; and it follows that if a statement is to be informative, it must be an empirical statement grounded in observational data. But empirical statements must, in order to be empirical, be confirmable or falsifiable in principle through conceivable observational data. And it follows that if any statement or proposition is not testable in this way, then it is either a logically determinate statement or a pseudo-statement (that is, a conjunction of words purporting to make an assertion but not actually doing so). In either of these last two cases, the statement (or pseudo-statement) will be non-informative—in the first case because definitionally true statements are conventional and arbitrary, and in the second case because a conjunction of words cannot be informative if it makes no assertion susceptible of being either true or false. Now the statement or proposition "God exists," as interpreted here, does not fall in the class of either logically or empirically determinate statements, and so, of course, it cannot be informative, although it clearly purports to be.

In response to this criticism, I will preface my comments by stating that I have no objection to the thesis that a straightforwardly empirical statement should be in principle confirmable or falsifiable in a limited practical sense on observational grounds. I have added the indicated limitation to take account of the fact that general empirical statements are never more than highly probable and are therefore not character-istically confirmable or falsifiable in a fully decisive fashion that pos-sesses logical finality. In fact, I regard it as wholly reasonable to contend that, for any empirical statement whatever, the grounds for deciding its truth or falsity are never logically decisive but merely practically feasible, since it will always be possible to conceive circum-stances which would alter the decision. Practically speaking, the prop-osition that my wife is in the kitchen is clearly confirmable or falsifiable just by my looking to see; but this is not logically decisive, since I might be dreaming or hallucinating, or I might even be experi-encing a visual failure or malfunction or whatever. So, if we are talking about logically decisive confirmation or falsification, empirical state-ments will not pass the test either. Yet this is not the real issue: For the question is not whether empirical statements are informative by being confirmable or falsifiable on observational grounds, but rather whether there is any plausible reason, in this epistemological context, for insisting that empirical statements are the only class of informative statements. In general, my whole discussion of epistemology, in the extended introduction that began the present work, constitutes the claim that the supposition that all genuinely informative statements are empirical is highly questionable if not actually false. Obviously, I

B. Response to this claim.
1. While empirical statements are practi-cally and in principle confirmable or falsifi-able on observational grounds (though per-haps never with final-ity),

yet the real issue is whether empirical statements are the only class of informa-tive assertions.
2. Such a claim is challenged by my whole previous episte-mology.

a) The verification/ falsification principle itself:

(1) is clearly not an empirical statement in the required sense,

(2) nor is it a logically determinate statement, since it seems to be a descriptive generalization;

(3) if it were logically determinate, it would, by hypothesis, be conventional and arbitrary, and could therefore neither eliminate alternative conventions nor settle any existential question.
b) If logical truth were objective and non-conventional, on the contrary, it would also be informative about reality.
c) But in the conventionalist context it appears that the verification/falsification principle would itself be a pseudo-statement.

2. If logical principles, as objective, are themselves grounded in God as Eternal Reason, then no argument based on such principles could consistently count against the claim that God exists.

cannot here reconstruct that whole prior argument—I am content to let it stand or fall, for any given reflective reader, on its intrinsic merits. But what I can do is to apply that earlier epistemological discussion to the present context.

For convenience, I will call that claim—that all informative statements must be empirical and therefore confirmable or falsifiable in principle on observational grounds—the verification/falsification principle. By hypothesis, the principle must itself be either an empirically determinate or logically determinate thesis, if it is to be cognitively significant (that is, be susceptible of being either true or false). But it is clearly not an empirically determinate statement, since there are, by its own assertion and also in general, no conceivable and determinate states of empirical affairs which could be inconsistent with it or count decisively against it, so that it is a formal requirement which admits of no possible exceptions. On the other hand, there are good reasons for holding that it is not a logically determinate statement either, if it is to be counted as a plausible thesis against its alternatives. In the first place, it appears to be a descriptive generalization about informative statements as empirical, so that it appears to be itself an empirical thesis, although I have already argued that this interpretation is incorrect. In the second place, if the verification/falsification principle is regarded as logically determinate, then, since such propositions are linguistic conventions and therefore logically arbitrary, the principle cannot be used as a plausible objection either against its own logical opposite or against any existential assertion, precisely because no logically determinate truth can eliminate an alternative convention regarding the status of logical truth, and also because no logically determinate truth can, as such, settle any existential question. If, on the other hand, logical truth were objective and non-conventional, then it would follow that its implications could indeed settle certain existential questions; but it would also follow that logical truth was informative about reality and existence. And that is clearly not the view being considered here (although it is in fact the view that I personally hold)—for then it would follow as well that some informative truths were not empirical in the stipulated sense. From all this it appears that the verification/falsification principle is neither empirically nor logically determinate (or if it is the latter, it is not an objection against its alternatives). Is it perhaps the case, then, that it is the very sort of purportedly informative, non-empirical assertion which, as a principle, it claims to be a pseudo-assertion, and is it perhaps therefore itself a pseudo-assertion by its own claim?

Suppose, now, that we revert to my own original argument for God from the possibility of the cosmos. In that context I argued that logical principles, ultimate rational categories, and essences—through which alone a cosmos could exist or be possible—were all best explained in their logical status by being regarded as grounded in God as Eternal Reason or Absolute Mind. If that contention is correct, and if objective logical principles have their ultimate locus in God, so that the principles of logical conceivability themselves imply God as their base, then how could any argument, constructed as it would be through such principles, conceivably count objectively against God's existence, since, if God did not exist, there would be no objective standard of logical conceivability? And let me extend that argument by talking about metaphysical theories in general. Such a comprehensive metaphysical explanation is, by its very nature, characterized by a capacity to provide a harmonious, integrative explanation of all actual and possible experiential facts, so that its adequacy will be precisely proportionate to the extent to which no actual or conceivable state of empirical affairs either is or could be inconsistent with it. Just to the extent that a metaphysical perspective fails to meet this all-inclusive degree of comprehensiveness, to that very extent its plausibility as an ultimate explanation is jeopardized. If we then add to this point an insight derived from my argument to God from the actuality of the cosmos, we get the following result: The fact that all empirical states are contingent (as are truths about them) is the very consideration which leads us beyond the chain of empirical causes and effects, however many may be the links in that chain, to God as their adequate, transcendent, and necessary cause. If a contingent empirical state cannot thus be conceived even to exist without the divine causality, how could the determinate character of any such effect even conceivably count against the existence of God as thus understood, much less count decisively? Yet there is a statable proposition which, if it were true, would count decisively against God's existence, namely, the proposition that "God does not exist." But on my explanation of the basis of logical conceivability, what is statable in this matter-of-fact way is not for that reason ultimately conceivable in any truly coherent sense. For if God did not exist, there would be nothing at all—no entities, no essences, no logical possibilities, and even no propositions, including this one! For myself, then, I can only conclude that the analytic-empirical criticism of theism, through logical conventionalism, provides no enduring basis for a reflective person to withdraw his commitment to the reality of God as that Eternal Reason in which logic, essence, and cosmic possibility have their transcendent locus and ground. This is not to deny that in practice one can certainly think or even act otherwise; but it is to question whether his doing so would be objectively possible if what he thus denied were not in fact the case. It goes without saying that, here too as in previous discussions, the logic is not absolutely final and overwhelming; but that there is any logical possibility at all is the very stake at issue, and in the end the reflective individual must decide whether he can coherently surrender the ground of logical possibility itself.

a) Metaphysical theories are in general plausible precisely to the extent that they provide an adequate explanation of all actual and conceivable states of affairs.

b) If the contingency of all empirical states and truths leads to God as necessary cause, how could any such state or truth count against God, since, if God did not exist, there would simply be nothing at all?

VIII. Hence, the analytic-empirical criticism of theism is clearly indecisive,

although in practice individuals can certainly think otherwise, and the argument, though highly plausible, is not overwhelming.

Metaphysical Naturalism and the Denial of Theistic Transcendence

Now I have argued not merely that the God of theism is the most plausible explanation of the *possibility* of there being any cosmos or

I. Explanation of
metaphysical natural-
ism:
A. Regards the natu-
ral world order as self-
explanatory and there-
fore the only reality.
1. This implies that
matter is the only sub-
stantial reality and
physical force the only
genuine causality.

2. Hence, there is
nothing transcendent,
so that God is either
non-existent or a natu-
ral entity.
B. Dismisses all the
arguments for a tran-
scendent God as both
invalid and indecisive.

C. Raises the question
whether the natural
order of the universe
can be reasonably re-
garded as ultimate.
II. Critical Response:
A. The naturalistic
claim is largely an-
swered by previous
arguments.
1. If the universe is
not even possible with-
out God as the locus
of its possibility,

2. and if the universe
is made up of contin-
gent parts or aspects,
so that the whole is
also contingent,
3. and if such a uni-
verse would have to
be a rationally unintel-
ligible, actually infinite
series of aspects or
successive states,
4. then the universe
requires a transcend-
ent ground.

world order, but also that God, so construed, is required to provide the most adequate account of the *actuality* of the existing cosmos as disclosed to our experience. Metaphysical naturalism, on the contrary, argues that the natural world order requires no transcendent causal ground of any sort, so that nature, taken in its most inclusive sense as the cumulative totality of things and events causally interrelated in space and time, is the only reality. It is further maintained, in such a perspective, that the ultimate constituent elements of all substantially real entities are material or physical in character, so that material force or physical energy is the operative principle of all genuine caus-ality, and whatever appears to be otherwise is either a derivative of physical energy or a determinate form of that energy. On such a view, of course, there is nothing real which transcends the natural order. If there is a God, it will have to be either the material universe itself or some identifiable aspect of it, so that it will be the natural cosmos that explains God and not the other way around. If we consider such a metaphysical naturalism in its broadest scope, it will sweep up into itself the denial of all the arguments for the existence of God which I have discussed—for, on such a view, not only is nature the only reality, but within nature itself purposive explanation is impertinent, and objective value is either an illusion or a dimension of purely natural causality. In this section, I shall concentrate solely on naturalism as an alternative to theistic transcendence, or, to put it otherwise, on the question whether the natural world order can reasonably be con-strued as self-existent and self-explanatory.

A considerable response to this question already emerges from our previous analysis. If God is the ultimate ground of the possibility of any natural world, precisely because he is the transcendent locus of basic rational principles, logical possibility, and the directive selection which explains why this particular natural order exists rather than some other among an indefinitely extended series of logically possible natural orders or universes, then of course it follows both that the universe which actually does exist is neither self-existent nor self-explanatory, and that God is therefore the necessary ground of the *actuality* of that universe as well. If, again, the actual universe is made up of particular and determinate parts causally related to one another either in an order of temporal succession or in an order of contem-poraneous connection, and if those parts are contingent in their reality so that the universe as a whole is contingent, and if an actually infinite series of contingent, causally related entities is, as I have argued, logically unintelligible and even self-contradictory—then it again fol-lows that such a contingent universe, by its very nature, requires a transcendent ground whose existence is necessary, so that the uni-verse itself cannot be the absolutely necessary being or (in religious terms) God. And I have, in fact, previously argued that all these conditions (in linguistic terms, all these if-clauses) are fulfilled in the case of the actual universe, whose existence and general character, I take it, are not here in dispute.

But there is, nevertheless, more that can be said in response to the naturalistic contention that the actual universe requires no causal explanation beyond itself. A naturalistic protagonist, for example, could argue that the crux of my argument to God from the actuality of the world order is the claim that if the world order were self-explanatory, then, since it would constitute an actually infinite series, such a series would have to be logically intelligible—which, however, it is not. But in that case, so the contender might insist, we should have to dismiss much of formal mathematics as the price of the soundness of the argument, since mathematics is replete with various infinite series of the same sort. Well, no, I do not dismiss mathematics, nor is there any need to do so. As elaborated in my original analysis of the argument, I rather contend that the so-called infinite series in mathematics is not the same sort of series as the actually infinite series would be if the universe were identified with such a series. Such a mathematical series is, in fact, an indefinitely extended series with a starting point defined by its principle of construction (different for different series). But the actually infinite series of the hypothesized naturalistic world order is quite different logically, since it has, by its very nature, no defined or even possible starting point—which is the very feature that is at one and the same time both self-contradictory and yet indispensable to the naturalistic world order as extended backward to a past that, by hypothesis, has no beginning. If I am correct about the self-contradictory character of such an actually infinite series, and if the natural universe is an order of temporal succession characterized by change, process, and transition; then it follows that the space-time universe must have had a beginning and therefore also a transcendent necessary cause, so that such a universe cannot itself be the absolutely necessary being or God. To put it succinctly, process and change are incompatible with the nature of ultimate, self-explanatory being, since whatever is in process is for that very reason contingent in its reality.

But from this claim, a critic might contend (indeed, actual critics from Democritus to A. N. Whitehead have contended), a still more significant difficulty arises—for God, as the transcendent causal ground of the contingent natural order, will have to be absolutely changeless and devoid of all process or transition. And how could a changeless first cause be the ground of the existence of a universe which is itself essentially changing and in process without that first cause, contrary to hypothesis, itself changing in the activity of originating the universe? In answer, the relation of the universe to God so construed is, of course, absolutely unique, so that we cannot expect full intelligibility from illustrations based on the relations of contingent things to each other. However, I think the general answer to this question is found in the thesis that it is precisely because God is transcendent and changeless that he can posit the existence of the space-time universe and be both present and causally operative at every point within it. Just as mathematical truths, for example, since they are changelessly independent of space and time, therefore can be fully true and relevant at every point within space-time; so also

B. If it is argued that there are analogous infinite series in mathematics:

1. The answer is that the so-called infinite series in mathematics is in fact an indefinitely extended series, rather than an actually infinite series of the sort involved in a naturalistic view. It is the latter sort of series that is self-contradictory, not the former.

2. It would follow that the space-time universe must have had a beginning (since it is essentially in process) and therefore also a transcendent cause.

C. If it is objected that a changeless causal ground could not originate a changing universe without itself changing:

1. The answer is that it is because God is transcendent and changeless that he can be present and operative at every point in space-time.
2. Illustrations.
   a) mathematical truths.

b) activities made possible by constancy of purpose or intent.

3. Nor does God change in the creation of the universe since the notion of temporal priority is inapplicable to him.

D. If it is objected that the causal principle appealed to in our argument is the imposition of a purely human requirement on objective reality, whereas an empirical principle of causality would be at least equally plausible:
1. The answer is that I have already defended causality as a synthetic *a priori* principle of objective reason.

2. Any argument to the contrary would appeal to just such a principle or else would itself be arbitrary as a purely human requirement.

3. In any case, the notion of causality, as applying only to repeatable sequences in experience, is implausible, since there are no literally repeatable sequences even in experience.

with God as transcendent ground. Or again consider an empirical and therefore admittedly imperfect example: My writing of this book is pervaded by process and change, but that process could neither originate nor continue, much less be brought to completion, without a sustained intent which pervades the whole process in the form of unchanging purpose; analogously, the world order, as a process, could neither originate nor continue without the unchanging divine causality. As for the suggestion that God would have to change in the activity of originating the universe, that contention is based on the confused notion that temporally before the creation of the universe God existed alone without the universe. But that notion is simply incorrect, since space and time have no existence except as forms of contingent being, so that the notion of a temporal priority for God, since by nature he transcends time and space, is clearly incoherent. It appears, then, that rather than the relation between a changeless cause (God) and the changing universe being logically unintelligible, it is rather the case that such a changing universe is itself fully intelligible only through such a relation to such a changeless ground.

Still, a hesitant mind may boggle. What if, as David Hume long since proposed, the notion of rationally adequate causality, presupposed by the argument to God from the actuality of the world order, is a kind of sophisticated illusion, a demand of the puny human intellect rashly assuming its own self-imposed requirements to be fulfilled by objective reality? What if, more humbly, we regard causality as a name for regular and repeatable sequences within empirical experience, so that it is an illegitimate move to transfer from that context where it is at home, so to speak, a limited principle of causal connection which we now expect to apply to the world order as a whole? In a sense, these questions have already been dealt with in my discussion of epistemology, in which I argued that the principle of causality (or of the relation between ground and consequence) is not merely a principle of empirical generalization, but rather a synthetic *a priori* principle of objective reason, a necessary presupposition of all possible thought and being—applicable indeed to empirical connections but in no sense exhaustively grounded in them or explained by them. Any argument to the contrary would inevitably be either wholly arbitrary and relative to mere subjective opinion, or else it would itself be grounded in, and in fact illustrate, the very principle of *a priori* causality which it purported to dismiss. So it is not a question of our puny human intellect but rather of objective reason. Or if it is a question of puny human intellect, then that sword will cut both ways by calling its own conclusions about causality into equally serious question. After all, it is the same puny intellect that proposes a purely empirical notion of causality.

Nor can we take with final seriousness the suggestion that, since the origin of the universe is, by hypothesis, an absolutely unique occurrence, a principle of causality which applies only to repeatable sequences within experience is inapplicable to it. For, strictly speaking, there are no literally repeatable sequences even in empirical experience. Every occurrence has a uniqueness about it which distinguishes it from all other occurrences, else it would be impossible to differentiate such occurrences from one another. And, hence, all inferences from one part of experience to another presuppose an analogical relation between those parts—a relation which is only different in degree and specifiable type from the analogy between all the parts of experience, on the one hand, and the transcendental ground of the whole experienced world order, on the other. And if, as I have claimed, the principle of causality is an ultimate category of reason, then it is *ipso facto* applicable to every conceivable object of rational apprehension. I conclude, therefore, that the objections to the argument for God from the actuality of the world order are at least inconclusive and pose no insuperable obstacle to the belief in the transcendent reality of God on this ground. If the world exists, so also does God!

E. Hence, it remains reasonable to contend that if the world exists, God exists as its ground.

The Chance Hypothesis and the Irrelevance of Purposive Explanation

Whenever, as in my third argument concerning the nature of God as disclosed in certain observed qualities of the universe, anyone attempts to argue from the pervasive and multiple facets of adaptive order which unquestionably characterize the space-time universe, perhaps the most widely posed objection is the suggestion that, while the presence of such adaptive order is obvious, there is no need to appeal to transcendent divine purpose and intelligently operative will to explain this order, since—given the ultimate material constituents of the universe and supposing their constant interaction through a past eternity—all this adaptive order could conceivably have occurred by chance without any operative factor of intelligent direction at all. Now to a larger extent my previous arguments, if plausible at all, have rendered this hypothesis of cosmic chance virtually impertinent. For the chance theory to be workable at all, a naturalistic explanation of the existence of the world order would have to be presupposed; but I have already tried to show that neither the possibility nor the actuality of the world order is plausibly explicable on naturalistic terms—so that, if I am correct about this claim, the chance hypothesis becomes irrelevant precisely because the dependence of the natural order on divine causality is already solidly grounded before the question of adaptive order even arises. If, then, the cosmos is already inexplicable without God as Eternal Reason and Ultimate Cause, it is far more reasonable to regard adaptive order as a clue to the nature of divine causality than to attempt to explain such order without reference to divine causality at all. It is quite true, of course, that if we argue in this fashion, we make the successive phases of our cumulative argument for God logically dependent on each other in the sense that the later phases are fully plausible only in conjunction with the earlier ones.

I. It is often argued that adaptive order in the universe is explainable by chance random motions without any appeal to purposive divine direction.
A. But if previous arguments show that the universe can be neither possible nor actual without divine causality, then it is preferable to regard significant order as a clue to the nature of God.

B. This response makes the purposive argument dependent on those previous arguments logically, but that merely illustrates the cumulative unity of the case for theism.

But there is no reason to regret this logical dependence at all, since it simply shows that the case for theism is not so many separately dangling argumentative threads, but rather a closely interwoven dialectical fabric with a strength which the combined threads serve to enhance.

Nevertheless, it is important to discuss the chance hypothesis on its own territory as well. Our teleological (purposive) argument moves from the complex fact of a particular order in the universe to intelligent will as an indispensable aspect of the cause of that order. But suppose the order had been different: Would it not be the case that, whatever the arrangement of the universe, the probability of that arrangement occurring, as over against all the other logically possible arrangements, is almost infinitely improbable in terms of chance? Or to put it positively: Is not any arrangement of the elements of the world equally as probable as any other, in terms of chance? Now if that is the case, so the argument runs, how is it plausible to argue from any particular order to intelligent will as its cause? That would be plausible only if there were some possible arrangements that would not require intelligent will as their explanation. And that, in turn, would be the case only if some arrangements were far less probable than others—but that is clearly contrary to the presumably obvious fact that, in terms of chance, any arrangement whatever is as probable as any other, and each, in relation to the others, is almost infinitely improbable. Now I submit that the clearer this objection to intelligent causality becomes, the less plausible it seems as an objection, for the objection admits that any arrangement of the elements of the world, in terms of pure chance, is almost infinitely improbable. And if that is the case, then it appears also to be the case that chance cannot reasonably be invoked as an explanation of *any* possible arrangement whatever. It is part of reflective thought to embrace the most probable rather than the least probable explanation. So we can turn the argument around and claim that the explanation of any particular arrangement of things in terms of directive intelligence is almost infinitely probable. Given such a state of things, is there any plausible reason to hesitate in deciding which way to go in understanding the cause of adaptive order in the universe?

The philosopher David Hume and his philosophical successors here have claimed that we are only entitled to infer intelligent causality for adaptive order on the basis of a past experience in which order and purposive design have been conjoined; and since we have, by the very nature of the case, no such experience of conjunction in the instances of adaptive order observed in nature, it is illegitimate to make the inference. Now this objection is virtually the same as one we confronted in discussing the empirical concept of causality in the previous section—for it assumes that causality can only be interpreted as referring to repeatable sequences in experience. Hence, all the criticisms I cited previously in regard to this notion are fully applicable here as well, and I will not undertake to repeat them. But I will raise the question whether, even in empirical experience, we legitimately infer

II. If it is argued that any arrangement of elements in the universe is equally improbable in terms of pure chance, so that no particular order can provide a clue to the causal ground of the universe:

A. The answer is that the premise of this argument acknowledges that the chance explanation of any particular order is almost infinitely improbable.
B. Hence, we can argue that the explanation through directive intelligence is almost infinitely probable.

III. As to the claim that order and purpose can be conjoined only on the basis of their experienced conjunction in previous experience:
A. The limitation of causal inference to repeatable sequences has already been questioned in the previous section.

intelligent causality only on the basis of a past experience in which adaptive order and purposive design have been conjoined for us in direct observation. On any normal reading of events, that claim seems obviously false. In countless instances on a virtually daily basis, we make precisely such inferences without any such direct observation. When there is any point in doing so, I legitimately conclude that ballpoint pens, watches, television sets, automobiles, refrigerators, and the like are all products of intelligent causality, although none of these cases has ever come under my direct observation, and I would clearly be right in regarding it as absurd for anyone to claim that I could not so regard such things without that direct observation. In fact, I would suppose it ridiculous to engage in such direct observation unless I was simply fascinated by such processes. No, the evidence for intelligent causality is based on the complexity of conspiring causes to produce a significant result of assignable value. And if I can infer from the intricate structure of a watch to the conclusion that it is a product of intelligent causality, I may as legitimately infer by analogy to the same conclusion about the intricate structure of the vertebrate eye. Adaptive contrivance provides a solid basis of inference in both cases. And if I proceed to compare my eye with even the most sophisticated camera that human intelligence has produced, the intricacy of the latter will clearly be dwarfed by the far more involved intricacy of the former, so that the inference to intelligent causality will be vastly more plausible in the natural case than in the case of the human artifact.

B. In any case, we regularly infer intelligent causality even without past experience of association, except in an analogous sense.

C. The real evidence for intelligent causality consists in the complexity of conspiring causes to produce a significant result of value.

But here the critic may appeal to a naturalistic evolutionary hypothesis to augment his case. Why not suppose that instances of natural contrivance, such as the vertebrate eye, have all been produced through a series of minute and successive variations over many generations, in such a way that the phases of development represent stages of increasing adaptive advantage to the organism with the result that such stages are preserved while less advantageous variations tend to die out? In that case, we would have a series of proximate causes which would together explain the occurrence of all cases of natural contrivance and therefore render any appeal to intelligent causality unnecessary. Now in response to this proposal I wish to make it clear at the outset that I have no intention of criticizing the evolutionary theory here as a biological hypothesis, since I have neither the interest nor the professional competence required for such a task—and in any case I would regard this task as quite impertinent for my purposes. The basic question is whether a series of intermediate proximate causes makes purposive explanation through intelligent causality superfluous; and I submit that it does not. Suppose, for example, that a physiologist were able to offer a complete descriptive analysis of all the bodily operations involved in the activity of writing this sentence, even to the extent of providing a detailed analysis of neurochemical changes in the brain and of brainwave functioning. Would that analysis of proximate, organic causes offer a complete explanation of the cause of my writing, so as to render explanation in terms of conscious purposive direction irrelevant? On any philosophically

IV. As to the claim that all cases of adaptive contrivance could be explained through the evolutionary production and preservation of mutations with adaptive advantages without any need for intelligent causality:

A. The issue here is not the evolutionary theory as a biological hypothesis, but rather whether proximate causes make purposive explanation impertinent.
B. The latter is clearly not the case, as any admittedly purposive human activity illustrates.
1. An extended example provided by my writing of these sentences.

undistorted account of the matter, the answer would almost surely be no. In fact, I am aware, through whatever physiological media involved (processes of which I am largely unaware), that I am consciously and purposively directing the whole activity and operation through my sustained intent to communicate certain ideas in this way. So it appears that explanation in terms of proximate, intermediate factors not only does not offer any complete explanation of the basic cause of my writing, but also provides no contribution whatever to the understanding of that fundamental purposive ground. For myself, of course, I am directly and introspectively aware of this purposive direction. For a separate observer of my activity, the same conclusion, though with a somewhat lesser degree of cognitive certainty, could be reached by inference from the complexity of conspiring factors to produce a significant result—so that for him the observed operation of proximate causes does provide, not indeed a complete explanation in physiological terms, but a reasonable basis for inferring a purposive cause. If I myself were asked to explain why I was writing or what the reason or cause of my writing was, I would simply assume the physiological media, and my entire answer to such an inquirer would be cast in purposive causal terms with no reference whatever to proximate physiological media. Quite analogously, in those cases of natural contrivance to which I have repeatedly referred, even a virtually complete analysis of physiological or material factors would in no sense eliminate the need for a purposive explanation even on the most radical evolutionary hypothesis. Such a physical analysis would (or should) then be viewed as a partial account of the means through which conscious purpose operated to produce the observable significant results, so that, in religious terms, evolutionary process would not eliminate God but rather serve as his instrument.

2. Hence, by analogy, even an exhaustive account of proximate causal factors through evolution does not eliminate the need for explanation in terms of intelligent causality.

C. If we grant the evolutionary theory in its strongest biological form:
1. Even though this concession is problematic, still it may be made for the sake of argument.

There are, of course, further ways of strengthening this general conclusion. Suppose we grant the naturalistic evolutionary theorist his wildest dream here and concede that all the cases of natural contrivance in the biological realm came about through successive variations in structure, each of which, to insure survival, possessed a recognizable gain in adaptive advantage. This is a gigantic assumption but nevertheless a necessary one (at least for most of the variations)—for if the changes thus produced had no such advantage, or had even a disadvantage, then, by such an evolutionary hypothesis, the forms so characterized would tend to be eliminated in the struggle to survive. It is indeed difficult even to imagine a succession of such steps that would account for the emergence of an eye, since many plausible candidates for these variations would seem to provide their possessor with no such advantage and might even be a positive hindrance. And there certainly is no fossil or other paleontological evidence, I am told, that even approaches such a complete list of advantageous variations for even a single hypothesized instance of such supposed evolutionary origin (although I do not insist even mildly on this point, since a well-founded judgment about it is quite beyond my professional competence). But let us not cavil about the concession even so; rather, let us grant the whole hypothesis for the sake of discussion. I should, then, certainly think that the broad proliferation of such adaptively advantageous variations—sufficient in number and extent to account for all the observable cases of natural contrivance in the biological realm— would itself constitute one of the most striking and impressive arguments for inferring the necessity of purposive direction, as an explanation, that it would be possible even to imagine. To suppose that all this took place by chance would be quite analogous to supposing that all the words, sentences, and paragraphs constituting this book had come into being where there were no such elements and had found their way, unguided by purpose, into their present form. If anything, the overwhelming strength of the inference to teleology or purpose, in the case of the evolutionary hypothesis, is by comparison so much more impressive than the case of the book that the latter would be cast into the shade, while the evolutionary hypothesis would take its place in the unambiguous light of the noonday sun—since here we are dealing, not with a single result like a book, but with that vast multiplicity of life forms which make up the entire biological realm of the natural world order. It is not therefore surprising that an intellectual giant like F. R. Tennant should have concluded that an evolutionary account of natural contrivance, far from calling teleology into question, serves instead to enhance it quite beyond any imaginable alternative example.

> 2. It would follow that the sum total of all these adaptive advantages would itself constitute virtually the most impressive case for teleology or intelligent causality imaginable.

There are any number of additional caveats registered as objections to inferring purposive direction from natural contrivance, and it is beyond my time and endurance to discuss them all, although I have made an effort in this direction in my earlier work, *The Resurrection of Theism*, by trying to discuss most of the objections I was aware of in the literature at the time. But to spin out, as it were, a few examples of this sort: Why, it has been asked, could it not be conceded that purposive explanation is called for, but that in cosmic teleology we are dealing with unconscious purpose or impersonal intelligent will, rather than with the conscious, personal intelligence of God? In answer, it seems plausible to contend that phrases such as unconscious purpose or impersonal intelligence analyze out into contradictions, if self-conscious awareness is essential to purposive direction and purposive direction is itself essential to intelligent operation. Alternatively, we could argue that it is precisely the evidence of purpose where there is no obvious empirical conscious direction of a natural sort (the parts of the eye clearly do not consciously cooperate together to make vision possible) that leads us to the supposition of purposive direction on the part of the person of God.

> V. Some supplementary objections.

> A. The purpose underlying natural contrivance could not be unconscious or impersonal, since that notion is incoherent.

Again, it has been claimed that the progressive and gradual realization of purpose through the use of complex means would be inconsistent with omnipotence as an attribute of God, since, if God is truly omnipotent, he could presumably act without means. But such an objection not only bypasses all the evidence for God as the necessary ground of all contingent being, it also fails to take account of the fact that for God to act at all, in positing the existence of any particular

> B. Nor is the use of means by God, in fulfilling his purpose, inconsistent with divine omnipotence rightly understood:

1. since any activity of God would be such a means, and the denial of this possibility would mean that God could do nothing;
2. since all these means are wholly grounded in divine causality.

C. Nor is the apparently limited extent of the realization of God's purpose any serious basis for significant criticism.

D. Nor finally is the analogy between divine and human intelligence so remote as to be meaningless, since the differences, though clear, may be viewed as logically accidental, rather than essential.

VI. Hence, I conclude that chance is not an appropriate substitute for purposive divine direction.

and determinate entity, would be to produce a means to the general end of his creating a contingent world order at all—so that, in the end, a God that cannot use means in process to achieve his ends is a God who cannot act in creation at all, or, more pointedly, a God who can do nothing. If, furthermore, as theism posits, all the means and ends of creation are aspects of God's timelessly necessary plan, then the implementation of these means and ends, wholly grounded as it is in the divine causality, puts no constraint on the omnipotence of God when that omnipotence itself is correctly understood.

I shall barely hesitate to answer the objection that if the purpose of God ultimately is the production and progressive development in righteousness of finite rational and moral beings like ourselves, then the very limited extent of the fulfillment of that goal is unbecoming to the Supreme Reality of God—as if quantity were in any sense a pertinent or relevant factor here, when in fact a single person possesses an intrinsic though contingent worth which makes his existence alone an appropriate end for God, and when, in fact, we do not know either how many persons among us are in some state of that progress or how many other orders of finite rational and moral selves God may have created.

Nor will I, finally, say much about the contention that intelligence in God must differ so radically from human intelligence as to make the analogy meaningless—for it is clearly open to us to hold that it is only accidentally, and not essentially, that human intelligence differs from divine intelligence. It is, for example, essential to intelligence that it have a structure in which complex means are, through determinate qualities of that intelligence itself, consciously directed toward the fulfillment of ends that are selectively willed. But it is not essential to intelligence that it be limited by time or characterized by process and succession—these last, and others like them, are accidental features of intelligence involved in our contingent human circumstance. Hence, the notion of the creation of man in the personal image of God, though it is a bold notion, is clearly neither absurd nor meaningless.

From all this I conclude, with sustained rational confidence tempered by what I hope is appropriate humility, that chance does not offer a plausible rational alternative for the explanation of natural contrivance, and that purposive direction, with the transcendent divine selfhood it entails, is the more credible explanation of the whole range of ordered adaptations which characterize the space-time universe, so far as it is accessible to human surveillance and understanding.

Emergent Evolutionism and the Naturalistic Explanation of Mind

In my argument from the unique features of human selfhood to God as the most plausible explanatory ground of that selfhood, I have made the claim, for a variety of reasons already developed in part, that the distinctive selfhood of man could not be reasonably or adequately explained as the product of purely physical or material causes, whether inert and inorganic or living and organic. But I have no intention of glossing over the enormous structure of contrary opinion without comment and critical discussion. It has certainly been widely argued both that life is explicable in terms of a sufficiently complex arrangement of what otherwise would be inert elements, and that mind or selfhood, even in the fullest sense, can be explained as an emergent from physical and biological components, so that any appeal to a transcendent spiritual ground of human selfhood becomes superfluous. It is no part of my present purpose to analyze the first element of this thesis, since the question whether life is explicable in physical terms within a limited natural context is both beyond my professional competence to discuss and, in any case, inconsequential for my argument. But whether selfhood is explicable in some analogous way is quite another question, the answer to which is crucial to my purpose.

If mind or selfhood is to be regarded as explicable in physical and biological terms, then it is apparent that the explanation will follow one or the other of two possible directions. Either finite mind will be interpreted as itself a wholly physiological phenomenon, though admittedly a uniquely and intricately complex one—or, alternatively, it will be regarded as a kind of resultant or by-product of physical processes, though not itself substantially physical in nature but perhaps even non-physical or immaterial. Views of the former type are commonly designated as varieties of metaphysical *materialism*, while those of the latter sort are described by various names such as *functionalism* (mental operations are a function of the physical organism though not themselves physical) or *epiphenomenalism* (mental operations are a sort of non-physical resultant of organic processes—floating, as it were, on their surface). Both types of perspective regard mind as a kind of emergent development from the physical and biological levels, and hence the phrase *emergent evolutionism* which, however, also usually connotes the development of the biological realm itself from non-living, purely physical elements. The materialistic view of mind, in turn, has been closely aligned in some of its versions with the classical psychological theory of behaviorism.

While materialism has had a long and complex history—extending back at least to the ancient Greek thinker Democritus who was a contemporary of Plato in the fifth and fourth centuries B.C.—I will simply bypass this historical paraphernalia and speak only of two currently significant types of materialism, on the hypothesis that all these views are basically variations on the same theme. One such perspective is generally referred to as *central state materialism* because it maintains that mental events are numerically identical with neurochemical states and processes of the central nervous system and especially of the brain—so that in fact there is no such entity as the mind apart from that central system itself, and it is rather the case that the term *mind* stands for a particular set of states and processes

I. The thesis that human selfhood is most adequately explained in terms of God as causal ground has been widely challenged.
A. Both life and mind are said to be fully explicable as the product of ultimately physical components:
1. The question of the mode of life's origin is impertinent in this context;

2. but the question of selfhood is crucial.

B. Attempted explanations of mind in physical and biological terms are of two main types:

1. *materialism*, which regards mental phenomena as wholly physiological in nature;
2. and *functionalism*, which regards these phenomena as non-physical by-products of physiological processes.

II. Two currently significant types of materialism are discussed as samples.
A. *Central state materialism*.
1. This view:
a) regards mental events as numerically identical with neuro-chemical states of the central nervous system,
b) and claims there is no such entity as the mind in any other sense.

2. Among supporting arguments are the following:
a) Since mental states can be drastically altered by externally in- duced changes in the central nervous sys- tem, it is plausible to explain these states as numerically identical with the components of that system,

so that there is no need to view the mind as an immaterial ent- ity.

(1) But since mental events can be initially identified only by a di- rect inner awareness which discerns no physiological compo- nents whatever, it seems clear that what is established here is not an identity but an extensive correlation between mental events and physical processes.

(2) In fact, since these correlations them- selves can be origi- nally established only through the testimony of an experiencing subject,

and since such a sub- ject's inner awareness involves no knowledge of physical compo- nents, while a physio- logical description discloses no mental contents either, it ap- pears that the identity thesis is seriously problematic.

which are intrinsic to the system indicated. A strongly supportive line of argument for this position is found in the fact that mental states are experimentally capable of being influenced and altered by intro- ducing modifications of a physical sort in the central nervous system. Mental experiences usually induced by external stimuli, such as ob- jects of vision, can be produced by directly stimulating parts of the brain without the presence in the field of sensation of the normal stimuli; and it is further the case that damage or disruption to the central nervous system introduces drastic alteration in so-called men- tal functions. Such innocuous and virtually indisputable descriptions are then regarded as most adequately explained by the numerical identity thesis that mental events and neurochemical states or changes in the brain are precisely the same thing under two different rubrics. And, of course, if this thesis is correct and the distinctive activities attributable to the self in its mental aspect are simply organic physical processes, then clearly the destiny and nature of the mind is the same as that of the physical organism—so that there will be no reason here for supposing that mind is a unique immaterial entity which, as contin- gent, requires explanation in terms of an immaterial and essentially spiritual cause or, in religious terms, God as absolute mind.

Yet, as I already indicated in my earlier exposition, this sort of position is not without serious difficulties. For one thing, the very way in which the theory is inevitably stated presupposes that mental events can be clearly identified, both by the theorist and by any reflective individual, only through a process of introspection or direct inner awareness which involves no awareness in that context of any physical or purely biological components whatever. For it is only on such a supposition that the suggestion that what appear as mental events are really identical with physical, neurochemical events is even intelligible. But the same supposition clearly indicates that these mental events are *not* experienced as identical with physical processes of any sort, so that what is really involved here is not an identity at all but rather an extensive correlation between mental events and physical proc- esses. The further fact that such correlations can only be established initially by the testimony of the experiencing subject, on the basis of his own inner awareness, makes the notion of such a correlation even more plausible. In fact, apart from such correlative testimony by an experiencing subject about his own inner mental experiences, not a single, original correlation between mental events and states of the central nervous system has ever been clearly established by any inves- tigator—although it is of course true that once general patterns of correlation have been established in this basic way, future predictions of such limited correlations can be made with considerable success from each side. If, therefore, an experiencing subject can have a detailed knowledge of the contents of his own mental awareness without any knowledge whatever of physical and biological compo- nents, and if a physiologist can have a detailed descriptive knowledge of states and processes of the central nervous system without any knowledge whatever of mental and psychological contents except from the corroborative testimony of an experiencing subject, then it appears to follow that the identity thesis—which regards mental ingredients as numerically identical with physical components—is in serious trouble.

But there is a well-known response to the type of criticism I have been developing, in the form of what is often called the *translation thesis argument*. This argument begins by acknowledging that the conventions of natural language and descriptive psychology for describing mental events are in fact throughout different from the correlative linguistic conventions of biological and physical science for describing bodily events, and especially for describing states and processes of the central nervous system. But then it is claimed that this admitted difference may easily be understood as a contrast, not between numerically distinct types of events, but rather between two distinct systems of linguistic convention for describing the numerically identical or same events—so that the failure of reciprocal knowledge (no knowledge of any mental event from a knowledge of correlative physical events, and *vice versa*), and the fact that mental events and physiological states have what appear to be mutually exclusive attributes (a thought, for example, has no velocity or spatial direction, while a motion or physical change does) need not be interpreted so as necessarily to imply that mind events and brain events are numerically distinct in any given case. Both of these circumstances are at least as easily interpreted on the supposition of an extensive difference of linguistic convention; and, in that case, the problem will be to continue both introspective and physical analysis until either a direct identity between mental event and physical event is disclosed, or rules of translation are discovered which permit confident movement between the two languages without essential dependence on the two distinct sets of observations and reports. Either of these results would, it is claimed, establish the identity thesis on which central state materialism rests.

In response to this ingenious proposal, I concede at the outset that the physiological dimension of this suggestion is so enmeshed in the details of anatomical complexity and technical jargon that it is quite beyond my competence to comprehend it, much less to analyze it, with my rather limited knowledge of anatomy. But fortunately that dimension is not crucial for what is being claimed in the translation thesis argument. In fact, the greater anatomical complexity simply expands the biological base of which I may, in fact, be completely ignorant, while still possessing a pervasively extended knowledge of my own mental states for the mere price of attentive and disciplined description. In any case, some provisional results seem clear enough. First, the suggestion that further introspection and physical analysis might ultimately expose the requisite identity seems highly questionable, since, by hypothesis and for lack of any neutral conventions for referring to the events in question, such further probing would necessarily involve the use of the admittedly distinct systems of linguistic convention—so that there would be, in principle, no plausibly identifi-

b) The *translation thesis argument* is a response to these difficulties.
(1) While it is true that the languages of mental description and physiological analysis are wholly different, it is still possible that these distinct languages are two ways of describing the same events.

(a) If that is the case, then some of the difficulties previously explained are readily accounted for as the expected consequences of the contrasting schemes of linguistic convention. *(b)* Hence either a directly discernible identity, or workable translation rules between the two languages, would establish the general identity thesis.
(2) Now, although the physiology of the central nervous system is exceedingly complex, an appropriate response is possible without anatomical detail.

(a) Since analysis must be carried on in one or the other of the two languages, the proposed possibility of a discernible identity is very implausible.

(b) As for rules of translation:
i) No significant progress has been made here;

ii) and if the identity thesis were established, there would be no unprejudiced way of deciding between mental and physical explanation.

iii) Also, the whole translation project seems impossible in principle, since neither a psychologist nor a physiologist could accommodate data proper to the contents of the other science.

B. *Linguistic behaviorism.*
1. This view denies that there are any inner contents of mental awareness, and affirms that what are wrongly called mental events are really modes of bodily behavior.

able way of recognizing any component of either mental or physical analysis as constituting the desired identity between mental and physical events in a particular case. Second, it is equally apparent that no really significant progress for establishing translation rules between the two languages has been achieved in any such way as to make direct inference possible without the extended use of analogies based on originally separate introspective and observational data. But suppose, however, that, in spite of what looks like an impossibility in principle, we actually found our Rosetta Stone and established the identity thesis. How, without sheerly arbitrary prejudice, would we decide that the real event was physical or biological, rather than immaterial and mental? How, in other words, would we decide between metaphysical idealism (what appear to be physical entities are really a disguised form of mental reality) and metaphysical materialism (what appear to be mental entities are really a disguised form of physical reality)? If we follow the translation model, we might indeed get a quite different result by reflecting that just as the same thing said in German or in French is itself neither German nor French except in a logically accidental sense, so the real event, describable in either mental language or physical language, would itself be neither mental nor physical except in a logically accidental sense. And then there would be the still more difficult task of gaining a genuine, if provisional, knowledge of this *tertium quid* or third thing without serious distortion by the prejudices embodied in existing linguistic conventions.

The fact seems to be, however, that the whole translation project bears the marks of impossibility in principle. Physical analysis will in principle discover only physical constituents—a radical transition in kind would be inconsistent with the whole project of physical description. And, by parity of reasoning, a mental analysis will in principle discover only mental constituents—a radical transition in kind would be equally unintelligible here as well. It is not that these tasks are so complex and difficult that we have not the stomach for them, however true that might be in any case. It is rather that, from the outset, the most sophisticated psychological introspector among us has no expectation whatever of stumbling onto an electron as an ingredient of mental contents—and the most disciplined physiologist among us has equally no notion at all of finding a concept or feeling among the contents of anyone's brain. To suppose otherwise would be rather like arguing that if one counted far enough, he would at last reach the highest number; or perhaps even like arguing that if one really understood the physics of light, sunsets or sunrises would never again appear as red or orange in his field of vision.

But a still bolder move is possible for the materialist or behaviorist. He can go on to question whether the whole problem has been raised correctly, or whether it may alternatively be the case that there are in fact really no introspectable contents of inner awareness that could even be identified as mental events—so that what we mistakenly refer to as mental occurrences are really modes of bodily behavior of one sort or another, a kind of talking to oneself either audibly or under one's breath, as it were. Theories of this sort have been quite common in various psychological perspectives and are generally referred to as varieties of behaviorism; but it is to a philosophical version of behaviorism that I wish to direct my attention. The version I have in mind is the one connected with the so-called ordinary-language movement in the contemporary tradition which I designate as analytic empiricism. The chief representatives of this *linguistic behaviorism* are thinkers in the vein of Ludwig Wittgenstein and Gilbert Ryle. It has been traditionally supposed, as I have previously indicated, that mental words (such as *think, remember, conceive, imagine,* and so on) refer to the contents of an inner awareness which is immediately accessible to each individual in his own case—although it is clear that no person under normal circumstances has this same direct access to any other individual's inner awareness, but can only judge of it by inferences from that individual's publicly observable behavior—what he says, how he acts, what his facial expressions disclose, and so on. But suppose that this tradition is mistaken and that mental words refer instead either to publicly observable modes of bodily behavior themselves or, in certain cases, to dispositions or tendencies to perform in certain publicly observable bodily ways when an individual is triggered to do so by appropriate circumstances. When, for example, I say that I know something ("saying" itself is, at least in principle, a publicly observable act), that means that, when I am prompted to do so, I can give a certain speech, or make certain marks on a sheet of paper, or generally give a certain publicly observable performance—and similarly for all other mental words. If this explanation were correct, then there would really be no individually private mental experiences, and the all-but-inevitable tendency for each of us to assume such a stream of exclusive inner awareness for himself would be a sort of linguistic confusion or category mistake. It would follow, furthermore, that so-called mental events were in fact numerically identical with those bodily dispositions and processes which, in our confusion, we had wrongly supposed were correlates or, in certain cases, even effects of inner mental activities.

Highly persuasive arguments have been proposed to support such a behavioristic explanation. None of us claims to have a wholly private language for referring to or attending upon our supposedly private mental states. On the contrary, we refer to these events in the vocabulary of some common conventional language such as English or French, although we can, of course, coin words for ourselves which function as synonyms for complex units in the conventional language, and we may even sense a peculiar individual flavor for conventional terms themselves. If, then, the words we use to refer to mental events are, on the whole, elements of a common language, and if, as seems obvious, each of us learns these words by imitating other persons and correlating sounds or marks with observable entities and modes of behavior, does it not follow that these terms actually refer to such publicly observable contents and not to inner mental events which

a) While mental words are commonly viewed as referring to inner mental contents directly accessible only to the subject experiencing them,

such terms are better understood as referring to either publicly observable modes of bodily behavior or to dispositions of the organisms to engage in certain types of such behavior on proper stimulus.

(1) Hence, there would be no private mental experiences— that supposition would be a confusion; (2) and so-called mental events would be identical with bodily dispositions and processes.

b) Among arguments for this view: (1) On the whole, each person refers to his supposed private mental events through a conventional, common language, the elements of which have been learned through imitative behavior.

(a) This fact suggests that such terms refer to these behavioral components.

are, by hypothesis, incapable of public observation? And if anyone claims that these words thus learned stand for mental events but are not identical with them, so that thinking and verbalizing are not the same, then there is a simple experiment that each person can perform for himself, which may convince him otherwise. First, try thinking through any thought by means of the symbols or words of some conventional language such as English or French. Now try thinking through the same thought without using any language at all, construing language to include any mode of thought which employs referential signs or symbols as vehicles of expression. It is presumed, of course, that anyone who construes language broadly enough and is perfectly honest with himself will fail in his attempt to perform the second part of the experiment. He will fail, not because he does not try hard enough or probe deeply enough, but rather because it is impossible, in principle, to think any thought without employing some system of referential signs—or in other words, a language. But, in that case, it would appear to follow that thought and language are not two different processes but the same process. And since language is invariably learned initially by connecting sounds and/or marks with modes of publicly observable behavior, does it not also follow that mental reference words actually stand for modes of publicly observable behavior and not for unique inner processes accessible in principle only to the individual subject of experience?

(b) Such a claim is strengthened by the fact that thought cannot be carried out except through the use of linguistic or referential signs whose significance is learned through association with modes of publicly observable behavior.

Let us suppose, however, that the traditional distinction between inner mental events and overt bodily behavior is correct, and that there is an identifiable set of overt bodily acts which, for any given person, are to be regarded as intelligently directed precisely because these acts are the sustained effects of inner, conscious mental operations such as formulating thoughts in propositions, making decisions of will, and recognizing and espousing appropriate criteria and goals for various types of overt activity which would be put into operation through the causal efficacy of these alleged inner mental processes. According to our analytic empirical critics, this proposed description is fraught with insoluble perplexities. To begin with, although most of us uncritically suppose that we do direct certain bodily activities in this way, none of us can even begin to give any account, either to ourselves or anyone else, of how these posited mental processes actually produce effects on bodily behavior. I decide, through a mental decision of will, to raise my arm and signal the bus driver to stop for me, and, barring any physiological malfunction, my arm goes up and makes the requisite motion. But how exactly do I get my arm to perform this way through the causal efficacy of my decision of will? If I actually do this as described and I am the only one eligible, through private inner scrutiny, to discern how I do it, should not the mode of this causality be clearly evident to me just by virtue of the all-but-countless instances of this sort of connection which fill even a single day of my life? Since, on the contrary, I have no knowledge of this causality, perhaps the whole account is mistaken, so that my arm moves, not as an effect of mental decisions, but through the actuali-

(2) The traditional view, that inner mental processes causally direct certain modes of bodily activity, is inconsistent with the fact that no one can give any account of how these mental processes actually produce or direct bodily activity.

zation of bodily dispositions as triggered by environmental circumstances and biological pressures.

But perhaps also an even more crucial difficulty emerges here. If what I call an intelligently directed activity must be preceded by subjective mental processes which that activity manifests, and if that inner mental activity is, at least on occasion, itself an intelligently directed activity, then it would follow that those intelligently directed mental processes must, for the same reason, be preceded by still other and prior mental processes and so on to infinity. But that of course would be absurd, since it would entail the conclusion that an intelligently directed activity required an infinite prior series of mental acts—which would be impossible in a finite period of time. The alternative would be to maintain that an intelligently directed activity would be possible without any preceding mental process of the sort supposed. But, in that case, the phrase "intelligently directed activity" need not imply unique mental antecedents at all, but would refer instead to a particular way of engaging in overt, publicly observable activity. And if that account is correct, mental reference words will again be clearly seen to refer to bodily behavior, or dispositions to bodily behavior, alone. This general argument—to the effect that if intelligent activity depends on antecedent mental acts, then an infinite series of such antecedents would be entailed—supposedly applies to all the species of allegedly unique mental activity: consciousness of one's own mental acts and contents, volitions or acts of will, in one's inner sphere of awareness, which are then productive of changes in bodily behavior or even in the orientation of one's own mental processes, introspective monitoring of the individual's privately accessible mental events, knowing construed as the correct description of these events inwardly disclosed—all these would be, as it were, swept away on the horns of the implied dilemma in which we are required to choose between an infinite regress of antecedents, on the one hand, and the admission that these mental terms are correctly applicable in cases where there clearly can be no such unique mental antecedents. If we add to all this the further facts that intelligence is often manifested in activities the rules or criteria of which are either unknown or unformulated by the agent (e.g., wit, aesthetic taste, or tactful manners), and that the appropriate performance of many skillful operations characteristically precedes any account of the theory or methodology of such operations (e.g., playing a musical instrument, painting a picture, or performing a difficult physical maneuver), then the argument against unique mental acts as a necessary condition of intelligent activity appears persuasive indeed.

If all these lines of argument succeed in rendering plausible the claim that mental words refer without exception to publicly observable modes of bodily behavior or to dispositions of the human physical organism to engage in such behavior, and if therefore all the functions of personhood or selfhood are explainable in physiological terms, then it will follow that there is no satisfactory way to argue from the unique spiritual selfhood of man to God as the transcendent cause of that

(3) If intelligently directed activity must be preceded by mental processes, then those processes themselves would have to be similarly preceded to infinity—which is absurd.

so that an "intelligently directed activity" would not require unique mental antecedents after all.

(4) This infinite-series argument applies to all the species of supposedly unique mental activity.

(5) Many clearly intelligent activities obviously involve no such mental antecedents as a ground of their status as intelligent.

c) If all the functions of personhood are thus explainable as behavioral or dispositional, then no inference to God, from the uniqueness of human personhood, will seem plausible.

2. In response to linguistic behaviorism:
a) The fact that mental events are mediated through observationally grounded language does not imply that mental terms refer to the modes of behavior through which such language is learned.
(1) Since the same thought can be expressed through different words, the thought itself is logically independent of the various word units that express it.
(2) Illustrative analogy provided by the relation of a musical theme to its modes of expression.

(3) Hence, language expresses thought but is not identical with it.

b) The fact, that no one can explain how his mental processes direct bodily activities, is not a real difficulty.

spiritual selfhood—since, for the sort of linguistic behaviorism we have been considering, there is no such uniquely spiritual dimension to be accounted for.

However, there certainly are plausible counter-arguments in response to this materialist claim. As to the contention that since supposedly private mental events are mediated through observationally grounded language, it therefore follows that there are no such unique mental events and that the words of that language actually refer to the publicly observable modes of behavior through which the words themselves are learned: This is a clear case of *non sequitur*, since the conclusion, though logically compatible with the premise or antecedent clause, simply does not follow. If, for example, the same thought can be expressed in two different languages through the use of entirely distinct words, it would appear to follow that the thought itself, though requiring some conventional means of expression, is not identical with any one set of these means nor with the indefinitely extended conjunction of all of them. In fact, it seems further clear that the thought itself constitutes a content that is logically independent of any and all admittedly conventional means or vehicles of its particular expression. Consider a musical theme—say, the theme of Beethoven's Ninth Symphony—it cannot be expressed except through some determinate musical medium. It can be hummed, or whistled, or played on the flute or guitar or harmonica, or even sung with its original German words or with some translation of them or even with the wholly different lyrics found in many standard church hymnals. But the theme itself is logically distinct from any or all of these various media of performance, and it would clearly be pure sophistry to argue otherwise. Analogously, even though my thoughts must be expressed through some linguistic medium (taking language in the broadest sense), it does not follow that the thoughts themselves are sheerly identical with these vehicles of conveyance. Quite the contrary, since the thought in a particular case can be embodied indifferently in any one or more of these conventional media and is itself therefore quite distinct from them, just as is the case with the theme of Beethoven's Ninth Symphony. It is therefore simply a mistake to conclude that because a thought requires a medium of expression, it is therefore identical with that medium. A parrot can recite a sentence, although there is no reason to suppose that the parrot is thinking the thought that the sentence expresses. Even a person can mechanically read a sentence in some language that he does not understand, without thinking the thought it expresses. And I, or anyone else, can say a sentence in English (which I do normally understand), without thinking the content it expresses, only perhaps to repeat that sentence with understanding the second time—all of which illustrate the point that thought and language, though intimately connected, are certainly not identical.

But what about the claim that if inner mental processes sometimes did causally direct and initiate bodily activities, then the subject or agent should be able to give a descriptive account of how he performs such activities, whereas no one can actually render any such account? The supposition is that the inability to render such an account implies that there is no such inner mental direction at all. But I think it is quite evident, upon careful reflection, that this supposition is incorrect. At the outset, it is intuitively obvious to me that I can, at will, decide to move my arm and then carry out the act myself—that, in fact, is precisely what I am doing as I write these words literally by hand (and arm). Yet, on any theory whatever (materialist, dualist, or idealist), I can give no neutral account of how I carry out this operation. There simply are many kinds of acts that I carry out just by performing them without the intervention of any mechanical or quasi-mechanical instrumentality. To see this point, I need only ask myself such questions as the following: How do I touch my wife's cheek with my index finger (not how do I move my finger into position)? Or how do I start to speak audibly after a period of silence (not how do I carry on the process once initiated)? Or how do I begin the series of fairly complex motions involved in getting up from the table after lunch (not how do I carry through the motions once they are under way)? With respect to all of these questions, two things are evident to me—first, that I actually do all these things voluntarily and with deliberate direction so that I could, in a given case, have acted otherwise; and second, that I can give no account of any method by which I do them. It seems apparent therefore that any complex activity involves elements which, although they may initiate means of operation, do not themselves involve any means of operation. How do I decide something, as distinct from preparing to make the decision? At the point of the actual decision, I just do it with no conceivable intervening means. How do I move my arm in consequence of such a decision? At the point of initiation, I just do it, again with no conceivable intervening means. And I suspect that the critic of my position does the same, else his book or article either would not have been, or will not be, written. It follows from all this that it is no criticism of the claim that bodily activities are sometimes initiated and directed by inner mental processes to say that if that were so, the agent should be able to give a descriptive account of the operation of that initiation and direction.

Yet there is another dimension of this issue to which I shall allude without detailed development or elaboration. In my previous response, I have for the sake of argument assumed the dualistic thesis, on which the critic's argument is based, to the effect that the mind (or mental events) and the body (or bodily processes and activities) are entirely different kinds of factors having no common property or attribute. Part of the perplexity I feel, when I wonder how a decision to move my body in a certain way is to be implemented, is due to the influence of this dualistic picture. The critic, of course, although arguing from the consequences of that picture, rejects it in favor of a materialism for which the only entity involved is the physical organism. But it is open to a defender of the reality of the mind or self to reject that dualistic picture on a radically different basis. Suppose we contend, for example, with Leibniz that while the mind is distinct from the

(1) We perform many acts directly and without means just by doing them.

(a) Some illustrations of this claim.

(b) Hence, any complex act involves elements that do not themselves involve means of operation.

(2) It is therefore not surprising that an agent can give no account of a means of inner direction.
c) Part of the perplexity about how the mind acts on the body is due to the mind-body dualism assumed in the discussion.
(1) The critic rejects this picture in favor of materialism.
(2) But it is possible to go the other way and regard the body itself as composed of elements which are centers of mental energy or spiritual force.

body, nevertheless the body itself is ultimately composed of centers of mental energy or spiritual force (monads, in Leibniz's parlance), and the mind or self is likewise a spiritual monad. On these terms, my original perplexity would be largely dissipated—for now I could construe the interaction between mind and body (an interaction which Leibniz questioned on systematic grounds that I will not elaborate here) as analogous to the interaction that goes on among my own mental processes themselves. While it is not germane to my present purpose to develop this concept in this context, I will nevertheless say that I find this perspective plausible indeed, and I see it as clearly making the concourse between mind and body more fully intelligible.

Now we have yet to deal with the claim that the mental direction of bodily activities would involve a regressive causal series that is logically absurd, so that we ought rather to regard mental reference words as referring, not to unique and private inner mental states, but to publicly observable modes of bodily behavior or to organic dispositions to engage in such behavior under the stimulus of appropriate circumstances. In response to this complex contention, I should like to state at the outset that the appeal of the dispositional interpretation of mental reference terms largely stems from the fact (which I have no wish to contest) that we characteristically learn what other persons are thinking through publicly observable modes of behavior in which they engage—what they say or write, how they respond to circumstances, what expressions appear on their faces, and so on. But that acknowledged fact hardly entails the conclusion that their thinking is itself identical with these modes of behavior, since these modes are clues to their thoughts rather than the thoughts themselves. This seems evident from the fact that we often misinterpret these clues and also from the fact that individuals can actually deceive us into understanding observable clues in a way that does not communicate their real thoughts—neither of which facts would be intelligible at all unless the thoughts and the observable clues were distinct rather than identical.

Perhaps more significantly, it seems clear that each of us is able to become aware of his own thoughts through a direct introspective analysis which completely transcends any dependence on tendencies to modes of publicly observable behavior. I do not need to observe myself in pain behavior (wincing, doubling up, and so on) to know whether I am in pain; I do not need to give any sort of performance for myself to know whether I understand Plato's theory of absolute ideas; and I certainly do not need to engage in any behavior, whether openly or in imagination, to know whether I remember the day in March 1983, when Arthur Godfrey died. And if, to offset the innumerable cases of this sort, the defender of the dispositional view interprets every case of self-knowledge of this sort as a kind of silent soliloquy which is in principle publicly observable—so that knowing that I know something is alleged always to involve "putting myself through my paces"—then the whole point of his view becomes vacuous, since there will then be no conceivable case of knowledge that could count

(3) This last view would make mind-body interaction more fully intelligible.

d) Does the mental direction of bodily activities involve a contradictory regressive causal series?
(1) While we normally learn what other people are thinking through observing their behavior, this does not imply that thinking is identical with this behavior.

(2) Modes of behavior are rather clues to thoughts—which is evidenced by the possibilities of misinterpretation and deception.

(3) Each person has a non-dispositional awareness of his own thoughts without behavioral clues;

the denial of such introspection would imply that there was no conceivable evidence against the dispositional view, which would then become an arbitrary thesis.

against the dispositional view, which then becomes a sort of incorrigible policy decision, rather than a thesis supported by experiential evidence.

But there are, of course, dispositional tendencies of which we are all aware in ourselves; and the dispositionalist theory of mental reference terms clearly depends on our being able to recognize such tendencies. However, it seems clear on reflection that the recognition of a dispositional tendency involves a non-dispositional mode of awareness in which that tendency is apprehended. Otherwise I should have to say that the recognition of a dispositional tendency in myself was interpretable as itself another dispositional tendency and that this interpretation again was another such tendency, and so on without logical limit. And in that case we would have the very sort of infinite regressive series which the dispositionalist charges against the person who defends unique and directly introspectible mental events. It therefore follows from this *reductio ad absurdum* argument that either no one can recognize a dispositional tendency, or else there clearly are non-dispositional modes of mental awareness of the very introspective sort that the dispositionalist rejects. And, whichever horn of the dilemma one accepts, the dispositionalist theory is in serious question, since that theory depends on the ability to recognize dispositionalist tendencies.

(4) The awareness of a dispositional tendency seems clearly non-dispositional, since otherwise it would itself require another disposition to recognize it and so on to infinity.

Of course, the dispositionalist charges the inner mental state theory with a precisely analogous infinite series, since he claims that, for that theory, an intelligently directed activity would have to be preceded or accompanied by an inner mental activity as its cause, and so on to infinity. But since that argument holds, as we have seen, with equal force against the dispositionalist's own view, then the dispositionalist can insist on this as a crucial objection to the other position only at the expense of sacrificing his own theory about mental reference terms. Now suppose that the dispositionalist can devise some ingenious way of escaping this dilemma. It will not really matter just what that device is in detail, or even whether it is objectively correct as an explanation, for then the inner mental state theorist will be able to devise a formally analogous explanation to get him "off the hook," as it were, and the whole issue will be neutralized. I shall, of course, not try to do the dispositionalist's homework for him; but I will try to devise my own response to the dilemma. I have long since contended that knowledge-claims, or more basically all cases of intelligible thought, are possible only through a structure of basic categories and interpretive principles which characterize the knowing mind logically prior to and independently of the data of experience. If so, then intelligently directed activity, through the causal operation of mental accompaniments or antecedents, would not generate an infinite regressive series, but would come to rest in those interpretive structures which make intelligible thought possible—whether or not the thinker is explicitly conscious of these structures in a particular case. In any case, there is something peculiar about a Ryle or a Wittgenstein appealing to arguments whose plausibility implies that logical incon-

(5) Thus the infinite-series charge holds equally against the dispositionalist view itself, so that the objection against the opposite view is not crucial.

(a) If the dispositionalist can devise any answer to this difficulty, so can the mental-state theorist.

(b) If, as I have argued, all intelligible thought depends on basic *a priori* structures, then any regressive series will come to rest in such structures and not be infinite in the way alleged.

(c) Logical objections are in any case arbitrary for anyone holding a conventionalist view of logic, although such objections can be objectively decisive for a synthetic apriorist.

sistencies are objectively decisive for settling a contested issue; for analytic empiricists of that sort regard logical principles as trivially analytic rules based on conventional agreement (presumably among logicians)—and that theory of logic, as we have earlier argued, would render all decisions based on logical principles relative and arbitrary. In contrast, for the synthetic apriorism that I have judged plausible, logical principles, such as the law of contradiction, are necessary presuppositions of all possible thought and being, so that arguments based correctly upon them do indeed become objectively decisive.

Finally, let us suppose *per contra* that, in spite of all these difficulties, the dispositionalist is right after all. What then would be the status of his dispositional theory itself as an interpretation of mental reference terms? It would clearly have to be regarded as a complex disposition of the dispositionalist's own organism to engage in certain modes of objectively observable behavior on the stimulus provided by physically conditioning circumstances. But, in that case, the whole theory would reduce to a perhaps interesting descriptive fact about the dispositonalist himself, rather than constituting any sort of objective truth-claim, much less any decisively objective criticism of any theory whatever.

From all these considerations, I can only conclude that the sort of linguistic behaviorism we have been analyzing provides no effective healing balm for the materialist view of the mind. And if the two types of materialism we have considered in some detail may be taken to provide sample paradigms or models of all theories of this sort, then I also conclude that the argument for theism, based on the uniqueness of human personhood or selfhood, still remains as a plausible ground of theistic belief even in the face of materialist criticism.

On the other hand, there is also the *functionalist* or *epiphenomenalist* view of the mind to consider. According to this view, which is closely connected with the general theory of emergent evolutionism, there actually are distinct non-physical mental events as elements of conscious experience; but these mental states, even though not therefore themselves material, are the by-product or resultant of biological processes going on in the human organism, so that those processes make such mental states possible. These mental events are therefore wholly the effect of the neurochemical processes that are their cause, so that mind, thus understood, can only subsist as long as the biological organism provides its causal ground; and since the mind is a completely determined effect of the physical processes that thus make it possible, it has no reciprocal causal efficacy of its own, no means, for example, of acting to produce any causal redirection or alteration of bodily processes. Mental functions are rather like causally inconsequential shadows cast by physically determined bodily processes, so that all genuine causal agency is carried out by the body without any intervention from the mind. Human beings think, of course, that mental purposes, decisions, and intentions do, to some extent, direct the course of bodily behavior and activity. But for this view, such a supposition must be an illusion as

e) If the dispositionalist theory were itself correct after all, the theory itself would be merely an organic disposition of the person holding it, and hence clearly not any objective criticism of any theory whatever.

3. In general, the materialist view of the mind does not constitute any decisive objection against the argument for theism from the uniqueness of personhood.

III. *Functionalism or epiphenomenalism.* A. This view holds that there are unique mental events, but that they are entirely the non-physical by-product of bodily states with no reciprocal causal power of their own.

vast and extensive as it is deceptive and mistaken. If, contrary to fact, a musical melody were conscious of itself as an activity, it would doubtless suppose that its sound vibrated the strings of the violin on which it was played; but we all know that it is the vibration that produces the sound and not the other way around. Quite analogously, thinking is the music of consciousness produced by the physical vibrations of the human body, as itself determined by its physical properties and environmental circumstances.

Initially, we may be disposed to regard the basic thesis of functionalism as virtually unintelligible. How can physical causes, which by nature can only redirect the motions of physical entities, conceivably produce immaterial, uniquely mental effects which are in no sense identical with the motions of the physical elements that produced them? But there are numerous empirical illustrations of causes producing effects that are qualitatively distinct from such causes. Water, for example, is neither hydrogen nor oxygen, yet it is clearly produced by their combination; the vegetables we eat are as clearly distinct from the human flesh they are used to produce; and the music we hear is obviously not the same as the vibrations which make our experience of sound possible. If causes can therefore produce effects so different qualitatively from those causes, it can be plausibly argued that mental states, although qualitatively distinct from neurochemical changes in the body, may also be produced by those physical changes. And if we add the fact that this dualistic view, distinguishing, as it does, physical processes from mental events, eliminates many of the perplexities that plague any version of strict materialism, then the position seems still more plausible. We further will be adopting a perspective which comports well with the fact that all cases of mental awareness which we can identify take place in conjunction with some operating physical organism. If the functionalist is right in all this, it will of course follow that the uniqueness of mind is wholly explainable as the effect of physical and biological processes, so that again there would be no legitimate inference from the unique personhood of man to God as the sole adequate cause of that personhood.

But, of course, I do not share the opinion that the functionalist is right. To begin with, I am not convinced of the intelligibility of the functionalist view as supported by the sort of cases cited in which causes produce effects qualitatively distinct from themselves. In the first two cases I mentioned, there is certainly a qualitative difference, but the qualities of both causes and effects are commonly understood as physical in each instance, so that there is a traceable physical continuity from cause to effect. Hence, the qualitative difference involved is radically distinct from, and contrasts with, the qualitative difference between physical states and mental states, where there is no such traceable physical continuity at all—since none of the descriptive qualities of bodily states are predicable of mental states, nor are the introspected qualities of mental states predicable, in any straightforward sense, of bodily states, as both types of states are commonly understood even by the functionalist himself. How can bodily states,

1. This view may seem unintelligible because of the qualitative contrast between physical cause and mental effect.
2. But:
a) Causes often produce qualitatively distinct effects.

b) This view eliminates many of the difficulties of straight materialism.
c) And mental awareness is regularly conjoined with some physical organism.

B. Critical response to this view:
1. The alleged intelligibility of the view is not really supported by the models of qualitative contrast between cause and effect, since typical examples display a traceable physical continuity absent from the relation between mental and bodily states.

whose characteristic activity is motion or neurochemical change, be intelligibly regarded as providing a complete account of mental states which, by hypothesis, are completely devoid of motion or neurochemical change in any non-metaphorical sense? This does not mean that causal interaction between the mind and body is impossible. It rather means that neither side (the mental or the physical) can provide an exhaustive account of states on the other side, since in that case there would be no distinguishable entities between which such an interaction could occur. Or, to put it more directly, if the functionalist account were correct, then mind-body interaction would itself be unintelligible. Of course, mind-body interaction can itself be questioned, but not for the functionalist, the essence of whose claim consists in contending that physical processes do act to produce non-physical uniquely mental effects.

2. If functionalism were true, we should have to deny all causal efficacy to conscious purpose.
a) But this claim runs counter to our own experience in consciously directing many of our activities.

Still, for the functionalist, the causal relation between the physical and the mental is, as we have noted, entirely one-directional, since, while physical processes produce mental effects, those shadowy mental by-products have no reciprocal causal power to reverse this causal line and produce physical effects in turn. Now the cost of this claim—essential to the functionalist position—is staggering indeed. It means that mind and its purposes have no active causal capacity to produce any result, since mental states are wholly the determined effect of physical processes. I, for one, cannot accept the illusion that this claim involves. On that hypothesis, although it is clear to me that my writing of this sentence is intelligently directed by my own sustained conscious purpose, I should, on functionalist terms, have to regard that clear insight as a bewitching deception. Put it this way: Either functionalism is clearly mistaken and a deception itself, or else conscious purposes never provide even a partial explanation of bodily activity. But this last I clearly recognize as patently mistaken, since I engage in all sorts of bodily activities under the causal direction of these activities by conscious purpose. A George Santayana or a Max Scheler might try to patch up this difficulty by suggesting that the mind does have the capacity, as I myself have earlier contended, to sublimate and direct bodily activities—but that the mind itself, as the functionalist maintains, has no causal power to carry out this sublimation or redirection, so that it must appropriate or borrow the active energy for this capacity from the animal drive of the organism itself as physical. But this last suggestion seems clearly mistaken, since the act of appropriating or borrowing energy from animal drive itself entails a causal operation which requires that the mind have intrinsic causal energy of its own to make such appropriation possible. While I do not doubt that I, as a spiritual self, use bodily energy to attain many of my purposes, that use itself is possible only if, as such a self, I possess intrinsically the causal energy to make my use of bodily energy conceivable. Therefore, if the self has the capacity to sublimate and redirect bodily processes, it cannot depend for all its active causal power on the bodily forces which it thus, within limits, is able to control.

b) Nor can the mind be viewed as borrowing the required energy from the physical organism, since the act of borrowing would require a causal energy intrinsic to the mind itself.

3. If all thoughts were merely determined effects of physical states:

But here a still more profound difficulty emerges for functionalism.

If thoughts and their sequences, as mental processes, are all equally determined effects of physical states, then it will follow here, as in the case of materialism, that there will be no way to identify the propositions which express those thoughts as either true or false, since all mental effects will be on an equal par as wholly the non-physical by-products of bodily operations. If the supposition, further, that physically produced effects would, without intelligent direction, constitute in certain cases the ordered steps of an extended logical sequence is simply incredible—then it will follow that there will be no way to account for the occurrence of such logical sequences in thought, no way to account for the recognition of the logical relations between premises and conclusions, or to determine their validity or invalidity. And if all this were the case, then, since functionalism itself is, as a theory, composed of thoughts which, by hypothesis, are the product of physical and biological processes, there will also be no way to claim reasonably that it is a true account of the relation between mental and bodily states, and no way either of recognizing the logical sequences in the arguments of functionalism as either valid or invalid. But of course all this is obviously ridiculous. Truth and falsity can, in principle, be distinguished, and the differences between valid and invalid inferences can be recognized, so that the functionalist position, which entails the impossibility of all this, must be seriously questionable, if not totally mistaken.

a) There would be no way to distinguish between truth or falsity,

b) no way to recognize or account for logical sequence,

c) and no way to claim that functionalism itself is true or its arguments either valid or invalid.

This conclusion is reinforced by an analysis of what, I suppose, the functionalist intends to accomplish by his own arguments. Presumably he intends that when a listener or reader mentally understands these arguments, that understanding will cause him to think differently about the relation between mental and bodily states. And that difference of thought will in turn cause such an individual to act differently as well—if he is not, as it were, numbed into silence, then he will thenceforth speak differently, write differently, and generally comport himself differently with regard to such questions. But all these intended results are inconceivable and impossible unless the mind has the intrinsic causal power to carry out all this redirection in both understanding and bodily activity; and yet it is just such intrinsic causal power that the functionalist denies to thought and the mind. It will therefore follow that philosophical or any other sort of arguments, about these or any other sorts of questions, will be totally pointless unless functionalism itself is basically and pervasively mistaken. To me, at least, and, I venture to say, to any other reflective person who fully understands even the core of such arguments, the conclusion seems obvious—functionalism will simply have to be set aside as inadequate and implausible, if not simply false.

4. The functionalist theory is inconsistent with the proponent's intent to change the thinking and actions of persons he hopes to influence by propounding the theory.

Therefore, neither materialism nor functionalism provides any reasonable explanation of the personhood or selfhood of man on purely physical or material grounds. And, if that is the case, then the argument which traces that selfhood to the Ultimate Personal Being of God, as its sole adequate causal ground, remains a credible basis for belief in God as thus understood. I do not, of course, claim that the

IV. Hence, neither materialism nor functionalism provides any reasonable alternative to theism as a plausible explanation of the uniqueness of human selfhood.

case, either for theism or against naturalistic explanation on this basis, is demonstrably certain. I merely claim that the theistic explanation is far more reasonable, with whatever difficulties that entails, than its naturalistic alternatives, with all the difficulties they entail. The conclusion is certainly not without risk; but it is not without foundation either.

Ethical Relativism and the Rejection of an Objective Moral Order

I. If there were no objectively valuable ends and no objective moral order, there would be no such ethical basis for theism as I earlier argued.

In my version of the moral argument for theism, I took as my contextual and provisional starting point the thesis that persons are intrinsically valuable as ends, and that therefore the community of persons constitutes the core of an objective moral order in which persons have objective moral duties and obligations toward themselves and toward each other as such intrinsically valuable ends. But suppose, in spite of the considerations I urged in support of the plausibility of this thesis, that its claim is some sort of basic mistake and that there are no intrinsically valuable ends in an objective sense, and therefore also no objective moral order at all. If that were the case, then any attempt to argue from intrinsic personal worth and objective moral truth to the Supreme Personhood of God as their ultimate locus and basis would of course be invalidated, since there would be no intrinsic moral worth and no objective moral order to serve as premises for such an argument.

A. Since there are moral beliefs, any critic would have to provide an explanation of them that did not imply moral objectivity.

Of course, it is factually indisputable that there are moral beliefs and that among these beliefs, for most reflective persons, is the belief that some moral beliefs express objective moral truths. So, of course, if the critic rejects moral objectivism and therefore also the intrinsic worth of persons as an objective value, he has the cognitive and intellectual responsibility to give some other account of these beliefs in such a way as to avoid grounding his explanation on any express or implied appeal to the concept of moral objectivity that he is attempting to criticize. Two principal ways of providing such an explanation are ethical emotivism and radical ethical relativism, although it certainly is not indisputably clear that the latter is logically distinct from the former explanation. *Ethical emotivism* is the thesis that ethical beliefs and the propositions stating them have no cognitive significance, since they are incapable of being either true or false and are therefore to be understood as merely (though importantly) expressive of the feelings and emotional preferences of persons employing such linguistic utterances. To claim, for example, that a person morally ought to tell the truth in a prescribed set of circumstances is not to make any cognitive claim at all, but merely to express one's preference for truth telling and truth tellers. This is not to say, of course, that a person never has any plausible reason for acting on this preference, but it is rather to

B. One such account is provided by *ethical emotivism.*
1. This view holds that ethical beliefs and statements make no cognitively significant truth-claims, but are rather emotively expressive and evocative.

claim that such reasons will be based on prudential self-interest and preference, rather than on any objective moral duty. If this explanation is correct, then, since on these terms moral expressions make no truth-claims at all, it follows that they make no objective or any other determinate sort of truth-claims at all.

I will say at once and without cavil that, in my opinion, this way of avoiding moral objectivism seems clearly misguided and mistaken. Historically (and perhaps even logically), ethical emotivism depends on a particular theory that conventionally (and therefore arbitrarily) prescribes the limits of cognitively significant statements by claiming that there are only two types of such cognitively significant propositions, namely, statements of empirical fact based ultimately on sense experiences and our ordering of them, and statements of formal logical equivalence based on conventionally adopted rules of logical structure and inference. Now, since ethical sentences, understood in the moral sense, are clearly neither synthetic *a posteriori* statements of empirical fact nor analytic *a priori* statements of conventionally grounded logical equivalence, it follows that they are not cognitively significant assertions making any sort of truth-claim. But of course this follows only if one accepts the doctrine of cognitive meaning on which the claim is based. This doctrine is part of the doctrine of one sort of analytic empiricism (usually called logical positivism, or logical empiricism). Now I have critically assessed this type of empirical epistemology in several earlier contexts of my overall analysis, and I have found such an epistemology decisively inadequate; nor will I repeat here my already much-labored criticisms. Suffice it to say two things in the present context: First, if the empirical epistemology on which the emotive theory of ethics is based is itself unsound, then unless there is some other basis for such an emotivism (I am aware of no plausible alternative basis), it must itself be judged unsound as an explanation of ethical statements. This is not, of course, to say that people do not often confuse their emotive preferences with moral truth-claims and then palm off those preferences as such. It is merely and rather to say that it is not logically inevitable that they do so, and that this admitted fact does not offer a plausible comprehensive explanation of moral statements. My final comment about the epistemological basis of emotivism would be to point out that the protocol statements, which limit cognitively significant statements to empirical statements and statement of formal logical equivalence, are not themselves plausibly interpretable as either empirical or logical statements of the sort prescribed. They are clearly not empirical, since there are no empirical data which, as such, would tend to conform or disconfirm the definitive universal claims of those protocol statements (it is not merely that by chance we have not discovered any such data—it is rather that there cannot logically be any such data by the very nature of the case). And if the protocol statements are formal logical definitions, then, for such a conventionalist logic, the statements will, by hypothesis, be the result of arbitrary and contingent choice, so that they will settle nothing objectively about the genuine logical status of

2. But this view seems implausible.
a) It depends on the claim that cognitively significant statements must be either empirical statements or formal logical equivalences of some sort.

b) But this empirical theory has already been judged inadequate.
(1) Ethical emotivism will therefore be as implausible as its epistemological basis.

(2) The protocol statements of such an epistemology are not themselves either empirical or logical in their own prescribed sense.

ethical or any other sort of statements. If, then, the protocol statements are neither empirical propositions nor logical definitions, are they then themselves non-cognitive expressions of the emotive preferences of the empirical critic himself?

Suppose then we turn to what I have called *radical ethical relativism.* For this position, there simply are no objective moral truths at all, as the moral objectivist claims. Instead, the propriety, validity, and truth-value of moral or ethical judgments are alike functions of, and relative to, individually and culturally variable states of opinion, preference, feeling, or response. Such judgments are by choice true for the cultural group or individual that propounds them, so that their truth is subjective, in the defined sense, rather than objective. Relativism, as thus clarified, is not to be confused with what is often called the situational relativity of limited moral principles. This last sort of relativity is quite compatible with moral objectivism, since one can consistently claim that there are objective moral principles, but that the way those principles are to be applied to particular cases will depend on the relevant circumstances of the particular case in question. In contrast, the radical ethical relativist holds that there are no objective moral principles at all.

There are two main lines of argument that are commonly urged in support of ethical relativism in this radical sense. The historical argument claims (on the whole correctly, in my opinion) that moral beliefs vary extensively from individual to individual, group to group, and culture to culture, in such a way that there is no universally conceded method of resolving this variation. It is then claimed that since moral beliefs and opinions vary in this (in principle) incorrigible fashion, it follows that it is reasonable to believe that there are no objective moral truths and that the truth status of moral beliefs is wholly relative to the variable opinions and preferences which, by hypothesis, are expressed in these beliefs. The unexpressed but implied assumption underlying this argument is presumably that, if there were objective moral truths, a universally conceded methodology for reconciling moral beliefs would at least be in principle achievable, if not already accessible—whereas, of course, this last is clearly not the case. The psychological argument for radical ethical relativism, on the other hand, claims that human beliefs (and therefore also ethical beliefs) are invariably the product of non-rational causal factors (for example, impulses, subconscious or conscious desires, personal idiosyncrasies, social and environmental conditioning), which therefore have no logical status as appropriate premises for the beliefs they causally produce. And, if that is the case, there will be no way to determine whether beliefs thus originated are objectively true or not, except by appealing to still other beliefs produced in the same non-rational way. It will therefore follow that, at the very least, it will be highly unlikely that such accidentally (in the logical sense) produced beliefs will be true; and in any event there will be no way to identify such beliefs as true. The same fate which thus attaches to human beliefs generally will of course attach to ethical beliefs as a sub-class.

In response to all this, it seems clear that the arguments for radical ethical relativism are formally invalid, since they are based on the questionable assumption that moral truths and moral beliefs have the same logical status and share the same logical fate. But this is evidently not the case. Beliefs can logically be false, while truths cannot logically be false; in fact, whatever the truth is about any issue at all, its status as thus true will be logically independent of what any finite person believes, prefers, or thinks about it. It is clear, therefore, that the most radical and incorrigible variation in belief about a given subject will have no logical tendency to establish the claim that there is no objective truth about that subject, although, of course, such a variation would be consistent with that claim. Would it be plausible, by analogy, to claim, for instance, that if there were no universal methodology for settling disputes among astronomers about the motions of the heavenly bodies, it would be reasonable to conclude that there was no objectively true description about those motions, much less that there were no heavenly bodies to move? Of course not: Truths and tenets (held beliefs) are forever logically distinct, so that the most radical variation of the latter would provide no basis for questioning the objectivity of the former. Since both the historical and psychological arguments for radical ethical relativism rest on a confusion of truth with belief, neither argument provides a plausible basis for such a relativism.

As for the psychological argument in particular, and quite aside from the confusion between truth and belief, if it establishes anything, it establishes far too much for the logic of its case. The thesis that beliefs are the product of non-rational causes, which have no logical status as premises for the beliefs they originate, is also itself a belief of the psychological critic; and if it destroys the objectivity of the truth-claims made by the subjects such a critic analyzes, it also destroys the objectivity of its own truth-claim. If, on the contrary, there is any method of avoiding such self-stultification, that method will be just as open to the moral objectivist as it is to the psychological critic, or to anyone else for that matter.

But there are, of course, other serious difficulties with radical ethical relativism. What such a relativist is really arguing is basically that nothing is objectively better than anything else, except in the clearly irrelevant and hypothetical sense that, given an admittedly arbitrary preference for certain goals of activity, some means are causally and objectively more efficient ways of achieving those subjectively relative ends than others. In that case, however, ethical relativism will be no better objectively than any other theory about the logical status of moral values, so that there will be no objective reason why the relativist or anyone else should believe this or any other theory about this or any other subject. The critic may indeed accept this consequence, but then his case for relativism will become irrelevant as a criticism of moral objectivism, since his whole theory will then become the subjectively relative projection of his own preference and will therefore be no more than an interesting but inconsequential

C. Critical response to these arguments:

1. Both arguments are formally invalid since they falsely assume that the logical status of truths and beliefs is the same, so that the most radical relativity of moral beliefs does not entail that there are no objective moral truths.

2. The psychological argument, since it is a structure of beliefs, renders its own truth-claim subjectively relative and arbitrary, so that it ceases to be a plausible criticism.

3. If nothing is objectively any better than anything else, then ethical relativism will be no better objectively than any alternative theory and hence not an objective criticism of moral objectivism.

piece of descriptive psychology. If, on the other hand, the critic argues that there is some objective basis for his relativism and that reflective persons ought therefore to believe it—possibly because, as a critic, he supposes it to be true—then he is clearly appealing to the very sort of objective value standard that his theory purports to deny, so that his claim again constitutes an existential contradiction. If we add to this point the fact that the whole enterprise of making morally responsible choices either reduces the institution of morality to triviality or else implies, as the basis of its genuine significance, the very sort of moral objectivity that radical ethical relativism denies, then the case for that sort of objectivity becomes even stronger. On the relativist's ground: There could be no ultimate moral concern, since its ultimacy would imply an absolute and objective moral principle; and there could be, further, no unconditional moral responsibility, since its unconditionality would imply absolute and objective moral authority. While these consequences do not logically demonstrate the invalidity of radical ethical relativism, they nevertheless display its comprehensive implausibility by indicating the staggering cost of such a commitment, to the effect that on this ground no human enterprise whatever could consistently be taken with objective seriousness.

In retrospect, I therefore conclude that neither ethical emotivism nor radical ethical relativism poses an objectively effective threat to the moral objectivism which our original argument took as part of the rational basis for a theistic metaphysic. Given that moral objectivity, the same original argument developed the plausibility of identifying intrinsic personal worth as the basis and locus of all objectively arguable moral worth, duty, and responsibility in the ultimate sense: All values less than personal being are clearly extrinsic and instrumental in nature and possess significance only as means for the actualization and fulfillment of personhood. Again, that same argument also made it clear that the intrinsic worth of finite persons is derived in nature by virtue of the contingency of finite persons, so that the ultimate intrinsic personal worth must find its actualization in the self-existent and self-explanatory Personhood of God as Ultimate Reality.

But it is just at this point that one of the most serious objections to an ethically grounded theism confronts us. If we suppose that God, as Ultimate Reality and therefore the ground of all contingent being, is the essence of absolute moral (and of course also non-moral) goodness, then how do we account for all the natural evil (suffering, pain, disease, physical death) and moral evil (the violation of objective moral principle and the resultant self-destruction and denial of the worth and moral rights of other persons on the part of personal agents)—evils which appear to abound on every side and in every dimension of human experience? And although it is a question virtually as ancient as reflective human personhood, it is not for that reason any less perplexing now than when, we may surmise, it first arose out of existential anguish. Yet the issue is no mere perplexity. Negative critics of theistic metaphysics have made out this so-called problem of evil as the ultimate logical conundrum for a theistic world-view, by claim-

Margin notes

4. Ethical relativism would render the whole moral institution of life trivial.

D. Hence, neither ethical emotivism nor ethical relativism is an effective threat to moral objectivism as a basis for theism: a summary of the theistic case on this basis.

III. The problem of evil for ethical theism.
A. Formulation of the problem.
1. If God, as ultimately real and essentially good, is the ground of all contingent being, how account for moral and natural evil in the world?

2. This problem is regarded as involving theism in logical inconsistency.

ing that there is a logical inconsistency among conceptual elements, all of which are essential components of the theistic perspective. How can the essentially good, all-powerful ground of the contingent world order have permitted his unobstructed causality to be sullied by the morass of natural and moral evil which encompasses that product of his creativity? If some of the elements are dropped—if evil is illusory, or if God is not essentially good, or if he is limited in knowledge and/or power—then the inconsistency can be eliminated; but then we would not have theism. As it stands, therefore, the theistic perspective is confronted with a moral and metaphysical scandal of the first magnitude!

It is clear that, however vast natural evil may be in its scope, it is moral evil that constitutes the real bugaboo, for natural evil poses a problem only because and if it is itself chargeable to moral agency— either the moral agency of God or that of finite persons as morally responsible subjects. For this reason, one of the most widely explored defensive tactics of theistic apologists has been the *free will defense*, as it is called. At the level of divine moral agency, could God consistently have created a world order which would both have eliminated moral evil and at the same time been consistent with the only sort of purpose that would be ascribable to divine creativity? If that purpose may be reasonably identified as the production and progressive development in righteousness of finite moral agents, then, from the standpoint of that finite moral agency, could God have created agents of this sort in such a way that this purpose would be realizable without endowing these agents with a radical free agency that, although not necessitating moral evil in any sense, the misuse of such free moral agency would be a genuine contingent possibility which depended on the self-legislated choice of finite agents rather than upon the logical predetermination of God? The free-will apologists argue that it is at least logically possible that God, although unlimited in real power and knowledge, could not consistently have created a universe in which moral agents would both be genuinely free and yet so disposed by divine creation as never to exercise their freedom in the commission of morally evil acts and their inevitably disastrous effects, since that latter disposition would be tantamount to the elimination of the genuineness of the freedom of such moral agents. It is assumed, correctly I think, that God's purpose in creation is plausibly construed here. What other morally worthy end of creation is even conceivable? And it is also assumed that progress in the development of moral righteousness is itself conceivable, again correctly in my opinion, only if moral agents are genuinely free in the radically contingent sense.

But the critic has a different line of analysis: If moral agents are genuinely free in the stipulated sense, then it is logically possible for such an agent to make morally right choices in an indefinitely extended series of situations calling for morally significant choices; and it therefore follows that there is a logically possible universe in which a determinate plurality of moral agents would always freely make morally right choices. Now if it can be assumed without discussion

a) Statement of the inconsistency.

b) Any solution might involve a dropping of some element essential to theism.

3. Moral evil a more difficult problem than natural evil.

B. The *free will defense* as a theistic tactic.
1. Could God have created a universe that would both eliminate moral evil and be consistent with reasonably identified divine purpose centering on intrinsically valuable finite persons?
2. It is claimed that genuine moral freedom is essential to this purpose, and that the elimination of the possibility of actual moral evil would be equivalent to the destruction of the required freedom.

C. The critical analysis of the free will defense.
1. Since a free agent could conceivably always make right moral choices, there is a logically possible universe in which all free agents always so choose.

and virtually by definition that such a universe, eliminating moral evil as it does, would be a morally better universe than one in which moral evil became actual, then—if God is omnipotent in the sense that he can do anything that is a logically possible and consistent object of agency (not, of course, in the sense that he can do logically contradictory and therefore impossible things)—God could therefore have actually created this logically possible universe in which evil would be eliminated, so that his not having done so represents a clear compromise of his goodness. In this way, it is claimed, the theistic metaphysic is logically inconsistent and therefore ethically falls apart before our eyes.

Now it is my opinion that the argument of the critic is seriously misconstrued. I agree that there are logically possible universes in which moral evil would be eliminated. But it is a mistake to suppose that God, by virtue of his omnipotence, can do anything that is a logically possible object of agency. It is rather the case that God, as omnipotent, can do anything that is a logically possible object of his own divine agency in the sense of being consistent with his nature as God and therefore as essentially good and committed to the morally worthy purposes which that goodness prescribes. There are, therefore, many logically possible objects of agency in general that it is impossible for divine agency to actualize. He cannot, for example, lie or commit an infraction of the moral standard constituted by his own essence, since that would contradict his moral nature as unconditionally good; he cannot literally (as distinguished from metaphorically) forget anything, since that would be inconsistent with his transcendent omniscience; and, generally, he cannot do anything which would contradict his nature in any respect, since he is by definition a self-existent and self-explanatory Being, all of whose limits are self-involved or self-imposed either directly or indirectly. Yet finite moral agents, by contrast, can do all of these things. They can lie and generally commit morally evil acts; they can all too readily become involved in lapses of memory; and, in general, they can (and often do) act against what their nature, rightly understood, would incline them to do. All these things are possible for finite moral agents precisely because of their finitude and their radical moral freedom. Quite differently from the case of God, the nature of finite agents does not function as a wholly explanatory ground of the exercise of that agency, and they are, in that sense and precisely as contingent beings, less perfect than God, whose agency is wholly self-determined. It follows from all of this that there clearly are logically possible objects of agency that are not possible for God, and also that there are logically possible universes that God cannot, just because of his perfection, create, even though he is omnipotent in the sense of being able to do anything that is a logically possible object of his unique divine agency.

If, now, God's purpose in creation involves the production of rational, moral agents characterized by radical moral freedom—and if that freedom, though a necessary ingredient of a universe in which the moral goodness of such finite agents is possible, nevertheless

2. God could therefore have created this universe.
3. That he did not do so is thus a clear compromise of his essential goodness.
D. Response to this critical analysis:
1. The criticism is flawed since it falsely assumes that God can do anything that is a logically possible object of agency:
a) But God can only do what is consistent with divine agency,
b) so that there are logically possible acts God cannot consistently perform.

c) Finite agents can do consistently many of the things that God cannot thus do precisely because of their finitude and freedom.

d) Hence, there are logically possible universes that God cannot create, even though he is omnipotent.
e) The creation of a universe in which moral evil is possible and becomes actual is therefore not inconsistent with either God's goodness or his omnipotence.

involves the possibility of their making wrong moral choices, since God's determining otherwise would destroy their very freedom—then it follows that God's creation of a universe in which moral evil was possible, and in fact became actual, is not inconsistent either with God's essential goodness or with his omnipotence, correctly understood. But the critic commonly responds to this claim by contending that God could have created some universe of which he foreknew (in the logical, not the temporal, sense) that all finite moral agents would always perform morally right acts. This contention, however, seems clearly false, since, in a genuinely free universe of finite moral agents, the question whether such agents will or will not commit morally wrong acts is by hypothesis up to those agents in the exercise of their freedom, and not up to the creative choice of God. If, in fact, God willed to create a universe in which evil was *ipso facto* eliminated, that determination would be the destruction of the freedom of the moral agents that universe could contain. To see this point, consider the following analogy: On the supposition that my wife and I are not going to have a fourth child (we have three, and it is not biologically possible for us to have another), does God know what our fourth child will be like, if in fact there is not going to be a fourth child? Clearly the answer is no, since such an insight is not a logically possible object of knowledge; and yet this circumstance involves no limit on the divine knowledge, which extends only to possible objects of knowledge. Analogously, does God know what a free moral agent will choose in a particular case, if in fact there is not going to be any such particular agent? Clearly again, the answer is no, since, as in the former case, there is nothing to know. If, on the contrary, there is going to be that particular agent as radically free, then God knows what that agent will choose in any and all particular cases, while at the same time what that agent thus freely chooses will be up to the agent and not up to God; but God logically cannot know what an agent will freely choose to do unless it is the case that the agent in question is going to exist as that agent. Of course, if, contrary to the whole hypothesis of radical freedom, creating a particular agent involves the determination of all his acts as conjoined necessarily with the nature of that agent, then clearly divine knowledge would extend to all those acts; but equally clearly there would be no question of radical moral freedom on such presuppositions. Again, therefore, the critic seems mistaken: The notion of God's choosing to create only those free moral agents whom he logically foreknows as making only morally right choices is a logically muddled notion. If I am really free in the radical sense, then what I choose, although made possible by God's creation of me as the particular person I am, is a contingency that is entirely up to me in the last analysis. God therefore cannot absolutely preclude moral evil on the part of genuinely free moral agents without precluding (inconsistently) that very freedom. And from all this I conclude that, on the terms stipulated, the free will defense stands. At the same time I fully realize that the philosophical price of the defense involves the dismissal of entire edifices of certain deterministic traditional

f) Nor is it reasonable to contend that God could have foreknown a universe in which free agents always made right choices, and could have created such a universe.
(1) For this would in fact eliminate freedom.

(2) The fourth-child analogy.

(a) Just as God cannot consistently foreknow the properties of a child that is not going to exist, so, without any compromise of omniscience, he cannot foreknow what a free agent will do if no such agent is going to exist.
(b) God can foreknow what an actual agent is going to do freely, but that will be up to the agent himself.

(3) The notion of God's creating only those free agents whom he foreknows as choosing rightly is thus a confused notion.

2. God can therefore not preclude moral evil by free moral agents without precluding freedom itself: the free will defense therefore clearly stands.

theologies—but I, for one, do not regard that price as in any sense an objectionable sacrifice, since paying it involves for me the only sort of objective moral order that I could sincerely regard as morally worthy of God.

Much more remains to be said about the problem of evil but especially about natural evil. In the last main section of my earlier book, *The Resurrection of Theism*, I have written what I still regard as my most effective treatment of this complex issue; and I have no intention of repeating myself at length in this present context. But I regard it as essential to make a few pertinent comments. To begin with, while I have no interest in glossing over the all-but-overwhelmingly staggering quantity of suffering on the part of sentient beings in the world of our experience, there are several reasons why I cannot regard all this as a decisive negative criticism of the ethical case for theism. First, physical suffering would be an insuperable difficulty for theism only if we supposed that some sort of hedonism were the correct moral philosophy—that, for example, God's only conceivable purpose in creating sentient beings would be to reward them with the uninterruptedly fullest quantity of pleasurable experiences that their natures would make them capable of. But that hedonistic moral thesis is itself highly debatable, and I have, in any case, long since parted company with such a view. If God's purpose in creating the universe is as I have construed it, then the most that can be required here is that the capacity for suffering should itself be understandable as an effective means to the realization of that purpose. And this condition is clearly fulfilled, since the capacity for suffering is an effective instrument for preserving the various forms of living beings. And, in the case of rational, moral beings like ourselves, that capacity is a significant means of disciplining moral character in the case of agents whose moral state has been sullied by the abuse of freedom on their part. Again, if we add that a generally law-abiding universe—while it makes physical suffering possible for beings whose activities are not fully accordant with that structured order—is nevertheless at the same time a necessary condition for the sort of intelligently directed activity through which alone moral ends are achievable (moral intentions could have no assured result in a generally irregular environment which might greatly increase the amount of suffering in any case), then we will be able to take a further step toward putting our capacity for suffering into perspective from a theistic point of view. And, finally, if we realize that much suffering, at least in human experience, is inflicted on sentient beings by our own wrong use of free agency, or is a result of an ignorance of causes which disciplined attention is capable of avoiding, then the difficulty for theism becomes still less of a perplexity. At the very least, considerations of the sort we have mentioned do succeed in reducing the terms of the so-called problem of evil to the point where the difficulty, although unquestionably genuine, does not constitute a decisive negative criticism of the ethical case for theism.

In overall retrospect, then, it would appear that a moral objectivism, ultimately grounded in the transcendent moral Selfhood of God, is a plausible and significant aspect of the overall case for a theistic metaphysic. But, more pointedly, it is my opinion that theism, as I have construed it, supplies the most fully intelligible basis for moral objectivism that sober and careful reflection has put forth. If we can take moral value and moral distinctions with genuine seriousness, it is because the moral order of being, in which that seriousness becomes possible in a more vibrant sense than is allowed by any alternative perspective, is ultimately possible and actual through the Absolute Moral Personhood of God. Whenever, therefore, anyone makes a genuine moral truth-claim, he is recognizing a dimension of reality which would be non-existent without the God of theism—whether or not the claimant recognizes that implication consciously.

A. The ethical case for theism is a plausible argument even in the face of criticism.

B. Moral objectivism and ethical theism therefore stand together.

The Culmination of General Revelation

In Relation to the Knowledge of God

I. Provisional conclusions.

A. Theism emerges as a highly plausible and pervasively probable explanation of existence, even though it is not absolutely demonstrated.

If we now balance the cumulative case for theism against the successive lines of criticism directed against that case, what plausible conclusions can we draw from that extended and difficult enterprise of balancing? It would of course be irresponsible and perhaps even ludicrous to suppose that it would be clear sailing to an impregnably secure intellectual port—to think, perhaps, that the whole issue had been finally and decisively settled in favor of theism. But it would, nevertheless, be intellectual and moral dereliction not to contend that theism emerges as a highly plausible and pervasively probable explanation of the meaning of existence—a perspective, in my opinion, far more plausible than the alternatives of metaphysics implied by the negative criticisms of theism. And hence I conclude: If a contingent world order is possible and actual; if the complexity of that cosmos is infiltrated with intelligently directed, purposive structure; if at the climax of that cosmos there are beings whose unique personhood is inexplicable in terms of impersonal causes; and if the community of such persons constitutes the core of an objective moral order of being—then all this is fully conceivable only if it is suspended on the nature and causality of God.

B. A summary statement of the argument.

II. Reiteration of the scheme of positions regarding religious knowledge.

And now perhaps we can return to the schematism of positions which emerged from our analysis of the problem of religious knowledge and the relation of thought to the Ultimate Religious Object. It may be recalled that the central issue of religious epistemology in relation to the understanding of that Ultimate Religious Object, or God, is the question whether that Object has an ontological status as genuinely real apart from the thought content through which it is apprehended, or whether, quite to the contrary, the whole being of the Religious Object is constituted by and identical with the human insight that, in varied and even contrasting ways, grasps that Object in thought, so that God has no other reality status at all. I have referred to this second alternative as *monistic religious idealism*, because it maintains that the idea of God and its objective referent are precisely identical in the sense indicated—and for this perspective, in whatever form, the sole reality of God consists in the ideas which man projects and construes, so that in any objectively independent sense, however understood, God simply does not exist. Yet, as we saw previously, the logic of this position is bolstered by an extended account of how the notion of God and belief in that notion are to be accounted for as exercising the pervasive and significant influence on human experience that they so obviously do. While there are distinguishable forms of monistic religious idealism (I have referred to projectionistic, psychoanalytic, and humanistic versions of this outlook), the basic claim that pervades them all is that religious beliefs are subconscious projections of the human psyche, both individually and socially, in such a way as to express wish fulfillment of some sort. The projectionism of a Ludwig Feuerbach and the humanism of a John Dewey view this projection as the ascription of idealized human selfhood to the cosmic order itself under the guise of an imagined divine reality—except that, while Feuerbach regards this process as sheer illusion to be dispelled by scientific understanding, Dewey regards the process as susceptible of a critical refinement which ideally would provide a criterion for validating the notion of God as the unification of ideal individual and social ends making for the realization of genuine human well-being, viewed as individual and social integrative harmony in which all destructive conflicts are in principle resolved and eliminated. The psychoanalytic approach of a Sigmund Freud, on the other hand, sees the idea of God as the projection onto the universe of suppressed infantile impulses surrounding the father-figure, in the human family, as a basis for cosmic security and directive social authority—all of which, with Freud as with Feuerbach, has the character of a bewitching illusion that brings human beings more disintegration than genuine well-being. But the assumption of all these views is the thesis that if religious belief is thus explainable as the product of natural causes of this psychological or any other sort, then that explanation entails the spuriousness of the content of that religious belief; still, as far as I am aware, no plausible arguments for this assumption are provided by this tradition in any of its versions.

I have already conceded in an earlier context that many of the elements surrounding religious beliefs, and even aspects of the beliefs themselves, may well be the product, at least in part, of such natural

A. The central issue is whether the Religious Object has a reality status that is independent of the thought content through which it is apprehended.

1. The denial of this is the thrust of *monistic religious idealism*, for which God has no independent existence.

2. The main argument for this position is the thesis that religious beliefs are subconscius projections, so that the content of such naturalistically produced beliefs, has no objective referent.

B. In response:
1. While many of the elements of religious belief may have originated in the alleged way, it would be a fallacy to suppose that this fact negatively settles the question of objective reference.

2. If genetic explanation settled negatively the question of objective reference, then all beliefs would be undermined by their genetic history—including the beliefs of the critic.

causes. But at the same time it seems clear on reflection that it is a fallacy of geneticism to suppose that the causes involved in the origin of an idea exhaust the significance of the content of that idea considered as making a truth-claim. The decisive question here is not how historically or even psychologically an idea has originated, but rather whether the idea, whatever its origins and however much a projection of those origins, has a content that refers to something actual or makes a plausible truth-claim. If, on the contrary, it was reasonable to deny the objective referent of a truth-claim by tracing the ideas that are elements of that truth-claim to explanatory natural causes which had no logical relation to the truth-claim itself—then, since any idea must presumably have such an historical and psychological genesis (it somehow originates in our consciousness), it would follow that all beliefs whatever would be negated in their objective reference by the fact that, as ideas, they admitted of just such genetic explanation. In that case, the ideas of a Feuerbach or a Freud or a Dewey, although directed against the plausibility of religious belief, would themselves be just as implausible by virtue of their own logically accidental genesis; and, hence, the whole argument would constitute an enormous existential self-contradiction—a fate that we have seen involved in many a negative philosophical criticism. It would appear to follow from this analysis that even if we grant the wildest and most bizarre genetic explanations of the origins of religious beliefs in God, theistically construed, we will have made no logically significant progress toward settling the question of the plausibility of the truth-claims involved in the content of those beliefs. The question, therefore, of the validity and soundness of the truth-claim that the God of an adequately construed theism exists can only be plausibly judged about by considering those identifiable grounds of the truth-claim which do have the status of logical premises in relation to the claim in question.

3. The genetic explanation of a belief simply does not settle the truth-claim of its content: which can only be settled by the consideration of logically relevant premises of the theistic truth-claim.

C. Our entire cumulative argument for theism is precisely the discussion of such premises.

Now, on the assumption that all this is a roughly correct analysis, it is appropriate to claim that it is precisely such logically relevant premises of the theistic truth-claim that our various arguments for the existence of God have been exploring. And if those arguments themselves possess the plausibility that I have claimed for them, then they constitute the very sort of relevant critical response to monistic religious idealism which has any promise of escaping the logical incoherence into which all such genetic criticisms of belief inevitably fall.

1. These arguments do not exhaust the case for theism, since every aspect of existence points to God, if theism is true.

Of course, it would be a gross intellectual and perhaps even moral impropriety for me to claim that the arguments put forth, even if they were given the fullest possible clarification instead of the merely suggestive treatment I have accorded them, in any sense exhausted the case for theism. I rather imagine that all the human efforts that have been invested in this enterprise through the ages of history have barely scratched the surface of an as yet largely untilled ground and unexplored territory. If theism, as I understand it, is true, then every contingent state of things, every logical structure of thought and being, every purposively ordered dimension of existence, and every genuinely valuable aspect of being—all alike constitute a vast network of trails, each of which when carefully traced out leads to the reality of God as its termination and, in another sense therefore, its beginning. Hence, I conclude that theistic dualism, as I have termed it in my analysis of religious epistemology, is a viable rational alternative and involves a more highly probable explanation in metaphysics than any other developed ontological perspective with which I am familiar.

As to the other alternatives embraced in my schematism of religious epistemology—ranging from monistic religious realisms through less inclusive forms of theistic dualism to the various versions of agnostic dualism—I indicated my main objections to such views in an earlier context. But, as I there indicated, I do not regard the issues at stake among those alternatives as crucial problems for the version of theism which I have defended. I sincerely believe them to be defective in a multiplicity of ways; but I can and do at the same time envision them as limited but significant dimensions of a comprehensive vision of the reality of God in an objective sense—dimensions which thus unitedly compose a solid but varied front against that structure of destructive negative criticism which would consign the whole body of religious truth-claims to deceptive illusion. Such perspectival generosity certainly does not blind me to the inadequacies of these philosophical allies, nor does it obscure for me the shortcomings of my own point of view. The implications and even straightforward claims of much of my whole analysis have involved, as I see it, serious criticisms of the perspectives which in the present context I view as philosophical comrades. And, as for the theoretical incompleteness of my own position, I have everywhere and repeatedly disavowed both demonstration and finality in favor of a probability which I find it wholly reasonable to embrace. As a man, I could hardly claim more; but as a rational being, I could hardly be satisfied with less.

> 2. But theistic dualism may be claimed as a viable alternative in metaphysics.
>
> D. Other alternatives of the schematism, though defective in various ways, can be regarded as limited aspects of a total theistic vision.

In Relation to the Predicament of Man

I find myself, therefore, as one specimen of representative humanity, at the core of an objective moral order of being that is grounded in God; and I find the obligation to actualize the intrinsic worth of my own personhood, as well as the personhood of others whose well-being it is in my power partly to implement, to be an unconditional moral claim which God, in his ultimate intrinsic Personhood, imposes on me as a rational, moral agent. The responsibility, I acknowledge, is simply staggering, since it requires of me a stability of moral character, a purity of moral motivation, and a consistency of commitment to moral principle which at best I possess only in the most undeveloped and embryonic form even at the climax of my most self-conscious moral moments; in a sense, the potentiality is there, but it lies on the bosom of my moral self largely unstirred and unactivated. Yet it would be a distortion to suggest that I am merely a moral flower waiting

> I. We can now envision an objective moral order of being grounded in God.
> A. In this context each finite moral agent faces an unconditional moral claim which at best is only fragmentary in its realization.

B. More pointedly, in-
dividuals are morally
defective through
varying degrees of the
rejection of that moral
claim.

1. This moral disinte-
gration is already
begun by the time
moral self-reflection
dawns.

II. The question now
arises as to whether
the purpose of God in
creating the universe
may have come to de-
feat through the exer-
cise of that very
freedom through
which alone that pur-
pose might have been
realized: this issue has
yet to be clarified and
resolved.

expectantly for the time of my blossoming; no, the fact is, I have in many respects already bloomed forth in an instability of moral character, an impurity of moral motivation, and an inconsistency of commitment to moral principle. Thus I find myself in a morally defective, if not positively rebellious, state as over against the unconditional moral claim of God. And I do not regard myself as any sort of isolated case, since I find myself in a community of human persons as morally shaky and inconstant as myself, as if we were all in a sort of solidarity of moral failure and revolt while yet under the moral authority of the God who claims us. And it is even more disturbing than I have indicated, since I find that by the time I became morally self-reflective enough to face moral issues with appropriate seriousness, I was already in a state of moral disintegration—whether from the subtle influences of a morally imperfect society on the impressionability of my childhood, or from the inherited tendencies of my imperfect humanity. It is as if I had started off with a moral disadvantage in which I was implicated, even though I was not personally responsible for it. In fact, measuring myself by any common moral standard distinguished from prudential self-interest, I find myself a moral failure on all fronts. Nevertheless, disinclined as I am to moral responsibility, I am a free and morally responsible agent in the context of the moral demands that are at present incumbent upon me.

But what, in all this, of God's purpose in creation? If that purpose is the production and progressive development in righteousness of the personhood of finite rational, moral beings like ourselves; and if at the dawn of moral self-reflection we seem already to find ourselves in a state of moral defection; and if, although responsibly free in the moral sense, we find ourselves, in the exercise of our capacity of moral choice, to be almost habitually choosing and acting in ways that make little or no contribution to the fulfillment of our unconditional moral duty before God as the ultimte locus of moral worth—then does all this mean that the divine purpose is lost and that the goal of creation must bow to defeat through the misuse of that very radical moral freedom by means of which alone finite moral beings could, through right moral choice, fulfill that goal? Is this, after all, the final irony of existence for us to have come so far toward the understanding of our human reality in relation to the whole of being, only to lose our way at last through a failure and blindness of our own making in the exercise of the very capacity through which we might have fulfilled our true purpose? To answer these questions it is perhaps necessary to shift our intellectual gears and move into a dimension of insight that discloses a different aspect of the self-disclosure and self-revelation of being.

In Relation to the Expectation of Reason

If a reasoned interpretation of the meaning of existence has led us to the understanding of the foundations of knowledge; and if the application of the ultimate interpretive principles involved in those foundations to the broad sweep of experiential data available to our thought has led us both to the reality of a transcendent personal God as the ground of all contingent being and the ultimate locus of moral worth, and also therefore to an objective moral order of being whose structural principles impose an unconditional obligation of moral self-actualization on finite moral persons like ourselves in a state of deep and pervasive moral defection in relation to such an unconditional moral claim—then it seems at least moderately plausible to suppose, on rational grounds of the sort that have already led our thinking to the present point, that the inclusive revelation of the whole of being will involve some further word of insight that addresses itself to the moral tension between that unconditional claim, on the one hand, and, on the other, the virtually universal moral defection of those finite moral selves through the exercise of whose moral and rational capacities alone the purpose of God in creating the contingent order of being might be brought to fruition. Of course, that moderately plausible supposition is not without numerous assumptions which are, in principle at least, viably disputable, if the disputant is willing to pay the epistemological price of contesting these assumptions. Basically, the contestable presuppositions focus on the claim that being is fundamentally and pervasively rational in the sense of being accessible to, and understandable through, those ultimate categories and principles of reason that make intelligible thought possible. It is, however, long past the point in our analysis where an extended and serious contest about this issue would be appropriate—for our whole epistemological approach is grounded on the assumption of the rationality of being in the sense just defined. If, therefore, a critic were to contest this admittedly ambitious claim, his own counterclaim would either be wholly arbitrary, or else it would itself be intelligible and arguable only in terms of the very sort of rational principles that it would be the point of his counterclaim to challenge—and that would involve the critic in an existential self-contradiction of the sort that we have frequently encountered along our previously trodden path. I shall, therefore, simply make the assumption of my original supposition with a cognitive boldness which perhaps matches the ambitiousness of my claim itself. I shall just expect existence, in all its facets, to be rational as a matter of course, although I shall not imagine that this presupposition in any sense erases or even significantly reduces the puzzlement I feel at the contemplation of that rational existence.

When I ask what sort of revelation of being to expect as addressed to the confrontation between moral demand and moral defection, I have no intention of hiding the fact that, as a committed Christian, I have some fairly definite notion of what to look for—nor do I have any reason to deny that this admitted notion provides me with equally definite guidance in carrying out the analysis. The question will not be whether such a notion is operative—that much is acknowledged—it will rather be the question whether the thesis propounded is arbitrarily imported from that notion, or whether, alternatively and preferably,

I. If reason leads to the reality of God, the moral order, and the universal defection of finite moral beings, it is plausible to expect an additional revelation which addresses the tension between moral obligation and moral guilt.

A. This expectation involves contestable assumptions:
1. that being is rational throughout,

although the denial of this assumption would be existentially self-contradictory or purely arbitrary;

2. that the Christian revelation claim itself provides a clue about what to expect,

although this guidance need not involve arbitrariness or question-begging.

the thesis, however motivated and guided psychologically, will display that degree of reasonableness which is both philosophically plausible and at the same time free from sheer question-begging.

B. If God's purpose is the realization of the selfhood among human beings, then human selfhood may be viewed as the highest revelation of God.
1. But in its highest form, it would be a selfhood which is free from moral corruption and therefore fully actualized.

Now then, if God's purpose in creating the universe is the production and progressive development in righteousness of finite rational and moral selves, we might reasonably expect (as indeed we have already argued previously) that personal selfhood would itself be the highest and most directive revelation of God. If, for example, human selfhood, as disclosed in our own being, is itself explainable as a contingent reality only through Divine Selfhood as its ground, then conversely human selfhood may be expected to be the most adequate vehicle for God's revelation. At the same time, however, it will not be human selfhood in the morally violated form, in which we ourselves represent it, that will most fully disclose the reality and character of God. It will rather be a human selfhood which—although springing, as it were, from the root of our common nature—so purges that otherwise despoiled nature of its moral corruption that human selfhood will as a result appear in that fully actualized state of moral actualization which alone and fully comports with divine purpose in the creation of human persons at the outset. The corruption of our selfhood is, after all, not an essential property of it, but rather an accidental quality of that nature which results from the wrong use of moral freedom. A human person who, in his individual actualization of our humanity rises above that accidental corruption and fulfills in himself the true goal of that humanity, is not therefore impossible in principle. The consequences of this expectation are of course enormous. Such a concept means that, however spoiled through our own moral practice, the humanity we share (our human nature, our human essence) is nevertheless primordially and in principle a potential vehicle of divine self-disclosure. and it even means that the selfhood of any of us, potentially and in principle, might, apart from its moral corruption, have been the individual locus of that disclosure, even though the morally defective state of our individuality clearly indicates that this potentiality in principle has not been actualized in any of our cases. What a profoundly revelatory reality, then, is personal selfhood, even in its historical finitude.

a) Nor is this impossible in principle, since corruption is an accident of human nature.

b) Thus the selfhood of any of us, apart from its corruption, might logically have been such a revelation.

2. But such a human selfhood could be transcended as revelation, if that selfhood were so conjoined with Divine Personhood that the gap between the two was closed in a divine-human unity of selfhood that was incarnation in the strictest sense.

On the other hand, a morally fulfilled human selfhood, which stands wholly on one side of the gap that separates finite persons from God as Ultimate Personhood, is still not the highest conceivable divine self-disclosure. That height would be reached if there were a human individual whose potential for actualized selfhood was at its innermost core so intricately and completely coalesced with Divine Selfhood that, although its human self-integrity was wholly intact, its unity with Divine Selfhood was nevertheless so entire that the gap between finite human selfhood and Divine Personhood was effectively crossed—so that it was in fact God himself whose personal Being engulfed and joined to itself inseparably the whole human potential for selfhood in that particular case. This would then be incarnation in the strictest sense—not merely a human self on one side of the gap, but a divine-human unity of selfhood that bridged that gap in a single complete personhood. Again, it would be not merely association between otherwise distinguishable personal centers, but a single personal reality that conjoined the fully human with the totally divine; and finally, it would be not a previously developed human selfhood which the Divine Self overwhelmed and displaced, but an integral divine-human selfhood whose personal oneness was in principle and in fact, an accomplished reality from the start.

Yet that highest conceivable divine self-disclosure would have to involve a further aspect if, as revelation in the ultimate and final sense, it were to address, at the same time, the universal moral predicament of our corrupted human selfhood. A first step in this direction has, in fact, already been taken. The notion of incarnation, as we have conceptually analyzed it, clearly illustrates the thesis that the corrupted state of our human selfhood is not intrinsic to the essence of that selfhood but is rather an accident of that selfhood. If uncorrupted human selfhood is therefore possible in principle as the concept of incarnation seems explicitly to indicate, then it is not unrealistic to suppose that the goal of eliminating the moral corruption of man, both individually and collectively, is at least an intelligible aspiration. Still, such a potential promise provides little more than a narrow ray of light in a vast ocean of moral darkness. Is there something more explicit that addresses itself here to our defective human condition?

If an incarnation were actual, then we would expect it to be directed toward the fulfillment of God's purpose in creating a universe which constitutes an objective moral order of being. And since that moral order is deranged in the moral state of finite moral persons like ourselves, we would also expect that incarnation to involve aspects which were relevant to the healing of our moral wounds—to be, in other words, not merely a final disclosure of the Divine Reality, but also the conclusive deliverance from our corrupted moral state. And there are reasons for thinking that this expectation also would not be disappointed. God Incarnate, by taking our human essence into complete and indissoluble union with himself in an individual life, would constitute himself as a sort of universally representative humanity, and would therefore, in an important sense, so identify himself with our humanity as to involve himself not only in our essence but also in our accidentally corrupted moral condition. If that, in turn, is a reasonable notion, it would disclose to the reflective individual the intent of God to act, in our essence, in such a way as to provide representatively on our behalf a comprehensive solution to the complex problems involved in human moral defection. After all, an incarnation that was merely informative and not morally regenerative as well, would be quite pointless in the achievement of God's moral purpose in creation for beings who, through the misuse of a moral freedom that might have been put to effective use in the progressive development of moral goodness, have nevertheless become spoiled samples of selfhood. If all these samples are to be finally cast aside, then the universality of such moral corruption would indeed make a travesty of divine purpose. It

C. But such an incarnation would also need to address the gap between God's purpose and the actual human moral condition:
1. not merely by exemplifying uncorrupted human selfhood (although that is important);

2. but also by constituting a deliverance from our corrupted moral state.
3. This expectation is itself reasonable, since God Incarnate would be a sort of universally representative humanity and would thus identify himself with our corrupted moral condition.
a) This would disclose God's intent to act representatively in repairing the moral breach, since otherwise the purpose of creation would meet defeat.

b) Thus a fully intelligible Incarnation would also be redemptive and regenerative.

II. The human moral predicament has two dimensions:
A. thus
1. objectively: man would be both responsible for fulfilling the moral ideal as an obligation,

and guilty and liable for making moral amends;

2. subjectively: man is in a morally corrupted condition whose habits further incline to wrong moral choices.

B. A mere example of pure selfhood (whether in ideal or fact) is not an adequate provision:

1. objectively,
a) complete conformity to the moral law is required of man even in a morally pure state, so that the mere restoration of that conformity after a moral lapse would not make amends for the lapse;

is therefore at least plausible to suppose that a fully intelligible incarnation will at the same time constitute a fully adequate redemption as a base for the moral regeneration of these otherwise spoiled moral samples and therefore as a solution to that moral predicament which threatens the divine purpose itself.

To see what such a redemptive solution would involve, we have but to spell out and analyze the facets of the moral corruption which the solution would be required to correct. For this purpose, I shall assume what I have previously argued: an objective moral order of being, grounded in divine goodness and imposing an unconditional moral claim on finite moral selves. On that presupposition, man's moral predicament would involve both an objective and a subjective dimension. Objectively, the moral self would be responsible for fulfilling that unconditional moral claim in morally relevant choices, acts, and disposition of character—and at the same time he would be objectively guilty and responsible for making moral restitution in relation to every morally wrong choice, every morally wrong act, and every degree and condition of habitual indisposition to the challenge and claim of objective moral goodness as grounded in God. Subjectively, the moral self, although free in the morally responsible sense, would—so far as he violated that objective moral claim in act, disposition, or state of character—clearly be in a morally corrupt condition in which, through the habits engendered by successive wrong moral choices, he would be fundamentally inclined to the further extension of the effective influence of those morally insidious habits. Illustrations of all this are hardly necessary for the morally sensitive individual. Each of us, in our most honest moments at least, can see in his own complex moral condition an all-too-clear mirror image and repetition of this description. Always free and responsible in the moral choices and acts we project, we are nevertheless and on the whole increasingly disposed to the exercise of those moral dispositions which we have ourselves formed and affirmed and which spell our moral condemnation through the progressive disintegration of our personal being.

It would be superficial to suggest that the mere example of unflawed moral selfhood, provided by either the notion or even the reality of Divine Incarnation, should provide all the motivating and efficacious resources required for our moral regeneration, so that the solution to our moral predicament is directly accessible to each individual through his own moral self-effort as inspired by such an example. That seems clearly not to be the case: On the objective side of the matter, even apart from the violation of the moral law in act, disposition, and state of character, the moral self is unconditionally obligated to moral conformity and fulfillment in all these respects—in a hypothetical state of complete moral innocence or even of accomplished moral conformity (the state concretely idealized in the concept of incarnation), our obligation to the divine moral claim is all-inclusive. If then we are in violation of that claim, in whatever aspects and to whatever extent, the mere restoration of moral conformity or even a complete, self-initiated moral regeneration would not meet the liability occasioned by the condition of moral violation—since that conformity and habitual disposition to moral goodness are morally required of the moral self quite apart from any such violation and even in the state of complete moral fulfillment. Even a moralist like Immanuel Kant, who thought of incarnation merely as an abstract moral concept, recognized this predicament in the mature reflections of his old age (*Religion within the Limits of Reason Alone*), but was able to provide no satisfactory solution to it even in his own eyes. A self-generated solution to the moral predicament, on the part of an individual in a state of moral corruption, seems to be out of the question in principle. Nor is it alternatively plausible to suppose that God, in his transcendent omnipotence, could, by a sovereign act of will, simply waive the unconditional claim of the moral law on conditions he might himself prescribe by equally sovereign decree—for the moral law is intrinsic to God's moral character as essential or Absolute Goodness. To waive the moral claim by mere decree would therefore be an act in violation (per impossible) of God's own character, and would show that there was no such unconditional claim at all—a result that would land us finally in the radical ethical relativism we have already rejected.

b) Nor could God merely waive the unconditional moral law without violating his own character as essential or Absolute Goodness.

On the subjective side, the predicament of the self-effort thesis is clearly not quite so drastic. Since we are ourselves responsible, through choice and act, for the habits that dispose us to the continuation of immoral practice; and since at any given point, as transcendentally free selves, we are not determined to particular acts and choices by our moral indisposition and can therefore always act against our fundamental inclination to immorality—it follows that in the exercise of our moral freedom we can, to some indeterminate extent, begin to reverse the inclining power of our old moral habits, so as to initiate the formation of new habits in their place. In principle, therefore, it is a conceivable moral possibility; but settled persistence in a course of morally right choice would seem itself to require a settled disposition to moral righteousness which, by hypothesis, is simply missing in the morally corrupted individual, so that what is in principle possible is sustained by a thread worn thin to the vanishing point by our characteristically settled disposition to moral wrongness. When we add to this consideration the fact that the most morally concerned among us, with all the self-effort and external motivation at our disposal along the whole front of our moral experience, have scarcely begun the task of moral self-transformation—so that our best endeavors constitute no more than a frail first step of moral infancy—we will then not be at all surprised at the bold thesis of that same Immanuel Kant who contended for the belief in immortality on the sole ground that it would take an uninterrupted eternity for each of us to fulfill the unconditional claim of the moral law through the only sort of moral progress that Kant could envision. No, what is here possible in principle is not realistically achievable. We need, instead, an inner moral revolution in which the structure of immoral habits is fractured and the skeleton, at least, of a new moral character is initiated. To this the

2. Subjectively: *a*) while it is possible in principle to alter character through the free redirection of moral choice, the actualization of this change presupposes a settled disposition to righteous choice which is realistically unachievable in view of our corrupted moral condition.

b) Hence, what is needed is a moral regeneration in which our fundamental disposition is basically changed—and the resources for this are not to be found in the corrupted self.

moral self must freely consent and with it he must progressively cooperate, but he seems scarcely able to bring it about without the moral power of resources that far transcend his own. So, in general, neither objectively nor subjectively is the solution to our human moral predicament accessible through individual self-initiation and self-fulfillment through the motivation provided by the concept of incarnation as the ideal of unflawed moral selfhood.

But what if the ideal of incarnation were historically actualized; and what if, in that historical reality, God Incarnate were to take on himself, as the vicar and representative of our humanity, the liability and guilt of our universal moral corruption in such a way as to satisfy that liability through such a complete identification with our human condition that the consequences of that identification constituted at one and the same time both a representative human fulfillment of the unconditional moral claim and also the unlimited divine provision for our moral regeneration? Such a notion would indeed require a certain adjustment in our common notion of individual moral responsibility, since we characteristically assume that the guilt and responsibility of any given individual can neither be vicariously assumed by another nor its liability satisfied or adjudicated by that other person. Such a transaction would involve an ascription of guilt where there was no individual personal act or inclination as its appropriate basis, and it would also seem to suggest that those persons whose guilt and responsibility were thus assumed had somehow been divested of an obligation that was quite properly theirs through act or inclination. Many a morally sensitive individual has indeed boggled at such difficulties; but there are plausible reasons for supposing that such hesitation is not wholly rational itself. The corporate structure of society as a whole is inevitably such that individuals, not personally responsible for various moral defections on the part of others, are inevitably faced with the consequences of those defections and at the same time collectively responsible for them. There are, for example, parental-responsibility laws. And it is also clear that no one commits moral faults in isolated separation from the various social structures of which he is himself a part, so that others not personally responsible for these faults are nevertheless collectively and in varying degrees stuck with their consequences. Nor is the personally responsible agent himself exempt from the disadvantageous consequences of his moral faults, even though such consequences are, in varying degrees, partly dissipated for him by their wider social distribution. What is evident in all this is the analogical plausibility of the notion of collective and organic guilt and responsibility, while at the same time it seems obvious that there is some association or corporate relationship that makes any such moral transfer plausible and reasonable.

In a sense, the analogy with the Incarnate God is apparent here, and yet, from another point of view, the case of God Incarnate is really quite different. On the analogous side, it is clear that God, so understood as vicariously rendering satisfaction and fulfilling liability, would not be personally and individually but only collectively and represent-

III. If God Incarnate, as representative humanity, satisfied our moral liability and provided for our moral regeneration through his identification with our human condition, then the case would be different.

A. This would involve a vicarious moral exchange, the notion of which itself seems to challenge moral propriety.

1. But the corporate structure of society is characterized by just such reciprocal moral involvement;

2. and the notion of collective and organic guilt and responsibility is therefore not as unreasonable as it appears.

B. God Incarnate as meeting our moral liability:

atively guilty and responsible for that moral defection for which he thus made amends. Again, there would be an association and corporate relationship involved, since God is the creator and thus metaphorical parent of the morally corrupted persons on whose behalf the moral liability is fulfilled, and since God, precisely as Incarnate, has so fully assumed our human nature as to be organically and corporately one with us, even in our moral predicament. But there is also a striking difference as well. The very notion of the Incarnate God implies the idea that in this fully divine and fully human person there is a representative identity with our humanity that far transcends the limited and variable senses in which we are corporately joined to one another, since we are never fully and completely conjoined in this way but only fragmentarily and incompletely—while the very notion of incarnation entails that very full and complete union with our human essence which is only imperfectly realized in ourselves. If we add to this fact the further difference that, on the whole, our corporate involvement with one another is, as it were, thrust upon us by our reciprocal social intermeshing—while the assumption of union with our humanity in the case of God is, by its very nature, a wholly voluntary assumption grounded in God's goodness and love as characteristically willing the well-being of those finite selves through whom alone God's own moral purpose can be realized—then the notion of a representative meeting of moral liability on the part of God in behalf of the individually and collectively guilty need no longer constitute a moral conundrum or perplexity for us. The previously argued claim—that, left to ourselves as individuals, our moral predicament of guilt would be hopeless and God's moral purpose in creating us rendered irretrievably lost—only serves to make the notion of representative moral satisfaction still more fully plausible. Nor, finally, would the personally and individually guilty be let off, as it were, scot-free. In the case of those who, by personal commitment to God as the true Good, become the beneficiaries of this representative fulfillment, that decisive commitment would itself become the starting point of a moral regeneration that would bind such individuals to an obligation of moral fulfillment that, in its outworking, would constitute the core of the entire personal career of individuals thus transformed by divine love—the bondage of guilt would be essentially broken only to be replaced by the bondage of a new and self-fulfilling responsibility.

I have already spoken to the anticipated criticism that all this is simply being read back into the dimension of rational plausibility from the historical and theological claim of traditional Christianity. I have indeed acknowledged that my background in Christianity did indeed supply me with a sense of direction as to what to look for. But I have also claimed that the crucial issue here is not about the historical or even psychological motivation that leads to the propounding of a proposal—it is rather about the intrinsic plausibility and reasonableness of the proposal, whatever its genetic background. But it is nevertheless the case that, broadly construed, the general idea of an incarnation, of an idea of the identification of the Religious Object,

1. is analogous to representative and collective guilt in society.

2. But it is also strikingly different, since:
a) the representative identity is far more complete,

is assumed voluntarily,

and is directed toward the recovery of God's purpose in creation;

b) the individual, who becomes the beneficiary of the representative fulfillment, is himself bound by a continuing self-fulfilling responsibility.

C. Nor can all this be criticized as read off from traditional Christianity in an arbitrary manner, since the general notion of incarnation is widespread in other religious traditions, however conceived, with the essence of our human nature, is an all-but-universal concept among otherwise very diverse religious traditions, some of which had little or no historical connection with the Hebrew-Christian tradition. It is true, of course, that the concept of Ultimate Reality in many of these traditions is quite different from the theistic understanding of God in Hebrew-Christian thought, so that the concept of an incarnation has a decisively different twist. In a pantheistic outlook (as in certain types of Hindu perspectives, or in Mahayana Buddhism, or in classical Taoism), everything (and therefore man as well) is an aspect of, and in some sense an incarnation of, the Absolute Reality—so that the idea of incarnation is a sort of universal human possibility or perhaps even reality, rather than involving the notion of a unique and historically unrepeatable union of God with human nature in a single individual. But even in these traditions, there is something special and at least conceptually (if not individually) unique in a Krishna or a Gautama Buddha that makes such individuals special cases. Even the notion, in classical Confucian thought, that the ideal of manhood is grounded in the moral qualities of the Tao or of the Great Whole is suggestive of a oneness between human nature and the Religious Ultimate that makes the potentiality of incarnation a conceivable one in that context. The differences are of course significant, but they are not overriding, and hence the similarities must also be recognized or perhaps even stressed. At the very least, the tendency for this notion of Incarnation, however diversely understood in context, to crop up in nearly all the developed religious traditions of the world clearly shows that the concept has a universally intrinsic plausibility that is by no means limited to the historical Christian tradition.

In any case, what I have so far proposed takes, at this stage, only the form of a rationally plausible framework of conception. The idea of a divinely initiated solution to the universal moral predicament of man, and the companion idea that the highest conceivable form of such a solution would take the form of an incarnation of the Ultimate—these are, at the very least, not incoherent or rationally implausible notions from the standpoint of discursive intellectual thought or conceptual reason. Christianity does, in fact, claim the fulfillment of all this in Jesus Christ as God Incarnate, but whether and to what extent and in what sense that claim is justifiable, on objectively plausible (though clearly not demonstrable) grounds, remains to be considered.

There is a final expectation of reason to which I have also previously alluded in more than one context. The notion of an authoritative scripture—or written and informative body of insights that constitute a divine revelation—is, if anything, rather more universal among religious traditions than the notion of Incarnation. And this fact is not really all that surprising. Whatever is a dimension of the self-disclosure or revelation of being is, in principle and so far as it is conceptually accessible, expressible in propositional form. In fact, it is in propositional self-expression that man most fully and adequately is capable of self-disclosure through the exercise of that aspect of his nature

---

Marginal notes:

although its interpretation varies with the general context in which it is put forth.

D. The idea of a divinely provided solution and revelation through genuine incarnation is thus not unthinkable or implausible in rational terms.

IV. It is a further expectation that revelation should take a written propositional form commensurate with conceptual reason as man's most elevated aspect.
A. Not only is this notion virtually universal,

which constitutes the most unique and elevated dimension of his being, namely, discursive intellect or conceptual reason. It is fully congruous with this understanding of man that a revelation of God to man should address, at its own abstractly highest level, that aspect in man which constitutes his most unique and elevated dimension as man, and that such a revelation should take the propositional form characteristic of the highest human self-disclosure. Hence, we confront the understandable and virtual universality of the idea of written revelation or authoritative scripture. Aside from this general philosophical insight into the universality of the concept of scripture or written revelation, there are, of course, a number of fundamentally practical reasons for the widespread dissemination of this notion. Written documents provide a form for the maintenance of developing religious insight, however originated, that provides a greater stability in the preservation of such insights and, at the same time, at least for the literate in any culture, a potentially greater accessibility in principle than any other form of authoritative understanding with which this written form might be plausibly compared. It is no secret, of course, that in Oriental and Semitic cultures a relative fixity of oral tradition, through instructors of various sorts, was an historically important form for the preservation of religious teaching—and that this form was fairly effective in cultures where, in the absence of widespread literacy, memory based on oral instruction was a far more keenly developed and exercised form for the preservation of insight than it could conceivably be in any developed contemporary culture. But, even under such circumstances, the written form of authoritative religious teaching came to be deemed important indeed—partly as a guiding framework for oral instruction and effective memory, and increasingly also as a substitute for both, since there is a concreteness and fixity about the written word that far exceeds that of oral tradition, with its inevitable tendency toward gradual transition in both the form and content of the teaching. And here we can cite as examples not only the Hebrew-Christian Scriptures themselves (stretching from the books of Moses, through the writings of prophets, psalmists and historical chroniclers, culminating in the gospel accounts of the words and teachings of Jesus, the historical record of the early Christian church, the letters of Paul and others, and finally the apocalyptic prophecy of the Book of Revelation—much of this was initially oral, but much was also in written form from the very first). There are also the sacred canons of both Hinduism and Buddhism, the classical treatises of Taoism, the Zend-avesta of Zoroastrianism, and many others. Even Confucianism, which is sometimes but, I think, mistakenly regarded as merely a moral system rather than a religion, came to have its five classics and its four books. So important has the written form of religious teaching seemed in all these varied traditions. Not that there are no problems with the preservation of written texts. Copyist errors, especially before printing, were humanly inevitable, and sometimes modifications were intentional. In the case of the New Testament, at least, whole different families of texts came to be dis-

but there are practical reasons for its prevalence as providing greater stability and accessibility.

1. Oral tradition, although widespread as a means of preservation, was itself embodied in written form to insure its relatively greater fixity.

2. Examples of the written form.

cerned. Yet, despite all this, the relative fixity of the written word stands largely unshaken as compared with oral tradition.

On the whole, then, we can conclude that philosophically, practically, and historically, the propositional, written form of divine self-disclosure is a reasonable expectation with respect to the idea of revelation. Yet that general plausibility settles no question of explicit substance on this issue. The origin, status, and authority of such sacred writings are differently understood in distinct religious traditions, and there are even strikingly different interpretations that proliferate the unfolding of any single tradition. The nature and basis of scriptural authority, even granted the obvious difference in identifying the writings that belong to Scripture, would be very differently construed in any Buddhist perspective as compared with an analogous understanding in any Christian perspective. And the contrasts of understanding within each of these traditions would perhaps be as extensive as between those entire traditions themselves. But, glossing over such contrasts, we confront, in addition, a diversity of revelation claims put forth by different religious traditions and embodying contrasting, if not at numerous points contradictory, conceptual frameworks for understanding the Divine Reality. The question then becomes—in regard to these competing written scriptural texts—which, if any, of these claimants provides the more plausible claim? How can the comparative plausibility of these claims be critically ranked? And, more concretely, what non-question-begging and therefore presumably rationally objective criteria can be used effectively to decide such issues with reasonable propriety?

As I much earlier pointed out in my discussion of religious epistemology, no such religious revelation can, without arbitrary presumption, be taken as logically foundational. Any attempt to opt for one revelation claim against another (or for that matter, any attempt to view them all in Hegelian fashion as each in its own context comparatively plausible but occupying a place in an inclusive hierarchy of revelation claims) will inevitably involve an appeal to criteria of assessment that are logically prior to that revelation and its claim to authority. My entire discussion of epistemology was a systematic and, I hope, critical attempt to formulate such objectively reasonable criteria. And my entire discussion of natural theology and its case for theism was, analogously, an attempt to provide a general metaphysical context for the effective operation of these criteria in the settlement of such issues regarding religious truth-claims. I have, of course, no reason to reiterate all that in the present context—I mention those earlier analyses merely to point out that all that previous philosophical spadework must now provide the philosophical garden and seed bed in which plausible decisions about these issues concerning religious revelation should now be attempted. The title of my book obviously discloses that I regard the Christian revelation claim, adequately construed, as the highest and most rationally plausible alternative here. But both my previous analysis here and my earlier publications (especially *Oriental Philosophy*) make it equally clear that I do not therefore

B. But the prevalence of the written word: 1. is very differently interpreted in different traditions and even in the same tradition;

2. and raises the question of conflicting revelation claims which call for rational evaluation.

a) Since no religious revelation can reasonably claim to be logically foundational, the relevance of epistemological criteria becomes clear.

b) While I opt for the rational plausibility of the Christian revelation claim, nevertheless I accept a graded hierarchy which recognizes elements of truth in all religious traditions.

simply dismiss all other revelation claims as mere chaff. I opt then for a sort of graded hierarchy which—although it is not Hegelian in dismissing all religious differences as accidental in relation to some sort of universal religious essence—nevertheless sees important elements of truth in all these contrasting and in many ways overlapping religious traditions. At the same time, I see all these limited but genuine insights as aspects of the whole Christian truth. And I am gratified by the thought that some of the finest proponents of those alternative religious traditions may be, and indeed are, willing to grant to persons like myself a comparable and reciprocal intellectual and spiritual generosity. Whether the Christian revelation claim, in the inclusive sense I have indicated, does possess a universal rational plausibility by embracing all genuine religious insight into its own comprehensive sweep of truth—whether, in Paul's words, all the treasures of wisdom and knowledge are in the end hidden away (although not therefore effortlessly discerned) in Christ as truth—that is the crucial issue which must now concern us.

Christianity and the Revelational Person: An Historical/Critical Case for the Incarnation of God in Jesus Christ

The Christian Concept of the Christ

The Biblical Witness

What, then, is a reflective individual to make of the Christian claim, concerning Jesus Christ, that he is God Incarnate and therefore both individually and historically fulfills that rationally plausible general concept of incarnation that I have previously analyzed? We do not, of course, start out on the answer to this question in a perspectival vacuum or wholly neutral terrain. Instead, we approach the question in a context of consideration in which the ideal of rational objectivity has been recognized as an appropriate epistemological stance, along with the structure-of-knowledge theory in which that ideal has been embedded in our analysis. And we also approach the question in the metaphysical framework of a rationally plausible theistic world-view. Hence, in analyzing the Incarnation claim of Christianity, I shall regard these previously developed claims as, both in principle and in practice, settled issues. It is not, of course, that they have been settled with absolutely final decisiveness—I have nowhere made any such claim— it is rather that these assumed stances have been argued as rationally preferable alternatives in epistemology and metaphysics. It is clear, in addition, that any individual, from whatever culture, who considers the Christian Incarnation claim, will himself bring with him an interpretive epistemological and metaphysical context in which he also

I. The Incarnation issue is approached with certain issues provisionally settled.

A. Thus:
1. rational objectivity in epistemology, and

theism in metaphysics, are assumed on the basis of previous analysis.

B. Any thinker:
1. employs such an interpretive framework, however different it might be;

will conduct his analysis, whether he does so explicitly and consciously or not. And his analysis will inevitably reflect the interpretive presuppositions involved in that context. It is not, therefore, that I am saddling myself with a burden of cognitive baggage of which other interpreters might, in principle at least, be free—it is rather that I am openly acknowledging a context which has a counterpart, however different, in every other interpretive approach. I am, of course, also claiming that the issues among these interpretive approaches themselves have already been considered and at least provisionally settled. Hence, it is not in a universe in which rational objectivity is an alien that I raise the Incarnation question, but rather in a universe in which reason, rightly understood through its own structural principles, is quite at home. And it is equally not in a universe in which the existence of God stands as a gapingly wide open question that I raise this same question, but rather in a universe in which numerous lines of reasoned analysis converge on God as the Ultimate Reality through whose transcendent Selfhood and divine purpose all contingent things whatever have the existence they possess. Hence the question is whether, in a rationally intelligible order of being at the capstone of which everything subsists through divine causality and purpose, the Christian Incarnation claim is plausible. Armed with a different interpretive context, the question might well take on a very different hue; indeed, in some such alternative contexts (say, one combining radical subjectivism with a naturalistic metaphysic), the Incarnation question would hardly be a serious issue, still less a viable option.

But the Christian Incarnation claim must also be cast up against a background provided by the specific historical context in which it arose—namely, the background provided by the Judaic context of the time of Christ as that context itself emerged from the thought world of the Hebrew Bible or the Old Testament. So it is not enough to have spoken of the expectation of reason, as we have already done; it is also pertinent and necessary to speak of the expectation of the Hebrew religious framework in which Jesus himself historically emerged. So much has been written about this background that it would be virtually impertinent and repetitious, not to mention practically impossible in view of my self-imposed spatial restrictions, to reiterate here in detail what is easily accessible in the work of biblical scholars whose volumes fill whole sections of theological libraries, if indeed the core of the requisite information is not at the fingertips of the average Sunday-school scholar or catechumen. But I will summarize, virtually without argument, what I take to be the salient and all-but-indisputable elements of that background for the purpose of providing this part of the context of the Christian revelation claim. It is first of all, then, clear that the metaphysical orientation of the Old Testament, through all its various historical phases and strata, is pervasively theistic. Indeed, it exhibits from first to last, in Law, Prophets and Writings, a rigorous monotheism which, in its most explicit form in the high prophets such as Isaiah, not only emphasizes the absolute unity of God, but also dismisses all the gods of the nations as mere idols of

2. and another framework might produce different results.

II. The Incarnation claim of Christianity also has a pertinent background in the thought of the Old Testament.

A. This setting:
1. involves a rigorous monotheism which rejects all idolatry;

human craftsmanship and perhaps even imaginative thought (Deut. 6:4; Isa. 44:6f.). There is no reason to deny that this explicit monotheism was not fully elaborated or understood from the earliest stages of Israel's history, and that the insight of the average Israelite was, in varying degrees, no doubt imperfect. The gods of other nations are frequently alluded to in the Old Testament; and the Lord Jehovah is even referred to as King above all the gods. And if we are ourselves sometimes confused about the exact import of these and other similar passages, it will not be surprising if many an Israelite thought of those other gods as real enough in their limited domain, but at the same time saw the God of Israel as towering above those other gods in his universal majesty. Yet it is clear that this confusion of monotheism with what is commonly called henotheism, even if it survived in the popular Israelite mind, was decisively swept away in the later stages of Old Testament thought (Isa. 45).

2. but this view may have been partly inexplicit at an early stage, so that henotheism was vaguely supposed by the average individual, although this possible confusion was cleared up at a later stage.

But there is a second and equally important strain in Old Testament thought for our purposes, and that is the element of Messianic expectation. With varying degrees of explicitness, in many historical and literary contexts, and with a steadily gathering and developing crescendo of anticipation which reached its climax in the high prophets and in the generally later stages of Old Testament thought, the Hebrew revelatory literature and tradition look forward to a single historical individual in whom God's revelatory, redemptive, and even sociopolitical purposes were to be, at first in principle and later in actualized completeness, decisively fulfilled. From the so-called protevangelium of Genesis 3:15, in which it was predicted that an individual offspring of "the woman" would crush, as it were, the head of God's archenemy depicted as a deceptive serpent, to Daniel's provocative vision of the son of man (Daniel 7) and the Anointed One (precisely, the Messiah, Daniel 9)—and including in its wake between these both the personalized description of God's wisdom in the Book of Proverbs, as well as the graphic picture of God's Servant in Isaiah, along with much else beside—all the streams of Old Testament anticipation converge on this promised individual, God's Messiah. Much that is quite specific is predicted of him: that he would be of the seed of Abraham, that his lineage would be through the royal line of King David, that he would even be born in Bethlehem in the land of Judah, and that he would meet with a tragic death from which he would emerge in victory. As to his vocation, the Messiah is finally to be the political ruler of world who would both reestablish Israel's place of prestige among the nations and at the same time also fulfil through his worldwide kingdom God's collective purpose for the whole of humanity. But on the other hand, the Messiah is also to be, in his death, a sort of human sacrifice, not only for Israel but for all the nations—a sacrifice that somehow bears the iniquities of the guilty and opens up a way of divine forgiveness for them (Isa. 53). Yet the decisive thing about the expected Messiah, for our purposes here, is that, while it is clear that he is to be full and integral humanity, at the same time he is somehow to be God himself appearing in that humanity (for example, Isa. 9:6,7; Ps. 110; Ps.

B. A second strain involves a developing and increasingly explicit Messianic expectation in the form of a single individual through whom God's purposes would be ultimately fulfilled in history.

1. God's Messiah is ultimately therefore to bring:
a) a political resolution through his reign,
b) and a provision for divine forgiveness through his death as a sacrifice.
2. But while he is to be fully human, he is also to be God himself appearing in that humanity.

a) This notion in-
volves a restructuring
of monotheism.

b) If, as is the case,
Jesus claimed to be
the Messiah, that
claim involves this
same element of deity,

and this implication
was recognized by the
Jewish leaders at the
trial of Jesus.

III. Historical and lit-
erary presuppositions
are essential here.

A. It will be assumed:
1. that Jesus of Naza-
reth was an actual his-
torical person, since
the emergence of
Christianity is not oth-
erwise explicable;

45:6,7). It is hardly my intent here to develop the full textual basis for any of this, much less for all of it—I should think any thoughtful reader of the Old Testament or Hebrew Bible would discern these as well as many other strains in the concept of the Messiah. The impor-tant implications of all this in the present context are clear enough. If the developed concept of the Messiah in the Old Testament depicts this clearly human instrument of God's purposes as somehow also himself God, then there appears already in the Old Testament itself an obvious question about the rigidity of Old Testament monotheism, since that last notion must be viewed as compatible with the notion of incarnation which we have already analyzed. Furthermore, it is equally significant that Jesus himself came on the historical scene in the context of such a notion of Messiahship as I have now briefly elaborated. And if it turns out, as historically seems to be the case, that Jesus appropriated the various elements of Messiahship to himself as the one in whom all these promises were to be fulfilled, then the full impact of this claim must not be ignored—namely, that Jesus was making no ordinary prophetic claim about himself, as if he were, though importantly, claiming no more than that he stood in the line of chosen prophets. No, the claim is far more drastic and staggering— for if he self-consciously claims to be the Messiah in the fullest sense, he is at the same time claiming, with whatever degree of plausibility, that he is, in a sense quite compatible with an adequately understood monotheism, God Incarnate. It can be reasonably contended that, at the blatantly mock trial that climaxed Jesus' historical career before his death, the leaders of his Jewish opposition clearly understood this implication. For when Jesus acknowledged (according to Mark 14:61– 63, one of the oldest historical sources) that he was the Messiah, the Son of the Blessed One, the high priest flew into a rage and accused Jesus of blasphemy. Such a charge would be intelligible only if the claim to Messiahship were at the same time a claim to deity. Whether it is plausible to accept this claim is an issue yet to be considered, but even now its implications are fairly obvious.

If, then, against the background I have described, we proceed to consider the self-testimony of Jesus, we can only do so on certain historical and literary presuppositions. There is, in fact, virtually no imaginable negatively critical thesis that some sophisicated exponent or other, often in academic context, has not cast up as an objection to even the most modest claim to any single piece of historical knowledge about the life and teachings of Jesus. The more extreme of these criticisms would make Albert Schweitzer's *The Quest for the Historical Jesus* seem, by comparison, to be virtually a piece of traditionally pious conservatism, even though Schweitzer's work was itself largely sceptical of many positive historical claims. I have no intention of dealing, for example, with the claim that no such person as Jesus of Nazareth ever even existed, and that therefore the whole form and content of the gospel materials, on which Christianity was based from the very beginning, were totally the product of the unbridled and highly imaginative inventiveness of first- (or second-) century religious enthusiasm on the part of the leaders of an otherwise obscure Jewish sect. Such a proposal has nothing whatever to support it other than the relatively *a priori* prejudice of the critics propounding it. Without the historical Jesus, the origin of Christianity is simply inexplicable even for responsible persons who reject the Christian truth-claim. Nor will I take very seriously the claim of somewhat more restrained critics who, though acknowledging the historicity of Jesus, regard all the gospel materials as providing us with scarcely any reliable information about Jesus—on the ground that these materials are already removed from any solid historical foundation by the pervasive presence in the materials of a pious framework which clearly has adapted the apparently historical elements to the religious and psychological needs of those committed to that framework. This position has, in support of it, the undeniable fact that the Jesus of the gospels is everywhere seen through the eyes of believing faith. But it is not indisputably evident that this fact necessarily, or even credibly, distorts the purportedly historical material. In fact, the existential concern of faith—suspending the personal and spiritual destiny of early believers who were close to the described events historically—on the truth of the core of those materials about Jesus might as believably operate in the exact opposite fashion by jealously and even fanatically guarding that historical core from any substantial distortion or corruption. In any case, in the absence of any plausibly identifiable historical core that in any sense contravenes the historical materials in the gospels, the supposition of the historical worthlessness of these materials can be confidently identified as an arbitrary prejudice with far less to support it than the positive interpretation which those materials engendered in the minds of those who, in consequence of that influence among others, became believers.

2. that the gospel materials contain a solid historical core of genuine information about Jesus even though it is seen through the eyes of faith.

Still I have no intention whatever of assuming, as my starting point here, any parallel arbitrariness on my part which would simply take the believing interpretation of the historical materials for granted. Instead, although I am clearly a believer myself and have no reason to hide or even obscure that fact, I will assume the far more modest thesis that the Gospel materials, especially in the Synoptics (Matthew, Mark, and Luke) and even generally in the Gospel of John, provide us with a substantial, though not necessarily flawless, account of events surrounding and composing the life and teachings of Jesus. At the same time, I will draw no substantive conclusion as to the historicity of the miracle accounts in the Gospels merely on the ground that these accounts stand as part of the record, since I acknowledge, for purposes of methodological procedure, that the obvious persuasive impact of these accounts raises for a reflective reader at least some justifiable question about their face value as bald historical accounts. Again, although I will assume that the Gospels provide us a generally accurate account of the teachings of Jesus, I will nevertheless not assume that every utterance attributed to Jesus represents a verbatim quotation of something he stated in precisely those words as nevertheless accurately translated into Greek out of some hypothecated Ara-

B. But it is not to be assumed methodologically that the records are flawlessly historical as they stand. 1. It will rather be assumed that the materials are substantially historical in the factual sense,

2. and that the sayings attributed to Jesus represent the thrust and meaning of his teachings, whether or not they are translated verbatim quotations.

a) There may be more translated quotation than is sometimes supposed by critics.

b) John will be regarded as historical in substance, although not necessarily in form.

IV. The gospel materials represent Jesus as fully human and at the same time as essentially divine.
A. This is particularly true of the Gospel of John and the First Epistle of John.

B. But the Synoptics, although less explicit, are nevertheless equally clear on Jesus' deity.

maic original—although I do take it for granted that Jesus characteristically spoke Aramaic. I shall simply leave the question open as to which of the sayings of Jesus are actual quotations, since for my purposes no point of substance hangs on this issue. I will rather assume merely that such sayings of Jesus represent accurately the thrust and meaning of what Jesus said or taught. On the other hand, there may be good reasons for supposing that we actually have in the Gospels far more translated quotations from Jesus than would commonly be assumed. The close parallelism of quoted matter in the Synoptics may well run back to earlier written or oral sources, but it nevertheless may be interpreted as reflecting a pervasive concern to preserve the precise wording of those earlier materials, which themselves may reasonably be believed to impinge historically on Jesus' actual words. As to the Gospel of John, I shall take the common view that the form of Jesus' sayings is there cast in the context of prolonged meditation on the ultimate significance of Jesus' words, and therefore appropriately given a literary structure befitting that reflective meditative stance. Yet I will here again regard the substance of the Johannine sayings as essentially representative of the content of what Jesus actually taught, although I will return to this issue in a later critical context.

It is everywhere clear that, quite apart from the self-testimony of Jesus preserved in the Gospel sayings, the writers of the Gospels and/or their sources—while indisputably depicting Jesus as genuinely and integrally a human being—nevertheless, in a multiplicity of ways, imply and assert that Jesus is divine. This is explicitly, perhaps even blatantly, true of the Gospel of John, whose literary prologue identifies the historical Jesus with the preexistent Logos of God, which in turn is declared to be God and to have taken humanity to himself in Jesus as the Logos incarnated (John 1:1–14). In the discourse of chapter eight, the writer ascribes to Jesus the claim to be identical with the "I Am" of the Old Testament—a clear reference to the special title of God disclosed to Moses at the burning bush (John 8:58; Exod. 3:14). Even if this discourse is not, on this point, historically grounded in an actual saying of Jesus (a point which I do not concede, but adopt for the sake of argument), it nevertheless reflects the clear conviction of the writer that Jesus is God in the highest Old Testament sense, and that this claim goes back to Jesus himself. John also depicts the disciple Thomas as confessing, when confronted with the risen Jesus, "My Lord and my God!" (John 20:28). In the First Epistle of John, doubtless from the same hand as the Gospel, it is openly asserted of Jesus Christ that "this one is the true authentic God and eternal life" (1 John 5:20). It is difficult to imagine how a clearer designation of the deity of Jesus could be affirmed than is indicated by these Johannine assertions, unless we consider the studied formulations of dogmatic theology itself.

It is precisely for this reason that it is often claimed that the synoptic Gospels, presumably closer to Jesus historically, disclose a different and decidedly less transcendent view of the person of Jesus. This claim is plausible in the sense that the synoptic references are more casual or incidental and less explicit; but at the same time they are no less clear and decisive as to the deity of Jesus as God Incarnate. This claim can be seen to be plausible both in terms of what the writers themselves say directly or indirectly about Jesus, and also in terms of what they ascribe to Jesus as having been said by him. Even if we suppose (in my opinion, incorrectly) that the sayings ascribed to Jesus have no substantial basis in what Jesus himself actually claimed, these sayings, at the very least, represent the view that the given writer clearly held concerning Jesus, since otherwise there would be no way to account for his including the account in his record. Now, of the three Synoptics, the Gospel of Mark is commonly regarded as the least dogmatic concerning Christology. But the astounding fact is that Mark begins his account (1:2, 3) by quoting a passage from Isaiah the prophet (Isa. 40:3) with a supplement from the prophet Malachi (3:1)—a passage which predicts a messenger who will prepare the way for the coming of the Lord God himself in a definitely historical sense. This passage Mark regards as fulfilled in John the Baptist as preparing the way for the coming of Jesus and for his open manifestation to Israel. This application would be both wildly irresponsible and virtually unintelligible if it did not imply for the discerning listener or reader that Jesus is the Lord God himself whose way had been thus prepared by the messenger John. And this careful scriptural citation is all the more significant in a book where such precise Old Testament references are comparatively rare. The Christ of the Gospel of Mark is, from the outset, therefore, no mere prophetic teacher (although he clearly is that also), but rather God himself appearing in history. Mark also provocatively ascribes to demons, whom he depicts as being exorcised by Jesus, the confession to and about Jesus that he is the Son of God in a clearly unique sense (3:11, 5:7). Whatever the historical status of such accounts, they clearly constitute a representation of Jesus with which the writer is in accord.

1. Mark:

a) Implied deity at the outset.

Just as importantly, the Markan Jesus not only claims to be the Messiah of Old Testament anticipation—an acknowledgement which he unhesitatingly accepts from his disciples (Mark 8:29–31)—while identifying the Messiah with the Old Testament Son of Man; but he interprets his Messiahship in the highest terms by admitting to the high priest that he is the Messiah, the Son of the Blessed One—an admission which, as previously noted, the high priest interprets as blasphemy from his own point of view, a thought which would be unintelligible unless he interpreted Jesus' admission as a claim to deity. The Markan Jesus (12:35–37) also refers to Psalm 110 as showing that the Messiah is not merely David's son (in an extended sense) but also David's Lord. This passage, which Jesus unmistakably applies to himself, makes it clear that, at least in Mark's eyes, Jesus interpreted his Messiahship in terms of Divine Lordship. And since it has already been made clear that the Old Testament asserts the Absolute Deity of the Messiah—and that this implication was understood by such Jewish leaders as the high priest—who can reasonably deny that Jesus, as

b) The Messianic claim, and the clear inclusion of the claim to deity.

2. Matthew and Luke:
a) Both reiterate the
Markan witness.

depicted here, specifically applied this implication to his Messianic claim?

The testimony of the other two Synoptic Gospels is at least equally clear. Much of the Markan witness is carried over and made, if anything, even more explicit, especially with reference to the Messianic claim. Both Matthew (23:63–65) and Luke (22:66–71) reiterate the Markan account of Jesus' acknowledgement of his Messiahship before the high priest and the council, with the same obvious implication that Messiahship carries the claim to deity along with it. Matthew himself, furthermore, represents Jesus as promising the nucleus of the disciples, as those who would carry on his mission after his own departure from the world in the literal human sense, that he would nevertheless be in their midst wherever two or three of them were gathered together in his name (18:20), and even generally that he would be with them always even to the very consummation of history (28:20)—a wholly incongruous promise unless the one who utters it is regarded as possessing the sort of spatial and temporal omnipresence that is unique to God. The same resurrected Jesus is depicted by Matthew as commanding his disciples to baptize believers into *the* name of the Father and of the Son and of the Holy Spirit (28:19)—an explicit Trinitarian formula which at the very least reflects the evident conviction of the writer, even from the most radical critical standpoint. As in Mark (2:1–11), Jesus is also represented in Matthew as having, in his status as Messianic Son of Man, the unique authority to forgive sins (9:2, 6), an authority that the Jesus of Matthew obviously views as a distinct divine prerogative (5:14, 15). Perhaps the climax of this Incarnation claim is present in Jesus' claim to be the final judge of the destinies of all men (Matt. 25:31–46).

b) Matthew clearly
implies Jesus' deity
also,

c) as does Luke, both
in his Gospel

Luke's witness is certainly to the same effect, both in his Gospel and in his representation of the primitive belief of the early church in the Book of the Acts of the Apostles. He too reaffirms the Messiahship of Jesus, not only in the context of Jesus' appearance before the council, but also in numerous other contexts (2:11, 26; 4:41; 9:20; 20:41; 23:2; 24:26, 46) which carry through the Messianic claim to the clear implication of deity. Here too Jesus, as Son of Man, is the forgiver of sins (5:24), the one to be seated at the right hand of God's power (22:69), and the determiner of the final destinies of men (9:26; 12:8; 21:36). All this is again carried over into the Book of Acts and further adumbrated: Jesus is addressed in prayer (7:59), is referred to as "Lord over all" (10:36), and is continually referred to by the title "Lord" with the highest conceivable implication. And, in Acts 20:28, the Apostle Paul is represented as speaking of "the church of [the] God which he took possession of through his own blood." This conjoining of God as agent with the human death of Jesus implies, for both Paul and Luke, the acknowledgement of the absolute Godhead of Jesus, since otherwise the conjunction would be totally unintelligible.

and in the Book of
Acts.

C. Since much of this
material is attributed
to Jesus in the gospels,
then, if that attribu-
tion is substantially
historical, the Incarna-
tion claim is also at-
tributable to Jesus
himself, with all that is
thus implied.

From these synoptic passages, the conviction of the writers as to the Messiahship and deity of Jesus is evident enough. But something else is also evident if we introduce the assumption with which I prefaced the whole discussion. If the sayings ascribed to Jesus in these sources, even though not necessarily verbatim quotations, are nevertheless substantially expressive of what Jesus himself claimed as to his identity, then, since a significant element of the citations involves such sayings, it follows that the self-testimony of Jesus in these sources is also clear. On that assumption, it is reasonably plausible to conclude that Jesus himself made the Messianic claim and the implied further claim to deity. If that is so, then we will have to reckon with the consequences of that conclusion. The resistance of critics has been very strong at this juncture—not only *can* my procedural assumption be disputed, but it *has* been so disputed by a veritable army of negative critics. The question is whether there is any reasonable (as distinguished from merely logically possible) basis for the dispute. There certainly is a theological and even psychological basis for it. If a critic begins with the prejudgment that the notion of incarnation is to be rejected out of hand, and if he nevertheless wishes to provide some historical foundation for this presupposition, he will attempt to go behind the sources as they stand in order to find prior documents and/or oral traditions on which those sources are themselves grounded. I shall not, in fact, contest the legitimacy of speculating about such sources; but what I will contest, in a later context, is the implied thesis that such historically more primitive sources would themselves be free of the Messianic incarnational claims. For the present I will be content to say merely that this implied thesis has only the initial prejudicial bias of the critic to support it, since the Gospels as they stand provide no clear foundation for any such thesis. Whether the historical and literary criticism of the documents will alter my judgment remains to be seen.

1. This implication has been extensively challenged by critics, though mostly on prejudicial grounds.

2. Whether source criticism would alter the point is yet to be considered.

That the rest of the New Testament confronts us with the same claim to Jesus' deity scarcely requires more than casual perusal in the present context. Support for this claim will be obvious to any reflective person who goes through the documents with even moderate care. The Pauline letter corpus certainly reflects this outlook by claiming that Jesus possessed the essential form of deity and a commensurate complex equality with God (Phil. 2:6–12), by declaring that in Jesus there dwelt the whole fullness of the Godhead or the Deity in its entirety (Col. 2:9), and by speaking of Jesus as "the God who is over all, blessed forever" (Rom. 9:5). And it is at least a Paulinist, if not Paul himself, who speaks quite unambiguously of "our great God and Savior, Christ Jesus" (Titus 2:13). It is furthermore worth observing in passing that in all of these texts the Christological inference is incidental in arguments with a different theme, so that the Christology implied must clearly have been common ground between Paul and the believers to whom he wrote.

V. The rest of the New Testament embodies the same incarnational claim, both implicitly and explicitly.
A. Paul's letters.

And what of other New Testament literary strata? First Peter (perhaps closely conjoined historically with the early parts of Acts) speaks of the Spirit of Christ as having testified through the Old Testament prophets (1:10–13), views angels and authorities as subject to Jesus as Messiah (3:22), and urges believers to "set apart in your hearts Christ

B. First and Second Peter.

C. James.

D. Hebrews.

E. Apocalypse.

F. Thus there is no basis in the New Testament as it stands for a subincarnational view of Jesus.

VI. The full humanity of Jesus is also emphasized in the New Testament materials.

VII. But there is no mere juxtaposition here: it is rather one and the same person who is both human and divine.

Jesus as Lord" (3:15)—a passage which clearly recalls Isaiah 8:13, where it specifically refers to the Lord Jehovah. In Second Peter (1:1) we read of "our God and Savior, Jesus Christ." In James, supposedly the most Jewish of the New Testament books, we find mention of "the Name"—obviously referring to Jesus and thus applying to him an Old Testament designation of Jehovah (5:14), and we hear Jesus spoken of as "the Glory" in a way reminiscent of the same title applied to Jehovah in Zechariah 2:5 (James 2:1). And, in Hebrews, Jesus is depicted as the one to whom God was speaking in Psalm 45:6 when he said, "Thy throne, O God, is forever and ever" (1:8), and as the Lord who created the world (1:10). The Apocalypse, finally, is a veritable crescendo in echoing the concept of the Incarnation of God in Jesus as the Messiah. In the Book of Revelation, Jesus is set forth as being, with God, the first and the last (1:8, 17, 18; 21:6; 22:13), and as jointly with God the object of the highest worship and adoration (5:13; 7:10; 21:22, 23)—this last passage parallels Isaiah 60:19 which refers to God alone as the everlasting light, so that the parallelism between God and the Lamb (Jesus) clearly implies the oneness of Jesus with God in the most exalted possible sense.

While what I have cited involves only a selective cross section of texts which could be greatly extended (as it has been in many a scholarly theological tome), it is sufficient to conclude that if we are to find anywhere a view of Jesus which, although accepting his full humanity, depicts him as something less than and quite distinct from God Incarnate in the most uncompromising sense, it will certainly have to be outside the New Testament in any of its present literary strata. For apologetic purposes, I have, of course, emphasized the biblical witness to the deity of Jesus as God Incarnate. But it is important not to overlook the equally biblical concept of Jesus as embodying full, genuine, and integral humanity, although, in a typically modern intellectual climate, this concept is simply assumed without extended analysis. Since that was not always the case, the New Testament strongly emphasizes the humanity of Jesus in a variety of ways. Hence, John speaks of the fact that the Logos became flesh (1:14) and, in his First Epistle, he makes this explicit acknowledgement of Jesus' humanity a test for distinguishing between alien spirits and the Spirit of God (4:2); and Paul speaks of Christ Jesus the Mediator as himself a human being (1 Tim. 2:5)—while at the same time the writer of Hebrews speaks of Jesus as having partaken of flesh and blood in the fully human sense (2:14). The incidental references in the New Testament are so abundant that it would be impertinent to spell them out in detail—and I shall therefore simply assume this aspect of the New Testament concept: There is in Jesus no mere theophany but an authentic human being.

At the same time, there is no question in that same New Testament of any mere juxtaposition of deity and humanity in Jesus in the sense of a merely intimate moral union that does not involve a single personal self-consciousness. It is one and the same person who in the wealth of his preincarnate state assumes the poverty of human existence that we might thereby become rich (2 Cor. 8:9); it is, again, the same person who empties himself in becoming man that he might endure the death of the cross (Phil. 2:5–8); and it is, finally, the Eternal Logos who becomes flesh and dwells among us (John 1:14; 1 John 1:1). And, in the Gospels, Jesus always appears as a single self-conscious person, a single ego, a single "I"; the Logos is not objective to the man Jesus, nor the man Jesus objective to the Logos—indeed, the Johannine Jesus speaks explicitly of the glory that he had with the Father before the world existed (John 17:5). While Jesus frequently speaks of his unity with the Father (which therefore implies personal distinctness), he never says, "I and the Logos are one." Any consideration therefore which involved a duality of personal principles in Jesus would clearly run counter to the whole grain of the New Testament conception.

The Theological Interpretation

But the biblical witness concerning the person of Jesus as God Incarnate scarcely constitutes a systematic theology of the incarnation; it rather provides the data and constitutes the problem of such a theology. To some extent, a beginning has been made on such a task by our previous analysis of the general concept of incarnation in its various facets, but that too is only a beginning, as it were. In the first several centuries of the Christian era the outlines for a biblically grounded, yet systematically and intellectually elaborated, Christology were developed by Christian thinkers faced with the task of communicating the Christian truth-claim to the Greco-Roman world with the fullest possible effectiveness. If that task was to be responsibly fulfilled, it would have to be through the adoption of a systematic and intellectual standpoint that would form a bridge of connection or common ground with the seminal minds of that world. At the same time, it was not the intent of Christian thinkers to go questionably or irresponsibly beyond the New Testament witness itself, so that the great creeds of Nicea and Chalcedon were put forth, not as in any sense a substitute for the scriptural materials, but rather as an attempt to understand those materials systematically in a philosophically and theologically effective framework.

For this task—never finally completed, of course, in any age of the Christian era—the main issues concerning Christology can be clearly expressed: How can we coherently conceive of Jesus Christ as possessing a real and complete human nature and at the same time the real and complete divine nature—yet co-existing in a single person in such a way that neither of these natures is compromised, in either genuineness or integrity, or even essentially modified? And this question branches out into others: Which side of this union supplies the central principle of self-consciousness in the historical Jesus? To what extent does the fact of this union modify the mode either of the existence or of the operation of these two natures separately and abstractly considered? Is the Eternal Logos or Eternal Son who becomes man in Jesus

I. The biblical witness calls for elaboration of the concept of incarnation in a systematic theological and philosophical context.

A. Such an explanation would aim at communicating the Incarnation claim to the intellectual climate of the time.
B. But it would not purport to go beyond a systematic explanation of the biblical materials themselves.

II. Clarification of the issues.
A. The problems are:
1. two natures in a single person,

2. locus of the unitary self-consciousness,

3. and possible modification of the natures during Jesus' earthly career.

essentially limited in either knowledge or power during the period of the historical life of Jesus?

In grappling with these issues, the Christian mind-set (if I may thus speak) successively considered and discarded a number of unsatisfactory explanations. All attempts to explain Jesus as originally no more than a man who, for whatever reasons, subsequently became invested with a unique divine mission or was even exalted to the level of virtual (but not full and essential) divinity (the Ebionite view and its modifications); all efforts to understand Jesus as the incarnation of a divine being who nevertheless was not God in the absolute sense (the Arian view); all explanations which did away with the personal distinction between Jesus and the Father (the Sabellian or modalistic position); all formulations which tended to destroy the reality or the completeness of either the divine nature or the human nature of the Incarnate Christ (for example, Apollinarianism in its view that the Divine Logos replaced the human spirit of Jesus; or the earlier Docetism which tended to deny the real humanity altogether—all these positions were eliminated from the central Christian understanding of the Incarnation. There could be no duality of persons in Jesus as God Incarnate, and no confusion of divine and human natures, much less any sort of third nature which was strictly neither human nor divine, yet somehow and inexplicably both.

The minimum resolution for all these issues was adopted at the Council of Chalcedon (A.D. 451)—a resolution which, although embryonic in a sense, became definitive and even normative for all subsequent Christological discussion that was to be regarded as genuinely reflecting the biblical materials concerning the person of Christ. The text of the Chalcedonian formulation is easily accessible in English translation to any concerned reader interested in perusing it, as it were, verbatim; and hence I will not repeat it here. But the formula makes the following points clear: (1) that Jesus is fully and completely God, and fully and completely man; (2) that his deity implies that he is of the same (and not merely a similar) essence as God the Father (so that this essence attaches equally to him and to the Father) and that his Sonship is an eternal relation to the Father; (3) that his humanity implies that he possessed a rational human soul or self and a physical human body such that he participated fully and genuinely in our humanity, although without sin and through unique virgin birth; and (4) that these two natures, thus united inseparably in one undivided and indivisible person, were nevertheless not essentially changed through this union. But even if we regard this formulation as an intellectually reasonable and coherent explanation of the New Testament affirmations concerning the person of Jesus, there is still much that remains if this provisional reasonableness is to be effectively rounded out and systematically completed.

How, for example, are we coherently to conceive of a single personality with two natures, each of which, when considered separately, would imply personality abstractly in itself? If there is a single personal self-consciousness in Jesus (a point which is, as previously noted,

B. Inadequate solutions:

1. Jesus as a highly endowed human being;

2. Jesus as the incarnation of a created divine being;

3. Jesus as a mode of God;
4. One or other of the natures as incompletely real.

B. Hence, no duality of persons and no confusion of natures.

III. The minimum resolutions at Chalcedon.

A. Summary of the resolution: as an essential starting point for systematic elaboration.

B. Problem of personal unity and dual nature.

crystal-clear in the New Testament conception), which nature contributes the essential principle or intrinsic core of this personal reality? And this question may plausibly lead to another: Can this union be explained by maintaining that what the Eternal Son (the Logos) assumed was not a particular human existence as such, but rather human nature in general? Of various proposals put forward historically in response to these issues, I regard the following as the most fully coherent and rationally intelligible. Since Jesus clearly spoke of the glory that he had with the Father quite apart from the existence of the contingent world order (John 17:5), we would naturally be led to conclude that the personal self-consciousness implied is that of the preexistent Logos or the Eternal Son. This in turn would mean that the human nature of Jesus, abstractly considered in and by itself (although of course it never actually had any such separate and abstract existence) is, strictly speaking, impersonal (the concept of *anhypostasia*—the *im*personal humanity of Jesus). On the other hand, this does not mean that the Logos assumed only human nature in general, as though there were any such abstract entity except in the sense of a universal essence. What the Logos assumed was a potential human individuality which never actually existed apart from its inseparable union with the Eternal Logos or Son. In this actualized union, the potential for personal consciousness which characterized Jesus' human nature, abstractly considered, was taken up into the personal consciousness of the Logos as that potential human individuality progressively became actualized. And it was thus in this sense of assuming the potential individuality of the human nature that Jesus is meaningfully understood as growing in wisdom (Luke 2:52). In the personal union of the two natures, therefore, the humanity of Jesus is never actually impersonal (the concept of *enhypostasia*—that is, the humanity of Jesus is not actually devoid of personality, but rather has personality in its sole actual existence through union with the Eternal Logos, who thus assumes the potential for personality which characterizes Jesus' human nature, abstractly considered. I should not, of course, care to claim that this explanation was the only logically possible account of the intelligibility of the union of two full and complete natures in a single indivisible personal self-consciousness in entire harmony with the New Testament materials. But I do claim that this account is one such possible explanation, and I am frankly unaware of any other such account which does not sacrifice either the rational intelligibility of the concept or the fidelity of the explanation to those New Testament materials.

One might also raise the question as to the extent to which the incarnate state may have, in some plausible sense, confined the Eternal Logos to the ordinary limits of human nature in the historical Jesus. The New Testament does describe the Incarnation as a sort of emptying, a *kenosis* (Phil. 2:7); and Jesus himself everywhere professes his entire subordination to the Father whom he even speaks of as in some sense greater than himself—and that in the very Gospel which most fully asserts his deity (John 14:28). Furthermore, the Gospel of Mark

---

1. The preexistent Logos as personal principle.

2. The impersonality of the human nature as such.

3. Potential human individuality, and not merely human nature in general.
4. The actual in-personality of Jesus' human nature in union with the Logos.

5. Yet this account not the only possible explanation of the unity of natures in a single person.

C. Problem of limits on the Eternal Logos;

1. New Testament limits on Jesus.

expressly (13:32), together with other passages incidentally, seems to imply some limitations on the knowledge of Jesus, at least in the period of his earthly career. Here again, numerous proposals have been put forward, some of which I will detail in a later context. But meanwhile I will again develop the response which exhibits, to my thinking, the most fully intelligible and biblically responsible character. This proposal maintains that, while the Eternal Logos is inseparably united to human nature in Jesus, this union does not in any respect modify either the essential attributes or the mode of the reality of the Logos and hence does not restrict him to those limits of humanity which would be inconsistent with the divine nature. One and the same Logos was both entirely incarnate and, without contradiction, entirely transcendent and unqualifiedly divine. The emptying of the Logos is simply the incarnation or assumption of human nature itself (he emptied himself by taking essential human nature). The subordination of the Son to the Father is an official functional subordination which in no way compromises the absolute Godhead of the Incarnate Logos; and the limits on Jesus' knowledge are not (inconsistently) restrictions of his divine omniscience, but rather restrictions of what it was God's will to make known in the Son as the Revealer of the Father. Whether other accounts of this issue exhibit a proportionate intelligibility and biblical fidelity, on quite different grounds, remains to be inquired. Meanwhile I merely claim that the account I have given does exhibit these qualities more fully than any alternative explanation with which I am familiar. The present issue therefore concerns the rational coherence, the logical self-consistency, of the concept of the Incarnation of God in Jesus. Whether, granted that rational intelligibility, the truth-claim of the Incarnation is to be granted as well on this along with other reasonable grounds is a quite separate and later consideration.

But in the meantime, of course, the concept of the Incarnation of the Eternal Logos in the historical Jesus involves clearly a reorientation of the concept of God with respect to the notion of unity. If, as previously clarified, Jesus, although fully God, nevertheless speaks of the Father as objective to himself, and the Father likewise speaks of the Son as analogously objective (Matt. 3:17; Mark 1:11; Luke 3:22; Matt. 17:5; Mark 9:7; Luke 9:35), then it is clear that the Divine Unity and the rigorous monotheism which that entails must, on pain of evident self-contradiction, be so understood as to be logically compatible with a plurality of centers of personal self-consciousness or (in the language of technical theology) hypostatical distinctions. Nor is the issue limited to the relation of the Son to the Father—for Jesus also speaks of the Holy Spirit as both perpetually representing and constituting his Divine Presence with believers after his own departure from the world, and at the same time personally objective to both himself and the Father (John 14:16, 17, 26; 15:26; 16:7-15). This plurality of personal distinctions, which is present clearly in the New Testament itself, Christians came universally to refer to as the Divine Trinity—a plurality which, from the first, they regarded as wholly compatible with uncompromising unity. While this notion has repeatedly been characterized as either beyond rational comprehension or even as rationally incoherent by both Christians and their critics, there is, in my opinion, no reason to take this allegation with ultimate seriousness. If the Trinitarian concept were actually incomprehensible or self-contradictory, then no one could coherently identify what he was committing himself to if he accepted it—since the two sides of the contradiction would reciprocally cancel each other out, and there would clearly be no determinate conception to accept but rather an incoherent one to dismiss as unintelligible.

How then are we, with full rational plausibililty, to balance the notions of Divine Unity and Divine Trinity? Much of the material for an appropriate answer to this question is already at our disposal in terms of my previous analysis. I have, for example, appealed to the principle of contradiction or rational coherence as an ultimate presupposition and precondition of all possible intelligible thought (a synthetic *a priori* principle of objective, universal reason); and I have also defended the doctrine that essences have a transcendent reality status that makes them logically independent of both finite knowing minds that apprehend them and of contingent particulars that instantiate them. In fact, I have argued that the ultimate locus of these transcendent essences is the Eternal Reason or Universal Mind of God, who himself possesses as attributes all those essences whose definitions would be consistent with God's character as an absolutely necessary and transcendent being, characterized by personal, intelligent will, and constituting essential or Absolute Goodness. All this I regard as reasonably (but, as always, not absolutely) settled. If, then, we apply these previous conclusions to the Unity-Trinity question, it will first of all be clear that God cannot be one and three in precisely the same sense or respect, since that would be self-contradictory and therefore inconsistent with the ultimate character of God as essentially rational. Deity, however, must itself have an essence, an intelligible and defining nature; and much of what I have argued in earlier sections of my overall discussion has been intended to clarify certain aspects of that Divine Essence. If, then, the concept of Deity has the Divine Essence as its object, then no being that lacks that essence in any respect can be truly Deity in an unqualified sense. God, therefore, may (indeed logically *must*) be construed as unqualifiedly one in essence or intelligible nature, since essences are themselves intrinsically self-identical. At the same time, the Divine Essence is unique in certain unparalleled respects which set it off logically and ontologically from the essence of all actual and possible classes of contingent entities. For the Divine Essence is self-actualized (since God is by nature a self-existent and self-explanatory being whose essence therefore implies necessary existence as an attribute), while no essence of any class of particular and contingent beings (actual or possible) is either self-actualized or self-actualizing (since the very meaning of contingency involves the concept of a being whose essence does not involve existence, so that, if a contingent being exists, it must have an extraneous ground of being). And since the Divine Essence is self-actualized, then it will have an-

D. A proposed conceptualization.

1. A starting point in the notions of rational coherence and transcendent essences in the mind of God as archetypes.

2. Unity and Trinity must be consistently construed.

3. God or Deity must itself have or be an essence.

a) God must be one in essence or intelligible nature.

b) But this essence is unique:

(1) self-actualized,

.

(2) existing in a certain determinate number.

other quality not ascribable to the essences of contingent entities. As self-actualized, the Divine Essence will, as a condition of that self-actualized status, have the ontologically necessary quality of existing in a certain determinate number—since otherwise the number of its instantiations would be a logical accident, and no self-existing being can conceivably have logically accidental qualities which would be inconsistent with its existence as absolutely necessary. Since, as already evident, I am not a deductive rationalist, I cannot deduce from the Divine Essence what that determinate number would be. But if, by virtue of historical revelation, we have reason to identify three centers of personal self-consciousness as actualizing the one Divine Essence (namely, the Father, the Son, and the Holy Spirit), then we can say, for the same reason, that the determinate number must be at least three, although I see no way of arguing on logical and rational grounds that it would necessarily be limited to that number, even if in fact I have also no reason to suppose otherwise. As to the essences of contingent entities, since they by definition do not imply existence at all, it follows clearly that they logically cannot imply existence in a certain determinate number, except in the obviously irrelevant sense that it is true of any essence that—if it is actualized or instantiated at all—it must logically be so in at least one particular instance.

c) Hence, the Divine Essence is set off from the essences of contingent entities.

These two unique qualities of the Divine Essence, as an essence, will serve to dispel any objection to my exposition on any such ground as that such an explanation would make the plurality of persons in the one Divine Essence wholly analogous to the plurality of particulars that might instantiate any essence, even of contingent entities—for that charge can be seen to be patently false in view of the differences explained. There are, of course, other standard objections. One would be that I am committing an error analogous to that of the Nicene fathers (or at least some of them), since I am assuming that the intelligibility of the Unity-Trinity relation is dependent on the doctrine of realistic essentialism which stems historically from the Greek philosopher Plato. I accept the charge as correct in substance, but I reject the contention that either I or the Nicene fathers in question are chargeable with a mistake on that ground. In fact, I would argue that nothing particular could either exist or be possible if there were no real essences, and that the historical connection of the doctrine with Plato, although noteworthy, is quite accidental to the substance of the doctrine, since—although Plato may have contributed much to our understanding of it (Augustine would agree)—he contributed nothing essential to its objective truth. One final objection, which I will mention only to dismiss as impertinent, is the claim that such explanations reduce the mystery of Divine Truth to the dimensions of human rational intelligibility. Quite to the contrary, such explanations, if they are plausible at all, indicate that human truth-claims can lay title to objective rationality only if the principles of reason they appeal to are themselves ultimately grounded in God as Eternal Reason. But this point is old ground revisited, and there is no need to plow or even cultivate it again.

4. This proposal: a) does involve realistic essentialism (but that is not a genuine objection);

b) and it does appeal to rational intelligibility as a norm, though the principles of reason are not merely human, but are grounded in God as Eternal Reason.

I shall not, indeed, claim that my analysis of the Unity-Trinity relation is the only logically possible ground for a defender of the plausibility of that relation to occupy. I certainly stand open to other possible explanations which might be construed to exhibit a parallel or even greater rational intelligibility—I am after all a merely finite thinker wielding a weapon of objective rationality which I suppose clearly to possess a far greater adequacy than attaches to any limited and effective use I may make of it. But what I do claim is that the account I have given provides one rationally coherent account of the Unity-Trinity relation which at the very least turns away any objection to the effect that the whole notion is rationally unintelligible. If my interpretive presuppositions are granted (and I regard them as clearly plausible), that charge can be fairly described as unfounded.

While therefore I have still not pronounced judgment regarding the Christian Incarnation claim as to its truth status, I nevertheless confidently claim that the conceptual context and content of this claim are clearly rationally coherent and intelligible. It is thus no collapse into irrationality or even incomprehensibility that leads me to the further consideration of that claim as possibly plausible. Quite to the contrary, in a theistic universe (which I presuppose from my earlier argument) I judge the concept of the Incarnation of God in Jesus to exhibit as full a degree of rational intelligibility as it would be plausible for the most stringent mind to expect.

> 5. Our proposal is not to be regarded as the only possible solution.
>
> a) But it does make the Unity-Trinity relation rationally intelligible.
>
> b) Whether the Christian Incarnation claim is true as a whole is yet to be investigated; but it is at least not incoherent or contrary to reason properly construed.

In Relation to His Vocation

As the Climax of Revelation

But of course, the question of who Jesus is stands inseparable from the question of what vocation Jesus fulfilled through his total life-activity. One thing indeed is clear enough: If we provisionally accept the Christian Incarnation claim as at least plausible in the sense of a viable option, then, consistent with my analysis of the general idea of revelation, Jesus, as God Incarnate, must be the highest conceivable form of divine revelation in comparison with which all other forms must be secondary and ancillary. The fullest revelation of any human person is, analogously, through that individual's real and actual presence to the recipients of his self-manifestation. Letters and other effects of action provide a basis for inference to certain truths about that person indirectly; but personal presence provides the terminus *ad quem* to which all such inferences point. Hence, God himself, personally present in Jesus as the Messiah, involves the highest possible self-revelation of God as precisely the terminus to which all indirect manifestation leads. This concept is made very clear in the New Testament. In the Gospel of John, for example, Jesus is referred to as the Logos or

> I. If Jesus is God Incarnate, then he is the highest conceivable form of divine revelation.
> A. All other forms of revelation are indirect and secondary as compared with direct personal presence.
>
> B. The New Testament witness to this claim.

1. John.

2. Hebrews.

3. Paul.

II. But other forms of divine self-disclosure are not less genuinely revelatory but merely less full and final by comparison.

Word who, as himself God, assumes human nature as the Logos Incarnate, and who thus decisively manifests or reveals the glory or character of God. In fact, one textual reading has John describing Jesus as the only-begotten God who sets forth or narrates God the Father (John 1:1–18). Again, the writer of the Book of Hebrews speaks of God as, after having spoken in many limited segments and in many different ways in the prophets, then with a sort of decisive finality speaking to humanity in his Son (that is, in Jesus as God Incarnate), whom the writer then describes as the shining forth of God's character and the defining nature of God's substantial reality (Heb. 1:1–3). And Paul, finally, declares that in Jesus there resides the whole fullness of the Deity completely and incarnately (Col. 2:9).

But while the New Testament in general and such representative passages in particular can thus refer to Jesus as the climax of revelation, this declarative emphasis does not imply that God's message through the prophets and apostles, in such a broad spectrum of styles and aspects, is any less than itself also revelation in a normative sense. It is not that the revelation in Jesus relegates all other insight about God to a status that is less than revelationary; it is rather that Jesus, as God Incarnate, climaxes, integrates, and fulfills the variety of divine self-disclosure which was itself revelatory throughout and from the very beginning. God, therefore, has spoken elsewhere as truly and authoritatively as he has spoken in Jesus; but he has not there spoken as fully or as finally. And it is not surprising therefore that First Peter sweeps up all previous revelation into the all-inclusive revelation in Jesus by boldly declaring that it was indeed the Spirit of Christ himself who testified previously in all that the prophets had said, particularly concerning himself as the fulfillment of their message.

As the Culmination of Redemption: The Concept of Moral Substitution

I. Jesus as universally representative humanity.

A. While every human being is by nature involved in every other, while yet a separate individual,

B. the case of Jesus is unique, since his human nature is realized only in union with the Logos, and is therefore more universally representative of all other human beings.

The Christian revelation claim contends that there is fulfilled in Jesus as Messiah precisely that expectation of reason which, as previously developed, led to the notion of God Incarnate as representative humanity. Because every single human being instantiates, or participates in, the essence of human nature, there is a sense in which each of us is representatively present in all the others, so that humanity constitutes as a totality a kind of corporate solidarity of reciprocal involvement and responsibility. But at the same time each of us is a separate individual human being with unique personal selfhood and cumulative personal moral achievement and responsibility—with the result that our reciprocal involvement and our individual liability are, as it were, simply distinguishable sides of one and the same coin. Yet the case of Jesus, as God Incarnate, is unique and unparalleled—for the human nature of Christ is, abstractly considered, *im*personal with no separately actualized individual self-consciousness; and that same human nature in Christ is, concretely considered, *in*personal because it possesses actualized selfhood only in conjunction with the Eternal

Logos. And, if that is so, then the individualized humanity of Jesus is sublimated and subordinated to his representative union with the whole of humanity, so that he is more truly representative of each and all of us than any one of us—separate human individuals that we are—could conceivably be of any of the rest of us. And that is precisely because in Jesus the Logos takes to himself precisely that common human nature which we all exemplify, but he takes that nature more universally just by reason of the fact that the principle of individual personal self-consciousness in Jesus is actualized only in union with the selfhood of the Eternal Logos. Hence, God the Logos assumes our humanity exactly in its universally representative capacity in a sense that could not be ascribed to any ordinary human self.

From this universally representative humanity, it follows that Jesus, as God Incarnate, exhibits a morally representative union with the whole of humanity that is so pervasive and complete that, by comparison, any ordinary person's reciprocal involvement with the whole of humanity, although genuine indeed, has merely the character of a shadow that is cast by that full representational union. As personally the transcendent Logos, Jesus stands in a unique, qualitative contrast to any and all human selves as creatures. But as the Logos Incarnate, Jesus takes the whole of humanity to himself in a universally representative union which voluntarily binds him to all of us more fully and completely than we are bound to each other. And that metaphysical reality is the basis of the New Testament concept that Jesus, in his life and especially in his death as the climax of his identification with our human destiny, can vicariously act as our moral substitute precisely in the fullness of his commitment to God's will and in the all-sufficiency of his sacrifice as a completely adequate satisfaction to the claim of unconditional moral obligation on us all. Of course, the New Testament refers to this vicarious moral substitution through a variety of metaphors, each of which emphasizes some different aspect or aspects of this sacrificial union. The death of Jesus is a ransom paid for the deliverance of moral captives (Mark 10:45; 1 Tim. 2:5, 6); it is the means of rendering inoperative the power of the devil and therefore delivering from the fear of their own death those who throughout their lives had been held in the grip of bondage (Hebrews 2:14, 15); it is the ground of our being released (possibly even washed) from our own sins in his own blood (Rev. 1:5); it is the bearing of our sins in his body on the tree (that is, the cross), so that we might ourselves die to those sins and come alive to his righteousness and be healed by the stripes of his punishment on our behalf (1 Peter 2:24); it is the fulfillment of all the rich anticipatory images of the sacrifices under the "old covenant"—sacrifices which could point to the adequacy of Christ's sacrifice but which could not themselves make amends for a single moral transgression (Hebrews as a whole, but especially chapters 9 and 10); finally, and perhaps above all, it is satisfaction, expiation, and propitiation which, as representative humanity, Jesus offers to the offended moral character of God, so that, through the adequacy of his sacrifice, those who are united to him through faith might be

1. Thus Jesus exhibits a full representational union that binds him to humanity more intimately than other human beings are bound to each other.

2. Through this union Jesus can appropriately act vicariously as our moral substitute in satisfying the claim of unconditional moral obligation.

II. Vicarious moral substitution in the New Testament.
A. Metaphors of redemptive union:
1. Ransom.
2. Deliverance from bondage to Satan.

3. Washing away sins.

4. Bearing of sins through Jesus' death as a punishment.

5. Fulfillment of Old Testament sacrifices.

6. Satisfaction offered to the offended moral character of God.

morally justified without any compromise to the unconditional moral claim of God's moral character on an individually and collectively guilty humanity (1 John 2:2; Romans 3:23–26). Much expository and theological ink has been spilled in attempts to balance all these metaphorical descriptions against each other. But the point is that they are metaphors of a non-metaphorical truth-claim to the effect that Jesus Christ as God Incarnate has, as morally representative humanity in his life and death, so made moral amends on our behalf as to make our forgiveness and moral restoration before God possible in the context of a fully maintained framework of moral objectivism grounded in the divine moral character. Hence, we can say with Saint Paul that it was no one less than God himself who in Jesus Christ was reconciling the world to himself while not charging humanity with its moral faults (2 Cor. 5:19).

B. The essential truth behind the metaphors: Jesus as morally representative humanity in making amends to God's moral claim.

But of course this objective moral transaction actualized in the incarnation and death of Jesus, although in one sense the culmination of divine redemption, was in a quite different sense only the beginning of a still larger achievement. The person who, through an act of believing identification with Jesus Christ as Redeemer, becomes the moral beneficiary of the all-sufficient sacrifice of the God-man, does not remain in a merely objective state of forgiveness and ethical justification over against the unconditional moral claim involved in the divine character. Quite to the contrary, and as the appropriate correlate of that objective moral relationship, he embarks subjectively on a radical personal transformation through which he is spiritually and morally regenerated, so that—although he remains the ontologically identical self that he was before this ethical rebirth—it is as though he has become a veritable new creation in the progressively developing moral renewal of that self, a renewal that begins as a small trickle of new life and then gradually expands to engulf the whole of his personal being (2 Cor. 5:17). The New Testament describes this change as activated by the indwelling Spirit of Christ and as constituting the individual thus reborn as a child of God and a member of God's spiritual family (Rom. 8:9–17). Yet, although the motivation for this transformation comes ultimately from God through a universal persuasive influence of the Divine Spirit (John 16:8–11), nevertheless this influence is not efficacious apart from the individual's free and self-initiated response through the act of repentance in which he decides to forsake the dominant influence of his morally corrupted character, and an act of faith in which he believingly identifies himself with Jesus Christ as Lord (Acts 2:38; 16:31). Nor is this cooperation between human and divine will in any sense limited to the initial moment of spiritual regeneration; it rather continues through the whole development of the individual's subsequent spiritual life as an always incomplete but nevertheless continually growing advance toward moral and spiritual maturity (Rom. 6; 8:12f.; Phil. 3:7–14).

III. The subjective consequences of Christ's redemption. A. The objective justification is correlated with a subjective moral transformation: a regeneration.

1. Though ontologically the same self,

2. the person becomes morally a different self through gradual change.

B. While the motivation comes from God, it is ineffective without the individual's free cooperation, both in its beginning and in its progressive achievement.

As the Core of Spiritual Community

But the spiritual development of the individual, through moral union with Christ and by means of the continual appropriation of his

Spirit's power, does not take place typically in a state of personal isolation from other human selves. Not only is there the obvious and unbroken involvement of the individual in the whole human community—an involvement that penetrates that community with the unfolding influence of the transformed individual's altered moral character—there is, as well, a spiritually constituted community to which such a person belongs precisely as a consequence of his spiritual union with Jesus Christ. For if each reborn person has become spiritually a child of God, he has by the same token become a moral sibling of all those who have taken that same step, so that together they are all brothers and sisters in the spiritual family of God, a family which itself belongs indeed and as well to the whole human community, but at the same time makes up a unique and special sub-class of that total community. All human beings *could*, of course, belong to that sub-class through an act of commitment to the Lordship of Christ—in which case the extension of the two communities would be identical. But only those *do* belong to that sub-class who have, in response to the divine motivation and initiative, actually carried through with that commitment in which God has been embraced, so to speak, as the true Good through which alone individuals are morally regenerated, or else, alternatively, who are eligible for membership in that divine family because they are, for some plausible reason, personally incapable of making that commitment in a self-consciously responsible way.

Nor is membership in the family of the reborn any sort of second option distinct from an individual's spiritual transformation—for the New Testament envisions spiritual union with Jesus Christ as tantamount to, and indistinguishable from, belonging to the family of God. Those who thus belong to this special group (a status open to all) are referred to as the Church or the Assembly, and are metaphorically designated as the spiritual body of Jesus Christ who is its Head. One cannot therefore belong to Christ the Head without thereby being a member of his spiritual body. Conversely, there is no body in the integrated, reciprocal and organic sense apart from the corporate unity provided by the Head, so that, in that sense, the Lord Jesus Christ is the Core and Fulcrum, as it were, of God's entire spiritual family, and without him there would be no such spiritual body or family at all, but merely, perhaps, a collection of morally similar but otherwise quite separate individuals (Eph. 1:22, 23; 4:15, 16; Col. 1:18; 2:19).

Because of my specifically apologetic and philosophical purpose, it is not my intention to develop in expository and theological depth any of the themes about the vocation of Jesus as God Incarnate. I have therefore limited my analysis to those aspects of Jesus' vocation which I envision as contributing significantly to that explicitly announced objective. And I leave to theological specialists the further and more intricate development of these concepts, decisively important as they may be. In any case, the real hurdle, from my point of view, is the issue concerning Jesus Christ as God Incarnate. If that issue is decided in the affirmative, then the recognition of Jesus as the climax of

---

I. The spiritually reborn belong not only to the human community, but also to a spiritual community through union with Christ.

A. This is the spiritual family of God as a special sub-class of the human community.

B. But all human beings *could* belong to that family through spiritual commitment.

II. Membership in this community is a dimension of the individual's spiritual transformation.

A. This is the Church as the spiritual body of Christ.

B. Jesus, as Head of the body, is the core of the spiritual community.

III. The apologetic limits of Jesus' vocation as analyzed here.

revelation, the culmination of redemption, and the core of spiritual community will follow in its wake. Indeed, if Jesus is not God Incarnate, he cannot be plausibly regarded as fulfilling any of these roles either.

In Relation to His Position as the Pivotal Basis of the Christian Truth-Claim

I. The concept of Jesus as God Incarnate having been thus elucidated, the question of its truth-claim may be raised.

A. But it is not a matter of demonstration here; it is rather a matter of reasonable probability.

A discerning and reflective reader might well observe that in the preceding analysis I seem to have assumed the very Incarnation claim that it was purportedly my intention to argue, since I have spoken with a style of descriptive facticity of all that Jesus Christ as God Incarnate makes possible. But I will set the uneasy mind of any such reader at immediate rest. For in all that analysis I have merely, although importantly, been developing the incarnation concept, both in general and in its New Testament context; and it is only now that I raise the decisive question whether that developed concept comports plausibly with objective reality. It is not, of course, any more than theism itself, a question that can be settled with demonstrative finality in any quasi-logical or quasi-mathematical fashion. It is instead an issue that we can approach, if at all, in an attitudinal atmosphere of contextual plausibility and relative probability, in an intellectual arena of rational persuasion and integral intelligibility.

B. The context of consideration involves:
1. A theistic world-view;
2. the coherence of the incarnation concept;
3. the traceability of the Incarnation claim to Jesus himself.

a) Any lesser claim is incredible, since it is devoid of historical support, and would presuppose implausibly that the claim was invented by the first-century disciples.

The overall context for raising the question has, for the most part, already been developed. It is a context characterized by a theistic world-view, on the one hand, and by the developed coherence of the concept of incarnation, together with its implications, on the other. Although the point can be challenged (and that challenge is yet to be considered), I will provisionally assume, on the basis of my previous analysis, that the Christian Incarnation claim goes back historically to Jesus himself in the sense that he implicitly and explicitly claimed, both to his disciples and to the religious and political leaders of Israel, that he was God Incarnate. The supposition that he claimed to be no more than a prophet, and that he made no supernatural, Messianic claim, is simply incredible. It finds, as we have seen, no support in the New Testament itself or in any other credible historical sources. And it presupposes that the Incarnation claim was wholly invented by first-century Jewish disciples who, by hypothesis, had no conceivable motivation for concocting such a legend, since they were rigid monotheists for whom any such notion would be utter blasphemy—a presupposition which even Karl Barth, with all his dialectical opposition to apologetical arguments as a threat to genuine religious faith, nevertheless regards as openly absurd, so that he sees this absurdity as the strongest of reasons for supposing that the claim was made by Jesus himself. At the outset, of course, the disciples did not clearly understand the claim themselves; but they gradually came to understand it through the overwhelming impact of Jesus' own personality, ministry, and sheer persuasive influence—so that Peter, as their spokesman, could answer Jesus' query about his identity by saying clearly that Jesus was the Messiah, the Son of the Living God (Matt. 16:16).

b) Yet the claim was only gradually understood by the disciples.

If then the acceptance of the Incarnation claim by the disciples can be plausibly explained only through the supposition that the claim is traceable to Jesus himself, the question then becomes for us, as it was for inquiring minds from the first, what to make of this claim on the lips of Jesus who was, after all, himself also a first-century Jew with the same monotheistic background as his disciples. We can make a beginning toward an appropriate answer by asking ourselves a still further question and attempting to answer it. On the assumption that the disciples of Jesus and therefore the initial circle of believers in Jesus accepted the Incarnation claim, on what grounds were these original devotees themselves persuaded of the truth of that Incarnation claim? This is a difficult and endlessly debatable question, but I will project a plausible answer which I think fits the New Testament records in the Gospels and elsewhere. As I already suggested, the disciples were themselves initially confused about the identity of Jesus (Matt. 8:27; Mark 4:41; Luke 8:25); but their vision progressively cleared, as I see it, through three lines of thought which ultimately achieved a united effect in their thinking. It must be kept in mind that they were Jews who accepted the divine authority of the Old Testament. For that reason, they were generally familiar with the Messianic concept in that source, whether their insight about it was fully clear or not; and they were perhaps also familiar with a varied group of predictive prophecies concerning the coming Messiah—that he would be descended from King David, that he would be born in Bethlehem of Judea, that he would be rejected by his fellow Israelites when he presented himself as their Messiah, and ultimately that he would suffer an ignominious death. It is, of course, very difficult to be confident as to how much of this background was clear in their minds and at what stage. But what we can be confident about is that they gradually came to see in Jesus the conjunctive fulfillment of these prophecies and therefore to recognize Jesus as the Messiah of Israel. Since I have already argued that the Old Testament depicts the Messiah as God Incarnate, it follows that at some stage (either before or after Peter's confession of Christ as Messiah) they put all this together, at first no doubt vaguely and gradually with greater clarity, so that they came to acknowledge Jesus as not only Messiah but also and therefore God Incarnate. If the spiritual leaders of the Jews recognized a Messianic claim as an Incarnation claim—so that anyone who falsely (in their eyes) made that claim could appropriately be accused of blasphemy (an accusation which would be sheer nonsense on any other supposition)—it should not be surprising that the disciples also recognized the implications of the Messianic claim with at least nearly parallel clarity, except that they of course accepted the claim so that no implication of blasphemy would follow in their minds. For the

II. The crucial issue: what to make of the Incarnation claim as made by Jesus.
A. The case of the first disciples seems to involve:

1. The recognition that Jesus fulfilled the Messianic prophecies of the Old Testament;

disciples, then, the first line of consideration was the culmination of Old Testament Messianic prophecy in the person of Jesus—with all that such an application implied about his ultimate identity.

2. The mighty works of Jesus as testifying to his unique spiritual authority;

Their second line of thought, which they saw as supporting the first in a multiplicity of ways, consisted in the remarkable works of healing, of power over the ordinary course of nature, and of control over demonic powers—works which characterized the public ministry of Jesus right from the first. They interpreted such works as a manifestation of the glory of God and as signs of Jesus' own spiritual authority. In fact, as the Gospels make abundantly clear, these signs initially provoked their questions about Jesus' ultimate identity, while at the same time they progressively reinforced their developing conviction that Jesus was the Messiah (for example, Matt. 8 and 9; John 20:30, 31). And Jesus himself attached this same significance to these signs in his remarks about them (John 10:32–38). So strong was the impact of these remarkable signs on the thinking of the disciples that, in their earliest preaching as recorded in the Book of Acts, they depicted what they regarded as the ultimate work of this sort (namely, the resurrection of Jesus from the dead) as a sign of his divine authority, not only to the Jews (Acts 2:25–36; 3:15; 4:10), but also among the Gentiles who, to some extent, lacked the religious background to fully understand the significance of such signs (Acts 10:40f.; 17:31). As for ourselves, of course, we can boggle in our efforts to understand such works of divine power, and we can be puzzled about the relation of such events to the generally uniform order of nature. In fact, we can even wonder whether such accounts are legendary rather than factual. This sort of puzzlement will, in part at least, be dealt with in due course; but there is no reason to detain ourselves about such questions here, since it is clear that, whatever significance such accounts have for us, we have no reason to suppose that the disciples had any such qualms either about the historicity of these events or about their implications for the understanding of the person of Jesus.

3. The direct personal impact of Jesus as both requiring and exemplifying:
a) the highest conceivable state of moral character;

These two lines of consideration were of great significance, no doubt, but they would have come to no lasting effect apart from the direct personal impact of Jesus on the disciples through their sustained association with him. It was, of course, in the context of that association that they came to apply the Messianic concept to Jesus and to regard his remarkable works as supportive signs. But it was something more than this. I am not thinking here of Jesus' physical presence—there are some reasons for supposing that he was not especially impressive in physical appearance (note the prophetic description of him in Isaiah 53)—nor am I thinking of his personal charm or attractiveness, although he doubtless exhibited that to perhaps an even striking extent; and I am not even thinking of his wit or his intellectual brilliance, since he made little attempt to impress people in these areas. What I am thinking of is, so far as the Gospel record goes, his profound insight into, and understanding of, human nature; his delicate sensitivity to, and moral censure of, the hypocrisy of the Jewish spiritual leaders; his rigorous moral expectation from all whom he confronted, so that he required of them unconditional conformity to the requirement of divine moral law even to the extent of a moral fullness that paralleled that of God the Father (Matt. 5:48); and above all I am thinking of the unbroken ethical love (not to mention personal affection) which he exhibited toward all who were ready to receive it—so much so that he baffled his own disciples by requiring of them that they love even their enemies (Matt. 5:44) and forgive those who personally offend them (Matt. 6:12–15). Perhaps the most astounding aspect of Jesus in this context is the fact that he himself uninterrupt-edly exhibited in his own moral character and behavior the whole scope and depth of the rigorous moral requirement which he held up to others as an ideal to strive for. Not merely his friends, whose understandable affection for him might well have led them to gloss over minor moral faults, weaknesses, or tendencies of an objectiona-ble sort, but even his enemies could confront him with no plausible moral accusation against his personal life—and rest assured that, had there been any moral skeletons in his closet, the Pharisaical propensity to personal criticism would have brought these moral faults out into the light of day for all to see. Instead, at the trial of Jesus, his critics had to depend on trumped-up charges and paid prevaricators. Closely conjoined with Jesus' high personal morality was his undisturbed psychological self-mastery and emotional stability. Not that he could not display an anger grounded in religious and moral indignation by driving financial entrepreneurs from the temple and by denouncing the Jewish religious leaders as inauthentic and hypocritical; nor that he was incapable of cursing a fig tree in order to communicate an object lesson to his disciples about faith. It is rather that in all such acts and under the most scurrilous attacks from his enemies, or even in the most threatening personal circumstances—during his arrest and at his trial, for instance—he maintained an unwavering calm and an unshaken self-control which made him appear as a tower of per-sonal strength when the most rugged around him were disintegrating in the same circumstances. Even at the hour of his agonizing death by crucifixion, Jesus could maintain the incredible composure to pray for the forgiveness of his executioners, to arrange for the care of his mother by a close disciple, and to assure a repentant thief and fellow victim of a place in paradise. No doubt it was this moral and personal stature of Jesus that, along with Messianic prophecy and signs of divine authority, clinched the whole case for the disciples so that the Incarnation claim finally became unassailable in their minds.

We are, of course, not the disciples in that direct historical sense; but nevertheless we have no convincing reason to question the general picture of Jesus' impact on them as depicted in the Gospel record and therefore also no reasonable ground to dismiss their understanding of his moral and psychological strength. Hence, when we try to under-stand the Incarnation claim as made by Jesus himself, it is not as if we had this issue to consider in abstraction from all the rest of our assured insight into his personal qualities. It is not just anyone at random who is making this claim; it is precisely Jesus as he totally

b) the most undis-turbed psychological self-mastery and emo-tional stability.

B. the case of a re-flective modern:
1. Even for us, there is no good reason to dis-miss that early under-standing of Jesus.
a) Jesus stands in constrast to others who have made simi-lar claims.

impacts our consciousness through the Gospel description we have developed. Others, before and since, have claimed to be the Messiah, but they did so out of personal confusion which their historical destiny finally made evident. Some, before and since, have, usually in some vaguely specified sense, even claimed to be God, but they did so out of a psychological and emotional instability that we have no reason whatever to ascribe to Jesus. Still others have, before and since, performed remarkable works, but they did so either through the power of the God whom Jesus himself manifested in a higher sense, or else out of context of morally flawed character which made their moral and spiritual alignment patently clear.

b) Nor is it reasonable to accept Jesus morally and reject his Incarnation claim:
(1) for deliberate deception would undermine his character,

Some among us wish to accept Jesus in his moral and psychological strength, while at the same time dismissing his Incarnation claim as impertinent. But that would be an utter inconsistency. If Jesus, knowingly and intentionally, perpetrated the claim to be God Incarnate while fully realizing that the claim was false, then that would imply that he was the worst of moral charlatans and deceivers. But it would at the same time fly in the face of the overwhelming pictures of Jesus' moral strength—a picture that, directly or indirectly, comes to us from those who, through long association with him, were in the best position to refute that claim if Jesus' moral character belied it. On the

(2) and self-deception would undermine his psychological strength.

other hand, if Jesus sincerely believed that he was God Incarnate when in fact he was not, then that would imply that he was the victim of a deep self-deception which could spring only from the most profound psychological confusion and possibly from positive insanity—but it would at the same time fail to explain all that we otherwise know about Jesus' psychological strength and emotional stability. We can, indeed, close our eyes to Jesus and ignore him, but we cannot coherently and consciously dismiss him as either a moral pervert or as psychologically self-deceived, much less as mentally ill or actually insane.

2. While no consistent account of Jesus is logically compelling and inevitable,

But if we are not thus to dismiss Jesus' Incarnation claim, what then are we to make of it while remaining consistent with all that we have reason to believe about his personal qualities, and while aiming at the most coherent total understanding of which our most carefully reflective thinking is capable? We are not, obviously, logically compelled in the direction of any particular answer to this question. Whatever response we give, it will always be plausible to counter that response with a contrary answer which, within some identifiable framework of thought, will have at least some appearance of plausibility or even a very strong appearance of plausibility. Yet, if we are not to bypass the issue altogether, we are constrained to make some

still some response is called for in view of all that we otherwise know about Jesus.

response which we at least can sincerely respect as reasonable and which we can confidently hope will make the same or a similar impression on the minds of other persons who consider what is at stake here with reflective care. Viewing the matter from this balanced and even-tempered standpoint, I can only declare the response which seems clear and coherent to me in the context of all relevant considerations: If our impression of Jesus' moral strength and psychostability is too well-supported and obvious to set aside, then the most reasonable explanation of his Incarnation claim would appear to be that he himself made that claim because he himself—from the depth of a consciousness fully committed to the highest moral ideal and fully conforming to that ideal, and from the stable bulwark of the most evident psychological soundness and health—believed that claim to be true. And the most reasonable explanation of his having had that belief under these inclusive circumstances would appear to be that the Incarnation claim was true, and that Jesus, who alone was in a position to have direct access to that self-awareness, therefore, knew unassailably that it was true. For ourselves, it is not that we cannot conceivably think otherwise—since we do not have the same direct access to the self-knowledge of Jesus, unbelief, a different interpretation, is always a logically possible option—but, viewing the coin from another angle, it is rather that we are justified in believing Jesus' Incarnation claim to be true, even though decisive finality is not epistemologically possible for us, because such a belief in the Incarnation claim is founded on the most coherent total explanation of all the relevant information at our disposal about the person of Jesus. So, while we cannot dismiss the unbeliever or his belief option as outside the limits of logical possibility, we can reasonably regard both him and his option as less fully capable of a comprehensively adequate explanation of all that is pertinent to this crucially important issue. Hence I conclude, with what I regard as the highest degree of probability under the circumstances, that Jesus was and is God Incarnate. As to the question whether this sort of reasonable probability is a sufficient basis for authentic religious faith, I can, at this juncture, only add the following comment to what I explained much earlier about this issue: Even if reasonable probability is not a fully adequate basis for the whole scope of confidence involved in the most mature religious faith, it is at least a wholly plausible starting point for the spiritual conception of the embryo of genuine religious life. And from that small beginning, a fully mature and wholly authentic religious life may ultimately develop through the use and absorption of many further spiritual nutrients accessible to a religious life thus initiated.

And now perhaps we can step into another dimension of insight that will strengthen our conclusion about Jesus' Incarnation claim. If Jesus is indeed God Incarnate, then we can accept with parallel confidence the thesis, already conceptually developed, that as such he can reasonably be viewed as so completely identified with our humanity as to be regarded as universally representative of our moral and spiritual concerns and therefore as with full appropriateness representing us in our obligation to moral self-realization and in our liability to make amends for our moral failure in character and action. In other words, we can now see Jesus far more confidently as the culmination of redemption, since that concept is now more fully plausible through the acceptance of the Incarnation claim. In a sense, that wholly adequate human redemption is in principle accomplished in the fact of the incarnation, in Jesus actually being God Incarnate. Yet,

---

a) The most plausible account of his claim is:

(1) that he made the claim because he sincerely believed it unwaveringly;

(2) that he believed it because he knew with direct awareness that it was true.

b) Unbelief is not logically excluded, but it is less fully coherent and therefore a less fully adequate explanation.

c) It is therefore concluded that Jesus is God Incarnate.

3. This probability is at least a starting point for genuine spiritual life.

III. If Jesus is God Incarnate:
A. then his status as universally representative humanity is more fully plausible, so that
1. he can appropriately make amends for our moral liability;

as we have seen, the New Testament emphasis is on the death of Christ as a propitiatory and representative sacrifice for the sins of humanity with a view to its moral restoration. I can only suggest a way of putting together these two lines of thought (incarnation and redemptive sacrifice): It is perhaps the case that Jesus' incarnation is not fully actualized except in conjunction with his death as the deepest dimension of his identification with our human lot; and it is perhaps the case as well that it is for this reason that Jesus' death, expressing as it does his assumed oneness with our humanity, is depicted as the culmination of accomplished human deliverance from our moral guilt and corruption through Jesus' universally representative humanity (Heb. 2:9, 14).

2. and his death is the completion of his identification with our humanity.

But it is important to view this redemptively representative role in a more specifically apologetic context. The climax of natural theology in Part One consisted in a view of reality as an objective moral order of being, grounded in God as essential or absolute moral and ontological goodness. Human beings, as rational, moral selves, have an unconditional moral obligation to conform to the objective moral law in the actualization of their moral personhood through act, principle, and state of character. Yet they have characteristically and universally failed in the fulfillment of this obligation through wrong moral choices and acts on the basis of unworthy principles, and with a resultant defective state of moral character. Hence, in their guilt and moral defection, they are liable to make amends or render satisfaction for their moral state, while nevertheless their moral predicament is such that mere restoration of conformity to moral law could not make the required amends, since that conformity is an obligation quite apart from moral guilt and corruption. If this analysis is correct (and I sincerely think it is), then it would appear that the moral predicament of corrupt humanity is insoluble and that God's purpose in creating a moral order of contingent moral selves would be brought to nought, since that purpose is reasonably viewed as the production and progressive development in moral righteousness of finite rational and moral beings like ourselves. But this resulting disaster is avoided if God, by becoming Incarnate in Jesus, accomplishes through his life and death an adequate moral satisfaction, adequate moral amends, representatively on behalf of the whole of humanity—for in that event the obligation would be fulfilled, the unconditionality of the moral law would be left uncompromised, and the satisfaction would be achieved by representative humanity in a morally appropriate sense. All this, of course, is exactly what the Christian truth-claim contends has been accomplished in Jesus. If, then, apart from some such universally adequate and appropriate remedy, God's moral purpose for humanity would be defeated, and if the supposition of an ultimate and universal defeat of divine purpose in a theistically grounded universe is contextually implausible—and if indeed Jesus did culminate his representative oneness with humanity through his death—then there is good reason to regard all this as a genuine redemptive accomplishment apart from which God's moral purpose, in the actual course of its realization, would be unfulfilled. By itself and in logical isolation, the

B. And apologetically: 1. if reality is an objective moral order with respect to which man is morally liable for defection in act, principle, and state of character, then, since man is incapable of making moral amends for his condition, God's moral purpose, at least for man, would be defeated;

2. but if God Incarnate in Jesus makes full and complete amends vicariously, this moral problem is solved;

3. yet by itself this solution is made merely possible; but in conjunction with theism and incarnationism, the possibility becomes a probability.

propriety of a thesis (the adequacy of Jesus' representative sacrifice) to solve a metaphysical problem (the possible defeat of divine purpose), in a rationally consistent fashion, would perhaps do no more than make the truth of the thesis possible. But, of course, this propriety is not by itself in logical isolation, since it is propounded in the context of a theistic universe in which God has become Incarnate in Jesus Christ. In that overall context, therefore, the purported propriety assumes a far greater degree of plausibility as providing positive foundation for the truth of the thesis. It is not, again, that it is logically impossible to think otherwise—here too unbelief, a different interpretation, is still a logically conceivable option—it is rather that belief in the truth of what I will now call the Christian redemption claim provides a more fully adequate and more totally coherent explanation. Indeed, apart from some such redemptive provision, not only would our human moral predicament be finally hopeless and irremediable, but divine purpose, at least in our human domain, would be finally frustrated and squelched. And that is why we can now claim that— given the actualization of the contingent possibility of wrong moral choice on the part of finite rational, moral selves—God's redemptive provision in Jesus Christ becomes a capstone without which the universal natural revelation of the being and character of God would itself be incomplete. And that is just one more reason why I have long since contended, in my analysis of the concept of revelation, that the unity of natural and supernatural (general and special, universal and particular) revelation is far more significant than any distinction that may reasonably be drawn between them.

a) Again, unbelief is still possible, but belief is more fully adequate and coherent.

b) Thus God's redemptive provision in Jesus becomes the capstone of natural revelation itself.

The Critical Controversy Concerning the Christ

In Relation to His Person

At the Level of Literary Criticism

I. The literary criticism of the Gospels as sources has challenged the historicity of our knowledge of Jesus.

A. Summary of the effect of this criticism.

Any conclusion as far-reaching in its implications for the meaning of life as the claim that Jesus is God Incarnate is bound to have been thoroughly investigated and challenged by critics of every imaginable stripe and in every pertinent area of human thought, especially in view of the enormous historical influence of Christianity on the world. One such area challenges the authenticity and historicity of the sole significant literary sources of whatever information we have about Jesus, namely, the New Testament Gospels, although to a lesser extent the rest of the New Testament writings are also involved. In general, the purported effect of the literary criticism of the Gospels on our knowledge of Jesus can be briefly characterized in five propositions: (1) The fourth Gospel (John) obviously represents an advanced stage of theological development in Christology and therefore cannot reasonably be used as a dependable source of information about the person of Jesus; (2) the synoptic Gospels (Matthew, Mark, and Luke) therefore represent an earlier form of tradition, and since Matthew and Luke embody virtually the whole of Mark in modified form, we may assume that this last Gospel (Mark) is one of their sources and that it therefore itself represents a still earlier stage of the tradition than the other two Synoptics; (3) in the passages common to Matthew and Luke, but not found in any readily identifiable form in Mark, we may recognize another early stage of the tradition which embodies, for the most part, the sayings of Jesus—the so-called Q document; (4) in addition, sections peculiar to Matthew and Luke respectively may well represent other early sources (called M and L) which underlie those Gospels as we now possess them; (5) there are, in all three synoptic Gospels, several distinguishable types of format in which the materials appear, and these types presumably arose, together perhaps with much of the Gospel content, quite as much (or more) from the preaching and instructional needs of the early Christian communities as from any reliable historical sources—so that the materials of even the earliest literary sources are traceable to an oral (or even written) tradition of these early communities which was itself largely determined by didactic motives, with the result that material thus formed should not be regarded as containing significantly reliable historical information. These five propositions involve two main types of criticism: a *source* criticism which attempts to analyze the Gospel materials into literary sources on which they are ostensibly based; and a *form* criticism which seeks a clue to the materials of even these sources in the literary forms which the sources embody and which presumably go back to a period of oral tradition before written sources of any appreciable sort existed. The assumption of this last type of criticism is that, in the period of oral tradition, the material circulated among Christian communities in separate oral units whose form and content came increasingly to reflect the didactic needs of these communities—so that at least the framework and even, for more radical critics, much or perhaps most of the content of the material should be regarded as legendary and ideal constructions with virtually no remaining authentic historical substance whatever.

B. Two types of criticism:

1. source;

2. form.

I have, of course, no intention of engaging in a detailed analysis and critique of these two basic forms of New Testament literary criticism, since my present interest is limited to the Christological implications of these positions. In that limited context, the pertinent questions are clear enough.

II. The pertinence of literary criticism to Christology.

A. Summary of the issues.

1. Does the tracing of Gospel tradition to its supposed pre-New Testament literary sources in any way require us to modify our understanding of the New Testament perspective concerning the person of Jesus, so that, perhaps, we might identify some stratum of New Testament tradition that embodied a purely human view of the person of Jesus?

2. Even if we were to concede to form criticism that the *structure* of the Gospel materials is in part (or even primarily) conditioned by the use of these materials in primitive Christian communities, is there any rationally plausible basis for pressing this position into the service of a scepticism which regards the *content* of the Gospels as also created by these communities and thus not finding its basis in the actual words and deeds of Jesus himself?

3. Is there any adequate ground for underrating the validity of the Johannine material, so that we find ourselves constrained to the view that the fourth Gospel is largely unhistorical in its content and therefore also in its view of Jesus' person?

4. If it turns out that these prior questions are reasonably answerable in such a way as to imply that Jesus' Incarnation claim is characteristic of the earliest plausibly identifiable strata of tradition, is there any viable way of explaining this claim apart from its assignment to Jesus himself?

B. Detailed consideration of the issues:
1. Whether source criticism uncovers a stratum in which Jesus is merely human:
a) On any plausible source analysis, the alleged sources still contain a view of Jesus as divine.
b) For example: the four-document hypothesis.
(1) Mark.

As to the question whether even the most radical literary source criticism succeeds in uncovering any layer of New Testament and especially synoptic tradition which confronts us with a purely human view of the person of Jesus, I think I can with full rational confidence claim that the answer to this question is unqualifiedly negative. No matter what alleged sources we may hypothecate by dividing up the existing Gospel materials on any even moderately plausible principles, these sources still confront us with a divine view of Jesus along with the recognition equally of his full humanity. If we accept provisionally the standard four-document hypothesis which divides the sources as Mark (or some earlier version of it otherwise unknown), Q, M, and L, this conclusion will become evident. I have already argued that the Incarnation claim is characteristic of Mark, and there is no need to repeat that argument here, although it certainly can be further strengthened. It is Mark, for example, who records Jesus' claim, as the Messianic Son of Man, to forgive sins (2:10). And it is Mark alone who records the objection of the Pharisees that only God can forgive sins (2:7)—an implication which Mark apparently accepts, not as an objection, but as asserting the very conclusion that Jesus possesses this intrinsic and uniquely divine authority. And, when Jesus, as described by Mark, tells the rich young ruler that by coming to him and following him he will fulfill the decisive condition for finding eternal life, then surely Jesus also, along with the writer, implies that he is the ultimate Good which constitutes this life (Mark 10:18–31). And, in this light, it is no accident that Jesus has, in Mark's account, previously cautioned the young man that the ultimate Good is to be found in God alone—the very Good which Jesus urges the young man to find in himself.

(2) Q.

The case is, if anything, even stronger for the so-called Q document. In Q, for example, Jesus clearly presents himself as Lord of the ultimate destinies of human beings, a claim that would be blasphemous nonsense apart from the supposition of Jesus' deity (Matt. 7:21; Luke 6:46). But the most striking implication of Jesus' deity occurs in the Q passage represented by Matthew 11:27 and Luke 10:22, in which Jesus claims not only that all authority has been delivered to him once and for all by the Father, but also that the Father alone has intimate knowledge of Jesus as his unique Son, and that he, the Son, has a reciprocally parallel intimate knowledge of the Father, so that it is only through Jesus the Son that anyone else can have an analogous knowledge of the Father. This mutually reciprocal knowledge, ascribed equally to the Father and the Son, and this unique mediatorial role of

Jesus as the one through whom alone others can know the Father, are both explicable in the most fully intelligible sense only on the supposition that Jesus is himself God in the highest sense.

The same outlook characterizes both M (the material unique to Matthew) and L (the material unique to Luke). In the unique birth stories, for example, Luke declares that the child to be born would be called the Son of God (1:35), and Matthew names him, from Isaiah 7:14, Immanuel, "God with us" (1:23). "God my Savior," of whom Mary speaks, is the very child she was to bear (Luke 1:47; 2:11); and the child whom the wise men seek to worship is clearly the Messiah (Matt. 2:2–16). For Matthew, Jesus is the Son of Jehovah called out of Egypt (2:15; cf. Hosea 11:1); and Luke describes the boy Jesus in the temple as "among the things of my Father" (2:49). Again, it is Matthew who refers to Jesus as the "great light" of whom Isaiah spoke (4:16; Isa. 9:1f.); and it is Luke who records Jesus' claim that the Messianic prophecy of Isaiah 61 is fulfilled in himself (4:17–21). It is Matthew who, in his version of the Sermon on the Mount, most fully ascribes to Jesus a self-contained authority to reinterpret the Old Testament in radical fashion—an ascription with the highest implications in a writer like Matthew, who uniformly attributes Old Testament Scripture to God himself (5:21f.; cf. 1:22,23). Again it is Matthew who adds to the great Q passage of 11:27 the invitation for all men to come to him for rest, satisfaction, and salvation (11:28–30)—an invitation whose incarnational implications I discussed much earlier. Luke, on the other hand, further depicts Jesus as the one, through whose acceptance in love, forgiveness of sin is received (7:47, 48). Again, in the Matthew account of the judgment (25:31–46), the Son of Man (with whom Jesus obviously identifies himself) comes in *his* glory with *his* angels to sit upon *his* glorious throne: and it is he who determines the ultimate destinies of individuals on the basis, finally, of their relation to *him.* Such a picture unquestionably confronts us with the implication of the Absolute Lordship of Jesus. Add to this the fact that the Zechariah passage (14:5), to which Matthew here clearly alludes and which he with equal clarity applies to Jesus, obviously refers in the original context to Jehovah God, and the evidence seems complete. Finally, it is Matthew who makes most of Jesus' careful distinction between "my Father" and "your Father" in reference to God (6:8, 9; 10:29, 32–33; 12:49–50; 25:34; 26:29). In fact, nowhere in the Gospels does Jesus use the expression "our Father" in such a way as to include himself with other human persons—a fact which strongly reveals his claim to an absolutely unique Sonship in utter transcendence of all creaturehood. Thus, in the special traditions of Matthew and Luke, we confront the same Incarnation claim that characterized Mark and the so-called Q document. Hence, the general answer to the question as to the effect of source criticism on Christology is clear: The search for pre-New Testament literary sources leads us *to* the divine Christ and *not at all away from* him. There is, then, no plausibly identifiable stratum of tradition in which we find a purely human view of the person of Jesus,

(3) M and L.

c) Hence, source criticism leads *to* the divine Christ as God Incarnate, not away from him.

so that source criticism, far from undermining the claim that Jesus is God Incarnate, serves on the contrary to support that claim.

2. Whether form criticism renders the information about Jesus historically unreliable.

It is a distinct and further question whether form criticism, even if accepted in modified form with respect to the structure and framework of the Gospel materials, can also be reasonably interpreted as supporting a scepticism which ascribes even the content of the earliest sources to the creative and virtually unbridled imagination of the early Christian communities—so that every bridge of connection with the actual words and deeds of Jesus is effectively cut off. Again, I think it confidently possible to answer that there is no sufficient, much less compelling, basis for such a negativism. Even if much of the *form* of the Gospel material was developed under the impact of the use of these materials by the Christian communities, there is no decisive reason to extend this explanation to include the essential core content of the material. If the early Christian communities created the very content of the Gospels, then what satisfactory account can be given to explain the origin of those communities themselves? If it is answered that the earliest believers attributed to Jesus, for example, words which were not his because they respected him as a teacher, would not this very respect have been among the strongest motives for preserving the actual words of Jesus to the highest possible degree in regard to the content of those words? And apart from an accessible tradition of Jesus' actual teachings, what explanation could be given of the origin of that very respect on which such a hypothesis is ultimately dependent? If, *per contra*, they had no such respect for Jesus as a teacher, it is difficult to see how they would be motivated to create a tradition of his words. Again, extreme form criticism of this sort appears to overlook the conservative influence that eyewitnesses of the deeds and words of Christ would naturally exert on the formation of tradition in the earliest Christian communities. We are, after all, not talking about centuries between the original communities and the New Testament form of the written Gospel. Indeed, we are barely talking about decades, so that such eyewitnesses as the original apostles and disciples would bring to bear a strong influence in maintaining the objective tradition that doubtless existed at the outset and found its original source in Jesus himself. Such eyewitnesses were, after all, the transmitters of their own experience in handing on that tradition—and, if there had been no such objective tradition, what effective ground would any early Christian have had for appealing to some words of Jesus as authoritative in the first place?

a) There is no plausible reason for ascribing the content of the materials to the inventiveness of early Christian communities.

(1) Such a thesis would leave the origin of the communities themselves unexplained.

(2) Respect for Jesus would motivate the preservation of his words, and without such respect, there would be no reason to create a tradition of Jesus' words.

b) The influence of eyewitnesses would support the preservation of the original oral tradition, without which there would be no reason to appeal to any word of Jesus as authoritative.

c) It is incredible to suppose that the early believers simply invented the whole substance of the gospel tradition,
(1) since the period is too short for legend to develop,

It is, furthermore, extremely difficult to think of the early Christian communities as literally going berserk (as on this hypothesis they must have) in their propensity for imaginative invention and virtually uncompromising misrepresentation, especially when we find in Paul's undisputed first letter to Corinth a keenly sensitive awareness of the distinction between what Jesus actually said and what he did not (1 Cor. 7:10, 12, 25, 40). And since, as I have just observed, the period between the actual life of Jesus and the Gospels in substantially their present form is so brief, the time span is simply not great enough for the growth of a widely accepted tradition, the main substance of which is all but entirely legendary. Indeed, it is quite reasonable to ask why there is any such thing as a *common* gospel tradition at all, if the form and content of the Gospel materials both originated through the creative imagination of widely separated communities that presumably created the very core of the traditions they respectively accepted. It appears therefore that an objective study of the forms of the Gospel materials gives no reasonable support to the thesis that the substance of these materials was created virtually *ex nihilo* by the early Christian communities. On the contrary, we may be confident that the Gospels are the embodiment of an objective tradition which finds its point of origin in the words and deeds of Jesus himself. And if those materials confront us, as I have previously contended, with the Incarnation claim as traceable also to Jesus himself, no properly qualified form criticism will be able to strip away that conclusion.

(2) and there would then be no way to account for a common gospel tradition.

d) If therefore the content of the tradition is genuinely historical, the Incarnation claim of Jesus stands unaffected by any plausible form criticism.

And what about the historical value of the Johannine witness to Jesus' Incarnation claim? The critical reasons for suspecting the historicity of the Johannine framework may be reduced to the following: (1) the *chronological* problem—the fact that the Gospel of John implies a much longer ministry for Jesus than we would be led to infer from the Synoptics; (2) the *stylistic* problem—the fact that the sayings of Jesus in this Gospel are cast in the same style and thought-constructs as the comments of the writer himself, a consideration which raises the question whether the sayings themselves may be, even in their content, constructions of the writer, rather than substantial representations of Jesus' own teachings; and (3) the *theological* problem—the fact that the self-testimony of Jesus to his deity in this Gospel, together with the didactic discourse of the writer to the same effect, is far more advanced theologically and explicitly traced out than is the case with the Synoptics, so that the validity of the testimony is alleged, to that extent, to be questionable.

3. As for the Johannine witness:

a) Reasons for doubt summarized:
(1) chronological;
(2) stylistic;

(3) theological.

The *chronological problem* is of no great concern for our present purpose, since it does not involve direct Christological implications. But the problem will, in any case, be largely alleviated if we bear several things in mind: First, that none of the Gospels seem cast, apart from the passion narrative, in a strict chronological framework, so that an objection of this sort will have no identifiable criterion on which to base itself; second, that distinguishable chronologies, even to the extent that they do exist, need not be interpreted as contrary or contradictory, but may plausibly be regarded as mutually and reciprocally supplementing one another; and third, that John, with whatever additional embellishments, clearly follows the broad general outline that pervades the common synoptic framework.

b The chronological problem is of secondary importance for Christology, and in any case is reasonably soluble on certain plausible assumptions.

As to the other objections, a few preliminary observations will be appropriate. At the outset, it seems evident that the writer of the Gospel of John *intends* to be historically correct in what he records, since the hypothesis of outright invention would be inconsistent with his express purpose of supporting Jesus' Messianic claim by actual historical events which the writer views as revelatory signs (20:30,31);

c) The author intends to be historical as evidenced by:

(1) his stated purpose,

(2) his fidelity to syn-
optic parallels,

And in the First Epistle, the supposedly same writer claims the historical foundation of his message to find its substance in that Logos of
Life "which we beheld and our hands handled . . ." (1:1). Again, wherever there *are* synoptic parallels (for example, in the passion narrative,
or in the miracles of John 6), the writer appears to follow the common
synoptic tradition with reasonable care—a plausible basis for supposing that in other respects also the writer purports to be faithful to his
considered sources and therefore embodies a valid historical tradition.

(3) the weakness of
the argument from
synoptic silence,

Any argument to the contrary would have only the absence of this
further tradition in the Synoptics as its basis—and silence is characteristically a questionable foundation for any such far-reaching historical
judgment. After all, the synoptic tradition may be fairly judged as itself
fragmentary; and it is at least questionable whether we can reasonably
proscribe the Johannine framework on the ground that it embodies a
sweep of tradition not also found in these other accessible sources.

(4) the early accept-
ance of the Gospel as
authentic,

Furthermore, if the Johannine discourses and narratives were entirely
out of line with the traditional core of materials, what accounts for
the early and virtually universal acceptance of the Gospel of John by
the Christian community at large? If the Rylands papyrus is correctly
dated, then by the early second century A.D. the Gospel had so far
extended its influence that a copy of it existed in a small provincial

(5) and the detailed
topological references.

town in Egypt. Finally, the many correct topographical references in
the Gospel would be surprising in a work that supposedly embodied
the preponderance of wholly imaginative projection and interpretation.

Nor is the *stylistic problem* of any decisive significance for the
question of historical reliability of substance. No doubt the writer
intrudes his own style into his account of the discourses of Jesus,
although of course we have no fully accurate way of knowing to what
extent this sort of intrusion may also be characteristic of the synoptic

d) The stylistic prob-
lem would affect only
the form and not the
content of Jesus'
words, since the latter
are not verbatim quo-
tations either here or
in the Synoptics.

materials. But this sort of development, in either John or the Synoptics,
is wholly compatible with the reasonable assumption that the accounts of Jesus' words in the Gospel materials are, with rare exceptions, not to be viewed as verbatim reports but rather as paraphrases
of the substance of Jesus' teaching. Certainly, to insist for any such
reason that substance of the discourses has no basis in the actual
words of Jesus would be entirely out of harmony with the previously
mentioned intent of the writer to present Jesus as he really was and is.

e) Since all the Gos-
pels present Jesus as
God Incarnate, the Jo-
hannine account is not
objectionable on that
ground, even if his
witness is more reflec-
tive and theological in
form.

As for the *theological problem*, it is greatly reduced by the already
argued thesis that all the Gospel materials and sources present us
with a view of Jesus as God Incarnate, so that it is scarcely appropriate
to express doubt about the historicity of a work which simply brings
out this implication in bolder terms. The Johannine account is doubtless born out of a long meditation on the meaning of the words and
deeds of Jesus. But on that account it is, perhaps, not less historical
but more, because it confronts us with a Jesus understood reflectively
by a slowly developing and profoundly matured Christian insight. That
such an insight would seek its basis in a substance entirely of its own
invention is virtually unthinkable in the interpretive context of a theis-

tic and wholly moral world-view. No doubt the narrative is often the instrument of the theological affirmation; but it seems evident as a minimal conclusion that the Johannine witness to Jesus as God Incarnate finds its historical basis in the actual self-testimony of Jesus, so that here too we return again to our perennial conclusion about the Incarnation claim.

The one remaining issue in this context is whether, in view of the answers to our previous questions, there is any plausible way of explaining the evident presence of the Incarnation claim in all the sources and strata of tradition that may be plausibly identified, apart from the ascription of that claim to Jesus himself as its historical source. For the most part, this question has already been answered in principle in my previous analysis. If the Christological witness which characterizes these earliest sources was not derived from Jesus himself, then the presumption would be that somehow the starting point for this common witness must have been a purely human Jesus quite devoid of any supernatural dimension that would go beyond his status as a prophet and teacher. From that starting point, two main alternatives have been suggested and developed. One is that of *apotheosis* or *progressive idealization*, according to which the profound reverence that the disciples and other early believers had for Jesus as a prophet and teacher was gradually (although within the scope of a relatively few years) transformed in their minds into an affirmation of his deity. The other alternative may be designated as a *mythical symbolism*, according to which the man Jesus is merely the historical symbol of the general truth of the universal oneness of the Deity and humanity, so that an already existing ideal of God-manhood—together with the metaphysical perspective that made such a notion intelligible—simply fastened, however inexplicably, on the historical Jesus, whose connection with this concept therefore is virtually an historical accident.

In response to either of these transitional proposals, my earlier discussion makes any such proposal extremely implausible, although not, of course, logically impossible. This sort of proposal has at the outset no identifiable historical support either in the New Testament or in any of the hypothecated sources that even a radical criticism can reasonably isolate. Again, as we have seen, it is unthinkable that the rigorously monotheistic Jews who were the earliest disciples of Jesus could have understood the Incarnation claim in either of these senses, both of which would have instantiated the essence of both idolatry and blasphemy for them. In view of their obvious respect for the Old Testament (a respect extensively reflected in the New Testament appeal to the Old Testament as divinely authoritative), they can only have understood the Incarnation claim in a sense which, in their understanding at least, would have been fully compatible with Old Testament monotheism; and neither apotheosis nor mythical symbolism could reasonably claim to meet this requirement.

As for the apotheosis theory specifically, I have already argued that the supposition that the early believers created the Incarnation claim leaves their existence as believers at all completely unexplained, and I

4. Nor is there any way of explaining the Incarnation claim apart from its ascription to Jesus himself.

a) Principal alternatives:
(1) *apotheosis.*

(1) *mythical symbolism.*

b) Neither of these proposals has any reasonable historical support, and both are incompatible with the monotheistic background of the early believers.

c) Apotheosis would leave the existence of the believing community itself unexplained.

need not repeat the details of that argument here, other than to say that a purely human Jesus, however impressive as a person, provides no plausible basis for the transition to the notion of deity. There have, of course, been cases of this sort of deification in world religion; but such cases (for example, Buddha in the Mahayana tradition) have required literally centuries for their crystallization and a radically different, non-monotheistic perspective for their breeding ground. The case of Jesus is therefore strikingly different on both counts.

d) Mythical symbolism:
(1) presupposes a pantheism that is inconsistent with the monotheistic context;

(2) and presupposes an extensive fabulation that does not fit well with the New Testament setting.

Mythical symbolism, in my opinion, fares no better as an explanation of the Incarnation claim. In the first place, the sort of world-view perspective that such an explanation presupposes can simply not be regarded as ascribable to the early believers. The concept of universal God-manhood belongs to a pantheistic view of reality that cannot reasonably be regarded as conditioning the thought of monotheistic Palestinian Jews of the first century. Furthermore, the general characteristics of the New Testament documents do not comport well with the notion of pure mythical fabulation. A fabulator would romanticize the whole setting of his description to the virtual neglect of the historical, while the New Testament is proliferated with concern about historical detail. And a fabulator would scarcely include with his description of deity an equal and coextensive account of Jesus' humanity in the sort of circumstantial and incidental terms that characterize that account in the New Testament as a whole and in the synoptic Gospels in particular. It is equally important that the New Testament witness to the deity of Jesus, clear as it is, is invariably cast in a framework in which that witness is assumed as the common belief of disciples everywhere, so that the primarily incidental form of the witness simply does not fit well with the sort of propagandistic persuasion that would characterize the work of a mythical fabulator.

(a) The Incarnation claim therefore goes back to Jesus himself, and that claim is most coherently explained on the supposition of its truth.

I think it therefore fair to conclude that the Incarnation claim goes back indeed to the historical Jesus, despite ingenious attempts to argue otherwise. And I have already argued at considerable length the implications of that claim as thus made by Jesus himself. The explanation that comports most adequately and coherently with all the information that we may reasonably claim to have in the Gospels and the rest of the New Testament about the person of Jesus is that which argues both that Jesus claimed to be God Incarnate because—in a state of untarnished moral commitment and unquestionable psychological soundness—he sincerely believed the claim to be true, and that he thus believed the claim because, in the depth of a self-awareness to which humanly he alone had direct access, he knew unhesitatingly that the claim was true.

I. Two types of Christological theory:

At the Level of Theological System

In discussing alternative Christologies, in the context of systematic and philosophical theological systems and from the admittedly limited standpoint of the sort of philosophical and critical apologetic with which I am here concerned, I find it illuminating to divide such theories about the person of Jesus into two types—*immanental* theories which attempt to explain Jesus' person and status as wholly a development from what is intrinsic and potential to universal human nature, so that what Jesus was and became is viewed as, in principle at least, a universal human possibility which, given the appropriate circumstances and genetic endowment, could have been realized by any human individual; and *transcendental* theories which, although fully acknowledging Jesus' authentic and integral humanness, nevertheless maintain that the core of Jesus' actualized personal selfhood cannot be wholly explained as the development of a merely immanent human possibility, but requires in addition a supernatural dimension and character, so that Jesus, although genuinely human, is at the same time decidedly more than human.

> A. *immanental*: Jesus as a development of human potentiality;
>
> B. *transcendental*: Jesus as more than merely human.

There is, of course on the immanental side, a favorable view of Jesus in the context of what I will call *naturalistic humanism—naturalistic*, in the sense that theism (or any other transcendental metaphysic) is denied, and nature alone, the space-time universe, is declared to be genuinely real; and *humanistic*, in the sense that the moral goal of mankind is the individual and social realization of an ideal of selfhood which is wholly intrinsic in basis and principle to human nature correctly understood. While it is not a foregone conclusion that a thinker operating in this interpretive framework would adopt a generally favorable assessment of Jesus, such an assessment has certainly often been propounded in this context. Since for this perspective there is no transcendent God in the theistic sense, the supposition that Jesus could be God Incarnate becomes unintelligible and is therefore dismissed on principle as pure mythology of the sort quite characteristic of various ethnic religions associated with the early stages of the development of civilization. In consequence of this stance, it thus becomes axiomatic that Jesus is viewed as purely human with no transcendent supernatural dimension to his person. But at the same time Jesus is regarded as strikingly exceptional in the degree to which he actualizes the moral ideal of human nature and in the impact of his ethical teachings as expressing this ideal and providing instruction for its realization—so that Jesus is both the exemplar and the expositor of the human moral ideal. Any supernatural context, which the Gospel materials associate with this moral ideal, is either dismissed as impertinent without further explanation, or else regarded as itself either an indication of Jesus' personal involvement in the religious milieu of his background or, alternatively, a legendary accretion that became attached to an ethic which in its original form, as actually taught by Jesus, had no essential dependence on this sort of religious-metaphysical context.

> II. Immanental views:
> A. *Naturalistic humanism.*
> 1. General definition.
>
> 2. View of Jesus.
>
> *a*) The Incarnation claim is here regarded as pure mythology.
>
> *b*) Jesus as the exemplar and expositor of the human moral ideal.

I shall pause only briefly in my critical assessment of this particular immanental alternative concerning the person of Jesus, since my previously argued claims, if accepted as plausible, already deprive any such view of its perspectival foundation. If my cumulative argument for theism—culminating as it does in the claim that an objective moral ideal is intelligible only in dependence on God as essential and Abso-

> 3. Critical problems:
> *a*) Metaphysical theism and transcendental ethics have already been argued.

(1) Jesus himself regarded ethics as theistically grounded.

lute Goodness—is itself basically correct in its contention, then both the naturalistic denial of theism, and the humanistic attempt to work out an objective ethic on grounds that do not exceed human nature and the natural realm in general are to that extent already to be seen as decisively inadequate both metaphysically and morally. In the Gospels, Jesus' association of moral principles with theism is no incidental feature of his moral teaching but rather wholly central to its thrust— so much so that he regarded the love of God with one's whole humanly responsive nature as the highest moral duty and as itself the basis of the subordinate but pervasively important duty to love one's neighbor or fellow human being. If Jesus could be as thoroughly mistaken about the very core of morality—as, for the naturalistic humanist, he must have been—that makes the exaltation of his moral teaching, forcibly extracted from its essential metaphysical base, far

(2) and he claimed to be God Incarnate.

b) Jesus would then have been fundamentally confused and therefore not a moral ideal from a humanistic standpoint.

less plausible. And perhaps more importantly, if, as I have argued, Jesus claimed to be God Incarnate when, in fact, that claim was false according to the naturalistic humanist, that fundamental confusion would argue a moral and/or psychological perversion in Jesus that would largely eliminate any serious respect for him as a moral ideal and exemplar. Of course, I do not accept these conclusions, but rather interpret Jesus' Incarnation claim in a radically different fashion. But what these conclusions show is that the naturalistic humanist has no legitimate or coherent right both to cling to his own metaphysical perspective and at the same time to respect Jesus as an outstanding moral exemplar and expositor.

B. *Liberal humanitarianism.*

1. General definition. *a)*Modified theism (or sometimes pantheism).

The immanental position that I will characterize as *liberal humanitarianism,* with respect to the person of Jesus, imbibes to a large extent the same sort of mistake. I call this perspective *liberal* because it was associated historically with the liberal tradition in Protestant theology which claimed a sort of transcendental metaphysic of either a theistic or quasi-theistic sort (sometimes even pantheistic), but attempted to eliminate from its understanding of Christianity any supernatural dimension aside from this general transcendental metaphysic. And I

b) Humanistic view of Jesus.

call the view *humanitarianism* because—quite in keeping with its intent to pare away reference points for any supernatural dimension as disclosed in the natural order itself—the position interprets Jesus once again as the fullest actualization of human selfhood and as therefore no more than human, although admittedly he represents

2. Historical exponents.
a) Schleiermacher:

humanity at its best. Thus, Friedrich Schleiermacher, often designated as the founder of Protestant religious liberalism even though his metaphysic wavered unsteadily between theism and pantheism, regarded

Jesus as the fullest actualization of God-consciousness.

Jesus as that historical human person who, in all his life, realized the human potential for God-consciousness (the feeling of absolute dependence as the subjective correlate of the Divine Reality which was the proper object of that feeling) to the fullest, humanly possible extent. In whatever sense Jesus was himself "divine," it was not a sense which made him, in his person, essentially different from other human beings; the difference was one of degree only. In a certain way, Jesus is unique as the full realization of this latent human possiblity, but his achievement is in principle an open-ended possibility for any human person, and it is through him as an example that the rest of us can move in the direction of a comparable but relative realization. More recent liberal theologians have used similar language to express in modern context a view of Jesus that is essentially the same as Schleiermacher's. For example, the so-called divine nature of Jesus is actually a symbolic reference to God's saving act through the merely but fully human Jesus (John Knox). Or God was incarnate in Jesus either through a paradoxical juxtaposition of the Divine Logos with the separately personal and merely human Jesus, or else in the sense that Jesus lived his whole life in conscious recognition that all was done in total dependence upon God's grace through a human selfhood wholly yielded to God (D. M. Baillie). Or, perhaps, Jesus is truly God in the sense that in him God truly and fully confronts us, so that what God manifested in Jesus, as fully human, was and is his own true self, and hence in and with Jesus God himself is present and revealing his true character (Hans Küng—but Roman Catholic, not Protestant). No doubt the language of such thinkers struggles to retain something of the biblical milieu of ideas concerning the person of Jesus; but I see in this sort of characterization nothing that essentially transcends the type of perspective classically represented by Schleiermacher so far as the person of Jesus is concerned. A special or even unique operation of God in and through the human Jesus, as exceptional and unparalleled recognition of God and submission to him on the part of Jesus, a real and climactically definitive revelation of God in Jesus—all these fall short of the full New Testament picture; all these are still not Jesus as God Incarnate in the fullest and most unqualified sense.

However impressed we may be, therefore, with the transcendent metaphysical emphasis of liberal humanitarianism on some version of theism, its perspective on the person of Jesus, although more exalted than that of naturalistic humanism, still does not go beyond the confines of a mere, although admittedly genuine, humanity. And if my overall argument is even moderately plausible, such a view scarcely provides an explanation of the fact that the Incarnation claim is not the product of the enthusiastic devotion and imagination of the early disciples, but must be traced to Jesus himself. Apart from some relatively *a priori* philosophical or theological requirement which makes a full and genuine incarnation impossible in principle, the only support for a view of Jesus as merely human, however exalted, is the recognition of Jesus as genuinely and fully human—a recognition that is wholly compatible with incarnation in the most elevated and uncompromising sense. It follows therefore that liberal humanitarianism is still left with the question as to how to explain the Incarnation claim as historically traceable to Jesus himself—not indeed the Jesus of some imaginative reconstruction whose primary basis is the perspective of some philosophically chosen world-view whose limits our previous analysis has already challenged, but the Jesus whose qualities and characteristics emerge from the New Testament records themselves as we have already considered them.

b) John Knox.

c) D. M. Baillie.

d) Hans Küng.

3. Summary characterization.

4. Critical problems:
a) The liberal view still construes Jesus as merely human:

and hence provides no explanation of the Incarnation claim as traceable to Jesus himself.
b) Such a view is supported only by:
(1) a philosophical assumption that incarnation is impossible,
(2) and the genuine humanity of Jesus.

C. Hegelian *absolute idealism.*
1. General definition.
a) Religious conceptions as symbolic expressions of philosophical truths.
b) All reality as a single Absolute Spirit.

c) The incarnation as the symbol of divine-human unity: hence, Christianity as the absolute religion.

2. Critical problems:

a) This perspective replaces the theism of the Christian tradition with a pantheism similar to certain Hindu and Buddhist views.
b) This in turn undermines the uniqueness of the Christian Incarnation claim.

c) If, as I have argued, such a monistic pantheism is implausible, then its explanation of the incarnation will be equally implausible:
and in any case it makes no connection with the Jesus of early Christian understanding.

No doubt the most obvious illustration of a philosophically determined characterization of Jesus, which makes virtually no significant connection with the New Testament materials, is found in the sort of understanding represented by the *absolute idealism* of Hegel and some of his intellectual successors. For such an outlook, religious conceptions in general are viewed as symbolic representations of truths which can, in principle at least, be non-symbolically stated in the prosaic propositions of speculative philosophy. Since Hegel's position takes as its core insight the notion that all reality is a series of dialectically related aspects of a single all-inclusive reality, namely, the Absolute Spirit; and since therefore the basic truth is the oneness of all determinate entities with that Absolute; and since the Incarnation claim of Christianity (whether traceable to Jesus or not) may be philosophically construed as symbolically asserting the metaphysical unity of humanity with the Absolute (or God, in religious parlance)—it follows that Hegelianism can characterize Christianity, with the Incarnation claim thus understood at its center, as the absolute religion, because it expresses the divine-human unity more clearly and effectively than the symbols of any other historically influential religious world-view such as the various perspectives of, say, Confucianism, Buddhism, or Hinduism. Hence, the historical significance of Jesus as an individual person fades away in favor of a metaphorical Christ-myth with purely symbolical importance—a myth, in fact, which pictorially expresses a truth about each and every human being, since we are all of us as one with God as Jesus himself.

Several implications are clear on the face of the matter. For such an absolute idealism, the theistic perspective, which clearly characterizes the Christian religious tradition in its main thrust, is replaced by a pantheistic stance for which all reality is included within the being of God—a stance not very different, allowing for distinctions of linguistic expression, from the ultimate monistic metaphysical perspectives in some varieties of Hinduism and Mahayana Buddhism. With that world-view shift, the Incarnation claim loses the uniqueness of that concept as applicable solely to Jesus in a sense in which it is not applicable to any other human beings, however impressive—so that now any human person has the potential and even the core actuality of God-manhood. For progressive Hindu and Mahayana Buddhist thinkers, Jesus also can be recognized as an incarnation of Vishnu or Brahma, or as an individual Buddha like Gautama, since all alike are manifestations of the universal Buddha essence. For these shifts of perspective, the real issue is whether this sort of monistic pantheism is a philosophically viable option. I have already spoken to that issue both in previous parts of the present discussion and in my earlier books, *The Resurrection of Theism* and *Oriental Philosophy*. Hence, I will not reiterate the details of my critique here. If my criticisms of such a metaphysical standpoint are themselves plausible, then the resultant inadequacy of that standpoint will entail the parallel implausibility of any such account of the person of Jesus, since it would depend on that inadequate metaphysical standpoint. In any case, it is clear that in this context we are, as it were, light years away from the Jesus of early Christian doctrine, and still further from the Jesus of history. The consequence is that, if we discuss the Incarnation claim in such pantheistic terms, we will not really be discussing the distinctively Christian Incarnation claim at all, but only a radically different notion which shares little more than the name.

If we now turn our attention to what I have termed *transcendental* theories of the person of Jesus from the standpoint of theological system, we are concerned with explanations which, while accepting the full and genuine humanity of Jesus, nevertheless regard any explanation of the person of Jesus in merely human terms as wholly inadequate. There is, of course, the broad sweep of Trinitarian explanations which constitute the mainstream of traditional Christology in the orthodox sense from the early fathers of the Christian church through Augustine, Thomas Aquinas, Calvin, and their theological colleagues, right down to Karl Barth and Emil Brunner. For all these thinkers, Jesus was and is God Incarnate in the sense that he is the Eternal Son and Logos of God, one in essence of deity with the Father and the Holy Spirit. I include my own analysis of the person of Jesus as one small assenting voice in this otherwise august and venerable company, although I do not claim that all these thinkers either did or would accept the details of my philosophical explanation of either Christology or Trinitarianism. But since my own perspective on these issues is one alternative version of this mainstream of thought, I shall not elaborate that traditional orthodox standpoint further. And if we are looking for alternative transcendental theories which at the same time accept the full humanity of Jesus, while they operate within the framework of a properly construed theistic metaphysic, then I think it would be fair to say that there are two main possibilities. These are, first, the *Arian* type of view which regards Jesus as the incarnation of a divine being who is, even in his transcendent state, not God in the absolute sense, but rather of similar instead of identical essence and substance with God in that highest sense; and second, the so-called *Kenotic* type of view which, while regarding Jesus as God Incarnate in the highest sense, so that Trinitarianism itself is purportedly in no sense compromised, nevertheless considers the Eternal Son or Logos as divested of either the possession or the independent exercise of the transcendent divine attributes (omnipresence, for example) during the period of the incarnate state or earthly career of Jesus.

While Arianism and Kenoticism have clearly contrasting views of the person of Jesus, they nonetheless spring from similar motives in part. Both are propounded as attempts to explain a variety of New Testament passages which clearly imply that Jesus is subordinate to God the Father, at least during the period of his earthly life (both views), and perhaps also in his transcendent state both before the incarnation and at the conclusion of Jesus' sojourn in the world (Arianism). I have no intention of merely glossing over passages of this sort, but neither do I intend to discuss them all in depth, since I have alluded to some of them already. But as a sample: The Gospels seem

III. Transcendental views:

A. Traditional orthodox Trinitarianism.

1. Historical representatives.

2. My own view as belonging in this category.

B. Two main alternatives:

1. Defined:
a) *Arianism.*

b) *Kenoticism.*

2. Both views aim at explaining the subordination of Jesus to the Father in the New Testament.

a) Illustrative passages.

clearly to put limits on the knowledge of Jesus, although at the same time emphasizing his more-than-normal human knowledge, even in comparison to the most perceptive among us (Mark 13:32; John 2:25; 4:16f.; 1:48f.). In particular, the Gospel of John, which emphasizes the divine and preexistent nature of Jesus more explicitly than either the other Gospels or even the rest of the New Testament, nevertheless also strongly emphasizes the subordination of the Son (clearly Jesus) to the Father (John 5:19–37), and even represents Jesus as saying that the Father is greater than he is (14:28). And the apostle Paul, whose clear testimony to Jesus' deity I have already affirmed, implies an analogous subordination when, after speaking of all things ultimately being subordinated to (or placed under) the Son, other than the One (God) who thus subjected all things to the Son, he goes on to declare that finally the Son would himself be subjected or subordinated to that One who thus subordinated all things to the Son, so that God might be all in all—a declaration which can linguistically be interpreted as implying a distinction between the Son (again clearly Jesus) and God.

There is further that open assertion by Paul in a different letter (Col. 1:15) that Jesus the Son is "the firstborn" of all creation—an admittedly imprecise, but for that reason puzzling, designation. And perhaps the most difficult passage occurs in the Apocalypse (the Book of Revelation) which, although alluding repeatedly to Jesus' oneness with God, nevertheless has the glorified Jesus refer to himself as "the beginning of the creation of God" (Rev. 3:14), although the meaning of the term here translated "beginning" is not explicitly clear without interpretation. There is, of course, no valid reason for suppressing these and other subordination passages; it is rather a question as to how they should be understood. Taken in isolation from the overall framework of New Testament teaching concerning the person of Jesus, such passages could indeed be taken as at least suggesting something like the Arian view that Jesus the Son, even in his preexistent state, was although a divine being, nevertheless a creature, while yet the highest of creatures. And, taken with less isolation of this sort, some of the passages could be taken to imply a subordination of Jesus to the Father, during his earthly career, which involved something rather less than the full possession and exercise of the transcendent divine attributes—as the Kenotic theory suggests in basing itself on the notion of emptying in Paul's Letter to the Philippians (2:7).

b) Problem of interpretation.
(1) In isolation these passages might support an Arian or Kenotic view.

How, then, should all this be understood? The issue is partly confused by the fact that Arianism, although originally emphasizing the genuineness of Jesus' humanity, ended up historically by denying that Jesus had a true and integral human soul or spirit, although a version of this view is certainly conceivable without that corollary. In any case, I shall fall back here on the criterion of rational coherence or systematic consistency—a criterion that I have long since thoroughly elaborated in my discussion of epistemology. And I shall also take it as plausibly argued that the New Testament, in all of its literary scope, clearly implies and sometimes explicitly states that Jesus is God Incarnate in the highest and most uncompromising sense. Now, since the

(2) But if these texts are taken in view of the New Testament concept of Jesus' unqualified deity, it is plausible to interpret the texts consistently with that claim.

(*a*) Relevance of the principle of rational coherence.

subordination of Jesus to the Father is characteristically expressed by
the very writers (John and Paul, for example) who most clearly contend for Jesus' deity—and since the supposition that such writers were
intentionally propounding a blatant contradiction seems highly implausible on the face of it—I will contend that the subordination of
Jesus to the Father can reasonably be understood in such a way as to
be fully consistent with Jesus being regarded as essential Deity in the
most unqualified meaning of that term. This contention is quite in
accord with the principle that, while we should recognize contradictions whenever they are clearly present, we should nevertheless not
introduce them in any context where a consistent and therefore reasonable alternative is clearly possible. Easily accessible biblical com-
mentaries are full of explanations which elaborate the exegetical
details of this contention; and there is no reason for me to take more
than a passing notice of this ample scholarly discussion. But if my
contention is correct, then such a coherent explanation of Jesus' subordination to the Father will simply eliminate the view of Arianism
that Jesus' preexistent reality should be understood in creaturely
terms. In general, Jesus' subordination should be understood as one
of office or revelatory-redemptive function, rather than as any subordination of essential nature. Thus it is in the official revelatory sense
that the Son does not know the time of the second coming, since it
was not God's will to reveal it. And it is in office rather than in essence
that the Father is greater than the Son. Again, it is as being only one
person of the Godhead that the Son will be finally revealed as subordinate to God in the full Triune sense; and, further, that Jesus is the
firstborn of all creation may be taken either as a reference to his
Eternal Sonship (begotten "before" or "apart from" all creation), or as
a quite different reference to his being the firstborn of the new spiritual creation through his resurrection from the dead (notice Col.
1:18f.); and finally that Jesus is the beginning of the creation of God
may also refer to that new spiritual creation—or the Greek word may
be taken quite differently in the sense of first or foundational principle,
so that the exalted Jesus is here referring to himself as the first
principle of God's creation. Exegesis of this sort is both possible and
responsible; and, perhaps more importantly, it fits in with the most
coherent total impact of the entire New Testament characterization of
the person of Jesus as God Incarnate.

But any purely creaturely view of the preexistence of the Son,
whether in Arianism or in any other historical context, is further
subject to a still more serious objection. If Jesus the Son is anything
less than essential Deity and therefore a creature in however an
exalted sense, then this view—both for Old Testament monotheism
and for the first Christian disciples who were themselves committed
to that monotheism—would be precisely idolatry and blasphemy in
clear violation of the first two commandments, especially when this
creaturely understanding is placed alongside the virtually undenied
fact that the earliest Christians worshiped Jesus in the clearly religious
sense. The tension between the New Testament understanding of God

(b) Subordination and deity viewed as consistent by John and Paul.

c) Jesus' subordination one of office or revelatory and redemptive function, not one of essence:

(1) Interpretation of texts in this light.

(2) Coherence with main thrust of New Testament.

3. Special problems:
a) The Arian view would have been idolatry and blasphemy for the early believers,

since it would have involved the worship of a creature.

b) The Kenotic view:

(1) is rationally incoherent since surrender or potentiality of attributes is inconsistent with the essence of Deity as conceptually understood;

(2) and the key passage does not imply such a view in any case.

and a wrongly understood view of God on Old Testament terms is already striking enough; but to understand that tension in an Arian vein would be to tear the New Testament understanding from its essential religious roots and make it a virtual historical impossibility.

The Kenotic Christology can, I suggest, be dealt with far more briefly, although I shall appeal to that same principle of rational coherence and systematic consistency. Exponents of this view acknowledge that it puts a great strain on the ideal of logical consistency to speak of either the surrender or the voluntary sublimation of the transcendent attributes of deity during Jesus' incarnate state on earth. It is even suggested that they are not literally surrendered, but are to be viewed as transposed, so that they are in Jesus in the form of concentrated potentiality. If this means that essential deity was not always or even characteristically manifest in the earthly career of Jesus, that notion of hiddenness creates no problem for the recognition of Jesus' full deity even during that earthly sojourn. But if anything more than such an Incognito Deity is meant, then I merely observe that a Deity divested of some of its essential attributes, or a Deity who possesses only a potentiality for actualizing those attributes, is really no Deity at all, since neither of these notions is logically coherent. The very nature of the attributes of a Deity, as self-existent, self-explanatory being, is such that neither divestiture nor potentiality can be predicated of those attributes with consistency. The Philippians passage (2:7) which speaks of emptying does not, in any case, reasonably admit of being interpreted in any such terms, since the passage makes clear that Jesus emptied himself by assuming the form of servanthood and by becoming an authentic human individual, rather than by surrendering any dimension of deity in some vague and unclarifiable sense. I can only conclude that a Kenotic Christology, which compromises the deity of Jesus in the way that is characteristic of such theories, becomes rationally incoherent and therefore also implausible precisely to the extent that its conceptual meaning is rendered explicit—so that no more here than in any Arian type of Christology is there any viable alternative to the Trinitarian perspective in the fullest sense.

I. The attack on the psychological soundness of Jesus.

A. This attack rejects either theism or incarnation as axiomatically incredible.

At the Level of Psychological Interpretation

Although a significant part of my previous argument concerning the person of Jesus involves the claim that he cannot reasonably be charged with the sort of psychological unsoundness which doubtless would have characterized him if his claim to be God Incarnate was grounded on a self-deception that enabled him sincerely to believe that claim when in fact it was false, it is nevertheless the case that the psychic health of Jesus has been repeatedly challenged by critics. I think it fair to claim in preliminary response that this charge has been largely based on some world-view perspective which made either theism as a metaphysical view, or the notion of a divine incarnation within a theistic perspective, both unintelligible in concept and impossible in principle. The basic and generally unjustified axiom of virtually every criticism of Jesus' psychological soundness is that since the notion of a genuine incarnation in the distinctively Christian sense cannot be taken seriously, it clearly follows that any human individual, who seriously and sincerely makes the sort of transcendent metaphysical claims that are ascribed to Jesus in the New Testament and particularly in the Gospels, must be regarded as the victim of serious mental imbalance, if not of outright, positive insanity—provided that the individual may reasonably be believed actually to have made such claims in the way indicated. With this allegedly incontestable axiom squarely in place, the argument then proceeds to show that Jesus did in fact claim to be the Messianic Son of Man, that he understood this claim to involve equality with God in the highest sense, that he fully expected both to be exalted to the place of divine authority after his death and also ultimately, if not immediately, to return to the earth again for the triumphant establishment of God's kingdom. The conclusion is then drawn that, since these claims represent a type of self-exaltation that is characteristically found in certain types of mentally ill persons, and since it is out of the question axiomatically that such claims could be taken seriously as possibly correctly attributable to any human individual, it follows that Jesus was mentally ill in some sense and that this diagnosis is the only explanation needed for his having made the transcendent claims in question.

1. Hence, anyone making an Incarnation claim sincerely must be mentally unbalanced.

2. Since Jesus made this claim in an apocalyptic and Messianic context, he must have been mentally ill, and no further explanation of his claim is required.

Of course, this general line of argument can be strengthened by various supplemental insights that may be culled out of the Gospel records. Members of Jesus' own household, perhaps even of his own immediate family, presumably regarded him as "beside himself" (mentally disoriented) very early in his ministry because of the public stir that his teaching and healing had created (Mark 3:21). Similarly, the religious leaders of Israel, hard-pressed to account for Jesus' authority to cast out evil spirits, charged Jesus with being demon-possessed himself (Mark 3:22; cf. John 10:20, 21). So the charge of mental imbalance emerged on the scene early indeed. Further, Jesus is also described in the Gospel records as having occasionally indulged in erratic emotional outbursts which, lacking any adequate provocation in circumstances, would testify to his being inwardly disturbed to an abnormal degree. For example, he cursed a fig tree because, although it had leaves which should have been the sign of ripe fruit, it had no such fruit (Mark 11:12–14, 20–25). On at least one occasion he became so provoked at the sale of sacrificial animals in the temple that, in an apparent loss of composure, he drove the animals out, overturned the tables of the moneychangers, and perhaps even drove the merchants themselves from the temple area with a scourge of ropes (Mark 11:15–17; Matt. 21:12, 13; Luke 19:45–46; John 2:14–17). And in the midst of a strong but controlled criticism of the Jewish leaders, Jesus seems to have quite suddenly flown into a virtual rage in which he turned directly on those leaders and abusively castigated them in an uncontrollably angry manner (Matt. 23:13f.; Luke 11:42f.). If incidents such as these are interpreted within the scope of the critical axiom which questions the very notions of incarnation and theism, they can clearly

B. Other marks of Jesus' mental imbalance:
1. This charge was made against him at the time of his ministry.

2. Erratic emotional outbursts comport well with the charge.

be interpreted as lending further plausibility to that framework of thought.

In responding to this charge of mental unsoundness on the part of Jesus, I can accept little solace from the attempt of no less a renowned scholar than Albert Schweitzer, who has attempted to respond to the same charge. His own work on the historicity of our information about Jesus, although largely sceptical of the Gospel materials, nevertheless retained as supposedly historical a fragmented picture of Jesus as an eschatological enthusiast or fanatic who was obsessed with the idea of the culmination of history, in the ordinary sense, through the setting up of the Messianic kingdom. This picture of Jesus as a religious enthusiast raised in many critical minds the question whether a person, who thus imbibed what both Schweitzer and his interpreters agreed was pure religious mythology, was therefore not a psychologically unsound, if not mentally insane, individual. Schweitzer responded by accepting the axiom of the critics of Jesus to the effect that, if Jesus had made all those transcendental claims about himself, he would indeed be correctly judged to have been mentally unbalanced. But Schweitzer then proceeds to claim that the sources for these claims, both Johannine and synoptic, are themselves of little or no genuine historical value, so that Jesus simply did not make those claims on which the charge of his psychological unsoundness had been largely based. Stripped of these transcendent dimensions, Jesus appears to Schweitzer as no more than a leading religious enthusiast of his time (a time when there were among the Jews many such enthusiasts), and therefore not really chargeable with any sort of mental illness, even though he had the admittedly peculiar traits of others whose enthusiasm he shared.

I cannot, indeed, take on the task of developing here a detailed criticism of Schweitzer's historical judgment—I will leave that to any New Testament scholars who may be disposed to undertake such a critique. But my whole previous analysis makes it abundantly clear that I reject his approach, since I have argued at length that the transcendental claims ascribed to Jesus in the New Testament materials are plausibly traceable to Jesus himself as their historical source. Indeed, it is difficult for me to find any reasonable basis for Schweitzer's claim that Jesus did not originate the substance of what I have called the Incarnation claim, unless we accept as valid the relatively *a priori* assumption of Schweitzer and his interpreters that such an Incarnation claim cannot be taken seriously—so that therefore Jesus, whom Schweitzer deeply respected as the merely human person he supposed him to be, cannot have made such a claim. The clearly subjective, idiosyncratic, and preferential basis of such an assumption should be obvious to any thoughtful and reflective reader.

But neither do I accept the argument of those who, in opposition to Schweitzer, argue that Jesus did make transcendental claims about himself and must therefore have been mentally unbalanced. The problem here is to assess Jesus' psychological state, not as a conclusion *from* his transcendental claims but rather quite independently of those claims, in order to decide whether to take his Incarnation claim with ultimate seriousness. Since it is the plausibility or otherwise of that very claim which we are trying to decide, it is sheer question-begging, and therefore unreasonable, to read Jesus' mental unsoundness right off the face of the very claim that is at stake. I have, after all, already argued that in a theistic and revelational context such as the one I have defended, there is nothing implausible or unintelligible in the abstract about the concept of divine incarnation. If that argument is essentially reasonable, then we cannot, without further ado, conclude that Jesus was mentally ill simply because he made that claim in the context of Old Testament Messianism. Hence, in assessing Jesus' psychological soundness or its opposite, we must set aside the Incarnation claim, and all its transcendent facets, and ask what the rest of our information about Jesus would lead us to conclude about his mental health. And it is here that we can welcome Albert Schweitzer back again—for, although he did *not* regard the Incarnation claim as historical, he did assess Jesus' mental health on grounds quite independent of that claim and, on the basis of that other information, argued against the other critics that Jesus, although a religious enthusiast, was not mentally unbalanced or psychologically ill. This is exactly the logically correct procedure; and if we set aside (but of course, in our case, without surreptitiously denying) Jesus' Incarnation claim, then the rest of what we know about Jesus' calm self-mastery and self-knowledge, about his deep understanding of other persons and his remarkable ability to increase their self-understanding, and about his sustained composure under stress, will decisively support the claim that he was, perhaps of all human individuals, the most sane and psychologically sound person we might ever consider. Nor will it be difficult, in the light of this view of Jesus, to explain those incidental facts in the Gospels that might otherwise raise a question about the state of his mental health. It is neither surprising nor decisive that some of the members of Jesus' household should have entertained the opinion that perhaps he was mentally unbalanced, in view of the public stir that he occasioned by his healing and teaching. Both would have been striking and wholly extraordinary to them, especially in contrast to the presumably ordinary impact of his earlier years, aside from the incident of his questioning the temple scholars (Luke 2:46f.). In any case, such a hastily drawn opinion under stressful circumstances settles nothing about Jesus' mental health. And, in view of the challenge that Jesus' ministry posed for the religious leaders of Israel, there is also nothing surprising about the fact that they adopted the tactic of charging him with demon-possession, a charge which Jesus himself answered with silencing effectiveness by pointing out that in his healing he was in fact opposing the work of Satan and his demons. The context also makes it clear that the judgment Jesus pronounced on the fig tree was intended as a lesson on the power of true faith, so that the incident provides no ground for the charge of even a lack of composure. If again we consider the explanation that Jesus himself gave of his reacting against the commercialism in the temple, it will

a) Since the plausibility (or otherwise) of that claim is the issue at stake, such a conclusion would be sheer question-begging.
b) An Incarnation claim is not unintelligible in a theistic and revelatory context.

(1) And here Schweitzer's defense is relevant.

(2) The rest of our information about Jesus fully supports his psychological soundness.

III. Explanation of texts previously cited.

A. The charge of insanity

and demon possession.

B. The fig tree.

C. The denunciation of temple commercialism.

be obvious that his response was based on righteous indignation at the pollution of his Father's house, and was therefore in no sense a symptom of personal disorientation. In view, finally, of the evident hypocrisy of the Jewish religious leaders, Jesus' declamation and renunciation of them seems, although strong, nevertheless wholly appropriate as part of his spiritual mission. In general, such incidents as these, balanced against an overall understanding of Jesus' ministry and his personal qualities, provide no plausible basis for questioning Jesus' psychological soundness, unless we approach the incidents with the axiom of the critics which I have already challenged. Jesus may therefore be fairly judged to have been characterized by complete mental health.

If now we proceed to add our earlier contention regarding Jesus' Incarnation claim, the conclusion will be that, in full mental balance and without any sort of psychological instability, Jesus claimed to be God Incarnate. And it follows from that fact that we must take that claim with genuine seriousness as to its implications. One way to take this thesis with requisite seriousness would be, of course, to draw the conclusion of Christian faith for which I earlier contended—namely, that the most comprehensively adequate way of explaining the Incarnation claim as traceable to Jesus himself would be to conclude that Jesus made the claim because he both believed and knew it to be true. Another preliminarily possible way to understand that same claim seriously would be to suppose that Jesus knowingly made the claim while inwardly rejecting it and regarding it as false. That alternative too has serious implications to which I now address my discussion.

At the Level of Moral Evaluation

Critics have claimed, and I agree with them on this point, that if Jesus intentionally made the Incarnation claim while inwardly believing, perhaps even knowing, that it was false, that alleged fact would have serious derogatory consequences for our assessment of his moral character. Such intentional deception could, it is claimed correctly, spring only from the deepest moral perversion in the inner selfhood of any person propounding it. As in the case of the psychological assessment of Jesus, however, we cannot start out with the relatively *a priori* thesis that, if any psychologically sound person made such an Incarnation claim, he could only do so while himself believing it to be false—so that such a person is for that reason alone morally perverse, since no sane individual could possibly take such an Incarnation claim about himself with inward seriousness. Here too such a transition of thought is logically implausible and arbitrarily unreasonable. We cannot fairly judge Jesus to be morally defective merely on the ground that he made the Incarnation claim with respect to himself, since it is the plausibility of that claim itself which we are attempting to assess. Any moral criticism of Jesus will therefore have to set the Incarnation claim as such out of consideration, and it will have to base itself on the rest of the information which the Gospel materials

D. Declamation of the religious leaders.

IV. The Incarnation claim was therefore made by a psychologically sound Jesus.

A. This claim could be taken as true in the sense of Christian faith.

B. Or it could be taken as hypocritically propounded by Jesus.

I. If Jesus made the Incarnation claim while believing or knowing it to be false, that would imply a serious defect of moral character.
A. But here again it would be question-begging to conclude that defect from the claim itself, since that claim is the issue at stake.

B. The assessment of Jesus' moral character must be made therefore apart from the Incarnation claim itself.

make accessible to us about the moral qualities of Jesus. On such terms, what serious moral evaluation of Jesus is available for consideration?

In an earlier context, I have already provided a general description of Jesus' moral character in a positive and favorable sense. And that impression of an impeccable moral state is, I think it fair to claim, the principal and overwhelming impact that is made upon even a casual reader of the Gospel records. Jesus, in his own moral teaching, imposed the highest standard of morality on both his followers and his critics by requiring that the former be as morally mature and complete as God's character itself viewed as absolutely pure morality—and by judging the latter, although they were the most conspicuous moral examples in all Israel, as falling far short of the required standard of ethical righteousness (Matt. 5:20). In turn, Jesus himself exhibited such a complete and unflawed conformity to the standard of moral righteousness exhibited in the principles of Old Testament morality that not even his worst enemies could bring off a single successful moral charge against him in either act or moral quality—so that they were reduced to employing hired liars at Jesus' appearance before their own tribunal (Matt. 26:59–62), and to falling back on a trumped-up and obviously false political charge at Jesus' trial before Pilate the Roman governor, who himself readily saw through the charge as fallacious (Matt. 27:11f.; Mark 15:9, 10; Luke 23:1–5), even though he gave in to their insistence that Jesus be executed. More importantly, the charge on which the religious leaders grounded their accusation of guilt in Jesus was precisely the Messianic claim itself as acknowledged by Jesus, a charge which they well knew would be regarded as empty by the governor. And that Incarnation claim, as we have explained, is no basis for a moral criticism of Jesus, since any such assessment of Jesus should have as its principle objective the decision whether the Messianic claim should be taken seriously. Even the earlier suggestion of the crowds who witnessed Jesus' ministry that Jesus was a deceiver of the masses (John 7:12) was a charge directed toward the question of Jesus' Messiahship and therefore clearly not a basis for proper moral assessment (John 7:26).

But the charge of moral defect, which could not be brought off successfully by Jesus' contemporaries, has nevertheless been attempted by later and even bolder ethical critics. These charges have been partly grounded on those instances of erratic behavior which came up in the investigation of Jesus' psychological soundness. If cursing the fig tree, and allegedly losing his temper at the commercialists in the temple and at the religious leaders of Israel, are not, when plausibly interpreted, reasonable grounds for challenging Jesus' sanity, perhaps they can nevertheless be interpreted as signs of moral instability. Again, Jesus has been accused of insensitivity to his parents both in thoughtlessly remaining in Jerusalem without their knowledge and thus causing them great distress (Luke 2:43f.), and in being presumably rude to his mother when she reported to him the depletion of the wine supplies at the marriage feast in Cana of Galilee (John 2:4).

II. The case for Jesus' moral soundness summarized.

A. His high moral teaching and rigorous moral demand.

B. His unflawed personal morality.

C. The Messianic claim, though impertinent here, was the primary basis of the charge at Jesus' trial.

III. The case against Jesus' moral soundness.
A. Lack of emotional composure.

B. Insensitivity to parents.

C. Sexual immorality.

More seriously, it has been charged by critics that the women who accompanied Jesus and his disciples in their travels (Luke 23:55f.; Matt. 27:55f.; Mark 15:40, 41) not only served Jesus by preparing food and making life generally convenient from a logistical point of view, but they were in fact "road women," in the worst sense of serving as objects of sexual pleasure and gratification to the whole traveling company—so that Jesus himself, though hypocritically teaching the most rigorous standards of moral purity, exempted himself and his disciples from that demanding requirement, and was therefore a man of discreet but nevertheless indulgent sexual experience. And there is finally the charge that Jesus' entire ministry was a deceptive hoax in which he deliberately attempted to pass himself off as the Messiah by aligning his activity with what he regarded as Old Testament (that is, scriptural) Messianic prophecies.

D. Jesus' ministry as a deceptive hoax.

A parallel series of charges has been directed at Jesus' moral teachings. It has been claimed, for example, that Jesus taught a sort of financial and material irresponsibility when he instructed his disciples to exercise no care about their present and future economic needs, and advised them instead simply to trust God for the provision of their necessities in this area (Matt. 6:25–34; Luke 12:22–34). If fact, he so far urged them to ignore the accumulation of earthly treasures or financial reserves that he counseled, perhaps even commanded, that they sell whatever stock of possessions they might have already accumulated and then distribute the proceeds as alms for the poor—and this on the clear ground that the true service of God was incompatible with the studied and deliberate goal of accumulating economic assets (Matt. 6:19–21, 24; Luke 12:33, 34). All this can, it is said, be fairly interpreted as advising an intentionally reckless abandon about making any provision for one's future needs of a financial and material sort. Yet, certainly, it is an evident moral duty to exercise a deliberate frugality in the management of one's financial resources, even though it is also an obligation to avoid any sort of niggardliness which would smother reasonable and balanced generosity to those whose needs we may be able to serve. Does this teaching of Jesus, perhaps, indicate an important lack of full insight on this significant moral issue?

IV. Defects in Jesus' moral teaching.

A. Material and economic irresponsibility.

B. Insensitivity to social and economic justice.

There is also some reason to suppose that Jesus lacked a sense of morally grounded social justice. The Sermon on the Mount, for example, so strongly urges the ideal of love for one's enemies that one is advised to ignore reciprocal penalty for what is clearly a moral violation of one's moral rights. A man is not to resist an evildoer, but is instead to submit to whatever violation of one's personal dignity such an individual inflicts (Matt. 5:38–48; Luke 6:27–36). And this apparently defective sense of morally justifiable personal justice carries over into the economic area of life, as illustrated by the parable of the workers in the vineyard. Here Jesus seems to approve the right of the owner of the vineyard to pay equally various hired workers who toiled in his vineyard for very different periods of time although presumably with comparable diligence—so that those who started work early in the morning and served all day were paid the same as those who worked a single hour at the end of the day (Matt. 20:1–16). And the point of this story is to suggest that, in the coming kingdom of heaven, God will deal in an analogous fashion with individuals in relation to their own achievement in personal diligence, as if we could expect no reasonable proportion between that diligence and anticipated compensation of whatever sort. But is not the concept of proportionate compensation, whether financial or otherwise, the very essence of social justice? And would not the passing over of the violation of one's personal resources and dignity, without any principled attempt at reciprocal restraint and punishment, be equally inconsistent with an adequate concept of that same ideal of justice? Again, it is asked, does not all this indicate an important defect in Jesus' moral teaching? And if, therefore, Jesus is thus seen to be at fault, not only in personal morality, but also in significant segments of his moral teaching, does not this raise a serious question about his moral character and insight—which would at the least cast some doubt on the sincerity and plausibility of his Incarnation claim, if indeed it did not lend considerable support to the claim that Jesus was morally flawed to the point of making possible a programmed deception which would destroy the viability of the Incarnation claim altogether?

In response to all this moral criticism of Jesus, I should like to point out that we have no record of Jesus' having ever been criticized on any of these grounds, whether personal or instructional, by his contemporary critics. There is no such record in the New Testament, and I am unaware of any such record in the extra-biblical contemporaneous literature of the time. This fact strongly suggests, if it does not actually show, that these criticisms are either wholly baseless and vacuous or else grounded on a misinterpretation of the materials at our disposal. It seems clear that, had a publicly controversial figure like Jesus been guilty of any such personally immoral acts as later critics charge—particularly the charge of sexual immorality—then his enemies, especially the Jewish religious leaders, would have a vested interest in apprising themselves of that information and exposing it in their public criticism of Jesus. But we have no such record of their having done so. And if, for example, there had been even the faintest rumor of the women who accompanied Jesus having been sexually intimate with him or his disciples, the Gospel writers would have had every reason to suppress any mention of the women at all. That our records contain the mention that these women accompanied Jesus and his disciples is therefore clearly an indication of the fact that the service of the women was culinary and logistic only, so that the sexual charge is a wholly irresponsible and unfounded interpretation.

As for the other charges of personal immorality, the alleged instances of erratic behavior (cursing the fig tree, for instance) provide no more evidence of moral instability than they did of psychological unsoundness, when the relevant passages are interpreted in the responsible fashion that I suggested earlier. Again, the supposition that Jesus was insensitive to his parents simply fails to take account of the fact that the incidents concerned illustrate instead the priority that

V. Response to the moral criticism of Jesus.
A. None of these criticisms were made by Jesus' contemporaries, although they would certainly have been pertinent, especially the charge of sexual immorality.

B. Other charges:
1. emotional instability;

2. insensitivity to parents;

Jesus placed on his spiritual ministry. We have no reason, for example, to suppose that Jesus acted irresponsibly in remaining in Jerusalem when his parents left for home, although we may indeed have good reason for supposing that the parents acted irresponsibly in not exercising greater surveillance over Jesus' whereabouts. Nor is there any reason to suppose that Jesus was rude to his mother in expressing some hesitancy about performing a remarkable deed that could (and ultimately did) precipitate a premature crisis in his ministry before the proper time. As for the contention that the Messianic claim was a deliberate hoax, not only is this the very sort of question-begging the logical implausibility of which I have already explained; but we may reasonably claim in response that the supposition that such a mass of Old Testament prophesies could be intentionally fulfilled in this deceptive manner, with no hint of such a deception being exposed, is simply incredible, especially in the light of the fact that many of the details of these prophecies would have been clearly beyond Jesus' power to control (his parentage and birth, the precise manner and circumstances of his death, for example). From all this, I conclude that these later critics have been no more successful in bringing off a plausible charge of personal immorality against Jesus than were his contemporary enemies.

And what about the alleged flaws in Jesus' moral teachings? I do not reject the interpretations on which these charges are brought as totally impossible on the face of it. But I do claim that alternative and more plausible interpretations, which would eliminate these charges, are both responsibly possible and more compatible with both the specific and general context of Jesus' teaching—so that the interpretations on which the charges are brought are therefore both comparatively irresponsible and implausible. To be more specific, when Jesus put a restraint on an individual's concern about worldly possessions, he was not advising financial irresponsibility, much less reckless abandonment in the management of one's economic assets. Instead, he was advising against that sort of obsessive preoccupation with the accumulation of worldly goods that would interfere with the completeness of one's commitment to God as the true Good, or with his trust in God as the ultimate Source of all his worldly assets. And when he advised the sale of possessions and the distribution of the proceeds to the poor, he was either speaking to the special circumstances of those who, through unparalleled self-sacrifice, were uniquely called upon to initiate the program of the kingdom of God in the world—or else he was putting a constraint on retaining more worldly goods for oneself than would be necessary in view of the obvious needs of those who would be helped by the distribution. In view of the all too easily prevailing tendency to depend on our material assets to a disproportionate extent, this last advice of Jesus is scarcely impertinent, especially in view of Jesus' doctrine that material goods are of merely instrumental significance and do not constitute the true worth of the person's life—particularly in a context where those goods have been acquired in an atmosphere of covetousness and competitive struggle which distracts the individual from his true spiritual goal (Luke 12:15 and context). In any case, it is conspicuously clear from Jesus' teaching elsewhere that he put a high (although not, of course, the highest) premium on the responsible management of economic resources, whether the individual is acting on his own behalf or as an agent of some other person. In his parable about the steward who squandered his master's resources in an unwise fashion, Jesus makes it evident that: (1) he regards the steward as socially and morally accountable for managing his master's assets responsibly; (2) he clearly agrees with the master in commending the steward for wisely planning for his own financial future in view of his imminent removal from his office of stewardship; (3) he affirms that believers and unbelievers have an equal moral duty for adequate economic management, and he therefore commands believers (the sons of light) to assume that responsibility as part (but by no means the whole) of their preparation for eternity; (4) one's faithfulness in economic planning prepares him for the wise management of spiritual values as well; and (5) it is nevertheless the case that economic assets are always subordinate and instrumental to an individual's commitment to God, so that one cannot, with moral propriety, place economic objectives on anything even approaching an equal par with God (Luke 16:1–13). From this important and well-balanced set of insights, it is certainly fair to conclude that anyone who interprets Jesus' Sermon on the Mount as either condoning financial recklessness, or as advising the neglect of careful economic planning, has misinterpreted Jesus' teaching by his own neglect of the general context of Jesus' moral instruction.

2. Responsible management of economic resources.

As for the issues concerning social justice, here again I do not dismiss the interpretations which ground these criticisms as totally out of the question, and I even acknowledge, with all candor, an initial disturbing perplexity about what appear on the surface to be the implications of these passages. But with equal and parallel sincerity I contend that there too the critics have failed to interpret Jesus' teaching in a fully plausible and reasonable manner, either by ascribing to him some doctrine that he did not intend to communicate, or by overhastily regarding as unjust some principle that is, after all, quite compatible with justice properly understood. When, for example, he commands love for one's enemies on the ground that God also extends certain of his blessings to both the just and the unjust, he clearly recognizes the injustice of acts and policies that are an affront or injury to the person and property of others. And since he teaches that God's concern for human beings precisely as such is not inconsistent with God's ultimate judgment on those who do not repent (Matt. 7:21–23; 5:17–20; Luke 6:24–26; 10:13–15; Matt. 11:20–24; 5:20; 23), he may fairly be interpreted by analogy as having urged upon his followers the sort of love for enemies which, while aiming at the promotion of their true well-being, was not incompatible either with a properly administered restraint on evildoers or with their being brought to account for perpetrated injustice. What, then, was Jesus actually teaching in these passages from the Sermon on the Mount? As I see it,

3. Love, as properly interpreted, fully compatible with the ideal of social justice in both the distributive and retributive senses.

he was teaching responsible love for all human beings whose state could be affected by our response to them, a genuine kindness which, while not without limits, would characteristically tend to offset or even dissolve the hostility of one who exhibits personal animosity toward another individual. Jesus may even be implying that social injustice is not ordinarily to be compensated by the taking of personal revenge, but rather by the ordered social structure for administering that retribution. It is especially interesting to note that the advice to refrain from personal vengeance is limited to each individual with respect to himself. There is no suggestion that we should refrain from obstructing the perpetration of such personal injustices on other individuals. On balance, therefore, it seems clearly to be a misinterpretation to suppose that Jesus was here teaching any generalized policy of allowing evident personal injustices to go unrestrained.

Equal compensation for unequal time is not unjust if:
a) it is contracted voluntarily;

We are left therefore with the charge that Jesus taught, or at least in principle approved, a sort of unjust inequity in the compensation of laborers for their work. The edge of this criticism is considerably turned by certain details of the story. One is that the original hired workers agreed at the outset on a fixed wage which was characteristically standard for the time, while all the later workers went to work in the vineyard with no explicit wage contract at all but with only the word of the owner that they would be justly compensated. In general, it is not unjust to compensate workers in accordance with their own voluntarily accepted contract. Another relevant point is that only the contracted workers lodged a complaint about the equal compensation, although the intervening workers also worked longer hours than the latest workers and were also compensated equally—which suggests

b) there is a difference of motivation and attitude;

that they recognized a just basis for the policy of the owner. But, more importantly, what the story illustrates is the socially perverse attitude of the contracted workers who obviously put a much higher premium and attention on their compensation than they placed on their own reciprocal obligation for diligence in the work they agreed to perform; and it was undoubtedly this which put them last in compensation. And it is evident from the context that it is this parallel that Jesus emphasizes in his instruction about the coming kingdom of God. When Jesus, in the immediately preceding context, had declared that it is difficult for those obsessed with wealth to enter the kingdom of God, Peter met him with the question as to what the disciples would get out of their surrender of everything for that same kingdom. Jesus' response was essentially that those who made such a surrender would certainly be amply rewarded, but that those who struggled, out of a self-preference inconsistent with complete surrender, for a position of high recognition in the work of God's kingdom, would end up last in compensation because their motivation was perverse (Matt. 19:23–30). This point he then illustrates with the story about the workers in the vineyard—those who struggle to be conspicuous and prominent will end up with a compensation equal to those who, in their comparative obscurity, could only concentrate on diligence in service.

And there is another side to this parable. Is it, after all, unjust to compensate equally workers who differ in time invested, provided there is, as in the present case, a rationale for the consequent difference of treatment? I am myself a professor in a graduate school. But I am aware that persons in my professional category are compensated differently in an economic sense, even though they are expected to carry analogous work loads. And I do not regard such a policy as unjust, provided (as is the case) that all serve voluntarily and that there is some rationale of distribution that can sincerely be regarded as generally fair and as providing the minimal needs of those at the bottom of the scale. Our whole society is based on this sort of structure; and it is not *a priori* clear that the principles of that structure are intrinsically unjust. In any case, it is at least reasonable to conclude that, on a fair interpretation of the story, Jesus does not teach any policy of social injustice. Here again, it is clear elsewhere in Jesus' teaching that this is the case; in the parables of the talents (Matt. 25:14–30) and the pounds (Luke 19:11–27), the workers are rewarded or compensated in proportion to the degree to which they wisely managed what was entrusted to them in their master's absence.

> *c*) there is a plausible rationale for difference of treatment.

It would appear therefore that, on a reasonable interpretation of the pertinent Gospel materials, the charges against Jesus' teaching on moral grounds may be fairly regarded as unreasonable and inconclusive. If that is so, then my previous argument, for the Incarnation claim of Jesus being plausibly interpretable as true, can by contrast be regarded as both reasonable and, if not absolutely conclusive, nevertheless highly plausible. If Jesus cannot reasonably be charged with either psychological or moral unsoundness—and if the only supportable alternative to these inconclusive charges is the supposition I have long since defended, that Jesus made the Incarnation claim from a psychologically and morally sound consciousness because he fully believed and, under the circumstances, also knew that the claim was true—then the truth of that claim becomes an entirely plausible alternative for ourselves as well. It is therefore a wholly defensible and rationally grounded conclusion that Jesus was personally God Incarnate. But the question still remains whether the main facets of his vocation can be viewed as at least equally and similarly grounded.

> VI. The moral criticism of Jesus is therefore unfounded.
>
> A. Hence the previous argument for the Incarnation claim is essentially reasonable.
> B. Jesus made the Incarnation claim because he both believed and knew it was true.

In Relation to His Vocation

No critical assessment of Jesus' vocation, in relation to revelation, redemption, or spiritual community, can be reasonably or fairly considered in isolation from insight about his person. If, on prior grounds, as I have argued, we can approach these issues not only in a presupposed theistic world-view context but also in a version of that context which accepts Jesus' Incarnation claim as true, then much of the criticism that has been propounded in these areas can be dismissed, as it were, out of hand as impertinent on the general basis of this

> I. If theism and incarnation are accepted as a context, much criticism of Jesus' vocation is rendered impertinent.

A. If Jesus is God Incarnate, then the revelation in him is in principle unsurpassable, since he would not be a merely human vehicle of disclosure;

theistic incarnationalism. This point is particularly, but not exclusively, applicable to the Christian claim that, in his vocation, Jesus is the climax and pinnacle of divine revelation. We could perhaps say of Isaiah, for example, that he was the prince of the Old Testament prophets and that the book identified with his name was even the climax and high point of Old Testament prophetic revelation. Yet, because Isaiah was only one member of a larger class of prophets which remains open to successors, and because he was, as to his person, a truly remarkable but nevertheless merely human being whose insight, even as grounded in divine revelation and inspiration, might conceivably be transcended by subsequent divine disclosure, we cannot reasonably say that the revelation vouchsafed through him is in principle unsurpassable—as if it were the case that no higher climax or pinnacle of prophetic revelation could be consistently conceived. But if, by comparison, Jesus, although clearly a prophet in Isaiah's class in any case, is also God Incarnate, then the considerations that limited the height and degree of prophetic revelation in Isaiah, or any other merely human prophet or vehicle of divine revelation, are themselves all, for that very reason, finally and decisively transcended, not merely in fact but in principle. In analyzing the concept of incarnation before even considering whether that concept was personally applicable to Jesus, I maintained that the notion of incarnation, on conceptual grounds alone in contrast to historical grounds, was in principle unsurpassable in the category of divine revelation, not merely because assuming our human nature would be a reasonably appropriate climax of divine revelation on God's part, but also and primarily because coming among us in our own nature as an integral human being is the highest conceivable form of revelation in a theistic framework of thought. If we can now conclude, as I have contended, that Jesus is God Incarnate in the unique sense which Christianity claims here, then Jesus, correctly and adequately understood, will himself in his person, activity, and vocation, both conceptually and historically, be the unsurpassable climax and pinnacle of divine revelation in the prophetic or any other category. This is not to denigrate

but this is not to question the possibility or genuineness of other revelatory forms.

either the authenticity or the importance of other human vehicles or other forms of revelation. It is not even to exclude on the face of it either the possibility or the actuality of some fragmentary revelation in the religious leaders of other religious traditions (it is, for example, to do no injustice to figures like Confucius, Gautama Buddha, or Mohammed). It is rather to see all these other forms and fragments in a total perspective in which they are every one subordinated to the, in principle, unsurpassable and final revelation in Jesus—not just arbitrarily because of the particular religious tradition to which he belongs, but because he is, in relation to all such traditions, God

B. As God Incarnate, Jesus can be universally representative humanity in a redemptive sense, to a degree that cannot characterize any merely human person.

Incarnate in a unique sense that cannot be transcended. That, in my case, is the heart of the Christian revelation claim and the central position for which I myself contend.

I have, in general, already addressed my discussion to some of the principal criticisms of the claim that Jesus, in his life and especially in his death, is the culmination of divine redemption. The claim itself I supported by arguing that Jesus—precisely because he was God Incarnate and precisely because his human nature was personal in the actualized sense only through the union of the personal potential of that nature with the eternally actualized personhood of the Divine Logos (so that Jesus was not a human individual apart from the Logos but was humanly personal only in union with the Logos)—that Jesus, I reiterate, was universally representative humanity to an extent that made it possible for him, in his person and in his acts, to render to God on behalf of humanity a wholly adequate vicarious or substitutionary satisfaction to the unconditional divine moral claim on human beings—so that all those who qualify as beneficiaries of his universal representation through faith are released from their moral guilt and reunited to God and the whole company of the similarly redeemed in moral and spiritual fellowship. I contended—in a degree of detail which I will not now reconstruct—that apart from this sort of moral provision, either the predicament of a humanity universally besmirched by moral guilt and defection would be hopeless, so that God's moral purpose in creation would be decisively defeated, or else the unconditionally obligatory framework of the objective moral order, grounded as it is in God's moral nature, would be inconsistently compromised.

> 1. Thus Jesus can plausibly make satisfaction to the moral claim on humanity without compromising the rigor of that claim.

As was earlier made clear, I intended this elaborated thesis to offset the standard criticism that this whole framework of thought solves the problem of moral obligation and guilt on grounds which are allegedly inconsistent with the concept of objective moral order itself—since the notion of such an order involves the concept of each individual's final responsibility and guilt for his own moral fault and defection, while the proposal I have elaborated as essentially Christian involves the notion of the moral transfer or imputation of all human moral guilt to Jesus and the reciprocal transfer of his personally achieved righteousness to those same morally guilty individuals. Perhaps the most outspoken defender, both of an unconditionally objective moral order and of the rejection of the Christian concept of vicarious moral transfer, was Immanuel Kant himself. So rigorous was his notion of individual moral responsibility that he rejected in principle and out of hand the traditional Christian concept of imputation. Moral accountability is strictly an individual matter for Kant, so much so that he interpreted the New Testament picture of Jesus' sacrificial death as a metaphorical symbol of each individual's rendering of moral satisfaction on his own behalf. Yet Kant is not without a certain personal agony about his own and every other human individual's moral predicament. Bound, as he insightfully sensed himself to be, to the unrelenting demand of absolute moral duty and obligation (on the reality of which, and not without foundation, he postulated the existence of God as a reasonable belief), grounded in the unconditional law of morality and yet at the same time keenly aware of the magnitude of his own moral guilt and corruption (if judgment is to begin at the house of a moral purist like Kant, where will the rest of humanity

> 2. Nor is the concept of moral transfer inconsistent with objective moral order.

> *a*) The rejection of moral transfer by Kant.

> (1) Jesus' sacrificial death interpreted symbolically.

> (2) Yet Kant is distressed as to how each person is to solve the problem of moral liability for himself.

appear on this scale of moral assessment?), Kant struggles with the question as to how each individual is to solve the problem of moral liability on his own behalf. His proposal clearly illustrates the meager plight to which humanity is individually and collectively reduced on such terms as Kant accepts. We can all take some consolation from the concept of pure moral selfhood—uncompromised in principle, propensity, and performance—to which, as a goal, every individual aspires through gradual and progressive moral self-transformation. I can think of myself as at last morally adjudicated in the status of the ideal selfhood for which I strive; but since, as Kant himself acknowledges, this goal is never actualized by any human person in any stretch of finite time however extended, this suggestion, while providing a balm of comfort, nevertheless constitutes no adequate moral solution. I cannot, furthermore, make any such adequate moral amends while I am in a state of principled and pervasive moral corruption, since all motives from which I act will be morally tainted by hypothesis. Nor can any progress in moral righteousness, after some turning point in my life, constitute the requisite fulfillment of liability—since that progress is not only partial and fragmentary, but is also impossible apart from a basic change of moral principle and motivation of which I am incapable in my corrupted state. It must be, therefore, that in that precise turning point, in which I renounce my moral corruption and experience a sort of death to desire and inclination as grounds of choice, I both make amends for all my personal moral guilt and at the same time adopt pure respect for the moral law as my subsequent maxim of moral decision and choice.

b) But Kant's proposed solution is wholly implausible.

Such a proposal as Kant's, with all the existential struggle that it evinces, is as inscrutable as it is inconsequential. The suggestion is inscrutable because Kant develops no intelligible way in which such a moral change of maxim and decision can be initiated except on grounds that presuppose that very tranformation or turning point as a basis—the choice of the moral law as a principle of choice is itself a choice that is only morally possible for the person already operating on that very principle. Kant himself acknowledges this difficulty and, as far as I can discern, contributes no consistent and significant solution to it. But even if this problem could be solved on Kant's terms, the proposed solution to the original difficulty is, I contend, inconsequential. The thesis that the initiation of a moral change, in which I set out on a course of moral self-transformation, somehow, as an act of mine, makes amends for my moral guilt can be stated more simply as the claim that if I restore obedience to the moral law in act, principle, and state of character, after a moral lapse of whatever scope, I will—in that very restoration —make adequate amends for that moral lapse to the unconditional demand of the moral law upon me. But I have already argued in an earlier context that this claim is itself a clear logical mistake. If, quite apart logically from any moral lapse and resultant guilt, I already owe total obedience to the moral law in the specified aspects, then no mere restoration of obedience, however complete (which Kant admits is never the case), can even conceivably

(1) The moral transformation which he proposes is itself possible only on the supposition (per impossible) of its own previous occurrence.
(2) The restoration of obedience after a moral lapse does not make amends for that lapse,

so that self-satisfaction for moral guilt is out of the question.

make amends for that moral lapse and guilt. To be in this predicament with respect to the moral law is, in effect, to be morally bankrupt as a result of my having already made choices that make any moral satisfaction by myself, on my own behalf, morally out of the question. I think it only fair to Kant to say that I believe he sees this difficulty quite clearly but finds himself operating in a framework of thought which makes its solution impossible, so that he not merely *does* not, but rather logically *cannot* face up to it.

There are, of course, other proposals for solving the moral predicament for which the Christian concept of vicarious moral satisfaction claims to provide a solution. But on the whole, we have already faced up to the bulk of such proposals, found them critically inadequate, and left them far behind in our thought. We might, for example, deny outright that the objective moral order which creates our moral predicament has any reality apart from our own projection of it (radical ethical relativism). Or we might make this rejection more subtle by claiming that, although there is such an objective moral order, its demands on us are far less rigorous than its advocates sometimes contend—since it is the function of moral laws or rules to provide us with ideal guidance rather than to hold us unconditionally responsible for conformity to their standards, so that moral law would become a sliding scale of requirement with no enduring and absolute basis. But all such proposals have already been dismissed in principle by my earlier defense of moral objectivism, my criticism of radical ethical relativism, and my argument that the transcendent ground of moral order is situated in the changeless and absolute quality of divine moral character. We have therefore come full circle on all such countermaneuvers, and we find ourselves once more confronted with that universal human moral predicament which finds its solution in Jesus as universally representative humanity—through whose vicarious satisfaction, to the unconditional claim of divine moral law, all who become the beneficiaries of Jesus' moral representation through faith can genuinely avail themselves of a solution to that human moral predicament and thus truly initiate that journey of moral transformation which, on Kant's terms, they had found themselves impotent to commence. Jesus is therefore indeed, as I previously argued, the culmination of moral and spiritual redemption. But there is, in a sense, a difference between his status here and his position as the climax of divine revelation. There can, as I suggested, be other and distinct forms of revelation, although they are all subordinated to Jesus as final revelation. But Jesus can only be the culmination of redemption if, in his universally representative satisfaction on our behalf, his achievement is at the same time the *whole* of redemption. There can be no question here of other forms of redemption which are merely supplementary to a final redemption in Jesus, since apart from his redemptive vocation we are one and all morally and spiritually bankrupt. Yet even this difference is clearly not absolute—for all those other forms of revelation, if authentic at all, are aspects of that totality of truth which is hidden away in Jesus as the Christ. It is, after all, as Peter

3. Other proposals for solving the human moral predicament have already been dealt with in principle. *a)* Compromising the reality or rigor of the objective moral order has already been critically questioned.

b) We are brought back therefore to Jesus' vicarious satisfaction.

3. Jesus is therefore the culmination of redemption in a sense which excludes all other possible forms of such redemption.

suggests (1 Peter 1:11), the Spirit of that same Jesus in and through whom all those other prophets speak and all those other forms of revelation constitute divine self-disclosure at all.

And what, finally, of Jesus' role as the core of spiritual community, the sovereign of all the truly regenerate, and the Head of his spiritual body which is called the Church in the most universal sense? If all of my previous conclusions about Jesus' vocation are accepted in relation to his being God Incarnate, there can scarcely be any really serious question about Jesus being the Head of the divine spiritual community composed of all those who are in a state of divine grace and forgiveness as beneficiaries of Jesus' redemption—and who, through the inward quickening of the Spirit of God in response to their own commitment, are in the process of being morally and spiritually transformed. If there is any relevant sort of criticism in this dimension of Jesus' vocation, it would turn on the question whether the centrality of a single historical individual, as constituting the basis of spiritual community, does not constitute a sort of exclusivism or particularism which would, at the least, leave large segments of the human community (which, in varying degrees, have been relatively out of contact with this historical tradition) out of serious consideration. If there is any such exclusionism, it might be objected, it would be at odds with the universal openness and unobstructed accessibility which ought to characterize a spiritual community that is founded in relation to an equally universal and unconditional divine moral claim.

One form of such exclusivism might be that of some organized social institution (also called a church, but in a particular rather than universal sense) that might be viewed as claiming that it was, as an organization with members, coextensive with the whole divine spiritual community. Whether there are any actual organizations that purport to make such a claim, and whether that claim, as carefully qualified, may be plausible or implausible, are questions that are simply outside the scope of my present concern with that Christian truth-claim which I clearly regard as itself cutting across any and all religious organizations or institutions of this or any other sort. But what is pertinent to my present objective is straightforwardly to contend at the outset that Christianity, as I understand it, has no essential connection whatever to any such organizational claim, but rather implies by its universality of openness that no religious organization or conjunction of such organizations is coextensive with the divine spiritual community which, as I understand it, cuts across them all in the same way that the Christian truth-claim itself intersects these same institutional structures. It is therefore, in principle and perhaps in actuality, the case that members of the true spiritual community are dispersed across the whole spectrum of such organizations, just as it is equally possible and even likely that all of these same organizations have as members some, perhaps even many, who are not genuine members of the universal Church or divine spiritual community at all. For the condition of membership in that community is, as I see it, not in any sense organizational but rather personal and spiritual in nature.

C. As God Incarnate, Jesus is also indisputably Head of the true spiritual community.

1. But this centrality of a single historical individual might be judged an objectionable exclusivism.

2. Institutional or organizational exclusivism is inconsistent with the Christian truth-claim as I construe it:
the divine spiritual community cuts across any and all such organizations.

3. It is another question whether there is an exclusivism of particular beliefs as a condition of membership in the divine spiritual community.

But there is another kind of possible exclusivism which may be far more problematic for a reflective critic who aims to employ rational objectivity as a criterion of assessment. Quite aside from particular organizations or institutions, is it essential to the Christian truth-claim to insist that, as a qualification for membership in the admittedly universal spiritual community, there is an identifiable set of historically (or even theologically) oriented doctrines or beliefs to which it is indispensable that one subscribe? Beliefs, for example, such as some of those that I have defended as pertinent to the elaboration of the Christian truth-claim itself—beliefs concerning the historical Jesus, or concerning his person as God Incarnate, or concerning his vicarious redemption? Granted that it is on the basis provided by these beliefs being regarded as truths that there can even be a spiritual community of the redeemed or that anyone at all can be a member of it, can we identify a minimum credibilia, a minimum set of beliefs, of which we can confidently say that a person must subscribe to them as a necessary condition of becoming a member of the spiritual community, or of being in a state of divine grace and forgiveness? We can even turn this question around and ask whether persons whose religious understanding has been conditioned by a religious tradition quite distinct from the Hebrew-Christian religious tradition—a tradition such as Buddhism, Confucianism, or Hinduism—may nevertheless, and quite apart from historically formulated Christian conceptions, be genuine members of the divine spiritual community. It is, of course, enormously important to be totally clear as to exactly what the question is that we are asking here, and it is perhaps even more important to distinguish it from a very different question with which it has been characteristically confused, with the result that neither question is appropriately answered.

a) Clarification of this question.

That different question can indeed be clearly formulated, however. It is the question whether anyone can be in a state of divine grace and forgiveness (and therefore a genuine member of the divine spiritual community) apart from the basis provided for that grace and forgiveness by the redemptive work of Jesus as God Incarnate. In other words, it is the question whether, quite apart from the redemption in Jesus the Christ, there is some other and distinct basis for being in a state of divine grace and forgiveness. There is, in turn, no question at all about the answer to this query from the standpoint of the Christian world-view. The whole implication of all that I have argued about the person of Jesus and his redemptive vocation is that—apart from God's activity in Jesus and the satisfaction that he made to the unconditional divine moral law through his position as universally representative humanity—the moral predicament of man, in his moral guilt and corruption, is completely hopeless, so that it is through and on the basis of this redemptive activity alone that anyone at all could be in a state of divine grace and forgiveness. Of course, it is, I think, in this precise sense that we should understand various New Testament claims to the same effect—the claim of Jesus, for example, that he himself is *the* way, *the* truth, and *the* life, so that absolutely no one

b) This question not to be confused with the question whether there is any grace and forgiveness apart from the redemptive work of Jesus the Christ.

(1) The clear answer to this question is that there is no alternative basis of grace and forgiveness.

(2) The biblical basis of this claim:

can come to God the Father (that is, enter into a reconciled and harmonious relation to God) except through the person and work of Jesus (John 14:6). There is likewise the claim of Peter that there is salvation or spiritual security in Jesus alone and in no other, so that through the whole of humanity there is no other individual in whom it is necessary that human beings, down to the very last person, enter into spiritual security, if they do so at all (Acts 4:12). Again, there is the claim of Paul that, just as there is one God, so also there is only one mediator between God and the whole of humanity, namely, the human being (or, in my terms, the universally representative human person) Jesus the Messiah, who once and for all gave himself as a wholly adequate amends or satisfaction for *all* human beings (1 Tim. 2:5).

as extended even to persons before the historical time of Jesus.

Nor is the unique and unparalleled mediatorship of Jesus universal merely in taking in the whole scope of humanity since Jesus' historical appearance. It is also universal in time by including that entire segment of humanity that preceded Jesus in the humanly historical sense, so that all those who were truly committed to God before that historical appearance of Jesus were nevertheless encompassed by divine grace and forgiveness through the vicarious redemption in Jesus—even though that redemptive vocation had not yet been historically fulfilled, and even though these previously admitted members of the divine spiritual community were totally ignorant (or, in some cases, no more than vaguely and imprecisely aware through prophecy that they did not clearly understand) of the historical form that God's redemptive provision would assume in Jesus (Rom. 3:25; Heb. 2:9; 9:14, 15). In

(3) Hence there is a genuine exclusivsm here, but it is not objectionable since no human person is excluded from Jesus' redemptive provision.

a sense, then, there is a sort of exclusivism here, since it is being claimed that salvation in Jesus is God's only objective redemptive provision for all the times and ages of man, for all the cultures and civilizations of the human species. But it is not a morally or logically objectionable exclusivism, since it is thus exclusive only by its total inclusiveness of all humanity within the scope of Jesus' redemptive satisfaction to the unconditional claim of divine moral law on all of that same humanity (1 John 2:2). Just because Jesus is the *one* Redeemer, it is the case that absolutely *no* human being is excluded from Jesus' totally unlimited saving provision.

c) If the provision in Jesus is intended by God to be universally applicable, then acceptance of it must be universally accessible.

Yet this question, thus clearly answered from the standpoint of the Christian world-view—although not the same as our original question about minimum subjective or personal belief—may nevertheless help us to achieve a reasonable answer to that original query. If every human being in all times and ages has been objectively provided for through the unique redemption in Jesus, and if this provision is in fact intended by God as for every such human being, then it must be possible for each human individual to become personally eligible to receive that provision—regardless of his historical, cultural, or personal circumstances and situation, and quite apart from any particular historical information or even historically formulated theological conceptualization—since a universally intended redemptive provision is not genuinely universal in the requisite sense unless it is also and for that reason universally accessible. This, I take it, is exactly the way that Paul argues (Rom. 1:18–23) when he claims that the people of all nations and civilizations, whether or not they have been apprised of God's historical revelation that reached its climax in Jesus, are nevertheless responsible and guilty before God if they reject God's moral and spiritual claim upon them, since there is a universally accessible knowledge of God in the manifestation of God through the whole realm of created beings, and even, as he adds later (Rom. 2:14–16), in the divine moral law that is written in their hearts and discernible by their moral consciousness. All this would be quite unintelligible if it did not imply that, through a proper response to this universally accessible revelation, individual human beings of whatever circumstances could so renounce their moral guilt and corruption and could so commit themselves to God and his claim upon them, as to become the beneficiaries of divine grace and forgiveness—a grace and forgiveness made possible only through Jesus' redemptive provision, of which, however, they would in a large variety of cases, be historically ignorant, or perhaps, in a parallel variety of instances, only weakly, dimly, and inadequately aware. That all this was certainly the case for individuals before the historical appearance of Jesus is clear enough; nor can we suppose that all those who reposed in God through genuine faith were somehow clearly aware of the prophetic expectation of the Divine Messiah. And it now seems equally clear that individuals since Jesus' historical appearance, but nevertheless deprived of any adequate awareness of it, should be quite as capable of reposing in God through an equally genuine faith, in order to become members of that same divine spiritual community.

All this is not to specify just which classes of persons, or under just what circumstances, may be reasonably considered by historically oriented Christians to have responded to God in this way and thus to have entered into God's spiritual family. In fact, it is to make no such definitive judgment at all, since it is, after all, God's prerogative to judge the spiritual state of persons, whatever historical insight may be at their disposal (2 Tim. 2:19)—so that it is clearly not our human prerogative to decide or even to attempt to spell out a list of personal properties on the basis of which we might be able to make such a spiritual judgment. The theologically most discerning among us are, as we all know, still far short of doctrinal perfection. And in spite of an admitted inadequacy of this sort, we nevertheless regard it as fully possible to be in a state of divine grace. Furthermore, while each individual can achieve for himself, through what Christians refer to as the inner witness of the Holy Spirit (Rom. 8:14–16), a sustaining confidence about his own spiritual condition, we can scarcely claim the ability to assume to ourselves the right to draw a cognitive theological line which we can use to decide who is, or who is not, in a state of divine grace. How can I reasonably decide the degree of theological or doctrinal misconception that is consistent with an individual's possessing genuine saving faith, when I am myself involved in a degree of theological misunderstanding which, by the very nature of the case, I cannot spell out in detail? If this line of reasoning is essentially sound,

(1) This point is explicitly argued by Paul in the New Testament.

(2) This was clearly the case for persons living before the time of Jesus, and therefore in principle for similarly situated persons since.

d) This does not provide a set of cognitive criteria for deciding which persons are, or are not, in a state of grace, since that is a prerogative that belongs to God alone.

e) Yet the historical truth about Jesus is decisively important: (1) as a supplement to general revelation, (2) and as a motivation to commitment,

(3) since it is through Jesus that anyone is eligible for divine grace.

4. Hence, although Jesus' redemptive work is the necessary basis of grace and forgiveness, it is at the same time universally accessible.

II. The critical problems concerning Jesus' vocation are therefore essentially solved.

then it is not unthinkable for even the most orthodox Christian believer to suppose plausibly that there are certain unidentified persons, involved in very different religious traditions than our own and having their minds clouded in varying degrees by errors quite different from our own—but who are, in spite of these conceptual shortcomings, nevertheless trusting in the true God as genuinely as ourselves.

Again, all this does not mean that the historical truth about Jesus and the gospel is either unimportant or non-essential. It is of the utmost importance that the good news of redemption through Jesus' life and death be disseminated to all mankind, in order to fill in with precision and clarity those aspects of God's universal revelation which would otherwise remain dim and shadowy, especially since this historical revelation will provide a strengthening buttress for motivating individuals in all cultures to spiritual commitment. But, at the same time, we cannot reasonably suppose that the incompleteness and inadequacy of Christian evangelism in disseminating the historical gospel universally leaves those thus left unevangelized without any access whatever to God. And of course the historical gospel is absolutely essential, since apart from the redemptive achievement of Jesus as God Incarnate, no human being at all, whatever his historical exposure, would be even conceivably eligible for divine grace and forgiveness.

In all this I have, in fact, been addressing two quite different audiences. On the one hand, I am trying to clarify the insight of sensitive Christian believers who imagine (incorrectly, as I think) that the universal accessibility of divine grace, quite apart from historical knowledge, somehow makes the redemptive work of Jesus less essential than it actually is—and I hope that apprehension has been eased, if not totally laid to rest. On the other hand, I have also been responding to those who have an obstructive question about Jesus being the Head of the divine spiritual community, on the ground that this role on the part of Jesus would involve a morally and spiritually objectionable exclusivism of some sort. But, if God's gracious forgiveness in Christ is, as I have contended, universally accessible to every human individual in every culture and historical epoch of mankind and in every state of historical understanding, then that fear also loses its disturbing grip. Jesus, indeed, as God Incarnate, is the exclusive Head of the divine spiritual community; but this exclusive position is paralleled by God's inclusive invitation to every human being to join his spiritual family. And if that is so, then it appears equally that the critical difficulties directed at the vocation of Jesus are as soluble in principle as we found those directed against his person to be. That Jesus is Lord therefore also means that he is indeed the Climax of revelation, the Culmination of redemption, and the Core of spiritual community. It remains to draw all of this together in a comprehensive conclusion as to his person and vocation.

A Concluding Christological Synthesis

Christology and the Christian Revelation Claim

We now find ourselves on what is perhaps the summit of my argument for the Christian revelation claim—for the thesis that Jesus, as God Incarnate, has accomplished a totally adequate and universally accessible redemption from moral guilt and corruption, on behalf of the whole human race in all times and ages and throughout all cultures and civilizations, is the heart of that Christian claim. If we accept this claim as essentially and fully true, then every other aspect of the Christian revelation claim will turn on and about this central thesis as a kind of unifying and integrating fulcrum, with respect to which all the rest will be settled in principle for us, so that it will then be a question of filling in the details of a comprehensive picture that is already completed in outline. And there is therefore also a sense in which this objective fulcrum for the Christian world-view is also a subjective turning point for the reflective individual who faces up to the full impact of the issues at stake in this question. If he settles this question by accepting the Incarnation claim of Jesus and then committing himself to God through an act of genuine religious faith, he will still have many lesser questions to decide—and in fact it is clear that he will never exhaust them all in the whole span of his temporal life. And yet he will be operating from that center from which each of these endlessly proliferating issues can be seen in a clear perspective from the standpoint of which he will be able to make genuine progress toward that fully adequate understanding which always eludes him in

I. The Incarnation claim and its redemptive corollary constitute the core of the Christian revelation claim as a whole.

A. On this basis, everything else will be objectively settled in principle.
B. And subjectively:
1. The acceptance of that claim, and commitment to God on its basis, will provide a center for answering further questions and progressing toward adequate understanding.

247

2. The rejection or by-passing of that claim:

a) Will either
(1) lead to the abandonment of the reflective task,
(2) or motivate the search for a different center.
b) But the alternatives are all obstructive for one reason or another.

final form, since in Jesus all the treasures of wisdom and knowledge will be hidden away for him. But if that same reflective individual either rejects the Incarnation claim of Jesus, whether provisionally or with finality, or else attempts to maintain a noncommittal neutrality with respect to it, he will either have to abandon the reflective task or find some alternative center from which he can attempt to gain what he may hope will be an analogously clear perspective for understanding the meaning of existence and achieving a reasonably satisfactory relationship to it. He can, for example, fall back on a theism which excludes the Incarnation claim—but then, like Immanuel Kant, he will have to struggle to make his peace with the unconditional divine moral claim which finds him both morally guilty and corrupt. Or he can, perhaps, adopt some pantheistic version of transcendental metaphysics—but then, possibly like Sankara in Non-dualistic Vedanta Hinduism, he will have to reconcile all the ignorance and the evil of human experience with the thesis that the whole of it belongs essentially to Brahma (or God), whom he also regards as incorruptibly good. Or he can, with a sort of resigned boldness, dismiss the whole of transcendental metaphysics, whether theistic, pantheistic, or any other sort, and fall back on a naturalistic view of the world which excludes all purpose as in any sense causally efficacious—but then, although no longer plagued by the objective claim of morality which he has also surrendered, he will nevertheless be haunted by the realization that on this turf he can no longer take his own highest thoughts and deepest aspirations with any seriousness, since they will all be materially determined by the sheer random and chance interaction of physical particles. It is, I contend, practically impossible to overestimate how much is at stake for the individual in the alternative between Jesus' Incarnation claim, on the one hand, and its multiple varied counter-options, on the other.

C. Yet the Incarnation claim:
1. is not demonstrated with finality;

2. but it is disclosed as a high probability, so that its acceptance, over its alternatives as less probable, is a reasonable and responsible act.

Still, I do not claim that the alluring reasonableness of the Christian Incarnation claim has been demonstrated with logical finality, as if all its counter-options were totally empty when clearly understood. The vision of world-view omniscience is reserved for God alone. For finite thinkers like ourselves, there is reserved the scale of increasing and decreasing probability together with the inevitable risk that accompanies it. So what I do claim is that the Incarnation claim of Jesus is invested with a degree of high probability which makes commitment to that claim, and all that it entails for life and eternity, a wholly reasonable and responsible act—far more so, as I think, than any of its viable alternatives. And, if that is the case, then clearly the acceptance of the claim that Jesus is God Incarnate is at the same time essentially the acceptance of the Christian revelation claim at its organizing center. If, as I earlier argued, God is supreme moral and spiritual personality, then it is reasonable to suppose that the highest form of God's revelation to humanity would consist of making our human nature the unique vehicle of Divine Personhood in the being of a single historical individual. Obviously, this momentous conclusion has extensive consequences for our understanding of Oriental relig-

II. This conclusion involves momentous consequences for Oriental religious-philosophical alternatives.

ious-philosophical perspectives and the alternative truth-claims that these traditions contain. What then, is the appropriate Christian response here, and how ought we to relate the Christian truth-claim to those other options?

Christology and Comparative Religious Philosophy

What, then, of Confucianism, or Buddhism, or Hinduism, to mention some of these other alternatives? In my earlier book, *Oriental Philosophy: A Westerner's Guide to Eastern Thought*, I have expounded at considerable length some of the main religious-philosophical perspectives in the Oriental traditions of China, India, and, to a certain extent in the case of Buddhism, Japan; and I have also developed extensive criticisms of those perspectives, but without any explicit reference of their relation to the truth-claim of Christianity. I have no intention of repeating, or even summarizing those critical comments in the present context. What I have written, I have written. But it is nevertheless important to spell out the implications of all this for the Christian truth-claim in general and for the Incarnation claim in particular.

It is, in my opinion, neither necessary nor reasonable for an informed Christian critic to assume a wholly negative stance toward these Oriental systems of thought, as if they contained no dimensions of truth and therefore nothing of enduring religious or philosophical worth. It is not necessary to take such a stance, since the recognition of genuine elements of truth in these viewpoints in no sense detracts from the inclusiveness of the Christian truth-claim. If all the treasures of wisdom and knowledge are hidden away in Christ—if he is the Eternal Logos who enlightens every human being that comes into the world—then we can recognize all such elements of truth in Oriental perspectives as facets of the one truth in Christ, so that there also is an element, however restricted or extensive, of genuine divine self-disclosure. It is, again, not reasonable to take such a negative stance, since much of the insight contained in these Oriental systems overlaps in conceptual content with the Christian understanding of existence. Here too we find a transcendent realm upon which the natural, empirically discernible realm of experience depends in a variety of ways. Here too we find an objective moral order which binds finite moral selves unconditionally, and here too we find a keen analysis of man's moral guilt and corruption with their resultant inner frustration and despair. Here too we also find much that is fragmentary, incomplete, and clearly inadequate from the standpoint of a rationally grounded theistic point of view; and in my cricitisms of these Oriental positions I have tried to open up a transition of thought which points away from these shortcomings to a theistic outlook. Yet, in spite of a penumbra of relative darkness and shadow, there is also a shining light in which God also speaks. This is, after all, a part of the context of that general

I. My previous clarification of Oriental alternatives will not be repeated here:

but its relationship to the Christian truth-claim needs to be explored.

II. A Christian critic need not take a wholly negative stance here: A. since elements of truth in these views may be regarded as facets of the truth in Christ;

B. and since these perspectives overlap the Christian outlook in content,

while also containing shortcomings which point to a fuller theistic outlook.

III. Does the Incarnation claim of Jesus have Oriental counterparts or parallels which can be defended

with comparable reasonableness?
A. If so, the result would appear to be a stalemate.

B. But none of the seminal Oriental religious figures made such a genuinely parallel claim.

1. Confucius.

2. Lao-tzu

revelation and that universal accessibility of divine truth, of which I have already spoken at length.

But what, in particular, of the Incarnation claim of Jesus in relation to the supposedly parallel claims of the other great seminal religious figures in these Oriental traditions? Is there here a sort of analogous Incarnation claim which must be successfully disputed if we are to maintain the unique Incarnation claim of Jesus? Do we not read of avatars or divine incarnations in Hindu religious literature, and did not Mahayana Buddhists come to think of Gautama Buddha as the human manifestation of the blessed Dharmakaya or Buddha essence? And could sincere apologists in these traditions make for these notions a reasonable defense that would parallel the Christian claim that Jesus was God Incarnate—with the result that we would confront here a virtually insoluble religious stalemate? Such an implicit criticism of the Christian Incarnation claim, a criticism based on misinformation and misconception about Oriental religious-philosophical perspectives has, I think, been quite widespread among reflective Westerners who have any concern at all about such issues. Yet the surprising thing for those enchanted by this sort of difficulty is that there is little or no genuine basis for this type of objection. Although there is some difference of opinions among Oriental scholars, it is generally admitted that none of the great seminal figures of the Oriental religious traditions made any such claim for themselves that would provide a genuine parallel, in conceptual context, for the purportedly unique (and, as I believe, genuinely unique) Incarnation claim of Jesus. Confucius, for example, was primarily a scholar and, to some extent, editor of earlier Chinese religious traditions which formed a basis for the ethical and moral maxims that are traditionally attributed to him. He even describes his own slow progress in moral self-fulfilment—a progress which, to the end, he viewed as incomplete and inadequate. Although he spoke in traditional terms of the Supreme Ruler, there is a serious question as to whether such language was for him anything more than a metaphoric reference to the objective moral order of the natural universe—so that, far from making any claim to be God Incarnate, Confucius did not make it clear whether he even believed in God in any non-metaphorical and transcendent sense. The traditionally credited founder of Taoism, Lao-tzu, whose very historical existence is in question, seems to have indeed believed in a transcendent metaphysical absolute—the Tao— if, indeed, we can take the so-called *Lao-tzu Book* (or *Classic of Reason and Virtue*) as representing in the main his teachings (whether he wrote the book or not). But here the Tao is construed pantheistically as the inner being of all things, including persons, which are themselves genuine and distinct entities only from the standpoint of a relative knowledge that must be transcended in the indefinable and indiscerptible Oneness of the Tao to which no determinate qualities can be correctly ascribed. As would be the case for all else that is recognizable, in this context of thought the Tao would constitute the true being of Lao-tzu also, but not in the sense of any sort of qualitatively unique incarnation. In fact, for a view in which the Tao is the sole genuine reality, no particular and transitory manifestation of it would be any more or less an incarnation of the Tao than any other, since all such distinct entities are ultimately to be construed as unreal from the absolute standpoint.

Something quite analogous may plausibly be said of certain Indian perspectives, both Hindu and Buddhist. Yes, there are Hindu avatars or incarnations of the absolute reality, Brahma; but here again this notion is situated in a pantheistic context for which Brahma includes all genuine reality, so that the idea of incarnation applies, in this sense, to all things and persons in general, and therefore to no particular person in any finally unique sense—although some things and persons are regarded as more fully manifesting Brahma than others. And in the historically most influential philosophy within Hinduism (the Absolute Non-dualism of Sankara), there is reiterated the same thesis that appeared quite independently in Chinese classical Taoism, to the effect that from the standpoint of the unqualified Brahma, to which no determinate property applies, the whole realm of distinct entities and persons is a sheer cosmic illusion (*maya*) or cosmic ignorance (*avidya* or nescience). Here again, therefore, no actual person with determinate qualities could be even a genuine, much less unique, incarnation of the Absolute which alone is finally real. There are, of course, Hindu perspectives which reject this doctrine of cosmic illusionism; but such views either maintain the pantheism which would compromise the notion of unique incarnation (Ramanuja), or else they make an ultimate metaphysical dualism out of the distinction between God and the world, so that the notion of a literal incarnation in an individual human being becomes impertinent, if not simply unthinkable (Madhva).

And what of Guatama Buddha—also rooted in the soil of India? Here there is a critical controversy about what the historical Gautama actually taught. But most scholars maintain that the Hinayana or Theravada version of Buddhism corresponds most closely to the original teachings of Gautama himself. If so, Gautama was a metaphysical agnostic who suspended judgment on the question whether there was a transcendent metaphysical absolute or divine reality. And it is clear on this basis that Gautama, thus understood, made no incarnation claim for himself, since he viewed himself as an example of the spiritual enlightenment which all could in principle achieve by genuinely accepting the four noble truths and sincerely following the eightfold path. But let us suppose, on the contrary, that Mahayana Buddhism (in some one or other of its principle schools) has the more correct view of the historical Gautama. In that case, there would indeed be the transcendental metaphysical Absolute—the Blessed Dharmakaya (the Buddha's Body of Pure Being), the universal Buddha Essence, the Absolute Suchness wholly unqualified by determinate properties. And here again, as in classical Taoism and in Hindu Absolute Non-dualism, there emerges that same doctrine of the sole reality of the Absolute and of the ultimate unreality, from the absolute standpoint, of determinate persons, things, and entities. Here again also, if

3. Hindu avatars.

4. Gautama Buddha:
a) in Hinayana Buddhism;

b) in Mahayana Buddhism.

the pure Buddha essence is the sole genuine reality, then, of course, in one sense, Gautama is an incarnation of the Buddha essence—as would be the case with every other person and entity. Yet, in another sense, since such particular things are finally unreal, it is not the case that either Gautama or anyone else is a distinct and unique incarnation of the metaphysical Absolute or the Buddha essence. It follows, therefore, that, whether we take Gautama in Hinayana or Mahayana terms, the notion, much less the reality, of a genuine incarnation eludes us.

C. Hence there is no competing alternative to Jesus' unique Incarnation claim, as situated in its theistic context.

There is thus no authentic parallel Incarnation claim among the seminal religious figures of the Oriental religious traditions—no genuinely competing alternative to the unique Incarnation claim as traceable to the historical Jesus. It is only in his case that the transcendent God, theistically rather than pantheistically construed, is depicted as uniquely assuming human nature in an absolute unparalleled sense. And if that is so, then the original difficulty about a competing Incarnation claim simply dissolves before our eyes; and we shall therefore have to deal with Jesus' claim precisely on these terms. Yet this is not

1. This is not to disparage these other figures.
2. There is much truth to be sought in these teachings.
3. The metaphysical perspectives of these concepts should be critically asessed by the same objective criteria used to ground theism.

in any sense to derogate or disparage these other religious leaders; it is rather to understand them on their own terms and in their own context. The moral and religious teachings of Gautama or Confucius, of Lao-tzu or Sankara, ought to be taken seriously—and there is much genuine insight to be uncovered in these sources. The metaphysical contexts of these teachings, whether pantheistic, naturalistic, or otherwise, should be carefully considered and critically assessed through the same epistemological criteria that I have attempted to use in working my way toward a theistic metaphysical context—not because those criteria are, as I tried to show, question-begging stepping-stones to an antecedently favored metaphysical scheme, but rather because those criteria can be correctly understood as necessary presuppositions of all possible intelligible thought and being. If we expect this sort of fair-minded, objectively reasoned assessment of our own perspective when it is viewed by an Oriental critic, we should be willing to give the same sort of consideration when we attempt to assess Oriental viewpoints. I have sincerely attempted to do just this in my book on Oriental philosophy to which I referred earlier. In my opinion, neither side of such a reciprocal and even-minded discussion has anything genuinely valuable to lose or anything ominously threatening

D. Yet, Jesus' Incarnation claim remains to confront the critic.

to fear from such an exchange. Still, this entire process will leave the Oriental or any other reflective critic with the Incarnation claim of Jesus to confront, both in the context of the theism in which that claim has been historically propounded and in the context of the perspective from which the critic himself is emerging in his attempt at objective assessment. The whole of my previous argument concerning Jesus and his claim makes it clear where I think a sincere and balanced

1. My view is that Jesus is explicable only if his claim is accepted.

consideration of that claim will end up. From such a process, it may reasonably result that Jesus, as an historical individual, is inexplicable and unintelligible, unless we accept as quite literally true the claim that he was (and is) God Incarnate. Obviously, this result is neither automatic nor guaranteed for any particular individual who considers the argument; but for every such individual who considers the argument seriously and with a fully informed awareness, the result stands as a rationally plausible option for personal commitment. That such a commitment, fully carried through, would be revolutionary is, at the very least, unquestionably an understatement.

2. But this result is not guaranteed for every thinker, although it does stand as a plausible option for any such thinker.

Concluding Estimate on the Critical Objections in Christology

What, then, emerges in retrospect from our extended involvement in the multifaceted critical controversy concerning the person and vocation of Jesus? Literary criticism finds no defensible historical trace of a Jesus who was merely human, unless it approaches the question with a psychologically unassailable prejudgment to that effect. Nor is theological systematizing any more successful in developing a conceptual context in which the Incarnation claim of Jesus is bypassed in principle. The psychological interpretation of Jesus may be plausibly seen as leading to the conclusion that it was in full soundness of mind that he claimed to be God Incarnate; and the moral evaluation of Jesus finds no stable foothold for regarding Jesus as any sort of deceptive charlatan or moral scoundrel. As I have often conceded, these conclusions have not been demonstrated with any sort of rigorous logical finality. But they have, I sincerely think, been shown to be more plausible, both individually and especially conjunctively, than any comprehensively inclusive alternative explanation of all our reliable information about Jesus. I can therefore only return to my earlier provisional conclusion about Jesus thus understood, but this time bolstered with a confidence that has grown out of what I hope has been careful and fair-minded consideration in detail. If Jesus made the Incarnation claim for himself out of a wholly sound and morally unassailable self-consciousness—in such a way that no reasonable line of criticism can dislodge this thesis successfully—and if nevertheless Jesus is not God Incarnate as he claimed, what then can a rationally coherent and objective interpretation make of him? Is this perhaps the ultimate and insoluble human riddle? Or is Jesus' Incarnation claim perhaps the ultimate metaphysical truth? If, as I contend, we settle for the last alternative, we will have little difficulty in viewing Jesus, not only as God's final revelation and redemptive provision for the whole of humanity, but also as the incontestable Head of the divine spiritual community which is his spiritual body. Yet there is also the propositional expression of all this in what Christians have come to call the Bible—the Book—as if there were no other. The Christian revelation claim, culminated in Jesus, will nevertheless not be completely filled out apart from a proper explanation of this propositional dimension.

I. A summary of results regarding the person and vocation of Jesus.

II. These conclusions, although not demonstrated, are more plausible than any viable alternative explanation of Jesus.

A. Jesus therefore is:
1. either the ultimate human riddle,

2. or else, as God Incarnate, he is the ultimate truth.
B. His redemptive and communal roles follow in due course.

1. the propositional form of revelation is yet to be investigated.

PART **III**

Christianity and the Revelational Word—
The Propositional Expression
of Revelation in Scripture

The Bible and Its Structure:
The Internal Nature
of Propositional Revelation

All truth, in its cognitive aspect as knowledge, is in principle propositionally expressible in linguistic statements in which certain predicates
are conjoined with certain subjects either universally or to a limited
extent (*all* . . . or *some* . . .), either subject to conditions (*if . . .
then* . . .) or not, and in some one of three principal modes of
predication—assertion, possibility, or necessity (*is . . . may be . . .
must be*). As complex as this sounds, what it asserts is that whatever
is true, and therefore the possible object of knowledge, can be intelligibly conceptualized and also linguistically stated. Of course, whatever
is false, in any coherent and descriptive sense, can also be intelligibly
conceptualized and linguistically stated as well, although there are
certain kinds of falsehoods that cannot be stated intelligibly precisely
because they express, or at least imply, some sort of contradiction or
incoherence. Since, as I earlier explained, the propositional expression
of conceptual apprehension is one of the most distinctive functions of
personhood, it is not at all surprising that language, in its cognitive
sense, while not the only effective means of personal self-revelation, is
nevertheless one of the most significant and important. Nor will it be
any more surprising if God, as supreme moral and spiritual personality, communicates his self-revelation to humanity through this same

I. All truth is, in prin-
ciple, propositionally
expressible.

A. Language, as a
unique function of
personhood, is also an
effective means of
self-disclosure.

B. Hence it is not in-
appropriate for God
thus to reveal himself.

257

1. The special case of Jesus' words.

2. The revelation claim of the biblical authors for their own linguistic expressions.

II. The scriptural revelation claim.
A. Summary of this claim.

B. Elaboration of this claim:

1. The claim is not one of total dictation, although some limited material is thus represented.
a) The claim is consistent with human research and preparation, as well as individual stylistic and expressional differences.

b) The product is thus both God's Word and the writer's word.

mode of propositional expression. If Jesus Christ is, as the Christian truth-claim contends, God Incarnate, then clearly his statements, so far as they are historically accessible to us in the New Testament documents, would be precisely such a divine propositional self-revelation, Indeed, much of the basis on which we built the argument that Jesus is God Incarnate consisted of self-testimony of Jesus about his own person and vocation. Yet this propositional self-expression, striking as it is, does not stand alone, since it is generally evident that the human authors of the Bible regarded their own writings, along with some of their oral expressions, as authoritative self-revelation from God—so that, if that claim is accepted, God's propositional self-expression would be extended far beyond the words spoken by Jesus as God Incarnate. In fact, of course, our access to the words of Jesus himself consists in the statements contained in more extended literary works (the Gospels, primarily) which Christians very early came to regard as themselves God's authoritative self-revelation through divinely guided human spokesmen.

More generally, the Christian revelation claim contends that the books of the Hebrew-Christian Bible (the Old and New Testaments), rightly interpreted in their total historical, cultural, and literary context, constitute precisely, and in a unique, unparalleled sense, such an authoritative self-revelation of God. The effect of this claim is that, through Moses or David, Isaiah or Ezekiel, Matthew or John, Peter or Paul, God was also speaking his authoritative word, not only in statements that purported to quote some divine utterance, but also in the narrative text of the human author himself, when that text is understood in context. It is virtually impossible to clarify this complex notion, even in a preliminary sense for clarifying discussion, without introducing a fairly sophisticated expression of what is actually being claimed. At the outset, it is clearly not being claimed here that every word of the biblical books was dictated to their human authors through an immediate divine operation upon them, as if they were mere secretaries or amanuenses, and as if all human research and preparation of other sorts for their writing were in principle excluded. Indeed, some biblical propositions are introduced as direct quotations from God, as it were—the Ten Commandments (Exodus 20), for example. But much of the biblical material is not in this form at all—it is rather a speech of Moses, or a prophetic declaration of Isaiah, or a letter of Paul to some individual or Christian congregation. In all this latter sort of material, there are clear stylistic differences among the authors, and even specific references to human research as a preparation (Luke 1:1–4). In whatever sense God spoke through the biblical writers, it was a sense wholly consistent with their normal human patterns of thought and speech, so that what they wrote, even though it was an authoritative Word of God, was also characteristically and equally their own word, communicated in their own cultural and linguistic, even their own idiosyncratic and individual, modes of expression.

If we ask, now, about how this result was actually achieved, the main-line traditional Christian answer to this question, as I understand it, has been to contend, on the basis of explicit statements and implicit suggestions in the biblical books themselves, that in the case of those biblical writings a supervening divine inspiration so guided the authors that what they spoke as thus guided and what they wrote in the Scriptures without exception was, when properly interpreted in its total context, an indefectibly authoritative self-revelation of God—while it was at the same time equally the word of the human spokesman, as expressed in his own style and through the linguistic patterns that were characteristic of his culture and would be therefore generally communicative to that historical audience to which that declaration was originally addressed. There is, of course, virtually endless debate about how to verbalize this complex notion—even among those who purport to accept that notion. I have, for example, used the phrase "without exception" to express the idea that the guidance of the Divine Spirit, while not characteristically involving anything like dictation, nevertheless extended to the writer's choice of words and sentences in the sense that these linguistic media would be the most effective expression of the thought communicated. Others prefer in this connection to use the word *verbal* to express the same notion—a term which I would rather avoid, since I view it as generating confusion by connoting for many persons the suggestion that the only mode of this verbal guidance would be something analogous to dictation.

Again, I have used the term *indefectible* to express the idea that the guidance of the Divine Spirit as extended to the biblical writers was such that, when correctly interpreted and to the extent that it is thus interpreted in full context, the resultant self-revelation of God is fully authoritative, and therefore devoid of fault with respect to truth, in relation to that which it purports to communicate. Others prefer to use the term *inerrantly* or *infallibly* to express the same notion. As I see it, the word *infallibly* is a plausible second choice for *indefectibly*, except that for many persons it calls up a theological tradition of interpretation which might distract their understanding from the true sense. The word *inerrantly*, on the other hand, while it certainly can, I think, be properly construed here, probably generates more confusion than it does illumination, since each person will bring his own sense to the understanding of this term, often without considering any precise clarification of what it is supposed to mean in this context. If the term *inerrant* is taken in the highest conceivable sense of scholarly precision or scientifically specified technical exactitude, so that all approximative expressions or all phenomenal descriptions or all conventional modes of communication or all summary statements of the sense of what was said by someone or other—together with virtually countless other commonly acceptable but technically inexact modes of parlance—are eliminated on principle as erroneous just on that account, then we will be operating in an ideal language framework which is not only worlds apart from the language patterns of the biblical writings but also quite foreign and elusive to our own most disciplined linguistic usage. Since the term *inerrant* is commonly suspectible to being interpreted in some such ideal fashion, or even in

2. This result is achieved through supervening divine inspiration, so that the product is an indefectibly authoritative divine revelation through human spokesmen.

10. The verbalization of the claim.
1. The extension of divine guidance to the writer's words and sentences.

2. The concept of full authority through correct interpretation.
a) The term *indefectibly* preferable to either *infallibly* or *inerrantly.*

b) The term *inerrant* is ambiguous in its implications for many readers.
(1) If it means scientifically specified technical exactitude,

(2) then it is not applicable either to the biblical writings or to other current forms of cognitive communication.

some lesser sense of expected precision which is still not that of the effectively communicative language of the Bible, much less that of our own casual or even carefully monitored conversation, I judge it strategically wise and prudentially expedient to avoid the term, as far as possible, because of the possible confusion which it might unnecessarily evoke, and because of the resultant distraction from the real issues which might therefore be neglected in the consideration of the Christian truth-claim.

D. The notion of ideally correct interpretation.
1. Since the objective divine authority of Scripture depends on its correct understanding, and since no actual interpretation can claim ideal correctness, no such interpretation can claim more than an approximation to objective divine scriptural authority.

Some important additional clarification is necessary, however, although it is perhaps somewhat more controversial among sober and reflective Christians. I have referred to the notion of ideally correct interpretation in relation to the total context, as a qualification of biblical statements considered as divinely authorative. It is important to acknowledge and even insist that, since not even the most sympathetic and thoughtful reader of the Bible can reasonably claim unexceptionably that he is in possession of this ideally correct interpretation—and since there is no way to be incorrigibly certain that one has adequately identified, much less sufficiently considered, the total relevant context in his careful interpretation of Scripture—it follows that no interpreter can do more than claim, for his own understanding of Scripture, an approximation to that divinely authoritative and objective truth that an ideally correct interpretation would in principle provide. This is, I suppose, an involved and yet indispensable way of saying that I cannot reasonably claim, for even my own most effective interpretation of Scripture, that same degree of indefectible authority which I objectively recognize in Scripture as understood through an ideally correct interpretation. Yet this admission is no cause for genuine alarm or even for moderately disturbing uneasiness. The notion of an ideally correct interpretation, although decisively important as both a characterization and a goal, is as elusive as the ideal of becoming a fully good person in the whole fabric of one's life. The fact that my best achievement, in either case, will never be more than an approximate realization of the goal, is no reason to hold back from the most disciplined effort that I can make in both cases. To suppose otherwise would be to misconstrue the whole context of my human performance in both situations.

2. But this is no reason for not aiming at the most adequate understanding of Scripture that is possible for us.

3. Since the biblical writings are primarily a self-revelation of God:
a) Neither the author nor his audience can be supposed to have had the ideally correct interpretation either, as the New Testament itself acknowledges.

In further clarification, I point out that—since on the view of biblical inspiration I have been elaborating, the resultant product in the biblical writings is primarily a self-revelation of God, however much it may disclose about the human author or his original historical audience—it follows that it is not necessary to suppose that either that author or his audience had, on however careful reflection, the ideally correct interpretation of the Scripture of which that author was the human writer. The New Testament itself acknowledges as much when it suggests (1 Peter 1:10–12) that neither the prophets who wrote of Christ's sufferings and subsequent glory, nor even the angels of God, had a wholly clear and adequate understanding (in my terms, an ideally correct interpretation) of what those prophets themselves had declared. Now a commonly accepted principle of biblical hermeneutics proceeds on the assumption that the one and only correct interpretation of any biblical text would be the one that the author himself historically understood by what he wrote, and that, if we could become aware of that understanding ourselves, we would be hermeneutically bound to understand that passage in the same way. If, however, I am right in supposing that we have no reasonable basis for supposing that the biblical writer himself had an ideally correct interpretation of what he had written—so that he might, on reflection, even have misconstrued its deepest and most decisive sense—then that frequently reiterated principle of biblical hermeneutics will be fairly seen to be incorrect. Whatever I can learn about what it was that Isaiah himself, on reflection, understood by what he had said under divine inspiration, that will provide a partial basis for my own attempted approximation to overall correct understanding. But I am in no sense bound to that original understanding of the prophet, even if (doubtless with great difficulty) I can discover it. I am provisionally bound instead to my own sincere, contextually informed, and linguistically plausible interpretation, guided by every genuinely relevant consideration which I can discover and reflect upon. I am, of course, also bound to what I recognize as God's address to me in his Word as discerned through such a comprehensive understanding. Indeed, it is in this way that a revelatory word, spoken through Isaiah in and to his own culture and civilization, is also a divine self-disclosure to every reflective human person in any culture and civilization. It is, after all, primarily God, and only in a lesser sense Isaiah, who is speaking—and primarily man as such, and only in a lesser sense those ancient Israelites, who should be listening.

b) Biblical interpretation is not therefore bound to the construction which the human writer put on what he wrote, even when that meaning can be discerned.

(1) The author's intent is one element to consider in my attempt at interpretation.

(2) But I am bound instead to my own informed and linguistically plausible understanding, as well as to God's address to me through it.

c) In this way God's revelation transcends its explicit historical background.

Now all this has been an elaboration and clarification of what is being asserted when it is said, as an integral part of the Christian truth-claim, that the Hebrew-Christian Bible is an indefectibly authoritative self-revelation of God. The subsequent issue involves the analysis and investigation of the basis of that claim, in order to discern whether, as a claim, it is an appropriate object of reasonable belief.

III. The question remains whether the scriptural revelation claim can be provided with a reasonable basis.

The Testimony of Jesus

As was the case with several previous questions, we do not approach the issue of the divine authority of the Bible in any vacuum of thought or, as it were, from scratch. Instead, we approach this problem in a framework of thought already reasonably well-structured: Ours is a theistic universe in which God is the ultimate, self-existent personal reality on which everything contingent depends for its existence and operation; ours is also a universe in which that same transcendent God has become Incarnate in Jesus the Messiah, who, in his vocation as universally representative humanity, has completely met on behalf of every human individual the unconditional claim of divine moral law on every such human being as guilty and liable before the judgment bar of that claim. It is true that we used the biblical materials, considered merely as sources of information, as a reference for estab-

I. The scriptural revelation claim is approached in a context.
A. This involves:
1. theism,

2. Jesus as God Incarnate, and as moral redeemer.

lishing our conclusion about the person and vocation of Jesus. But this material was in no sense appealed to as authoritative divine revelation—it was rather employed as generally reliable historical source material, so that no circular begging of the question is in any sense entailed. And, of course, the case for a theistic perspective in general was developed without any dependence whatever, in the logical sense, on the biblical reference matter.

By the time of Jesus and the writing of the New Testament, the scope and content of the Hebrew Bible was at least so far settled that in the writings of the New Testament and in non-biblical writings of the same general era, the Old Testament as a whole was referred to repeatedly as simply "Scripture" or "the Scripture" ("Writing" or "the Writing") in such a way as to imply that its scope and generally accepted divine authority among the Jews was virtually a matter of common agreement—although it is possible that the collection of authoritative books remained peripherally open until about the end of the first century A.D., especially among members of the Jewish community outside Palestine. If now we again advert to the Gospel materials as merely sources of information about what Jesus taught or implicitly believed himself, we can also raise the question as to how he viewed the authority of the books that we now refer to as making up the Old Testament. Nor will this be any mere historical curiosity for us in a context in which we already presume Jesus' status as God Incarnate to be an established and wholly reasonable thesis (not of course, as I have repeatedly acknowledged, a logically demonstrated conclusion in the most rigorous sense). If Jesus is God Incarnate and if he has a clearly evident view of the authority of the Old Testament, then his plenary divine insight, on this or any other topic on which his views are known, will establish for us a solid basis for commitment to whatever view Jesus may be reasonably regarded as having held, as disclosed in the available sources. To suppose that Jesus was God Incarnate in the sense which I have argued, and to entertain seriously the notion that he might nevertheless have been personally committed to a developed viewpoint that was in fact false—such a combination of suppositions would simply be logically unthinkable.

And what did Jesus believe about the divine authority of the Old Testament, so far as we can discern from the Gospel materials? The libraries of universities and theological seminaries are, on an average, well stocked with ponderous tomes which discuss this question in scholarly detail and depth; and it is not my intention to discuss at length here what is already at the fingertips of any sincerely interested person. What is clear is that the Jesus of the Gospel materials held unexceptionably, both in his explicit teachings and in his frequent allusions, to what I can fairly refer to as the highest plausibly conceivable view of the divine authority of the biblical writings of the Old Testament. As to his explicit teaching on the subject in arguing with the Jews about the propriety of referring to himself as the Son of God in a unique sense, he reminds them of an Old Testament statement (Ps. 82:6) and then cites a premise, common to himself and his opponents, to the effect that the authority of Scripture is so pervasive that it cannot be set aside in even a single instance (John 10:35). And in commenting on the authority of the Law (a common designation, not merely for the Pentateuch, but for the Old Testament Scriptures as a whole), he states that not even the smallest letter of the alphabet or the segment of a single letter of that alphabet can be properly excluded from the Scriptures in which they occur (Matt. 5:17, 18)—a reference which clearly implies that the Scripture (of course, rightly understood) is authoritative right down to the letters and parts of letters of which those writings are composed. As for citations of, and allusions to, Scripture, Jesus with great frequency is represented as claiming the authority of Scripture by citing some passage or other with the simple formula, "It is written," as if the text, rightly understood, would through its authority settle whatever issue was in question (Matt. 4:4, 7, 10; Luke 4:4, 8; 24:25f., 44–46). Furthermore, Jesus was not averse to reminding his critics that they were in error because they knew neither the Scriptures nor the power of God (Matt. 22:29)— thus plainly to suggest that they would be prevented from error through a proper knowledge of the Scriptures. To these same critics, who denied the resurrection of the dead and accepted only the authority of the Pentateuch or Books of Moses, Jesus cited God's word to Moses that "I am the God of Abraham, and the God of Isaac, and the God of Jacob . . ." (Matt. 22:32–33), and then argues that since God is not the God of the dead but of the living, and since the patriarchs named had indeed died physically long before Moses' time, it follows that those patriarchs were therefore alive with God and hence awaiting the resurrection. Quite apart from the issue about the resurrection, the point is that Jesus here argues from the merely implied present tense of the Hebrew text ("I, the God of Abraham . . .")—an indication of how precisely and fully Jesus regarded the authority of Scripture.

> 2. Citations and allusions.

Other allusions abound. Jesus refers, for example, to a statement of David in the Book of Psalms (110) as having been spoken by David in the Holy Spirit (Mark 12:36; Matt. 22:43). And in reasoning with the Pharisees about Old Testament teaching on divorce, Jesus cites a narrative portion of Genesis (1:27; 2:24), not represented as a saying of God in that context, as nevertheless something that God the Creator said—thus implying that, on his view of Scripture, whatever stands written in that Scripture is in some basic and inclusive sense a statement of God, although of course it must be understood in context (Matt. 19:4). The upshot of all this is that the Jesus of the Gospels held a view of scriptural authority tantamount to the one I have represented as the traditional Christian understanding of that authority, to the effect that the Scriptures are throughout, and in their express statements and words, a divine self-revelation.

> C. Jesus clearly regarded the Scriptures as fully authoritative divine revelation.

But, of course, since this conclusion is so momentous in its consequences, those who boggle at these results have, as might be expected, attempted to avoid their evident implications. Some of the standard counter-proposals are, in fact, already logically excluded for those who have conceded the general thrust of our previous argument as a

> III. Attempted evasions of this conclusion.
> A. Some such evasions are already excluded:

1. That Jesus believed
and taught an erro-
neous view:

a) Mere humanism;

b) Kenoticism.

2. That Jesus believed
but did not actually
teach an erroneous
view.

B. Two evasive theo-
ries require critical re-
view.
1. That the view of
Scripture was merely
ascribed to Jesus by
the writers who them-
selves believed it.

a) Jesus' reconstruc-
tive suggestions in the
Sermon on the Mount
are said to support
this claim.

whole. If Jesus is, as I have claimed, reasonably believed to be God Incarnate, so that I am *ipso facto* bound by the requirement of logical consistency to accept whatever his belief was about any question just to the extent that I can confidently determine the content of that belief, then any suggestion that Jesus did indeed believe in the indefectible divine authority of Old Testament Scripture, but that he was mistaken in that belief and so decisively ignorant of the truth about this issue, must be dismissed on principle. And it will not matter whether the suggestion takes the form of regarding Jesus as no more than a remarkable human being who nevertheless understandably imbibed the prevalent misconceptions of his culture and religious background, or the more moderate form of a Kenotic Christology which contends that, although Jesus was God Incarnate, he was so far divested of the possession or effective exercise of his transcendent divine attributes as to be capable of a variety of commonly accepted but mistaken notions. For the former view simply dismisses Jesus' Incarnation claim at the outset, and the latter view involves the sort of objectionable inconsistencies that I pointed out in discussing the Kenotic theory in connection with my analysis of the concept of Jesus' person. Even the still more moderate thesis—that Jesus believed in Old Testament authority in the sense I explained (or some closely similar sense), but that he cannot be charged with error because he did not dogmatically teach that view—will also have to be dismissed: For not only is Jesus' actual teaching on the subject, as preserved in the Gospel materials, clearly opposed to this suggestion; but it is also the case that any such distinction between belief and specific teaching is simply inapplicable to a person who is God Incarnate in the sense I have tried to argue. God, whether Incarnate or not, cannot have any mistaken beliefs consistently with his omniscience. In fact, if belief means probable and, in principle, revisable opinion (as it frequently does for human subjects like ourselves), then the distinction between belief and knowledge is simply inapplicable to God, even in the case of what for us would be reasonably true beliefs.

But there are two evasive suggestions that, on the surface at least, appear not to be eliminated in principle by the acceptance of Jesus' Incarnation claim as true. The first is an old thesis in a new guise as adapted to the present issue: Just as it was argued, in regard to the Incarnation claim itself, that somehow a hypothecated historical Jesus, behind the Gospel materials, did not make any such claim, but that it was ascribed to him by the inventive imagination of the early believers, so here it is suggested that the historical Jesus did not hold the high view of Old Testament authority which is ascribed to him in those same Gospel materials, but rather that this conception was interwoven into his otherwise (and drastically limited) authentic teachings by the Gospel writers who did in fact imbibe this mistaken conception of scriptural authority. This suggestion, it is claimed, has some support even in the Gospels themselves. In the Matthew version of the so-called Sermon on the Mount, Jesus is represented by the writer as several times placing counter-proposals against specifically cited Old

Testament instructions (Matt. 5:21, 27, 31, 33, 38, 43). Is it not reasonable to discern here at least a glimpse of a fairly extensive set of reservations that Jesus had with regard to Old Testament authority?

In response to this claim—that Jesus did not actually hold the high view of scriptural authority—I suggest that the general answer to the claim is not essentially different from the appropriate answer to the criticism of Jesus' Incarnation claim along similar lines. Suspending for the moment the passages in the Matthew version of the Sermon on the Mount, there is simply no basis in the Gospels, as they stand, for a Jesus who takes anything less than the highest view of Old Testament authority. If it is suggested that possibly in the written sources that underlie our present Gospels—say, for example, in accordance with the four-document hypothesis we confronted previously (Mark, M [peculiar Matthew material], L [peculiar Luke material], and Q [material common to Matthew and Luke])—there might be an historical basis for a Jesus who had no such view of Scripture, that suggestion turns out to be essentially as unsubstantiated here as it did in the case of the Incarnation claim itself. This point has been well argued by a scholar of no less stature than B. B. Warfield himself in his monumental work, *The Inspiration and Authority of The Bible*, from which I transcribe a list of parallel references to biblical authority in the teaching of Jesus as recorded in more than one of the present Gospels: Matt. 4:4, 7, 10 (Luke 4:4, 8, 12); Matt. 11:10 (Luke 7:27); Matt. 21:13 (Luke 19:46; Mark 11:17); Matt. 26:31 (Mark 14:27); Matt. 19:4 (Mark 10:6); Matt. 21:42 (Mark 12:10; Luke 20:17); Matt. 22:32 (Mark 12:26; Luke 20:37); Matt. 26:56 (Mark 14:49; Luke 24:44). Since these passages reflect, even on a fairly radical view of pre-Gospel sources, what may be supposed to have been contained in those sources concerning Jesus' view of scriptural authority—and since they indicate the same high view of Scripture, on the part of Jesus, that we find in the Gospels themselves—it is reasonable to conclude that we cannot plausibly identify any sources which do not depict Jesus as subscribing to that same elevated perspective. The supposition, therefore, that the historical Jesus did not actually hold this view may therefore fairly be ascribed to the inventive imagination, not indeed of the early believers or Gospel writers, but rather of the critics themselves. Perhaps more plausibly, that supposition may be ascribed to the unsupported and, in my view, insupportable thesis that Jesus could not possibly have held such a view of Scripture, because the critics, while rejecting that view themselves, nevertheless wish to maintain their respect for Jesus as a religious teacher.

As for the argument based on Jesus' alleged qualifications concerning scriptural authority in the Sermon on the Mount, several observations are pertinent: First, that in the immediately preceding context (Matt. 5:17–19) Jesus made it clear that nothing he was about to propose should be viewed as calling into question the authority of the Scriptures themselves, rightly understood, so that he cannot reasonably be regarded as having the alleged reservations about scriptural authority. Again, in the passages in question, Jesus cites the Scripture

b) But this explanation is implausible.

(1) It is not supported by the Gospel materials as they stand.

(2) Nor is the view supportable by resolving the synoptic Gospels into their sources.

(3) Jesus was not challenging Old Testament authority in the Sermon on the Mount.
a) Instead he was challenging the interpretation of the Old Testament by Jewish teachers.

portions on which he comments with the formula "It has been said . . . "—perhaps intimating that what he had reservations about was not anything that stood written in Scripture, but rather the oral interpretation of these Scriptures by the Jewish teachers, over against whom he counterposed his own interpretation of those Scriptures. Further, Jesus' remarks about those Old Testament passages themselves are clearly extensions and reinterpretations of principles whose application he considered, not as perennial, but as restricted to the particular circumstances of the Israelite nation under the Mosaic and generally theocratic legislation. This last point is especially illustrated in Jesus' teaching on divorce (Matt. 5:32–32), since he elsewhere makes it clear that Mosaic instruction on divorce, while authoritative enough in its context, was a contingently permitted exception to an earlier and more exacting requirement of God, which Jesus clearly grounded in the divine authority of Scripture and which he also clearly regarded as taking precedence over that contingent exception which he viewed as relative to the hardness of heart (the unforgiving spirit) of the Israelites at the time (Matt. 19:3–9). Hence, what Jesus' reinterpretation of the Scriptures shows here is not that he had any reservations about their authority in context, but that he saw his own interpretation as precisely an extension of, and fully parallel to, that Old Testament authority. On this whole question, I might make the final comment that, if the critics have such profound reservations about the accuracy of the Gospel writers in ascribing the high view of Scripture to Jesus elsewhere in their writing, what plausible reason would those same critics have, on their own suppositions, for leaning so confidently on what they take to be (mistakenly, as I suppose) Matthew's representation of Jesus' alleged qualifications of Old Testament authority?

b) But Jesus did see his own interpretation as an extension of Old Testament authority.

But there is, as I earlier intimated, a second line of evasive argument which has been used to bypass Jesus' view of scriptural authority. It is suggested that, while it is clear that Jesus adverted to the high view of Scripture in his teachings, he did so, not because he himself accepted this view, but rather because he was placing himself by accommodation on the premises of his hearers (who did accept that view), in order to show them, through a sort of *argumentum ad hominem*, that, even on their own premise of indefectible Old Testament authority, their insight was extremely limited and, on occasion, perverse. This hypothesis would explain, presumably: (1) Jesus' consistent appeal to scriptural authority, in view of his listeners' beliefs: (2) his own serious reservation about that authority; and (3) the critics' own high esteem for Jesus as a teacher in view of the critics' parallel reservations on, if not outright rejection of, that same authority. In response, however, I do not find this thesis any more plausible, on examination, than the preceding one. In the first place, the subscription of Jesus to scriptural authority so fully pervades and permeates the whole body of his teaching, on such a wide variety of subjects and in such fundamental fashion, that the accommodation thesis is simply implausible on its face. For Jesus to have subscribed so unexceptionally to biblical authority, without himself believing in it, would have amounted to the

2. That Jesus, in subscribing to Old Testament authority, was accommodating himself to his hearers for the sake of argument. *a*) Explanation of this view.

b) Critical problems: (1)Jesus' commitment to scriptural authority is too pervasive for such a view, unless we regard the whole as a massive and perverse deception.

perpetration of a deception so massive that we would have to challenge the moral integrity of his character and therefore our entire previously argued view of his person as God Incarnate. Against any such move I simply juxtapose my entire case for the Incarnation claim itself. And there is another side to this coin: It is simply unthinkable that Jesus could have argued in this vein of accommodation without explaining his true view of the matter to his disciples, who most assuredly would have preserved that explanation; or, alternatively and on the darkest view of the matter, without such a supposedly calculated fraud coming to light at some point—a disclosure that would also certainly not have fallen on deaf ears. Yet there is not a single scrap of evidence that either of these eventualities occurred. No hint of any such lower view of Scripture appears anywhere, either in the Gospels (including John) or in the rest of the New Testament—but everywhere, as I shall argue, there is the same high view of Scripture that we have found to be characteristic of Jesus himself. And again, there is also no evidence of any criticism of Jesus, even on the part of his religious enemies, for his having had anything less than the highest view of Old Testament authority. In fact, Jesus appealed to that authority, not only when discoursing with his critics, but quite as emphatically when instructing his own disciples and followers, to whom he would surely have explained his own true view. Thus he makes extensive appeal to the Scriptures in the so-called Olivet discourse in which he prophesies about the end of the age (Matt. 24; Mark 13; Luke 21), and he views his own impending death, in describing it to his disciples, as a fulfillment of Scripture (Matt. 26:31, 54; cf. Luke 24:25–27, 44–48). And, even in arguing with his critics, Jesus would scarcely have told them that the source of their erroneous insight was their failure to understand either the Scriptures or the power of God, if he had not himself held to the unexceptionable authority of those same Scriptures (Matt. 22:29; Mark 12:24). For all these reasons, therefore, the accommodation theory is thoroughly implausible and cannot reasonably be used to avoid the conclusion that Jesus himself accepted unstintingly the indefectible authority of the Old Testament writings as a revelation from God. And if he held that view, while at the same time he was (and is) God Incarnate, it is wholly reasonable for a reflective person who himself subscribes to these two beliefs (that Jesus had the highest view of scriptural authority, and that Jesus is God Incarnate) to accept himself the same view of that authority.

But, of course, an equally, if not more fundamentally, important part of the Christian truth-claim concerning Scripture, relates to the books of what came to be called the New Testament—books which, since they were written as a consequence of Jesus' historical career, can hardly be expected to have had the same sort of detailed vindication for their revelational authority as the Gospels themselves make clear that the Old Testament possessed, since obviously the New Testament, even in its earliest parts, did not exist during Jesus' historical career. Yet there are general intimations in what Jesus did say and teach about his own ministry and its extension through his disciples—

---

(2) Jesus' true view would have been taught to his disciples and preserved—but there is no evidence of such a different view anywhere in the New Testament.

(3) On the contrary, Jesus appealed to Scripture as authoritative when instructing his own disciples.

(4) Jesus' objection to his critics, that they did not understand Scripture, implies his own confidence in it.

C. Hence, Jesus held the high view of Scripture, so that it is wholly reasonable to accept his view.

IV. Jesus and the New Testament.

A. Jesus anticipated a supplemental authoritative revelation through his disciples, that would definitively clarify the revelation in himself.
1. He claimed for his own teaching an authority parallel to that of the Old Testament.

2. His listeners recognized this authority.

3. Jesus envisioned that authority as becoming invested in his disciples as subordinated to him.
a) This was implied clearly in Jesus' teachings.

b) It was also understood by the disciples (especially the apostles) themselves.

c) Hence, a developing concept of revelational authority vested in the apostolic leadership.

intimations which clearly suggest that he anticipated an authoritative revelation, through his disciples, that would embody in definitive form an expression of the meaning and implications of the climax of divine revelation in himself as God Incarnate. I have already argued that Jesus, as God Incarnate, is the climax of divine self-revelation. And it is clear enough from the Gospels that: (1) he claimed for himself a teaching and instructional authority that embodied no mere extension of interpretive commentary on the Old Testament, but rather an originative and reinterpretive authority that, in its expressed content, paralleled and extended the revelational authority of the Old Testament itself—that is, for example, the evident impression left by the style of the Sermon on the Mount in which Jesus cited Old Testament Scriptures (as improperly understood) and then juxtaposed his own emphatic "But *I* say unto you . . . " with the obvious intent of claiming for his own instruction an authority fully parallel to that of the scriptural source (Matt. 5:31–44), an authority which he generalized, in later discourse with his disciples, by claiming that all authority, both heavenly and earthly, had once and for all been delivered over to him (Matt. 28:18); (2) that those who listened to Jesus' teaching—not merely the disciples but the multitudes—recognized this clear contrast of authority between Jesus' teaching and that of the Scribes and Pharisees, whose teaching was regarded as interpretive, provisional, and therefore revisable (Matt. 7:28, 29); and (3) that Jesus envisioned his own teaching and declarative authority as becoming invested in his disciples, although of course in a sense fully compatible with their subordination to him (Matt. 16:17–19; 18:18–20) through his promised presence among them after his departure (Matt. 18:20; 28:20)—a derivative but genuine authority which he clearly implies when, after claiming all authority for himself, he includes in the mission grounded in this authority, for the disciples, the task of teaching (Matt. 28:20). Of course, the disciples (and especially the apostles whom Jesus specifically chose as their leaders) envisioned themselves as charged with the responsibility for preserving with the greatest care, at first orally and later in writing, the teachings of Jesus whom they acknowledged as the Divine Messiah. The Gospels themselves (and whatever written and oral sources antedate them and are reflected in the Gospels) are evidence enough of that. But they also saw themselves as vested with the subordinate but revelatory authority to which I just now alluded. That they preserved, in the Gospel literature, the passages I just now cited (along with other similar intimations) is analogously evidence enough of that (cf. also Jesus' charge to the disciples in Luke 24:46–49). It is no mere coincidence that Luke, both in his Gospel (24:49) and more explicitly in the Acts of the Apostles (1:8f.), represents Jesus as promising the disciples a fullness of the Holy Spirit which would invest them not only with divine power but also with the capacity for authoritative witness. Nor is it any less striking that Luke represents the apostles, throughout his history, as speaking in the authority of that promised Holy Spirit. In all this there is, at the very least, the developing concept of a revelational authority which has its source in Jesus as God Incarnate, but which, in subordination to that source, is vested in the apostolic leadership of the earliest circle of believers. That this revelational authority came to be viewed as attached to books which, at apostolic instigation, expressed that authoritative teaching in writing is precisely what might have been expected.

What is thus intimated and suggested in the synoptic tradition becomes fully and explicitly clear in the Johannine literature (the Gospel and the First Epistle). Whatever view we hold about the authorship of the fourth Gospel and the Epistle, it is clear that this literature expresses a widespread understanding of the teaching of Jesus toward the end of the first century A.D. (or, according to some scholars, considerably earlier). Hence, it also reflects the thinking of the first-century Christian community on the topics that this literature covers, so that, for my purposes here, it is not necessary to settle the disputed issues about the precise authorship and origin of the literature itself. In any case, Jesus is here depicted as promising his disciples in his farewell discourse that, after his departure from the world and in consequence of his mission in the world, the Holy Spirit of God would assume a special role for his disciples by representing and reconstituting Jesus' own presence with them and his operation among them (John 14:16–18). One aspect of this special role of the Spirit was to be instructive in the sense that the Spirit would teach them all things that were pertinent to God's revealed presence among them, and especially that He would bring to their memory with accuracy all the essential things that Jesus himself had said to them during his earthly pilgrimage among them (John 14:25–26). The decisive thing to notice here is that Jesus puts the instruction of the Holy Spirit entirely on an equal par with his own words by implying that the Spirit would continue his own (Jesus') teaching. Later in the discourse, this same point is made with more forthright explicitness: Jesus tells them that the Spirit (now referred to as the Spirit of truth) will guide or direct them into all essential truth, since He will not speak on any independent authority in which He might be construed as a source of insight distinct from that of Jesus, but will rather speak with the same voice of authority as Jesus himself by instructing them in that same revelational insight—an insight in which Jesus declares himself to be fully equal with God the Father (John 16:13–15—note especially: "All things that the Father has are mine . . . hence, [the Spirit] will take from that which is mine and relate it to you"). Now since Jesus is God Incarnate so that his teaching has full divine authority, and since the teaching of the Holy Spirit reconstitutes the revelation in Jesus, then it follows that what the disciples and, more specifically, the apostles teach, as thus vested with the Spirit's influence and guidance, has a revelational authority quite on a par with that of Jesus himself, although, since they are human beings subject to fallibility, this authority extends, not to every remark they make or to every opinion they express, but only to what they teach under what I will call the plenary direction of the Holy Spirit. There is thus, as it were, a direct line of revelational authority here, emanating from Jesus as God Incarnate,

d) All this is made still clearer in the Johannine literature.

(1) The promised Holy Spirit is to continue Jesus' own teaching presence among the disciples.

(2) In this role, the Spirit will guide them into all essential truth by speaking with the same voice of authority as Jesus himself.

(3) Hence what the apostles teach, under the full guidance of the Spirit, has an equally full revelational authority:

thus the line of revelational authority.

channeled through the influence of the Divine Spirit, and extending to that segment of apostolic instruction which was declared in complete subordination to that influence of the Spirit. This same concept of revelational teaching authority is further extended in the First Epistle of John. Indeed, it virtually pervades that letter from the beginning through the writer's claim that he is declaring what he has heard and seen about the Word (the Logos) of life—a clear reference to Jesus as God Incarnate (1 John 1:1-3; cf. John 1:1-18). In fact, he claims that his teaching is based on the Divine Word within him (1 John 1:10), and that it is essentially continuous with that word and commandment which they (the believers) had from the outset of their Christian experience—possibly a reference to the general apostolic teaching of the gospel. The writer makes a special point of instructing his believing hearers to "test the spirits" to see if they are from God, and he offers a twofold criterion: (1) whether the content of any insight recognizes Jesus as God Incarnate; and (2) whether his own Spirit-guided testimony is accepted (1 John 4:1-6). This, he declares, is the standard for distinguishing between the Spirit of truth and some misleading spirit of error.

In reflective retrospect on all of this, it is difficult to escape the conclusion that the apostolic revelational authority, under the plenary guidance of the Divine Spirit, is taking definitive written form in the Gospel and Epistle themselves. For there, in the Gospel, is indeed the preservation of the words of Jesus which the promised Spirit was to call to mind; and here, in the Epistle, is the Spirit-guided extension of that same revelational word. In this sense, buoyed up by the intimations of Jesus in the Synoptics and his explicit teachings in the Johannine literature (especially in the Gospel), we recognize in principle a clear illustration of the written form of that apostolic teaching authority which Jesus himself recognized as an extension of his own revelational ultimacy. And if we find in the rest of the New Testament writings an analogous claim to revealed authority, either in explicit statement or in suggestive intimation, it will not be unreasonable to suppose that Jesus, prophetically and in principle, anticipatively recognized those writings as an extension of his own revelational authority which he in turn regarded as wholly on a par with those Old Testament Scriptures that he clearly accepted as indefectibly authoritative divine revelation.

As I pause on the threshold of this conclusion, and before I turn to a consideration of the revelation claim of the biblical writers themselves with regard to their own and other biblical books, I want to consider in transition a possible perplexity that might disturb some of my more reflective readers. Christian believers have often taken some (or all) of the New Testament passages to which I have appealed, as applying to the Holy Spirit's guidance of all believers indiscriminately, rather than to the more restricted apostolic teaching authority which I have interpreted as a bridge from Jesus' revelational authority to the analogous but subordinate revelational authority of the New Testament writings. If that exegetical move were to be taken, we would, of

---

(4) The fulfillment of this authority is clearly exemplified in the First Epistle of John.

(5) It is therefore reasonable to conclude that apostolic revelational authority is taking definitive written form in the Gospel and Epistle themselves.

(6) The rest of the New Testament may be taken as an extension of this form.

e) Thus Jesus may be supposed to have anticipatively recognized the New Testament as an extension of his own revelational authority.

B. A transitional problem: whether the passages cited apply to the Spirit's guidance of all believers.

course, confront a difficult dilemma. Either we should have to extend this high view of revelational authority to all that is declared by Spirit-guided believers of all ages, or we would have to make a far less ambitious claim for the apostolic teaching authority in either its oral or its written form. Whichever horn of the dilemma we select, the results would be all but disastrous for my argument that Jesus implicitly recognized the revelational authority of the New Testament as essentially and in principle an extension of his own revelational authority, even though the books in question did not exist during Jesus' earthly career. To suppose that a parallel revelational authority extended to all Spirit-guided believers in all ages would simply fail to take account of the logically contrasting opinions of different believers—contrasts which have, of course, led to the sectarian diversification of Christendom. The New Testament itself does, of course, clearly recognize a genuine guidance of the Spirit extended to all believers (1 John 2:26–27; Rom. 8:9f.); but this guidance should be viewed as quite compatible with a fallibility on the part of believers in general as to just what insights are to be regarded as emanating from the Holy Spirit—hence, the instruction already noted (1 John 4:1) that the spirits must be tested (implying that confusion here is possible in principle), and hence also the intimation of Paul that even believers prophesying in the name of God may need the counterbalancing and correction of the prophetic insights of other believers (1 Cor. 14:29–33). If, in view of all this, we acknowledge a similar fallibility in the teaching of even the apostles as plenarily guided by the Holy Spirit, then the line of revelational authority clearly intimated, as I have argued, by Jesus himself will have decisively broken down.

1. If the passages do so apply, that would clearly weaken the argument for apostolic authority, since Spirit-guided believers in general are clearly fallible in their opinions about what insights should be ascribed to the Holy Spirit.

This is, of course, an enormously complicated issue on which I can, as always, only urge what I sincerely believe to be an informed and correct opinion, since I obviously regard myself as fallible in principle even when I think I am being guided by the Holy Spirit. Operating in this attitudinal framework, I can only venture to suggest that, in my opinion, it is simply a mistake of biblical interpretation to regard the passages on which I have based the concept of unique apostolic teaching authority as if those passages applied indiscriminately to all believers in all the times and ages of Christendom, at least not in the same distinctive sense in which they apply to the apostles themselves. I think, therefore, that these scriptural intimations and explicit claims, primarily on the part of Jesus, are correctly understood as applying principally to the apostles in what they wrote or said under the plenary guidance of the Spirit which the passages seem to imply. Yet, even in the case of the apostles, such authority does not extend, as I earlier explained, to anything and everything they said or wrote, or to any and every personal opinion they may have entertained. Instead, this authority extends only to what the apostles declared in the full and unique guidance of the Holy Spirit. The apostle Paul himself seems to have had a clear knowledge and awareness of this distinction, since, in one and the same letter (1 Corinthians) he claims, on the one hand, that the words in which he writes to them are words not taught him

2. My sincere opinion is that these passages apply primarily to the apostles.

a) But the authority entailed applies only to what the apostles spoke or wrote under the full guidance of the Spirit.
(1) The apostle Paul seems aware of a clear distinction between a clear word of the Lord and his own personal opinion.

by any sort of merely human wisdom, but rather taught by the Holy Spirit (1 Cor. 2:10, 13—not, I take it, in the sense of dictation, but in the sense of the Spirit's plenary guidance and direction). And, on the other hand, Paul acknowledges that, on a certain question about marriage, he has no definitive word of the Lord to deliver to them, but he nevertheless gives his opinion, which he distinguishes from the word of the Lord, while stating that he *thinks* that in giving it he is being generally guided by the Spirit of God (1 Cor. 7:10, 12, 40). Admittedly, these passages are viewed in different ways by equally scholarly interpreters. But, as a minimum, they are fairly interpretable as at least containing an admission by Paul that not all of his opinions are sanctioned by full divine inspiration. At the same time, however, since no other such admission occurs in Paul's New Testament letters, these passages indirectly imply that elsewhere in his letters Paul was speaking with full apostolic teaching authority.

I have, in fact, already intimated my basis for the opinion I have about passages which I take as supporting apostolic teaching authority in a revelatory sense. The passages imply an authority of such a nature that, when the condition of plenary guidance by the Holy Spirit is fulfilled, the resultant teaching or declaration, correctly understood, is incompatible with its fallibility in substance—while, on the other hand, the general guidance of the Spirit, extended to all believers indiscriminately, is quite compatible with this sort of fallibility in the substance of what believers in general offer as a teaching or opinion, even when they think sincerely that they are being guided by the Spirit of God. I therefore conclude that my general line of argument for the revelational authority of apostolic teaching, in the qualified sense I previously explained, stands on reasonably solid ground; and I also conclude, although perhaps with a somewhat lesser degree of plausibility, that part of the fulfillment and operation of this apostolic revelational authority is found in the New Testament books themselves, as illustrated by the Gospel and the First Epistle of John in my analysis. With these points at least plausibly settled, I finally conclude more generally that we can claim the support of Jesus, as God Incarnate, not only for the Old Testament Scriptures, but also, implicitly, anticipatively, and in principle, for those books of the New Testament which, although they did not exist as books during Jesus' earthly career, were yet to be written under the aegis of an apostolic teaching authority which Jesus himself promised would have a revelational status parallel to that of his own words and to that of the Old Testament as well. It now remains to consider, therefore, the claims made by the scriptural writers themselves regarding the revelational authority of their own writings and that of the rest of the biblical authors.

The Testimony of the Scriptural Writers

It is hardly necessary, in view of our conclusion about the perspective of Jesus about Old Testament revelational authority, to provide an elaborate account of the claim for such authority on the part of the

(2) At least Paul did not regard all of his own opinions as divinely authoritative.

b) The passages in question imply an authority in teaching substance which excludes fallibility, although such fallibility is not excluded by the Spirit's general guidance of all believers.

3. The argument for apostolic teaching authority:
a) is therefore reasonably solid,
b) as is its extension to the New Testament books.

C. I therefore conclude that the support of Jesus can be claimed for the extension of his own teaching authority to the New Testament books through the apostles.

Old Testament writers themselves. Yet even the most casual examination of these writings, with this issue in mind, discloses unquestionably that neither Jesus nor his contemporaries in Israel foisted upon the Old Testament writings any view of their indefectible divine authority that was foreign to those writings or their authors themselves. The creation account itself (Gen. 1 and 2) is replete with reports of what God is reputed to have said, both in connection with the project of creation and to the human beings who were the capstone of that creation on earth (Gen. 1:3f., 27f.; 2:1f.). This context of divine self-revelation to man seems henceforth to be normative for human experience. God is represented as having spoken, not only to Adam and Eve, but to their children (Gen. 4), to Noah (Gen. 6–9), to Abraham (Gen. 12f.), and so on as well to the other patriarchs of Israel, and finally, at great length, to Moses (Exodus 3 and throughout the rest of the Pentateuch). In the account of the last words of King David, author of many of the Psalms, he is recorded as having said that he spoke, on particular occasions, in an oracular fashion—that the Spirit of the Lord had spoken through him, and that God's word was on his tongue (2 Sam. 23:2). With the prophets, this sense of divine self-revelation is, if anything, even further extended. Thus Isaiah in his vision claims both that God spoke to him and that, through divine appointment, he himself spoke the word of the Lord (Isa. 1:1, 10; 6:8f.). Jeremiah presents his prophecies repeatedly as the word of the Lord coming to him (Jer. 1:4; 2:1; 7:1 *et passim*); nor is it essentially different with Ezekiel (1:3), or Daniel (2:28), or Hosea (1:1), or Joel (1:1), or any of the writing prophets right down to and including Malachi, the last of them (1:1). In general, the atmosphere pervading the Old Testament as a whole is an atmosphere of divine self-revelation which takes definitive form in the writings themselves. The discovery of the Book of the Law in the Temple during the reign of Josiah, king of Judah (2 Kings 22–23) and the spiritual revival that resulted from its reading as divinely authoritative provide a striking example of the sense, in Israel, of the revelational status of the word of God in written form.

If, in the light of that general characterization, we now turn to the references regarding Old Testament authority as contained in the New Testament writings, a single-minded and unexceptionable view of the divine authority of Scripture confronts us virtually everywhere in those later books. As a start, the New Testament texts, containing the testimony of Jesus himself to scriptural authority, are of course implicitly an indication of the respect which the writers themselves had for those same Scriptures. But, beyond that, the New Testament authors themselves regularly revert to the indefectible authority of the Old Testament in all that they themselves teach and declare. The general declarations on this point are so widely discussed as to require, for my purposes, no more than passing mention and limited comment. Thus the writer of Second Timothy (presumably Paul, but in any case representing his perspective) speaks of the sacred writings and then, collectively (all Scripture) or perhaps distributively (each and every Scripture), refers to the whole of this literature as God-breathed and

I. The Old Testament writers clearly claim revelational authority in the same sense in which Jesus ascribed it to them.

A. Sample indications:

1. The period of creation.

2. The patriarchs.

3. King David.

4. The prophets.

5. General atmosphere of divine self-revelation in written form.

B. The New Testament witness to Old Testament authority.

1. The testimony of Jesus as reflecting the view of the writers.

2. General declarations in the New Testament.

a) 2 Timothy 3:16–17

therefore profitable for teaching, for refuting error (hence, their status as the standard of truth), for correcting faults, and for disciplined instruction in righteousness (2 Tim. 3:16, 17). And the writer of Second Peter speaks of that more sure prophetic word (doubtless referring to the Old Testament as a whole) and then declares that it is the case for this entire prophetic Scripture that it did not originate from any private interpretation of a merely human sort—since in no case was this prophetic word brought by merely human will or inclination, but rather specially selected men from God spoke with decisive authority

as a result of being carried along themselves by the Holy Spirit (2 Peter 1:19–21). A higher view of scriptural authority than that expressed in these texts is scarcely imaginable; and the upshot of it all is that the authority of Scripture, correctly understood, is precisely the authority of God himself. And it is perhaps equally significant that

these same writers refer to other books of the New Testament itself as falling in the category of "Scripture," with all the authority that, as a quasi-technical term, this title implies. The writer of the first letter to Timothy cites scriptural authority to support a point of teaching, by using the introductory phrase, "For the Scripture says . . . " (1 Tim. 5:18); and then he proceeds to quote, first a passage from the Old Testament Book of Deuteronomy (25:4)— which, as part of the Pentateuch, was regarded as possessing the very highest divine authority—and then a passage from the Gospel of Luke (10:7). The writer of Second Peter, in turn, refers to certain persons whom he regards as having misinterpreted some difficult passages in the letters of the apostle Paul and then he states that these individuals twist and pervert these passages as they also do "the other Scriptures" (2 Peter 3:16). Both writers make it clear therefore that they routinely apply the title "Scripture" not only to the books of the Old Testament, but also to the growing body of writings which would ultimately become the New Testament. And if that is the case, then it is reasonable to suppose that, in those previously mentioned didactic passages about the divine authority of Scripture, they also included the books in that growing aggregate as parallel in revelational status to the Old Testament itself.

But the case for Old Testament authority, in the minds of New Testament writers, is inadequately represented if it is confined to such explicit declarations as we have considered. Throughout the New Testament as a whole, there is a complex interweaving of incidental

intimations of Old Testament authority—a phenomenon so pervasive that it illustrates how thoroughly the deference to that authority pervaded the whole mind-set of these writers. A detailed analysis of these phenomena is out of the question here, and I therefore content myself with a few exemplary illustrations. Thus the writer of Acts represents Peter as referring to the Scripture which the Holy Spirit spoke previously through the mouth of David (Acts 1:16); and the writer of Matthew repeatedly refers to the fulfillment of this or that Old Testament passage which he describes as spoken by the Lord through the writer, or even simply as spoken through the writer with the reference to divine action clearly implied (Matt. 1:22; 2:5, 17; 3:3; 4:14; 12:17;

13:35; 21:4; 27:9). In a number of New Testament passages, the narrative portions of the Old Testament are represented as spoken by God, when, in the original context, no direct word from God is mentioned (for example, Heb. 1:6–9; Deut. 32:43 LXX; Ps. 97:7; 104:4; 45:6–7)—and conversely, Scripture itself is personified and represented as speaking when, in the original context, God is referred to as the speaker (Rom. 9:17; Exod. 9:16; Gal. 3:8; Gen. 12:3; 18:18). The evident implication of both of these usages is that "Scripture says" and "God says" are interchangeable in the minds of the writers, so that for them any portion of Scripture, correctly understood, had the full authority of God himself. Again, there is the hanging of a decisive argument of Paul on the sheer grammatical number of a noun in the Old Testament text (Gal. 3:16)—an indication that Paul viewed the authority of the Old Testament as extending even to the form of the words. It is hardly necessary to give specific references for the numerous texts in which Old Testament authority is cited with the simple phrases: "Scripture says," "It says," or simply "It stands written." If we parallel this reference formula with the repeated habit of New Testament writers in falling virtually incidentally into the phraseology of the Old Testament, even when they are not explicitly citing it (a habit which any person can confirm for himself just by leafing casually through a Greek New Testament in which Old Testament quotations and allusions are printed in boldface type), we may be able to get a keen sense of the degree to which the minds of the New Testament writers were utterly pervaded by God's Old Testament Word. All this, and much beside, has been so thoroughly investigated by biblical scholars that I have no hesitation in claiming that, as in the case of Jesus, so in the case of the biblical writers, we confront the same high view of the indefectible authority of the Old Testament Scriptures, properly interpreted, as divine revelation. And this conclusion is, after all, hardly surprising when we are dealing with writers who, for the most part, were brought up in the theological climate of Jewish religious life in the first century. When we add to that circumstance the fact that they acknowledged as God Incarnate, as Lord and Savior, one who himself held as well the same view of Scripture, we should obviously expect no less of the New Testament writers themselves. And since they saw both the teaching of Jesus and the extension of it in apostolic authority as on a revelational par with the Old Testament as Scripture—a teaching and extension which, in general, they purported to embody in their own writing—it will be no more startling if we find that those New Testament writers claimed analogous revelational status for what they themselves wrote under the plenary guidance of the Holy Spirit.

And this is precisely what we find to be the case—not in the sense of a labored claim constantly and explicitly reiterated, indeed; but in the sense that the divine authority of the New Testament writings is extensively intimated by the writers themselves, and in the sense that the same authority is explicitly claimed whenever that issue was pertinent in any particular context of these writings. The apostle Paul, for example, makes frequent reference to his apostolic authority and the

4. The same high view, of the indefectible authority of the Old Testament, pervades the New Testament.

a) This is not surprising in view of Jesus' own testimony.

b) An analogous revelational claim is extended to the New Testament writings.

II. The authority of the New Testament books.
A. Specific intimations.

1. The Apostle Paul.

resultant revelational status of what he wrote in his letters, a status which, as I have indicated, is already acknowledged in the New Testament itself by the writer of Second Peter. Thus, Paul characteristically begins his letters with such a designation of his apostolic authority (Rom. 1:1,5; 1 Cor. 1:1; 2 Cor. 1:1; Gal. 1:1, and so on). In the last cited opening of his letter to the Galatians, Paul explicitly ascribes his apostleship to Jesus Christ and God the Father, and denies that his authority as such either emanated from or through any merely human source. When, in that same opening context, he claims such authority for his declaration of the content of the gospel of Christ that he pronounces a curse on any who would proclaim a different gospel—even on himself or a heavenly angel if either claimed any change in that gospel—his claim to revelational teaching authority is put in the strongest terms, a claim that would be absurd on any other terms (Gal. 1:8, 9). He then proceeds to explain that he received his understanding of the gospel by and through direct revelation from Jesus Christ (1:12), so that, in his teaching, God was revealing His Son Jesus through Paul—an explanation which further strengthens his revelational claim. In his first letter to the Corinthians, Paul takes up an analogous claim. After advising the Corinthian believers that his message and preaching among them was not based on any merely human wisdom but rather came through an open demonstration of God's Spirit and power, he explicitly tells them that the wisdom which he speaks (present tense—so as to include his word in this letter—1 Cor. 2:6f.) has been disclosed to him by the revelation of God's Spirit, so that its very words are words that result from the teaching of the Holy Spirit in contrast to any words that might have been taught by any human wisdom alone (1 Cor. 2:7–13). Paul's claim to revelational authority for his apostolic position and teaching is clear enough in all this. But we are not to conclude that he had some degree of authority that the other apostles lacked, since he speaks of the company of believers as a building built upon the foundation of the apostles and prophets, and having Jesus the Messiah himself as the chief capstone which holds the whole building together (Eph. 2:19–22)—so that there Paul sees himself as merely one of those apostles who parallel the revelational authority of the Old Testament prophets, yet in complete subordination to the Headship of Jesus. In this sense, the authority which Paul claims for himself as a divinely appointed apostle he also claims in principle for the apostolic office in general. And he climaxes this point in the same context by again referring explicitly to God's revelation of the gospel to him personally (a revelational status which he specifically claims for what he writes—Eph. 3:3, 4), and then by extending this revelational authority to God's holy apostles and prophets in general (Eph. 3:5).

This extension of apostolic authority is evident elsewhere in the New Testament, even if we cannot cull out explicit teaching on the subject from every single book. The letters attributed to Peter also begin with the apostolic designation (1 Peter 1:1; 2 Peter 1:1). And in the first of these letters the writer proceeds to claim that it was that

2. The Epistles of Peter.

same Spirit of Christ, who spoke through the Old Testament prophets and who now speaks, with parallel revelational authority, through those who proclaim the gospel of Jesus (1 Peter 1:10–12)—a word which the writer also identifies as the word of the Lord mentioned by the prophet Isaiah (1 Peter 1:23–25; Isa. 40:8). Again, in the second letter, the author claims that, in making known to believers the power and coming of the Lord Jesus Christ, he did not do so as a result of tracing out sophisticated legends, but rather spoke as an eyewitness of the majesty of Jesus and God the Father's word to Jesus on the mount of transfiguration (2 Peter 1:16–18). And when, continuing in the first person plural (thus referring to apostles in general), he claims to possess a well-established prophetic word on the basis of his status as an eyewitness, it is wholly reasonable to suppose that he refers, not merely to the Old Testament revelation, but perhaps even more specifically to the word which he and the other apostles authoritatively proclaimed (2 Peter 1:19). That he moves directly to the well-known declaration about scriptural authority (1:20, 21) would therefore indicate how in his mind the categories of the apostolic eyewitness, the prophetic word, and the Scripture had already assumed the conjunctive status of a single and inclusive revelational authority. And it is virtually the same thought that dominates his mind when in a later context he urges believers to remember decisively as authoritative the words that had been spoken previously by the holy prophets and by the command of the apostles of their Lord and Savior (2 Peter 3:2).

I have already indicated, in an earlier context, the strain of implied apostolic authority in the Gospel and First Epistle of John, so that it is not necessary to repeat that analysis here. But if we turn to the Apocalypse (the Book of Revelation)—whether or not we regard it as part of the Johannine literary corpus—the claim to the revelational authority of what is written is evident on the face of the entire writing. Here the writer, John, opens his book by identifying what he writes as a revelation from Jesus Christ who in turn received it from God (the Father) and then sent and expressed it by means of signs to his servant John, whose testimony about the things he saw therefore constitutes the word of God and the testimony of Jesus Christ (Rev. 1:1–3). And John then repeatedly refers to his commission from the Lord Jesus to write with revelational authority (1:11, 17; 2:1, 8, 12, 18; 3:1, 7, 14; 21:5), not to mention his frequent allusion to the status of what he writes as a divinely disclosed vision (4:1; 5:1, 11; 5:1, 5, 8; 7:1; *et passim*). Again, at the conclusion of the book, the words themselves are said to be faithful and true as what God has thus sent through his angel to show decisively to his servants (22:6, 7; cf. 22:16). So strong is the writer's claim of revelational authority that he pronounces a curse on any one who either adds to, or subtracts from, the words that are written in the book (22:18, 19).

Some mention may appropriately be made of other New Testament writings as well. Luke opens both his Gospel and his account of the Acts of the Apostles with formal prefaces, in the first of which he makes reference to things most fully believed among Christians, be-

3. Gospel and First Epistle of John.

4. The Apocalypse.

5. Luke.

cause they were transmitted to them by those who were original
eyewitnesses of Jesus and became servants of the word of God—to
which Luke adds that his own account will enable his immediate and
doubtless representative reader (Theophilus) to know the certainty
that attaches to the words in which that reader has been instructed in
the gospel of Christ (Luke 1:1–4). In the preface to Acts, Luke refers to
his previous treatise as an authoritative account of what Jesus *began*
to do and teach; and then he refers to the commandment which Jesus
gave to the apostles through the Holy Spirit—apostles whom Jesus
charged to *continue* his task of authoritative teaching and action (Acts
1:1–3,8), an account of which Luke himself here intends to initiate (cf.
Acts 2:42). I have already referred to the statements in Matthew in
which Jesus is represented as implying and initiating special apostolic
teaching authority; and since Matthew and Luke draw heavily, in their
account, on the material in Mark, it is plausible to assume that they
regarded that source as invested with precisely such authority. Jude
also, after representing his own book as an apologetic for the defense
of the content of Christian belief as once and for all having been
delivered to the saints (v. 3), clearly adverts to the basis of that definitive form of faith when he admonishes his readers to remember
decisively the words that had been previously spoken by the apostles
of the Lord Jesus Christ (v. 17). And when James, further, urges his
readers to receive the implanted word of God which is able to save
their souls, and then commands them to be doers of that word and
not hearers only, it would be odd not to suppose that he included his
own instruction to them as a part of that Divine Word to which they
were to submit (James 1:21–25). The writer of Hebrews, finally, opens
his treatise by referring to God's diverse and multiple revelation to the
fathers (presumably the Old Testament patriarchs who represent Israel in general) in the prophets—a revelation which he then parallels
with God's decisive revelation in His Son Jesus (Heb. 1:1–4). This same
revelational theme is continued in a later context (Heb. 2:1–4) in which
the writer again reiterates the comparison between the Old Testament
word of God, on the one hand, and the new word which took its
inception in being spoken by the Lord (Jesus)—to which the writer
adds that this word was confirmed to us by those who heard Jesus'
teaching, a confirmation supported by signs, wonders, and various
mighty acts, wrought by God himself, along with specific distributions
of the Holy Spirit. This confirmation is clearly that which occurred
through the teachings of the apostles and the signs God performed
through them, since it is precisely the apostles who heard Jesus in this
virtually official capacity as witnesses. After an extended discussion of
this new revelation in Jesus, whom the writer designates as the Apostle
and High Priest of our confession (an established and authoritative
form of declaration) (Heb. 3:1), our author summarily refers to that
disclosure as the word or logos (Heb. 5:11; 6:1)—a term which suggests, as did the term *confession*, an established and authoritative
spoken or even written form of expression; and the same concept is
expressed by a synonymous term in the same context (6:5), a term

6. Jude.

7. James.

8. Hebrews.

which identifies this word, concerning Jesus and his salvation, with the spoken pronouncement of God. I take all this to refer in general to the relatively fixed form of apostolic teaching which clearly has revelational status. But since it is an account of this very revelation in Jesus that the author has himself expressed in writing in the earlier chapters, I see it as wholly reasonable to take this reference to God's word as applying to the writer's own account as itself an expression and extension of that same apostolic teaching with precisely the same revelational status which that designation implies.

In all that I have said regarding the complex revelational claims in the New Testament—whether those claims are made by Jesus or the writers themselves, and whether they refer to the Old Testament or to that growing aggregate of acknowledged literature that finally became the New Testament—I have, of course, not even attempted to give anything even approaching an exhaustive analysis of what is there to be discussed. But I have said enough to point the way to some plausible general conclusions as a basis for further argument. It is evident enough that both Jesus and the New Testament writers fully accepted the claim of the Old Testament writers themselves, in general and in specific claims, to the effect that those writings constituted, as correctly interpreted, an indefectibly authoritative revelation of God. It is all but equally evident that Jesus conferred on his disciples, and more especially the apostles, a teaching authority which both he and they envisioned as enjoying parallel revelational status with the Old Testament itself. And it is even plausible to suppose that Jesus anticipatively intimated that this revelational teaching authority would extend to the written form of its expression in books written under the aegis of the apostles. It is, furthermore, hardly disputable that the New Testament writers frequently recognized that apostolic teaching authority in both oral and written form. We may add to this the well-supported thesis that the New Testament writers characteristically claimed the parallel revelational status of their own writings. Again, in at least two instances (1 Tim., 2 Peter) New Testament writers referred to other writings of the New Testament itself as having the technical status of authoritative Scripture, even though the collection of New Testament books was not completed, much less finalized, at the time.

In part, I have already argued the central conclusion that follows from all this: If Jesus was himself God Incarnate, and if he explicitly argued the indefectible authority of the Old Testament, while as explicitly conferring revelational teaching authority on his apostles—and at the same time intimating the extension of this authority to its written expression—then it should follow that for all those who accept the Incarnation claim as itself true, there is a parallel obligation to acknowledge Jesus' perspective on what I will now designate generally and inclusively as Scripture (including both the Old and New Testaments) as correct in both substance and principle. If we then go on to acknowledge the explicit revelation claims of the New Testament writers, both about those writings themselves and about apostolic teaching authority—acknowledge them, that is, as equally correct claims—we

B. General conclusions regarding the New Testament witness.
1. Specific results.

2. The central conclusion:
a) Jesus' perspective on Scripture extends to both Testaments and implies an obligation to acceptance.

b) The revelational claim of the New Testament writers themselves, as an extension of Jesus' claim, constitutes a parallel obligation.

c) This whole argument, while not a demonstration, is a plausible basis for reasonable commitment.

C. A possible critical objection: that the whole New Testament revelation claim was either a self-deception or a fraud.

1. But there is no evidence of the implied mental disorder or moral perversion.

2. The balanced insight and precision of the New Testament writers simply belies any charge of mental disorder.

a) To regard the revelation claim itself as evidence of mental imbalance, would be sheer question-begging.

will only be recognizing in more determinate form what is already anticipatively intimated by Jesus himself, so that we are as bound to their claim as we have already seen ourselves to be bound to his. We can, of course, boggle at this conclusion. It is certainly not logically inevitable or inescapable, and the elements of the case for it are loosely conjoined in a fashion that does not exhibit the rigorous precision of an axiomatically defined formal logical system. Yet it would be a clear misconception to suppose that any such precision is even in principle achievable in the case of such intricate historical issues. What we have here instead is an extended fabric of developing plausibility, through the whole of which there runs an unbroken thread of reasonableness characterized by a degree of probability high enough to justify rational commitment on the part of any seriously reflective person. We could, of course, resurrect, in the case of the apostles and the New Testament writers, charges not unlike those that critics have brought against Jesus himself—charges to the effect that the whole apostolic community, in conjunction with the human instruments of its written expression, was either the victim of a contagious self-deception that could only be the product of profound mental disorder, or else was surreptitiously engaged in the perpetration of an enormous religious fraud that could spring only from the deepest moral perversion. Since the apostles and New Testament writers (the two classes overlap, of course) were, in themselves as individuals, fallible and even corruptible human beings and invested with all the implied frailties, these hypothetical charges are somewhat less implausible in their case than we have seen them to be in the case of Jesus himself. Yet the charges are, for all that, nevertheless highly implausible. Aside from the already mentioned fact that these men are merely envisioning themselves as the instruments of a revelational authority that Jesus himself conferred, there is no evidence, in their case, of either the mental disorder or the moral perversion that would be required to support the charge. The supposition that this sort of mental disorder was disseminated over such a variety of persons as represented by the New Testament authors, yet with the same religious result (or delusion, as a critic might say), is simply unbelievable on the face of it, especially when we find no plausible evidence of mental imbalance in the writings themselves. Quite the contrary, in fact: On the whole, the New Testament writers exhibit such a balanced insight into human nature, and such a profound and developed understanding of the person of Jesus the Messiah and his redemptive vocation, and even such a developed sensitivity to the careful statement of facts (at least as judged by the standards of their cultural milieu), that there is simply no indication that there is in their case even a hint of the sort of unbalanced judgment or distorted perspective that would inevitably accompany such a massive mental disorder. Of course, if one supposes at the outset that a revelation claim on the part of any individual is *ipso facto* a conclusive indication of his mental dysfunction, there is then no issue to discuss. But since the plausibility or otherwise of such a revelation claim is precisely the issue at stake in this discussion, such a supposition would be sheer prejudicial question-begging of the most objectionable sort, especially since our previous analysis has rendered the general concept of divine revelation fully reasonable in principle. It is sometimes said that Paul's experience of Jesus on the Damascus road has the earmarks of an epileptic seizure; but this suggestion, even if true, is no necessary indication of mental imbalance, nor does it in any sense detract from the revelational character of the experience. Or it is sometimes claimed that the visionary character of the imagery in the Apocalypse is itself an expression of the fanciful and uncontrolled imagination of a mentally disturbed person. But this is to dismiss by initial assumption the plausibility of a genuinely revelational vision, which again is the very point at issue here—so that once more the question is being begged at the outset. On the whole, then, the hypothesis of mental disorder, as an explanation of the revelation claim of the New Testament writers, is a highly implausible claim.

b) Nor do Paul and the writer of the Apocalypse provide any such evidence.

There is, if anything, less basis for the charge of deliberate deception as based in moral perversion. As with Jesus, so with the apostles and New Testament writers: Not only is there no independent evidence of this sort of hypocrisy in the writings, but the authors themselves everywhere held up the highest sort of moral standards, a standard which they interpreted to be as applicable to themselves as to the readers they addressed. Furthermore, these men had their very lives and social reputations at stake in both their commitment to Jesus as Lord and their claim to be the recipients of the sort of divine authority and revelational insight that Jesus promised them. To suppose that they merely posed, with respect to either the commitment or the claim, when they had consciously collaborated in the knowledge that both were spurious, is simply incompatible with the sacrifice and risk that all this entailed for them. Such charlatanry, in any case, would be impossible to disguise on the part of such an extended group of persons, all of whom were, throughout their careers as religious teachers, more or less continuously exposed to a varied and widespread public scrutiny. Such a ghastly truce of deception would almost certainly have been detected, and even more certainly exposed. Doubtless there has been many an Elmer Gantry (a morally corrupted clergyman in one of Sinclair Lewis's novels) in the history of religion and even of Christianity; but then we know, on the whole, who the most important among them were. Furthermore, by the very nature of the case, few, if any, of them kept that secret entirely to themselves. For all these reasons, it is scarcely reasonable to challenge either the genuineness or the sincerity of the New Testament writers. There is no real shadow of perverse deception here—these men really believed in Jesus as God Incarnate, and they really believed that they were the recipients of Jesus' promised revelational authority. If that is true, and if this genuineness and sincerity cannot be charged to any mentally disturbed state of mind which the New Testament writers purportedly shared, then—given the theistic, incarnational, and revelational framework in which we are shaping our discernment here—it is wholly reasonable to conclude that the New Testament writers expressed that

3. There is still less evidence of moral perversion and sham.

a) The high moral standard of the writers.

b) The personal risk of their commitment and claim.

c) Such deception would have been exposed.

d) Hence, the genuiness and sincerity of the New Testament writers cannot be seriously questioned.
4. It may be plausibly concluded that the New Testament revelation claim was made because the writers believed it to be true as the most adequate explanation of their own total experience.

revelational claim, which we find expressed in their writings, because they knew through their own receptive experience of divine direction, and through the impact of Jesus' own revelational claim upon them, that their own claim to that effect was in fact true, as the most fully plausible account of their own total experience and reflective thought about this issue. And if that is the case, then, even though we cannot under the circumstances have the same direct basis for the vindication of that claim that they themselves in that event possessed, the acceptance of the truth of that revelational claim will also be the most fully adequate and coherent account of our own experience and reflection

D. In general conclusion, the Scriptures of both Testaments, rightly interpreted, constitute an indefectibly authoritative divine self-revelation.

about this same question. I therefore conclude that the Scriptures of both the Old and New Testaments, correctly understood in their total context, constitute an indefectibly authoritative divine self-revelation of God. To conclude more, at this juncture, than this admittedly general conclusion would doubtless be to overstate the case; but to conclude less, at this same crossroad of thought, would be to draw back unnecessarily from the most comprehensively adequate and rationally coherent account of the pertinent grounds for thought on this difficult and complex question.

III. But this general conclusion leaves much that is so far unsettled.

Still, it is of the utmost importance to delineate carefully at this point in our argument just what in general is—and what in particular is not—settled by this conclusion. What is settled, at least provisionally and with high probability, is the general and plenary revelational authority and truth of the biblical writings as a collective and varied, developing, and extended divine self-disclosure. On the other hand, there is much that our conclusion does not settle, and perhaps even more that, for my purposes, it need not settle. For one thing, the

A. The precise literary limits of the two Testaments are as yet undetermined.
1. The developing aggregate of written Scriptures for both Testaments was recognized as divinely authoritative long before any final canonical list was fixed historically.

literary limits of neither Testament are as yet clearly settled for us. I have already indicated that, at a time when the New Testament was not itself complete in its traditionally accepted literary sense, writers of certain New Testament books were referring to still other New Testament books as inspired Scripture. For those writers at least, the literary limits of the new written revelation, which expressed in that form the apostolic teaching authority conferred by Jesus, were still open in the sense that no final list of such books either existed or was universally acknowledged. No doubt a similar situation had characterized the accumulation of written revelation in Old Testament times. Certainly and obviously, the people of God did not need to wait for some formalized canonical list, however determined, in order to recognize a developing core of written revelation in the Books of the Law or the Prophets, or even in the so-called Writings. Even if we accept the traditional date for the finalization of the Old Testament canon (fifth century B.C.), during most of the period in which written revelation was recognized as divinely authoritative among the people of God (I make no attempt at a precise definition of that category), no such final and universally accepted canonical determination had been made. The core and central thrust of written revelation were evidently clear enough, but the precise limits defining and identifying the books included in that category were indeterminate in any official religious sense—the whole was a developing aggregate. If, indeed, we may assume that the final canonization of the Old Testament literature was primarily, although perhaps not exclusively, a Jewish matter, then there is, according to some scholars, a plausible basis for supposing that—even after the traditional date of final canonization—controversy continued among the religious leaders of the Jews concerning just which books were to make up the total canonical collection. Apparently this question was settled with a considerable degree of finality by around 400 B.C. for the adherents of orthodox Judaism in Palestine. But among the Jews in the Dispersion, especially in Alexandria (Egypt), it appears to have been a different question, since the so-called Septuagint translation of the Old Testament into Greek appears to have contained certain writings (called apocryphal) which were excluded from the Palestinian Hebrew Bible, although this point is not certain since all extant copies of the LXX (as the Septuagint was called) are of much later Christian origin. What is reasonably evident is that controversy concerning the canon continued well into the Christian era, and that this controversy did not come to any definitive close until about the end of the first century A.D., when, at a council in Jamnia, Jewish scholars settled on the Hebrew Bible as containing either twenty-four or twenty-two books (corresponding to the differently arranged thirty-nine books in most Protestant Bibles of the last century and a half)—although even this did not end all controversy among the Jews. It is important to note as well that a considerable number of the Old Testament apocryphal books were eventually accepted as canonical by numerous early Christian fathers, and these books are still acknowledged by Roman Catholic doctrine.

The details of all this are not important for my purposes here; but what this controversy illustrates is that, even in the period in which both Jesus and New Testament writers were appealing to the indefectible authority of the Old Testament, the precise limits of that collection had still not been settled with finality. And if that is the case, then two important points emerge: First, that the scope of written revelation that the New Testament writers adverted to as authoritative, although clear enough in its main content, was still indeterminate at the fringes; and second, also more significantly as I see it, the case for the revelational authority of the Old Testament in general does not depend in any decisive way on the plausibility of any final canonical list of books as defining the precise literary limits of that authority. This second point holds also for the New Testament as well. The core of its revelational authority was acknowledged and appealed to virtually from the time that any of these written expressions occurred under the aegis of the apostolic teaching authority. The fact that controversy concerning certain books continued well into the Christian era, before universal unanimity defining its precise literary limits was achieved for all practical purposes, does not call that revelational core into any serious question, nor does it either confuse or adversely affect the general plausibility of the case for the revelation claim of the New Testament

a) Controversy concerning the Old Testament canon continued even into the Christian era.

b) The issue was made more complex by the apocryphal books of the Old Testament, about which controversy among Christians continues to the present.

2. Hence, the witness of Jesus and the New Testament writers to the Old Testament did not presuppose that the canonical limits were precise, so that it is not essential to the case for its revelational authority that these limits be precisely fixed.
3. This point applies, with some qualification, to the New Testament as well;

so that for both Testaments the precise fixing of canonical limits, although important, is not essential to the case for revelational authority.

as a whole. This does not mean that the question of canonicity, for either the Old Testament or the New Testament, is not important; it merely means that the settlement of it is not decisive for the issue at stake concerning the revelational authority of the Hebrew-Christian Bible. As an individual Christian believer, I have, of course, certain definite convictions about the Old Testament apocryphal writings; but as a philosophical apologist for the Christian revelation claim as a whole, and since I intend this apologetic to be as Catholic as it is Protestant and as Protestant as it is Catholic, I prefer to pass by this issue and regard it as a manageable family disagreement which does not significantly affect my case, inasmuch as the question of biblical authority in general and the question of canonicity are simply not identical issues. Scarcely a dozen miles from the place where I am writing these words, there lies situated southern Indiana's beautiful but sprawled-out Lake Monroe. On the map which attempts to specify with precision the shoreline of that man-made body of water, the general identification of the lake is clear enough on the whole; but there are clearly identifiable sections of that precisely defined entity which, when you drive by them in an automobile, are observably open fields and even stands of tree clumps. This does not mean that Lake Monroe cannot, as a whole, be observably identified, of course; but it does mean that its exact shoreline is imprecise. Analogously, the indeterminate fringes of canonicity do not mean that God's written revelation cannot be identified as a whole either; but it does mean that, in a sense and during much of the period in which its authority was clearly in place, the perimeters of that revelation were (and perhaps even remain) indeterminate.

But there is still much more that is not settled by our previous general conclusion concerning the indefectible authority of the biblical revelation. From a sophisticated (and in my view, wholly reasonable) theological point of view, the quality of indefectible authority applies only to the original autographs of these writings, and not to any subsequent transcribed copies, oral recitations from memory, or translations into other languages or dialects—into any or all of which inadvertent copyist errors and even interpretive glosses might easily creep. But, in fact, of course, for neither the Old Testament nor the New Testament, do we have any original autographs. Instead, we have some copy fragments which go back in some few instances to within a century or a few decades of the hypothecated date of the original; we have larger sections removed by several centuries from those same originals and complete texts which in certain cases, postdate the originals by upwards of a thousand years or more. As a result of the prolific copying of these writings, we have, in many cases, entire families of manuscripts (all copies, of course), which are distinguished from each other by peculiar and distinctive textual variants of one kind or another. Rather full information about all this is all but universally available in theological and literary libraries and collections; and it is entirely outside my purpose to provide any detailed discussion or

4. The question of precise canonical limits may therefore be left open for my apologetic purposes.

a) God's written revelation can thus be identified as a whole.

b) But its exact perimeters are perhaps indeterminate.
B. The problem of original autographs.
1. The revelation claim applies primarily to the autographs, and must be qualified for all subsequent copies and translations.

a) But we have no original autographs of Scripture books, but only fragments and copies variously classified.

analysis of it. Yet these general facts have clear implications for what is of significant concern for my argument.

It has often been suggested by critics that, since we do not have the original autographs, the thesis of the indefectible authority of those writings is an empty and inconsequential thesis. But I think that this suggestion is clearly misconstrued along two lines: First, the study of so-called lower or textual criticism has, in virtually universal scholarly opinion and through enormous scholarly effort, so extensively and minutely compared extant copies of the biblical writings that our present texts of both the Old and New Testaments (and even of the LXX—which was, as noted, itself a translation), as available in scholarly editions, are judged to be so close an approximation to the original writings that the possible differences are negligible for all practical purposes. As a result, we need be gripped by no paralyzing fear to the effect that currently available Hebrew and Greek texts are filled with extensive deviations from the originals. We can be reasonably confident that no matter of substance would be significantly affected by whatever differences may possibly remain. Yet there is another reason why a claim about the autographs is neither empty nor inconsequential. Since, as my own previous argument indicates, our present texts, fairly interpreted, make the claim of indefectible revelational authority—an authoirty that is ascribed ultimately to the guidance and direction of the Spirit of God—and since God, by his nature as omniscient, cannot conceivably be characterized by any defect of understanding or insight, then the very quality of the divine personal character itself is presumably at stake in a revelational claim for writings that, although inscribed by human authors, were nevertheless produced, according to that claim itself, by plenary and unexceptionable divine guidance. Hence, even though the original autographs of Scripture may be forever lost to our grasp, the claim of their indefectible authority is of high significance.

On the other hand, the fact that we do not have the original autographs of Scripture is itself significant from another point of view. It means that, as in the case on canonicity, here too and from a somewhat different perspective, we must work with a preserved form of revelation which, although determinate enough on the whole, is once again surrounded by a fringe of imprecision, indeterminacy, and approximation, since we cannot claim that our text does anything more than exhibit a highly probable degree of correspondence to the original. Yet here too, as in the case of canonicity, we can proceed with a confidence that we can clearly identify revelational content on the whole, even if we cannot entirely remove the dust of textual imprecision from its surface. This acknowledgment will also help us to solve, in principle at least, another problem that has been a perplexity to careful students of the biblical writings.

We may suppose that the imprecision of textual copies was much more characteristic of earlier historical epochs, when the controls of high scholarly standards were far less defined and far less realizable than they seem to be at present. And we may assume with even

b) Yet the claim for the autographs is important:

(1) because critically reconstructed texts are generally recognized as very close approximations to the original texts, so that no substantial content is in serious question;

(2) because the character of God is at stake in the claim for the autographs.

2. The absence of the autographs means that here too (as with the canon) the preserved form of revelation, although determinate as a whole, has a fringe of indeterminacy.

a) Such textual variations have a bearing on the differences between the Septuagint translation and our best Hebrew texts of the Old Testament.

greater confidence that a preserved copy of some translation, of what is itself already a copy of some earlier writing in a different language, will therefore be doubly exposed to the intrusion of copyist errors, interpretive glosses, and deliberate emendations for whatever reasons. It should not surprise us to learn therefore that even the best text of the LXX (Septuagint—a translation of the Hebrew Bible into Greek, made about two and a half centuries before the time of Christ) exhibits numerous deviations of meaning and translated language from the best text of the Hebrew Bible as we possess it, or even in any of its historically identifiable forms in the past. All this would hardly consti-

(1) New Testament writers are familiar with the Septuagint (especially Paul) and frequently use it in their citations and allusions.

tute a problem if it were not for the fact that all New Testament writers display a familiarity with the LXX, in whatever recension of its text was available to them at the time—and some of them (especially Paul) appeal primarily to this Greek translation in making allusions, citations, or even arguments. This whole issue is exceedingly complicated; but it has been estimated by certain scholars that about 80 percent of the citations and allusions to the Old Testament in the New Testament as a whole are taken from the LXX with only minor variants. This is hardly surprising under the circumstances, since the vast majority of converts to Christianity, in the decades of the first century, during which the New Testament books were written, were Greek-speaking individuals for whom the Hebrew text would on the whole be unusable. And since the LXX posed no linguistic barrier and was far more accessible to the readers of these writings, it was wholly plausible, at least in general, to appeal to its authority. It is not surpris-

(2) These writers sometimes cite the LXX, even when it deviates from what we judge the Hebrew text to have been.

ing either, in this light, that the New Testament writers, as far as our knowledge of all these related texts is concerned, sometimes cite the LXX, even when that translation represents a deviation from what we plausibly judge to have been the reading of the available Hebrew text at the time. Sometimes, indeed, the writer appears to improve the text of the LXX through a use of the Hebrew text; and sometimes other Greek translations of certain Old Testament books appear to be cited

(3) This phenomenon appears to put a strain on the case for the indefectible authority of the books in question.

instead of the LXX. Now, if we assume that the Hebrew text available at the time was in fact closer to the original of which it would presumably be an historically distant copy (a copy of a copy of a copy . . . and so on), it would appear to follow that the citation of the LXX, when it differed with the hypothecated Hebrew original (presumably as unavailable to the New Testament writers as it is to ourselves), would put a strain on our sense of the indefectible authority of the New Testament book in which the citation occurs. For my purposes, it is scarcely

(4) Some examples of this phenomenon.

necessary to map out full details about this problem, but it might be helpful to supply some paradigm examples of the crucial difficulty. In his speech to the believers at the Jerusalem Council, James is repesented by Luke (Acts 15:17) as quoting or citing a passage from the prophet Amos (9:11, 12)—but it is clear that James (or perhaps Luke) is following the LXX where it differs from the posited Hebrew original, which presumably reads "that they may possess the remnant of Edom," while the LXX seems to have read "that the rest of men may seek the Lord." However the variation of the texts is to be explained (possibly as a misreading of two Hebrew words in making the Greek translation), the problem still remains for James's citation (or Luke's). Again, in Ephesians (4:26) Paul quotes the text of LXX, for Psalm 4:4, as "Go on being angry and do not continue to sin," where the Hebrew text appears to have read, "Tremble, and do not sin." Finally, the writer of Hebrews cites Psalm 40:6 from LXX as ". . . a body you did prepare for me," while the Hebrew text appears to read, ". . . my ears you have pierced" (Heb. 10:5). There are, of course, other analogous examples of this same general phenomenon.

In response to this difficulty for our concept of biblical authority, it is important at the outset not to exaggerate the scope or the magnitude of this sort of difficulty, as if the New Testament itself were as a whole virtually bulging with quotations from the LXX which misconstrued the Hebrew text, or even as if the LXX itself were in general a pervasively and substantially serious distortion of the Hebrew from which it was translated. On the contrary, I think it fair to say that neither of these conditional clauses is fulfilled in fact (although the second is of little or no concern to my argument), and that no question of significant substance is adversely affected in any serious way by those LXX passages (cited in the New Testament) which appear to differ from the Hebrew original. The difficulty, so far as it is genuine, is considerably alleviated if we consider the fact that we are not finally certain how many textual emendations (copyist mistakes, interpretive glosses, deliberate alterations) have crept into any of the three texts involved (the New Testament, the LXX, the Hebrew original of the Old Testament), so that our conclusions must be tentative at best. Again, a given LXX citation in the New Testament, even where it differs verbatim from what we judge to have been the Hebrew text, often represents a plausible paraphrase or interpretation of the original and therefore constitutes no genuine problem. That is quite possibly the case in the Hebrews (10:5) passage, since the reference to piercing is an allusion to the custom of pinning a slave to his master's doorpost with an awl as a symbol of the slave's subjection, so that the LXX speaks interpretively of the body whose subjection is symbolized by the piercing of the ear. This appears to be the case as well with Paul's LXX citation of Psalm 4:4, since trembling is an observable symptom of the anger about which the apostle gives his exhortation. It is also the case that many of the citations in question are merely allusions which introduce LXX phraseology into the expression of the New Testament writer—a wholly understandable phenomenon in the case of writers whose minds were doubtless permeated by the language of the LXX, so that this phenomenon manifested itself in the expression of their own thoughts. As for the quotation ascribed to James in Acts 15 by Luke, finally, we must not assume that the divine guidance of Luke in writing his account guarantees anything more than the substantial accuracy of what must have been a paraphrase and precis of James's actual speech. Nor must we assume that the actual speech itself, in abstraction from its accurate representation in the text, has as such the status of indefectible revelational authority, since it was

b) In response to this problem:

(1) The issue is not to be exaggerated.
a) The phenomenon itself is quite limited in scope.

b) Emendations are possible in all three relevant texts.

c) The LXX text may often be a plausible paraphrase or interpretation.

d) Many of the pertinent passages are merely linguistic allusions.

e) The Acts 15 citation by James is a special and explainable case.

not taken as such in the context where we read merely that the apostles and elders acceded to James's opinion (Acts 15:22), and not at all that his declaration settled the question by dint of its indisputable revelational authority. As I have previously argued, not everything said by a member of the apostolic circle may be reasonably assumed to have had that divine status. It is even likely that Luke himself, recollecting James's citation of this passage naturally filled in its exact phrasing from the LXX with which both he and his readers might be expected to be so familiar; no loss of substance would be occasioned if that were the case. What all these explanations illustrate, then, is the relative modesty and tenuousness of the problem that I am discussing about biblical authority.

However, I do not claim that every such variation of a LXX citation in the New Testament from the Hebrew text is appropriately explainable in this piecemeal fashion, although I hold that this type of explanation *may* indeed be applicable to all such cases and is therefore possible in principle. Yet I will not base my argument solely on this quite respectable possibility. Instead, let us suppose that, after all such explanations have been exhausted, there remains an unyielding residue of intractable passages which are not plausibly soluble in this way, and that in these cases there is a clear deviation from the apparent meaning of the Hebrew text in the LXX passage cited by the New Testament writer. Aside from the fact that we do not know with precision the original reading of any of these three texts, or the reading available for the Hebrew text at the time that the LXX was produced, or the reading of the available Hebrew and LXX texts at the time the New Testament passages in question were themselves written—and quite apart from the evident subjectivity and historical relativity of our own concept of what does or does not constitute a deviation of this sort, though all of these considerations are clearly pertinent to the issue in question—it is scarcely reasonable to define biblical authority in such a way as to include the perfection of either the scholarly methodology or the literary form and expression of the biblical writers as an indispensable corollary, if we define the content of perfection by our own current standards of expectation, which, after all, are themselves susceptible of criticism. Even the most arduous defenders of biblical authority (among whom I admittedly include myself) interpret the indefectibility of that authority in such a way as to be quite consistent with the use of round numbers, the employment of phenomenal language which differs from that of some definable standard of scientific precision, the presence of numerous kinds of grammatical solecisms (incomplete sentences, disagreement in grammatical number between subject and predicate of a clause, for example), the use of paraphrases in representing purportedly quoted matter, and other similar but generally accepted devices of common speech. There is, in my opinion, no plausibly defensible reason for not including in this list certain inadvertences of quotation from the Old Testament by New Testament writers, when no matter of substantial content is significantly affected, so that this methodology, loose as it may be, is wholly

(2) Even in cases not explainable by the ways illustrated, there is no serious problem. *a*) Our ignorance of the precise readings in question, and the subjectivity involved in identifying a deviation, are both pertinent points.

b) Biblical authority does not imply perfection of scholarly method or literary form by current standards.

i) That authority is quite consistent with various commonly employed impressions of expression.

ii) Inadvertences of quotation may be of this sort.

compatible with the indefectible authority of what is being expressed by the writer. In fact, it is even reasonable to include this type of consideration as a factor in the proper interpretation and understanding of the New Testament text, since it is, after all, not just any interpretation of the text that is supported by its indefectible authority, but only its proper interpretation in view of its total context.

Recall, for example, that the apostle Paul, or any other New Testament writer who made extensive use of LXX in quoting the Old Testament, was characteristically addressing contemporary audiences who, because they spoke Greek as a primary language, would have been familiar with the Old Testament, if at all, in its Greek translation. If Paul had, in a typical case, quoted a translation from the Hebrew text which differed noticeably from the LXX with which his readers might be supposed to have been familiar, such a device would clearly have confused them and diverted their attention from whatever issue was at hand. Now consider further that Paul himself, although doubtless familiar with whatever recension of the Hebrew text was available to him at the time, probably was even more familiar with the LXX in its then available form, so much so that its phraseology pervades his allusions to the Old Testament. It would be quite appropriate for him to use that translation as a quotation source, even under the directive guidance of the Holy Spirit. And if the inspiring Spirit had directed Paul's writing in such a way as to controvert the Hebrew text itself, with which Paul was familiar, in favor of an original text which was known to the onmiscient Spirit but unfamiliar to Paul from his version of the Hebrew text, we can imagine the intellectual and psychological pandemonium that would have resulted for Paul himself. Under such circumstances, the use of the currently received text, whether Hebrew or Greek, was clearly the appropriate instrument of the writer and the understandably condescending medium of the inspiring Spirit as well, since the conceivable alternatives would run contrary to the revelatory intent of both the writer and the inspiring Spirit. If we add to all this that as with Paul, so with ourselves, in that we too can only cite biblical authority in those recensions of the text that are available to us—and that nevertheless we accede to that available form of authority, even though we acknowledge a gap between it and the original text—the so-called difficulty about New Testament quotations from the Old Testament diminishes virtually to the vanishing point, if indeed it does not entirely disappear. This particular problem, on which I have labored at length, may well serve as a model for a conceivably broader issue. It has often been contended that the view of scriptural authority which I have argued takes a position of indefectibility which is not entirely congruous with the phenomenal characteristics of the biblical writings themselves, since they appear to contain numerous inadvertences similar to the one I have been discussing about quotations. But the real problem, in all such cases in general, is that the critic is bringing to the consideration of the biblical writings a standard of scholarly expectation and precision which is quite foreign to the milieu of those writings themselves, and quite foreign also to the concept of

c) The use of the currently received text of either the LXX or the Hebrew Testament would be wholly appropriate to the circumstances of the New Testament writers.

d) We ourselves use current textual recensions, while recognizing a gap between them and the original.

3. In general, the indefectible authority of the biblical revelation is not compromised by phenomenal inadvertences as judged by our own idealized standards of precision, since the correct interpretation of Scripture involves the recognition of such culturally contingent modes of expression.

indefectible revelational authority, when that concept is itself properly and reasonably understood. Of course, that concept must be understood in such a way as to be congruous with the descriptive phenomena of the writings. But that is, as I see it, only another way of saying that the biblical writings constitute an indefectibly authoritative divine revelation only when they are properly and correctly understood in the full light of their historical, cultural, and literary context, since the descriptive phenomena of the writings are themselves an important aspect of that context. If, on the contrary, we interpret the indefectible revelational authority of Scripture in terms provided by the expected standards of modern scholarship and technical precision, we probably deserve the resultant confusion with which such an interpretive blunder understandably clouds our minds.

C. The problem of alternative revelation claims: Could a similar argument be used to support such claims?

There is a final issue that is not settled by our general conclusion concerning biblical authority. If we are going to argue, as I have, that the revelation claim of the biblical writers is appropriately understood as true, since there is no plausible basis for charging them either with psychological perversion or with pervasive moral depravity, then we may raise the question whether a similar type of argument might be used to vindicate the revelational status of other writings regarded as authoritative in other religious traditions. Consider, for example, the Vedas and the Upanishads of Hinduism, the Five Classics and the Four Books of Confucianism, the Lao-tzu and Chuangtzu Books of Taoism, the Tripitaka of classical Buddhism, and the Koran of Islam—not to mention such treatises as the Book of Mormon, Science and Health, or Divine Principle. Can we reasonably regard the writers of all these purportedly authoritative religious writings as in every case either psychologically unsound or morally depraved? And if not, are we then to accept them all as of equal religious authority along with the Bible of the Hebrew-Christian tradition?

1. The acceptance of the biblical revelation claim need not entail the rejection of all other such writings as devoid of religious truth, since general revelation would lead to the expectation of widespread religious insight.

I think I have already made it clear that, as I understand it, accepting the Bible as indefectibly authoritative divine revelation need not imply the rejection of all these other writings as totally devoid of religious truth. If, as the New Testament clearly teaches, there is a universal ministry of the Holy Spirit to all human beings, and if Jesus is the Logos of Divine Reason who enlightens every person who comes into the world, and if there is a general revelation that is universally accessible to the whole of humanity, then we should expect that in writings which represent the best efforts of any religious tradition to understand the Ultimate Reality, there would be much genuine truth along with whatever elements of misunderstanding might surround that truth with a penumbra of shadows. That this expectation is, in varying degrees, fulfilled in fact should be surprising to no reflective and informed individual.

2. Alternative revelation claims are made in contrasting contexts which lessen the analogy among the claims.

Yet such a general revelation is not the whole response to the issue of alternative revelation claims. The revelation claim of the biblical writings is, of course, made in a certain context—the context of a vindicated theism, the context of a justified and reasonable belief in Jesus as God Incarnate, and the context in which, finally, Jesus himself, so construed, affirms the indefectible authority of Scripture. As this context is increasingly rendered explicit, the alternative revelation claims, involving, as they characteristically do, a distinguishably different perspectival context, provide an increasingly lessening parallel to the unique revelation claim of the Hebrew-Christian Scriptures, however authoritatively those other writings may be regarded in their own perspectival context. For example, the respected writings of Confucianism, along with those of Taoism, are not regarded as in any sense the authoritative self-disclosure of a transcendent personal Divine Reality. There is no such view of God as personal Creator in either of these religions in their classical form, since the Great Whole of Confucianism is simply the total natural universe regarded as an objective moral order, and the Tao of Taoism is a pantheistically construed Ultimate Being (or Non-Being) which is wholly devoid of determinate qualities, but of which the apparent distinctions and determinate entities of the phenomenal world order are so many surface manifestations. For such perspectives, the idea of an authoritative personal self-disclosure in propositional form to specially selected human instruments is simply out of the question, so that the authoritative writings of these religious traditions, although highly respected and regarded as spiritually normative, do not constitute a genuine parallel to the Christian revelation claim. The situation is not essentially different for the Vedas and Upanishads of Hinduism. Again, these writings appear in a pantheistic context for which the Creator-creature distinction of a properly construed theism is virtually, if not totally, obliterated, although there are personalistic versions of the concept of God or Brahman (the qualified non-dualism of Ramanuja, for example). Again, the writings themselves are not construed as personal divine self-disclosure, but rather, in the case of the Upanishads in particular, as the account of experiences of spiritual vision on the part of religious seers whose personal identity is largely unknown and in any case of little significance. Here again, the "revelation," although possessing ultimate spiritual authority for its sincere adherents, is not revelation in any sense that provides a competitive parallel to the Christian revelation claim in its context. As for the Koran of Mohammed, it is clear that it is itself built upon the historically prior Hebrew-Christian revelation itself, however misconstrued its understanding of that revelation may be. Even for Moslems themselves, the Koran does not provide a competitive alternative to the Christian revelation claim, but rather an extension and supplementation of it. This is even more pertinently the case with the Book of Mormon, Science and Health, and Divine Principle. All three, even in the minds of those who accept them as religiously authoritative, are regarded as extensions of the Hebrew-Christian revelation itself, rather than as options which would discount that revelation. Whether this self-understanding of the Koran and of the last-mentioned religious treatises is correct is quite another question, which must be settled in principle by considering whether the doctrines of these books are congruous with those of the biblical revelation, whether the category of revelation is applicable to them in the sense and to the degree that it has been argued to be applicable to

a) Examples:
(1) Confucianism and Taoism.

(2) Hinduism.

(3) Islam.

(4) Some current alternatives.

b) Claims to extend the biblical revelation are to be assessed by their coherence or otherwise with that revelation and its theistic context.

the biblical writings, and whether the general philosophical stance of these treatises is coherent with the sort of theistic perspective that provides the world-view context for the biblical revelation itself. The investigation of these issues is beyond the scope of my present purposes, although I have provided in principle the thought framework for carrying out such a task. But, in any case, it is not plausible to regard these purported revelation claims as competitive parallels to the Christian revelation claim, since they profess to be based upon it. And it is certainly not necessary, or even reasonable, to regard the seminal originators of these traditions as either mentally disturbed or morally perverse and insincere, if we question the plausibility of their revelation claims on grounds of the sort mentioned above. Without challenging the genuinely religious character of their experience (the Holy Spirit is universally influencing humanity to respond to God's claim upon it), we can challenge the propriety of the conceptual framework in which they interpret that experience. If Christians, who suppose themselves as speaking in the name of God, are subject to judgment in what they say through various corrective standards of the sort I have indicated all along, the same standards of plausibility and reasonableness may, with the same philosophical right, be applied to the interpretations of religious experience which we find in the treatises here in question. Finally, as for the Tripitaka of classical Buddhism (accepted as authoritative by both Hinayana and Mahayana Buddhists), there is here no sense of inspired personal self-disclosure, since these writings lack the metaphysical concept of a Divine Reality which such a sense would presuppose. In fact, one of the main reasons that Buddhism was regarded by Hindus as heterodox rather than orthodox was that Gautama rejected the ultimate spiritual authority of the Scriptures of Hinduism because he questioned even the attenuated notion of revelational vision which those writings involved.

What follows from all of this is that the difficulty about alternative revelation claims, if it is interpreted as a threat to the Christian revelation claim, is reduced to modest or perhaps even negligible proportions indeed. Many such supposed alternatives lack the world-view context for providing a genuine parallel to the Christian revelation claim—and where there is some semblance of parallelism in context, the purported alternatives are considered by their adherents as extensions of the Christian revelation claim itself. If it is a question of the comparative and relative adequacy of clearly distinguishable world-view contexts, then the whole of my previous analysis provides, in principle, an epistemological method for resolving such questions, as well as a defense of theism as the most adequate metaphysical alternative available for reflective religious thought. It is hardly necessary therefore to rework that same philosophical soil again.

The Theological Interpretation:
Alternative Views of the Revelation-Status
of the Hebrew-Christian Scriptures

From my immediately preceding analysis, I conclude that the biblical writings, properly interpreted in their total historical, cultural, and

---

(1) In any case, these are not genuine competitive parallels to the biblical claim.

(2) There is no need to challenge the genuineness of such religious experiences, even if we challenge their interpretation.

c) Nor does Buddhism provide a genuine competitive parallel to the biblical claim.

3. The problem of alternative revelation claims is therefore virtually nonexistent, while the related problem of the adequacy of general metaphysical contexts has been the main concern of my whole project.

literary context, constitute an indefectibly authoritative, propositionally expressed, self-disclosing revelation of God as the transcendent
personal ground of all contingent reality. In what I have said, I have
tried to argue, clarify, elaborate, and appropriately qualify this claim
in relation to a selective cross section of relevant and important issues.
I view my perspective about all this as a viable version of what I will
designate as the classical orthodox viewpoint on these questions.
While I do not claim that it is the only possible, much less the only
actual, version of this orthodox stance, it is nonetheless the only
version I will discuss in detail, since I regard it as, at least in general,
typically representative of Christian orthodoxy on the whole, whether
Catholic or Protestant. In fact, except in contexts where it would
seriously jeopardize the completeness of my analysis, I have deliberately avoided taking any explicit stand that would be incongruous
with this typically representative character. But there are, of course,
within Christendom, loosely construed in the broadest historical sense,
some clear alternatives to the classical orthodox perspective regarding
the biblical revelation claim. I think it important to provide a brief
analysis and critique of two main classes of such alternatives. The
first, which I will term the *liberal* perspective, has been primarily a
development within Protestantism connected with the work of such
thinkers as Immanuel Kant, Friedrich Schleiermacher, and Albrecht
Ritschl. The second, which I will term the *neo-orthodox* perspective,
was also spawned by Protestantism and is associated with more recent
thinkers such as Karl Barth, Emil Brunner, and John Baillie.

The liberal outlook on revelation and biblical authority, as I understand that position, maintains, in general, that the biblical writings are
revelatory of God to the extent that they contain much religious truth,
as identified by some previously defined criterion of such truth—but
that the truth thus recognizable is set in a context of thought and
linguistic expression which is, in varying degrees and over a wide
range of subject matter, at the same time pervaded by elements of
error (partly in non-religious spheres of thought, but partly also in
religious conceptualization itself), from which that essential core of
truth must be distinguished by extensive and painstaking reflection.
The biblical writings, then, cannot be in either word or thought wholly
identified with the word of God (genuine religious truth); but they can
be said to contain that word in those propositions and thought contexts which do embody genuine religious insights—so that to that
same degree the Bible may be considered a revelation of the Divine
Reality, however that may be construed. The crucial factor here is the
recognition and clarification of the criterion or standard for understanding the nature of religious truth and distinguishing it from error.
That criterion will differ for different liberal thinkers. For the *religious
empiricism* or *experientialism* of a thinker like Schleiermacher, the
essence and principle of religious truth is the experienced awareness
of absolute dependence on God as the Infinite All (pantheistically
construed), so that religious propositions, concepts, and doctrinal
structures are correctly understood, not as factual assertions, at what-

I. Summary of pre-
vious results as one
expression of the clas-
sical orthodox view-
point concerning the
Scriptures.
A. While there are
clearly other orthodox
positions in this area, I
regard mine as typi-
cally representative of
this type of view.

B. Two alternatives to
such an orthodox view
are important enough
to consider.

1. The *liberal* per-
spective.

2. The *neo-orthodox*
perspective.

II. The liberal view of
Scripture.
A. Summary defini-
tion of the general
outlook: the Bible con-
taining some genuine
religious truth but set
in a context of error.

B. The criterion of re-
ligious truth:

1. For *religious
empiricism*: religious
statements as con-
structs of religious ex-
perience whose truth
is a function of their
capacity to generate
such experience.

ever level, but as constructions upon religious experience whose genuineness is a function of their capacity to generate and sustain that experienced awareness itself—with the result that the Bible (or any other religious document) is an authentic revelation of the Infinite precisely to the extent that it performs that function of experiential provocation for any individual or group. On the other hand, for the sort of *religious ethicism* propounded by thinkers like Kant and Ritschl, the essence of religious truth and the criterion of its genuineness is the conformity of its expression to unconditionally authoritative and objective moral law (for Kant, the categorical moral imperative), so that any historical and revealed faith, such as biblical Christianity purports to be, is a genuine religious revelation to the extent that it expresses this moral law and motivates its implementation in human moral experience—with the result that the propositions and doctrinal patterns of the Bible are authentic religious insights to the extent that they are plausibly interpretable as symbolizing and subserving this moral function.

2. For *religious ethicism:* religious truth as expressing and implementing moral law.

C. Critical problems.
1. My previous analysis already covers this.

To a considerable degree, I have already assessed such perspectives as these in principle through my initial discussion of the criteria for assessing religious truth-claims, so that my critique of religious perspectives of this sort hardly needs to be repeated in the present context, since that critique is relevant here as it stands. Of course, the experientially efficacious and morally motivating roles of religious propositions and concepts are significant aspects of them; but by themselves they cannot function as adequate criteria of religious truth-claims, much less as identifications of the essence of those claims and their content. Very different conceptual frameworks in other respects might well function with comparable effectiveness in provoking general religious awareness or in motivating commitment in principle and practice to unconditionally authoritative and objective moral law. In that case, such criteria would provide no basis for a reasonable choice among those conceptual frameworks. But more pertinently to our present concern, while both Kant and Schleiermacher, not to mention Ritschl, regarded their philosophies as recognizing and defending what was essentially true in historical Christianity, their views of revelational authority run clearly counter to the perspective expressed by the biblical writings themselves and especially by Jesus as historically represented in these writings. To challenge the view of Jesus on this point is at least logically, although not necessarily in practice, to challenge the central core of the Christian revelation claim to the effect that Jesus is God Incarnate and therefore himself God's final and unsurpassable revelation. Nor can we legitimately separate Jesus from the view of indefectible biblical authority which the biblical writings, considered even as mere historical sources, ascribe to him, since we know no other Jesus than the one presented to us in the New Testament picture. Hence, if Jesus held such a view of scriptural authority, then to challenge that view, in favor of any such liberal perspective as we are here considering, is at the same time to challenge the authority of Jesus and therefore also his

2. The experiential and moral aspects of religion are inadequate as criteria of religious truth.

a) No basis for choosing between perspectives that function equally well in these respects.

b) Such views run counter to the views expressed by Jesus and the biblical writers.
(1) This is tantamount to challenging the core of the Christian revelation claim that Jesus is God Incarnate,

(2) since there is no plausible way to separate Jesus from the view of Scripture as indefectibly authoritative revelation.

status as God Incarnate. But that ground we have already covered more than once. It is clear, of course, that historically none of these thinkers accepted the Incarnation claim of Jesus in any sense analogous to the form in which I have defended that claim—but that only illustrates how far removed from the core of essential Christianity any such liberal reinterpretation of revelational authority really is.

The neo-orthodox outlook on revelation and biblical authority, as I understand that position, maintains in general that revelation is not to be construed as statically identical with any book, doctrine, or conjunction of propositions, but is rather to be regarded in its primary occurrence as, subjectively, personal encounter with God in the sense of a reciprocal exchange between two personal subjects (God and the individual), and as, objectively, the Divine Event in which God becomes incarnate in Jesus Christ, so that revelation is God himself in his unique Word, Jesus as Messiah. Yet in both of these aspects, revelation since the time of Jesus himself is characteristically mediated to human beings through the prophetic and apostolic witness in Holy Scripture, which, although not actually itself revelation in the primary sense, is nevertheless the normative witness for revelation as encounter. The Scriptures and especially the New Testament have this normative status because the apostles are the mediating link between the historical Jesus and subsequent generations, so that the Scriptures, as the apostolic word preserved in written form, constitute the enduring character of that mediating link in accessible form. In a sense, we can even say that the biblical writings—as such a witness to revelation as event (encounter and incarnation)—actually become revelation in propositional form when through their witness the event of revelation as encounter is actualized for a given person. At that moment, and in the biblical words through which the encounter occurs, the Bible becomes the Word of God, although it does not statically retain that status outside the living context of that encounter. The authors of Scripture were, for this perspective, inspired in the sense that what they wrote was written under the guidance of the Holy Spirit. But that guidance did not either guarantee or result in their preservation from all error—even the doctrinal aspect of Scripture is subject to error and inconsistency, so that these doctrines, mutually supplementing and correcting one another in interaction with our own reflection, point to the center of revelation as primary event, yet without constituting that event itself. Even though we cannot therefore speak of verbal and plenary inspiration in quite the traditional orthodox sense, we can nevertheless claim that the writings themselves, and not merely the authors, are inspired. Baillie and Barth do not even object to the phrase "verbal inspiration," if it is rightly understood from their standpoint. Within the context of revelation as encounter, the biblical word which the Holy Spirit uses to actualize that encounter is characterized by verbal inspiration, even when the word, as humanly understood, may contain errors; but we cannot correctly transmute that dynamic verbal inspiration into any sort of "verbal inspiredness"

III. The neo-orthodox view of Scripture.
A. Summary definition of the general outlook: revelation as personal encounter and the Divine Event in Jesus as God the Word.

1. This revelation is characteristically mediated through the biblical witness which, although not itself revelation, is the mediating link to revelation.

2. The biblical word becomes revelation to the extent and at the moment that it thus mediates encounter.

a) The authors were guided by the Holy Spirit so that what they wrote is inspired as pointing to the event of revelation itself, although this does not guarantee freedom from error, however defined.

b) The biblical word used by the spirit is characterized by "verbal inspiration," but not "verbal inspiredness."

as a permanent and objective quality of biblical words apart from the moment of revelation.

B. Critical problems: 1. This position is, in certain respects, similar to the position I have myself argued, and hence it is a partially adequate position.

In response to this neo-orthodox perspective on scriptural authority, it is clear that this position, as I have represented it, bears an extensive affinity to the position which I have myself elaborated and argued. Here also we find an emphasis on God Incarnate in Jesus Christ as the climax of revelation; here also we find a pervasive emphasis on the normative status of the biblical word as enshrining the apostolic connection between Jesus and subsequent history; and here also we find a divine inspiration which attaches, although in a stringently qualified sense, to the biblical writings themselves. In these respects, somewhat differently understood to be sure, I see in the neo-orthodox perspective a partial reconstitution of an approximately adequate position.

2. But there are two principal difficulties. *a*) That Jesus is the highest form of revelation does not imply that there can be no other form of objective revelation.

However, I see here two essential points central to the neo-orthodox outlook which seem to me to be subject to serious misconception and therefore appropriate criticism. It is certainly correct to say that it is God himself who confronts us in authentic divine revelation. But it scarcely follows, from the acknowledged fact that Jesus, as God Incarnate, is the climax and highest form of revelation, that there can be no other form of divine revelation which, although lacking the form of identity with God that characterizes the Incarnate Christ, is nevertheless for all that still authentic revelation, much less that such a revelation cannot be in conceptually apprehensible, propositional form, as the biblical writings purport to be. The God who himself confronts us in encounter and Incarnation is only recognizable as such through the medium of intelligible concepts which are in principle propositionally expressible. If encounter is genuine, it logically must involve contact with objective divine truth, in conceptual-propositional form, since there is no other means of recognizing or clarifying a content of conscious experience. And if that is the case, then that truth, as objective, does not depend on its relation to a given individual as such for that status, so that this truth constitutes a revelation of God quite apart from any given individual's experience of encounter. There is therefore, in principle, no reason to deny propositional revelation in the objectively enduring sense, merely on the ground of its distinction from a personal experience of encounter, since that experience itself is possible only in conceptual terms that are themselves propositionally expressible.

(1) Even God, as apprehended in revelation, must be recognized through concepts which are propositionally expressible, so that there is no reason in principle for denying enduring propositional revelation.

(2) The biblical word could only become revelation for the individual in encounter if it was already God's Word objectively and in itself, since encounter does not change the objective content of the word.

This point is virtually admitted in the neo-orthodox emphasis on the normative character of scriptural propositions as a witness to revelation and even as becoming revelation in the moment of encounter as actualized through biblical words. Unless those words constituted an objective self-disclosure of God quite apart from encounter, they could not reasonably be regarded as becoming propositionally revelatory through such an encounter, which, after all, does not change the objective content of those words as rightly interpreted. If then it is meaningful to speak of the Bible as ever becoming God's Word for the individual (that is, assuming the status of revelation for that individual), it can only be because it is antecedently meaningful to speak of the Bible as being God's Word objectively and continuously in itself, and as therefore belonging quite properly in the category of revelation.

If this conclusion is not accepted, it is perhaps because these thinkers suppose that the biblical writings contain statements which, on any plausible interpretation of them, contain various kinds of errors, which characterize the statements objectively but are in some unspecified sense transcended or sublimated in the experience of encounter. And since it would be quite incongruous to ascribe those errors to God in any straightforwardly objective sense, it would have to be the case that the words of Scripture do not constitute objective divine revelation in any straightforwardly objective sense either. Apart from the baffling question as to how propositions which are objectively erroneous, on any reasonable construction of them, could be transformed into the authoritative revelation of God during the moment or experience of encounter without becoming different propositions— and apart from the question as to how, on such terms, any even approximately sound theology is to be possible in principle, much less in practice—I can only say that much of my previous analysis has already responded to this issue about alleged errors in the biblical writings. If such errors are identified and accepted, then it will, in my opinion, be on the basis of some rigorously defined standard of precision and exactness which, although quite proper in technical science or formal academic scholarship, is inappropriate as applied to the biblical writings. Of course, it is logically possible to define a concept of error with respect to which those writings would indeed include incidental or perhaps even substantial errors. But those same standards would doubtless also dismiss as erroneous most of the content of our own ordinary truth-claims which both we and our hearers sincerely accept as correct in substance when rightly interpreted. If it is reasonable to grant to the biblical writers at least the same measure of generosity as we daily accede to each other, then it is, I think, quite reasonable to turn the neo-orthodox thesis around and maintain that the biblical writings, correctly interpreted in their total historical, cultural, and linguistic context, are an indefectibly authoritative and objective revelation of God. What we include in the elucidation of that context is a complicated question open to scholarly pursuit with the leisure that normally characterizes such investigations. In the meantime, we should acknowledge that our own theories about that context are always subject to revision, just as is the case with our own efforts to approximate a correct interpretation of Scripture, so that, although the objectivity of scriptural revelation is always accessible to us, our own comprehensive interpretation of that revelation is always susceptible of improvement or even, at times, drastic reconstruction. The advantage of this turnaround, as I have called it, is in part that we now have a perspective on biblical authority which wholly accords with the testimony and promise of Jesus to the same effect, and which is entirely consistent with the self-testimony of the biblical writings themselves—that after all are regarded by neo-orthodox thinkers as

b) If the biblical word is in principle subject to error on any reasonable interpretation of it, serious problems arise.

(1) How could words, erroneous in themselves, become God's Word in encounter?

(2) I have already dealt with this problem of error.
a) The supposition of such error involves the application of a standard of precision foreign to the biblical writings, and even to our own ordinary truth-claims.

b) We can therefore claim, by a logical reverse, that, rightly interpreted in context, the biblical writings are free from such errors.

c) Contextual interpretation and our theories about it are always subject to improvement or reconstruction.

d) The striking advantage of our turnaround is that it gives us a view which harmonizes with that of Jesus and of the biblical writings themselves.

the normative witness to revelation and even as revelation in itself through the experience of encounter.

IV. Liberal and neo-orthodox perspectives do not therefore provide a viable alternative to the classical orthodox view.

I conclude, therefore, that neither the liberal nor the neo-orthodox perspective on biblical authority provides an actually plausible alternative to my version of classical orthodoxy here, even though both views contain substantial and genuine fragments of a reasonable perspective, as I have indicated. Meanwhile, I rest with tentative but genuine confidence in the main position I have developed and argued, since that is, after all, from an intellectual point of view, the only sort of confidence appropriate to a fallible human investigator, who is at the same time a sincerely reflective individual.

The Canon of Scripture

I. The plausibility of the scriptural revelation claim requires criteria for determining which books fall into the category of authoritative revelation.
II. The Old Testament Canon.

A. Jesus' witness to the authority of the Old Testament implies his approval of the methods and criteria used to determine its limits.

If the collection of God-inspired books which make up the Hebrew-Christian Bible is to be regarded as an indefectibly authoritative divine revelation in the sense that I have contended and attempted to clarify, then it is important to recognize that, for such a claim to be genuinely plausible, there must be identifiable criteria for determining—in principle at least and, so far as possible, in fact and practice—which books are to be properly construed as belonging to both the Old Testament and the New Testament collections. In a sense, this problem is not as difficult for the Old Testament as it is for the New, if we accept as genuine and plausible the recognition of the authority and revelatory status of those books as taught by Jesus himself, his disciples, and the New Testament writers generally—a case which I have already made earlier in my analysis. The unswerving confidence in the Old Testament which Jesus exhibited implies his approval of both the collection of books at the time (so far as that can be itself confidently determined) and the methods by which the contents of that collection had in general been determined before the earthly career of Jesus. If therefore we can identify the criteria and principles that were *de facto* in practice for making this determination in pre-Christian times, we will be able reasonably to assume not only Jesus' approval of those methods but also their actual correctness as criteria, since we have already argued the ultimate teaching authority of Jesus as God Incarnate. As plausible as this seems, the determination of those criteria is nevertheless extraordinarily difficult in practice. For one thing, although, as I have argued, Jesus everywhere affirmed scriptural authority, he himself appears to have provided no real clues as to the methods used, prior to his earthly career, for determining the limits of that Old Testament collection. For another thing, the Old Testament itself, particularly in its later portions, clearly recognizes the divine authority of the earlier Mosaic law books and the books of the former and latter prophets, but very little is said about the procedure for defining the principles used in that recognition. Finally, there is an

1. But:
a) Jesus gave no real clues about those methods.

b) The Old Testament itself is not very informative either.

elaborate rabbinical tradition about how the sacred books (or, as they said, "books that defile the hands"—because of their divinely inspired character) were to be recognized and identified, but we can hardly assume without question that their elaborate theories about the matter correspond to an accurate account of how the determination was actually carried out. Yet we need have no great hesitation about identifying the Old Testament collection in general, even though we may be uncertain about those actual criteria, if we accept the authority of Jesus himself as to the general content of that collection, since he referred clearly to its main divisions in the Hebrew Bible by speaking of the Law, the Prophets, and the Psalms (Luke 24:44), and he also quoted or alluded to passages in all of these divisions as divinely authoritative. I have myself already argued previously that, even if we cannot determine with final precision exactly what books were included in these divisions as referred to by Jesus, we need have no significant question about the divine authority of the collection as a whole, despite its possibly indeterminate fringes.

> *c*) The rabbinical tradition about canonicity does not necessarily correspond to actual historical procedure.
>
> 2. Yet the identification of the Old Testament collection, as a whole, is clearly recognized in Jesus' references to its divisions and books.

Even in view of these difficulties about principles of recognition for the canon or collection of books, several things are nevertheless quite clear from the historical circumstances surrounding the origin of the Old Testament books. It is evident at the outset that the recognition of these writings (and, in many cases, of their previously delivered oral contents—as in the speeches of Moses and the public orations of the prophets) as divinely authoritative did not have to wait for any formal or even informal decree by some assembled body of public officials, whether religious or political. The teachings of Moses were clearly accepted as divinely revelatory immediately upon his delivery of them, on the obvious ground that he was himself recognized as a prophet of God (Deut. 18:14–22). In fact, in one of these very speeches, Moses, speaking on behalf of God, provides a criterion for distinguishing between a true prophet of God and a false prophet, namely, whether what the prophet proclaims actually takes place or comes true (Deut. 18:20–22). If we add to this passage certain accounts about disputes with false prophets and judgments upon them in Jeremiah (23:9–40; 28:1–17; 37:19) and Ezekiel (13:1–19), we can recognize in this concern about the genuineness of a prophet and his prophecy a clear hint about the centrality of the prophet in determining the scope of divine revelation. And it is perhaps not too much to say that here the Old Testament itself supports the later rabbinical thesis that the authoritative books as well were recognized through their relation to the prophetic office. If a book was written by a prophet of God or at his instigation and under his supervision (cf. Jer. 36), then it was divinely authoritative and would "defile the hands"; if it was not thus written or based on the word of a true prophet, it was not. The assumption is that here, with prophets of God in general as with Moses, the declarations of authentic prophets were recognized as authoritative immediately upon their pronouncement, at least by the spiritually discerning among their hearers in Israel. The public acknowledgment of the authority of certain Old Testament books during the reign of Josiah in

> B. Preliminary clarification.
>
> 1. The recognition of books as authoritative did not have to wait for an official list.
>
> 2. There is a line of emphasis on the prophetic office as crucial to the canonicity of given books and pronouncements.
>
> *a*) Biblical hints.
>
> *b*) The rabbinical thesis.
>
> 3. Various public acknowledgments of biblical books did not constitute the criterial basis of their acceptance as divinely authoritative.

Judah, and even their reaffirmation by a living prophet at the time (2 Kings 22; 23:1–3), hardly constituted the basis of that authority in any sense, but rather reasserted an authority already long established. The same is true of a similar public recognition at the time of Nehemiah (10:28–29), and analogously, the clear indications in the Book of Ezra to the effect that he was a teacher of the law and had access to both the book of Moses, as it was called, and the words of the prophets as well (Ezra 6:18; 7:6, 10, 12–14, 25; 9:4, 11). All this, while it may reinforce the traditional thesis that Ezra and his associates were responsible for collecting or even editing these books, certainly does not entail that this process conferred on these writings any divine authority which they did not already possess. The same may be said for whatever was contributed to the public recognition of these books by the so-called men of the Great Synagogue and the far-later rabbinical councils at Jamnia a century or so into the Christian era. It therefore appears that the general criterion for the recognition of divinely inspired books in the Old Testament period was precisely the origin of those books or their essential contents from the exercise of the authentic prophetic office. And if that is the case, then Jesus' documented acceptance of the general Old Testament collection, as determined by this prophetic principle, implies his clear, if unexpressed, approval of that principle or criterion itself.

This thesis about the standard for the recognition of Old Testament books receives a sort of additional retroactive support, as it were, from the parallelism that it bears to the principle of apostolic teaching authority which was crucial for the recognition of a wholly analogous divinely revelatory status for the growing nucleus of authoritative books that became the New Testament. And this point I have already argued in a previous context by contending that Jesus conferred on the circle of his apostles a teaching authority that linked the revelation in Jesus himself as God Incarnate with the oral proclamation of the apostles and its written expression and extension in those books which were either written by apostles or by persons under their aegis and supervision—books which ultimately constituted the New Testament. Here too, as with the Old Testament books in general, the divine authority of the new books thus originated did not await their public recognition by the dissemination of canonical lists or the approval of such lists at councils of Christian leaders, however important and informative those lists may have been for historical purposes. As I noted in an earlier context, within the New Testament itself, certain books actually refer to earlier books as scripture wholly on a par with the writings of the Old Testament. Thus Paul (or in any case, a Paulinist responsible for the pastoral Epistles) refers to the Gospel of Luke (10:7) as parallel in scriptural status to the Old Testament book of Deuteronomy (1 Tim. 5:18); and the writer of Second Peter (3:15, 16) clearly intimates the scriptural status of those letters of Paul with which he was familiar. This sort of reference again suggests, analogously with Old Testament revelation, that these books were recognized as having revelatory status immediately upon their promulgation to this or that

---

Margin notes:

4. The general criterion appears to have been the origin from the authentic prophetic office, for which we may then claim Jesus' approval.

III. The New Testament canon.
A. The apostolic teaching authority parallels that of the Old Testament prophetic office.
1. This apostolic authority previously argued.

2. Here again the recognized authority did not wait for canonical lists and councils.

a) The recognition of the scriptural status of certain books by other New Testament books implies their recognition as authoritative immediately on promulgation.

Christian community, and, as I previously argued, on the basis of their having been written either by apostles or under their direction and approval. It therefore appears that the New Testament revelation was a growing collection of books, whose recognition as authoritative divine self-disclosure had as its criterion the exercise of the apostolic office of teaching that had been conferred by Jesus himself on the apostles as special recipients of the directive guidance of the Holy Spirit into revealed truth. Hence, we discern here a symmetrical parallelism with the exercise of the prophetic office in the case of the Old Testament books, so that this analogy actually strengthens our conviction concerning the apostolic link between Jesus and the writings of the New Testament, since Jesus approved the exercise of that parallel prophetic authority in relation to the Old Testament revelation.

There were nevertheless disputes about the revelational authority of certain books finally included in the New Testament, so that still in the time of Origen of Alexandria (third century A.D.) it was common to distinguish between books universally viewed as Scripture and others that were, in varying degrees and in various geographical areas, opposed as not having this status. The fact that, where pertinent information is available, the criterion appealed to in the main was the apostolic origin or supervision of the books in question not only illustrates my general thesis about the crucial role of the apostolic office in this issue, but it also suggests that the disagreements about a given book turned on the question of apostolicity—so that when that issue was settled in the case of any particular book, there was no longer any serious and sustained question about its revelational status, even though adverse value judgments about particular New Testament books on the part of specific individuals have continued down to modern times. In any case, when, about the end of the fourth century A.D. (Third Council of Carthage, A.D. 397, and Council of Hippo, A.D. 419), virtual unanimity on the twenty-seven books of our present New Testament was achieved, that consensus, rather than bestowing on these books some degree of authority which previously they might be supposed to have lacked, on the contrary merely (but importantly) recognized the authority that the books already possessed by virtue of their now clearly recognized apostolic origin or sponsorship. Whether this decisive office of apostolicity ceased at the death of the original apostles, or continued as vested in their duly constituted successors, is an issue which is quite beyond the scope of my concern here, so that I am content to leave that question as another of those family disagreements among different groups of Christians—disagreements which may be pursued at leisure but which, fortunately, do not significantly affect the plausibility of the New Testament revelation claim.

Is it plausible to recognize still other criteria of canonicity beside apostolicity? It is clear that, since conciliar approval, if properly construed, is itself based on the standard of apostolicity, it cannot be regarded as a basic criterion itself. And it seems equally clear that, since a criterion of canonicity is a means of identifying which books

b) This was on the basis of apostolic origin or supervision.

c) The apostolic teaching office therefore serves as a basic criterion.

B. Disputes about certain New Testament books continued at least through the fourth century A.D.

1. What we know about their resolution suggests that the disagreements turned on the question of apostolicity as a criterion.

2. When unanimity was achieved, it was the recognition of an authority already possessed through apostolic origin or sponsorship.

3. Whether this apostolic authority continued through successors, is left unsettled here and is not decisive for my case.

C. Are there other criteria of New Testament canonicity?
1. Not conciliar approval.
2. Not divine inspiration.

3. Not the inner witness of the Holy Spirit:

are divinely inspired, the purported or even genuine inspiration of a given book could not itself function as such a criterion. A serious supplemental criterion, proposed by some of the Protestant reformers (notably, Calvin) is the inner witness of testimony of the Holy Spirit to individual believers who compose the publicly recognizable spiritual community of Christians. I have no doubt that the Holy Spirit does in fact confirm the authority of Scripture to individual believers through the illumination of their minds by means of their contemplation of those same Scriptures. But I do not regard this readily ackowledged

a) because that witness itself requires a test of operation;

b) because this is too subjective in practice;

c) because the criterion would reduce to individual decision what should be communal.

4. Apostolicity, as objective criterion, can subsume these other proposed tests under itself as aspects.

role of the Spirit as criterion of canonicity: First, because the influence of the Holy Spirit itself requires, for believers in general, a test of its operation—we are to test the spirits to see whether they are of God; second, because the difficulty involved in interpreting the guidance of the Spirit for the community of believers as a whole renders a criterial appeal to this influence far too subjective for it to function as a test in relation to an issue where the highest possible objectivity is of basic importance; and finally, because a criterion of exclusively inner witness of this sort relegates to purely individual decision a recognition function which ought rather to be the project of the Christian community at large as an organic totality. I prefer therefore to say that the inner witness of the Spirit supplements and psychologically strengthens the conviction of an historically vindicated and objective canonicity in terms of the criterion of apostolicity. Around this criterial center as a focal point there turns a wheel of reciprocal support through the development of a consensus inwardly bolstered by the Holy Spirit's testimony to the individual through the Scriptures themselves, and outwardly acclaimed by cumulative historical unanimity reflected in

5. Yet apostolicity, although approximating objectivity, does not make absolute finality possible.

canonical lists and embodied in conciliar pronouncements. While therefore the criterion of apostolicity, involving as it does an historicity which cannot wholly transcend tentativity, does not lead to absolute finality and unrevisability, it does provide the only sort of reasonable approximation to objectivity which is realistically possible in relation to such questions—and for the rationally reflective and adequately informed, that should suffice.

The Coherence of Scripture

With Itself Organically: The Internal Unity

I. The biblical writings represent a wide variety of literary types from different authors and under varied historical circumstances.

Anyone who investigates the Hebrew-Christian Bible in a descriptive frame of mind will find it an extraordinarily varied collection of individual books which represent a broad range of literary types, reflect an extensive variation of subject matter, and repose, as it were, in strikingly different historical and cultural settings. Furthermore, the authors of these books represent the whole sweep of social hierarchy, from kings on the one extreme to farmers and fishermen on the other—all of whose personal idiosyncrasies and varied circumstances intrude themselves in various ways and to different degrees on the structure and form of what they wrote. We could hardly expect, under such conditions, to discover in the biblical writings any extended mechanical uniformity of the sort that might characterize a formal logical or mathematical system, much less any such deductive logical structure as would characterize that type of system. If therefore the notion of coherence is to be defined in any such strictly mechanical and formal fashion, it will hardly do to refer to the conjunction of perspectives reflected in the different books and sections of Scripture as coherent in that sense. But if we take a broader construction of the notion of coherence—so that we think of it in terms of a sort of reciprocal organic unity of insight that is compatible with differences that supplement each other and constitute in that way a complex and cumulative understanding from which, rightly interpreted, contradiction and substantial inconsistency are nevertheless eliminated from the thought structure as a whole, in spite of elements of complementary tension that contribute to that wholeness—then in that sense the biblical writings are pervaded by a coordinating strain of intrinsic unity in outlook which is all the more striking in view of the varied circumstances in which the parts of this literature originated historically. This inner unity, understood in the way I have suggested, does actualize the sort of coherence that we should expect in a comprehensive divine revelation which emerged in the cumulative stretch of history during which the biblical writings were produced. From one point of view, this complex unity might be compared to the multifaceted aspects that would go into the adequate description of some mature person whose thought and life are characterized by many overlapping but nevertheless distinguishable dimensions. Through all the variety and even contrast the integrative harmony of a single personal life would shine through; and hence analogously, in the Bible, the unity of divine personal reality also irradiates the broad scope of history and individual human authorship through which the divine self-disclosure is expressed.

On the other hand, although God is himself a timelessly actual reality from which change, potentiality, and imperfection are wholly eliminated, the biblical revelation itself is addressed to individuals and to an inclusive humanity whose insight and understanding are achieved through a temporally developing accumulation of mutually reinforcing and equally developing phases of conceptual advance which are characteristically achieved only through long struggle and interaction with many paths of thought which in the end turn out to be blind alleys on the whole, even though they contain some rays of genuine light. And just as the growth of a human person to maturity of understanding in general involves many phases of insight along the way—which, although illuminating and appropriate at the time, are fragmentary and incomplete as compared with still later phases of that understanding which incorporate and transcend those earlier

A. Hence, they do not reflect any strictly formal, deductive, logical coherence.

B. But they are coherent as expressing an organic unity of insight which, rightly interpreted, excludes substantial inconsistency.

1. This is the type of unity we should expect under the circumstances,
2. and it is analogous to the unity of a single personal life.

II. Since individuals and humanity as a whole go through stages of understanding which successively transcend and include the earlier stages, phases in a more inclusive and integrated sweep of insight—so it will not be surprising if God's self-disclosure in the Bible is characterized by successive stages of insight which are themselves gradually being transcended and incorporated within later stages of more inclusive insight in such a way that the whole process matches the corresponding development patterns of those individuals and that humanity to which, through successive phases of growth and cultural development, God condescends to reveal himself. And all this is just what we find in the biblical writings—a gradually unfolding view of God in which much that is only implicit in earlier historical epochs emerges explicitly in the clearly delineated theism of the high prophets of the Old Testament (Isaiah and Jeremiah, for example). There is a pervasive metaphor and symbolism of God's nature and activities in creation and self-disclosure which are to be understood in the light of more specifically doctrinal and didactic passages in other and usually later parts of Scripture; a varied scheme of sacrifices, as transitionally mediating between God and man in earlier times, but progressively interpreted as prefiguring and anticipating the wholly adequate mediatorial work of Jesus as God Incarnate, so that those earlier shadows and images are rendered impertinent through the later light and substance which they dimly mirrored from the first; and a pervasive level of relatively uncomplex direction toward a right moral and spiritual relation to God, a level discernible with a clarity, however incomplete and provisional, which would be accessible even to the least sophisticated and reflective amongst us—yet this extended strain of insight is encompassed by a varying context of intricate conceptualization and doctrinal complexity which continue to challenge our most erudite scholars. In this whole progressive and multifaceted revelation, God condescends to make himself, as it were, accessible to humanity in all the successive epochs of its developing maturity, and, at the same time, to individuals in whatever stage of maturing insight in every such epoch of history and civilization.

And it would, I think, clearly be a mistake to suppose that, at any stage of this developing self-revelation on the part of God, even the most spiritually discerning necessarily saw through the whole intervening process to the final secret of divine self-disclosure. If, at any given stage, some among the people of God misunderstood some provisional fragment of truth by identifying it with the final whole— if, for example, some among the Israelites mistakenly thought of God as merely the God of Israel supreme among the other gods whom nevertheless they construed as actually existing; or if, in further illustration, some took an anthropomorphic representation or metaphorical characterization of God as if it were literal truth; or if, finally, there were, among the people of God in Old Testament times, some (or even many) who had little or virtually no understanding, of the proper conception of God's Messiah, through whom salvation was to be actually accomplished and universally accessible—all this would in no significant sense disturb the organic and intrinsic unity of the scriptural revelation whose earlier phases are adequately understandable in principle only through a correct insight into its later phases. Nor would the fulfillment of all these if-clauses necessarily detract from the genuineness of the personal faith commitment of those who imbibed such provisional fragments as if they were final prosaic truth, since, as I have contended all along, the authenticity of personal faith is not contingent on perfect understanding. After all, even the most philosophically and theologically mature among us undoubtedly imbibe for ourselves numerous shadows and images that we variably but mistakenly identify with light and substance, since we also are lacking in perfect, final insight.

b) nor undermines the genuineness of individual faith at any provisional stage of understanding.

Biblical and theological handbooks of a certain type are often replete with cases in which the biblical writers are supposed to have contradicted one another or held irreconcilable views of the same doctrinal theme. But I suggest that such conclusions are based on a rigorous definition of precision and logical compatibility which is far removed from the complex thought world of the Bible as a whole. Substitute for such a definition the organic conception of coherence which I have attempted to elucidate, and most, if not all, of these purported difficulties will vanish in the light of this more plausible interpretative framework. Instead of contradictions, we will begin to see contrasting tensions which supplement and reinforce each other by bringing out different facets of a comprehensive unity of truth. Or, at a less exalted level, we will recognize the imprecise patterns of ordinary speech habits which are nevertheless correct if properly construed. Thus, for example, Genesis 1 and 2 supplement one another as accounts of creation, as do Kings and Chronicles as accounts of the historical period they describe. Likewise, the synoptic Gospels and John bring out different phases of the life and ministry of Jesus, and arrange and select their subject matter in relation to partly distinct purposes of explanation; the resurrection appearances of Jesus do not confront us with alternative accounts between which we are forced to choose, but rather with fragments which together constitute a larger whole; and Paul and James, correctly understood in conjunction, are both right on the question whether salvation is by faith alone or, in a clearly identifiable sense, also partly by works.

D. If the organic conception of coherence is substituted for a precise formal notion of coherence:

1. Alleged contradictions will be reinterpreted as contrasting tensions which supplement each other, or as imprecise forms of discourse which are correct if properly understood.

2. Some illustrations of these tensions.

The detailed analysis of all this I leave to others with a greater flair for intricate exposition and analysis, since that sort of project is quite beyond the scope of my intent. But the upshot and point of it all is clear enough: If biblical inspiration and authority are understood as I have contended they should be, and if biblical books and passages are correctly interpreted in the light of their total context, and if coherence is itself understood in the organic sense which I have elaborated—then the biblical writings, taken as a conjunctive whole, exhibit a striking inner unity of insight which is not only compatible with the thesis of the revelational status of those writings, but is, in addition, a part of the basis for seeing, behind the surface variety of those very writings and their human authors, the directive guidance of the single, but itself infinitely complex, mind of God himself.

3. Apprehended in the way I have suggested, the biblical writings reflect a pervasive unity of insight which is consistent with their revelational character, and which witnesses to the directive guidance of God's mind.

With General Revelation Systematically:
The External Correlation

I. The knowledge of God from natural revelation can be employed as a complex criterion of assessment:

If, as I argued virtually from the outset, there is a structure of accessible knowledge about the nature of the contingent world order in its multiple dimensions, and about the relation of that order to its ultimate causal ground—and if that ultimate causal ground is most adequately and reasonably understood as transcendent personal mind or God construed in the theistic sense—then that whole structure of knowledge, accessible as it is, in my opinion, quite independently of any logical subordination to any particular claimant to the category of special historical revelation, provides a criterial framework with which any purported revelation must exhibit an extended congruity and coherence of overlapping subject matter, if that revelation claim is to be viewed as in any sense rationally vindicated. And it will also follow that, among alternative revelation claims—so far as they are judged to be genuinely competitive and logically opposed rather than merely supportive and complementary in a reciprocal sense—that claim which, other things being equal, exhibits the more inclusive and multiple applicable congruity with that logically prior metaphysical insight or general revelation will for that very reason be the more plausible revelation claim from a rational point of view. As I have long since indicated, revelation claims are not necessarily logically competitive; and they clearly are not so far as their conceptual content genuinely overlaps or so far as the notion of revelation itself, in any proposed alternatives, is so differently construed that there is no viable logical front along which the alternatives may join issue—precisely because the interpretive frameworks within which the contrasting notions of revelation are understood are themselves so different conceptually. These interpretive frameworks precisely as such, however, can be logically assessed in terms of their congruity and coherence with general revelation as properly construed. And here again, the greater the congruity and coherence of such a framework with that structure of universally accessible metaphysical knowledge, the greater its claim to objective plausibility as well.

A. first, for alternative revelation claims, so far as they are actually competitive;

1. The greater the congruity of a revelation claim with the natural knowledge of God, the more plausible the claim.

2. But such claims are not always genuinely competitive.

B. second, for general interpretive frameworks in which revelation claims are themselves understood.

II. None of the major revelation claims or interpretive frameworks of religious traditions are radically competitive.
A. But there are differences that must be critically evaluated.

B. The determination of comparative plausibility requires an epistemological method which was clarified at the outset of my analysis.

As I understand it, none of the well-developed revelation claims of the major religious traditions of the world, nor the interpretive frameworks within which they are propounded, are radically competitive in the strict logical sense. There are, of course, discernible and even serious differences that call for logical and conceptual adjudication—but there are always also areas of common conceptual territory, so that we simply do not face a situation in which the reasoned acceptance of a given interpretive framework or a revelation claim within it implies the total falsity, much less the pervasive nonsensical character, of all its conceptual alternatives. It is rather a case of greater or lesser plausibility, of more or less adequate total perspectives, of different degrees of reasonableness—all of which might conceivably be arranged on a scale or in a hierarchy. But, of course, the comparative assessment of these alternatives and the provisional determination of their position in such a hierarchy require the use of an epistemological method or set of criterial principles. The structure and categories of that method I have elaborated and argued (in the only sense in which such an issue can be plausibly argued) at the very beginning of my whole analysis, so that it is in no sense relevant to resurrect those old themes in the present context. I shall therefore simply point out that, since this methodological issue was provisionally resolved in the first part of my work, I have employed the interpretive principles which I there attempted to display as rationally basic, even though I do not regard my position as final or absolute in any ultimate sense; and I view my propositional formulations of that position as even more susceptible of appropriate revision and restatement.

Equipped with that epistemology, I then proceeded to argue for a theistic metaphysical world-view, on grounds independent logically of any particular religious or theological framework and of any particular historical revelation claim. And it is precisely that theistic perspective which I here propose as a criterial framework for arranging revelation claims in a sort of logical hierarchy. It is, however, not my purpose actually to set up that hierarchy in any inclusive historical sense. The sheer magnitude of such a task is appalling just to consider, and its execution is in any case not essential to my argument. Instead I propose to argue that the Christian revelation claim exhibits a more extensive congruity and coherence with the general metaphysical perspective I have defended than any other viable alternative revelation claim with respect to its genuinely competitive elements, although at the same time I recognize that some of these elements of correlation characterize other revelation traditions as well.

The personal theism that emerges in the progressive conceptual development of the biblical writings extensively parallels the conclusions about the existence and nature of God that appear in the properly formulated arguments of natural theology. In both, God is the self-existent and transcendent ground of the contingent world order which is his creative product and therefore distinct from himself. In both, God, as personal intelligent will, directs the course of events toward the fulfillment of morally and spiritually significant ends in the context of an objective moral order whose principles are themselves grounded in God's moral character. And in both, God's specific and overarching purpose in creation is the production and progressive development in righteousness of rational, moral selves, made in his image and possessing a derived intrinsic worth which is wholly compatible with a spiritual selfhood and continuing destiny that are independent at their core of the organic human body which is the expressive instrument of those selves. The belief in an objective moral order is characteristic, of course, of virtually all the world's principal religious traditions; but it is often cast in a non-theistic or even pantheistic context, rather than in the context of personal theism, as I have defined it. The belief in the enduring spiritual selfhood of man, beyond the present worldly scene, is somewhat less universal, as is the sense of a divine purpose pervading history and specifying its ultimate goal.

1. But they are more fully and coherently contained in the biblical revelation claim.
2. That claim also provides an unparalleled solution to the problem of moral guilt and corruption through the redemption in Christ.
a) This tension is recognized elsewhere.
b) but no plausible solution is proposed apart from the Christian concept of redemption.

C. An extended personal application.

D. The Christian revelation claim:
1. not only exhibits a greater congruity with natural revelation,
2. but it incorporates into itself the fragments of truth found in other religious visions.

IV. Summary on the Bible and its structure.

But all these elements are more fully and conjunctively embodied in the context and substance of the biblical revelation claim; while in addition there is a unique redemptive core in the Christian perspective through which a solution, in both principle and practice, is provided for the tension between the unconditional claim of objective moral law and the actually defective moral condition of finite moral selves, as a consequence of their wrong moral choices and the resultant corruption of their moral character. Alternative revelation traditions recognize this tension but, as I argued earlier, provide no rationally plausible or effective solution to it, except for the recommendation of a self-transformation which, incredibly difficult at best and practically impossible at worst, hardly solves the problem of objective moral guilt. On the contrary, the Christian thesis—that Jesus, as God Incarnate and as universally representative humanity, vicariously makes moral amends on behalf of collective humanity—provides a solution to the moral impasse between human guilt and the divine moral claim, apart from which the moral and spiritual predicament of humanity may plausibly be judged as hopeless. Earnest effort at the task of moral self-discipline and at the shaping of sound moral character is of central importance, of course; but it is a realistic goal only in a context for which the problem of objective moral guilt is rationally soluble.

All this can be put on a personal level. Surely, when I look at myself in the mirror of the Buddhist Sutras, or the Hindu Vedas and Upanishads, or the Lao-tzu Book, or the Confucian Classics, or the Koran, and so on, I see aspects of my true self and principles that define my moral inadequacy and even glimpses of the one true God who claims me. But when I look at myself in the mirror of the biblical revelation, all that I see elsewhere is brought into clearer focus through its light, however much that light may itself be set in relief by the contemplation of those other visions—and I see, in addition, a path to moral reconciliation with God and my fellow human beings, as well as a spiritual resource for the moral transformation which all those other visions urge upon me in conjunction with the Christian revelation itself. This personal construction is, of course, not an argument by itself, but it individualizes and intensifies the sense of congruity and coherence which the biblical revelation claim exhibits in correlation with the universally accessible metaphysic of theism.

If, then, the Christian revelation claim does in fact involve this sort of congruity and coherence more fully and extensively than alternative revelation claims which nevertheless embody fragments of genuine truth, all that is a plausible reason for the acceptance of that claim as a framework which integrates all those authentic fragments into an inclusive totality of Divine Truth in Jesus as God the Logos Incarnate. Such a commitment need express no disdain for those alternative visions, but may even enable us to see them as they really are; while without that commitment our sight might be obscured by a commingling darkness of inadequate conceptualization and understanding.

Perhaps now we can rehearse in retrospect what emerges from our analysis of the Hebrew-Christian Bible and its structure. It seems fair to conclude that, given the testimony of Jesus and of the biblical writers themselves as to the indefectible authority of the Old Testament as a divine self-disclosure in propositional form, and given the parallelism between the apostolic teaching authority, promised and bestowed by Jesus himself as God Incarnate, with the prophetic office that defined in its exercise the general boundaries of that Old Testament revelation, then it is reasonable to suppose that the most adequate explanation of all these lines of analysis—centered as they are on the teaching authority of Jesus himself—is the thesis that both the Old Testament and the New Testament, properly interpreted in their total context, do indeed constitute an indefectibly authoritative divine revelation. The assumptions concerning Jesus, his disciples, and the biblical writers in general—assumptions about their moral character and psychological state such as would be required as a basis for challenging that conclusion about biblical authority—are so fully implausible (even if they are logically possible) that they cannot be taken seriously on sober reflection. The assumptions I refer to are those that would view Jesus himself, his disciples, and all the biblical writers as, both separately and collectively, either mentally unbalanced to the core or surreptitiously conjoined in a profoundly depraved enterprise of moral skulduggery. I have argued, plausibly I think, that neither of these assumptions is plausible as an interpretation of all the historical and psychological data pertinent to the issue in question.

A. The Hebrew-Christian Scriptures as an indefectibly authoritative divine revelation.

1. This claim is centered in the teaching authority of Jesus himself, through the apostolic and prophetic teaching authority.

2. The assumptions required to discount this claim have been shown to be fully implausible.

At the same time, I have acknowledged that, in identifying the boundaries which determine the collection of books that constitute the biblical writings, we can confidently identify an extensive central core of books which clearly belong in this category, although we may freely recognize, without any serious difficulty for our revelational thesis, that the exact perimeters of that literary collection cannot be identified with absolute and unquestionable precision but rather should be viewed as provisionally and yet plausibly sketched out. The principles of recognition (the criteria of identification) are clear enough as defined by the prophetic office for the Old Testament and the apostolic office for the New, even if the exact limits identifiable by means of these standards remain partly indeterminate for our thinking.

B. While the central core of biblical writings is clearly identifiable, the exact perimeters of the collection may reasonably be regarded as partly indeterminate for our thinking.

If we add to these considerations the striking internal organic unity of insight that is progressively unfolded in the biblical writings, and the equally remarkable completeness of their congruity and coherence of what can be known about God and his relation to the contingent world order quite apart from the biblical revelation itself, then the overall plausibility of the biblical revelation claim achieves an extensive systematic reasonableness that reaches far beyond that which could fairly be claimed for alternative revelation claims so far as they are genuinely competitive. At the same time, those alternative claims need not be dismissed as either totally worthless or fundamentally spurious by those who sincerely recognize the biblical revelation

C. The internal unity of Scripture, and its congruity with natural revelation, make the biblical revelation claim more plausible than its alternatives: but this claim is fully compatible with recognizing elements of the true light of Jesus the Logos in those other revelation claims.

claim as essentially and pervasively correct. If Jesus, as the Logos of God Incarnate, is the radiating light of reason for every human being (John 1:9), we should expect that light to be universally disseminated in varying degrees, even if that same light always stands in contrast to the darkness it penetrates.

The Bible and Science:
The External Relation of Scripture
Propositions to Scientific Truth-Claims

The Nature and Limitations of Scientific Methodology

The concept of science with which I am concerned here does not employ that term in the broadest conceivable sense, as if science were a designation for whatever could be reasonably regarded as knowledge in some specifiable sense. If I used the term in that all-inclusive extension, and if religious truth-claims, properly construed, could, on being rendered reasonable through a discernment of their basis as sound, be referred to as constituting knowledge, then religious knowledge, thus understood, would simply be a subdivision of science and knowledge in general. And if, in particular, the biblical revelation claim were accepted as reasonable, so that its truths constituted knowledge in an identifiable sense, then biblical truth would itself be a category of religious knowledge as a subdivision of science. And then both religious knowledge and biblical truth, as a species of it, would be unique, no doubt, in some respects—but in others it would be comparable in certain formal and structural respects to other subdivisions of science such as history, physics, or psychology. Now I find this way of construing science to be confusing and misleading, at least in terms of the questions with which I am preoccupied in the present context. For one thing, this way of understanding science is likely to be transmuted into the thesis that whatever is not scientifically explainable—

I. The concept of science, in this context, is not identified with the whole of knowledge, of which religious truth would, in that case, be a subdivision and aspect, different from but comparable with other parts of science.

A. This way of defining science is confusing:
1. first, because then all insight that did not conform to a much narrower view of science could mistakenly be eliminated from the status of knowledge;

through scientific concepts and methodology construed in terms of a much narrower notion of science as mathematical-logical formalization, empirical description, and theoretical explanations of phenomena in terms of principles that result from the conjunction of that formalization and description—simply is not or (more strongly) *cannot* be knowledge in any appropriately identifiable sense. In this way, knowledge (that is, science—confusedly understood through the improper conflation of these two different notions of it) would be restricted to the logically formal and the empirically descriptive. When the matter is put in this way, we clearly recognize an old acquaintance: the logical empiricism or logical positivism of the analytic empirical tradition in philosophy. Since I have already dealt critically with this perspective much earlier in my analysis, it is hardly necessary to rehearse all that again. Suffice it to call up the gist of that prior criticism by suggesting that, if knowledge were restricted in this way, then the statement that it was so restricted could not itself be knowledge, since it is neither a statement of formal logic nor an empirically meaningful and verifiable description.

2. second, because it would lead to a tight compartmentalization of subdivisions which would obscure the extensive overlapping of subject matter,

But there is yet another reason why I find questionable the all-inclusive view of science, with all its neat subdivisions. And that is on the ground that it leads to the implied supposition that these subdivisions are more or less tight compartments with very little, if any, commerce or relationship between them in either methodology or subject matter. As far as subject matter is concerned, religious perspectives contain much that is historical, psychological, physical, or whatever; and religious perspectives and concepts are of concern to historians, psychologists, physicists, and other so-called scientists. In fact, the actual overlap of subject matter in various areas of knowledge is far more complicated than these incidental examples suggest, so that the slightest sober reflection should dispel the tight-compartment theory

and the pervasion of basic methodological principles through the whole of knowledge.

with regard to subject matter. As for methodology, I have myself defended from the outset the thesis that there is a universal methodology of knowledge which is in general applicable to all dimensions of cognitive insight, and I have criticized what I have called the internal-criterion view, according to which the criteria of truth-claims are internal to each particular context of thought, so that there are no universal criteria of truth and knowledge which cut across all areas of insight. Here again, there is no reason to rehearse music that has, as it were, already been played. But what is important to mention here is that the universal criteria of knowledge are philosophical in nature, rather than narrowly scientific in the restricted sense. In all areas of knowledge and insight, these universal criteria will be pertinent and applicable; but the application of them to various areas of thought will be variable and relative to the concerns and objectives of that area.

B. Science will therefore be more narrowly construed as mathematical formalization, empirical description, and their conjunction in the theoretical explanation of causal connections.

In the light of these considerations, what notion of science is it functionally useful to employ? While this issue is extraordinarily complicated, and since I have no intention of making any substantial contribution to the philosophy of science as such, I will simply elect to use the term *science* in the narrow and restricted sense in which it includes, as I earlier mentioned, mathematical formalization, empirical description, and the variable conjunction of these two in the construction of theoretical (and therefore also hypothetical) explanations of phenomena in terms of interrelated causal networks. At the same time, I will include not only areas characterized by a very high degree of mathematical formalization (not only mathematics and formal logic themselves, but also physics, chemistry, statistics, and the like)—but, in addition, areas where mathematical formalization is minimal and empirical generalization is predominant (sociology, psychology, biology, history, and the like). I will also take the position already implied that even science in this narrower sense cannot function without employing the universal criteria of knowledge, even though its techniques of mathematical analysis and empirical description and generalization may be highly specialized and technical in nature, in comparison with the use of the analogues and parallels of these techniques in other areas of investigation.

> 1. The scope of science thus defined.

> 2. The dependence of science on universal criteria of knowledge.

If science is construed in the fashion I am suggesting, what account of its limitations is it reasonable to provide in the present religious-philosophical context? One of the fundamental assumptions of scientific explanation is the principle of the so-called uniformity of the natural, empirically discernible realm—to the effect that natural processes are characterized by a sort of regular order, such that the patterns of occurrence in these processes are expected to repeat themselves under similar circumstances and perhaps even in circumstances where that similarity exhibits a degree of merely analogous resemblance that falls short of precise similarity in every relevant respect. From this standpoint, the natural order is viewed as a vast and inclusive network of causally connected and recurring patterns, such that generalization about these connections and patterns are regarded as causal laws which formulate the regular and repeatable sequences of that natural order itself. At the lowest level of generalization, these laws are simply shorthand summaries of the patterns and connections of an immediately observable sequence. But since analogous explanations can be sought for the enduring stability of these shorthand summaries, it follows that at higher levels of explanation we confront increasingly complex and far-reaching theoretical principles of explanation whose justification consists, not in any direct observation of sequences, but rather in the fact (or claim) that if these theoretical principles are assumed, we can deduce from their application the propriety of lower generalizations they were designed to explain, and finally the propriety of the low-level empirical generalizations which are originated in direct empirical observation. In a sense, all this constitutes, in rather intricate fashion, a causal explanation of why ordinary occurrences take place as they do. But, in another sense, explaining an event by subsuming it under a principle of regularity merely describes the fact that such events occur, so that no explanation of why such events occur in that way is really provided. If we go on to a higher level of generalization, that in turn will merely be a description of the lesser principles that are subsumed under it, and so

> II. The limitations of science in the present context.
> A. Scientific explanation, as an increasingly generalized hierarchy of descriptive summaries, may purport to explain why events occur, but they are really only organized statements to the effect that they occur as they do.

on without assignable limit. Hydrogen, for example (or a specific volume of hydrogen), is observed to expand when it is heated. Why? Because hydrogen is a gas, and all gasses expand when they are heated. Why? Because gasses are composed of molecular units whose relative motions are increased and accelerated with rising temperatures. Why? . . . At each level, the explanation not only recedes further from observation, but it also replaces one level of description by another without supplying at any level a finally satisfactory explanation of *why* any of the descriptions hold. Hence, the so-called laws of science are descriptive (because they describe occurrences at successive levels of generalization), but they are in no sense *pre*scriptive in the sense that these theoretical explanations function as causes of the events they are concocted to explain. If therefore we call these principles, at any level, "laws," it is of the utmost importance to keep in mind that they are not laws in the sense of prescribing, causing, or even influencing anything that occurs, since at every level such laws or principles are merely descriptions of what occurs, not explanations of the causes of their occurrence in the sense in which a cause is construed as actually bringing about the occurrence. It is therefore a wholly confusing impropriety if, analogously with political laws, rules of games, and other similar structures involving stipulated procedures, we speak of natural laws being violated, either because we suppose such violations to be impossible in principle, or because we regard certain actual events as clearly occurring in violation of these laws. For, since the so-called natural laws are in no sense prescriptive (as political laws, rules of games, and so forth, clearly are), there is simply nothing there to be violated in the sense implied. All this is not to say that the formulation of these principles of natural regularity is either unimportant or useless. The basic motive of science, from a functional point of view, is prediction on the assumption of regularity with a view to control over natural occurrences in the pursuit of our interests; and the formulation of empirical generalizations about such occurrences clearly subserves that goal. But it is significant to point out that, if law reigns supreme in the contingent world order, it must be some other kind of law beside that of descriptive regularity.

Perhaps an equally significant limitation of science and its methodology, in the sense in which I have understood them here, is the evident implication that scientific explanation, while certainly of basic importance in its own dimension, does not constitute either the totality of explanation in general or the sum of all genuine truth. In a way, these limitations are implicit in my previous analysis: It has already been contended that there is a sense in which scientific explanation of phenomena as purely descriptive is not complete explanation even of those phenomena, since it does not provide an account of the cause of things being as they are, but merely of the fact that they are. And it has also been argued that even the conjunction of all mathematical formalizations and all empirical descriptions and generalizations could not constitute, when propositionally stated, the whole of truth, since the claim that such was the case would itself not be a proposition that falls under these categories. From the combination of these two insights, it follows that both explanation and truth extend beyond science, so that any attempt to dismiss propositions falling outside the dimensions of science as cognitively meaningless, in the sense of making no truth-claim whatever, is a wholly unjustified and in principle unjustifiable enterprise. Even if, for example, scientific explanation wholly bypasses the explanation of certain states of affairs in terms of the causal efficacy of purpose or teleology, that does not mean that this type of explanation is to be discounted in principle. If teleological explanation is non-scientific (on the view of science we are here considering), that does not mean in principle that it is either unscientific or anti-scientific. Again, if ethical, metaphysical, and even certain types of theological propositions are neither formal/logical propositions, as in mathematics and pure logic, nor empirical descriptions or generalizations, they may, if properly formulated, express genuine truth-claims, and they cannot therefore be merely jettisoned without further consideration. If propositions of all these types fall outside of science as rigorously construed, that merely means that truth and explanation extend far beyond science, even though they unquestionably include it.

2. Statements that fall outside of science cannot be dismissed as non-cognitive on that ground alone: for example—teleological, ethical, metaphysical, and theological propositions.

A third limitation of science is that it cannot, through the use of its methods and the subject areas interpreted by the application of these methods, proceed to defend, either in part or in whole, any given world-view perspective or inclusive metaphysical philosophy without transcending its character as science. Individual scientists can of course formulate and defend world-view perspectives; but that is possible because, in addition to being scientists, they are also total human beings and can therefore function, as characteristically they do, in other roles beside those of science. Hence, when a scientist does propound a world-view, its propositions are not scientific statements in any rigorous sense, and its methods, procedures, and assumptions are not those of science as such either. Instead, such a scientist is doing philosophy, and the propriety of his project is not determined by the plausibility of his or anyone else's science, but rather by philosophical methods that fall outside the scientific arena properly construed. It follows that there is no logical alliance between genuine science and any particular philosophical world-view. Numerous individuals with an interest and even a respectable expertise in both science and philosophy have tried to contend that some version or other of metaphysical naturalism has a sort of affinity with, and therefore a strong support from, genuine science, quite in contrast to other metaphysical perspectives which are viewed as bereft of any such affinity or support. But if I am correct in my analysis here, any such contention can now be seen to be a farce, if indeed its impropriety has not been long since unmasked. Of course, and very importantly, that does not mean that world-view perspectives have no obligation to develop a coherent view of the relation of scientific truth to the whole of truth; quite the contrary, in fact—and a world-view may exhibit an aspect of its comparatively greater adequacy by being

C. Science can neither defend nor criticize any world-view perspective through the use of scientific method.

1. Scientists can formulate and critically assess such perspectives, but as a philosophical rather than a scientific enterprise.

2. Hence, there is no logical alliance between genuine science and any particular philosophical world-view.

3. Yet theories of the relation between science and philosophy are an important part of philosophy itself.

capable of, and actually carrying out, a more totally plausible view of that relation. Science may not be the whole of truth; but it is an important part of that whole, with the entire scope of which any comprehensive philosophy is called upon to deal.

The Relation Between Scientific Theories and the Biblical Perspective

I. It follows from the previous analysis that, when religion and science are so construed, there is no logically possible conceptual conflict between them.

A. But individual proponents of them may have possible and legitimate quarrels:

1. either because religion and science are misconstrued;

2. or because they are actually debating philosophical perspectives on philosophical grounds.

B. It is possible for the religionist to do legitimate science, and vice versa;

but the real opposition is between viable world-view alternatives.

If the previous analysis of both religion and science is accepted as reasonable, it will follow at once that not merely is there no necessary antagonism between religion and science, but there is, if religion is construed in its world-view dimension and science is construed in a rigorous fashion, no logically possible and direct opposition between them in the conceptual sense. In general, religious truth-claims as such, in the respect that I have in mind, are not propositions of genuine theoretical science; and scientific truth-claims are not world-view propositions. Religion, thus construed, has no logically possible quarrel with science properly delineated; and science in turn has no such quarrel with religion either. But this does not mean that individual proponents of religion and science have no possible or even, in numerous cases, legitimate quarrel. And that quarrel may take in general one or other of two forms. The first is a form based on confusion and occurs when either the religionist or the scientist takes the position (mistaken, as I suppose) that some genuine religious world-view truth-claim actually does contradict a proposition of genuine science, or else that some statement of the latter actually does contradict some thesis of the former. The second form is based on a clear understanding that any genuine quarrel is actually philosophical in nature, so that the opposition is between the religionist, as propounding a given world-view perspective, and the scientist who, as a total human being like the religionist, propounds, quite outside the dimensions of his science as such, a contrasting world-view perspective which disagrees in certain respects with that of the religionist. In general, this means that all the real controversies are philosophical in nature and must be addressed at that level. But it is also possible (although I have the impression that it is both rare and extraordinarily difficult in the genuine sense) for the religionist to enter science as himself a scientist and attempt to discredit the genuineness of another person's alleged science on truly scientific grounds—or for the scientist to assume the guise of the religionist with entire sincerity and full awareness in order to attempt to discredit the plausibility of another's religious truth-claims on genuinely philosophical grounds. If all this can be openly recognized, then at least the battle lines can be clearly drawn, and the warfare, although it doubtless will continue, can be carried out on the proper field of confrontation. When that happens, it will appear, I think, that it is not really a warfare between science and religion, but rather one among viable (or at least discussable) world-view alternatives in philosophy. This conclusion does not mean, as I previously indicated, that religion and science have no overlapping areas of concern regarding general areas of subject matter. Both may be, and often are, interested in history, the dimensions of human activity, the motivations that influence human behavior, and so on. But they can truly disagree here only if the religionist acknowledges the world-view dimensions of his own perspective as the focus of the opposition, and if the scientist steps outside the dimensions of his science and takes up a world-view perspective of his own to defend. The case will not be altered even if neither openly and clearly recognizes the true face of the situation, although it certainly will clarify the circumstances if both do realize what they are actually about in their opposition.

Suppose, now, that these conclusions are applied to the biblical outlook characterized as embodying, at least implicitly, a world-view perspective of the organically unified type that I clarified earlier. Since that perspective is in general religious-philosophical in character, then there can be, in that perspectival sense, no real controversy between the biblical world-view and genuine science. For the understanding of science that is involved in any given perspective of this sort is not itself actual science but rather a philosophy of the character of science—not unlike, in structure, the analysis of science that I am myself now involved in developing, an analysis which, although about science and its presuppositions, is clearly not scientific in content. And any objection to the biblical perspective on the part of the scientist as an individual will be from the standpoint, not of his science as such, but rather of an alternate world-view perspective with which he challenges the biblical perspective as formulated by some particular interpretive tradition. Yet this general scheme requires certain qualifications by reason of the overlapping subject matter with which both science and the biblical perspective are obviously concerned. The biblical propositions contain, for example, a wide range of historical truth-claims about particular persons and events stretching over a comparably wide cultural range and extending over a long temporal period. If we are to include history, in its truly scientific and descriptive aspect, as a part of genuine science, then of course the determination of the factual character of the historical accounts in the Bible will fall under the jurisdiction of history in its descriptive aspect just so far as pertinent data are available for making the determination (which often such data are not). But what characteristically and perhaps even inevitably happens is that a fabric of world-view interpretation is woven into the factual content of a given historical account, both in the Bible and in some purportedly scientific analysis of the same account and its descriptive history, so that the old confusion is generated again, and the genuinely scientific aspect is in varying degrees obscured. Whether, for example, Jesus was an actual historical person, when he was born and when he died and under what circumstances, whether in fact he appeared alive on various occasions to his disciples after he had died—all these are genuine historical issues to be settled

C. Yet religion and science do have overlapping areas of concern.

1. But the religionist and the scientist can truly disagree only in a world-view context, 2. whether or not this is consciously realized by the participants.

II. There can thus be no real controversy between the biblical world-view and genuine science.

A. Genuine disputes are between world-view perspectives (and even different philosophical accounts of the nature of science and its relation to religion).

B. But this scheme must be qualified due to overlapping subject matter.

1. While the factuality of historical accounts is properly scientific concern, world-view aspects are characteristically woven into the factual account, so that the old confusion is again regenerated. 2. An illustration concerning an historical account of Jesus.

a) Attempts are sometimes made to settle genuine historical issues on world-view grounds, so that the discussion is no longer scientific.

by historical methods, even though, at the same time, they are of great significance to the biblical perspective as a world-view. But if an allegedly scientific investigator tries to settle such issues on grounds that are themselves rooted in some world-view—if, for instance, he argues that the resurrection of Jesus did not take place on the ground that any such event is empirically impossible in principle in view of his own belief in the unexceptionable regularity of the natural order— then such an investigator is no longer doing scientific history at all, but is instead pitting world-views against each other, so that whether his claim is correct or not no longer falls under the jurisdiction of

b) Non-scientific issues lie outside the limits of history as science rigorously construed.

history of a science. On the other hand, questions such as whether Jesus had a transcendent existence before his birth into the world, whether he was God Incarnate, whether in his life and death he acted as universally representative humanity in a redemptive sense, and whether, if he was resurrected, that event was uniquely attributable to divine power and constituted a divine affirmation of Jesus' person and mission—all these and other queries like them in type are simply outside the limits of historical investigation in the rigorously scientific sense, although they may be philosophically viewed as a part of re-demption history in a strikingly different and non-scientific (though

c) The attempt to argue historical issues on philosophical grounds may some-times be plausible, but it is not historical science.

not unscientific) sense. It is, of course, important to add that, if the grounds urged by a defender of the biblical perspective—in support either of his position about the genuinely historical issues previously mentioned, or of his views about the clearly interpretive and world-view questions now being considered—are in fact themselves clearly world-viewish and philosophical in character, then his arguments, while they may legitimately support his claims philosophically, are nevertheless not legitimate history in the rigorously scientific sense. Philosophically oriented arguments may on occasion make it ration-ally plausible to believe or disbelieve certain historical propositions in circumstances where scientific history is impotent to decide the issue on genuinely descriptive grounds; but he plausibility is grounded in philosophical congruity, not, as such, in historical science.

3. Biblical statements about overlapping subject matter are not cast in the language of technical, postula-tional science, but in the language of phe-nomenal appearance expressed in culturally relative terms.

More pointedly, it should be obvious to the reflective reader of the Bible that the propositions of Scripture, which overlap historical, cos-mological, biological, psychological, physical, chemical, astronomical, or any other science in subject matter, do not provide an alternative scientific account to those given by these sciences so far as they restrict themselves to genuine science, although those propostions do clearly provide, when properly interpreted, an alternative perspectival and philosophical interpretation in contrast to opposing perspectives which themselves have a world-view character. For one thing, as I have contended in earlier contexts, the language of the Bible in these overlapping areas of subject matter is simply not that of technical, postulational science. It is rather that of phenomenal appearance, cast in the terms commonly used for such matters in the culture of the time and expressed in a large variety of literary forms which would be

a) Some biblical illus-trations.

quite foreign to technical science in any period of its developed for-mulation. Thus, the biblical writers speak of sunrise and sunset (just as we do ourselves in common parlance); they refer to psychological functions in terms which, taken at their face value, would imply that these functions are operations of bodily organs such as the heart, liver, kidneys, and bowels; they use round numbers and rough approximations which lack the precision and exactness of a more studied scientific context; and the writer of Genesis speaks of the creation under the imagery of the seven days of a human work week, and later says of the Noahic deluge that its waters covered all the high mountains under the heavens, because that would have been the appearance to the human observer, had he scanned everything to the horizon of his vision. These illustrations are but a limited sample of a much more extended character of the biblical writings; and what they illustrate seems clearly to be that the writers were not using the language of descriptive science and therefore did not intend to be providing an alternative scientific account. Yet the whole of it, when fairly understood in its total cultural, linguistic, literary, and historical context, is plausibly interpretable as correct in relation to the claims actually being made by the writers. In general, the biblical accounts simply do not theorize about proximate, secondary, and instrumental causes or means in any sense comparable to the attempts at such theorizing on the part of technical science.

b) Thus the biblical writings do not provide alternative accounts, although they are correct when properly interpreted.

My thesis on this issue has, of course, extended consequences. It means, for example, that the biblical account of creation is misconstrued if it is taken as a scientific cosmology, and that the biblical account of the origin and hierarchy of living things is equally misconstrued if it is taken as a scientific biology. The intent of the biblical account is to ascribe, through a literary framework of imagery, the entire cosmos and the whole spectrum of living things to God's creative activity—while at the same time it is a mistake to see all this as an account of the proximate means that God employed to implement creation in detail. This does not settle the controversy between, say, theistic evolutionism and direct creationism as accounts of the origin either of life in general or of human life in particular. It merely claims that the resolution of such issues is not the intent of the scriptural account. Parallel accounts could be given in the areas of psychology, astronomy, and other such disciplines of science; but I spare myself and the reader the labor of such details, since the principle and result will be the same. If my conclusions about all this are correct, it will also be a mistake to try to foist upon the Scripture writers any occasional prevision of the insights of a science far later than that of their own historical epoch, as if their revelation claim were to be supported by a series of striking burst into modern "scientese" which could only be ascribed to the Divine Omniscience. Any such supposition would simply reintroduce that prolific confusion which I have all along been attempting to resolve in principle. In any case, the science of our own age is hardly final; and the critics of some later epoch might well find the Bible's conformity to our present science—by then partly outmoded—to be an objection to the biblical revelation claim, rather than a significant support for it, although in either case that same old

C. Consequences of the view here taken.
1. The Biblical accounts of the creation in general and of living things in particular are not to be taken as scientific theory.

2. So with other areas of scientific concern.

3. The Scripture is not to be interpreted as previsioning modern scientific theory.
a) That would reconstitute the old confusion.

b) The conformity of Scripture to present science might constitute a later objection in terms of the same confusion.

confusion would be carried along. Let science be science—and not philosophy masquerading under a different name. And let the Scripture be divine revelation perspectivally understood—and not philosophy misconstruing itself as rigorous science!

III. Thus there is no reason to question the scriptural revelation claim on scientific grounds.
A. From the biblical point of view, science, as science, is a wholly legitimate enterprise.
B. But it should be purged of its association with anti-religious philosophy, so that the real contest between world-views can be seen in its true light.

It is, of course, often said that the biblical revelation claim cannot be accepted precisely because its propositions are allegedly incompatible with those of science. But that contention can now itself be unmasked as based on a serious, pervasive, and even insidious confusion which does no service either to the biblical world-view or to genuine science. From the standpoint of a properly construed and biblically oriented philosophy, science is, as science, a wholly legitimate enterprise whose historically mistaken bondage to anti-biblical philosophy (or any other sort of philosophical perspective as such) may now be reasonably pronounced dead. In fact, a committed believer in the biblical outlook may well regard science, purged of that erroneous association, as itself resurrected into its true nature as science, and he may then say of science thus understood, as Jesus said of the resurrected Lazarus: "Release him, and let him go!" At the same time, genuine science will do well to pursue its work outside the poisoned attitude of an anti-religious or even anti-Christian motif, and to allow the battles between the biblical perspective, in its multiple philosophical versions, and its genuinely opposed alternatives to be fought with their true and proper weapons.

The Evidential Support of the Scriptural Revelation Claim in the Area of Scientific Subject Matter

Empirical Science and the Problem of Miracle

I. The supposition of a conflict between the biblical view and the science is particularly tenacious in relation to the idea of the miraculous.

It hardly needs repeating that, on the position I have elaborated, there can be no real conflict or antagonism between the biblical world-view perspective and genuine scientific explanation, when both are properly construed. Yet certain purported antagonisms have historically proved to be extremely tenacious and hence very difficult to resolve in practice. The main context of this lingering and seemingly stubborn tension has to do with the notion of miracle and one of its principal species in the form of prophecy as the prediction of the future. The notion of divine acts as providing evidential support for the biblical revelational claim appears to be an important aspect of the biblical outlook. And if these acts, regarded as authentic historical occurrences, are understood as deviations from the order of natural law, whether as violating the principles of that law or transcending them in some identifiable fashion, then, since the formulation of natural law and the explanation of all events through it may be regarded

A. This problem arises because miracles are often construed as deviations from natural law as the proper concern of science.

as the proper domain of science, it seems to follow that the occurrence of such events would be incompatible with the ideal of scientific explanation. The impression of such an antagonism is noticeably reinforced by certain definitions of the concept of miracle which have been propounded both by supporters of the idea of the miraculous and also by critics of that idea. If, with David Hume, we define a miracle outright as a violation of natural law, and if we then regard such laws as descriptive generalizations regarding natural occurrences, so that we identify these laws solely by the observation of repeatable sequences in experience, then it will follow that a miracle is impossible by direct experience on the part of any observer, since anything that occurs is presumed *ipso facto* to be explainable in terms of some principle of natural regularity properly formulated and qualified on experiential grounds. If, with Thomas Aquinas, we define a miracle as an event whose occurrence is beyond the conjunctive and intrinsic powers of any combination of natural agents, then a miracle will by definition lie outside the scope of scientific explanation, since its occurrence will be possible only through the operation of a unique divine agency which stands in contrast to explanation in terms of natural agents as the proper domain of scientific explanation. If, with still other thinkers, we regard a miracle as a supervention on lower levels of reality through whose intrinsic operating principles the event could not occur—a supervention, that is, of the operating principles of some higher level of reality, so that a miracle in the religiously pertinent sense will be a supervention of transcendent divine law on various aspects of the natural order construed as lower levels of this sort—then we will still be viewing the natural order itself as a rigorous order of laws whose operation would be drastically altered or suspended by the supervention. And once again such miraculous events would stand outside the domain of scientific explanation, since presumably that sort of explanation could not, in principle, extend to the formulation of the immanent operating principles or laws of divine activity. All of these conceptions serve to polarize the contrast between those events regarded as miraculous, on the one hand, and the sort of ordinary events which are susceptible of scientific explanation, on the other hand. And they all carry with them, as I see it, the assumption that any event for which a scientific explanation, in terms of formulated principles of natural regularity, can be plausibly given could not be a miracle in the specified sense— with the result that as scientific explanation expands, the realm of the genuinely miraculous is progressively diminished and might, in theory, finally disappear. Even if we regard these first-class miracles, thus construed, as supplemented by second-class miracles which, although in principle scientifically explainable, nevertheless present a striking illustration of divine agency at least for those unfamiliar with that scientific explanation, the tension between the miraculous and the scientifically explainable is nevertheless retained.

For my part, I regard any and all of these conceptions of miracle as the proliferation of that old confusion which I have all along been

B. This antagonism is increased by certain definitions of miracle: 1. as the violation of natural law construed as observable regularity;

2. as occurrences that are beyond the intrinsic power of natural agents;

3. as the supervention of divine law on lower levels of reality as constituting the natural order.

C. Such conceptions polarize the contrast between the miraculous and the scientifically explainable, with the implication that whatever is explainable by the latter is excluded from the former.

D. All such definitions proliferate the old confusion.
1. The biblical writings do not contrast God's mighty acts with natural events, or regard them as violations of the natural order.

2. The natural order itself is sustained by immanent divine agency, although contingent things have a derived intrinsic causal efficacy.

3. The cosmological argument entails the conclusion that God's agency pervades all contingent being.

4. The descriptive view of natural law leads to the same conclusion.
E. Hence, there is no inviolable structure of natural law, since all natural events and agencies are sustained by divine causality.
II. An adequate concept of miracle.
A. Since miracles are not violations of natural law or agency, there is no conceivable antagonism here between miracle and science, which itself is describing the operation of divine causality.

attempting to dispel. And I think that this can best be seen if we weave together certain threads of our previous analysis which compose a unitary fabric with the biblical writings themselves. If one searches those writings for any suggestion, much less specific thesis, that the biblical writers regard the mighty acts of God as standing in contrast to the structure of natural occurrences—and especially if he looks for some vindication of the notion that these acts violate or suspend an otherwise fixed realm of nature—he will certainly find little reward for his efforts; for that concept of miracle is, in my opinion, simply foreign to the biblical thought world. The New Testament, for example, refers to these divine acts as signs, or wonders, or deeds of power; but there is, so far as I know, no suggestion that these acts are an intrusion into an otherwise inviolable natural order. Instead, the biblical writings regard the natural order itself as continuously sustained in its existence and operation by the operation of an immanent divine agency or causality which pervades the whole of that order down to its last detail. This does not mean that contingent entities (persons or things) have no intrinsic causal efficacy of their own. It does mean, however, that they exist and possess that efficacy only through the uninterrupted operation of divine causality as making that contingent being and power possible (cf. Ps. 19; Acts 14:17; 17:24–28; Heb. 1:3; Rom. 1:20; Col. 1:15–17, and so on). Now combine this biblical notion with two other insights I developed previously. Consider, first, the cosmological argument, from the fact that any particular thing exists or particular event occurs with God as the sole adequate causal explanation of that thing or occurrence through however many proximate means or instruments—that argument, I suggest, quite apart from any dependence on the biblical witness, makes it equally clear that God's causal agency pervades the whole contingent order of things, so that, for example, I could neither be the person I am nor perform any function of activity except through the sustaining causality of God. Then add to this doubly propounded thesis my more recent contention that the principles of regularity, which natural occurrences illustrate, are not really laws in any prescriptive or causal sense at all, but only in the descriptive sense that these principles generalize the natural occurrences that, in a very limited sense, they purport to explain. The combination of these insights leads to the conclusion that there is no rule of natural law, no inviolable structure of unexceptionable regularity to be violated or suspended, no wholly intrinsic power of natural agents to be supplemented or set aside by an act of divine causality that stands in contrast with that agency—for it is the divine causality itself that accounts for the observable regularity of natural occurrences, for the derived intrinsic power of natural agents, and hence for the rule of law in the only sense in which it may be reasonably construed.

And now we can perhaps piece together the main elements of an adequate concept of miracle. Negatively, a miracle is not a violation of natural law, or an event beyond the power of natural agents, or an occurrence requiring the supervention of transcendent divine law for its explanation, since divine causality in the specified sense is required as the ultimate explanation of *all* occurrences, as I have indicated. And there is therefore, in this framework of thought, no conceivable antagonism between miracles as acts of God and the ideals of a genuine science whose function can now be envisioned as the formulation of descriptive generalizations which specify, in a limited sense, the operational structure of immanent divine causality. More positively, a miracle (a sign, wonder, or deed of divine power) is an occurrence, or conjunction of occurrences, which, because of its striking contrast to ordinary occurrences and because of its moral and purposive propriety in relation to God's providence, calls the special attention of an appropriately prepared observer to the operation, in this particular case, of an immanent divine causality which in fact is universally operative. It is, of course, indisputably the case that, for the qualified observer, the impact of the operation of that divine causality can take place even if that observer construes the relation of divine causality to the natural order in some partially or wholly inadequate fashion (such, for example, as that of the theories I am here contesting). What makes an observer qualified is his readiness, on whatever grounds, to construe events in terms of some possible relation to divine causality. The one disqualification would be the insistence in principle on the absolute exclusion of operative divine causality from explanation at any level whatever. Thus, for a given qualified observer, any conjunction of occurrences which confronted him with the stark reality of divine causality in operation could for that reason take on the hue of the miraculous.

And all this has a clear implication about the relation of a given miraculous event to the enterprise of scientific explanation. Since the miraculous character of such an event no longer is understood as in competition with the scientific explanation of it, it follows that a properly construed scientific explanation of it, no matter how thorough, in no sense discredits the quality of the event as miraculous. In fact, the Bible itself provides occasional insight into the fact that God's operational causality acts through the functioning of second causes which are the appropriate subject matter of scientific explanation. Thus, in the Exodus account of the crossing of the Sea of Reeds, we are told that God Himself drove the sea back throughout an entire night by means of a strong east wind, so that the Israelites could cross, as on dry land, what had previously been a stretch of open water (Exod. 14:21,22). Here there is no contrast between God's mighty act of deliverance and the operation of the natural causality of the wind, but rather the conjunctive operation of both in what is nevertheless a profoundly miraculous event to the Israelites who are thus saved from the Egyptians. Therefore, we are certainly not surprised at the writer's statement that when the Israelites saw the great power of God against the Egyptians, they were themselves moved to deeper reverence and trust in God who had thus acted (v. 31). What they actually saw, of course, was the water held back by the wind so that they could cross on dry land, the Egyptians thrown into confusion in attempting to do

B. The definition of miracle as an event that calls particular attention to divine causality.

C. The concept of a qualified observer.

1. The essential qualification.

2. The only disqualification.

D. Hence, a scientific explanation can logically never discredit the quality of any actual event as miraculous.

E. An extended biblical illustration: the crossing of the Sea of Reeds.

the same, and the waters rolling over those same Egyptians and sweeping them helplessly away. And to them, qualified observers as they were, that was precisely seeing the great power of the Lord displayed, so that it was perfectly appropriate for the writer to say, in conjunction with his account of the operation of these natural causes, that it was the Lord who swept the Egyptians into the sea (Exod. 14:27).

F. The view of miracle here propounded:

1. does not settle the historicity of any particular event;

2. but it shows that the miraculous is wholly consistent with scientific and natural law properly construed.

This theoretical and conceptual understanding of the miraculous and its relation to the natural order does not, of course, settle anything about the actual historicity of any particular event which strikingly displays God's power in some specific set of circumstances. What the account does settle is the point that, in a theistic universe for which the natural order itself is causally dependent on God for its total existence and operation, there is no objection in principle against the possibility of miracles, either on the ground that such events can be explained through the operation of natural causes and are not therefore actually miraculous, or on the ground that such events could not logically occur, since their occurrence would be incompatible with the law-abiding character of the natural order itself. Such objections, from the point of view I have elaborated, can now clearly and justifiably be

G. Nor is it a reasonable objection that, on these terms, any event could be miraculous.

1. That claim is correct in principle, but it is not an objection apart from the old confusion.

regarded as based on serious confusion and misconstruction. It is sometimes claimed that, on the view of the miraculous which I have propounded, miraculous events would provide no distinctive evidential support for the reality of divine power, since any conjunction of events whatever could, in theory, provide for some qualified observer a wholly comparable reminder of divine power. In a sense, this claim is correct; but it is hardly intelligible as an objection to the position, unless the old confusion about a tension between the miraculous and the scientifically explainable is surreptitiously smuggled in as a disguised premise. If all contingent causality is possible only through the operation of divine causality and in pervasive dependence upon it, then it is hardly an objection to conclude that, in principle, any conjunction of events might for some qualified observer be construed as

2. In any case, certain types of events have been especially provocative reminders of divine causality.

a miraculous display of God's power. However true this may be, certain types of events have for a large cross section of observers involved such an extraordinary contrast to the standard routines of common human experience that these events are viewed as particularly striking reminders of God's omnipresent reality and operation.

III. The resurrection of Jesus as the crucial miracle.
A. The New Testament emphasis.

If we consider the train of biblically recorded events commonly construed as miraculous, it seems clearly to be the case that the most central and impressive event of this sort is the bodily resurrection of Jesus after his death on the cross. The Book of Acts and the Epistles of Paul make it especially evident that the disciples and apostles, in preaching the gospel of Christ, emphasized as crucial to their message that the resurrection of Jesus was a mighty act of God which vindicated not only Jesus' Messianic claim but also the full adequacy of his redemptive achievement through his vicarious sacrificial death as universally representative humanity—so much so that Paul could speak of that event, before the intellectuals of Athens, as a universally persuasive and motivating assurance that God had offered to all men, regardless of their religious and cultural background (Acts 17:31). Many of the miraculous signs recorded in the Bible are such otherwise unknown occurrences that there is no way to assess their plausibility as actual occurrences except by viewing them as authentic because of their place in the biblical record, itself viewed as indefectibly authoritative divine revelation. Nor is this logical move intrinsically unreasonable in principle. If as I have argued, it is reasonable, on grounds quite independent of these miraculous elements, to acknowledge the Bible as divine self-disclosure, then that overall reasonableness will support the plausibility of the actual occurrence of the events that compose a part of the biblical record, when, of course, that record is properly interpreted in context. But, in the case of the resurrection of Jesus, the situation is strikingly different. For this event, regarded as an actual occurrence and interpreted as divine vindication of Jesus' mission, is virtually the historical condition of the very existence of the Christian community from the first, since without it the band of disciples would doubtless have ceased to exist as a group by reason of the overwhelming discouragement that would have been occasioned by the irreversible loss of the one on whom they had pinned all their hopes. Nor is there any believable possibility of fraud here. So sincere and so unexceptionable is the confidence of that first circle of disciples in Jesus' resurrection, that any supposition of a joint deception here cannot be taken seriously, since the disciples had everything to lose and nothing to gain if they unitedly proclaimed the resurrection of Jesus when in fact they knew it was all a lie. In fact, not only is the reality of the resurrection the only plausible explanation of their belief in it, but that unwavering belief is the only plausible explanation of the continued existence of the community of believers itself. Of course, all sorts of ingenious theories have been concocted to explain away the event without acknowledging its actual occurrence—that the disciples stole the body of Jesus, that Joseph removed the body and thus provided a base for the alleged myth of the empty tomb, that the resurrection appearances were individual and group hallucinations, that it was only the spirit of Jesus that appeared, that the women who came to the tomb after Jesus' death made a mistake about its location, and so on. I think it fair to say that voluminous scholarly treatises have been written to discount any and all such explanations by showing that they simply do not exhibit a plausible congruity with the reliable information we clearly have about the fate of the believing community after Jesus' death. All of these theoretical constructions, both ancient and modern, have in common that they suppose the actual corpse of Jesus to have been reposing in some nearby location at the very time that the disciples were proclaiming his resurrection. But the enemies of Jesus had such a vested interest in discounting his Messianic claim that they would, both literally and figuratively, have left no stone unturned in their effort to produce the corpse and thus forever silence the Christian zealots. Add to that the obvious point that the preservation of a secret deception about the resurrection, on the part of the

B. Numerous biblical signs are such that the question of their historicity can only be investigated indirectly and contextually:

but the case of the resurrection is an exception.
1. The resurrection as the condition of the existence of the Christian community after Jesus' death.

2. The unreasonableness of explanation in terms of fraud.

C. Alternate explanations of the resurrection.
1. Some views listed.

2. None of these views explain all the reliable information about the fate of the believing community after Jesus' death.
a) The problem of the corpse of Jesus.

b) The implausibility of joint fraud.

early disciples, would have been a secret so difficult to keep in such a wide circle of adherents that the likelihood of such joint fraudulent deception reduces virtually to zero. Yet there is not a shred of evidence that any early believer ever bolted from that first community of disciples and denounced the gospel on the ground that Jesus had not risen from the dead after all. Under the circumstances, the evidence for Jesus' bodily resurrection seems therefore stronger than that for

3. The rejection of the resurrection is generally based on the assumption that such events are impossible in principle—but this contention is based on a confusion.

any reasonably comparable ancient event. But I will labor the point no further, except to say that if the historical reality of the resurrection is rejected by whomsoever, it will not be from a genuine and objective lack of reasonable supportive evidence. It will instead be from a relatively *a priori* assumption that such events are impossible in principle—and I have already provided reasonable grounds for regarding that assumption as itself grounded in conceptual confusion. Given,

D. Given our present context, the resurrection of Jesus is a profoundly motivating assurance of God's power.

therefore, the theistic context I have argued, and the reasonableness of Jesus' Incarnation claim; and given, as well, the plausibility of the claim that Scripture is an indefectibly authoritative divine revelation—and all this is the framework in which we now operate—the bodily resurrection of Jesus is a wholly appropriate and profoundly motivating assurance of divine power, and therefore an entirely reasonable belief even on the part of the most sober-minded and reflective among us.

Historical/Psychological Science and the Problem of Prophecy

I. Predictive prophecy, as a species of the miraculous, is analogously explainable.

An unusually provocative subset of the miraculous in general confronts us in the phenomena associated with predictive prophecy. It is evident enough that both the Old Testament and the New Testament contain passages which purport to predict the future. And it is equally plain, as I contended in discussing the prophetic office in an earlier context, that the biblical writings represent the success of such prophecies, through their fulfillment, as a sign of the divine origin of the particular prophetic message as a whole. Now since such predictive prophecies, so far as they are genuine and occur in the religious context appropriate to them, are correctly regarded as miraculous,

A. Such events do not violate the order of natural regularity.

then the general explanation of such prophecies will be the same as the parallel explanation of miracles as a class. It will therefore be a mistake here also to view predictive prophecies as violating and opposing the order of natural regularity—and we can simply "plug in" the whole of our previous analysis of the concept of miracle at this

B. The revelatory significance of prophecy would not be lessened by any explanation of its occurrence through intermediate causes.

point. Nor is it the case that the propriety of such prediction as a revelatory sign will be lessened for qualified observers, if it turns out that a faculty of predictive insight is an intrinsic human potentiality which is actualized in certain aspects of the biblical revelation. While there is continued debate about such issues, at least some respected psychological investigators have conducted tests with individual human subjects who appear to the investigators to have a verified, if impermanent, capacity to predict future events concerning such relatively trivial events as the order of a deck of cards yet to be shuffled, or the arrangement of a collection of books yet to be placed on a shelf. I do not regard myself as competent to assess the interpretation of either these experiments or their interpreted results in parapsychology. But I merely use this information as an illustration of my thesis that the explanation of prophecy as involving the operation of an intrinsic human capacity, however far that explanation could reasonably be extended, is in no sense inconsistent with the recognition of that prophecy as a sign of divinely grounded knowledge and therefore also of genuine revelatory status. We should indeed expect that the inspiring Holy Spirit would take up as instruments all the intrinsic capacities of the biblical writers that were pertinent to their position as means of divine revelation, since, after all, the very existence of those writers and the operative efficacy of all their faculties are grounded, for a theistic position, in divine causality.

Yet the old confusion persists here also. Numerous literary critics of the Bible operate on the (for them) unquestioned assumption that genuine prediction of the future is impossible in principle on the ground that the occurrence of such prediction would run counter to the regular order of nature with respect to the ordinary means of acquiring information—means which would limit prediction to those probable conjectures about the future which are deducible from our present knowledge of empirical circumstances as interpreted through some structure of theoretical explanation. (In this way, for example, we can predict the relative positions of planets and the occurrence of solar and lunar eclipses at particular future times.) Since the predictive prophecy in the Bible far exceeds in its scope what could be confidently deduced by causal inference from present circumstances, it is assumed that the actual occurrence of such predictions would be incompatible with the ideals of scientific explanation. Given this interpretive framework of assumptions, biblical critics then proceed to limit their conclusions about the dating and contents of biblical books on the sheer assumption that genuine predictive prophecy is impossible in principle. If, for example, the Book of Isaiah contains, in its last twenty-seven chapters, predictions about historical events that occurred after the time of the original Isaiah, then Isaiah could not have written those chapters—which are therefore assigned to a later and otherwise unknown author (usually called Second or Deutero-Isaiah). Or if the Book of Daniel contains prophecies about events in the second century B.C., it could not have been written before that time and hence, was certainly not written, at least with its present detailed content, by the historical Daniel who lived several centuries earlier. Or if certain events in the life of Jesus correspond to predictive passages in the Old Testament to a degree that goes beyond mere coincidence, then it must be, in view of the evident previous existence of the books in question, that this correspondence was contrived by Jesus and others in a sort of massive and deceptive plot that would enable Jesus to pass himself off as the generally expected Jewish Messiah, with whatever personal and political advantage that might bring him. Ex-

---

1. Parapsychology as a possible illustration.

2. We may expect the inspiring Spirit to use intrinsic human capacities where pertinent.

II. The persistent confusion.
A. Literary critics commonly regard predictive prophecy as impossible in principle because opposed to scientific explanation.

1. The assumption elucidated.

2. The application of the assumption to biblical criticism.

amples of this sort could be multiplied, but these illustrations are sufficient to clarify the principle. The whole fabric of this reasoning is, of course, miswoven from the start. Scientific laws cannot limit occurrences, since they are merely descriptive generalizations; and the ascription of a genuine predictive prophecy to divine agency is wholly compatible in principle with its being scientifically explainable in principle through the expansion and actualization of intrinsic human capacities which are themselves existent and functional only through divine causality from a theistic point of view. While these points do not settle the whole critical question about the illustrations cited, they do make it clear that the unquestioned assumption of the impossibility of predictive prophecy is based upon a confusion about both scientific explanation and the occurrence of the miraculous with which that explanation is alleged to be imcompatible.

There are, of course, numerous biblical prophecies that obviously remain unfulfilled—prophecies about the end times, for example, and especially about the second coming of Jesus in glorious triumph and about the future resurrection of the dead. Quite apart from the question as to how these prophecies are to be interpreted on the assumption of their genuinely predictive character, it is certainly not necessary, as if in the name of science, to dismiss them (and other similar unfulfilled predictions) as the rampant delusions of eschatological fantasy. Since, as I have contended, scientific explanation, as purely descriptive, makes nothing that is logically conceivable impossible in principle, neither does it render impossible either genuine predictive prophecy or the yet-to-transpire events which it anticipates. The question of the genuineness of prophecy must therefore be approached, and can only be approached appropriately, in an interpretive framework from which our now timeworn confusion has been ejected.

Again, as in the case of miracle in general, the focus of prophetic genuineness centers on Jesus himself, at least in the sense that in his case the antiquity of the predictions is so indisputable, their extent so wide-ranging, and their detail so specific that in this context the question of the genuineness of predictive prophecy faces a clearly decisive test. So many treatises have been written on the specific Old Testament prophecies which were fulfilled in the person of Jesus that I do not regard it as pertinent to my argument to spell all this out in depth and detail. The task has been so well done by biblical scholars that its reintroduction here would be analogous to reinventing the wheel. That the Messiah would be born in Bethlehem (Mic. 5:2; Matt. 2; Luke 2),

from the tribe of Judah (Gen. 49:10; Luke 3:23, 33; Heb. 7:14), and of the lineage of David (2 Sam. 7:13f.; Matt. 1:1; Acts 2:25–31); that he would be rejected by his own Jewish people (Ps. 118:22; Isa. 53:3), and would die a humiliating death through crucifixion along with thieves (Ps. 22; Isa. 53: esp. v. 12); that he would be buried in a rich man's tomb (Isa. 53:9; Matt. 27:57–60) and afterward rise from the dead (Ps. 2:7; 16:10; Acts 2:25–32; 13:33–37); and that he would ascend into heaven (Ps. 68:18; Acts 1:9f.) and take a position of authority at God's right hand (Ps. 110:1; Heb. 1:3)—all this and much more was obviously predicted and equally obviously fulfilled in the person of Jesus as the Messiah. Nor is the charge that all this was the working out of a fraudulent and deceptive plot worth boggling over for more than a moment's time, since many of the predictions were beyond the voluntary control of Jesus on the assumption of his mere humanity (he could hardly have contrived to be born in Bethlehem of a particular ancestry, for example)—and since such pervasive fraud, as I argued earlier, would be wholly incongruous with what we otherwise know of Jesus' moral impeccability and his uncompromisingly exacting moral demand on moral selves in general. I think it wholly reasonable to claim therefore that in the plethora of prophecies concerning Jesus, and in their evident fulfillment, predictive prophecy both meets and passes its decisive test. And for the qualified observer, this complex of prophetic anticipation and actualization, however subject to scientific analysis and explanation, provides once more a striking and unambiguous sign of the divine causality.

If therefore we construe the nature of science correctly and thus rid ourselves of what I have been calling the old confusion, and if accordingly we understand the miraculous as in every instance a striking reminder of universal divine causality for the qualified observer, then the ancient warfare between the Bible and genuine science will indeed be seen to be based upon a pervasive but nevertheless curable misconception. Science therefore will be denied access to no area of investigation which belongs to its character as authentic science in contrast to misconstrued philosophical prejudice; and the biblical revelation will hence be free to lay aside, hopefully for good, an antagonism with science which rightly understood, never really existed at all. As a result, it may at last be possible to view the real warfare as a controversy between philosophical world-views, so that at least we will be engaged in the right battle, whether or not we find ourselves always to be fighting on the right side.

C. The incredibility of fraud or deception.

D. Here, as with miracle in general, the divine causality is strikingly exhibited to the qualified observer.

IV. General conclusion:
A. The alleged opposition between the Bible and science is thus based on a confusion.

B. The real conflict is between philosophical world-views.

The Bible and Christian Religious Experience: The Progressive Realization of Scriptural Truth-Claims in Personal Life

The Apologetic Significance of Christian Religious Experience

I. The definition of religion and its implications for religious experience.

A. Religious experience will be a variable conjunction of the aspects of religious response.
1. Religious beliefs will be essential to religious experience and even more basic than its affective and volitional elements

It seems a world of thought, long since visited, when I defined religion as the total life response of man to what he regards as ultimately significant and decisive for human life and destiny, both individually and collectively. But the intervening world of analysis and reflection, while greatly expanding on that concept, has left it intact as a whole. And since the distinctively human response to any conscious experience is characteristically *affective* (involving a range of feelings and emotions), *volitional* (involving a range of decisions, acts, and both intrinsic and formed dispositions to act), and *intellectual* (involving a range of beliefs, whether implicit or explicit in form), it follows that religious experience, as a species of conscious experience in general, will consist of a variable and developing conjunction of these three dimensions in relation to the ultimately significant, by whatever name that object of unconditional concern may be designated. If this analysis is sound, then religious beliefs will constitute an essential aspect of every genuinely religious experience. And there is clearly a sense in which the intellectual aspect of religious experience is more fundamental and more extensive than either the affective or the volitional aspects, since we can only become explicitly conscious of feelings and volitions through intellectual discernment and conceptualization, while the awareness of intellectual beliefs and contents themselves, although characteristically conjoined with affective and volitional elements, has no analogous dependence upon them as a condition of their possibility as ingredients of conscious experience. There can therefore be no religious experience which is entirely severed from an interpretive conceptual framework—part of which, as I argued from the beginning, is intrinsic to a person's very existence as a rational mind (*a priori* categories and structures of reason), and part of which conjoins with those intrinsic structures whatever elements of a particular world-view outlook the individual may have imbibed from extrinsic sources (intellectual and religious training, for example) or from sober reflection on the meaning of existence. Since the determinate content of religious experience is largely brought to that experience by this interpretive framework or structure, I have earlier concluded that religious experience itself cannot as such be the ultimate criterion of religious truth, since these criteria are supplied by the interpretive principles which function as a necessary condition of the existence of religious experience in the first place. Hence, I have adopted a view that I have designated as *interpretive contextualism*, according to which the determinate content of a religious experience, as conceptually apprehensible, is a function of the interpretive structure that is brought to that experience as one of its essential ingredients. If that is the case, then the truth-claims of a religious perspective cannot in principle be objectively validated by their emergence from the religious experience itself, however genuinely religious it may be, but can only be tested through a reasoned assessment of the plausibility of the interpretive structure which makes the religious experience possible at the outset.

Now it is just this sort of interpretive structural framework that I have been developing throughout my entire previous analysis. I argued, for example, that discursive, conceptual, intellectual knowledge is possible only through a structure of synthetic *a priori* categories or principles which characterize the mind of each individual person dispositionally, prior to and therefore independently of any actual experience. I also argued that the function of these interpretive principles was to make actual thought and experience possible and, ideally at least, to provide a basis for moving toward an inclusive explanation of the meaning of existence in general through the reasoned understanding of thought and experience. Then, having argued that being as such is a self-disclosing revelation, I proceeded to argue successively for a theistic world view, for the Incarnation claim of Jesus as God Incarnate and the consequent adequacy of his redemptive provision for the whole of humanity through his universally representative human status, and finally for the revelation claim of Christianity to the effect that the Hebrew-Christian Bible, adequately interpreted in its total context, is an indefectibly authoritative divine self-disclosure.

B. Religious experience within such a context can provide a motivating basis for increased confidence in the interpretive structure itself.

1. Thus the personal satisfyingness of a religious experience which help to actualize selfhood, can provide a supplemental ground for the reasonableness of the framework, since that is an important function of any viable world-view.

2. Yet this test could not stand alone as a criterion of religious truth.

C. Success and failure in terms of this functional test.

Given the overall reasonableness of this interpretive structure, a genuinely religious experience of a particular individual—an experience which could provide no logically independent support for any religious truth-claim merely as such—could nevertheless constitute, through its occurrence within an interpretive structure analogous to, if not identical with, the one I have elaborated, a powerful reciprocally motivating influence for bolstering one's confidence in that interpretive structure itself. Such an individual could then regard the subjective and personal satisfyingness of his ongoing religious experience, contributing as it would to the cumulatively integrative wholeness of his personal selfhood, as itself an additional supportive ground of the independently arguable reasonableness of the interpretive framework which made that religious experience itself possible. If we are constrained to regard the recognition and realization of actualized personal selfhood in the moral and integrative sense as an essential ingredient of any genuinely plausible world-view whatever, then a world-view which, although containing that principle, did not in its acceptance by an individual make possible for him a personally satisfying religious experience which furthered the achievement of personal wholeness in an enduring and decisive way—such a world-view, I suggest—could reasonably be regarded by that individual as so far forth defective as a world-view. Conversely, a world-view that did contribute to the achievement of that goal of realized and intrinsically valuable selfhood could, by parity of reasoning, be quite as reasonably regarded as so far forth adequate in that respect. For a variety of reasons that I discussed much earlier, this sort of test could not stand wholly on its own as a criterion of truth (I have rejected religious pragmatism as inadequate in religious epistemology). But, in conjunction with a complex of logically independent grounds of reasonableness (such as my entire previous analysis purports to provide), this sort of functional criterion can and does contribute to the strength of that reasonableness. There are, of course, numerous individuals who claim to have found Christian commitment unworkable in the sense I am here discussing. However, quite apart from the fact that an indeterminate number of these may have hedged their commitment with so many reservations as to make it functionally inoperative for that reason alone, I think it fair to claim that the number of genuine failures is overwhelmingly dwarfed by those who have found unqualified spiritual fulfillment through commitment to the Lordship of Jesus the Messiah as God Incarnate. I too am "resting in my sweet, sweet Jesus," and therefore count myself among those whose confidence in the Christian revelation claim is immeasurably bolstered by my personal religious experience.

It is in the sense I have been explaining that genuine religious experience provides an ancillary apologetic support for the world-view that makes it possible, and that Christian religious experience provides an analogous but (as I see it) comparably stronger support for the Christian world-view and its revelation claim as I have contended for it. Of course, all sorts of negatively critical attempts have been made to explain away the uniqueness and genuineness of religious experience by interpreting it as based on psychological illusion (Freud) or economic class interest (Marx) or whatever; but I have long since argued against all such religious projectionisms, and since there is no need to rehearse those arguments again, I am content to rest my case on that score. Still there are other thinkers who, accepting the sort of reasoning I have given previously about religious experience, although not without peripheral reservations, nevertheless think with responsible and informed sincerity that there is more to be said about the role of religious experience as an apologetic support for some general or even specific type of world-view.

I have in mind here a thinker such as Rudolf Otto, whose book, *The Idea of the Holy,* is certainly among the most profoundly stimulating discussions ever to have come to my attention. Otto argues that there is a non-rational mode of religious awareness which pervades all genuine religious experience and provides a sort of religiously *a priori* structure for all such experience, quite apart from the variable interpretive schemes through which that experience may be apprehended in conceptual, rational terms—although he thinks that there is a discernible correlation between the aspects of this non-rational religious awareness and the conceptual structures through which they are understood. I am not concerned here with the details of his analysis. What I am concerned with is his subsequent thesis that religious experience as such, in both its non-rational and conceptual aspects, has certain unique features which he sees as more plausibly supporting a theistic world-view, or even a Christian theistic world-view, than any other identifiable and viable religious alternative. Thus, for example, the object of numinous (non-rational religious) awareness is universally construed as both capable of responding to human personal need and also as itself constituting that religiously holy and intrinsically moral good through which that spiritual need is experientially met. But the capacity for this sort of reciprocal response is more adequately construed, in the conceptual sense, in terms of a personal view of God like that of theism, than in terms of any impersonal understanding of the religious ultimate, however understood, since it is precisely personal being that is capable of this type of response. More specifically, Otto contends that every developed religious outlook exhibits a correlation between the non-rational and the rational elements of religious response, in which the rational dimension provides a schematism or conceptual counterpart for apprehending the non-rational dimension—so that, for example, the enticingly attracting and alluring aspect of the numinous (the Religious Object) is thus schematized by the concepts of goodness, mercy, love, and (in general) grace in the sense of unmerited forgiveness. Yet the rational elements can never subsume the non-rational feeling aspects entirely, nor can the non-rational elements function effectively without the rational aspects. There is rather a wholesome tension and integrative harmony between the two which prevents genuine religious experience from reducing to sheer intellectualism and mere theology, on the one hand,

D. Alternative explanations of religious experience have already been dealt with in earlier analysis.

III. Is there a further and stronger apologetic role for religious experience?

A. Rudolf Otto's proposal.

1. The non-rational *a priori* structure of religious experience and its correlation with interpretive conceptual schemes.

2. This structure itself as supporting a Christian theistic perspective.

a) The numinous object adequately understood through categories of personhood.

b) Every developed religious outlook achieves a correlation between the rational and the non-rational factors of religious response.

(1) These two aspects are interdependent.

(2) The degree to which these aspects are harmonized provides a criterion for assessing the adequacy of the outlooks themselves.
(3) Otto views Christian theism as approximating this ideal balance.
c) The recognition of this criterion is not unreasonable.
(1) While the criterion could not stand alone,

(2) it could supplement overall coherence and explanatory adequacy.

d) But this provides no plausible basis for dismissing or ignoring other perspectives which have their own contribution to make to the unity of God's truth.

B. I have no objection to Otto's overall thesis here.
1. My own analysis perhaps contributes to the conceptual aspect of Otto's claim, while my neglect of the non-rational aspects is not a sign of their unimportance.

2. Otto's claim, that the categories of the non-rational factors of religious experience suggest theism, is a plausible contention.

and from sinking into total fanaticism and unbridled emotionalism, on the other. Since the symmetry and balance of this relationship differs from one religious outlook to another, as Otto sees it, therefore the degree to which this harmony is effectively achieved in a given religious outlook affords a comparative criterion for ranking the adequacy of the outlooks themselves as religious world-view perspectives. Theism in general and Christian theism in particular achieve a proportioned unity of these elements which transcends the lesser degree of balance in alternative religious traditions, according to Otto; but unfortunately he does not work out the details of this argument for particular religious world-views other than Christianity. Still, in principle, the recognition of this criterion as such is not intrinsically prejudicial or unreasonable; and if in fact and upon detailed analysis the Christian theistic perspective actually achieves this symmetrical and integrative harmony between the rational and non-rational aspects of religious experience—and does so to a degree that puts it in marked contrast to perspectives that fall noticeably short of this conceptual ideal—then, while that consideration alone is not decisive as such, it nevertheless adds to the overall character of systematic coherence and comprehensive explanatory adequacy that I have myself been arguing throughout my whole analysis. Yet all this must not even smack of intellectual or religious snobbery, much less provide any sort of proud disdain toward other religious perspectives. A totally adequate outlook should recognize all the facets of truth and genuine insight as aspects of an inclusive unity of God's truth. No matter what the historical traditions in which that truth and insight are disclosed in varying degrees of clarity. And a perspective which lacks some measure of overall harmony and balance may nevertheless provide such a depth of insight on particular points that no developed religious world-view will be completely comprehensive without incorporating that depth into its own maturing understanding.

As must be evident already, therefore, I have no objection in principle to this general thesis which Otto puts forth, although I regret the embryonic form in which he leaves the matter. In a certain qualified sense, my own comparative defense of the adequacy of the Christian theistic outlook at least makes a sustained contribution to the conceptual dimension of Otto's claim. And if I have exhibited a relative neglect (though clearly not a total one) of the non-rational and emotive aspects of religious response, that in no way stems from any supposition of their unimportance—it is just that my philosophical and conceptual concerns had already given me quite enough business to cope with. In any case, as I view the matter, Otto's main point would be that, if a reflective person analyzes conceptually (so far as that is legitimately possible) the non-rational factors of religious experience along with their rational schematic correlates, he will find quite objectively that the descriptive categories of religious experience as such involve certain suggestions about the being and character of the Religious Object which point more effectively toward a theistic, if not an explicitly Christian, understanding of God than they do toward any other framework of religious insight. And with that main point I am basically inclined to agree, even if I do not regard this consideration as having quite the strength of many other lines of argument I have introduced, and even if I am disappointed by a tendency in Otto which I have not even considered here—the tendency, in spite of his clear efforts to the contrary, to allow the non-rational dimensions of religious experience to overbalance and outrun the rational. Certainly a purely intellectualistic religious experience cannot long survive in individual personal life. But it is equally true, I think, that a purely emotional and effective religious experience cannot either exist or be identified without the conceptual structures through which alone those non-rational factors can be recognized.

3. Otto seems clearly right in regarding the intellectual and non-rational factors of religious experience as interdependent.

The satisfying and personally fulfilling quality of Christian religious experience can therefore bolster an individual's confidence in the adequacy of the world-view perspective which made that experience in its determinate form possible by providing an interpretive framework for its occurrence as a total experience. In that sense, such a pragmatic support may and does provide a supplementary argument for the reasonableness of that world-view itself. But cut off from the conceptual support and context of such an interpretive framework, the satisfaction provided by religious experience is too individually idiosyncratic and thus too subjectively variable and imprecise to provide any objectively significant support for any particular religious perspective in terms of its comprehensive philosphical adequacy. Still that does not mean at all that the satisfyingness of religious experience is not an important or even for some individuals a decisive motive for religious commitment—a motive in comparison with which the intricacies of systematic philosophy, even if it is Christian in its aim, may seem as meager fare indeed.

IV. General conclusion.
A. The satisfying character of religious experience can supplement the reasonableness of the interpretive scheme.
B. But apart from the interpretive scheme, this factor is too subjective and individual to provide independent and objective support, even though it is an important or even decisive motive for religious commitment.

The Subjective Reality of Christian Religious Experience

It is all well and good to theorize about Christian religious experience as a supplemental apologetic consideration which contributes to the total cumulative argument for what I have called the Christian revelation claim. But that abstract contention will remain a skeleton without solid flesh unless its vagueness and generality are filled in with an account of what that experience involves as a living reality for individual persons, and of how the Scriptures function as a normative provocation to personal spiritual realization. Fortunately, an enormous descriptive and illustrative literature already exists to fill this gap—a literature which begins with the Bible's own illustrations and teachings about spiritual life; a literature which stretches from the post-scriptural life analyses of the Christian fathers of the first centuries of the Christian era through the *Confessions* of St. Augustine, the *Imitation*

I. My theoretical account calls for extension by an account of religious experience as a lived reality.

A. An extensive literature exists to fill this gap for Christian religious experience.

of Christ as expounded by Thomas à Kempis, and a veritable sea of other similar writings; a literature which invades the inner sanctums of systematic theology and psychology of religion, and then widens to engulf the whole extent of the sacred music of the Christian church in all the lyrics that may be sung to that music. And all of these are not only accounts of religious experience and encounter, since their mere reflective and expectant consideration is a sort of provocative contagion for stimulating the rebirth of that lived experience in each individual who is responsive to its challenge. The whole is like an enormous, universally inviting evangelical witness, suspended upon the biblical writings themselves, and reaching out continuously to the whole world in such a way as to exclude none from its call.

If the Bible is, as I have contended, an indefectibly authoritative divine revelation, it is to be expected that characteristically through its words, directly or indirectly, humanity should confront the claim of God and experience His immediate reality to an extent that is at best no more than mirrored by other provocations to divine encounter. It is there incomparably that I see God at work for the moral and spiritual redemption of humanity, and there also that I see myself with a frankness of assessment that even the most searching independent self-analysis can only distantly mimic. And while seeing myself in terms of my personal moral inadequacy and consequent alienation from moral harmony and fellowship with God, I also see myself in terms of what I can nevertheless become in contrast to all this through a personal commitment to Jesus as God Incarnate and through a decisive rejection of the vestments of my presently defective moral status in favor of what I can thus become. In theological and also biblical language, I see myself as guilty before God because of my sinful choices, actions, and dispositions of character; but I also see myself as one who can be regenerated and transformed through faith in Jesus the Messiah whose universally representative satisfaction to the claim of divine moral law on humanity I now appropriate as my own. And I even see, through Scripture statement and example, that if and when I spread the wings of repentance and believing commitment, I will not be left to fly wholly on my own strength to the loft of spiritual regeneration—since I see also the promise that the Holy Spirit of God will himself be the decisive agent of my new birth, which at the same time I discern as only but very importantly the beginning of a new life in which, empowered by God's indwelling spiritual presence, I cooperatively and progressively move toward a maturity of reconciled fellowship with God in Christ and with my fellow human beings so far as they are themselves even touched by this same vision.

But then I look around me at those limited forms of the divine spiritual community which I find at my disposal through churches and other adjoining religious institutions and organizations. And I see there an expanding and triumphant host of persons who are already advancing through some stage or other of this envisioned spiritual regeneration. Encompassing all this, both in the Bible and outside it, both among my contemporaries and in that circle of the committed

Margin notes:

1. This literature provokes religious response,

2. and invites all individuals to commitment.

B. The biblical writings as a means of confronting God's claim.
1. A personalized analysis of this role.

2. The social extension of this role.

preserved for me from history in the heritage of the written word, I sense in and through it all a surging and swelling power which is bent on sweeping me through the door of spiritual decision into the living reality of what, until now, has been for me only visionary anticipation. It may not be too much to say that, buoyed up by all this, I hear the voice of Jesus himself saying to me, not now merely from a page of Scripture, but rather as my eternal contemporary: "Come to me, you who are struggling under life's burdens and about to collapse and I myself, not another (though I have spoken through a great multitude of others), will give you true rest!" Of course, I cannot really see what is on the other side of that commitment until I make it; but I see enough to assess my options as they truly are and then make a free and responsible choice. For all this is a motivating invitation and not an irresistible compulsion. I am not really swept against my will into the sustaining current; but its waters are breaking at my feet, and the rest is up to me, as it is up to you.

3. The subjective impact of the biblical witness.

Of course, I am not blind to the other side of this so far provocative coin. I also see a discernible and steadily expanding sprinkling of persons from all sorts of backgrounds who purport to have tried Christian commitment but for one reason or another (or even for no reason) claim to have found it both unsatisfying and unfulfilling, so that they have turned their backs on that earlier and clearly tentative decision. And I see all around me professing (and, as often as not, actual) believers for whom their faith is peripheral rather than central to their lives, so that their commitment is incidental, if not actually flippant. Swelling their number are those whose moral change through faith has been so incompletely and fragmentarily actualized that, wittingly or not, they are forced to hide behind a facade of variable hypocrisy in order to mask, with however little success, their virtually uninterrupted moral foibles. Then there are the multitudes for whom the Christian religion connotes a merely social and cultural organization which attracts them through the promise, real or imaginary, of financial, political, or other wholly self-seeking and prudential benefits—after all, what better context in which a lawyer might enlist clients or an insurance agent muster customers? And across this whole spectrum of human and purportedly Christian samples, I notice at least some among all the mean, petty, disruptive, and even annoying violations that these people, quite as much as individuals external to the institutional church, heap not only upon the outsiders but often indiscriminately on each other as well.

II. The case against the motivation of Christian religious experience.
A. The case developed.

And if I expand the horizon of my vision to include the whole of history and civilization since the time of Jesus, I see even more disorienting sights. I see all the useless and morally indefensible battles and wars that have been fought in the name of Christianity, all the outright murders that have been justified on Christian religious grounds—not only Bruno at the hands of the Inquisition, but also Servetus at the hands of Calvin and the Christian city government over which he presided, plus unnumbered others from all the quarters of Christendom. I see all the economic and social injustices inflicted on the virtually helpless by professing Christians vested with the political and financial power to do so, whatever the mitigating and exonerating circumstances might appear to be. More alarming still is the double fact that even the most saintly persons I have known admit that, restrained as their actual conduct has habitually been, they discern in themselves the seeds at least of a disposition which, if fanned into flame, would in principle be capable of all these same travesties and others like them. At the same time I see an analogous disposition in myself which, however blunted and sublimated by moral and spiritual regeneration, would be equally capable of analogous provocation to expression along all the lines of moral demeanor.

B. The mitagation of the negative case:

And yet I see in many of these same people a moral and spiritual power which, however embryonically and incompletely realized at any given point, is nevertheless making some discernible progress toward the individual and collective conquest of all this moral tragedy in the context of the divine spiritual community. And I see, at least among the saintly I mentioned, a power of restraint which squelches the temptation to moral and spiritual transgression on the appearance of its first inflaming spark. Yes, I even see some whose growth in righteousness through the Holy Spirit has reached a stage of such moral maturity that, as far as I can tell, only the vestiges remain of what was once for them a constantly recurring struggle, so that now they have made a comprehensive habit out of moral and spiritual virtue of

The crucial role of Jesus himself.

character. Above all, I see the triumphant person of Jesus in whom even those vestiges of moral defection are absent altogether and to the core. Should I, after all, have been looking beyond all the others to him in the first place, since it is in him, and not in them, that I would

C. The lingering indecision.

place my trust and find my rest through spiritual commitment? On the other hand, I cannot completely quell the indecision that emerges for me from contrast between the promise of spiritual life through faith in Jesus as God Incarnate, on the one hand, and the meager and restricted extent of the actualization of that spiritual life in the actual human community of the allegedly and even genuinely redeemed, on

1. Spiritual commitment as involving a risk.
2. The alternative to taking the risk as involving personal disintegration.

the other. So it is, after all, not a wholly obvious and easy matter to make such a decisive choice. It is, in a sense, a genuine risk to step into the waters of the Jordan and launch out for the spiritual Canaan! But the alternative to taking this risk is to remain in the same state of personal disintegration in which I find myself now—to go on pitting myself against my fellow human beings who are as prudentially self-seeking as I am myself; to further alienate myself (if that is imaginable) from the God whose invitation urges me to the acceptance and achievement of moral harmony and fellowship with himself; to cut myself off from that divine human community whose members, however imperfect in their spiritual realization, are nevertheless making some significant progress toward that goal and therefore constitute the one framework of moral and spiritual solace in which the promise of moral and spiritual life is beginning to make a genuine impact. It is, in short, to go on relentlessly, if ever so slowly, toward that self-destructive isolation and solitude which will eventually constitute the hell of my own making.

This life-transforming if mind-boggling and risky choice is therefore up to me in the end. But here I find myself at last as taking my stand with Pascal and, in a sense, even with William James: I have after all nothing of real value to lose by a total commitment to the God whose very being is the locus of all ultimate goodness and true value in any case. And if I continue to follow a path of self-willed refusal, or even suspension of judgment, I will only be multiplying a personal loss which, in the light of the gospel, I clearly see as all but engulfing me even now. To make a choice, therefore, which at worst can occasion me no real loss, and which at best promises me all the real value and humanly realizable goodness there is to be had, that choice seems as reasonable, as compelling, and as momentous as any decision I can imagine myself as ever being called upon to make.

3. The intrinsic reasonableness of the risk.

The Individual Prerequisites for Christian Religious Experience

If the beginning of a spiritual pilgrimage in Jesus the Messiah is a matter of individual personal choice, then clearly the prerequisite for intiating that journey is precisely an individual personal decision in which I commit myself to the Lordship of Jesus, accept the claim and invitation of God upon me, and renounce in principle the wholly self-seeking disposition which has previously dominated my life and experience. Not that in so doing I do not implement my genuine self-advantage. It is only my false self that I turn my back on, only the destructive self-seeking, blinded by moral defection, that I renounce. My genuine self is preserved, sustained, fulfilled, actualized, and redeemed through the entire transaction—it is, after all, I who respond, I who repent and exercise believing faith, I who enter into the instigated regeneration of God's Holy Spirit. In a provisional sense, therefore, I sacrifice myself through spiritual commitment; but the self I sacrifice I now see to have been only a shadow, while the substance of my true self remains—expanded and drastically altered, no doubt, but clearly the same ontological individual.

I. Personal decision as initiating the spiritual pilgrimage.

A. The renunciation of the false self and the preserved transformation of the true self.

Yet it is no simple matter to spell out with confidence the specific elements of this commitment through which, in theological language, an individual enters into a state of gracious forgiveness. Basically, it is an intellectually guided decision of moral will; but, as I have previously argued, we cannot specify with precision the exact minimal content of that intellectual dimension. In its fullest form, it would be a commitment to Jesus as God Incarnate, viewed in the explicitly apprehended totality of fully enlightened theological understanding—but few enter into genuine believing faith with anything even approaching this sort of insight, and none realize the ideal completely. In its most

B. The intellectual aspects of the commitment.

1. Although these aspects can be ideally characterized, they cannot be precisely spelled out as conditions for all individuals.

characteristic form, this intellectual dimension would be the acknowledgment of Jesus as Lord and Savior in the context of at least an elementary understanding of God and his relation and revelation to the contingent world order. But even this cannot be incorrigibly sketched out as a minimum condition, since it is clearly not the adequacy of one's theological understanding which qualifies him for admission into a state of gracious forgiveness before God, but rather the genuineness and authenticity of one's decision and commitment to God, however imperfectly understood. Perhaps it is therefore best to say that each human person capable of making any substantive decision is also capable of some individually variable intellectual insight which can direct his decision of moral will and validate the genuineness of that decision as a prerequisite for the regenerated and forgiven status that the promise of spiritual life in Christ involves. And that is quite enough, since it is after all God alone who can with finality apply the criteria of genuineness to spiritual decision and commitment; and according to the New Testament (Rom. 8) the inner witness of the Holy Spirit makes it possible for each such redeemed individual to be confidently assured of his own inclusion within the circle of the truly redeemed. It should therefore be no cause of regret that we cannot define the perimeter of that circle with a precision that belongs to God alone. Let us each then appropriate that assurance to himself through personal commitment and the evidence of the Spirit's inner regenerative working; and let us at the same time leave the judgment of the spiritual state of other individuals to the prerogative of God whose jurisdiction it truly is.

2. But each individual capable of the decision is also capable of an intellectual insight which will support that decision as authentic.

II. God alone is the judge of the genuineness of spiritual commitment.
A. Personal assurance is possible for all the committed.

B. But the judgment of the spiritual state of others is not our proper concern.

Concluding Synthesis on the Revelational Word

I. A summary of the reasonableness of the scriptural revelation claim.

In retrospect, the acknowledgment of the Hebrew-Christian Bible, when rightly interpreted in its total context as an indefectibly authoritative revelation of the one true God, is evidently a wholly reasonable intellectual and philosophical thesis, even if it exhibits as coherently and plausibly more adequate than any other pertinent alternative on this issue, something less than the absolute demonstrableness that is conceivable in a formal logical conclusion. In view of the Bible's revelational claim as centered on the witness of Jesus himself, in view of the internal organic unity of the Biblical writings, in view of the fact that, properly construed, the Bible and genuine science exhibit no real logical opposition, and in view of the reaffirmation of biblical revelation in Christian religious experience—in view, I suggest, of all this, the conclusion that the revelational claim of Scripture is true is as reasonable as honest reflection could exact responsibly of such a claim. Still, it must not be forgotten that the acceptance of this thesis as an intellectual conclusion, while in my opinion right and proper, is not the same thing as that personal spiritual commitment which the Bible

II. But the acceptance of this claim is not the same thing as the personal spiritual commitment to God which Scripture itself urges on each individual.

itself urges on every human person in the name of God and through the redemptive achievement of Jesus as God Incarnate. That also has its intellectual and conceptual aspect; but it involves as well something more and decidedly distinct, since it requires a fundamental surrender of moral will in which the individual yields and submits his very being as a person both to the Lordship of Jesus and to the one true Good which is God, however vaguely and indistinctly that individual may construe this in his explicit consciousness.

Epilogue: A Summary Reflection

I. The pursuit of a comprehensive religious-philosophical world-view as an open-ended task never actually completed.

In a sense, the journey on which we embarked at the outset never reaches its terminus—for the development of a comprehensive religious-philosophical world-view is by nature open-ended and incomplete as a human project. It is indeed a struggle toward a goal of comprehensive adequacy and coherent reasonableness, but that goal recedes from even the most diligent and perspicuous among us precisely because closer scrutiny endlessly uncovers a greater and expanding intricacy in the goal itself—so that, to borrow a phrase from Rudolf Otto, the project and the goal can indeed be thought, and thought with ever-increasing clarity and rational discernment, but it cannot be finally thought through or thought out in any finite time or any finite exercise of our keenest intellectual powers. The self-completed and perfect vision of the whole of truth, in all its detail and systematic adequacy, is reserved for God alone, for whom indeed it has never been a project but rather an eternal and omniscient intuition. It follows from all this that, when we think we have reached the end of our pursuit, we find, if our insight is unobstructed, that we are really back at the beginning again, except that now the ground has been broken, the path partially smoothed out, and the direction less obscured by peripheral shadows. Here too, as with much else in human life, it will be easier the next time around, until we discover that the goal itself has widened to close the gap between our never-ending present task and our previous difficulty in pursuing it.

II. But in another sense, the task is completed.
A. Books must end, although without the illusion of finality.

Still, there is a different sense in which the task is, after all, completed: Books, unlike human careers and projects, cannot go on indefinitely, but must end at a certain time and on a certain page, however fragmentary and provisional they may seem to their authors. And that is all well and good, just so there is no subtle illusion vested in that final word, as if the completion of the book somehow signaled the end of the thinker's task, whether that thinker is the writer or the reader. There is, furthermore, another dimension of our project that calls for completion: Since the exigency of our human situation calls for action, and since significant action is possible only through decisions of value and principle, we can ill afford to wait for total and unrevisable vision before committing ourselves to that limited vision we have as we progress, and to that clarion call and invitation of God which we see as crucially summoning us, since meanwhile, as Kierkegaard has reminded us, the ship of our limited earthly existence is all the time making headway through waters that we shall never traverse again. And from that standpoint there will be no second time around. At some viable existential juncture, then, we must choose our spiritual destiny—and then, in the stability provided by that commitment, we can proceed to inquire, at whatever leisure remains for us, into the philosophical ramifications of the choice, always alert to the fact that such reflection may itself call for some change of course.

B. Spiritual commitment cannot wait for finality of vision.

I hardly think it necessary to spend more than a sweeping glance on the long course of our journey here. He who has survived this far will by now be able to make a more detailed rehearsal for himself. I have defended rational objectivity through the application of interpretive principles of reason to an expanding front of experiential data. I have contended that being itself, in all its facets, is a progressively unfolding self-revelation. I have argued that the rational analysis of being leads to the God of personal theism as the self-existent, self-explanatory ground of the contingent world order, and as the Ultimate Good which grounds and orders all limited genuine values. I have claimed that Jesus Christ is the human incarnation of the one true God, who, through his status as universally representative humanity, has vicariously satisfied the unconditional claim of the divine moral law on morally defective human beings. And finally, I have urged that the Hebrew-Christian Bible, properly understood in its total context, is an indefectibly authoritative revelation of the one true God manifested in Jesus the Messiah. For the systematic exposition of all this as a philosophical perspective, I have claimed, from a human standpoint, no more than a comparative rational plausibility which I sincerely regard as involving a more adequate and comprehensive explanation of the meaning of existence than any analogous alternative explanation with which I am familiar. Through it all, I have tried to exclude no fragment of truth, from whatever quarter it may have emanated, but have instead envisioned the whole of all truth as brought to its fullness in Jesus the Eternal Logos of God. It is therefore enough, and it remains only to express one last time here the invitation of the gospel of Jesus the Messiah to every human person in every human culture— an invitation which I deem as fully reasonable, and, at the same time, as rich with the promise and reality of true spiritual life.

III. The sum of the whole matter.

Amor vincit omnia!

Bibliography of Suggested Readings for the Exploratory Reader

Introduction:
Philosphical Prologemena
Concerning Religious
Knowledge
and the Concept of Revelation

Aquinas, Thomas. *Basic Writings of St. Thomas Aquinas.* Edited by A. C. Pegis. 2 vol. New York: Random House, 1945.

———. *Summa Contra Gentiles.* 5 vol. South Bend: Notre Dame University Press, 1975.

Augustine. *Basic Writings of Saint Augustine.* Edited by Whitney J. Oates. 1948. Reprint. Grand Rapids: Baker Book House, 1980.

Ayer, A. J. *Language, Truth, and Logic.* 2d ed. New York: Dover Publications, 1946.

Baillie, John. *The Idea of Revelation in Recent Thought.* New York: Columbia University Press, 1956.

———. *Our Knowledge of God.* New York: Charles Scribner's Sons, 1959.

Barth, Karl. *The Knowledge of God and the Service of God According to the Teaching of the Reformation.* Translated by J. L. M. Haire and I. Henderson. New York: Charles Scribner's Sons, 1939.

Bavinck, Herman. *The Philosophy of Revelation.* Grand Rapids: Wm. B. Eerdmans, 1953.

Berkeley, George. *Principles of Human Knowledge.* In *A New Theory of Vision and Other Writings.* New York: E. P. Dutton & Co., 1950.

———. *Three Dialogues Between Hylas and Philonous.* In *A New Theory of Vision and Other Writings.* New York: E. P. Dutton & Co., 1950.

Bradley, F. H. *Appearance and Reality.* 2d ed. New York: Oxford University Press, 1969.

Brunner, Heinrich E. *Revelation and Reason: The Christian Doctrine of Faith and Knowledge.* Translated by Olive Wyon. Philadelphia: Westminster Press, 1946.

Burtt, Edwin A. *In Search of Philosophic Understanding.* New York: New American Library, Mentor Books, 1965.

———. *Types of Religious Philosophy.* rev. ed. New York: Harper and Row, 1951.

Butler, Joseph. *The Analogy of Religion.* New York: Frederick Ungar Publishing Co., 1961.

Calvin, John. *Institutes of the Christian Religion.* Translated by Henry Beveridge. 2 vols. Grand Rapids: Wm. B. Eerdmans, 1953.

Dewey, John. *A Common Faith.* New Haven: Yale University Press, 1934.

Farrer, Austin. *The Glass of Vision.* Glasgow: The University Press, 1948.

Feuerbach, Ludwig. *The Essence of Christianity.* Translated by George Eliot. New York: Harper and Row, 1957.

Freud, Sigmund. *The Future of an Illusion.* Translated by W. D. Robson-Scott. New York: Liveright Publishing Corp., 1955.

Hackett, Stuart C. *Oriental Philosophy: A Westerner's Guide to Eastern Thought.* Madison: University of Wisconsin Press, 1979.

Hegel, G. W. F. *The Phenomenology of Mind.* Translated by J. B. Baillie. New York: Harper and Row, 1967.

Hume, David. *An Enquiry Concerning Human Understanding and Selections from a Treatise of Human Nature.* Chicago: Open Court Publishing Co., 1949.

James, William. *The Will to Believe and Other Essays in Popular Philosophy.* New York: Longmans, Green, & Co., 1903.

Jaspers, Karl. *Reason and Existenz.* Translated from 3d German ed. New York: Farrar, Strauss, & Co., 1955.

Kant, Immanuel. *Critique of Pure Reason.* Translated by Norman Kemp Smith. New York: St. Martin's Press, 1965.

———. *Prolegomena to Any Future Metaphysic.* Chicago: Open Court Publishing Co., 1949.

Kierkegaard, Søren. *Concluding Unscientific Postscript to the Philosophical Fragments.* Translated by D. F. Swenson and W. Lowrie. Princeton: Princeton University Press, 1941.

Kuyper, Abraham. *Principles of Sacred Theology.* Grand Rapids: Wm. B. Eerdmans, 1954.

Leibniz, G. W. *New Essays on Human Understanding.* Translated and edited by Peter Remnant and Jonathan Bennett. abr. ed. London: Cambridge University Press, 1982.

Macintosh, Douglas C. *The Problem of Religious Knowledge.* New York: Harper and Row, 1940.

Montague, William P. *The Ways of Knowing.* New York: Macmillan Publishing Co., 1925.

Niebuhr, H. Richard. *The Meaning of Revelation.* New York: Macmillan Publishing Co., 1955.

Pascal, Blaise. *Pensees.* New York: E. P. Dutton & Co., 1931.

Phillips, D. Z. *Faith and Philosophical Inquiry.* New York: Schocken Books, 1970.

Plotinus. *The Enneads.* Translated by Stephen MacKenna. 2d ed. Revised by B. S. Page. New York: Pantheon Books, 1957.

Ricoeur, Paul. *Fallible Man: Philosophy of the Will,* Part 2, Book 1. Chicago: Henry Regnery Co., 1965.

———. *Freud and Philosophy: An Essay on Interpretation.* Translated by Denis Savage. New Haven: Yale University Press, 1970.

Royce, Josiah. *The Religious Aspect of Philosophy.* New York: Harper and Row, 1958.

Santayana, George. *Scepticism and Animal Faith.* New York: Dover Publications, 1955.

Schleiermacher, Friedrich. *On Religion: Speeches to Its Cultured Despisers.* Translated by John Oman from the 3d German ed. New York: Harper and Row, 1958.

Temple, William. *Nature, Man, and God.* London: Macmillan Publishing Co., 1934.

Thornton, L. D. *Revelation and the Modern World.* Westminster: The Dacre Press, 1950.

Tillich, Paul. *Dynamics of Faith.* New York: Harper and Row, 1957.

Urban, Wilbur Marshall. *Language and Reality.* New York: Macmillan Publishing Co., 1939.

Van Til, Cornelius. *The Defense of the Faith.* Rev. 3d ed. Philadelphia: Presbyterian and Reformed Pub. Co., 1967,

Part I: Christianity and the Revelational Cosmos—A Philosophical Case for a Theistic Metaphysic

Anselm. *Proslogium; Monologium; An Appendix in Behalf of the Fool by Gaunilon; and Cur Deus Homo.* Translated by Sidney N. Deane. Chicago: Open Court Publishing Co., 1948.

Bergson, Henri. *The Two Sources of Morality and Religion.* Translated by Audra, Brereton, and Carter. New York: Henry Holt & Co., 1935.

Berkouwer, G. C. *General Revelation.* Grand Rapids: Wm. B. Eerdmans, 1955.

Blanshard, Brand. *The Nature of Thought.* 2 vol. London: George Allan and Unwin, 1939.

Brunner, Emil. *The Divine Imperative: A Study in Christian Ethics.* Translated by Olive

Wyon. Philadelphia: Westminster Press, 1947.

Feigl, Herbert. *The "Mental" and the "Physical": The Essay and a Postscript.* Minneapolis: University of Minnesota Press, 1958.

Ghose, Aurobindo. *The Life Divine.* New York: Greystone Press, 1949.

Hackett, Stuart C. *The Resurrection of Theism.* 2d ed. Grand Rapids: Baker Book House, 1982.

Heim, Karl. *God Transcendent.* Translated by E. P. Dickie from 3d German ed. London: Nisbet & Co., 1935.

Kant, Immanuel. *Critique of Practical Reason.* Translated by Lewis W. Beck. Indianapolis: Bobbs-Merrill, Co., Liberal Arts Press, 1956.

———. *Foundations of the Metaphysic of Morals.* Translated by Lewis W. Beck. Indianapolis: Bobbs-Merrill Co., Liberal Arts Press, 1959.

———*Religion within the Limits of Reason Alone.* Translated by T. M. Greene and H. H. Hudson. Chicago: Open Court Publishing Co., 1934.

Kung, Hans. *Does God Exist?* Translated by Edward Quinn. Garden City: Doubleday and Co., 1980.

Lecomte du Nouy, P. *Human Destiny.* New York: Longmans, Green, & Co., 1947.

Leibniz, G. W. *Theodicy.* Translated by E. M. Huggard. Abr. Ed. Don Mills, Ontario: J. M. Dent and Sons, 1966.

Patterson, C. H. *Moral Standards.* New York: Ronald Press Company, 1949.

Sorley, W. R. *Moral Values and the Idea of God.* 2d ed. Cambridge: University Press, 1921.

Stout, G. F. *God and Nature.* Cambridge: University Press, 1952.

Taylor, A. E. *Does God Exist?* New York: Macmillan Publishing Co., 1947.

Tennant, F. R. *Philosophical Theology.* 2 vols. Cambridge: University Press, 1935.

Part II: Christianity and the Revelational Person—An Historical-Critical Case for the Incarnation of God in Jesus Christ.

Adam, Karl. *The Christ of Faith.* Translated by Joyce Crick. New York: Pantheon Books, 1957.

———. *The Son of God.* Translated by Philip Hereford. New York: Sheed and Ward, 1934.

Aldwinckle, Russell F. *More than Man: A Study in Christology.* Grand Rapids: Wm. B. Eerdmans, 1976.

Baillie, Donald M. *God Was in Christ.* New York: Charles Scribner's Sons, 1948.

Boisen, Anton T. *The Exploration of the Inner World.* New York: Harper and Row, 1962.

Bonsall, H. Brash. *The Person of Christ.* 2 vols. London: Christian Literature Crusade, 1967.

Brunner, Heinrich E. *The Mediator.* Translated by Olive Wyon. 2d ed. Philadelphia: Westminster Press, 1947.

Bultmann, Rudolf. *Jesus and the Word.* Translated by L. P. Smith and E. H. Lantero. New York: Charles Scribner's Sons, 1958.

———. *Jesus Christ and Mythology.* London: SCM Press, 1960.

Bundy, Walter E. *The Psychic Health of Jesus.* New York: Macmillan Publishing Co., 1922.

Cave, Sydney. *The Doctrine of the Person of Christ.* London: G. Duckworth, 1962.

Cullmann, Oscar. *The Christology of the New Testament.* Rev. ed. Philadelphia: Westminster Press, 1963.

Dodd, C. H. *The Interpretation of the Fourth Gospel.* Cambridge: Cambridge University Press, 1953.

Dunn, James D. G. *Christology in the Making.* Philadelphia: Westminster Press, 1980.

Gogarten, Friedrich. *Christ the Crisis.* Translated by R. A. Wilson. London: SCM Press, 1970.

Goguel, Maurice. *Jesus and the Origins of Christianity.* 2 vols. Translated by Olive Wyon. New York: Harper and Row, 1960.

Guitton, Jean. *The Problem of Jesus.* New York: P. J. Kennedy and Sons, 1955.

Heim, Karl. *Jesus the World's Perfecter.* Translated by D. H. van Daalen. Philadelphia: Muhlenberg Press, 1961.

Hengstenberg, Ernst W. *Christology of the Old Testament and a Commentary on the Messianic Predictions.* Translated by Theodore Meyer. 2d ed. Edinburgh: T. and T. Clark, 1854–1858.

Jones, Geraint. *Christology and Myth in the New Testament.* New York: Harper and Row, 1956.

Kung, Hans. *On Being a Christian.* Translated by Edward Quinn. Garden City: Doubleday and Co., 1976.

Mackintosh, H. R. *The Doctrine of the Person of Jesus Christ.* New York: Charles Scribner's Sons, 1921.

Orr, James. *The Christian View of God and the World.* 3d ed. Edinburgh: Andrew Elliot, 1897.

Pannenberg, Wolfhart. *Jesus—God and Man.* 2d ed. Translated by L. L. Wilkins and D. A. Priebe. Philadelphia: Westminster Press, 1977.

Pittenger, William N. *Christology Reconsidered.* London: SCM Press, 1970.

Schweitzer, Albert. *The Psychiatric Study of Jesus.* Translated by Charles R. Joy. Boston: Beacon Press, 1958.

———. *The Quest of the Historical Jesus.* Translated by W. Montgomery from the 1st German ed. New York: Macmillan Publishing Co., 1962.

Stalker, James. *The Christology of Jesus.* New York: A. C. Armstrong and Son, 1899.

Strachan, R. H. *The Historic Jesus in the New Testament.* London: SCM Press, 1931.

Taylor, Vincent. *The Person of Christ in New Testament Teaching.* New York: St. Martin's Press, 1966.

Temple, William. *Christus Veritas.* London: Macmillan and Co., 1924.

Warfield, Benjamin B. *Christology and Criticism.* New York: Oxford University Press, 1929.

———. *The Lord of Glory.* Grand Rapids: Zondervan Publishing House, n. d.

———. *The Person and Work of Christ.* Edited by Samuel G. Craig. Philadelphia: Presbyterian and Reformed Publishing Co., 1950.

Well, G. A. *Did Jesus Exist?* London: Elek Books, 1975.

Woolf, Bertram Lee. *The Authority of Jesus and Its Foundation.* London: George Allen and Unwin, 1929.

Part III: Christianity and the Revelational Word—The Propositional Expression of Revelation in Scripture

Baillie, John. *Invitation to Pilgrimmage.* London: Oxford University Press, 1942.

Barnes, Ernest W. *Scientific Theory and Religion: The World Described by Science and Its Spiritual Interpretation.* New York: Macmillan Publishing Co., 1933.

Barth, Karl. *The Doctrine of the Word of God.* Translated by G. T. Thompson. Edinburgh: T. and T. Clark, 1936.

Bettex, F. *Modern Science and Christianity.* London: Marshall Brothers, 1903.

Campenhausen, Hans, Freiherr von. *The Formation of the Christian Bible.* Translated by J. A. Baker. Philadelphia: Fortress Press, 1972.

Dickie, Edgar P. *Revelation and Response.* New York: Charles Scribner's Sons, 1938.

Dodd, C. H. *The Authority of the Bible.* New York: Harper and Row, 1958.

Everest, Alton F. ed. *Modern Science and Christian Faith.* 2d ed. Wheaton: Van Kampen Press, 1950.

Filson, Floyd V. *Which Books Belong in the Bible? A Study of the Canon.* Philadelphia: Westminster Press, 1957.

Geisler, Norman L., ed. *Inerrancy.* Grand Rapids: Zondervan Publishing House, 1979.

Harris, Robert L. *Inspiration and Canonicity of the Bible.* Grand Rapids: Zondervan Publishing House, 1957.

Huxley, Thomas. *Science and Christian Tradition.* New York: Appleton, 1896.

Kenyon, Frederick G. *The Bible and Modern Scholarship.* London: J. Murray, 1948.

Kline, Meredith G. *The Structure of Biblical Authority.* Grand Rapids: Wm. B. Eerdmans, 1972.

Otto, Rudolf. *The Idea of the Holy.* Translated by J. W. Harvey. London: Oxford University Press, 1923.

Orr, James. *Revelation and Inspiration.* New York: Charles Scribner's Sons, 1910.

Peacocke, A. R. *Creation and the World of Science.* Oxford: Clarendon Press, 1979.

Pinnock, Clark H. *Biblical Revelation—the Foundation of Christian Theology.* Chicago: Moody Press, 1971.

Preuss, Robert. *The Inspiration of Scripture.* Edinburgh: Oliver and Boyd, 1955.

Ramm, Bernard. *The Christian View of Science and Scripture.* Grand Rapids: Wm. B. Eerdmans, 1954.

————. *Special Revelation and the Word of God.* Grand Rapids: Wm. B. Eerdmans, 1961.

Robinson, H. Wheeler. *Inspiration and Revelation in the Old Testament.* Oxford: Clarendon Press, 1956.

Rowley, H. H. *The Unity of the Bible.* Philadelphia: Westminster Press, 1953.

Rust, E. C. *Nature and Man in Biblical Thought.* London: Lutterworth Press, 1953.

Schleiermacher, Friedrich. *The Christian Faith.* Edited by H. R. Mackintosh and J. P. Stewart. Edinburgh: T. and T. Clark Ltd., 1928.

Seeberg, Reinhold. *Revelation and Inspiration.* New York: Harper and Row, 1909.

Standen, Anthony. *Science is a Sacred Cow.* New York: E. P. Dutton and Company, 1950.

Warfield, B. B. *The Inspiration and Authority of the Bible.* Philadelphia: Presbyterian and Reformed Publishing Co., 1948.

White, Andrew D. *A History of the Warfare of Science with Theology in Christendom.* 2 vols. New York: D. Appleton and Company, 1896.